Advance Praise for *George Marshall*

"George Marshall was the model of what a general and statesman should be: wise and nonpartisan and honorable. That is why it is so timely that this judicious biography brings him back to life for us. Using papers and material that have become available in the past three decades, David L. Roll helps reveal Marshall's human side and how it relates to his public image and momentous achievements."

> —Walter Isaacson, *New York Times*–bestselling author of *Steve Jobs* and *Leonardo da Vinci*

"David L. Roll's well-researched, well-written and enthralling book explains perfectly why Winston Churchill called George C. Marshall the 'Organizer of Victory.' The psychological insights are penetrating about this courtly, modest Pennsylvanian who nonetheless had a core of tempered steel."

> —Andrew Roberts, *New York Times*–bestselling author of *Churchill: Walking with Destiny*

"In this engrossing biography, David Roll pinpoints the sources of George C. Marshall's greatness: character, integrity, and a deep devotion to the well-being of his country. Put simply, Marshall possessed in abundance qualities that today have seemingly all but vanished from American public life."

> —Andrew J. Bacevich, professor emeritus of history and international relations, Boston University, and *New York Times*–bestselling author of *America's War for the Greater Middle East: A Military History*

"David Roll's *George Marshall* couldn't come at a more crucial time. There's a growing conviction among Americans that their country no longer produces strategists and statesmen of Marshall's stature. Thanks to new sources on the general's life and the military establishment through which he rose, this thorough, balanced, and wise book goes far in assessing that claim."

> —John Lewis Gaddis, Pulitzer Prize–winning author of *George F. Kennan: An American Life*

"David Roll's majestic new biography of General George Marshall will reintroduce twenty-first century readers to one of the most important figures of the twentieth century: the soldier and statesman who devised the strategy that won World War II. The first major study of Marshall in a generation, Roll skillfully explores papers, diaries and documents never before available to portray a modest, moral man who served ten presidents, his nation, and the world."

> —Susan Page, Washington bureau chief of *USA Today* and author of *The Matriarch: Barbara Bush and the Making of an American Dynasty*

"A book as necessary as it is great. At a time when Americans are struggling to define what real leadership looks like, David Roll's brilliant new portrait of George Marshall offers valuable clarity."

—General Stanley McChrystal, U.S. Army Ret.

"In this time of national demoralization, when a small-minded president casts a shadow over our highest office, David Roll's biography of General George C. Marshall reminds us that the country has also been served by the best and the brightest. Roll's highly readable book captures the many challenges that Marshall faced and overcame by brilliance and resilience. This book should be read by anyone who wishes to renew faith in America's greatness."

—Robert Dallek, author of *An Unfinished Life: John F. Kennedy, 1917-1963*

"A hugely significant book on an American leader to whom freedom around the world owes an enormous debt. This exhaustively researched, penetrating biography provides important new perspective on a soldier-statesman whose character of service and contributions over a fifty-year career make him worthy of comparison to the most substantial figures in American history. Based on letters and papers available for the first time, David Roll provides a portrait of Marshall that is far more penetrating and nuanced than past biographies and establishes very clearly that George C. Marshall was an extraordinary defender of the republic at one of the most perilous times in our history."

—General David Petraeus, U.S. Army Ret.

"This splendid, freshly researched and lively biography gives us a full portrait of one of the most talented and admirable leaders the United States ever produced. David Roll, with a telling eye for personal detail, humanizes the stoic Marshall and reveals his true genius as a soldier, strategist and diplomat across fifty years of war and global turmoil. This is an important, even urgent, book."

—William I. Hitchcock, author of *The Age of Eisenhower: America and the World in the 1950s*

"David Roll's *George Marshall* is a tonic for our troubled times. Roll brings to life the decency and strength of character that made Marshall one of America's greatest soldiers and statesmen, showing how, for all his brilliance, Marshall always put his country first, rather than himself. He was reticent, disciplined, measured in his opinions, and magnanimous in his treatment of others—qualities that are so obviously missing from many of today's leaders."

—David Ignatius, *New York Times*-bestselling author of *The Quantum Spy*

GEORGE MARSHALL

★ ★ ★ ★ ★

Defender of the Republic

DAVID L. ROLL

CALIBER

DUTTON CALIBER
An imprint of Penguin Random House LLC
penguinrandomhouse.com

Copyright © 2019 by David L. Roll

Library of Congress Cataloging-in-Publication Data
Names: Roll, David L., author.
Title: George Marshall : Defender of the Republic / David L. Roll.
Description: New York : Dutton Caliber, 2019.
Identifiers: LCCN 2018055675| ISBN 9781101990971 (hardback) |
ISBN 9781101990995 (ebook)
Subjects: LCSH: Marshall, George C. (George Catlett), 1880-1959. |
Marshall, George C. (George Catlett), 1880-1959—Military leadership. |
Marshall, George C. (George Catlett), 1880-1959—Political and social views. |
Generals—United States—Biography. | United States. Army—Biography. |
Statesmen—United States—Biography. | Political leadership—United States—Case studies. | United States—History, Military—20th century. | United States—Politics and government—1901-1953. | United States—Foreign relations—20th century. |
BISAC: BIOGRAPHY & AUTOBIOGRAPHY / Military. |
HISTORY / Military / World War II. | HISTORY /United States / 20th Century.
Classification: LCC E745.M37 R65 2019 | DDC 973.918092 [B]—dc23
LC record available at https://lccn.loc.gov/2018055675

Printed in the United States of America
1   3   5   7   9   10   8   6   4   2

Book design by Francesca Belanger
Maps by Jeffrey L. Ward

For Mike and Charlie, friends indeed

Contents

List of Maps

Prologue

SACRED TRUST

The bricks of the Old National Pike, the road that ran westward through the center of Uniontown toward Ohio and beyond, had been painted red, white, and blue for the occasion. Triumphal arches decorated with patriotic bunting had been erected at each block. Even in the late August heat, thousands of townspeople had turned out to welcome home the boys of Company C, veterans of the Spanish-American War. They had spent months in the sweltering jungles of the far-off Philippines, fighting Spaniards, Filipino *insurrectos*, and malaria. Once the soldiers were relieved, they were shipped back across the Pacific to the West Coast, then across the continent by rail to Pennsylvania. When their train finally chugged into town—but only after a stopover in Pittsburgh, where they had been honored by the president himself—their friends and neighbors roared in delight. One eighteen-year-old, about to begin his third year at the Virginia Military Institute, watched from the crowd as the infantrymen paraded over the painted bricks and under the adorned archways. Deeply affected, he glimpsed a life far beyond the rich coalfields and beehive coke ovens that surrounded the place where he had grown up in the rugged hills of southwest Pennsylvania. It was then, on that last day of August 1899, that he decided to become an officer in the United States Army.[1]

George Catlett Marshall Jr., the young man who would go on to reshape the army and oversee it through its greatest challenge, could easily have never committed to a life in uniform. Marshall's father, George C. Marshall Sr., was a gregarious businessman who viewed the army as a dead end that offered a subsistence salary, few opportunities for rapid advancement, and no social standing. His mother, Laura Bradford Marshall, the quiet and reserved daughter of a physician who was an avid abolitionist, agreed with her husband, primarily because a career in the army meant that the favorite of her three children would leave the area, rarely return, and might be ordered into harm's way. Still, knowing that military school could lead to myriad

1

opportunities, Marshall's parents had chosen to send George Jr., at the age of sixteen, to VMI to acquire discipline and a practical education, not to help him obtain a commission in the army.

In April 1901, two months before he was to graduate from VMI and eight months shy of his twenty-first birthday, Marshall made a bold move to seize control of his future. Armed with letters of recommendation from the superintendent of VMI and a Republican close to the president, Marshall boarded a train to Washington, DC, where he lobbied Attorney General Philander Knox, his father's acquaintance from nearby Brownsville, Pennsylvania, and scored an interview with John A. T. Hull, the chairman of the House Military Affairs Committee. Then, without any appointment, Marshall simply strolled into the White House, joined a procession upstairs, and eventually found himself alone with the president of the United States. "Mr. McKinley in a very nice manner asked me what I wanted," recalled Marshall, "and I stated my case." Several days later, Marshall's name appeared on the secretary of war's list of Pennsylvania candidates selected to sit for a competitive examination that was required in order to receive a commission. Though hard evidence is lacking, Marshall believed his selection "flowed" from his lobbying efforts in Washington.[2]

Marshall sat for the three-day examination in late September at Governors Island in New York Harbor. Despite poor performances in math subjects and grammar, he received one of the highest average scores, including perfect marks for physique, moral character, and "antecedents" (meaning distinguished relatives, notably Supreme Court Chief Justice John Marshall). Commissioning was delayed until after he reached the age of twenty-one. Instead of the Artillery Corps, his first choice, he was assigned to the infantry. With no training whatsoever, Second Lieutenant Marshall shipped out of San Francisco aboard the army transport *Kilpatrick* to join the 30th Infantry in the Philippines. "Flicker"—the nickname a young Irish girl had bestowed on George when he was a sandy-haired, freckle-faced boy running carefree through the streets and alleys of Uniontown—became a distant memory. For the ensuing fifty years he would defend his country as soldier and statesman.

*   *   *   *   *

General George C. Marshall, who served under ten presidents, occupies a singular place in the history of the twentieth century, yet his significance is fading from public memory. His achievements, and particularly his character, must never be forgotten.

As a soldier, Marshall influenced the course of each of the two world wars that swept away the European system of power, colonialism, and international order. As a statesman, he husbanded the policy of "containment" of Soviet aggression, and faced up to the limits of American power in Asia. He lent his name and reputation to the Marshall Plan, arguably the most significant initiative in American diplomacy since the Louisiana Purchase. These moves triggered the divisions of Europe and Korea, the forty-year Cold War, and the rise of China, while a nuclear holocaust was avoided. No one person comes close to matching Marshall's ubiquitous yet selfless presence throughout the history of the last century.

Recalling George Marshall's power to influence people and events, former secretary of state Dean Acheson wrote that "the moment [he] entered a room everyone in it felt his presence. It was a striking and communicated force."[3] Legendary Speaker of the House Sam Rayburn remarked that Marshall had "the presence of a great man. He doesn't dissemble . . . He would tell the truth even if it hurt his cause. Congress always respected him. They would give him things they would give to no one else."[4]

While Marshall's accomplishments and the respect he commanded during his professional life were unrivaled, the answer to the question of why he matters today lies in the values and principles that shaped his character. Marshall lived by a moral code that emphasized self-control, perseverance, integrity, truth, honor, and duty. He was a humble man. Even the instructions he left for his funeral reflected this: "Bury me simply, like any ordinary officer of the U.S. Army who has served his country honorably. No fuss . . . And above everything, do it quietly."[5] Like most of the World War II generals, he could have made a fortune writing an autobiography or memoir. He declined all offers, preferring to let the record he left behind speak for him. Marshall abhorred any activity that attracted attention to himself. And he certainly did not want to offend or embarrass any of the people he had associated with during his decades of service.

Thirty years have passed since the last two praiseworthy and widely read biographies of George Marshall were written.[6] In large part, these works were based on Forrest Pogue's monumental four-volume biography of Marshall. Much has been revealed since then, bringing new perspectives, shifts in attitudes, and revisions upon revisions from all sides relative to Marshall's successes, failures, and significance. Five of the seven volumes of Marshall's annotated papers were not even published until *after* the release of these two biographies. Diaries, letters, films, interviews (including several conducted by the author), and documents moldering in the British National Archives have emerged that were simply not available to or unearthed by Pogue and subsequent biographers.[7] From all of the materials that have emerged since 1990, Marshall's critical role in four wars during the twentieth century—three hot and one cold—becomes even more vivid than the portrait drawn by Pogue in his multivolume work.

This book tells the story of Marshall's education in the uses of military, diplomatic, and political power, an education that Marshall found both humiliating and instructive when President Franklin Roosevelt set aside his "Europe first" strategy in 1942, largely for political reasons. The story unfolds within a selection of pivotal episodes, beginning with then major Marshall's angry and impertinent encounter with General Pershing during World War I, continuing with his confrontations during and after World War II with Roosevelt, Churchill, Truman, and Stalin, and ending with Marshall's testimony before Congress in 1951 supporting the firing of national hero General Douglas MacArthur in the midst of the Korean War, a performance that eviscerated MacArthur's presidential prospects.

George Marshall has almost always been portrayed as coolly impersonal, austere, stoic, and aloof—as if he lacked feelings and was something less than a whole person. There is no question that Marshall often appeared that way to those outside his inner circle. But his marble-like constancy was of his own making. Unmasked in the presence of close friends and family, he was warm, relaxed, and reasonably talkative, prone to telling—and sometimes repeating—stories about army life that he, at least, regarded as witty. Thanks to Marshall's correspondence, a trove of which was donated to the George C. Marshall Foundation in 2012, the pages of this book present, for the first time, a more authentic description of Marshall's inner life, a life that found completion in his relationships with his two wives, a headstrong stepson, a precocious young girl, and a handful of intimate friends.

* * * * *

From the time he was commissioned as a second lieutenant until he resigned as secretary of defense in September 1951, Marshall refused, as a matter of principle, to participate in any kind of political activity, much less accept nomination for a political office. He did not even vote. When asked what party he preferred, he glibly answered, "Episcopalian." Perhaps because he was keenly aware that war and politics were inextricably related, Marshall believed that involvement in partisan politics might conflict with his obligation as a military officer to subordinate himself to civilian authority and would undermine his effectiveness as secretary of state and defense. He counseled General John J. Pershing not to run for president in 1924. His advice to his protégé, General Dwight D. Eisenhower, who was elected president in 1952, was disregarded.

When Marshall was army chief of staff during World War II, he held forth on why generals and admirals should steer clear of politics, implying that they should do so even after they have resigned from service. The American people, he was quoted as saying, had conferred a "great asset" on the professional officer corps, in that they harbor no fear that the military will seek to alter or overthrow the government. This is a "sacred trust," he declared, that must be protected and preserved. "We . . . are a member of a priesthood really, the sole purpose of which is to defend the republic."[8]

Chapter 1
Harvest of Death

George Marshall's ascent to power and prominence began on January 27, 1914, "under the shade of a bamboo clump."[1] Nearly five thousand U.S. Army soldiers had just completed an amphibious landing on the island of Luzon in the Philippines and were gathering to attack Manila, some sixty miles to the north. Marshall, then a thirty-three-year-old first lieutenant, was sitting in the mud with his back against one of the trees, surrounded by officers awaiting orders. The wide brim of his felt campaign hat was tipped up, revealing closely cropped sandy hair and deep-set blue eyes. Staring intently at a map, he slowly and confidently dictated orders detailing a choreography of infantry, cavalry, field artillery, signal corps, Filipino scouts, field kitchens, surgical tents, wagons, and hundreds of pack animals. They were to move north day and night on mucky trails through patches of jungle, fields of sugarcane, towering razor grass, and mountain passes. One of the officers who witnessed Marshall's performance that day was Henry "Hap" Arnold, a West Pointer who would rise to become head of the army air force during World War II. Arnold was so impressed that in a letter to his wife he wrote that he had "met a man who was going to be chief of staff of the army some day."[2]

Over the next eight days, Marshall's invasion forces outwitted the enemy defenders and captured successive objectives on the way to Manila. It was just an exercise, a mock invasion and attack, but those who were there spread word throughout the officer ranks that Marshall was a military genius, one of the most promising future wartime leaders in the army.

* * * * *

Instigated by the War Department in Washington, the 1914 maneuvers had been designed to test the army's readiness to defend the Philippine archipelago against a possible invasion by Japan. Following victory in the Russo-Japanese War of 1904–05, and the complete annexation of Korea five years later due to the assassination of a prominent Japanese statesman by a Korean, Japan had become the preeminent power in the Pacific. The Philippines, symbol of U.S. imperialism, stood directly in the path of Japan's increasingly aggressive designs to dominate East Asia. To simulate a Japanese attack, a "White Force" was to land at Batangas Bay, south of Manila, and try to overwhelm the "Brown Force" charged with defending the capital.

Given the importance and high-profile nature of the maneuvers—the largest ever in the Philippines—it was unlikely that a mere first lieutenant like Marshall, no matter how competent, would command the White Force. In fact, General J. Franklin Bell, head of the Philippine Department, had initially selected a hard-drinking colonel to take charge. "A courtly gentleman, a very nice fellow," recalled Marshall, although he couldn't—or preferred not to—remember his name. Referring to the man's propensity for strong drink, Marshall wrote that the colonel would ride beside him in a "spring wagon" with a "zinc-lined suitcase," and every time they stopped he would open the suitcase and "refresh himself against the Philippine heat."[3]

Under the colonel—his name was William Cathcart Buttler—the first stage of the attack, the amphibious landings by the White Force, had to be delayed a week due to a snafu in procuring an adequate number of landing boats. Marshall, an adjutant assigned to the colonel's staff, stepped into the chaos and coolly secured the boats, arranged to have stalls built for the pack animals, and organized the amphibious landings. The umpires for the maneuvers, having lost confidence in Colonel Buttler, proposed that he be removed from command. At some risk to his own career, Marshall presumptuously suggested that to save face the colonel be left in nominal command, but that he, Marshall, be allowed to act as Buttler's alter ego in planning and leading the attack, along with Marshall's close friend, Captain Jens Bugge, the White Force chief of staff. The umpires agreed. The next day Bugge suffered a malarial attack and had to return to Manila. The umpires and General Bell had no choice. Marshall was the only one with knowledge of the White Force plans, forces, and officers. With the War Department in Washington and the garrison in Manila watching, the maneuvers had to go on. First Lieutenant Marshall was in sole command of almost five thousand men.

Except for Marshall's failure to commit enough of his forces to the first day's objective, his performance was regarded by the umpires as outstanding. Under pressure day and night for two weeks, he was imperturbable. With courtesy and self-effacement, he cut through the reluctance of colonels and other senior officers to accept orders from him. The clarity and precision of Marshall's field orders evidenced his grasp of the situations he confronted and his attention to tactical details. The landings of the men, animals, food, and equipment on the beaches at Batangas went smoothly despite the fact that the boats could not stand in closer than three-quarters of a mile and there was no dock. On the way to Manila, Marshall kept his units intact so that attacks on the enemy defenders could be made in strength. He managed three successful mock battles and several skirmishes and cavalry forays, reaching the capital on February 4.

One superior officer wrote in Marshall's efficiency report that he was the best leader of large bodies of troops in the entire American army. Another gushed that "there are not five officers in the Army as well qualified as [Marshall] to command a division in the field."[4] Although the umpires ended the maneuvers without declaring Marshall's White Force a clear winner, the tales that grew out of his performance, and the dazzle that surrounded his name, guaranteed him a reputation in the small officer corps of the Regular Army that few if any of his rank could equal. Beneath the overblown legend, however, certain facts stood out: Marshall's White Force executed a successful amphibious invasion, and then proceeded to outsmart and overwhelm the Brown Force defenders, thus providing the army with vital lessons for the future. Much later, when a confrontation with Japan was far more than a possibility, these lessons were incorporated into the army's war plans.

Whether or not Marshall's performance deserved all of the plaudits it received, there is no doubt that an aura surrounded him, an emanation of controlled power. "His figure," wrote Dean Acheson, "conveyed intensity... It spread a sense of authority and calm." Physically, Marshall was lean, erect, square-shouldered, and tall for his era, slightly under six feet. He had a way of carrying himself that conveyed order and self-restraint. His face was pleasing and dignified, though with a long, thin upper lip and receding chin he could hardly be described as handsome. Professionally, Marshall was stern, deliberately reserved, yet he exhibited "nothing of the martinet."[5] In social situations he was typically genial, friendly, and sometimes even warm and charming. Yet his emotions, including his explosive temper, were usually masked, his fears and vulnerabilities well hidden.

Marshall tried but could not conceal his susceptibility to the effects of the enormous stress he was under throughout the war games' days and nights. After the maneuvers were suspended, he was hospitalized in Manila for about two weeks, suffering for the second time from what the doctors of that era called "neurasthenia," a catchall term for a variety of nervous conditions short of insanity such as chronic fatigue, anxiety, depression, and nervous breakdown.[6] Where he fit into this spectrum is unknown. Following these episodes, Marshall realized that he was working himself to death and resolved to take better care of himself. For much of the rest of his life, he made an effort to ride for an hour most mornings before breakfast, play tennis or catnap in the afternoons, and relax after dinner viewing a movie or reading. And if he could find time to hunt or fish, he would escape for a day or two with Hap Arnold or another army pal.

While recuperating, Marshall wrote a rare but revealing letter to his older brother Stuart. Marshall detested braggarts, yet to his brother he boasted at length about how he took on "the entire burden" of commanding the White Force, "chewed the other side up, captured two of their six cavalry squadrons, and smashed up their infantry." In the same letter he wrote that his wife Lily "looks very well," had "gained a number of lbs.," and that they were looking forward to resting for "several weeks or a month" in a "celebrated hotel" near Mt. Fuji in Japan.[7] Had it not been for some emotionally searing comments that Stuart had made years earlier, there would be nothing particularly remarkable about this letter. After all, it is not unusual for a younger brother, no matter how self-effacing, to seek approval from his older sibling, or write about a romantic interlude with his wife. Yet this letter sought more than approval. It summoned a painful past.

Marshall would never forget a conversation between Stuart and their mother that he overheard in 1897, when he was sixteen, living with his family in Uniontown. Marshall had been begging his parents to send him to the Virginia Military Institute. From a room adjoining the kitchen, he heard his brother, who had graduated from VMI in the class of 1894, attempting in vain to persuade his mother that Flicker should not be allowed to attend the Institute because he "would disgrace the family."[8] Stuart was referring to Flicker's feckless attitude toward school, his shyness, and his fear of failure and rejection. As Marshall recalled later, "The urgency to succeed came from hearing that conversation; it had a psychological effect on my career... I decided right then that I was going to wipe [Stuart's] face, or wipe his eye."[9]

Nor would Marshall ever forgive Stuart for the "unkind, unfair remarks" he made about Lily Carter Coles, the flirtatious, titian-haired beauty with whom Marshall fell in love as a senior at VMI, the year he headed his class of thirty-three as First Captain, the highest-ranking cadet.[10] In February of 1902, after he had graduated and received his commission in the army, Marshall married Lily in the parlor of the little Gothic cottage at 319 Letcher Avenue near the south Limit Gate of VMI in Lexington, Virginia, where she lived with her widowed mother. The night after their wedding, at the New Willard Hotel in Washington, DC, Marshall learned for the first time that Lily could not risk a pregnancy due to a heart condition (Marshall called it a "mitral regurgitation").[11] The substance of Stuart's hurtful remarks about Lily, and when he articulated them, is unknown. It is known that Stuart courted Lily when he was at VMI. One historian speculated that Stuart disliked her because she had rejected his marriage proposal.[12] During the late 1920s, Marshall confided to his goddaughter that Stuart "opposed everything I wanted to do, including my marriage to Lily. He attempted to run my life and was unpleasant about it, but when he made unkind, unfair remarks about Lily, I cut him off my list."[13]

Though out of character, Marshall's boastful letter to Stuart in 1914 was his way of "wiping" his success in his brother's face—a not-so-subtle reminder that he had become a credit, not a disgrace, to the family. References to nesting in a celebrated hotel with Lily were yet another means of rubbing it in—telling Stuart that he was wrong, that he and Lily were happily married. This would be one of the last letters that Marshall would write to Stuart. He would be estranged from his brother for the rest of his life.

After Marshall was discharged from the hospital in Manila, he and Lily set off on a four-month journey to Japan, Manchuria, and Korea, courtesy of the army's generous sick leave policy combined with Marshall's accumulation of regular leave. As guests of the Japanese army the couple spent a month in Manchuria, where Marshall toured on horseback the already forgotten battlefields of the Russo-Japanese War, prophetically noting in his thirty-three-page report "the sublime spirit of self-sacrifice for the cause of the Emperor displayed by the Japanese soldier."[14] On the return trip to Japan, Marshall stopped to investigate the terrain on the south side of the

Yalu River before he and Lily continued by train to Seoul. Thirty-six years later, when he was secretary of defense, this area would be a flashpoint in the Korean War.

* * * * *

On June 28, 1914, when Marshall and Lily were nearing the end of their trip, an act of terrorism in the turbulent Balkans improbably triggered what came to be called the Great War, later known as the First World War. The terrorist, a nineteen-year-old Bosnian Serb named Gavrilo Princip, shot and killed at point-blank range Archduke Franz Ferdinand, heir to the throne of Austria-Hungary, and his consort Sophie when their carriage came to a momentary halt opposite a café in Sarajevo. Princip and his coconspirators hoped that the murder of the future king would foment an uprising leading to the freedom of the South Slav people from Austro-Hungarian rule and the creation of a Greater Serbia. Instead, they were the spark that kindled the first of the twentieth century's two world wars, at the center of which was German power.

If Princip was the spark, the fading empire of Austria-Hungary, called the Dual Monarchy, was the chaff that ignited the fire. Rather than dealing on its own with the tiny kingdom of Serbia, home of the conspirators, it decided to seek the support of Germany. In the judgment of historian John Keegan, it was this decision that "transformed a local into a general European crisis."[15] Once Germany signaled its support for war against Serbia, the fire began to spread. Russia mobilized for war. Germany declared war against Russia, then against France, Russia's ally. The blaze raged out of control. When Germany demanded that its armies be permitted to pass through Belgium to attack France, Great Britain, a guarantor of Belgian neutrality, declared war against Germany.

Within six weeks of the double assassination, Germany's Kaiser Wilhelm II, emperor of a powerful new nation less than half a century old, was at war with the three other great powers in Europe—Russia, France, and Great Britain. Except for France, it was a family affair since Czar Nicholas II of Russia and Britain's King George V were cousins of the kaiser. Not to be left out, Austria-Hungary declared war on Russia and Britain, and France declared war on the Dual Monarchy. From his window overlooking Horse Guards Parade in London, British foreign secretary Sir Edward Grey lamented, "The lamps are going out all over Europe. We shall not see them lit again in our lifetime."[16]

In the fall of 1914, the German army sliced through neutral Belgium and Luxembourg into France, at one point reaching the Marne River, a short distance from Paris. Racing to the front, many in taxis, French soldiers rallied, pushing the Germans more than thirty miles back to the line of the Aisne River. Farther north, in Belgium, twenty-five-year-old Private Adolf Hitler fought as an infantryman with the 16th Bavarian Reserve Infantry Regiment on the Menin Road in the First Battle of Ypres, known in Germany as the Massacre of the Innocents because 40,000 German enlistees were killed in the first twenty days—Hitler's regiment alone was reduced from 3,600 to 611 men. On December 2, the future Führer was awarded an Iron Cross, Second Class, for protecting his commander's life when a French shell hit their dugout, killing several German soldiers. It was, he later said, "the happiest day of my life."[17] Weeks later, when Hitler's comrades emerged from their trenches during the spontaneous "Christmas truce" of 1914 to shake hands and sing carols with enemy troops in no-man's-land, he strongly disapproved, believing that nothing should interrupt the slaughter.

In 1915, a bloody stalemate took hold on the Western Front, marked to this day by the remnants of vast zigzagging networks of opposing trenches that stretched 466 miles from the border of neutral Switzerland in the south to Nieuport, Belgium, on the North Sea. Other fronts developed, including one in the Balkans and another at Gallipoli, a disastrous defeat for the British blamed on First Lord of the Admiralty Winston Churchill. To the east, in Prussia and the flatlands of Poland, the Germans battled the armies of Russia. A host of smaller nations, including Japan and Turkey, entered the war, transforming it from a war among European powers to a world war. Due to the unprecedented killing and maiming power of massive artillery bombardments, machine guns, poison gas attacks, flamethrowers, and tanks, and the seemingly endless supply of manpower and diabolical death machines, the number of killed and wounded on all sides was mind-numbing. On the Western Front alone, the casualties in the battles of Verdun, the Somme, and Passchendaele exceeded 2.4 million, snuffing out the lives of a generation of French, British, and German men. Neither side was able to pulverize the other into submission.

For the first twenty-eight months of the Great War the official policy of the United States, as decreed by President Woodrow Wilson, was strict neutrality. Wilson was viscerally opposed to becoming involved in foreign wars, famously (and controversially) declaring in one of his speeches, "There is such a thing as a man being too proud to fight."[18] Yet inevitably, America was slowly drawn in. Newspapers printed tales of atrocities by the "Huns," some invented by the British, who begged the Americans to join the fight. U.S. corporations sold war matériel and bankers provided financing to the western Allies. The Germans, feeling the effects of the British naval blockade, struck back at shipping from the U.S. to Great Britain and France, deploying their deadly U-boats to sink merchant ships and sometimes even passenger liners—which Americans called unrestricted submarine warfare. The sinking of the British liner *Lusitania* and the English Channel passenger ferry *Sussex* in which almost 1,300 civilians lost their lives, including more than 130 Americans, provoked outrage in the United States. The Wilson administration sent notes of protest to Kaiser Wilhelm's government and threatened via a deliberate news leak to break off diplomatic relations. The Germans backed down, at least for the time being. They made a public promise not to sink liners and merchant vessels without early warning, thus depriving their submarines of the vital element of surprise.

Former president Theodore Roosevelt ignited a "preparedness movement" that swept the country. It became fashionable for well-heeled college men to volunteer to spend the summer at camps run by the army, learning how to become officers. In 1916, President Wilson, sensing the public's mood, supported increased appropriations for a navy "second to none" and a National Defense Act that would expand the Regular Army to 175,000, create a Reserve Officers' Training Corps (ROTC), provide enhanced presidential powers over munitions production, and increase the size of the National Guard to 450,000.[19] Wilson and majorities in Congress believed this legislation was needed not only to better prepare the nation's military for possible war in Europe but also to pressure the Germans to continue to abide by their promise to refrain from unrestricted submarine warfare. Moreover, the legislation was designed to strengthen the National Guard that had performed so abysmally when it was called upon to join General John J. Pershing's "Punitive Expedition" in northern Mexico.

With Pershing and his 8th Cavalry already at war with Pancho Villa and a heightened prospect that the U.S. might enter the war in Europe, George

Marshall was itching to get back to the States. He had hoped that his champion in the Philippines, General Bell, a former army chief of staff and Medal of Honor recipient, would help him get into the Mexican expedition. Bell did arrange for Marshall and his wife to return to America in the summer of 1916, but he had other plans for his protégé. For the next several months Captain Marshall (the National Defense Act of 1916 opened the way to Marshall's promotion, retroactive July 1) was immersed in the preparedness movement, working mostly on the West Coast to set up officer training camps. As a testament to Marshall's powerful influence over them, a group of trainees in Monterey, California, gave him the nickname "Dynamite."[20]

Shortly after Wilson was elected to a second term on the slogan "He kept us out of war,"[21] the kaiser, with the hope of knocking Britain out of the conflict, announced that the German government would reinstate unrestricted submarine warfare against all U.S. and Allied shipping. German leaders knew that this would probably impel America to enter the war, but they calculated that they would have time to capture Paris and negotiate an armistice before U.S. troops could reach the battlefield. Almost immediately, the president addressed Congress and broke off diplomatic relations with Germany. The rush to war began.

In late February 1917, British intelligence stoked war fever in America by releasing the so-called Zimmermann Telegram, a secret intercept in which Arthur Zimmermann, the German foreign secretary, proposed an alliance with Mexico. According to the telegram, if Mexico sided with Germany in war against the United States, Germany would help it regain Texas, New Mexico, and Arizona, territories it lost during the Mexican-American War. With the unanimous backing of his cabinet, Wilson asked for and obtained from Congress a declaration of war against the Central Powers (Germany, Austria-Hungary, Turkey, and Bulgaria) in order, he proclaimed, to make "the world safe for democracy." Wilson signed the declaration on April 6, 1917. Little more than a month later Congress passed the Selective Service Act, which provided for the conscription of a citizen army of "doughboys," a term of uncertain origin that was commonly used to describe the young Americans who fought the Germans in the Great War.[22] All males between the ages of twenty-one and thirty who resided in the United States were required to report to their local precinct stations. Nine and a half million men registered for the draft on June 5, 1917.

Less than two weeks after war was declared, General Bell ordered Marshall to move east, where he was to serve as Bell's aide-de-camp. His immediate task was to select candidates for officer training and to organize training camps.

* * * * *

It was at Governors Island in late May that Captain Marshall first encountered fifty-seven-year-old General Pershing, a man who would have a profound influence on him for the remainder of his life. A few days earlier, Pershing had met briefly with President Wilson and Secretary of War Newton Baker at the White House to confirm his appointment as commander of all United States land forces operating in Europe, the United Kingdom, and Ireland—to be called the American Expeditionary Forces, or AEF. Pershing's formal letter of instruction, drafted by Baker, gave him complete discretion as to when to engage his troops; however, he was to bear in mind that the "forces of the United States are a separate and distinct component" of the Allied forces, "the identity of which must be preserved."[23] Pershing hoped to obtain some guidance from his commander in chief as to war aims, cooperation with the Allies, or overall strategy. He got absolutely nothing from the aloof president other than his "full support."[24] Astonishingly, this was the *only* meeting between Wilson and Pershing during the entire war. No American war before or since has been fought with less interaction between the president and his commanding general.

In heavy rain and fog on the morning of May 28, 1917, Marshall accompanied Pershing, who was dressed in "civilian clothes and a straw hat," to a secluded dock on Governors Island. A ferryboat took him "over to the *Baltic*, an ocean liner [of the White Star Line] which he boarded for his trip to Europe."[25] "I was in a most depressed frame of mind over being left behind," Marshall later remembered. He had narrowly missed being attached to Pershing's staff. Returning from the dock, Marshall stopped by his quarters to dry off. He and Lily watched through the window as Pershing's ad hoc staff of 191 officers and enlisted men shuffled down the dock in the rain, "dressed in civilian clothes, coat collars turned up . . . not an imposing group," wrote Marshall. "Lily remarked, 'They were such a dreadful-looking lot of men, I cannot believe they will be able to do any good in France.'"[26] General Pershing and his staff (which included Captain George Patton) were the vanguard of the host of American men and boys who would comprise the American Expeditionary Forces.

Despite trying to disguise themselves as civilians, the departure of Pershing and his staff was an open secret. Boxes of supplies had languished on the pier for days marked "General Pershing's Headquarters." Journalists across the country had been tipped off. When the *Baltic* sailed in the late afternoon, a salute by the signal guns on Governors Island, reserved solely for generals and other notables, announced the departure to the entire harbor.

* * * * *

At three a.m. on June 11, 1917, Marshall was standing at the window of the former North German Lloyd Line shipping office in Hoboken watching a steady stream of infantry of the 1st Division, mostly raw recruits, plodding slowly in the rain from the meadowlands where they had detrained, through a courtyard and into the covered docks. Two days earlier Marshall had been overjoyed to learn from General William Sibert, Pershing's newly selected commander of the 1st Infantry Division, that he would be sailing to France with the division as its operations officer. Sibert had been impressed with Marshall's performance at the Monterey training camp in the summer of 1916 and was pleased to take him on when General Bell, prompted by Marshall's plea to get into the fight, gave his consent. To break the silence in the shipping office, Marshall turned to the port boss, a German immigrant, and said, "The men seem very solemn."

"Of course they are," replied the sullen Lloyd Line employee. "We are watching the harvest of death."[27]

The next day, along with General Sibert, his staff, and the 2nd Battalion of the 1st Division's 28th Infantry Regiment, Marshall boarded the transport *Tenadores*, a recently converted fruit liner of the Latin American trade. After delays due to the installation of antisubmarine guns and heavy fog, the odoriferous *Tenadores* finally steamed out of New York Harbor through a gap in the submarine chain and into the open Atlantic, bound for Saint-Nazaire on the French coast. Marshall had had less than thirty-six hours to gather and pack his field gear and transfer his heavy workload for General Bell to another officer. He scrambled to arrange for Lily to take a train to Lexington, Virginia, where she would live with her mother for the duration. Years later, Marshall recalled his last-minute dash into New York City to purchase "three suits of Jaeger underwear which . . . enabled me to go entirely through the First World War without a cold."[28]

The *Tenadores* was the first of the troop transports to cruise up the Loire River on the sunny morning of June 26, 1917, nose slowly into the basin at Saint-Nazaire, and tie up at the pier. The destroyers and cruisers that had safely convoyed them across the Atlantic stood out to sea. The gangplank was lowered. Behind General Sibert, Captain George Marshall was the second soldier in the 1st Division to descend and set foot in France. They and the doughboys who followed them onto French soil were, in the words of General Pershing, "the advance guard of America's fighting men."[29] The 1st Division, the "Big Red One," was destined for glory.

The small gathering of citizens who watched them disembark, mostly women dressed in mourning black, were silent and somber. "[T]he general aspect was that of a funeral," wrote Marshall.[30] "[E]veryone seemed to be on the verge of tears."[31] He could see the despair in their eyes. He knew that the "much advertised French offensive of April 17th"—the offensive that would supposedly "win the war"—had failed disastrously, with the French suffering 163,000 casualties. And he had heard rumors that elements of the French army "were practically in a state of mutiny."[32] But it wasn't until later that Marshall realized how low morale had sunk all along the Western Front. The French had lost two million men since the beginning of hostilities. Numerous divisions were content to defend, but unwilling to attack. Farther north the British Expeditionary Force suffered a humiliating defeat at the battle of Arras. German U-boats threatened to starve Britain into submission. After three years of grinding trench warfare, the western Allied forces and their citizenry were at the edge of exhaustion.

The Germans were likewise fatigued, their armies having taken millions of casualties and their people cut off from food and fuel by the British naval blockade. However, they had one more card to play. By the summer of 1917, with the abdication of Czar Nicholas II, the loss of confidence in Aleksandr Kerensky's provisional government, and the rise of the Bolsheviks, it had become clear that the Russian army would soon withdraw from the war, thus releasing more than a million German troops from the Eastern Front to fight the Allies in the west. Knowing his comrades were about to be bolstered by veteran forces, General Erich Ludendorff began preparing plans for a massive all-out offensive to be launched in the spring of 1918 at key points along the Western Front with the objective of winning the war before the American forces were strong enough to make a difference.

The French and British high commands, their own troops depleted, weary, and demoralized, also knew that the Russians would soon withdraw. They were aware that the Germans would probably mount a last-ditch, war-ending offensive in the west, but they didn't know when or where it would begin. Consequently, almost from the moment General Pershing became commander of the AEF, his allies began pressing him to send arriving American doughboys into seasoned French and British units for training and use as replacements. Pershing fiercely resisted. Backed by his instructions from Secretary Baker and President Wilson, he insisted on preserving the identity of the American forces: they would train and fight as a separate component of the Allied forces. Pershing's intransigence was based on more than national pride. He was convinced that under standards set by him and tactics taught by his officers, an all-American army could be trained to fight more aggressively and suffer far fewer casualties than those of the British and French armies that had been worn down for three years in static trench warfare. Pershing, at least at the outset, was a proponent of "open warfare," a tactical shift whereby decisive victory would be won, he believed, "by driving the enemy out into the open and engaging in a war of movement."[33] His stubborn stance carried grave risks. As General James Harbord, commander of the 2nd Division at Belleau Wood and Soissons, wrote, Pershing would be "cursed to the latest generation" if his refusals to place his doughboys under European command caused the Allies to lose the war before the Americans were ready to fight under their own officers.[34]

Acutely aware of the risks, General Pershing was under enormous pressure. Marshall experienced firsthand the supreme commander's impatience with what he regarded as the slow progress of the 1st Division's training program. As operations officer and at times acting chief of staff of the 1st Division under General Sibert, Marshall's job was to set up sites for training, organize the construction of barracks and kitchens, and see that the raw, green soldiers of the division were trained, equipped, and made ready for battle against an enemy that had been fighting for three years. It was an incredibly demanding set of tasks. Adding to Pershing's impatience, Georges Clemenceau, who was about to become the French premier once again, was pressing the division to speed up its training.

One day in October, General Pershing and his staff, on short notice, arrived by train at the 1st Division's training area about thirty miles south of Saint-Mihiel to observe an exercise to be conducted by the 2nd Battalion of the 26th Infantry. With General Sibert delayed, Marshall met Pershing at the train. The general, already having second thoughts about Sibert's competence, was angered that he wasn't there. In a sour mood, Pershing and his entourage watched the exercise. As Marshall later recalled, "[t]here was a lot of shooting . . . a lot of dashing around . . . a lot of grenade throwing and general hullaballoo, and then it was all over."[35]

"Assemble the officers," barked Pershing. He turned to Sibert, who had just arrived, having not witnessed most of the exercise. "Conduct the critique," Pershing ordered. Sibert haltingly got off two or three sentences, but "it didn't go fast enough for General Pershing." Pershing rudely interrupted him and then, according to Marshall, "[h]e just gave everybody hell." In front of the assembled officers, he administered a severe dressing-down to Sibert. He went on to denigrate the readiness of the entire division, complaining that its officers had not followed instructions from headquarters, specifically and somewhat trivially focusing on how they were using "new names" for such things as "ammunition dumps."[36]

As Pershing turned to leave, Marshall reached out and grasped his arm. "General Pershing, there's something to be said here, and I think I should say it because I've been here longer."[37] Pershing, taken aback, paused. Marshall's anger was bubbling to the surface. As one of his aides remembered, when Marshall was angry, "his eyes flashed and he talked so rapidly and vehemently no one else could get in a word."[38] For the next few minutes, Marshall crisply ticked off several reasons why the division's training progress had been inhibited, aiming much of the blame at Pershing's own headquarters staff. With impertinence, Marshall looked directly at Pershing and said, "The only thing you've gotten out was to change the name of the dump . . . and now you are criticizing us for the names you changed." Pershing's chief of staff tried to brush him off, saying, "I'll look into it." Marshall shot back, "You don't have to look into it." Pointing to a packet of papers, he continued, "It's right here in the orders. It is a fact."

"I was just mad all over," recalled Marshall. He went on to drive home one final point. "We've worked very, very hard. The men have had no advantages and they don't expect any. But they ought to get a fair deal at any rate." To this, Pershing could only say, "Well, you must appreciate the troubles we have."

"Yes, again, General," Marshall responded, "but we have them every day and many a day and we have to solve every one of them by night." The encounter was over. Marshall's "bosom friends" believed his career "was finished," and he'd "be fired right off."[39]

To the contrary, Pershing—who was not offended by constructive criticism—was impressed. For Marshall's career this turned out to be a pivotal encounter. His courage in speaking truth to power caused Pershing to confer even more power and authority on him. The general began to seek Marshall's advice, pulling him aside to discuss privately matters of training, strategy, and troop morale. In early January 1918, Marshall was promoted to lieutenant colonel (temporary). Throughout winter and into spring, private sessions between the two became more frequent, their relationship deepening. Marshall had encountered no other superior officer with whom he "could be frank to the degree" he could with General Pershing.[40]

During that winter Marshall was taught an important lesson, one he vowed never to forget. When Pershing finally relieved General Sibert in December, Marshall was "outraged." Convinced that the decision was grossly unfair, he broadcast his views throughout the division, directing his vitriol not at Pershing but at the headquarters staff at Chaumont. Sibert's replacement was General Robert Lee Bullard, a slim, hard-driving, fifty-seven-year-old West Pointer from Alabama afflicted with bouts of disabling neuritis. He was well aware of Marshall's talents; indeed, he had planned to appoint Marshall chief of staff of the division. Yet when he learned of Marshall's angry and indiscreet criticisms, he changed his mind. In Marshall's words, Bullard wanted a more "moderate person" who didn't get "'het up' to the extent I did." Marshall remained chief operations officer, a position that rendered him ineligible for rapid promotion to brigadier general. Years later he said it was this experience that taught him to control his "temper through all the vicissitudes which I had to go through, political and otherwise." The lesson was no doubt delivered and understood, but there would be occasions throughout his career when Marshall simply could not control his anger.

* * * * *

German general Ludendorff's long-awaited spring offensive began at dawn on March 21, 1918. His objective was to split the British and French armies, roll up the British flank against the Channel, open the road to Paris, and "bring about an early decision."[41] In the first week, German armies crossed the River Somme, took 90,000 Allied soldiers prisoner, and pushed the front forty miles to the west, within striking distance of Paris. Four 120-foot-long Krupp guns on rails hurled more than 300 barrel-sized shells into the panicked city, killing 250 Parisians and wounding 650. Marshall worried that the attack might bring the war "to a sudden conclusion."[42] With disaster looming, the British finally gave in and agreed with the French to the principle of unified command—an historic decision not lost on Marshall, who would press for the same during the final days of 1941.

On March 26, Marshal Ferdinand Foch became "supreme commander" of the British and French armies on the Western Front, although his actual authority, never fully defined, was limited to that of a coordinator. In view of the crisis, Pershing decided to make a dramatic gesture. On impulse, he drove to a farmhouse near Clermont-sur-Oise that Foch was using as his headquarters. In halting French, Pershing offered to place his troops under Foch, saying, "All that we have is yours; use them as you wish."[43] Marshall later wrote that this was the moment when "General Pershing rose to greatness."[44] This is an overstatement. At the time, Pershing had just six divisions in France, one of which—the 1st Infantry Division—was trained and battleworthy. Moreover, he had no intention of allowing his troops to be amalgamated into those of the British and French. At most, Pershing agreed to allow Foch and his commanders to select the sector where the Americans would fight, but he insisted that his divisions would remain intact and that they would fight as part of an American army. Since the only division that could be committed reasonably soon was the 1st, Pershing's offer to Foch was a boost to the morale of his European allies, but a single American division could not turn the tide of the war.

As commander in chief of the entire French army, it was General Philippe Pétain's prerogative to select the sector of the front where the 1st Division would fight. Pétain, an erect, soldierly-looking man from Calais, sometimes called "the Lion of Verdun," had made a favorable impression on

Pershing when he first arrived in France. At the end of March, after Ludendorff's first great offensive had run its course, Pétain recommended and Pershing agreed that the 1st Division should be moved into the Montdidier sector, at the point of Ludendorff's farthest western advance. The Big Red One was to be the first American division blooded in the Great War.

On a chilly, overcast Tuesday morning, April 16, 1918, hundreds of officers of the 1st Infantry Division, as well as a group of French artillery officers, surrounded Lieutenant Colonel George Marshall in the grass courtyard behind a château in the town of Chaumont-en-Vexin. The château was the temporary headquarters of the division commander, General Bullard. Marshall, as chief of operations, was delivering preliminary remarks

about the forthcoming movement of the 1st Division to the front and into battle. Everyone was awaiting the arrival of General Pershing and his words "of confidence and encouragement."[45]

Pershing entered the courtyard. An officer bellowed "Attention," then "At ease." The commander of the AEF certainly looked the part. Pershing's stiff-backed posture was impeccable, his chiseled features and manicured mustache memorable. He stood five foot nine in polished knee-high leather boots. He was wearing a Sam Browne belt and an overseas cap, an alternative to the campaign hats worn since the Spanish-American War. Pershing was often called "Black Jack," a nickname from the days when he commanded the "buffalo soldiers"—the all-black 10th Cavalry Regiment.

Marshall had just finished explaining that the division was about to depart for the village of Cantigny in Picardy, the tip of a huge salient that represented the westernmost penetration by the Germans in their recent offensive. In private talks, Pershing and Marshall had discussed the Cantigny salient, concerned that the Germans would resume their attack in that sector "in order to administer a damaging blow to American morale."[46]

Pershing asked that the courtyard be cleared of all non–U.S. officers. Aware that this would be the first major engagement by an American army in the war and that a defeat or setback would deal a crippling blow to the spirits of the Allies and the people back home, Pershing chose his words carefully. "Centuries of military and civil history are now looking toward this first contingent of the American Army as it enters this great battle . . . Our people are hanging expectant upon your deeds . . . I assure you . . . of our strong beliefs in your success and of our confidence in our hearts that you are going to make a record of which your country will be proud."[47] With that, Pershing's brief but famous "Farewell to the First" speech came to an end.

At dawn the next morning the 28,000 men of the 1st Infantry Division began a three-day march toward the sound of the guns. Waiting in the hilltop farming village of Cantigny were three veteran German infantry regiments that had recently been deployed from the Eastern Front. They had established strong defensive positions along the west-facing edge of the village—barbed wire, freshly dug trench lines, armed bunkers, command posts in cellars, and sniper nests in buildings and trees. Water-cooled Maxim machine guns with overlapping fire were capable of blasting almost every inch of the downward-sloping wheat fields in the no-man's-land to the west.

Behind the German troops, strategically emplaced in wood lines, on hills, and in elevated towns, were upward of ninety batteries of German artillery—guns of all sizes—that could range in and accurately hurl explosives and mustard gas shells on targets close in and miles away.

Under constant artillery fire, the American doughboys of the 1st Division's 28th and 26th Infantry Regiments moved into shallow shell craters and ditches at night and relieved the French Moroccan troops who had been badly mauled while holding the line. "Trenches were shallow and scanty," wrote Major Theodore "Ted" Roosevelt Jr., son of the former president, "and dugouts were almost lacking."[48] Engineers were called in to work at night to dig and build the sector's trenches, parapets, dugouts, command posts, and communications systems. Casualties from artillery, machine guns, gas, and small unit raids mounted. Marshall and the other members of General Bullard's staff bunked down at division headquarters in Mesnil-Saint-Fermin, three and a half miles behind the front lines, in a brick wine cellar beneath a manor house. Most nights, however, Marshall could not be found in his bunk. Knowing that he would eventually be called upon to plan an attack on Cantigny, Marshall needed to explore the terrain of the prospective battlefield. Because of artillery fire it could not be done during the day. Therefore, it became Marshall's custom to depart headquarters at one o'clock in the morning, drive toward the front about a mile, and leave his automobile and driver "in the shelter of a shell hole."[49] Under random artillery fire, he would pick up a guide and walk to the front, where he would check and adjust troop dispositions. Between the faint gray of first light and sunrise, when he could make out the ground and its features, Marshall would venture far out beyond the front line into no-man's-land and map the terrain in his head. Discovery by enemy patrols was a constant danger. As the sun rose, he hustled back to the car, which by that time would be attracting the attention of the German gunners.

"Days passed," wrote Marshall, without an order for a "hostile advance." Then, "out of a clear sky came orders for us . . . to prepare an operation to capture the heights of Cantigny, without the assistance of any French divisions." It would be "a new and distinctly American operation," the first of the war.[50] And it would involve the most difficult of military challenges—a frontal assault against a heavily fortified position on the high ground. As chief operations officer, Marshall had to plan every detail of the attack. All eyes would be on Cantigny. American prestige and morale were on the line.

Far from the "open warfare" advocated by Pershing, the Cantigny operation had a "strictly limited objective"[51] and would be conducted on a relatively narrow front (roughly 2,200 yards), so narrow in fact that the main assault would be carried out by a single infantry regiment, in this case the 3,700 men of the 28th Regiment. The 28th, soon to be known as the "Lions of Cantigny" and then the "Black Lions," were commanded by Iowa-born Colonel Hanson Edward Ely, "a giant of a man," who distinguished himself at West Point not in the classroom (he was near the bottom of the class of 1891) but as a skilled boxer.[52] The mission: shrink the salient. The objective: capture Cantigny, move the American line about a mile east, and hold the high ground against German counterattacks.

To prepare his attack plan, Marshall needed specific information as to German dispositions in and around Cantigny. Accordingly, he made sure that patrols would be sent out each night to capture German prisoners and to identify locations of enemy machine guns, sniper posts, and other strongpoints. When the patrols returned, officers filled out reports, sometimes with map sketches, and forwarded them to Marshall's team of intelligence officers and planners. One intelligence officer, Lieutenant George Redwood, was famously adept at obtaining valuable information. Sam Ervin, a North Carolinian who served with Redwood and would become a U.S. senator, wrote that "fear was a word with which [Redwood] had no acquaintance." Over a span of "twelve successive nights," Redwood, a German-speaking Harvard graduate from Baltimore, blackened his face with burnt cork and ventured very near and sometimes into the town of Cantigny, often alone. He returned at daylight with sketches and map coordinates of machine gun and artillery emplacements. Occasionally, he came back with a bottle of wine.[53]

The assault on Cantigny was set to commence at dawn on Tuesday, May 28. As zero hour approached, the plan of attack, Field Order No. 18, took shape.[54] With the input of the division's artillery commander, General Charles Summerall, Marshall's blueprint laid out instructions that coordinated the placement, timing, and movements of "aerial observers, artillery, infantry, engineers, tanks, and flamethrowers."[55] According to plan, the

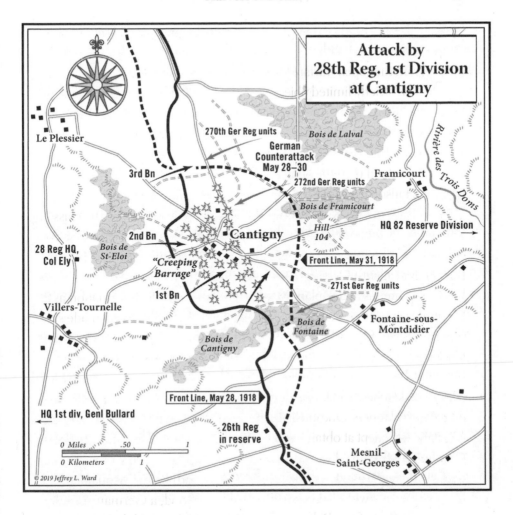

Attack by
28th Reg. 1st Division
at Cantigny

Le Plessier

270th Ger Reg units

Bois de Lalval

German
Counterattack
May 28–30

3rd Bn

272nd Ger Reg units

Framicourt

Rivière des Trois Doms

Bois de Framicourt

2nd Bn

•Cantigny

Hill
104

HQ 82 Reserve Division →

28 Reg HQ,
Col Ely

*Bois de
St-Eloi*

"Creeping
Barrage"

Front Line, May 31, 1918

1st Bn

271st Ger Reg units

Villers-Tournelle

*Bois de
Fontaine*

Fontaine-sous-
Montdidier

*Bois de
Cantigny*

Front Line, May 28, 1918

HQ 1st div, Genl Bullard ←

26th Reg
in reserve

Mesnil-
Saint-Georges

0 Miles   .50   1

0 Kilometers   1

© 2019 Jeffrey L. Ward

operation was to begin with a massive artillery bombardment of Cantigny and the surrounding area. At zero hour, the first stage of a "creeping barrage" would fall a few hundred yards out into no-man's-land and the 28th Regiment would emerge from its staging trenches and go over the top. The infantry, machine gun companies, flamethrowers, and twelve top-heavy French Schneider tanks would follow the creeping barrage, which would advance one hundred yards eastward every two minutes. When the troops reached the village of Cantigny the barrage would pause and then advance every four minutes until reaching the eastern end of the fields on the other side of the town. At that point, hopefully having attained their objective, the doughboys were to dig trenches, lay barbed wire, and set up machine gun emplacements. Their orders were to hold the ground against the certainty of repeated counterattacks by experienced German defenders.

Once Marshall's plan was approved by Colonel Ely and General Bullard, the 28th Regiment was pulled out of the front line on May 23 and trucked back twelve miles to rehearse. Doughboys in the 18th Regiment who relieved the 28th at the front were tasked with digging and preparing the assault trenches. Marshall split his time during the next four days, supervising aspects of the rehearsal at the rear, making sure the trenches were properly prepared at the front, and attending to the artillery, particularly coordinating the positioning of one hundred supplementary guns (thirty-seven batteries) of French Corps artillery. In the midst of this work, an ammunition dump containing small arms ammunition and water cans for the assault forces was blown up by a German shell, necessitating frantic efforts to resupply the dump before zero hour. On the morning of May 26, Marshall learned that Lieutenant Oliver "Judd" Kendall, an engineer officer, was missing and likely captured by the Germans the previous day while carrying heavy entrenching tools along the jumping-off trenches. His dispatch case contained a map "giving the location of all the trenches and dumps which had been prepared for the assault."[56] The risk to the entire operation was obvious, yet it was not called off. After the war, Kendall's body would be found in a shallow grave, his throat cut.

Late that afternoon Marshall suffered a painful ankle fracture when his horse stumbled and rolled twice on top of his right foot while it was caught in the stirrup. Characteristically, Marshall blamed himself for the mishap rather than the horse. A doctor taped up his ankle, and eventually it was wrapped in a plaster cast. With his foot propped on a chair, or him hopping on the other foot with the help of crutches, Marshall continued to work for the next week, "sixteen to eighteen hours a day," rarely sleeping for more than an hour or two and never taking his clothes off.[57]

Marshall received more news threatening the success of his plan on the morning of May 27. Word came from headquarters that General Ludendorff had launched the third of his spring offensives to end the war, this one a powerful attack aimed southward from the Chemin des Dames ridge toward the Marne River. Again, Paris was threatened. Within hours Marshall learned that the French would be withdrawing some of the artillery that would be supporting the Cantigny attack as early as noon the next day. "This was a heavy blow," wrote Marshall, "as we were to depend on these guns to suppress the enemy's artillery fire," particularly when the German infantry counterattacked.[58]

That evening, just hours before the attack, Marshall summoned reporters to 1st Division headquarters. The newsmen had been complaining about excessive secrecy, so Marshall decided to give them the details of his plan and full liberty to go where they pleased. James Hopper of *Collier's* magazine, who had won accolades for his reporting of the 1906 San Francisco earthquake, asked Marshall to explain what he meant by "full liberty." With a straight face, Marshall said his only rule was that Hopper "should not precede the first infantry into Cantigny."[59] Laughter filled the fetid air of the wine cellar.

Pitch-black darkness gave way to barely perceptible light on Tuesday morning, May 28, known to survivors as "Cantigny Day." Nerves and fear had kept the doughboys awake. Platoon leaders made sure their men were geared up in accordance with Marshall's detailed operations plan, ready to move forward to their starting positions. To say they were overburdened is an understatement. In addition to a rifle, Marshall's plan specified that a typical infantryman would carry 220 rounds of ammunition, two hand grenades, a rifle grenade, a Bengal flare, two steel canteens full of water, a bulky gas mask, and a backpack crammed with two days' rations, four sandbags, a shelter half, and a heavy pick or shovel that poked out of the top.[60]

His lower leg encased in a cast, Marshall hobbled out of Colonel Ely's bunker to observe the opening bombardment. He was about six hundred yards behind the front near Bois de St. Eloi, a small patch of woods. The morning was warm and clear. At 5:45 a.m., "the world turned to thunder," wrote a forward artillery observer."[61] Spread over three miles, almost four hundred American and French artillery batteries, belching yellow cordite smoke and flame, hurled thousands of shells toward their preregistered targets. The air vibrated. Within minutes, recalled Marshall, "Cantigny itself took on the appearance of an active volcano, with great clouds of smoke and dust and flying dirt and debris, which was blasted high in the air."[62] The shelling, designed to kill, maim, and demoralize the German defenders and to suppress their artillery, went on for an hour. The pilot of a single German plane, flying high above the American front, sent wireless messages warning of a massive attack, but received no responses.

At 6:40 a.m., the bombardment ceased. General Summerall's smaller guns, the 75mm howitzers, began laying down the creeping barrage. Five minutes later, responding to the whistles and shouts of their platoon leaders, the first of three waves of khaki-clad American doughboys mounted ladders and steps dug into the sides of their jumping-off trenches and went over the top. They were following a script largely written by Lieutenant Colonel George Marshall. America's first full-scale assault in the Great War had begun.

Between the line of untested troops and the wall of the protective barrage lay fields gently ascending to the village and beyond. Hopper, the *Collier's* correspondent, described it as a "beautiful plateau … a clean and virgin No Man's Land untainted yet of the terrible stench of mortal man, carpeted with flowers, with grass, with wheat, with red poppies, yellow buttercups, and purple thistles—the ideal battlefield of an ideal battle."[63] Few if any of the doughboys who survived the three-day battle of Cantigny would describe it as "ideal." However, with the help of the clumsy French tanks that drove German machine gunners under cover and the flamethrowers that cleared the cellars and bunkers, the village itself was in American hands within the first hour. Marshall was relieved. "The success of this [first] phase of the operation was so complete and the list of casualties so small that everyone was enthusiastic and delighted."[64]

The enthusiasm was short-lived. While the first phase was still in progress, French high commanders, responding to attacks on Château-Thierry, less than sixty miles from Paris, ordered the withdrawal of even more batteries of their artillery. Marshall discovered that "at least one French regiment [of artillery] had started its withdrawal without firing a shot." Without those heavy French guns to degrade German counterattacks, the ability of the Americans to hold their ground in and around Cantigny was in grave doubt. "Troubles" were surely coming, predicted Marshall.[65]

Around noon, as American soldiers in the fields east of Cantigny were furiously digging in, the troubles began. From Colonel Ely's command post Marshall noted in his battle report that "very heavy enemy shelling began on our new first line, together with terrific machine-gun fire."[66] Deprived of adequate suppressing fire by their own artillery, the doughboys were subjected to "continuous bombardment by 210-mm. guns." According to

Marshall, "[a] 3-inch shell will temporarily scare or deter a man; a 6-inch shell will shock him; but an 8-inch shell, such as these 210-mm. ones, rips up the nervous system of everyone within a hundred yards of the explosion."[67] Shells large and small were levying a heavy toll, yet with communication wires severed by the bombardment and runners unable to operate in daylight, it was difficult to assess the extent of casualties.

As expected, the Germans struck back in the late afternoon, launching their heaviest and most determined of several counterattacks. Despite standing orders from headquarters to hold their positions, scattered reports came in to Ely's command post indicating that two battalions of the 28th Regiment were falling back. Given the violent bombardment and reports of "extremely heavy losses in officers and men," Marshall believed that "resistance against a strong counterattack was practically impossible."[68] In fact, at a little before six p.m., an "order to withdraw"—likely invented—was being passed man to man throughout the ranks of Ely's entire 3rd Battalion. As German shells plowed into the doughboys' positions, it wasn't long before they started to pull back in groups. Some panicked and began to run. Lieutenant George Redwood, the intelligence officer so skilled at infiltrating German lines, was at an aid station being treated for a shoulder wound when he heard a pause in the bombardment and could tell that the Boche were counterattacking. He hastened to the front lines and began urging the fleeing men to turn back. While Redwood led "a retreating company (Comp. K) up to their line of resistance . . . a high-explosive shell burst near him killing him instantly," remembered one sergeant.[69] For his gallantry, Redwood was posthumously awarded a Silver Star and a second Distinguished Service Cross.

The Americans streamed back to their previous lines outside the village, where they halted and regrouped. To the northeast a platoon leader observed a mass of field-gray German infantry, the first wave of another counterattack, as it began to emerge from a forest and out onto the open plateau. His signal flare arched skyward. Summerall's artillery responded with a devastating barrage that pulverized the second and third waves in the woods. Those in the first wave who managed to get inside the barrage were cut down by small-arms fire. Similarly, an observer in Major Ted Roosevelt Jr.'s battalion of the 26th Infantry Regiment that was protecting the southern flank on the road to Fontaine spotted yet another counterattack and called in artillery. By dusk the German counterattacks, at least three that day, came to a standstill. The doughboys of the 28th Infantry Regiment of the 1st Division had lost two or three hundred yards of ground, but they had a firm grip on Cantigny.

For the next two days the German heavy artillery continued to hurl explosive shells of all sizes, interspersed with volleys of gas canisters, and its infantry continued to mount counterattacks against the exhausted doughboys dug in east of the village. The concentrated bombardment "exceeded any experience [the men] were to have later on in the great battles of the war," wrote Marshall.[70]

The men of the 28th were battered and wearing thin. From the first evening of battle Colonel Ely had repeatedly urged General Bullard to order a reserve regiment to relieve his depleted unit. Under pressure from Pershing to keep reserves fresh in case they were needed at Château-Thierry, Bullard refused Ely's requests. Ely was beside himself with rage. On the second evening of battle, after fighting off two more German counterattacks, he phoned a message to Bullard: "Front line pounded to Hell and gone, and entire front line must be relieved tomorrow."[71] Near midnight Ely sent his intelligence officer, Lieutenant Joseph Torrence, back to division headquarters to make a personal plea for relief. The officer descended the stairs into the old wine cellar and found Marshall and a gang of orderlies answering phones. Marshall summoned Bullard, who arrived and ordered a hot breakfast for Torrence. The lieutenant delivered an impassioned pitch for immediate relief. He needn't have wasted his breath. By that time, as Marshall knew, Bullard had already authorized the 16th Infantry Regiment to move into Cantigny and relieve the 28th.

On the morning of the third day, the Germans counterattacked again, and again they were repelled by the American doughboys, whose lines had been strengthened by units of the 16th and 18th regiments. It was the enemy's "final determined effort to take the town."[72] The Germans were spent. For the first time in several days, the guns were quiet.

"We held Cantigny," Marshall exulted. "The Germans never afterwards reoccupied the village."[73]

In their failed effort to hold on to the Cantigny salient, the Germans sustained approximately 1,700 casualties, a minuscule number in comparison to losses in the great battles of the war. They could have moved reserves forward and mounted more counterattacks. However, in light of the need for manpower to support their more important offensive in the south aimed at Château-Thierry and the Marne, the German high command elected not to throw additional forces against the Americans at Cantigny.

For the AEF, the cost of capturing and holding Cantigny was a little more than 300 men killed and about 1,300 wounded, a casualty total slightly less than that incurred by the enemy. In Marshall's judgment the losses suffered "were not justified by the importance of the position itself, but were many times justified" by the positive effect on the "morale of the English and French Armies."[74] General Pershing agreed, calling it an "electrical effect," demonstrating to his Allies "the fighting qualities [of the AEF] under extreme battle conditions."[75] If the 1st Division had failed to take and hold Cantigny, an intelligence officer observed, "the French would certainly not have entrusted a portion of the defense of the Marne to two other American divisions a week later."[76]

Marshall's biographers barely mention his critically important role at Cantigny, nor the significance of the battle in the context of the Great War. It seems obvious, however, from Marshall's ten-page account of the Cantigny operation—in particular, the emotive language he used in describing the "ordeal of personal combat" he and his fellow soldiers experienced—that he regarded the battle as a defining moment in his life as a soldier. Over a fifty-year career spanning three shooting wars, it was only at Cantigny that Marshall was actually in combat—under hostile artillery and small-arms fire for hours and operating behind enemy lines at night. All around him he saw soldiers maimed and killed. He did not carry a rifle. He did not lead troops in battle. But it was during this ordeal that Marshall for the first time became convinced that he had the nerves, stamina, and temperament to make command decisions under the most difficult battlefield conditions. Having been at the elbows of the division and regiment commanders throughout the battle, he must have participated in virtually all of the key command decisions. If General Bullard and Colonel Ely could do it, he believed he could do it too—only better.

But it was not to be. A little more than three weeks later, Marshall penned a letter requesting that he be given a troop command, preferably a regiment. Cantigny had fired his ambition to lead men on the front lines, under fire, directly engaging the enemy. He sent his letter up the AEF chain of command through General Bullard, who passed it along without specifically approving it. In fact, he doomed Marshall's chances by pointing to his "special fitness" for staff work and suggesting he be given "wider" responsibilities as an operations planner on Pershing's staff. Bullard sealed Marshall's fate—and perhaps unwittingly saved his life—when he wrote that he doubted anyone else in the army possessed "equal" talent.[77]

Ironically, Marshall's request to lead in battle got him booted to the army stratosphere, far from the front. On July 12, he received orders to depart the 1st Division and report to the Operations Section at Pershing's headquarters in Chaumont, where his boss would be Colonel Fox Conner, AEF's legendary chief of operations. Marshall was "disappointed and bitter." Men older than he who had not been "jerked off to Europe" so early had been temporarily promoted and put in charge of divisions. The "final blow" came when Pershing's chief of staff ordered that Marshall could not be "detailed away" for troop command. "They had me pinched," said Marshall.[78]

For the remainder of his army career, Marshall would serve at the highest levels of war strategy and planning, all the while harboring an ambition to lead troops in battle. Cantigny was the source of this internal struggle.

The day after he received his order, Marshall reluctantly bade farewell to his comrades in the 1st Division, "the men with whom I had been so intimately associated for over a year in France." He was deeply moved. Marshall treasured the relationships he was leaving behind. "It was hard to preserve one's composure," he wrote. "I can see them now—gathered in the broad doorway of the château. The friendly jests and affectionate farewells . . ." He foresaw with some sadness the direction his life was taking, away from the comradeship among fighting men, and into the isolation that inevitably accompanies power. Several days later almost every officer who stood in that doorway was dead or grievously wounded in the Soissons counteroffensive.[79] If Marshall had had his way, he would likely have been among the fallen.

CHAPTER 2

Rumours of Peace

I t was "the hardest nut" he had to "crack in France," wrote Marshall—and his "best contribution to the war."[1] He was referring to an assignment he received from General Hugh Drum, Pershing's chief of staff, a task with no precedent in the history of warfare that would be regarded as next to impossible to achieve by even the most experienced and brilliant of battle planners.

Marshall had spent most of August 1918 planning the first major American offensive of the war, an attack by sixteen divisions of the newly organized First Army to eliminate the so-called Saint-Mihiel salient south of Verdun—a 200-square-mile bulge in the front that the Germans had held since 1914. Once the salient was eliminated, the plan called for the Americans to drive the Hun back toward the German border to the strategic city of Metz.

On September 8 or the morning of the 9th (Marshall couldn't remember which), General Drum summoned Marshall to his office at Ligny-en-Barrois, a small town about twenty-five miles west of Saint-Mihiel. There has been a change of plans, he explained. The First Army was to launch *two* attacks instead of one. The Saint-Mihiel operation would jump off as scheduled on September 12, but only seven of the sixteen divisions would make the initial attack and the objective would be limited to pinching the salient off from the main German line. There would be no drive to Metz. As soon as the bulge was substantially reduced, those troops not needed to hold the line at Saint-Mihiel would pull out and link up with the rest of the First Army that was in the Saint-Mihiel area. That army would then move sixty miles northwest and mount its second attack—the much larger Meuse-Argonne offensive—on the morning of September 26. This huge American operation, supported by the French Fourth Army converging from the west, would be coordinated with powerful attacks farther north by British, Belgian, and French armies, part of Marshal Foch's "continuous offensive" strategic plan that was designed to win the war by preventing the Germans from having any time to rest and regroup. Marshall's orders from Drum were to plan, organize, and implement the movement of approximately 600,000 men; 2,700 guns; 93,000 horses; and 900,000 tons of supplies and ammunition in slightly less than two weeks. To avoid detection by the Germans the sixty-mile move by foot, horse, truck, and light rail would have to take place *only at night*.

Marshall regarded his assignment as an "appalling proposition."[2] Many of the artillery batteries and some of the troops in the Saint-Mihiel assault would have to withdraw as early as the evening of the first day of the attack in order to reach the staging areas for the Meuse-Argonne offensive by the night of September 25. Yet it was expected that it would take a minimum of two days to reduce the Saint-Mihiel salient. Also, how could the movement of an army of more than half a million men avoid detection by the enemy?

Marshall had less than twenty-four hours to come up with a plan. He decided to sneak away from the interruptions at First Army headquarters and take a walk along the Marne-Rhine canal that ran through Ligny-en-Barrois. He recalled the next hour as "the most trying mental ordeal experienced by me during the war." He managed to compose his mind by sitting in silence beside "one of the typical old French fishermen who forever line the banks of canals and apparently never get a bite." Still without a solution, he returned to his office, spread a map out on a table, and reviewed the list of divisions to be assigned to the offensive. Inventing an adage, "the only way to begin is to commence," he began dictating. Inside of an hour he had drafted a preliminary plan for the movement of First Army divisions, guns, and equipment to the Meuse-Argonne assembly points while at the same time providing for the defense of the ground gained at Saint-Mihiel. With trepidation, he sent his plan to General Drum that evening. The next morning Drum summoned Marshall to his office. "That order for the Meuse-Argonne concentration you sent over last night is a dandy," said Drum. "The General [Pershing] thought it was a fine piece of work."[3]

* * * * *

Knowing he needed to be rested and sharp, Marshall tried to sleep through the four-hour artillery bombardment at Saint-Mihiel that began around 1 a.m. on the morning of September 12. At 5:30 a.m., the assault troops of the First Army, preceded by a rolling barrage, converged on and broke through the barbed wire entanglements on the west and south faces of the salient. After the morning fog cleared, Marshall was at First Army headquarters as reports from the pilots of observation planes streamed in, indicating that the initial stages of the attack were successful. The French had placed more than a thousand of their aircraft, the largest concentration of airpower at that point in the war, under the command of Colonel Billy Mitchell. In the afternoon it became apparent that the Germans were putting up only halfhearted resistance, trying to cover a tactical withdrawal due to insufficient manpower. Thus, by the end of the second day the First Army had reduced the salient. Six of the divisions held in reserve were never deployed.

By the war's standards, U.S. casualties were light, only about 7,000 killed or wounded. Except for an imperious general by the name of Douglas MacArthur, all of the American field officers who fought at Saint-Mihiel were delighted. Not content with having reduced the salient, MacArthur argued eloquently for a continuation of the attack, his eye on the heavily fortified city of Metz only ten miles to the northeast. Yet his entreaties to take the key city were turned down by the "highest authority," much to his disgust.[4] MacArthur probably didn't know it, but it was Marshall who wrote General Pershing "vigorously opposing" pleas, such as those by MacArthur, to resume the offensive.[5] The U.S. Army's part in Marshal Foch's "continuous offensive" strategy could not be changed, even though Marshall probably agreed with MacArthur that Metz could have been taken. The troops at Saint-Mihiel had to be pulled out and shifted northwest in time to participate in the far more important Meuse-Argonne offensive.

MacArthur had met George Marshall at Fort Leavenworth in 1909–1910 when he was commanding a company on the post and Marshall was a gifted instructor in the Army Staff College, having graduated first in his class at Leavenworth's Infantry and Cavalry School. MacArthur's biographer, William Manchester, without citing his source, wrote that "even then" the two "rubbed each other the wrong way."[6] Assuming there is some truth to Manchester's assertion, there is no evidence that MacArthur blamed Marshall for the Metz rebuff, which MacArthur regarded as one of the great mistakes of the war.

Once Marshall was confident that the First Army's divisions at Saint-Mihiel were achieving their objectives as planned, he turned his attention to the movement of troops and equipment to the Meuse-Argonne, the largest and most complex logistical operation of the war. The artillery, especially the heavy artillery, took the most time to move and had to be in place by the time the infantry arrived. Therefore, Marshall began ordering the withdrawal of batteries from the Saint-Mihiel area as early as the night of September 12. Next, he coordinated the movement of some nine divisions in the vicinity of Saint-Mihiel and elsewhere in eastern France. The last to move out were units of the seven divisions that had fought or were fighting at the Saint-Mihiel salient. These troops, having been bloodied in battle, would not arrive in time to participate in the initial assault waves of the Meuse-Argonne offensive. Instead, U.S. infantry divisions with little or no combat experience would lead the attack on September 26.

There were only three narrow dirt roads from the Saint-Mihiel region to the launch of the Meuse-Argonne offensive. Over these often muddy paths, columns of troop-carrying trucks, chain-driven ammunition trains, horses and wagons hauling gun carriages and supplies, and miles of foot-slogging infantry, all moving at different speeds and only at night, had to cross through lines of hundreds of thousands of French troops moving up from the Belfort region (near the Vosges mountains) to support the American offensive west of the Argonne Forest. Colonel George Crile, an Ohio-born surgeon in the AEF medical corps, painted the scene with vivid word strokes in his diary. "[A]t night all is activity. Prowling—skulking—preparing—stalking—500,000 armed human beings—with acres of guns—and paraphernalia covering the earth—a blanket of destruction 10 miles deep—30 miles long gliding by inches—skulking by inches. Upwards of hundreds of thousands of fellow human beings, dragging—tugging this vast carpet of destruction toward the enemy; thrusting its sharp explosive edge into the enemy." Crile would later cofound the Cleveland Clinic, known throughout the world as a premier research and medical institution dedicated to saving the lives of millions. Yet on that September night in 1918, the famous surgeon, in his own words, celebrated the "marvelousness of this sheet of death which moves only at night." Suffused with bloodlust, he admitted not only that "Hun hunting is a wonderful sport," but also that "man hunting" itself "throws a dullness on all other sports."[7]

For the reserve divisions south of the Saint-Mihiel salient, the first challenge was to march west under constant bomb attacks from the air and cross the river Meuse. Describing the night crossing by a field artillery regiment,

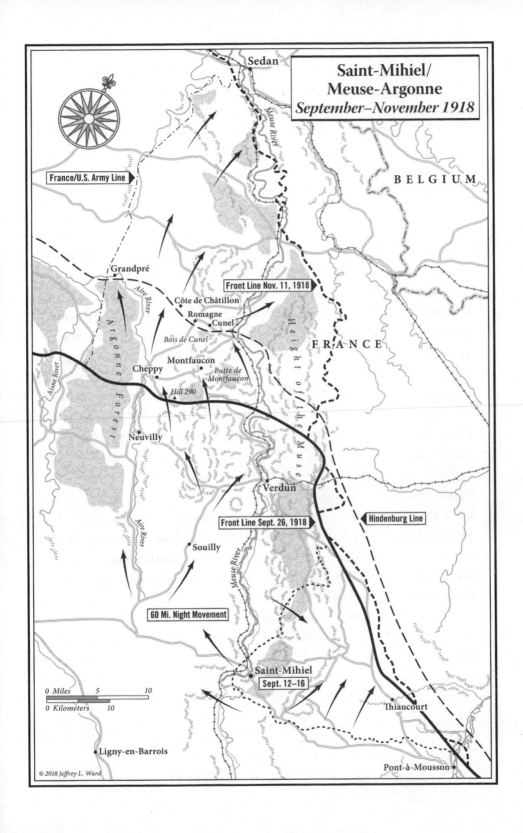

Saint-Mihiel/
Meuse-Argonne
September–November 1918

BELGIUM

FRANCE

Sedan

Meuse River

France/U.S. Army Line

Grandpré

Aire River

Aisne River

Front Line Nov. 11, 1918

Côte de Châtillon

Romagne

Cunel

Bois de Cunel

Montfaucon

Cheppy

Butte de Montfaucon

Hill 290

Argonne Forest

Height of the Meuse

Neuvilly

Aire River

Verdun

Front Line Sept. 26, 1918

Hindenburg Line

Souilly

Meuse River

60 Mi. Night Movement

Saint-Mihiel
Sept. 12–16

Thiaucourt

0 Miles 5 10
0 Kilometers 10

Ligny-en-Barrois

Pont-à-Mousson

© 2018 Jeffrey L. Ward

Captain Bob Casey wrote that his lead horse got tangled up in a spiked anti-cavalry trap (*cheval de frisse*). That incident "started a riot" and the "milling of the horses threatened to blockade the bridge." An artillery piece that had to be shoved aside in order for the regiment to pass over the bridge was lifted by manpower back onto the road so that the "panic stricken nags could be hitched to it again."[8] This was but one of hundreds of accidents and holdups that took place along the choked roads and bridges.

Venturing out at night, Marshall witnessed firsthand the traffic jams and collisions, as well as the heated arguments and fights between officers and military police. Some of the most difficult traffic snarls were caused by the fact that American divisions had to pass through columns of French troops and equipment moving across to the west to join the French Fourth Army. At the same time they were forced to share the few roads with some 220,000 other French soldiers who were being withdrawn from the Meuse-Argonne front (to be replaced by the Americans who would mount the assault). The problems were exacerbated by the language barrier and made even worse because most of the truck and ammunition train drivers were French colonials (many Vietnamese). Marshall quickly realized that he needed to establish a working relationship with French authorities. Fortunately, a meeting was arranged in Ligny between now colonel Marshall (his promotion to full colonel finally came through) and Major Joseph Doumenc, chief of the French Automobile Service, who controlled both the road system leading to the front and the drivers. "With remarkable little difficulty and . . . a minimum of friction," Marshall wrote, he and Doumenc worked out procedures to govern the remainder of the troop movements. "It was my fixed policy," said Marshall, "to make every minor concession" so that he could prevail on the more important matters.[9]

Within the river of men slogging north was a future president of the United States, thirty-four-year-old Captain Harry Truman. He was in command of the "Wild Irish" Battery D of the 129th Field Artillery, which was to support the 35th ("Santa Fe") Division in the upcoming battle. His job was to make sure that his column of 193 soldiers, one Catholic priest, Father L. Curtis Tiernan, and twelve carriages consisting of "four guns, six caissons and two fourgon wagons" made it to Hill 290 on the edge of the Argonne Forest by September 25.[10] Of the weeklong march under Truman's command, one soldier remembered that "the weather was bad, rainy, and we would sleep in the daytime in thickets or in woods and then take off at dusk and march all night." Truman and Father Tiernan, one of his closest pals, who had a knack for scavenging a bottle of whiskey now and then, often walked at the head of the battery chatting about "the history of the world and I don't know what all." Truman reportedly told Tiernan that if all priests were like him, "there wouldn't be any Protestants."[11]

One night Marshall was forced by an aching tooth to spend a half hour with an army dentist in Ligny. While brandishing his drill over Marshall, the dentist sought to engage him in conversation about rumors concerning a huge new offensive. Given his vulnerable position Marshall offered pleasant responses without revealing anything of consequence. At a moment when the drill was in Marshall's mouth, a "German aviator dropped a bomb" into an adjacent courtyard, wrote Marshall. "[T]he explosion almost resulted in the loss of my tongue, as the dentist was a trifle gun shy and I was none too calm."[12] This was one of only two occasions when Marshall came close to being a casualty of the Meuse-Argonne offensive.

In the midst of the movement, First Army headquarters was shifted north to the town hall of Souilly, the building General Pétain had used as his headquarters during the battle of Verdun in 1916. (The road outside came to be called the Voie Sacrée, or Sacred Way, because of the critical role it played as a supply route during the Verdun battle.) From a second-floor office, the same one used by Pétain, Marshall spent his days and nights issuing orders in person and by telephone to officers posted on the roads and at railheads and supply depots. Chain-smoking his way through packs of Chesterfields, he tried to keep straight in his sleepless head the names of dozens of villages and the routes of more than thirty light- and standard-gauge railroads being built by First Army engineers.

There was one important area in which Marshall's logistical foresight fell short—horses. The First Army's movement was heavily dependent on horsepower, yet the animals were starving, "dying so fast" that officers faced "difficulty keeping all the vehicles on the move," wrote Major Roy Myers of the 114th Field Artillery Regiment. With their relatively slow digestive systems, horses need from sixteen to twenty hours to obtain nourishment from the hay and oats they consume, but no one in Marshall's organization made arrangements for the storage of food at the camps where the animals would stop after a full night's march. "The loss of horses by starvation was one of the most deplorable features" of the movement to the Meuse-Argonne offensive, complained Myers.[13] Given the tight schedule, it was said that the American veterinarians' only medicine for the famished animals was the revolver. Myers lost almost half of his horses on the march and the rest were so weakened that they couldn't pull the caissons.

Though the men who endured rain, mud, delays, and infuriating lapses in coordination during the northward slog from Saint-Mihiel might have disagreed, the implementation of Marshall's plan, many aspects of which were revised and improvised on the spot, was regarded as a stunning success. By early morning of September 25, all of the artillery batteries and infantry assault units were in place, ready to fire and fight. Dozens of evacuation hospitals, field kitchens, oil and gas storage tanks, supply centers, and ordnance depots had been established and provisioned behind the lines. Awestruck officers began referring to Marshall as a "wizard." The Marshall legend, born in the Philippines, was burnished. It spread throughout the AEF and beyond. Charles Repington, an astute military correspondent for the *Times* of London, not one to heap praise on the Yanks, wrote, "It was a fine piece of Staff work and no other Staff could have done it better."[14]

*   *   *   *   *

The Meuse-Argonne offensive was designed to strike at a key point that would result in the destruction of the entire German supply system on the Western Front and thus end the war. The vital point—the strategic hinge— was a railroad net in and near the city of Sedan on the Meuse River that connected the two main rail routes essential to Germany's ability to supply its armies. Of all the Allied forces along the Western Front in September 1918, General Pershing's First Army was closest to Sedan. Therefore, it was given the job of "cracking" the hinge by advancing thirty miles north to the outskirts of Sedan through a narrow defile walled off by the German-held heights of the Meuse on the right and the dense Argonne Forest on the left. As General Drum, Marshall's boss, explained in a lecture shortly after the war, "[t]he German could not lose on this front [Meuse-Argonne] or his whole army would be ruined." According to Drum, the proposed offensive would force the Boche to rush their best troops to defend the Meuse-Argonne defile. The Americans would be in for a ferocious battle. However, the strategy would have the benefit of relieving pressure on the British,

Belgians, and French who would be attacking elsewhere and pushing the Germans back at the same time.

"The terrain features," lectured Drum, "were the most difficult of any on the Western Front." In addition to the walls on the right and left of the twenty-two-mile-wide defile, there were three "interior barriers that blocked passage," including the Butte de Montfaucon in the center, the highest point on the battlefield, "the most ideal defensive terrain I have ever seen or read about."[15] Farther north lay the Hindenburg Line (Germans called it the Krunhilde Stalling), a defensive redoubt consisting of a honeycomb of entrenchments, mazes of concrete pillboxes and machine-gun nests, and miles of barbed wire entanglements. Marshall did not have an opportunity to study the order of battle until the night before the attack. The plan called for nine American infantry divisions to make the initial assault (225,000 soldiers), backed by six U.S. divisions and one French cavalry division held in reserve. Most of the troops were green and inexperienced. Only three of the assault divisions had been in serious combat (but not a major attack), and two of them were worn out and needed to be replaced. Elements of a fourth had fought alongside the British. Of the remaining five divisions, three had served at a quiet training sector of the front and two had never been present at any front. The most experienced divisions in Pershing's First Army, those that had been under fire at Saint-Mihiel, would not be ready to resume fighting for another four or five days.

On September 26 at 2:30 a.m., 2,775 U.S. and French echeloned artillery pieces announced the onset of the Meuse-Argonne offensive with a shattering roar. The rain had given way to a clear moonlit night. Flying in a Spad XIII fighter, Captain Eddie Rickenbacker of the 94th Aero Squadron, who would shoot down twenty-six German planes during the course of the war, observed that the battlefield below looked like a "giant switchboard which emitted thousands of electric flashes as invisible hands manipulated the plugs."[16] On Hill 290, about half a mile from a partially ruined stone church that would be used as a field hospital, Harry Truman's Battery D was responsible for preparing the way for the 35th Division, rated as one of the weakest and least experienced of the frontline divisions. For three hours Battery D fired at the rate of one thousand rounds per hour from its four 75mm guns. "My guns were so hot," recalled Truman, "that they would boil wet gunnysacks we put on them to keep them cool." In a dense fog the troops of the 35th division, along with the eight other assault divisions, jumped off as scheduled at 5:30 a.m. into the heavily defended Meuse-Argonne defile, marching at quick step behind Truman's rolling barrage.[17]

From a woods outside the town of Neuvilly a half mile east of Truman's Battery D, two companies of Colonel George Patton's 1st Tank Brigade roared forward to lead elements of the 35th Division up through the valley of the Aire River east of the Argonne. Marshall had met the brash tank commander a year before when they paraded together on horseback down the Champs-Élysées on Bastille Day, sporting shiny new Sam Browne belts. Now Patton watched as his French Renault and Schneider tanks crept out with the infantry. As commander of the brigade he stayed behind, huddled in his command dugout, yet missing the action was not in his nature. By 6:30 a.m., he could sit still no longer. Patton gathered his staff and raced on foot through the smoke and lifting fog to a crossroads south of the village of Cheppy, where he finally came upon several of his tanks bogged down in a German trench system. Heavy French Schneider tanks soon found themselves in the same predicament. Patton could see that a massive traffic jam was developing. German artillery and machine guns began registering and zeroing in.

Almost twenty miles to the right, near the Meuse River, twenty-seven-year-old Captain Louis Johnson, a lawyer-politician who had just resigned as majority leader of the West Virginia House of Delegates, observed the opening bombardment from an intermediate ordnance dump on the "Sivry-La Peche-Bethelainville Road, under the dubious protection of some old and tattered French camouflage."[18] Johnson was responsible for supplying ammunition to the troops and artillery batteries of the 80th ("Blue Ridge") division, another one of the six untested assault divisions. To Marshall's regret, his career and that of Johnson's would intersect again in 1938, when Johnson, as President Franklin Roosevelt's assistant secretary of war, endangered the chances that Marshall would be appointed chief of staff by conducting an unwelcome lobbying campaign on his behalf.

At headquarters on the morning of September 26, Marshall was well aware that the success of the initial stages of the assault depended on surprise and speed. He knew via U.S. intelligence that only five or possibly six German divisions were defending the Meuse-Argonne defile because the Boche were under the mistaken impression that most of the U.S. First Army divisions were still in the Saint-Mihiel area, preparing to advance on Metz (as MacArthur had pressed for in vain). Marshall was also aware that once the First Army launched its attack the Germans could easily move four new divisions to the front within a day, another two on the second day, and nine more by the third—a total of twenty divisions. Pershing's plan, therefore, depended upon a drive during the first day—or two days at the very most—all the way to the Hindenburg Line killing grounds, an advance of almost ten miles. The goal was beyond ambitious. It was a gamble.

In the opening few hours the nine American assault divisions, protected by dense fog and smoke, met only light resistance. Yet the low visibility caused units to become separated, and the smoke was mistaken for gas attacks, which added to the confusion and delay. When the sun finally broke through, dug-in German machine-gun emplacements and snipers began to inflict heavy casualties, especially among the most inexperienced divisions.

One of the early wounded was George Patton. Around noon, his tanks were still mired in a German trench line under withering fire. Patton got mad and "decided to do business."[19] He jumped into the trenches, hit one of his men with a shovel, and made the soldiers dig a passage out. Five tanks got across the trench line. Cussing and yelling, "Let's go get them," Patton rallied about 150 panicked infantrymen in the 138th Regiment of the 35th Division and led them forward up a hill.[20] As they neared the crest where all would be exposed to heavy machine-gun fire, the doughboys hit the ground and took cover on the reverse slope. Patton looked back and shouted, "Who comes with me?"[21] Only six rose up. Three started to follow. One of them went down. At the crest it was just Patton and Private Joseph Angelo, his orderly. They were completely exposed. Patton was armed only with a holstered pistol and a walking stick. He later recalled that he felt terrified, "trembling with fear when suddenly I thought of my progenitors and seemed to see them in a cloud over the German lines looking at me. I became calm at once and saying out loud 'It is time for another Patton to die.'"[22] Seconds later a bullet struck Patton in the left thigh. The slug, he wrote to his wife, "came out just at the crack of my bottom about two inches to the left of my rectum [leaving] a hole about the size of a dollar."[23]

By the end of the day, the First Army had advanced some five miles, far short of Pershing's objective. The Germans, realizing that the attack in the Meuse-Argonne was a major American offensive, moved four divisions into the valley. On the second day, the green 79th Division finally captured a major strategic objective in the center, the 1,200-foot Butte de Montfaucon, but still the Americans were well south of the Hindenburg Line. During the next two days additional German reserves that were rushed to the front managed to slow down and then completely halt American momentum.

Pershing had lost his gamble. Word spread that the American offensive was on the verge of failure. On the afternoon of September 30, Marshall was ordered to arrange for the forward movement of the Big Red One, his old division that had taken Cantigny, from its reserve position and relieve the fatigued 35th Division (Marshall said it suffered "more of a nervous exhaustion than physical").[24] Shortly thereafter he was asked to shift two more veteran divisions up to the front to relieve two of the other most inexperienced divisions (the 37th and 79th). Gradually and grudgingly, the Germans gave ground. Overall, Marshall fed more than a million troops into the Meuse-Argonne meat grinder.

*   *   *   *   *

While German troops managed to slow down the Americans in the Meuse-Argonne, their two principal leaders, steady but aging Field Marshal Paul von Hindenburg and brilliant General Erich Ludendorff, foresaw the makings of a catastrophe for Germany. In coordination with Pershing's First Army, seven other British, French, and Belgian armies were simultaneously attacking German forces along the Western Front. The Germans were outnumbered, exhausted, and running out of manpower. Fresh American troops were arriving in France at the rate of 200,000 per month. Germany's allies were collapsing. In early October, Hindenburg and Ludendorff began to press Germany's political leaders to seek peace negotiations before their armies were defeated, which they believed was inevitable. At the same time, they sought to distance themselves from any responsibility, as evidenced by Ludendorff's October 1 message to staff officers: "I have asked his Majesty [Kaiser Wilhelm] now to incorporate those in government whom we have to thank for our situation. We will now see these gentlemen entering office. They must conclude the necessary peace. They have to swallow the soup they have cooked up for us."[25] According to Ludendorff and the German high command, left-wing socialists were the culprits who "cooked up" the "soup" that the proud and undefeated German army found itself in. Within a few short years Adolf Hitler and his Nazi Party would adopt and build on this narrative, adding Jews, Bolsheviks, Slavs, and other groups to the socialists who supposedly stabbed German Aryans in the back.

Ludendorff and Hindenburg persuaded the kaiser to face up to eventual defeat and reorganize the government so that the European Allies and the United States would be more amenable to a peace settlement. It was agreed that the two military leaders would be made completely subservient to civilian control and that the cabinet would include socialists. A new chancellor, Prince Maximillian von Baden ("Prince Max"), a democrat and reformer by instinct and reputation, was appointed. On October 5, President Wilson, who thus far had delegated the conduct of the war to his war secretary and others in his cabinet, received a message from Prince Max proposing an immediate armistice and peace negotiations along the lines of Wilson's "Fourteen Points" speech in January, an idealistic but vague outline of how to end the war and assure a durable peace. Wilson was tempted to engage in negotiations, but hesitated. He knew that the British and French, who had borne the brunt of the fighting, would object if he offered any concessions to the Germans. And he was mindful that public opinion would view the German proposals as a clever ploy to extricate themselves from a murderous war that they started—and were on the verge of losing—by appealing to the liberal proclivities of the American president (some regarded Wilson as "a dangerous visionary").[26] On October 14, the United States delivered a message to Germany making clear that an armistice would be up to the judgments of the military commanders and providing no indication that the European Allies subscribed to Wilson's Fourteen Points.

Pershing, and most likely Marshall, knew that the Germans were at last looking for a way out, but neither was aware of the diplomatic exchanges between governments. They remained focused on breaking through the Hindenburg Line, the key to clearing the Meuse-Argonne and destroying the vital railroad net near Sedan.

*　*　*　*　*

On the morning of October 4, wrote Marshall, the First Army gathered "itself for a renewed general assault."[27] For an entire week Marshall's beloved 1st Division, having been moved to the center of the defile, spearheaded a ferocious slugging match aimed at a group of hills on the Hindenburg Line called the Côte de Châtillon. Lead units reached the outer wire of the line on October 11, but at a terrible cost. The division's four infantry regiments, any one of which Marshall would have given up his exalted staff job to command, sustained 7,500 casualties. Some 1,800 officers and men of the Big Red One alone were killed in action, the greatest losses of any division in the Meuse-Argonne campaign. The 1st Division was spent.

Pursuant to orders written by Marshall, the 42nd "Rainbow" Division, having been pulled out of the line at Saint-Mihiel and moved north by truck and bus, replaced the shattered 1st Division on the afternoon of October 11. The next evening, Douglas MacArthur, commander of Rainbow's 84th Brigade, received a surprise visit at his farmhouse headquarters from General Charles Summerall, by then the commander of V Corps, which consisted of the Rainbow and two other divisions. He looked "tired and worn," having come in out of a cold rain. According to MacArthur, after he poured the corps commander a cup of hot coffee, Summerall burst forth with a startling challenge. "Give me Châtillon," the general demanded of MacArthur, "or a list of five thousand casualties." Equal to the drama, MacArthur paused and then replied, "All right, General, we'll take it or my name will head the list."[28] Given MacArthur's penchant for hyperbole, there is reason to question the accuracy of these statements. Yet William Manchester, MacArthur's prize-winning biographer, as well as others, repeated this exchange from MacArthur's *Reminiscences* without critical comment, perhaps because Summerall, the only other person present, never took issue with them.[29]

Beginning on October 14, General MacArthur's leadership under fire was documented by less biased sources and requires no embellishment. Exploiting a failure by the Germans to protect their flanks on the high ground (their barbed wire entanglements "dribbled out at the ends"), MacArthur taught his officers to attack each hill in the Châtillon in small units, crawling, clawing, and side-slipping up and around the flanks, then springing forward with grenades and rifle fire to envelop machine-gun emplacements from both sides.[30] By nightfall on the first day, the 168th Infantry (MacArthur's self-proclaimed "Iowa pig farmers") held a slim grip on one of the first hills. Day and night MacArthur was often up front with his troops, exposed to enemy artillery and machine-gun fire, so far out that General Summerall recommended him for the Congressional Medal of Honor. On the morning

of October 16, MacArthur's Iowans approached the heights of the Châtillon through a ravine. Supported by deafening machine-gun fire, they scrambled up the right side of the hill while the "Alabama cotton growers" of the
167th Infantry Regiment made their way up on the left. Major Lloyd Ross,
leading the Iowans, found a break in the wire. He and his doughboys reached
the crest first and discovered the Alabamans coming up the other side. The
fighting atop that hill was savage. Two German counterattacks were repelled, one by the 5th Field Artillery, the other by the firepower and courage
of the Iowans and the Alabamans. By the end of the day they killed the last
of the German defenders who had not fled or surrendered. MacArthur's
84th Brigade had broken through and was behind the Hindenburg Line. For
his leadership and bravery MacArthur was awarded his seventh Silver Star
and second Distinguished Service Cross. He and the 84th delivered the
"decisive blow" in the Meuse-Argonne, crowed Pershing. "The importance
of [the breakthrough] can hardly be overestimated."[31]

*   *   *   *   *

Demoralized and outnumbered, the German defenders in the Meuse-
Argonne began to buckle. Pershing, the only Allied military leader to openly
advocate "unconditional surrender," marshalled his forces for the final assault that would end the war.[32] With additional troops pouring into France,
he split his thirty-nine divisions into two separate armies, assigning the First
Army to three-hundred-pound General Hunter Liggett and a newly organized Second Army to General Bullard. Liggett quickly snapped up Marshall and made him chief of operations of the First Army, a job that ordinarily
would be filled by a brigadier general. On October 20, Marshall was ordered
by Liggett to prepare plans for a massive attack by all of the American forces
west of the Meuse. Because the assault would take place continuously "without rest or reorganization," Marshall called it "a 'steamroller' operation."[33]
Pershing's armies, he wrote, were "crouching for the final spring."[34]

   At 5:30 a.m. on November 1, the "steamroller" planned by Marshall began moving out along an eighteen-mile front. Within a few hours he knew it
was a success. Boche resistance melted; indeed, all along the Western Front,
German troops seemed to be in retreat. Ludendorff resigned. At Kiel on the
Baltic Sea, crews of the German High Seas Fleet refused to raise steam for
a showdown battle against the British fleet. The mutiny spread to other

German ports. Socialist-inspired riots broke out. In Berlin, a republic, later known as the Weimar Republic, was proclaimed from the Reichstag. Prince Max appointed a socialist leader as his successor. The kaiser's support among the high command eroded and he was being pressured to abdicate. Germany was on the road to a parliamentary democracy. At a hospital near Stettin in Pomerania, Corporal Hitler was recovering from a mustard gas attack that left him burned and temporarily blinded. He and many other Germans were convinced that the collapse of the military and the revolution in Germany were due to treachery. His apocalyptic ideology was to take shape in the next few years.

All along the Western Front the crisp autumn air hummed with "rumours of peace," especially among the German soldiers who were falling back, well aware that they were losing the war. On a sector that was for a day "so quiet and still," a single German soldier fell. "His face had an expression of calm, as though almost glad the end had come."[35] So wrote Erich Maria Remarque in *All Quiet on the Western Front*, the most famous novel of the Great War. He was writing not just for the German soldier but for all soldiers in all wars. In this war thousands more would fall on both sides of the front before the end would finally come.

Though the war was winding down, Colonel Marshall was still hard at work in his upstairs office at Souilly. On Tuesday afternoon, November 5, he was formulating a plan to pivot the left flank of the American First Army out of the way so that the French Fourth Army, as ordered the day before by Marshal Foch, would have a clear path to move in and recapture Sedan. At about four p.m., Major General Fox Conner, AEF's operations chief, climbed the stairs to Marshall's office and asked him what he was working on. When Marshall began to explain, Conner interrupted, saying that the French Fourth Army was lagging behind schedule, which would give the enemy time to regroup and reorganize defenses around Sedan. Why not let the Americans capture Sedan right away since they were directly in front of the town?

Marshall and Conner discussed the pros and cons of the situation for a half hour or so, Marshall pointing out that the city itself no longer had any strategic significance since U.S. and French heavy guns were already in range of the critically important rail line outside of Sedan. Then Conner rather abruptly announced, "It is General Pershing's desire that the troops of the First Army should capture Sedan, and he directs that orders should be issued accordingly." Marshall was taken aback, believing this might cause a rift with the French. Since he had a close working relationship with Conner, he laughed and said, "Am I expected to believe that this is General Pershing's order when I know damn well you came to this conclusion during our conversation?" Conner wasn't laughing. He replied, "That is the order of the Commander in Chief, which I am authorized to issue in his name. Now get it out as quickly as possible."[36]

Marshall wasn't sure what to do. He knew enough about the history of Sedan and what it meant to French prestige to question the wisdom of Conner's order. In 1870, Sedan was the place where, after a crushing defeat, Napoleon III surrendered to Prussian King Wilhelm I, thus conferring pre-eminence on Germany and changing the balance of power in Europe. As a matter of national pride the city needed to be recaptured by a French army, as Marshal Foch, supreme commander of the Allies, had made clear the day before. On the other hand, Marshall was confronted with a direct order by his superior, who said he was speaking for General Pershing, head of the AEF. Was Pershing even aware of what Conner was up to? Was Conner in fact carrying out Pershing's instructions? What about Marshal Foch? This was serious business.

Marshall asked for delay. He proposed that issuance of the order be put off until six p.m. so that Hunter Liggett, commander of the First Army, or his chief of staff, Hugh Drum, could be located to approve Conner's order. If they couldn't be found by then, Marshall would telephone the order to attack Sedan to the field commanders. Conner reluctantly agreed and left Marshall's office.

A few minutes before six, General Drum showed up. He approved the order, but added a parenthetical—"Boundaries will not be considered binding."[37] This permitted the American First Army to cross into the zone that Foch delineated for the French Fourth Army. It also allowed American corps and divisions to disregard their own boundaries. Marshall promptly telephoned the order. Once it was passed down to the zealous and competitive American field officers, they goaded their doughboys into a series of foot races, including all-night marches, to capture Sedan—notwithstanding its lack of strategic or tactical significance. Predictably, chaos and recriminations broke out. "I did not authorize a free for all," commented Marshall, "but that is what happened."[38] Divisions cut across the advances of other divisions, sometimes into their fields of fire. Supply trains were delayed by troops crossing in the rear. Roads were jammed. Units got lost. The headquarters of the French Fourth Army complained that American troops were in their zone. Liggett was outraged to learn that Marshall and Drum had gone along with Conner. He suspected that Pershing, who had axes to grind with Foch, was behind the whole mess. Memoirs published by Pershing and other generals long after the war spread blame with liberality.[39]

On the chilly night of November 5–6, columns of the 1st Division were marching across the Rainbow Division's sector on a road leading to Sedan. A patrol of the Big Red One's 16th Infantry led by a Lieutenant Black spotted a soldier carrying a riding crop and wearing an impossibly long silk muffler, creased riding breeches tucked into polished knee-high boots, and a mashed-down garrison cap. Assuming with good reason that the man could only be a German officer, Black arrested him at pistol point. Within a few minutes the young lieutenant was persuaded that he had captured Brigadier General Douglas MacArthur. With profuse apologies MacArthur was quickly released, but the story, with accompanying snickers, was widely repeated. At the time MacArthur treated this assault on his dignity as a joke. Later, after an appeals board decided he was ineligible for the Medal of Honor and he suspected he was under investigation for not dressing according to army regulations, MacArthur's "paranoia" got the better of him.[40] He blamed these and other perceived slights on an enmity against him "on the part of certain members of Pershing's GHQ staff" whom he regarded as paper pushers and yes-men who could never lead men in combat.[41] MacArthur and his aides derisively called these staff officers the "Chaumont crowd" after the location of Pershing's headquarters. For the rest of his career MacArthur would harbor grudges toward those in the Chaumont crowd, one of whose members was, of course, George Marshall.

Pershing shrugged off the entire Sedan debacle, regarding MacArthur's arrest as just one of the innumerable foul-ups that happen in the fog of war. With Marshall's help Pershing placated the French commanders, assuring them that the Americans would rapidly withdraw from their sector as soon as the French Fourth Army came up to take Sedan. And while the French were moving into Sedan, Pershing urged his First and Second Armies, by then more than a million strong, to "press the enemy as vigorously as possible."[42] There was to be no letup.

* * * * *

Meanwhile, armistice talks were beyond the rumor stage. President Wilson was fully engaged, having been acting as an intermediary for several weeks. Terms were drawn up and agreed on by Wilson's envoy, Colonel Edward House, and representatives of the Allies at Versailles on November 1. Four days later Wilson's secretary of state, Robert Lansing, notified the German government that the Allies had authorized Marshal Foch to "receive" a delegation of representatives and "communicate to them terms of an armistice."[43] On the evening of November 7, Foch waited in the mist with British officers as a train slowly pulled into the tiny station of Rethondes in the Forest of Compiègne and stopped with a hiss of steam. Six German representatives stepped out. Surrounded by guards, they walked a hundred yards through a grove of trees to Foch's personal train. Once settled in, Foch began by asking the Germans, through his interpreter, the purpose of their visit. The head of the delegation, regarding the question unnecessary and the answer obvious, replied that they had come to receive the "proposals of the Allied Powers" for an armistice. As if rehearsed, and it likely was, Foch feigned anger and ordered his interpreter to "[t]ell these gentlemen that we have no proposals to make to them." The Germans looked confused. In a sharp tone Foch revealed the game he was playing. "Do you ask for an armistice? If you do, I can inform you of the conditions subject to which it can be obtained."[44] The Allied Powers were laying down nonnegotiable conditions, not proposals.

In light of the weakened state of their armies and the revolutionary mood of their people, the German representatives had little choice. They responded in the affirmative. Thereupon, French General Maxime Weygand read aloud the main clauses of the armistice conditions previously agreed on at Versailles. Among other things, the Allies demanded that the agreement be signed on or before Monday, November 11, 1918 (hostilities to end at eleven a.m. that day); that German armed forces be withdrawn from France and Belgium (including Alsace-Lorraine); and that the U.S. and Allied powers be permitted to march into and occupy Mainz, Coblenz, and Cologne, cities inside Germany on the Rhine. The face of one of the German representatives "turned deathly pale." The eyes of another "filled with tears."[45]

On the evening of November 7, a lower-level member of the German delegation was entrusted with a copy of the armistice conditions. Under a white flag of truce, he made his way through the front lines and north to the town of Spa in Belgium, where he delivered the conditions in person to the kaiser and his supreme command. The remaining members of the German delegation, uncomfortably confined in Foch's railcar, spent the next two days trying, without success, to soften the terms. With the November 11 deadline looming, tensions rose as they awaited word concerning the fate of the kaiser at Spa and instructions from Prince Max in Berlin.

In the town hall at Souilly, Marshall continued to draw up orders for the movement of reserve divisions to the Second Army in preparation for a Franco-American attack to be launched on November 14, southeast of Metz. "The air was filled with wireless messages that indicated a break-up in the German Army and the trembling of the nation," he wrote.[46] At the officers' mess—army-speak for meals and the place where they are eaten—Marshall was amused to hear the English and French attachés talk casually about how the German colonies should be divided among the Allied powers, one insisting that the United States "should take Syria." Tongue in cheek, Marshall remarked that the U.S. was "opposed to any colony that had a wet or dry season, and an abnormal number of insects," adding that "Bermuda was the only colony" America would consider. Marshall and the other American officers were "flabbergasted" when the English attaché "violently objected," believing that Marshall was actually serious.[47]

On Sunday, November 10, the group in the Compiègne forest learned that the kaiser had finally abdicated, having been persuaded that he had lost his following in the military. He and his son the crown prince were being driven from Spa to Holland (the kaiser would remain there in exile until his death in 1941). That evening Prince Max sent a message from Berlin authorizing the German delegation in Marshal Foch's railcar to sign the armistice agreement. In the early hours of November 11, the agreement was signed.

Marshall fell into bed at about two a.m. Four hours later he was awakened—for the second time that night—by a telephone call. Pershing's senior aide informed him that all fighting was to cease at eleven a.m. Marshall immediately got on the phone to make sure that fighting units received the cease-fire message and to halt previously ordered troop movements to the front. At 10:30, he joined the other headquarters officers in a stately house at 49 Voie Sacrée for a late breakfast. A few minutes before eleven, there was a "tremendous explosion in the garden," wrote Marshall, that blew him and the others out of their chairs onto the floor. Marshall "thought [he] had been killed." Aside from his head getting slammed against the wall, he and the others were not injured. They learned later that a bomb had been accidentally released by an American plane as it was landing just beyond the garden wall. Marshall dryly noted that they had all been saved from "a little tragedy" just minutes before the armistice went into effect.[48] He was happy the war was about to end—he didn't think he had enough luck left to survive a third encounter with an aerial bomb.

Wireless operators and runners raced to get word to the infantry and the gunners at the front. The shelling continued from both sides until the minute hand reached eleven. "The quietness that followed was awesome," Private Frank Groves recalled. "[T]here was no singing, no shouting, no laughter; we just stood around and looked and listened."[49] Harry Truman, whose Battery D was near the tiny village of Hermeville, said that his men "looked at each other for some time and then a great cheer arose all along the line. We could hear the men in the infantry a thousand meters in front raising holy hell . . . Celebration at the front went on the rest of the day."[50] That night, troops on both sides set off their "entire pyrotechnic supply of rockets" and "there were camp fires all along the lines."[51]

In Washington, President Wilson handwrote an announcement to the world. "A supreme moment of history has come. The hand of God is laid upon the nations. The eyes of the people have been opened and they see. He will show them favour, I devoutly believe, only if they rise to the clear heights of His own justice and mercy."[52]

* * * * *

As events unfolded, the new era of enduring peace that Wilson envisioned would not dawn. Indeed, the cessation of hostilities in 1918 scarcely interrupted the thirty-year tumultuous revolution in world affairs that began in 1914 and ended at the conclusion of the Second World War, when the age of European hegemony finally ended. The November 1918 armistice did, however, put a stop—all too briefly, as it turned out—to four and a half years of unimaginable human carnage. It is estimated that at least fifteen million combatants and civilians perished in the "war to end all wars." Perhaps another twenty million were wounded, many scarred for life. The citizens of France and Britain had reason to speak of a "lost generation," since a third of the men between the ages of nineteen and twenty-two when war broke out did not survive.

By comparison, American casualties were light: 53,402 deaths in combat; 63,114 deaths due to other causes (e.g., illness, accidents); and 204,002 wounded—a total of 320,518 casualties. U.S. casualties in the forty-seven-day Meuse-Argonne operation totaled 122,063, including 26,277 killed, almost half the total of Americans killed during the entire war. The Meuse-Argonne offensive had the highest casualty rate and was the deadliest battle in American history.

Pershing believed the armistice was premature and therefore a mistake. He recoiled at the thought that German troops might march home in triumph and blame the armistice on left-wing politicians, as many of them did. He was willing to sacrifice more American blood to defeat the German army on the battlefield, even if it meant pursuing them all the way to Berlin. Marshall, on the other hand, was not at all sure that the armistice was a mistake. Five years after the war, he expressed concern that if the Allied powers had continued to pursue and degrade the German army as it retreated inside German borders, they would have ended up having to take over Germany, "a very difficult and lengthy task," he wrote.[53]

* * * * *

When the Great War ended, Marshall, almost thirty-eight, was still a colonel, though the wartime promotion was temporary. He had served throughout the fighting in staff positions, while many of his peers who commanded troops, notably General MacArthur, and even some of his subordinates, had surpassed him in rank. If the war had lasted another month or so, General Pershing's recommendation in October that Marshall be promoted to brigadier general almost certainly would have been approved. As it turned out, Congress froze promotions after the armistice. It would be eighteen years before he received his first star.

Setting aside his rank, Marshall emerged from the war with a reputation for competence as a staff officer that, in the words of Forrest Pogue, was likely "unexcelled by any other officer his age in the Army."[54] He became a master in the arts of planning battles and managing the training, organization, and movement of large bodies of troops. He earned a doctorate in the science of logistics. Of equal importance, Marshall was known for his ability to bridge cultural differences and work smoothly with British and French commanders who far outranked him. Years later Fox Conner counseled young Dwight Eisenhower to seek out an assignment under Marshall because in future wars "we will have to fight beside allies and George Marshall knows more about the techniques of arranging allied commands than any man I know. He is nothing short of a genius."[55]

While Conner correctly foresaw the future, Marshall knew that the United States military establishment tended to reward leadership of troops in battle more than rear-echelon staff work, no matter how brilliant. For this reason he was frustrated over having been deprived of command assignments during the war and discouraged about the prospects for advancement in peacetime. Marshall had experienced intense artillery and machine-gun fire at the front without cowering in fear or running to the rear. No one ever questioned his bravery. He had the temperament to make sound decisions in the midst of chaos, stress, and physical and mental exhaustion. But he had never led a charge with saber, bayonet, or revolver. He had demonstrated moral courage, but did he possess physical courage? Did he have the mettle to inspire and lead combat troops in the heat of battle? Though the answer is probably yes, the question can never be answered with certainty. Organizing armies and planning and managing battles from headquarters was simply not the same as leading men over the top at the front. Marshall himself recognized this truth when he wrote in *Infantry Journal* a few months later that "control of troops closely engaged with the enemy is the most difficult feat of leadership and requires the highest state of discipline and training."[56]

Marshall always regretted that he never led troops in battle, worried that this shortcoming would inhibit his advancement. He would wait twenty years before a commander in chief had the wisdom to entrust him, an officer who had never fired a gun at the enemy, to lead the nation's armies in war— this one a global war against Germany, Italy, and Japan, the most catastrophic war in history.

What were the key lessons that Marshall learned from the Great War that he would endeavor to put into practice in the Second World War? Perhaps the most important was the demeanor of General Pershing. At the lowest point, after the Germans launched their all-out offensive in the spring of 1918 against

war-weary, depleted, and depressed British and French allies and untested
Americans, Marshall would always remember, as he wrote in his memoir, that
Pershing "radiated determination and the will to win." It wasn't so much his
"speech" but "his manner and expression" that fired the officers and doughboys.[57] Marshall would strive to emulate Pershing's iron will during the Valley
Forge days of World War II. The second most important lesson was a sense of
the qualities he would look for in promoting officers to lead troops in the next
war. As listed in a letter Marshall wrote in November 1920, they include common sense, physical strength, marked energy, determination, and cheerful optimism.[58] The emphasis on physical strength and energy meant that many if not
most older officers would have to be passed over or retired. Marshall valued
character over intellect, conservatism over flamboyance, and the loyal team-
player over the adventurous individualist. He avoided yes-men and conformists,
preferring those who, like Pershing and himself, were unafraid to express dissent and open to criticism without taking offense.

From Pershing, Marshall also learned that in an allied coalition one should
strive to minimize the dispersion of forces to other fronts and instead concentrate overwhelming power against the enemy. Marshall was aware that British
and French commanders constantly pressed Pershing to assign—that is,
divert—his individual combat units to their armies, thus jeopardizing his goal
of building and maintaining an independent American army powerful enough
to defeat the Germans. In the next war, Marshall would resist dispersion and
argue for a buildup and a massive frontal assault aimed at the heart of Germany. Like Pershing, he did not always succeed in preventing dispersion, and
his frontal assault strategy may have been premature. Nevertheless, he
preached a military doctrine that had been drummed into him at Pershing's
headquarters, the same principles taught by Prussian military theorist Carl
von Clausewitz, and exhibited on the battlefield by generals such as Napoleon
Bonaparte and Ulysses S. Grant. Other lessons Marshall learned included the
importance of appointing a single theater commander (Marshal Foch), and
that with adequate training, even green troops can succeed in their first taste
of real combat (the 91st, 33rd, and 80th Divisions at Meuse-Argonne).

* * * * *

After the armistice, Pershing and a cadre of officers and regulars, including
Marshall, remained in France to perform occupation duties and to assist in

demobilizing the doughboys and sending them home. In addition, Marshall was asked to work out a plan to resume the war in the event peace talks in Versailles collapsed. On April 30, 1919, following a ceremony in the Place de la République in Metz in which Marshall and several others received the Croix de Guerre, Marshall was at a luncheon surrounded by a group of French generals with whom he had worked during the war. They "had had a lot to drink," admitted Marshall. As he stood arm in arm with them, General Pétain, well acquainted with Marshall, approached with a mischievous smile. "I'm very glad to see you on such intimate terms with my fighting generals," he said.[59] General Pershing stepped forward and joined the fun. He announced that Marshall had just agreed to sign on as his personal aide.

Marshall had indeed accepted the offer an hour or so earlier, outside on the plaza. He was to serve as Pershing's official adviser in an executive capacity on matters of substance, and would act in his place from time to time. It was, of course, a considerable honor. Whether or not Marshall liked the idea of once again functioning as a staff aide, he knew that his close association with the famous general would be invaluable to his career. Thus began a five-year assignment, one of Marshall's longest tours in the army. When it was over, Marshall would write an affectionate note to Pershing saying that his years with the great general "will always remain the unique experience of my career."[60]

Throughout the summer of 1919, Marshall accompanied Pershing on trips to revisit battlefields, and to be feted at parades, dinners, dances, and gala receptions in France, Italy, and England. In Paris, Marshall was introduced to Pershing's chief civilian aide, Dwight Morrow, a partner in J.P. Morgan & Co., the largest and most powerful commercial bank in the United States. Morrow, whose daughter Anne would marry Charles Lindbergh, reportedly offered Marshall a job at Morgan at an annual salary of $30,000 (more than $435,000 today). Marshall graciously turned him down.

In London, Marshall stood with Pershing and Winston Churchill in Hyde Park, watching an American "victory" regiment march by in review.[61] Churchill turned to Marshall and remarked, "What a magnificent body of men never to take a drink."[62] Churchill was, of course, referring to the fact that Prohibition in America was about to go into effect. The next day, as the American retinue prepared to lead the great Victory Parade on horseback, Marshall agreed to trade his docile horse for a "fractious and vicious" steed that another general could not control. For more than seven miles on the parade route, Marshall's horse bucked constantly and tried to "kick everything in reach." Inside the narrow Admiralty Arch leading to the Mall, the animal reared, "lost his footing and went over backwards." Marshall "fell clear" and rolled out of the way. He was able to get back into the saddle before the horse got up. "As it turned out," he happily reported, "I entered the Arch on a horse, and came out of it on a horse—and did not even lose my place in the line-up."[63] His only injury was pride and a small broken bone in his hand.

On September 1, after two years in France, he was finally headed home. As Pershing and Marshall prepared to board the swift liner *Leviathan* at Brest, Marshal Foch personally bade the American general farewell. "We have cemented our ties of friendship," declared Foch, "and if ever in the future we shall find it necessary to unfurl our banner, then we know that we shall continue as brothers-in-arms."[64] No one could have predicted it at the time, but twenty years later to the day, September 1, 1939, the Second World War commenced, France unfurled her banner once again, and George Marshall was sworn in as chief of staff of the United States Army.

*   *   *   *   *

The *Leviathan* slid by Ambrose Light and into New York Harbor on the morning of the 8th of September. During the crossing Congress had conferred the title "General of the Armies" on Pershing, an honor previously bestowed on only one other American general—George Washington. Thousands lined the streets as Pershing and his staff, including Marshall, motored up to City Hall in Manhattan. George spotted Lily among the crowd of officials. Though there is no firsthand account of their reunion, they must have been overjoyed to see each other. The two spent the next four nights at the elegant Waldorf-Astoria Hotel on Fifth Avenue getting reacquainted, regaining their prewar intimacy after two long years of anxious separation.

In light of Lily's heart condition, questions have been raised concerning the depth of the childless couple's intimacy. A letter turned over to the Marshall Foundation in 2012 provides a rare glimpse into their relationship and goes a long way toward answering these questions. The letter, dated November 18, 1917, was written by George to Lily while he was in France. Most of its seven handwritten pages were devoted to life insurance and income for her and her mother to live on in the event of his death. Marshall's concluding lines, however, were deeply personal: "Dearest, I love you very much; I want you very much; and I would give my soul to have you close in my arms this afternoon. You are all I think about and long for. I even think a mud hole would be pleasant with you in it. Your husband."[65] Given the mores of the time and Marshall's exceptional reserve, the letter's euphemisms suggest intimacy of a sexual nature—despite the fact that Marshall knew it would be reviewed by a censor (it is marked with a censor's stamp). From the opening lines it is clear that George and Lily exchanged numerous personal letters during the Great War, yet this is the only intimate note known to have survived.[66]

In Washington, DC, painters were putting the last touches on what was called "Pershing's Victory Arch," a huge temporary wooden structure modeled after the Arc de Triomphe that spanned Pennsylvania Avenue at 15th Street just a block from the White House. On September 17, General of the Armies Pershing rode slowly at the front of the 1st Division, roughly 25,000 men. Marshall, ever the organizer, tightened up the parade so that they "came by in masses," and "took about a third as long" as they did when they marched in New York. It was "impressive," recalled Marshall, "[b]ut the people were most impressed of all by one mule licking the soup that was coming out of the back of a rolling kitchen."[67] A photograph shows Marshall riding a white horse behind Pershing near the reviewing stand in front of the Riggs Bank. President Wilson was absent; he was out west, trying to mobilize popular support for Senate ratification of the Treaty of Versailles and its covenant of the League of Nations.

Among the parade-goers was thirty-seven-year-old Mrs. Katherine Boyce Tupper Brown. She was in Washington visiting her cousins from the Boyce branch of her family and had turned out "to see the men come up Pennsylvania Avenue." Recalling the event years later, Katherine said, "I can hear that roar now—and General Pershing riding in front . . . And I saw him [Marshall] then but, of course, I didn't know anything about him— never heard of him."[68] In little more than a decade, Mrs. Brown would be the most important person in Marshall's life.

CHAPTER 3

I Will Find a Way

Though untouched by the ravages of war, the America that thirty-eight-year-old Colonel Marshall returned to was in crisis. In the autumn of 1919, the economy was sliding into a second postwar recession. Labor unrest was endemic, made worse by the release from service of four million draftees, still in uniform, desperately looking for work. The flood of immigrants from Europe and the great migration of African Americans from the rural South to northern cities increased competition for scarce jobs and depressed wages. Prices remained high. The result was an unprecedented outbreak of ethnic hatred, violence, and blatant discrimination. Lynchings by the resurgent Ku Klux Klan and race riots in major cities were commonplace. White citizens feared that foreign terrorists and Bolsheviks were behind the waves of lawlessness, strikes, and signs of anarchy.

George and Lily leased an apartment at 2400 16th Street in the Northwest section of Washington, DC, a unique establishment that operated more like an exclusive club than a typical apartment building. Known simply as "2400," the owners carefully selected tenants on the basis of whether they "fit in" rather than on the strength of their bank accounts. When the Marshalls joined 2400 near the end of September, the residents were still buzzing about events of the past few months. The "Red Summer" of 1919 began in the District of Columbia with the bombing of a townhouse on R Street owned by U.S. Attorney General A. Mitchell Palmer (across the street from the home of Franklin and Eleanor Roosevelt) and climaxed when a mob of whites, aroused by newspaper tales of a "negro sex fiend," set off a four-day race riot in which thirty-nine Washingtonians lost their lives and more than 150 were clubbed, beaten, and shot by mobs of both races. Together with the race riots in Washington and other cities and the violent labor strikes taking place across the country, the attempt to kill Palmer and his family gave rise to the "Palmer Raids," a national crackdown on labor organizers, suspected Communists, and foreign-born "radicals." Thousands were arrested.

Hundreds of aliens were deported. From the White House, where rumors were emerging that President Wilson had suffered a stroke and that his wife was running the executive branch, there was nothing but silence.

The friendly "clublike atmosphere" of 2400 was a refuge from the racial tensions that simmered in Washington. Soon after George and Lily moved in, the colonel found himself sharing an elevator with a precocious eight-year-old named Rose Page, who was living with her family in the building.[1] As Rose later recalled, she had heard from her best friend Eleanor that the "lithe and tall" army officer was a "whiz with children," so she decided to initiate a conversation.[2] The following Sunday, Rose and Eleanor joined Colonel Marshall, still in uniform and carrying a riding crop, for a fast walk down into Rock Creek Park. When the girls got their shoes and socks sopping wet while jumping from rock to rock in the creek, Marshall laughed and taught them to hang them to dry on forked sticks. "[H]is strikingly blue eyes were lively and full of fun," and his "easy relaxed manner" made Rose feel equally at ease.[3] So began what Rose described as a "mutually affectionate relationship."[4] For forty years, Colonel Marshall—she would always address him that way—would be her loyal friend, confidant, mentor, moral compass, and godfather to her children.

It wasn't long before Marshall received his first exposure to congressional oversight of the military, along with a dose of army politics—the disagreeable facts of life he was to deal with for the rest of his career. Pending before both houses of Congress were bills to reorganize the army, the centerpiece of which was a proposal by army chief of staff General Peyton March, backed by Secretary of War Newton Baker, to establish a postwar standing army of half a million men. General Pershing, the individual who had built, trained, and led the largest army in the nation's history, was angry that March proposed the reorganization without consulting him. Pershing could see that the war-weary, Republican-controlled Congress was in no mood to finance a large standing army, especially since the League of Nations, whether or not the U.S. became a member, was being set up to prevent future wars.

Having decided to propose his own plan, Pershing asked Marshall to confer with Fox Conner and devise an alternative. Over several days at Bandreth Park, an Adirondacks hunting compound built by the grandfather of Conner's wife who made a fortune selling laxative pills, Marshall and

Conner drafted a new plan for Pershing. The key idea that made it work—universal military training—came from Marshall's close friend Colonel John McAuley Palmer, an expert on army organization who was assigned temporarily to the Senate as a special adviser. Palmer's proposal was to require every young man in America to undergo several months of military training, followed by a four-year army reserve obligation. With this trained manpower, a standing regular army of between 275,000 and 300,000, almost half the size proposed by Baker and March, would be large enough to protect the country, mobilize the reserves, and wage war if necessary. Borrowing Palmer's words, a citizen army in reserve would be more "in harmony with the genius of American institutions" than a large standing army.[5]

Beginning in late October of 1919, General of the Armies Pershing testified before the committees on Military Affairs of the Senate and House concerning his alternative plan for the reorganization of the army. At his side were Marshall and Conner, who drafted his prepared statements and briefed him on questions he might face. Recalling the three days testifying before the committees, Marshall noted that the congressmen were astonished to see that Pershing had "no hesitation" in pausing to accept advice and suggestions from two subordinates in the midst of his testimony. "It was one of [Pershing's] great strengths that he could listen to these things."[6]

Deftly shooting down the idea of a 500,000-man standing army, Pershing defended universal military training on the ground that it would promote good "citizenship" and teach both rich and poor that everyone owes an "obligation to their Government."[7] Yet it was apparent from the questions that the concept would run into stiff opposition from liberals, farm groups, organized labor, and others as being the essence of militarism. Among other opponents were the racists. Congressman Percy Quin, a Democrat from McComb, Mississippi, lectured Pershing, informing him that when the "black man" receives military training he is a "menace to the white race," and comes "back home with all that virus in him." Pershing and Marshall were accustomed to the blatant racism that prevailed at the time, but Quin took it to a new level. Pershing pushed back, pointing out that "few, if any, of the colored men who were in the Army have been engaged in any of the recent racial troubles."[8] Marshall no doubt agreed with Pershing.

The opponents succeeded in watering down and effectively eliminating the universal military training provisions. As amended, the Senate and

House army reorganization bills were reconciled and enacted into law the following June as the National Defense Act of 1920. The Act provided for an authorized strength of 17,726 officers and 280,000 men, and a structure for a standing regular army, general staff, organized reserve, and war plans division, which Marshall would eventually inherit in 1939. Marshall, however, would never give up on what he regarded as the unifying principle of national service.

While Congress was grappling with the details of army reorganization, a related and more widely publicized debate was coming to a head. The issue was whether a two-thirds majority of the Senate would give its constitutionally required "advice and consent" to the Treaty of Versailles, including the covenant of the League of Nations, that had been approved by President Wilson and thirty-one other nations in June. Marshall attended the fiery Senate debate "one morning, but that was all." At the time, the "general idea" of the League of Nations as a guarantor of world peace appealed to Marshall. He was disappointed that President Wilson's rigidity—his absolute refusal to compromise with senators who had reservations—doomed U.S. membership in the League. Marshall had heard the gossip in the dining room of 2400 and elsewhere that Wilson had suffered a paralyzing stroke, but he was unaware that the president's judgment was impaired. On November 19, 1919, and again on March 19, 1920, the Senate returned the treaty to the disabled president with a note indicating its inability to provide its advice and consent.

Into the late spring of 1920, the president clung to his dream that the Senate could still be moved to provide its consent without reservations. Notwithstanding his flaccid left arm, drooping jaw, and immobility, he convinced himself that he would recover enough strength to lead the country. With an election looming in November, he began to seriously contemplate running for a third term. This was "his greatest delusion of all following his stroke," wrote historian John Milton Cooper Jr. "By any reasonable standard, Wilson was not functioning as president."[9]

Pershing too was beginning to harbor thoughts of launching a bid for the White House. He was an American hero, one of the most popular figures in the nation. Having run the war, he believed he could function as president. Marshall, however, was convinced that generals, past and present, should not engage in partisan politics, that the proverbial man on horseback posed a threat to democracy and civilian control. "A group came from Tennessee" to convince

Pershing to stand for the Republican nomination, recalled Marshall, and he sent them away without even consulting the general. "He [Pershing] was furious with me," remembered Marshall.[10] What's more, Marshall doubted whether Pershing had the temperament for the back-scratching compromises that had to be made by politicians. Remembering the tarnished legacy of Ulysses Grant, Marshall believed Pershing's reputation for integrity would eventually be sullied by scheming supporters, money, and backroom deals.

Marshall need not have worried. Since Republican leaders already had a strong bench of experienced candidates, they were not interested in drafting Pershing to run in 1920. At the party convention in the Chicago Coliseum, Senator Warren Harding of Ohio was nominated as the Republican standard-bearer (after twenty ballots) and Calvin Coolidge became the vice presidential nominee. Pershing turned down feelers from the Democrats and finally gave up the notion of running for president.

In June 1920, Marshall pulled off a coup for the Virginia Military Institute, his alma mater. Since Pershing was scheduled to speak to West Point graduates, Marshall persuaded him that he should also visit VMI because so many of its men served in "lead positions in the army" during the Great War.[11] With Marshall as his guide, Pershing spent two days in Lexington, handing out diplomas to the class of 1920, paying his respects to the south-facing statue of Stonewall Jackson in the town cemetery, and delivering remarks at a reception in the Lee Chapel of Washington and Lee University, where Robert E. Lee's recumbent effigy was displayed on the floor above his burial vault. Pershing probably suppressed a smile when VMI officials insisted that he also view the mounted skeleton of Traveller (with the two *l*'s), Lee's revered wartime horse, and Traveller's stable, where the doors were always open to allow his spirit to roam freely.

Shortly after his visit to Lexington, Pershing was on the receiving end of numerous complaints from northerners who objected to his trip to the final resting place of General Lee. Pershing ordered Marshall to answer all the letters. "You got me to go there, now you attend to the letters objecting to my having gone."[12]

* * * * *

Marshall was well aware that the shrines to Jackson, Lee, and the "lost cause" of the Confederacy were controversial. Born on the last day of 1880, only fifteen years after the Civil War ended, he had grown up in western

Pennsylvania among veterans who had fought for the Union. Both sides of his family were from the northern border of Kentucky, the town of Augusta on the Ohio River. In an interview, Marshall made it clear that he was not from the South, that he did not regard himself as a Virginian. He was even reluctant to admit that he was related to Chief Justice John Marshall, a noted Virginian.[13]

Marshall was indisputably a northerner, and his fellow cadets at VMI, almost all from the South, never let him forget it, mocking his Pittsburgh accent and placing contemptuous emphasis on "Union" in the name of his hometown. Throughout his army career, his close friends and associates, many of whom were West Pointers, came from all sections of America. During the Great War, he was guided by the memoirs of Philip Sheridan, the Union general who used scorched-earth tactics in the Shenandoah Valley and played a large part in driving Lee to surrender. Marshall often recalled a speech by a former Confederate that he described as "almost treason in its enthusiasm for the Lost Cause and its condemnation of the North."[14] Indeed, no evidence exists that Marshall sympathized with the southern cause. Nevertheless, many of those who have written about Marshall contend or at least suggest that because of his four-year exposure to VMI's southern traditions and its reverence for the Confederacy, he was an adopted son and lifelong defender of the Old South.

There is no question that the VMI experience had a profound influence on Marshall. He told an interviewer in 1957 that during the time he was at the school he was "greatly influenced by the traditions concerning General Lee and General Jackson." Yet in the same interview he said it was the "self-control" and "discipline" that the Institute "ground in[to]" him, as distinct from its southern traditions, that stayed with him throughout his career.[15] Historian Mark Stoler wisely observed that it would be more accurate to say that VMI "nurtured" Marshall's "natural strengths . . . by placing such a high value on them."[16] If Marshall had attended West Point instead of VMI, he would have emerged with virtually the same self-control and discipline that was ground into him at the Institute.

Another significant trait that Marshall perfected at VMI was loyalty, especially to his superior officers. This too had little to do with the South and the cult of the lost cause. A few weeks after the Valley Railroad dropped Marshall off in Lexington to begin his "rat year," the first year at VMI, a group of upperclassmen barged into Room 88 on the third stoop of the barracks where Marshall was living with his roommates. Like cadets at West Point, the upperclassmen were bent upon the practice of hazing a first-year cadet. Their target this time was Marshall, an awkward sixteen-year-old from the North with a Yankee twang. They jammed the butt end of a naked bayonet between the floorboards and sadistically ordered him to squat over the blade. Weakened from a bout of typhoid fever that had delayed his arrival at the Institute, Marshall could not hold the position for long. He slipped sideways. The bayonet gashed his buttock. He was stitched up in the infirmary, but never uttered a word to anyone about the real cause of his wound. His stoic loyalty was spread by word of mouth throughout the cadet corps and was rewarded with respect.

Though he received relatively high marks in drill regulation and the civil engineering courses that he majored in, Marshall, nicknamed "Pug," was a mediocre scholar. His poorest grades were in German and math. Due to a permanent injury to a tendon in his right elbow when he was a boy, he promised his mother that he would not play football at VMI for the first two years. In his third he made the team and played in the fall, but the season was cut short by an outbreak of typhoid fever. In the autumn of 1900, his fourth year, Pug Marshall was apparently a standout at left tackle, even though he weighed less than 150 pounds. One of Marshall's biographers wrote that he ran fifty yards for a touchdown against Washington and Lee, but Marshall said in a later interview that he couldn't remember "exactly that."[17] With regard to VMI's 5–0 victory over Virginia Polytechnic Institute (now Virginia Tech), the *Rockbridge County News* reported that "the tackling of G. Marshall in breaking up the interference was of the highest order, and a prominent University of Virginia athletic man said he was the best tackle in the South."[18]

In terms of its effect on the course of history, the most important quality that VMI enabled Marshall to develop was not discipline, self-control, loyalty, or athletic prowess. It was leadership. More precisely, and in his own words, what Marshall "learned most" at VMI was how to address and solve "the problem of managing men."[19] VMI's superintendent Scott Shipp recognized and rewarded Marshall's nascent management potential, conferring on him the leadership of his class of cadets—First Corporal for his second year, First Sergeant in his third year, and finally First Captain in his senior year. Marshall took advantage of each opportunity to lead and manage. His authority and responsibilities varied but increased each year, from forming up the company and marching the "detail to guard mount" each morning as First Sergeant, to serving as officer in charge of the entire cadet corps at every meal in the mess hall as First Captain.[20] Marshall learned to discipline himself for attention to detail and judicious command. He knew he would be judged severely by his classmates if he slacked off in any aspect of his tasks. Cadet Marshall willed himself to exercise, or appear to exercise, authority without causing resentment, and he came to know when to confer a compliment, when to discipline with a few carefully chosen words, and when to remain silent. He realized that his classmates would periodically test his leadership by engaging in a prank or circumventing a rule. And on occasion they would challenge his authority. Marshall developed a sense of the extent to which he would allow such challenges. Similarly, he began to learn whether (and when) it would be appropriate to confront those in the VMI administration with authority over him. It was his job at VMI to manage each such situation. It would be his life's work to manage individuals, groups, armies, crises, government officials and departments, and an almost infinite variety of situations.

What was it about Marshall that caused cadets at VMI, and generals, admirals, and political leaders in later years, to allow themselves to be managed and led by him? David Brooks said it was because Marshall knew "how to exercise controlled power."[21] Mark Stoler wrote that Marshall's natural "austerity, discipline, and distance from his peers" was seen as a "form of charisma."[22] Both explanations bring us closer to answering the question, yet neither is wholly satisfactory. Those who personally experienced Marshall point to his reserve, his coolness of manner, his self-restraint, and his ordered mind as the source of his power and charisma. Still, even with these firsthand recollections, there is probably no combination of words, no metaphor, that adequately describes the elements of Marshall's personality that caused so many to respond positively to his leadership. All that can be said for certain is that the VMI system and its superintendent were enablers that allowed Marshall's commanding presence to flourish. By the spring of his final year, he seemed to be well on his way to understanding the problem of managing men.

When Marshall attended VMI, there was almost no opportunity for the cadets to interact with women. There were only four days during the long school year when classes did not meet—Christmas and New Year's Days, Washington's Birthday, and May 15, the anniversary of the Battle of New Market in 1864 in which VMI cadets fought and died in the Civil War (ten cadets "died on the field of honor," forty-four were wounded, including then superintendent Shipp). Cadets without demerits, which included Marshall, were allowed to stroll into Lexington on Saturday afternoons for a maximum of two hours. The odds of developing a relationship with a young woman were long.

In Marshall's case the odds were lengthened by his lack of experience. Marshall's older sister Marie said she could remember only "one affair," prior to Lily Coles, when George tried to court a girl. During high school in Uniontown, George met "a very beautiful girl" at Mt. Chateau, a nearby resort, and fell "madly in love." The girl was "[n]ot too interested in George," which made him very "unhappy."[23] A VMI yearbook photo shows Marshall, grim-faced and braced ramrod straight in full dress uniform, next to his "date," Katharine Fauntleroy of Staunton, Virginia, at the Final Ball on July 4, 1900.[24] Nothing more is known about their relationship, if there ever was one. Late in life Marshall told of three other encounters with girls, all of which took place when he was a boy. Each ended with the girls teasing and making fun of him, leaving him with memories of humiliation and pain.

On an evening in September 1900, George Marshall met Lily Carter Coles for the first time. He had walked by her green and white gingerbread house near the Limit Gate many times, occasionally stopping to catch a glimpse of her through the window playing the piano—"some of the airs my mother had played to which I had become devoted." On this particular evening, he was invited in, probably by Mrs. Coles, Lily's mother, who saw him outside listening in the shadows. Lily appeared. She was almost as tall as George, full-bosomed with a narrow, corseted waist. Her warmth and wit put George at ease. He was fascinated, and immediately attracted to her. She too was intrigued by the shy, serious First Captain of the cadet corps. Within days they began seeing each other, at first as much as the strict VMI regimen would permit and then beyond the rules. To spend more time with Lily, George began sneaking out of the barracks after hours, risking his three-year record of zero demerits. "I was very much in love," Marshall said

years later, "and I was willing to take the chance."[25] Everyone in the corps
knew the two had become "steadies." Rules permitting, George could be
seen driving with Lily around the parade ground and in Lexington in her
horse-drawn "Stanhope trap [a light phaeton], where the lady sits up on a
slightly raised seat and has a whip with a long lash."[26] Before long, they were
engaged to be married. At the Final Ball in June 1901, they were the most
popular couple, although Lily's heart condition precluded her from dancing. Lily and her mother were at the graduation ceremony on the parade
ground when First Captain Marshall marched at the head of the Corps of
Cadets.

Knowing that he had to secure a salary before he could support Lily (and
eventually her mother), it was near the end of 1901 before Marshall received
word that he had passed the examination for an officer's commission in the
U.S. Army. When he was finally commissioned on February 3, 1902, he was
told that he had only ten days before he was to report for active duty. The
wedding was thrown together in haste. On the frigid afternoon of February 11, twenty-one-year-old George Marshall, his family, and Andy Thompson, his best friend from Uniontown, gathered in the little house on Letcher
Avenue with Lily's mother and brother. The priest from the Episcopal
church in Lexington was there to perform the ceremony. The bride—a stunning woman, the belle of Lexington—was dressed in white. She was at least
four years older than George, although she would never admit it. The group,
many of whom had never met, engaged in nervous small talk for the first
twenty minutes or so. Lily broke into the conversation. Taking charge, she
turned to Second Lieutenant Marshall and said, "Come on, George, let's
get married."[27]

* * * * *

In the summer of 1921, George and Lily, even more in love after nineteen
years of marriage, moved out of 2400 and across the Potomac River to the
heights of Fort Myer, adjacent to Arlington Cemetery and the Lee-Custis
Mansion, the former home of General Lee. Newly inaugurated president
Harding had appointed General Pershing to succeed Peyton March as army
chief of staff, which meant that Pershing's "official residence" became Quarters One, a pressed brick house on the crest of a bluff overlooking the city of
Washington. As Pershing's chief aide, Major Marshall, newly promoted,

and his wife were assigned to Quarters no. 3, a few houses south of Pershing's on tree-lined Grant Avenue. For the next three years, Marshall worked
next to the West Wing of the White House in the former State, War, and
Navy building, today known as the Eisenhower Executive Office Building.
When Pershing had matters to discuss with Harding, General Charles
Dawes, head of the Budget Bureau, and other administration officials, Marshall would almost always accompany him to the White House, exposure
that was invaluable to his career and reputation. Much of the time, however,
especially in the later years of his term, Pershing was not in Washington,
instead spending time in Manhattan, vacationing in France, or working on
his memoirs. Without a war to fight, Pershing began to lose interest in managing the affairs of the peacetime army. Or perhaps the rumors were true—
that he was in love with a young Romanian-born woman, a talented painter
whom he met in Paris during the war. Whatever the reason, Pershing delegated an extraordinary amount of authority to Marshall. In the words
of Larry Bland, editor of several volumes of Marshall's papers, Pershing
provided Marshall "with a graduate course in politics, government, and
management."[28]

The politics and government part of Marshall's job must have been dis-
couraging. Using the time-honored practice of legislating via appropriations,
by 1923 Congress had reduced the size of the regular army to 132,000 men
(the authorized strength was 280,000), not that much larger than the
100,000 limit that Germany was allowed by the Treaty of Versailles. Congress was reflecting the mood of the American people, moving toward isolationism and limiting immigration to a trickle. The prevailing view was that
so long as the U.S. avoided "entangling alliances," and closed its borders to
foreigners, war was unlikely. After all, the League of Nations, the limits on
warships agreed at the Washington Naval Conference of 1921-22, and the
1925-26 non-aggression pacts by Germany and the other Western European powers (the Locarno Treaties) appeared almost to guarantee that
peace would reign for at least the next twenty years.[29]

Nevertheless, Marshall continued to preach preparedness. Despite the
League and other international agreements, he believed that, human nature
being what it is, somehow, somewhere another war would break out and
America could be drawn in. Thus, in 1923, he once again called for

universal military training, warning that "if we fail in the development of a citizen army, we will be impotent in the first year of a major war."[30] He advocated for a large citizen army reserve not only because it would enable the U.S. to mobilize faster in the event of war, but also because it might act as a deterrent to future aggressors. Marshall did not want the nation to be caught short again as it was on the eve of the Great War.

Although the Marshalls had moved across the Potomac River, they maintained a close relationship with Rose Page, the girl they had befriended at 2400, inviting her for "sleep overs" at Quarters no. 3. In her memoir Rose described an evening with them in their bedroom when she was about ten or eleven. "Before she went to bed," wrote Rose, "Lily floated around," dressed in a chiffon negligee. Marshall burst into the bedroom smelling of toothpaste and bay rum. After the two of them made room for Rose in their double bed, George leaned over to kiss Lily, yawned, and then cried out, "Oh Min, this bed feels good to I." Rose squealed with laughter and asked where that outburst came from. Marshall said it was a line from *The Gumps*, his favorite comic strip. "It's part of what Andy's always saying to his wife when he's going to bed." Later, George would carry Rose in his arms to the room they had set aside for her.[31]

In June 1924, as Marshall sat behind the wheel of his new Oakland, driving Rose over to Fort Myer, he told her that he, Lily, and Lily's mother, Elizabeth, would be leaving for China for a three-year tour of duty with the elite 15th Infantry Regiment. Rose was crushed. She wrote that Marshall gave her advice that lasted a lifetime. "Don't act like a dumbbell. You have sense enough to understand that few things last, good or bad." The day before they left, George and Lily drove to 2400 to say goodbye. Rose sobbed uncontrollably. George hugged her and said, "I wish I could spare you hard times always. God bless you, Rosie."[32]

Three months later, Lieutenant Colonel Marshall (promoted a year earlier), Lily, and her mother, Mrs. Coles, disembarked in the riverport city of Tientsin, headquarters of the U.S. 15th "Can Do" Infantry Regiment, not far from the battles among the mercenary armies of three Chinese warlords (*tuchuns*) for power in northern China. There was no such thing as a functioning central government in China. Along with military units from Britain, France, Italy, and Japan, the mission of the 15th was to defend the city, police the strategically critical Beijing-to-Mukden railroad, and protect the lives and property of U.S. and foreign nationals in the region, including hundreds of Christian missionaries. At the time Tientsin was a thriving commercial city in northeast China of almost one million people, second only to Shanghai.

Marshall was originally assigned to the 15th Infantry as an executive officer. Yet before he had a chance to unpack he was told that the commander of the regiment had been posted back to the States and his replacement would not arrive for several weeks. Marshall, therefore, became acting commander of the 850 officers and men in the regiment's two battalions. For the first time, he felt entitled to tuck a swagger stick under his arm. As the new commander, he was also informed that one of the three Chinese mercenary armies had fallen apart after a defeat in the north and was retreating toward Tientsin in search of food and plunder. It was being pursued by the army of a second warlord while the third *tuchun* moved into the vacuum and seized Beijing, the capital city. Having barely arrived in China, Marshall found his command—his first command of troops in harm's way—already being put to the test.

Counting the pursued and the pursuers, tens of thousands of armed Chinese soldiers were flooding south toward Tientsin on trains, riverboats, mules, horses, and on foot. His forces completely outnumbered, Marshall's challenge was to avoid bloodshed, persuade the Chinese mercenaries to go around instead of into the city, and to disarm them if possible. He set up five posts outside Tientsin and manned each with an American officer and five troopers, plus a team of Chinese citizens to interpret and assist. As the fleeing Chinese soldiers approached the posts they were offered bowls of rice, boiled cabbage, and hot tea in exchange for their weapons. Captain Matthew Ridgway, who would later prove to be one of America's greatest combat generals, was instructed by Marshall to divert the Chinese troops by "'bluff, expostulation or entreaty,'" but "under no circumstances to fire unless . . . fired upon."[33] It worked. There was no shooting. The Chinese troops skirted the city and continued south. In response to Ridgway's oral after-action report, Marshall "merely nodded" his approval.[34] Writing a friend, Marshall said of the encounter, "We got thru without untoward event and I snaffled a nice letter of commendation out of the affair which is worth my three years in China."[35] There were a handful of other confrontations between troops of the 15th and those of the warlords, but this was the most dangerous incident during Marshall's years in China and the only serious one that took place while he was in command of the entire regiment.

After the arrival of a permanent commander, Marshall reverted to his desk job as executive officer and settled into garrison routine. George and his two ladies, Lily and "Mud" (Lily's affectionate name for her mother), resided in a comfortable ten-room house, staffed by five Chinese servants, on Woodrow Wilson Street close to the office quarters and redbrick barracks occupied by the 15th. "We quite adore it over here and find life so easy," wrote Lily to a friend in the States. "We are actually accumulating some lovely things for our house . . . Viewed merely as a three-year shopping trip, our tour here would be well worthwhile."[36] Marshall's junior officers loved being around Lily. "You always knew exactly what Mrs. Marshall thought about you," remarked one of them, "because she told you frankly. She was not one of those Army wives who carry tales to the commanding officer."[37]

George also enjoyed the easy lifestyle and was able to spend more time with Lily than ever before. Their years in China were probably the happiest of their marriage. But while his life at home was fulfilling, his job tested his patience. In the presence of Lily or the children of other officers he was relaxed and affable; at his desk, or with troops in the field, he continued to have trouble controlling his temper. According to Mark Stoler, when Marshall was in China, he "had a reputation for excitability, abruptness, and being something of a martinet," qualities that became less pronounced years later after his thryroid operation.[38]

To be sure, he was a perfectionist, always seeking ways to improve his performance. As executive officer for U.S. Army forces in China, Marshall had to maintain peaceful relations with the warlords and their commanders in the field. In order to be effective, he knew he needed to learn to understand and speak their language. With typical focus and determination, he immersed himself in language classes provided by the regiment. Within a year, much sooner than most others in the classes, he was able to carry on causal conversations, conduct negotiations and court-martials, and discuss treaty rights in Chinese "with a fair degree of fluency."[39]

When Major Joseph Stilwell arrived in September 1926 for his second tour in China, Marshall discovered a fellow officer with whom he could practice and improve his Chinese. The two had met in 1918 when Stilwell was an intelligence officer and helped plan the Saint-Mihiel offensive. During their eight months together in Tientsin, Marshall and Stilwell developed a close professional and personal relationship. Though they had vastly different personalities, Marshall came to regard Stilwell as an ideal infantry officer. He respected Stilwell's pragmatic intelligence, his evident leadership skills, and his blunt, albeit profane and caustic manner of speaking, which would earn him the sobriquet "Vinegar Joe." Stilwell's lifelong bond with Marshall—he was one of the few who called him "George"—would be tested after he was sent to China for the fourth time during the Second World War.

During the last months of Marshall's posting in China, he became aware of what came to be known as the Northern Expedition, a seminal event in Chinese history. The Northern Expedition was a military campaign led by Moscow-trained Generalissimo Chiang Kai-shek, the objectives of which were to end the rule of the warlords in the north, drive out imperialist powers, and unify China. Chiang was the chief protégé of Dr. Sun Yat-sen, the first republican leader of China who dreamed of unification, but died in 1925. Allied with the Communist Party of China and with an army trained by German officers and equipped with Russian and German weapons, Chiang kicked off his drive north in July 1926. With each success Chiang consolidated control over the National Revolutionary Army and its political affiliate (collectively referred to here as the "Nationalists"). At the same time, his distaste for his Communist allies increased. However, Chiang could not end the alliance because, in the words of Oxford historian Rana Mitter, "the Soviets were bankrolling the Expedition."[40]

In Tientsin, the news from the south was sketchy, with some reports indicating that Chiang's Nationalists were threatening Shanghai and its colony of westerners, whom they regarded as foreign imperialists. Marshall was dispatched to Beijing in December to meet with U.S. diplomats. In a December 26, 1926, letter to Pershing, Marshall reported that "[officials] in Peking have their wind up pretty badly," fearing that the Nationalists will "leap into control of North China" soon and disregard treaties allowing the U.S. and other nations to conduct business and occupy military enclaves in China. The "old fellows," as Marshall called the American diplomats, may have had their wind up, but they did not impart a strategy for how the Western powers should deal with the critical situation in China, the worst since "Boxer days," when 189 Protestant missionaries were killed by militants of the Boxer Rebellion, nor did they advise Marshall that the 15th should be prepared to fight the Nationalists in order to protect U.S. interests in China. Based on his letter to Pershing Marshall came away from his meetings in Beijing with the hope that the foreigners, meaning the U.S. and other nations with enclaves in the country, would have "sufficient tact and wisdom" to let the situation evolve and avoid provocations. Yet he doubted that matters could be handled peacefully, so long as Western politicians continued to make public statements favoring support for the Nationalists that in Marshall's view would only encourage "violent and unreasoning outbreaks" against foreigners.[41]

By the end of March 1927, the chief U.S. diplomat in China was predicting that serious trouble was likely to occur in Beijing and the "Tientsin area in the not too distant future."[42] However, since Marshall's tour of duty with the 15th Infantry was scheduled to end in May, he would not remain in China long enough to come to grips with the anti-foreign threats posed by Chiang's Nationalists and Mao Zedong's Communists, much less the years of civil war that lay ahead. Perhaps it was only a glimpse, but as events unfolded, Marshall's initial experience in China was enormously valuable. Though his life in Tientsin was insular, he had seen enough to gain an understanding of the complex problems posed by the sheer enormity of China and the "bitter hatred" that seethed in the hearts of her people.[43] There was no way, he believed, that Western military power, or diplomatic efforts for that matter, could control the deep divisions and murderous politics of the parties vying for dominance. Marshall's understanding of the chaos that reigned and the limits of power was no doubt aided by his mastery of the language, probably the signal achievement of his first posting in China. Though his command of the language would atrophy, he would resurrect his understanding of Chinese politics and culture twenty years later when he returned as President Truman's special envoy.

After nearly three years overseas, Marshall was ready to return to the United States. On May 10, 1927, Marshall, accompanied by Lily and Mud, departed China, bound for the States and a faculty position at the National

War College in Washington. Lily looked forward to living in one of the beautiful houses on the grounds of the War College at the tip of Buzzard Point in Washington (today Fort McNair). When their ship arrived at San Francisco, Marshall learned that Shanghai had fallen to the Nationalists. A few weeks later Chiang launched a brutal coup against his so-called allies, the Communists, believing they were plotting, with Moscow's tacit support, to eliminate him. Thousands of Communists in Shanghai and other cities were kidnapped, tortured, and murdered. The rest fled to rural bases under the leadership of Mao Zedong who set up the headquarters of the Chinese Communist Party in a cave in Yenan. After achieving partial reunification of the country, Chiang established his government, the Republic of China, in the central city of Nanking, where his military and economic control was strongest. Except for an uneasy coalition between 1937 and 1941 for the purpose of resisting the Japanese invaders, the followers of Chiang and Mao would fight one another for control of mainland China for the next twenty-one years.

Back on American soil, Lily did not feel well. She tired easily. During the slow cross-country drive in George's comfortable Packard, she grew weaker. A two-week rest at her mother's house in Lexington failed to restore her vitality. When Lily and George finally reached Washington, they moved temporarily into an apartment on Florida Avenue, awaiting the arrival of their crated furnishings from China. While Marshall prepared his lectures for the coming term at the War College, Lily's condition worsened. George was terribly worried. In early August he checked Lily into Walter Reed Hospital for tests. The doctors determined that her thyroid gland was diseased and it was aggravating her preexisting heart condition. Surgery was necessary. While in the hospital Lily ate little, lost weight, and grew even weaker. She was in no condition to undergo a serious operation. George, Lily, and the doctors felt that if she was moved to her own bed in the white-columned house on the grounds of the War College, furnished with their China treasures, her spirits would be lifted, her appetite would improve, and she would begin to regain weight. In a letter to Lily's "Aunt Lottie" (Mrs. Thomas Coles), George wrote that once he brought Lily home to the three-story house on Colonel's Row, she "gained nine pounds" and her basal metabolism tests improved so much that the doctors felt she was in as "good condition for an operation as she probably will be." At the same time, he confided that she was "so weak" that she could not sit up on her own, and suffered "increasing suffocation due to the pressure of the swollen thyroid gland on her wind pipe."[44]

The risky operation was much more serious and consumed twice the time that the army surgeon expected. Apparently the goitrous thyroid had penetrated deep into Lily's chest. George was not allowed to visit Lily until two days after the operation and then only for a few minutes. Morphine kept her in and out of consciousness for five days. In a letter to his friend John Palmer, Marshall wrote that Lily was suffering from "prolonged periods of suffocation."[45] Gradually she improved. By early September she was able to pen a relatively long letter to her Aunt Lottie and a couple of cousins, describing her ordeal as "the most horrible experience of my entire life." Repeating what her surgeon said, Lily wrote, "I could only have lived a few months if I had not had the operation."[46] George's afternoon visits lightened Lily's lonely days in the hospital. "George is so *wonderful*. He puts heart and strength in me."[47] She was optimistic but realistic about how long it would take for full recovery. "Towards spring I hope to be very *much* alive & able to take up life where I left off."[48]

Early on the morning of September 15, Colonel Wiliam Lordan Keller, chief of surgery, came to Lily's room and told her she could go home the next day. Excited at the news, perhaps overexcited, Lily sat down at her desk and began writing a letter to her mother. She never finished. Her heart stopped. A nurse found her slumped over her desk, dead.[49] The last word Lily wrote was "George."[50]

A guard at the War College named Throckmorton called Marshall out of his morning lecture and led him to a telephone in a small office. "He spoke for a moment on the phone," said the guard, and "then put his head on his arms on the desk in deep grief." For a few minutes, Marshall's legendary reserve escaped him. Asked by the guard if he could do anything, Marshall gathered his emotions and replied quietly, "No, Mr. Throckmorton. I just had word that my wife, who was to join me here today, has just died." Thus, within the space of a few minutes, possibly because of the presence of someone he barely knew, Marshall's self-control and formality returned. It is not known whether Marshall completed his lecture, but he might have. Later that day Colonel Frank Hayne, Marshall's friend from China, and another officer were called to the big house overlooking Potomac Park, where Marshall had spent the afternoon alone. The two were seated in the living room when Marshall walked in, "obviously under great emotional strain and white as a sheet." Marshall sat at his desk, wrote a brief note, and handed it to one of the officers. The note read "Make all arrangements for the funeral. Don't ask me any questions." He left the room without another word and went upstairs.[51]

A brief Episcopal funeral service was held at the Old Post Chapel at Fort Myer on Saturday morning, September 17, 1927. Afterward, a crowd stood in the rain at the gravesite inside the gates of Arlington National Cemetery. Rose Page, age sixteen, was there with her mother. In her memoir Rose noted that "Colonel" Marshall "stood bareheaded with his back to me; he had a fresh haircut—how inappropriate, I thought, to notice." He passed by, holding Mrs. Coles's arm, "looking straight ahead, and when I saw his face, I wept for the first time since Lily died." A few days later, Rose spent an hour or so alone with Marshall. At first they engaged in small talk followed by awkward silences. Rose wrote that Marshall's face was "haggard . . . eyes lifeless." Eventually, she took his hand in hers. "When he spoke, his voice was scarcely audible, on the narrow verge of breaking. 'Rosie, I'm so lonely, so *lonely*.'"[52]

General Pershing was not far from Paris on the day of Lily's funeral. He and Marshal Foch were on the slopes of Mt. Valerein in Suresnes, dedicating a small American cemetery in a chill rain. To his protégé and younger friend, Pershing wrote, "[n]o one knows better than I what such a bereavement means . . ." and went on to express his sympathies.[53] Pershing was referring to the profound loss that he had suffered years earlier. Marshall was well aware of Pershing's personal tragedy—everyone in the army knew about it—but Pershing had never before brought it up. In August of 1915, while the general was in El Paso, Texas, a fire engulfed his quarters at the Presidio in San Francisco, burning to death his wife and three of his four children. Marshall understood that Pershing's reference, albeit oblique, to his deepest and most private hurt was his way of reaching out to tighten the bonds of friendship between them. Marshall was clearly touched. In reply, he reciprocated, revealing his emotions as he would with no other man. "The truth is," wrote Marshall, "the thought of all you had endured gave me heart and hope. But twenty six years of most intimate companionship, something I have known ever since I was a mere boy, leaves me lost in my best efforts to adjust myself to future prospects in life. If I had been given to club life or other intimacies with men outside of athletic diversions, or if there was a campaign or other pressing duty demanding concentrated effort, then I think I could do better. However, I will find a way."[54]

CHAPTER 4

Hands on Benning

I n the weeks following Lily's death, George Marshall returned each night alone to the big house on the grounds of the War College. There were reminders of her in almost every room. Marshall continued to grieve—he wore a black armband for months—but it was not in his nature to be depressed. Nor did he descend into self-pity. He was, however, growing restless, so anxious to escape his sedentary existence in the War College classrooms and the places that reminded him of Lily's last days that he thought he "would explode."[1]

Marshall had promised General Pershing that he would "find a way," and he did. Taking advantage of his contacts throughout the army hierarchy he made it known that he desired a new assignment outside of Washington, one that would challenge him intellectually and physically. It didn't take long for the army to come through for one of its own. In Marshall's letter of October 26, 1927, to Lily's Aunt Lottie, he informed her of a "violent change in my affairs," namely that he had just been appointed assistant commandant of the Infantry School at Fort Benning, a sprawling 97,000-acre army base located along the Chattahoochee River on the western edge of Georgia, a few miles from the city of Columbus.[2]

Given his reputation and connections, Marshall had a range of more attractive-sounding options. Why did he choose Fort Benning, down south among the yellow pines and cotton fields of rural Georgia? The short answer: the job description. It was this that appealed to Marshall's ambition and called on his strengths. As assistant commandant, Marshall would be in charge of the Academic Department of the Infantry School, the "university" for the army's company-grade infantry officers, and the "graduate degree" programs for senior officers as well as the officers of the National Guard and reserve. He would have a virtual free hand in selecting the instructors and designing the curriculum for teaching small-unit tactics, tank and air support, and battlefield mobility, an opportunity to experiment with new ideas for preparing the officers who would lead the nation in the next war that he had been thinking about ever since the last war. Marshall was convinced that the existing curriculum was antiquated, having witnessed situations in France and in China where highly intelligent officers wasted hours—and lives—writing out detailed orders in the midst of battle, as they had been trained to do, instead of reacting quickly with oral commands. Recalling one of those instances that he had observed in China in 1926, Marshall wrote to a friend, "I then and there formed an intense desire to get my hands on Benning."[3]

* * * * *

Accompanied by his sister Marie, Marshall drove south through Virginia, North Carolina, and Tennessee to Fort Benning, his first exposure to the Georgia countryside and the Deep South. By late 1927, the Georgia economy, heavily dependent on the state's cotton crops and textile mills, was already in a deep depression, well before the 1929 stock market crash and the onset of the Great Depression of the 1930s. Overproduction, man-made fabrics, technology, and foreign competition had caused cotton prices to plummet. In the mid-1920s, the effects of the boll weevil and a three-year drought drove legions of white farmers into sharecropping and low-paying jobs in the cotton mills. African Americans, who had been working the land as sharecroppers and tenant farmers since Reconstruction, were barely subsisting. Tens of thousands were forced off the land entirely, compelled to seek menial jobs in towns or migrate to cities in the North. From Virginia on down through Georgia, lynchings and legally sanctioned "whites only" signs spawned hate and fear between the races. It was an open secret that Georgia state legislators and the executive branch, including Clifford Walker, the outgoing governor, were members of or closely aligned with the Ku Klux Klan, which was chartered in Georgia in 1915.

Economic and racial issues seemed far from Marshall's mind when he and Marie arrived at Fort Benning around the 10th of November. In a letter to Aunt Lottie on the 13th, his only observation was that the roads across Georgia "were not so good." In fact, a guidebook written during the Depression characterized the road system in Georgia as "a travesty."[4] The letter included Marshall's sketch of the renovated 1850 farmhouse, magnolias, and gardens on the old Bussey Plantation that he would occupy at Benning ("the most attractive I have had") and noted that he was fortunate to have "inherited a fine colored orderly" and a "good cook," plus a "fine Cadillac car and driver that goes with the job."[5]

Marshall's intention from the moment he drove through the gates at Fort Benning was to revamp the curriculum and the techniques of teaching. However, to head off knee-jerk opposition and passive resistance, he began gradually, starting with the formation of a committee to assess and rethink the entire program of instruction. Without issuing edicts or orders, Marshall led but did not force the committee's deliberations and recommendations. His leadership emanated from lessons he learned in the Great War, his infrequent but carefully chosen suggestions, and his commanding presence. Slowly a consensus around a few guiding principles emerged. The next war would be a war of movement—offensive maneuver—supported by tanks and airplanes. Because in war the unexpected was to be expected, officers must be free to innovate and improvise, to use their imagination and think on their feet. Methods for teaching infantry tactics should be so simple "that the citizen officer of good common sense can readily grasp the idea." Above all, counseled Marshall, "speed of thought," and "speed of action," will be "essential to success."[6]

These principles were fed into the bloodstream of Benning. Instructors were not allowed to lecture from written texts or extensive notes. If they could not teach with spontaneity, they knew they would be replaced. Classes in tactics were moved outside and into the field. Students practiced leadership by taking turns commanding elements of the all-white 29th Infantry, described by Marshall as a "war-strength regiment" of some 3,500 men who were headquartered at Fort Benning.[7] In addition, Marshall arranged for a tank battalion to be attached to Benning and for demonstrations of air support by a squadron from nearby Maxwell Field. Class sizes were reduced so that every student could be given hands-on experience. To mimic the fog and confusion of war, accurate maps were banned. Training exercises took place at night in unfamiliar terrain at random places throughout Benning's 152 square miles. Student officers were confronted with surprises and adversity. They were encouraged to come up with creative and unorthodox solutions, to fearlessly disagree with their superiors. School solutions were verboten.

Marshall soon had his "hands on Benning." He would slip into the back row of classrooms or step out of the shadows during night exercises to offer his comments. Often he would appear unexpectedly in the midst of a tactical problem and pick out a student to compose an oral order on the spot. Then he would solicit a critique by the others, weighing in with his concluding thoughts. For the instructors, officer-students, and the soldiers of the 29th Infantry, the "spirit of Benning" began to emerge. Marshall made it clear that everything was subject to challenge. Student officers responded, engaging with their instructors as never before, which in turn energized and motivated the instructors. It wasn't quite an atmosphere of intellectual ferment, but there seemed to be a new seriousness of purpose at Benning, a "noticeable change in the discipline at the school," as one officer observed.[8]

The spirit of Benning did not, however, inhabit the 841 all-black soldiers of the storied 24th Infantry Regiment who were also headquartered at Benning. Except for a letter in which he described those soldiers as "a peace strength regiment," Marshall virtually ignored their existence.[9] In fact, the 24th Infantry—whose men had fought with bravery and distinction in the Spanish-American War and the subsequent Philippine insurrection—served as an indentured labor pool at Fort Benning. Many lived in rough wooden shacks in Block 45 east of the stables that they built for themselves, working as ordinary day laborers, constructing roads, barracks, and sports facilities and performing jobs as servants and gardeners for the white officers and their families. African American soldiers risked bodily harm, sometimes even their lives, if they frequented the streets and stores of all-white downtown Columbus and its residential neighborhoods. Blacks who refused or were slow to "move on" were attacked and beaten, sometimes by the white soldiers stationed at Benning.[10] Because the 24th Infantry had been involved in bloody race riots while training for the Great War in Texas, the regiment was not sent to fight in France and its access to rifles and ammunition at Benning was tightly controlled.[11] While it is possible that Marshall took steps to improve the living and working conditions of these soldiers during his years as assistant commandant, there is no evidence that he did. It is no excuse, of course, but in this regard Marshall's attitude of indifference toward the black soldiers of the 24th was similar to that of the others who commanded at Benning in the era of Jim Crow and blatant discrimination against all African Americans in the Deep South.[12]

During Marshall's four and a half years running the Infantry School at

Fort Benning, 50 of his instructors and 150 of his students were destined to become World War II generals. Marshall regarded his hand-picked instructors as "the most brilliant, interesting and thoroughly competent collection of men I have ever been associated with."[13] Among them were: Major Omar Bradley, in charge of weapons instruction, the revered "GI's General" who would go on to command an army group in France after the Normandy invasion; Lieutenant Colonel "Vinegar Joe" Stilwell, whom Marshall brought back from China in 1930 to head the tactical instructors and who would command troops in the China-Burma-India theater and serve as Chiang Kai-shek's chief of staff; Captain "Lightning Joe" J. Lawton Collins, who would earn his nickname at Guadalcanal and become a corps commander in Europe; and Walter Bedell "Beetle" Smith, who would serve as Eisenhower's "proactive chief of staff," ambassador to the Soviet Union, and number two to Allen Dulles at the CIA. Marshall's students included future combat generals such as Matthew Ridgway, Norman Cota, James Van Fleet, Courtney Hodges, Jacob Devers, and Terry de la Mesa Allen. These strong-willed soldiers, as well as dozens of others, all products of the "Benning Revolution," would be known as "Marshall's men," the backbone of the U.S. Army in the next war.

Years later Marshall recalled Benning as "magical," for it "caught me at my most restless moment, and gave me hundreds of interests, an unlimited field of activity, and all outdoors to play in."[14] No doubt his days and evenings were packed with activity, but he was essentially a lonely, private man. Marshall's father had died years earlier, he was estranged from his brother, his mother passed away in late October of 1928, and Lily's mother died the next year. All that remained of his close family was his sister Marie, who lived far north in Pennsylvania. During the summer of 1928, Marshall's goddaughter Rose visited for several weeks. On their last evening together he confided, "I dread returning to an empty house."[15]

* * * * *

On countless nights Marshall rattled around the old house, surrounded by dozens of photographs of Lily. In part to offset his loneliness he was frenetically active during the day. When not managing the Infantry School, he organized and participated in tennis matches, twice-weekly cross-country fox hunts for the officers and their wives, and strenuous point-to-point riding competitions, often at night, for the men. Under Marshall, Benning had a reputation as the "horsiest post in the Army," although Beetle Smith and Omar Bradley "hated horses."[16] Marshall was known for staging pageants for visiting dignitaries, consisting of imaginative acts to show off the sports activities at Benning rather than a solemn review of marching soldiers. These pageants were quirky but unforgettable additions to the legendary spirit of Benning. Without Lily's natural warmth and gracious presence, the all too frequent social occasions were awkward for Marshall, and especially for the officers and spouses in attendance. Although normally taciturn, Marshall tended to talk compulsively, trying too hard to engage those around him in an attempt to conceal his loneliness. With an air of confidence and command that permeated his conversation, he sometimes came off as a tiresome know-it-all, a bit of a stuffed shirt.

To adults not in Marshall's inner circle, which included all but a few, his manner and appearance in social settings could be off-putting. Except for children, he rarely addressed anyone by his or her first name. Those who told even a remotely off-color joke or story in his presence would be met by silence and a disapproving glare. Since Lily's death Marshall had lost weight, which was particularly evident in his tight, drawn facial expressions. Shortly after arriving at Benning he gave up alcohol, explaining that it was due to Prohibition. In truth, Colonel Morrison Stayer, one of Marshall's key instructors who also became his trusted doctor, had convinced him to stop both drinking (usually whiskey) and smoking (he was a heavy smoker for years) because of a thyroid condition that was causing an irregular pulse and may have contributed to his explosive temper. In the late 1920s and early 1930s, when army officers and their wives typically imbibed despite Prohibition and smoked to excess, Marshall's abstinence may have curbed conviviality even if he did not actively discourage them from indulging. Dr. Stayer was unable to control Marshall's stress-induced facial tic, which spontaneously contracted a corner of his mouth, pulling it into a grimace that was often mistaken for a smile. The spasms originally appeared when Marshall was under particular stress during the Great War and would reappear throughout the rest of his life.

Notwithstanding Marshall's distinctive traits—some would regard them as strange or eccentric—most who came in contact with him felt that he was completely devoted to his mission and to their welfare. Well out of his earshot, both adults and children often referred to Marshall with affection as "Uncle George."

As an antidote to his loneliness and to escape from Benning, Marshall often called on his driver to chauffeur him into Columbus for shopping, Episcopal Church services, and luncheon meetings of the Rotary Club of Columbus, which he had been invited to join a few weeks after arriving at Benning.[17] In the late 1920s, Columbus was essentially a mill town, located at the fall line of the Chattahoochee River, home to eight textile mills and an ironworks that employed low-paid factory workers. Between 1920 and 1930, its population jumped 28 percent to a total of more than 40,000, about a fifth of which were African Americans, mostly grandchildren of former slaves.[18] The black citizens lived north of Macon Avenue, sometimes called "the Macon-Dixon Line." They had not forgotten that as late as 1921 the mayor and the police chief of Columbus openly acknowledged their connections to the Ku Klux Klan, the racist vigilante organization that had more than 500 members in the city. Nor had they forgotten the lynchings of several blacks by the Klan or its sympathizers in and around Columbus during the previous twenty years, including the highly publicized murder of T. Z. "Teazy" McElhaney. In the summer of 1912, a mob of white citizens brazenly dragged Teazy, a black teenager, out of the courthouse in Columbus, minutes after he was sentenced to "only" three years for accidentally killing his white boyhood friend (the jury found him guilty of involuntary manslaughter), and shot him multiple times. Wives and daughters of many of the most prominent white businessmen in Columbus (including members of Rotary and the daughter of General Henry Benning) were outraged by the murder of McElhaney. They signed and circulated a petition calling for the arrest and trial of the perpetrators.[19]

At the time Marshall began frequenting Columbus in late 1927, the members of the Rotary Club consisted almost entirely of white Protestant businessmen and professionals, many of them the movers and shakers in Columbus. It was a committee of the club's leaders that had traveled to Washington in 1919 to convince Congress and the War Department to establish a permanent army base just outside Columbus on the theory that it would help revitalize the city's economy. They recommended that the post be named after Henry Benning, a Confederate brigadier general from the Columbus area. Since then, there had always been a close relationship between Columbus and the leadership at Fort Benning. Through the men he met at Rotary, Marshall became friends with many married couples his age and quickly fell into the town's social and sporting circles. One couple he surely met was Savannah-born Julian LaRose Harris and his brilliant wife, Julia Collier Harris. Julian Harris was a fellow member of Rotary. As the firebrand editor of the *Columbus Enquirer-Sun*, Harris was among the most well-known men in the city. Since the early 1920s, when Harris and his wife moved to Columbus (having lived and worked as journalists in New York and Paris), they used the newspaper's editorial pages to fight for social progress and equal rights for African Americans in the South. In 1926, their newspaper won the Pulitzer Prize for its exposure of the Ku Klux Klan, its stance in favor of antilynching laws, and its advocacy of improved education for blacks. It was the second newspaper in the South to win a Pulitzer for public service and the first ever in Georgia.[20]

Harris and his wife's views on racial issues found considerable support among affluent Rotary Club members and others with college educations living in the upscale areas of Columbus (Dinglewood, St. Elmo, Overlook), the same social groups that Marshall was acquainted with and some of the same women who signed the petition protesting the lynching of Teazy McElhaney. There are no documents establishing that Marshall and Harris were friends, but there can be no doubt that Marshall was well aware of the causes Harris and his socially active wife were fighting to advance via their editorials. Through his exposure to the Harrises, along with mutual friends at the Rotary Club and the crowd that he hunted and socialized with, Marshall acquired at least some appreciation of the injustices faced by African Americans in the Deep South. His later attitudes toward the treatment of African American soldiers were shaped by these experiences.

One couple who befriended Marshall was Thomas Charlton Hudson, chairman of the First National Bank of Columbus, and his Philadelphia-born wife, Edith Folwell Hudson. In the late spring of 1929, the Hudsons learned that recently widowed Katherine Boyce Tupper Brown and her teenage daughter from Baltimore would be visiting an old friend who lived nearby. Because the Hudsons had gotten to know Katherine years earlier, they offered to host a dinner party in honor of Katherine and her daughter. In putting together the guest list, Edith, with Tom's encouragement, suggested that Lieutenant Colonel George Marshall, age forty-eight and single, would be the perfect man to pair with Katherine, who was forty-six and presumably ready to emerge from a year of mourning her deceased husband.

Katherine was initially reluctant to attend the party, but Edith assured her it would be a small affair, consisting of only a few friends and George Marshall, whom she described as a "very interesting man from Fort Benning." On condition that Tom Hudson—not some "stranger"—would pick her and her daughter up and bring them to the party, Katherine agreed to attend.[21]

A few days later, Katherine arrived at the Hudsons' stone house on Dinglewood Drive, today listed in the National Historic Register. In the living room, she recalled seeing Colonel Marshall "standing in front of the fire place—I'll never forget. And, you know, George had the way of looking, right straight through you—he had these very keen eyes, blue eyes, and he was very straight and very military." When George declined a cocktail, Katherine remarked, "You're the first military man I ever met in my life that didn't drink . . . I knew two in Baltimore and they're both carried out of everything they go to." He smiled and laughed. So did she. "I like a cocktail as well as anybody," replied George, "but I don't break the laws of the United States." Maybe it was the way he said it, but Katherine was not put off by Marshall's "holier than thou" statement, which also happened to be a fib. In fact, as she told her interviewer, "He just fascinated me because he talked so well—I was utterly fascinated." On his part, George was impressed by her striking presence—the confident way she carried herself—and her voice, the voice of a trained Shakespearean actress, as he would soon learn. The bantering conversation flowed easily through dinner. Katherine's daughter left early for another party with a couple of the younger guests. George asked, "May I take you home this evening?" Katherine demurred. "Let me take you home," he insisted, assuring her that he knew exactly where her friend, Mrs. William Blanchard, lived. He helped Katherine into his car, "and he drove and he drove and drove." They continued to talk. After an hour or so, Katherine shot a knowing glance at Marshall, and said, "You don't know your way around Columbus yet?" George replied, "Extremely well, or I could not have stayed off the block where Mrs. Blanchard lives."[22]

The next day Marshall took charge, dispatching his chauffeur to pick up Katherine and her daughter in Columbus and drive them out to Benning for a horse show and reception. Rather than introducing Katherine to his army colleagues, George kept her to himself, lavishing her with all of his attention. She had never met anyone as worldly and experienced as Marshall, and he had never encountered a woman as glamorous, intelligent, and sophisticated as Katherine. By the end of the afternoon, it was obvious that they were mutually attracted to, if not enamored with, each other. They departed, she to return to Baltimore where her two young boys were in school, with an understanding that they would exchange letters and perhaps see each other again.

*　*　*　*　*

Katherine's story, which she only partially revealed during her initial encounter with Marshall, was most unusual, and no doubt one of the reasons why he was so intrigued with her. She had been born into a family of wealth and writers. The wealth on the Tupper side originated with Ker Boyce (cotton, finance, dry goods) and his son James Boyce (coal, railroads), two of the richest men in the South, and was inherited in part by Katherine's father, the Reverend Dr. Henry Allen Tupper Jr. On her mother's side, much of the money allegedly came from Josiah Solomon Pender, a painter and poet who owned a fleet of ships that ran the Union blockade to and from Beaufort, North Carolina, and Bermuda during the Civil War. Katherine's father, by trade an itinerant Baptist preacher who took no salary, preferred to travel the world and write books about Latin America, mission work, and democracy. Her grandfather, H. A. Tupper Sr., spoke upward of ten languages; a "very cultured man," recalled Katherine, and "a writer in a way," though he did not write books.[23] Her sister, Allene, wrote several plays, including *The Creaking Chair*, which starred Tallulah Bankhead in a 1924 production, and her younger brother, Tristram, was a prolific author of fiction and short stories as well as a screenwriter.

Most likely because her grandfather had been a trustee, Katherine and her sister attended Hollins Institute (now Hollins University), an all-women's two-year college in Roanoke, Virginia, founded in 1842.[24] Beginning in her early teens Katherine had performed in plays and pageants, but it was at Hollins that she developed a passion for acting on the stage. After graduating at age twenty in 1902, she returned to her family's home in Manhattan at 26 Gramercy Park, where her father was pastor of Calvary Baptist Church in Brooklyn. Instead of traveling in Europe or seeking a husband, Katherine courted her father's disapproval by enrolling in the American Academy of

Dramatic Arts, the premier (and only) performing arts school in the country, then situated in Carnegie Hall. For two years she focused solely on acting. "I did not care about anything else in the world," she later recalled, "a stage struck person I was!"[25] At graduation she was awarded the leading part in *Mrs. Dane's Defence*, the story of a "woman with a past," opening at the Empire Theater on Broadway.

Katherine attracted the attention of David Belasco, the leading writer, director, and theatrical producer in America, known as the "Bishop of Broadway" because he dressed in black like a priest. Belasco offered her a role in one of his plays. Her father put his foot down, compelling her to sign a paper saying she would not appear onstage. During the early twentieth century it was considered disgraceful for a young woman from a good family to become a stage actress. Although prostitutes and their customers were no longer as prevalent in the dark upper tiers and back rows of theaters as they were in prior years, the old associations lingered. Acting was still regarded as an immoral profession. The Christian clergy, particularly the Catholics, spoke out about the depravity of the theater and of the men and especially the women who worked for a living onstage. Henry Tupper was proud of Katherine's talent and success, but he could not risk his reputation as a prominent Baptist minister, lecturer, and writer.

Katherine was relentless. She persuaded her father to allow her and her sister Allene to study abroad in London. While Allene would learn to paint by painting, Katherine gave her father the impression that while she would "study" acting, she would refrain from appearing onstage. Reverend Tupper accompanied his daughters on the ship to England and found a flat for them on Torrington Square in London that belonged to two older Scottish ladies who promised to act as chaperones. He agreed to pay the rent and his daughters' living expenses. Suspecting that Katherine had a broad interpretation of the word "study," Tupper said he would end her allowance if she appeared onstage. As soon as he departed for New York she dropped her surname, in part to protect the reverend's reputation. Employing her middle name, Boyce, she began networking. It didn't take "Katherine Boyce" long to obtain an audience with Frank Benson, founder of a repertory company of actors and actresses known as the Bensonian Company that toured the cities and towns of Great Britain, Ireland, and Australia. Frank Benson and his Bensonians had achieved fame for reviving many of the Shakespeare plays that had not been produced for generations. He managed the Stratford-upon-Avon Shakespeare Festivals between 1886 and the Great War.

Once Katherine explained her background and training to Benson, he invited her to audition. She performed lines of the dying Camille, the young woman "kept" by her various lovers in the play adapted from a novel by Alexandre Dumas. "He sat there and looked at me for a long time," remembered Katherine. Then he said, "You know you'll have to study English," meaning that she would have to expunge her Yankee accent. Aside from her accent, Benson believed she had real promise. Agreeing to take her into his "school" that traveled with his company, he cautioned her that it would take time and hard work, but if her English improved sufficiently, she would be fed "parts, bits as you can do them" onstage. Benson assured her that his English teacher, Monsieur Burton of the Comédie-Française, would give her his "special attention for the next three months."[26] Regarding the cost of the school, Katherine frankly explained that when her father found out she was appearing onstage he would cut off her allowance. Benson thought it over and agreed to take her on for nothing.

Katherine joined the Bensonians on the road at York. Since they would be living on a single allowance, Allene agreed to set aside her painting lessons and travel with her. Katherine remembered their first night, "an awful place" with one small bed and a chair. Allene started to cry, accusing her sister of having "gone crazy." Katherine pointed out the window to the York cathedral. "You see that tower?" she said. "I'm going to get there." [27]

And she did. Monsieur Burton, whom she came to loathe, worked her "nearly to death . . . until three o'clock in the morning." Katherine's first speaking part was the voice of the ghost in *Hamlet*. She had to climb up a ladder behind the scenery and throw her voice "very distinctly." In another early role, her task was to catch Lady Benson gracefully "when she fell in *Macbeth*." Katherine received her first big break when one of the company's actresses left to get married. After a successful tryout in front of Benson, the two sisters spent the next season "all over Ireland" where Katherine played leading roles in three comedies—*She Stoops to Conquer*, *The Rivals*, and *The School for Scandal*—and five Shakespeare plays, including Rosalind in *As You Like It*.[28] Benson was pleased and asked her to return to England for a third season. At the time, Katherine was the only American in the company. One of Benson's actors, Clarence Derwent, wrote that she was a "very pretty young girl," one of the most "popular" members of the company. He remembered Katherine for her "sparkling brilliance as a conversationalist," a talent that caused Benson to "take a special interest in her progress."[29]

Everything pointed toward a bright future on the English stage for Katherine. When Benson offered her a seven-year contract she did not hesitate to sign. She looked forward to being the first American to play at the festival in Stratford-upon-Avon. She had "cut loose" from America and expected she would never return.[30]

The bottom fell out in Glasgow. One night as Katherine took the stage she felt a "terrible pain" in her shoulder that radiated down through her side. She tried to play through it, but soon the stage managers had to bring down the curtain. She rested for a few days and traveled with the company to Newcastle upon Tyne, where she was to play Jessica in *The Merchant of Venice*, an easy part that would allow her to sit down much of the time. Again, the unbearable pain returned. Katherine was taken directly from the theater to a nearby sanatorium where she stayed for almost three months. The doctors diagnosed her as suffering from "tuberculosis of the kidney."[31] Her condition did not improve. She had no choice but to leave the company and return home.

Katherine's doctor in New York, and probably her father as well, insisted that she be examined by Dr. Howard Atwood Kelly in Baltimore, the nation's foremost gynecologist and one of the four professors of medicine who founded Johns Hopkins Hospital.[32] Dr. Kelly debunked the TB diagnosis. Believing Katherine was "just completely exhausted," he advised her to rest at the Tuppers' summer home, the Overlook Mountain House, a 300-room hotel and resort high in the Catskill Mountains of New York near Woodstock that her father purchased in 1906 (the ruins of Mountain House can be seen today). Katherine arrived in the early spring before the tourists ascended and lived with the year-round caretaker and his wife. From Overlook Mountain's 3,000-foot elevation Katherine took in breathtaking views of the Hudson River. The physical pain and discomfort subsided, but it would take years before she got over the disappointment of having to leave England.

Throughout the year or two of Katherine's recuperation, an "oil man" from the West Coast courted her sister Allene. Their wedding took place at Mountain House on September 16, 1908. Among the groomsmen was Clifton Stevenson Brown, a young man whom Katherine and Allene had known as teenagers in Baltimore. At a party that week Clifton confessed his love to

Katherine and asked her to marry him. She turned him down, saying she was not ready for marriage and planned to return to the stage. About a year later, Katherine received a letter from Victor Mapes, a director who had opened a theater in Chicago, asking her to take a leading role in one of his new plays—*Aren't You and Belinda Engaged?* Accompanied by Allene, whose marriage already was falling apart, and her brother Tristram, Katherine moved to Chicago to resume her career.

It happened again. The same shooting pains that brought Katherine to her knees in Glasgow returned. As the curtain went down on her third or fourth performance in Chicago, Katherine recalled that she "couldn't move." She was carried out of the theater. "[T]hat was the end. They sent me right back up in the mountains."[33]

Once more Clifton Brown came up to Mountain House from Baltimore. By that time he was building his law practice, establishing a reputation as an appellate specialist. He renewed his efforts to persuade Katherine to marry him. As Katherine recalled, he said, "You're throwing your life away, Katherine; you haven't the strength for that life ... let me take care of you. You're not going to live if you keep this thing up."[34] Eventually she relented. They were married by Katherine's father in a "quiet" ceremony at the Tuppers' Gramercy Park residence on September 11, 1911.[35] Katherine was almost thirty years old. For the next sixteen plus years she and Clifton, living in Baltimore, were, as she remembered, "just as happy as we could be."[36] Thoughts of returning to the stage faded as Katherine, the supportive wife of an increasingly successful and well-regarded lawyer, managed their home on Calvert Street and the lives of their three children, Molly, Clifton Jr., and Allen.

On a warm Saturday evening in the summer of 1928, Mr. and Mrs. Clifton Brown were out on the lawn at their country club, drinks in hand. A friend turned to Clifton and said, as Katherine later recalled, "You better beware of that man, he's just crazy as a loon." Clifton responded, "What in the world can he do to me?"[37] Katherine knew who they were talking about. Louis Berman, one of Clifton's clients, had been refusing to pay Clifton's bill for legal services despite court orders and a judge's threat earlier that week to put him in jail if he didn't pay. Berman claimed the $2,500 bill was excessive, even though Clifton had spent years obtaining a judgment in his favor for $37,000. Clifton's next move was fateful. He sued his client, a step most attorneys view as risky. Bad things often happen when a lawyer sues his or her client. Clifton went to trial to collect his fee and won. Berman brought two appeals and lost.

On the Monday after drinks at the club, June 4, 1928, Katherine called Clifton at his office in downtown Baltimore. She was excited to tell him about her purchase of a second summer cottage on Fire Island. No answer. She called again. No answer, even though Clifton's secretaries and partners should have been there. The doorbell rang. Two men were at the door. Clifton was dead, gunned down in the hall outside his office door. Katherine's husband and the father of her three children was gone. That afternoon, a huge headline, along with photos of Clifton and Katherine, announced the murder on the front page of *The Baltimore News*. Recalling the pain of the two occasions when she had to quit the stage, Katherine thought that once again, "life had stopped for me."[38]

The murderer was Louis Berman, Clifton's client. Berman was convicted of first-degree murder, but avoided the death penalty by claiming insanity. Katherine was moved when Berman's bereft widow wrote her "the most beautiful letter," saying her husband was insane, that she knew Katherine had three children and felt deepest sympathy for her.[39] For the next twenty years Berman haunted Katherine by repeatedly bringing habeas corpus proceedings in a vain effort to obtain his release from prison.

Katherine was lost. After the murder she spent several sleepless months at Allene's country house in Connecticut. Knowing she had to get a grip on herself, she decided to go to a place far away where she didn't know anyone. With Molly, her oldest child, and a New York friend, Katherine booked passage on an ocean liner, having arranged to leave her two boys with friends in Baltimore. They steamed through the Panama Canal to Los Angeles, then sailed on to Hawaii. She leased a cottage for three months on Waikiki Beach. Waikiki brought back her health. On the way back to Baltimore, Katherine received a telegram from Mrs. William "Etta" Blanchard, her Hollins roommate, inviting her to visit Columbus. Without giving it much thought, Katherine accepted. This decision had life-altering consequences, both for her and for George Marshall. It resulted in a relationship that anchored Marshall for the rest of his life.

*   *   *   *   *

The letters that passed between George and Katherine after they first met in the spring of 1929 have been lost, or more likely destroyed. George may have broached the subject of marriage, or perhaps even proposed, or he may have waited until they were together again in 1930, when Katherine returned to Columbus to stay with Etta Blanchard.[40] As Katherine recalled, she warmed to the prospect of marrying George, provided that each of her boys, who had not met him, gave their consent (Molly, in school in Florence, Italy, was already fond of Marshall). And she warned Marshall that she would not neglect her children for anyone. Katherine decided that the best way to test whether marriage would work was to invite George to spend a month or so with her and the boys during the summer at her place on Fire Island, a slim barrier island off the coast of Long Island. When Katherine told the boys that she had invited Colonel Marshall to visit Fire Island, they suspected that marriage was on her mind and that a stepfather was in the wings. Clifton Jr., age seventeen, had no problem with the idea. Allen, a sensitive and willful fifteen-year-old who was most affected by his father's sudden death, was at first resistant. According to Katherine, his response to the notion of Marshall joining the family was "I don't know about that, we are happy enough as we are." The next morning Allen went to Katherine's room and told her he had changed his mind and that it was "all right" to ask Marshall to come to Fire Island. Later, he wrote the following letter to Marshall. "I hope you will come to Fire Island. Don't be nervous, it is OK with me. (Signed) A friend in need is a friend indeed. Allen Brown."[41] Marshall, who probably was somewhat nervous, was touched deeply by Allen's vulnerability and honesty. As will be seen, he would form an unbreakable bond with Allen. George and Allen would not only be "friends indeed," he would come to love Allen as though he were his own son, the son he never had.

Marshall spent five weeks with Katherine and the two boys at her cottage in the tiny village of Ocean Beach on Fire Island. By the end of his stay she was convinced that the marriage was the right decision for her and her children. Marshall was overjoyed, writing General Pershing that he would be acquiring "a complete family."[42] The couple agreed that the wedding should take place in Katherine's hometown of Baltimore, not at Benning. Oddly, the wedding ceremony was set for a Wednesday afternoon—October 15, 1930. This was because Marshall had planned two lavish wedding receptions at Fort Benning for more than a hundred of his instructors and students on the next two days.[43] Wednesday was a particularly inconvenient day for Clifton Jr. and Allen to be in Baltimore because they were attending boarding school at Woodberry Forest in Virginia. In Marshall's letter to

Pershing asking him to be his best man, Marshall said that things were so "active" at Benning that he would take the train up to Baltimore for the wedding and return with Katherine the same day.[44]

Writing with considerable understatement, Katherine described her wedding day as "a rather hurried affair." It certainly could not be called romantic. No invitations were sent, though Katherine had notified a few close friends by telephone and letter. When she and her boys arrived at Emmanuel Episcopal Church at 2:30 p.m., Cathedral Street and the front sidewalk were jammed with a crowd hoping to catch a glimpse of General Pershing. The chapel was full. Katherine's oldest son, Clifton Jr., walked her down the aisle. At the altar Allene stood next to Katherine as the maid of honor, her only attendant. Pershing, in business attire, posed ramrod straight beside George. The vows were spoken; the ceremony was brief. Outside the church, George in a dark suit looked young and craggy. Katherine was elegant in a fur-trimmed coat and flapper hat. The crowd at the train station waiting for Pershing and the wedding party was huge. Pershing returned north to Washington. The newlyweds, the two boys, and Lily's brother, Edmund Coles, gathered in the drawing room car to relax and celebrate. As the train rolled south, Clifton Jr. and Allen got off at Orange and Coles departed at Charlotte. George and Katherine spent their wedding night in a Pullman sleeper.

During her first few weeks at Benning, Katherine was bewildered by unwritten army protocol at social events, and overwhelmed by George's insistence that she join him on jarring eight-mile afternoon horseback rides. She soon became accustomed to her new home, and began to enjoy life with George in the creaky old farmhouse. With Katherine and her teenage children Marshall seemed unusually contented, fitting into family dynamics as a kindly stepfather. The tensions that typically accompany such relationships, particularly at the outset, did not surface. When Molly visited, sometimes with her friends, Marshall played tennis with them and chose to ride with her group, which was fine with Katherine. He particularly enjoyed mentoring Allen, a budding athlete, taking him on hunting and fishing expeditions to the remote areas of the post and encouraging him at football and wrestling. Allen casually began calling Marshall "George," whereas the two older children always addressed him more formally as "Colonel." As he was with Lily, George was Katherine's courtly protector, always solicitous of her "well-being and her health."[45] George and Katherine were entering their fifties, so they probably did not experience the youthful passion of their first marriages. By all indications, however, they were a deeply devoted couple, evidencing a tenderness and respect for each other during their time at Benning and the stressful years thereafter that would test their marriage.

Marshall's instructors and students hoped that his marriage would have a mellowing effect on the assistant commandant. One biographer concluded that Marshall did in fact become "less driven," and more of an extrovert.[46] Omar Bradley, who worked closely with Marshall as chief of the weapons section at Benning, disagreed, writing that Marshall "remained his same formal, aloof self." Bradley's observation is closer to the mark. Because Katherine and her family abated Marshall's loneliness, Colonel Marshall probably saw less need for engaging in the kind of forced socialization with his subordinate officers and their wives that followed Lily's death. Bradley confirmed this point, writing that after the marriage, he and his wife "seldom saw the Marshalls socially."[47]

On December 31, 1930, Marshall celebrated his fiftieth birthday with a "house full"—Katherine, her two boys, and their friends. He boasted to Pershing that he took Allen on an "eighteen mile wild cat hunt" during the holidays.[48] Marshall was at the peak of his intellectual and physical powers. His years at Benning were the most creative and arguably the most significant of his entire career. It was Marshall the innovator who revolutionized the curriculum at the Infantry School, teaching and training the next generation of combat leaders to focus on mobility, simplicity, ingenuity, and experimentation. In his back pocket, or more likely in his head, Marshall kept a "black book" listing the names and noting the traits of hundreds of instructors and students who passed through during his years at the school. Later, Marshall would call upon his black book both to weed out ineffective officers and to select the commanders who would lead America's citizen army to victory in World War II. He would be the first to admit that he made some serious mistakes. But for the most part the record would show that Marshall's judgments, formed at Benning, were sound.

*   *   *   *   *

As George and Katherine were packing their household belongings in May 1932, preparing to leave Fort Benning for a new assignment, New York governor Franklin Delano Roosevelt was moving into a new cottage at nearby

Warm Springs, the resort and farm along the slopes of Georgia's Pine Mountain that Roosevelt purchased when he was seeking a cure for the polio that had paralyzed him below the waist. Warm Springs had been a vacation spot for wealthy residents of Columbus, many of whom maintained cottages there. Under Roosevelt's tutelage, it also became a polio rehabilitation center. In the midst of his campaign to become the Democratic Party's nominee for president, Governor Roosevelt was huddled at Warm Springs with advisers and journalists, working on a speech to be given at Oglethorpe University in Atlanta, the last he would deliver before the convention. The Great Depression that had crippled the U.S. economy for more than two years was deepening. Almost 25 percent of the workforce, some thirteen million workers, stood idle. Revolution was in the air. It was at Warm Springs, just forty-five miles up the road from Benning, that Roosevelt and his advisers settled upon the message that would clinch the nomination and win the presidency: the people demand a leader who will take immediate action to defeat the Depression; Governor Roosevelt is that leader; with imagination, confidence, and enthusiasm, he will take drastic actions on the day he becomes president; above all, he will act.

While Marshall steadfastly avoided any involvement in partisan politics, he was a shrewd observer of politicians and the political process. He met Roosevelt for the first time in 1929 when the governor stopped to visit him at Fort Benning.[49] There is no evidence concerning his initial impression of Roosevelt or the substance of their conversation, yet there can be little doubt that Marshall was aware of FDR's subsequent bid for the presidency in the spring of 1932, including his resounding 8-to-1 victory in the Georgia Democratic primary. And he had to have read or heard the frank and widely publicized phrases for which Roosevelt's Oglethorpe speech of May 22, 1932, is still remembered: "This country ... demands bold, persistent experimentation. It is common sense to take a method and try it. If it fails, admit it frankly and try another. But above all, try something."[50] These words, the heart of Roosevelt's New Deal, capture the same kind of out-of-the-box thinking that Marshall advocated during his time at Benning.

*　*　*　*　*

In the summer of 1932, as George and Katherine were getting settled at Fort Screven on Tybee Island near Savannah, where Marshall assumed command of a battalion of the 8th Infantry Regiment, America's economy continued to slide into the maw of an unprecedented worldwide depression. In a misguided effort to reduce the deficit, Congress, under president Herbert Hoover, enacted cutbacks in army and navy appropriations, including mandatory furloughs without pay and freezes on promotions and pay raises. At the same time, the world was becoming a much more dangerous place. The earliest hot spot ignited by the global depression was Manchuria in northwest China. There, extremist Japanese army commanders, preparing to transform the region into a food-producing area for Japan's farmers since the domestic agriculture sector had declined disastrously, blew up a Japanese-controlled railroad near Mukden in September 1931 and blamed it on the Chinese. The incident was used as a pretext by Japan to take over the whole province by force. Preoccupied with the Depression, America's diplomatic reaction was timid, and the League of Nations refused to impose sanctions on Japan. This weak response encouraged the Japanese government to withdraw from the League and foreshadowed wider aggression by Japan that would spread to the rest of China and the European colonies in East Asia.

In Germany, former corporal Adolf Hitler engineered a political revolution by captivating German voters, especially the country's six million unemployed, with his message of national redemption. Hitler was a singularly gifted speaker and performer. Between 1928 and 1932, his Nazi Party shocked the German establishment by increasing its share of the vote in the Reichstag (parliament) from 2.6 percent to 37.4 percent. By the end of July 1932, it was by far the largest of a handful of political parties in the Reichstag with 230 seats. Six months later, while Roosevelt was preparing for his presidency, Field Marshal Paul von Hindenburg, the president of Germany's crumbling Weimar Republic, was persuaded by right-wing advisers to ask Hitler to become Reich chancellor (supposedly a coalition cabinet would curb Hitler's extremism). Few realized it at the time, but this was a momentous political miscalculation that would lead into an abyss of war and genocide. It wasn't as if Hitler hid his intentions. He had spoken and written of restoring Germany to greatness by casting off the shackles of Versailles, destroying Jews and Bolsheviks, rebuilding the armed forces, and acquiring by force more "living space" for the German people at the expense of Poland and the Soviet Union. But the politicians discounted his stated intentions as overblown rhetoric and they underrated his abilities. After all, Hitler was just a demagogue who had emerged from the lunatic fringe, with no credentials and no experience indicating that he could effectively take over and run the government of Germany, let alone assume dictatorial powers.

Marshall had received firsthand reports in the winter of 1931–32 on the military situation in Germany, including the extent to which German armed forces were (and were not) complying with restrictions on expansion imposed by the Treaty of Versailles and subsequent postwar agreements.[51] However, once he left Benning for Fort Screven and subsequent posts he was dependent on the U.S. press, mainly *Time* magazine, for information about Hitler's Germany.[52] It was not until January 2, 1936, that Colonel Marshall received a detailed assessment from a source in Berlin on the state of Germany's military under Hitler, who by then had secured total power. In a confidential letter, Major Truman Smith, the military attaché in Berlin and a former Benning instructor, informed Marshall that "the most powerful if not the largest army and air force in Europe is coming into existence under a strict veil of secrecy." By the fall an army of 600,000 would be trained and ready. Smith correctly predicted "trouble," but probably not until 1939 when Germany, he wrote, will "expand in Eastern Europe" unless stopped by the "western nations." Smith further wrote that it wouldn't surprise him if France and England gave "Germany a free hand to help herself to Russian territory," in which case it would take an army of three million men to stop her. He concluded by providing Marshall with a description of some of the fifty new weapons, vehicles, and army units that the German army was developing.[53]

For the first time Marshall had solid information indicating that Hitler was preparing for war. There is no evidence suggesting that Marshall thought Hitler's aggressive designs would threaten the security of the United States. However, Smith's letter gave him a sense of what he and those he had taught at Benning might be up against if, for some unfathomable reason, they were drawn once again into a European war.

CHAPTER 5

God Help Us All

I n mid-May 1938, George Marshall, by then a brigadier (one star) general in command of the 7th Infantry at Vancouver Barracks, was ordered to report to the War Department in Washington. He was to be temporarily assigned as head of War Plans with the understanding that he would be made deputy chief of staff. The timing was propitious. While Marshall was entering the final stages of his rapid but by no means predictable ascent to become chief of staff of the United States Army, Truman Smith's warning that Adolf Hitler's powerful army and air force would cause "trouble" in Europe was about to come true.

With the move to the nation's capital, the Marshalls would leave behind what Katherine remembered were "two of the happiest years of our lives."[1] In addition to commanding troops, Marshall was responsible for the boys working in some thirty-five Civilian Conservation Corps camps in the Pacific Northwest, duty for one of FDR's most successful New Deal initiatives that buttressed Marshall's faith in the value and effectiveness of a citizen army. Katherine often traveled with her husband on trips to inspect the CCC camps. Together, they took time to fish, hike, and picnic along the magnificent rivers and streams in Oregon, Washington State, and Montana.

In linen suit and straw boater, Marshall reported for duty at the Old Post Office Building on Pennsylvania Avenue in July 1938. It was apparent to everyone that a global crisis was brewing. Hitler, the German chancellor, was intent on seizing part, if not all, of Czechoslovakia, even at the risk of war. He had flouted the Treaty of Versailles by marching into the Rhineland buffer zone, and had consolidated his power over the continent by establishing the "Rome-Berlin Axis" with Benito Mussolini, the fascist dictator of Italy. The Führer had joined hands with Japan, and later Italy, in an alliance against the Soviet Union called the Anti-Comintern Pact, and in March he annexed Austria. Hatred of Jews was at the core of Nazi ideology. Destruction of businesses, evictions from homes, theft of personal property, arrests, and beatings forced thousands of Jewish citizens to flee Germany and Austria, leading to a refugee crisis in Europe. In Asia, Japan's full-scale invasion of China that began in 1937 continued to rage, with reports of mass rape and butchery of civilians by Japanese soldiers.

Due to pressure from isolationists in Congress, and his concern about being too far out in front of public opinion, Roosevelt tempered and sometimes backpedaled his warnings about the growing threat to America's national security and the need for military preparedness. His proposals to boost the strength of America's armed forces were modest at best. Meanwhile, the two political appointees who headed his War Department, Marshall's civilian bosses, had locked horns in a bitter feud, a situation that Roosevelt tolerated, and perhaps even encouraged.

The feud began in 1937 during FDR's second term when he was faced with the political decision of whom to appoint as his secretary of war. The leading candidate was short, plump Harry Woodring, a one-term Democratic governor of Kansas who had been defeated by Alf Landon in 1932. Woodring had been an early supporter of Roosevelt and enjoyed a strong relationship with the president. A stylish dresser, he and his younger, attractive wife had become a socially prominent couple since their arrival in Washington. Following the death of Secretary of War George Dern in 1936, FDR had tapped Woodring as temporary secretary. Under Woodring, the War Department seemed to be running smoothly, and he worked well with Congress and the army brass, including Chief of Staff Malin Craig. Still, the president seemed to have lingering doubts about making the arrangement permanent.

The other candidate was Louis Johnson, a veteran of the Great War who had survived the Meuse-Argonne offensive. Standing six feet two and weighing more than two hundred pounds, Johnson was an ambitious, large-boned Virginian who had been born above the family corner grocery store in Roanoke. He studied law at the University of Virginia, where he was literally and figuratively the big man on campus—a heavyweight boxing and wrestling champion, leading debater, and president of his class. After the war, Johnson presided over the West Virginia law firm of Steptoe & Johnson, and rose to become national commander of the million-member American Legion, one of the most powerful lobbying organizations in the 1930s. During the 1936 presidential campaign, he headed the Veterans Committee of the Democratic National Committee and provided strategic advice to FDR on veterans' bonus issues, helping Roosevelt win his second term.

Following the election, Johnson, an ardent advocate of airpower and military preparedness, orchestrated an intense lobbying effort to try to secure the secretary of war appointment. He made clear to Roosevelt's confidants that he had no interest in the assistant secretary position. Johnson's hopes soared when the press began reporting that the president would probably *not* choose Woodring. There was truth to those reports. Roosevelt was in fact wavering. Johnson's energy and commitment to expanding the army air corps were attractive attributes. However, the president surprised Johnson and many insiders when he reappointed Woodring and sent his name to the Senate for confirmation.

In the weeks after the president's decision, Roosevelt's aides, no doubt at his insistence, redoubled their efforts to persuade Johnson to accept the number two position. West Virginia senator Matthew Neely, Johnson's most influential supporter and friend, was contacted by former head of the Democratic National Committee Jim Farley, one of FDR's key political advisers and at the time his postmaster general. According to Neely's notes, Farley said to him, "You can tell Louis I think within three or four months he will be made Secretary if he will take the post [assistant secretary of war]."[2] This was enough for Johnson. Knowing how Farley and Roosevelt operated, Johnson interpreted Farley's words as a signal, if not a promise, from the lips of the president that he would soon replace Woodring as secretary of war. On June 13, 1937, Johnson accepted the assistant secretary position. He was sworn in on June 28, a year before General Marshall arrived.

Farley later denied any suggestion that his words amounted to a commitment from the president. FDR too claimed that he never authorized such a deal, and there is nothing other than circumstantial evidence that he did. Whether Johnson was misled, or whether he simply chose to hear what he wanted to hear, will never be known for sure. Regardless, he was convinced the secretaryship was his. "Almost in the same breath with which he took office," wrote syndicated columnist Drew Pearson, "he informed intimates that he had been appointed for the express purpose of replacing Woodring in a few months."[3]

Naturally, Johnson's drumbeat of statements to department officials, both civilian and military, that he was about to be named secretary infuriated Woodring. Taking advantage of provisions in the National Defense Act of 1920, which gave the assistant secretary independent responsibility for procurement and economic mobilization, Johnson deliberately sought to undermine Woodring's authority. He believed the Act gave him the right to bypass the secretary and consult directly with the president. What's more, he was at odds with Woodring on the fundamental issue that divided the nation: how to respond both to Hitler's aggression in Europe and Japan's brutal war in China. Woodring reflected the views of the isolationists, while Johnson was an outspoken supporter of military preparedness—though not yet an interventionist. Johnson was firmly committed to building the strength and capability of the U.S. Army for the purpose of deterrence or to wage war if America's security were to be threatened. The vast personal and ideological differences between the two men caused them to disagree so often and so violently that they would not even speak to each other for weeks on end.

The president was not only responsible for this infighting, he tolerated it. When Roosevelt appointed Johnson as assistant secretary he was well aware that the man's dedication to rapidly building the strength of the army and the army air corps would offset, if not overwhelm, the cautious, penurious Woodring. Such a juxtaposition was consistent with Roosevelt's practice of selecting top officials to administer government agencies who would act as counterweights to one another. By pitting opposites against one another, Roosevelt guaranteed that he, not his feuding appointees, would end up resolving major policy issues.

By the time Marshall arrived, the atmosphere in the War Department was poisonous. On his first day, he was greeted by General Malin Craig, the current army chief of staff who for the past year had been caught in the cross fire between Johnson and Woodring. "Thank God, George," Craig said to his old friend from the Great War, "you have come to hold my trembling hands."[4]

Marshall was well aware that the deputy chief of staff post was not a traditional stepping-stone to the chief of staff appointment. Nevertheless, the top job was within his reach, and he would have only one shot. Craig's four-year term was set to expire on August 31, 1939, when Marshall would be a few months shy of fifty-nine. Mandatory retirement age was sixty-four; a prospective chief of staff had to be young enough to serve for four years before reaching that age. If Marshall was not appointed to replace Craig, he would be disqualified from consideration for a subsequent appointment. To make matters more daunting, of the five general officers eligible for the position, Marshall ranked fifth in seniority.

Fortunately for Marshall, one matter over which Woodring and Johnson did not disagree was whether Marshall should be promoted to deputy and then appointed chief of staff. They both supported him, although for different reasons. But this did not ease the difficulty of his temporary job as head of War Plans, nor his path to become chief of staff. Nearly every day Marshall was asked to comply with orders, often conflicting, from his two civilian superiors, whom he knew were implacable enemies. If he sided with one, it would appear he was allying against the other. The president also presented a challenge. If, to curry favor with Marshall, Johnson or Woodring lobbied Roosevelt to appoint Marshall as chief of staff, or spread rumors that Marshall would soon be appointed, it could hurt Marshall's chances, for Roosevelt did not like to be pressured. He might even suspect Marshall himself was behind such a campaign. As long as Woodring and Johnson occupied the two top slots at the War Department, Marshall had to walk a political and bureaucratic tightrope—one which he could fall off of at any moment.

* * * * *

As summer of 1938 faded into fall, Hitler's desired war in Czechoslovakia seemed imminent. The pretext was the lofty principle of self-determination. Three million ethnic Germans in Czechoslovakia's Sudeten region, called the Sudetenland, near the Bavarian border were clamoring to rejoin their countrymen in the Reich, thundered Hitler. If the Western powers resisted, war would once again break out in Europe. The French, who had agreed to protect Czech borders, called up 500,000 reserves. In Great Britain, where the pledge to defend Czechoslovakia was less direct, gas masks were distributed and air-raid shelters were dug in London parks. On September 12, Roosevelt was in his specially fitted railroad car with his closest adviser, Harry Hopkins, listening to a radio broadcast of Hitler's Nuremberg address to the soldiers of the German Wehrmacht. Roosevelt, who understood German, listened as Hitler threatened to make war in the east and announced, for the first time, that he was building a wall of fortifications on Germany's western frontier. "I have never heard Adolf so full of hate, his audience quite so on the borders of bedlam," wrote CBS correspondent William Shirer. "What poison in his voice."[5]

Soon after hearing Hitler's speech, FDR asked Hopkins to quietly travel to the West Coast and assess the production capacity of the U.S. aircraft industry. In addition to being the president's most trusted adviser, Hopkins was also head of the Works Progress Administration (WPA), a New Deal agency whose mission was to put Americans to work on infrastructure projects. Roosevelt felt Hopkins was the right man to make recommendations to expand production under a program the WPA could help finance and implement. The president was coming to the conclusion that France and Britain were likely to capitulate to Hitler's demands not only in Czechoslovakia but elsewhere in Europe primarily because they could not come close to matching his airpower. He was already thinking about a plan to mass-produce planes in the U.S. and sell them to the French and British. Hopkins returned from his trip with ambitious recommendations. He believed that "the War Department should present a big program" to Congress not only for airplanes but also for the "manufacture of modern armaments . . . and the employment of men in all arsenals . . ."[6]

* * * * *

Off Cape Hatteras in the Atlantic, another storm was brewing. This one was barreling up from the south at an unprecedented speed of sixty miles per hour. Some 400 miles north, Katherine Marshall was spending the last days of September at Cliff Cottage, her summer house on Fire Island, with her daughter, Molly. Her two boys, now in their early twenties, had gone back to their jobs in New York. Most of the summer residents had departed. On a cold and rainy Wednesday, the morning papers reported that British prime minister Neville Chamberlin would likely fly to meet Hitler again, this time with a proposal for an orderly transfer of the Sudetenland to Germany. At three in the afternoon, with little warning, the Great Hurricane of 1938— the "storm of the century"—made its first landfall on Fire Island, slamming into the low barrier dunes with winds at 90 miles per hour, gusting as high as 150. Katherine and Molly spent part of that terrifying night huddled in their cottage, the storm surge crashing against the walls and the surf coursing around the cement foundation. Wading in waist-deep water, they sought refuge in a neighboring cottage. Hundreds of houses disappeared. The storm claimed upward of 650 lives, eight on sparsely populated Fire Island. Katherine and Molly survived, uninjured.

The next morning Marshall commandeered an army bomber and pilot at Bolling Field and flew low over the island. "From the air," Marshall wrote Pershing, "I saw the cottage had not been destroyed, though most of the houses in the vicinity had collapsed or been demolished."[7] At Mitchel Field on Long Island he transferred to a small two-seat open cockpit trainer and landed on the debris-strewn beach in bright sunlight near Katherine's battered home. Katherine would never forget the sight of her husband in flight gear and goggles as he loomed in the doorway and then wrapped her in his arms. She recalled crying out, "Why you are the most beautiful thing I ever saw in my life."[8]

A week later, in Munich, Hitler and Mussolini sat down with Neville Chamberlain and French prime minister Édouard Daladier and they agreed that the German army could occupy the Sudetenland, including all of its fortifications and major industries. A significant part of Czechoslovakia was now in Nazi hands, and with no Czech representatives in the room to argue. Hitler promised that this was his last demand. Roosevelt's instinct was proven correct: Great Britain and France gave in to Hitler and capitulated. With the threat of war in Europe temporarily subsided, on the afternoon of September 30, an enormous crowd gathered on the tarmac at London's Heston Airport. Standing in a driving rain, they erupted in cheers when Chamberlain emerged from his plane and opened his black umbrella, ever after the symbol of appeasement. That evening the prime minister appeared in an upper-floor window of No. 10 Downing Street. Waving a paper in his hand that contained Hitler's signature, he shouted to the crowd below that he had brought "peace with honour" back from Munich. Infamously, he added, "I believe it is peace in our time."[9] In the House of Commons Winston Churchill declared that the Munich agreement was a "total and unmitigated defeat . . . This is only the beginning of the reckoning."[10]

Like Churchill, Roosevelt was convinced that the world had not heard the last of Hitler's territorial demands. He cabled Chamberlain, "Good man," but privately Roosevelt told his cabinet that the Western European allies "would wash the blood from their Judas Iscariot hands."[11] Throughout September the president, along with Harry Hopkins, Aubrey Williams (deputy WPA administrator), and Tommy Corcoran (presidential adviser), had been secretly formulating plans for a dramatic expansion of aircraft production in the United States. The most effective and least expensive way to protect the nation without going to war, reasoned Roosevelt and his team, would be to produce a vast armada of warplanes in America and sell them to France and Great Britain.

The official in the War Department best suited to lead this effort was Assistant Secretary of War Louis Johnson. By statute he was in charge of procurement for the army air corps; what's more, he was a longtime champion of airpower who was familiar with executives in the industry and had for months supported increasing production. But before Roosevelt could deal directly with Johnson, he had to find a way to work around Secretary of War Woodring. Roosevelt knew that Woodring would vigorously oppose his aircraft expansion program, arguing that its purpose—arming allies in Europe—would likely drag the United States into war, that it would be far too expensive, and that it needed to be balanced against increases in ground forces.

Roosevelt devised a stratagem to bypass Woodring. The midterm elections of 1938 were set to take place in early November. Since Woodring was an effective surrogate for the administration, the president asked him to hit the campaign trail on behalf of Democratic congressmen who were New Deal supporters (FDR's efforts in the spring primaries to "purge" conservative Democrats had largely failed). Woodring readily agreed. During almost all of October he was out of Washington. In his absence Johnson was acting secretary of war.

No one realized it at the time, but the president's move greatly enhanced the odds that Marshall would become chief of staff. On October 14, Roosevelt summoned Johnson to the White House and placed him in charge of the aircraft expansion program. A breathtaking goal of 15,000 planes per year was casually mentioned, but the president did not elaborate on his idea of selling a large portion of those planes to the French and British. The next day Johnson called a meeting in the War Department to establish objectives and assign responsibilities. As the staff was gathering for the War Council meeting, Johnson startled Chief of Staff Malin Craig by asking, "What about a deputy chief of staff?" The deputy had responsibility for the army budget and the post had been vacant for two weeks. Craig had been procrastinating. Not wanting to act until Woodring returned, Craig responded,

"We'll work that out." Johnson, who had been deeply impressed by Marshall's intelligence and organizational abilities since first meeting him at the Vancouver Barracks in January, pressed the matter. He needed to have Marshall in the deputy slot as his numbers analyst and adviser. In the presence of the other officers and with a menacing tone, Johnson declared, "There is not going to be any War Council meeting until that thing is worked out." Craig, realizing Johnson was serious, left the room and returned a few minutes later to announce, "The orders have been issued."[12]

The appointment came at a time when the president's plans to vastly expand aircraft production promised to test the army's shoestring budget. As deputy chief of staff, Marshall would be in the room when advice was given and decisions were made that affected the funding of the entire U.S. Army and Army Air Corps. This meant that Marshall would soon have face time with both the president and his closest aide, Harry Hopkins.

A month later, Monday, November 14, 1938, Marshall was ushered into the White House for a top secret meeting in the Cabinet Room. His colleagues from the War Department—acting secretary of war Johnson, Johnson's executive assistant Colonel James Burns, Chief of Staff Malin Craig, and head of the army air corps General Hap Arnold—took their seats at the long table. Almost all of the other chairs were occupied by cabinet officials and administration aides, including Hopkins. Woodring, by this time back in Washington, was conspicuously absent; in fact, he had not even been invited. Marshall found a seat in a side alcove. At two o'clock President Roosevelt was wheeled in to the head of the table. He was all business and did most of the talking. He began by stating that in light of German military power, particularly its more than two-to-one air superiority, "the United States now faced the possibility of an attack on the Atlantic side in both the Northern and Southern Hemispheres." The only weapons that stood a chance of deterring Hitler's territorial ambitions, he argued, were warplanes, not ground forces. Referring to the Führer's threat to take Czechoslovakia by force of arms, the president reportedly said, "Had we had this summer 5,000 planes and the capacity to immediately produce 10,000 per year, even though I might have had to ask Congress for authority to *sell or lend* them to the countries in Europe, Hitler would not have dared to take the stand he did."[13] Based on these unchallenged assertions, Roosevelt announced that he had decided that the U.S. must greatly expand its capacity to produce warplanes in order to deter

further aggression; and that he planned to ask Congress for authority to produce 10,000 planes immediately plus capacity to produce 20,000 planes per
year, at a cost of $500 million. At no point did the president indicate that he
actually intended to sell these planes to the British and French to help them
deter or defeat Hitler. Turning to Johnson at the conclusion of his remarks,
FDR asked how soon he could prepare a plan to implement his proposals.
"By Saturday!" responded the ever confident acting secretary.[14]

The president continued around the room, seeking approval from the
gathered officials and aides. "Most of them agreed with him entirely," Marshall recalled, "[and] had very little to say, and were very soothing." When
Roosevelt spotted Marshall, whom everyone in the room knew was a candidate to become chief of staff, he said, "Don't you think so, George?" In
fact, Marshall believed the proposal was amateurish and militarily unsound.
Further, he was mildly irritated by Roosevelt's use of his first name, since
they barely knew each other. Marshall responded politely, some said coldly:
"I am sorry, Mr. President, but I don't agree with that at all." Roosevelt gave
Marshall a startled look. With that, he adjourned the meeting, a mere half
hour after it began. "[W]hen I went out," recalled Marshall, "they all bade
me good-by and said that my tour in Washington was over."[15]

It was a remarkable moment, one that most who were there would never
forget. Twenty years earlier Marshall had confronted Black Jack Pershing,
the most powerful general in the army, with his version of the truth. Now he
had rebuffed the president of the United States. He later explained that he
thought FDR's proposal to produce 10,000 planes for $500 million did not
take into account the recruitment and training of pilots, the munitions required, and the infrastructure needed to support a large air armada. Moreover, if Congress was going to appropriate that much money to the army,
Marshall and Craig wanted it to be used to create more of a balance between
ground and air forces. After all, in the fall of 1938, America's regular army of
174,000 ranked eighteenth or nineteenth in the world. Even if Roosevelt
had made it clear that he intended to sell most, if not all, of the planes to the
British and French, Marshall would probably still have responded negatively
because the planes, not to mention increased ground forces, would be
needed by the U.S. to deter and defend against an attack on the Western
Hemisphere, the possibility of which Roosevelt had just put forth in his argument to the group assembled in the Cabinet Room.

There is no evidence that Marshall had second thoughts about the fact that he was the only one in the packed room to openly disagree with Roosevelt, nor that he believed that he had hurt his chances to be appointed chief of staff. Indeed, he later suggested that the incident in the Cabinet Room may have improved his odds because the president knew that "I would tell him the truth so far as I personally was concerned."[16] Recent Marshall biographers have suggested that he may have deliberately opposed the president in order to get attention.[17] This is sheer speculation—Marshall would not have jeopardized his career by attempting such a ploy.

Marshall did, however, initiate a lobbying effort to persuade the president of the need for a balanced buildup of the nation's defense capability. Knowing that he did not yet have the necessary stature, he enlisted General Pershing to approach Roosevelt. On Armistice Day, Pershing discussed the matter with FDR in person. To underscore his arguments, Marshall prepared for Pershing a three-page letter that the General of the Armies signed and sent without alteration to Roosevelt on November 25. Based on the president's noncommittal response in early December ("I am having a study made"), Pershing's efforts had little effect.[18]

Two weeks later Marshall was once again in the White House, along with Johnson, Burns, and Craig. They were in hot water with the president. Roosevelt had expected to receive from them a plan to implement his aircraft production proposal. Instead, Johnson had interpreted FDR's request as an opportunity to ask for much more than airplanes, a first step toward all-out preparedness. Johnson had directed Craig and Marshall to draw up plans not only to build a fully equipped and manned air corps but also to upgrade and increase army and reserve ground forces. The total cost was $2.1 billion. The president was irate. "I sought $500 million worth of airplanes and I am being offered everything except airplanes," he railed.[19] The discussion was heated, although there is no record of how Marshall reacted. In light of what happened to Marshall's career in the next few months, however, he must have done or said something to impress Roosevelt.

* * * * *

A day or two after Christmas 1938, Marshall received word that Harry Hopkins, newly appointed secretary of commerce, would like to call upon him. Over the years Marshall had corresponded and spoken by telephone with

Hopkins when military and New Deal budgetary issues overlapped, but the two men were virtual strangers. All Marshall knew about Hopkins was that he had been an effective administrator of the WPA and was very close to the president.

Roosevelt was once asked by a political rival why he kept that man—meaning Hopkins—so close to himself. "That man asks for nothing except to serve me,"[20] he responded. But it was more than a singular willingness to serve. Hopkins was shrewd. He was said to have a "mind like a razor [and] a tongue like a skinning knife."[21] Recognizing that Hopkins knew how to cut through bureaucracy and get things done, FDR drew Hopkins into his inner circle, relying on him more and more to help pick the talent and solve the problems that would help prepare the country for war. The closer Hopkins came to Roosevelt, the more Republicans and other outsiders regarded him as a spectral figure in the administration—slightly sinister, kind of a back-room Rasputin.

Marshall wasn't sure why Hopkins had asked to meet with him. Was he sizing him up for the chief of staff job? Or did he have something else on his mind? Of one thing Marshall was certain: this was to be no casual encounter. Hopkins began their meeting by probing Marshall's objections to Roosevelt's proposal to vastly increase the production of airplanes. The conversation soon turned to a broad-ranging discussion of the shortcomings in the nation's air and ground forces. Like Hopkins, Marshall was a quick study. It was obvious that he had complete command of the facts, yet he didn't waste words. By the end of an hour, Marshall's fact-based arguments outlining the woeful state of America's preparedness shocked Hopkins so much that he urged Marshall to fly at once to Warm Springs or Hyde Park and discuss this matter with FDR. Marshall politely declined. He did not want to jeopardize his chances to be appointed chief of staff by stepping outside the army's chain of command. Yet, as the discussion wound down, he believed he had gained a powerful ally and probably the president's ear on the urgent need to adopt a balanced approach toward increasing the strength and capability of the army and army air corps.

During the next two weeks Hopkins persuaded Roosevelt to restore a measure of balance to his request for national defense appropriations. On January 12, 1939, the president sent a message to Congress requesting that a total of $550 million be appropriated to the army, roughly 60 percent to be allocated to the production of warplanes (3,000 instead of 10,000) and the other 40 percent to army ground forces (for guns, munitions, and incentives to expand industrial capacity). Given the looming threats to national security, the amount requested was scarcely adequate, but at least it was a start and it established the principle of a balance between ground and air forces.

In the words of playwright Robert Sherwood, who was one of Roosevelt's speechwriters, Marshall's brief meeting with Hopkins between Christmas and New Year's of 1938 "was the beginning of a friendship that was deep and enduring and important."[22] On the surface they couldn't be more different. Fueled by Lucky Strikes and caffeine, Hopkins was a ramshackle character, an informal Iowan with tie askew, feet perched atop his government desk, and phone pressed to his ear. Marshall was the opposite, proper and reserved almost to a fault. Hopkins, first divorced and then widowed, dated glamorous women and hung out at nightclubs and the racetrack. Marshall preferred quiet evenings at home with his wife, sipping a watered-down highball. Yet they each shared qualities of selflessness, a commitment to reform, an ability to get at the heart of complex problems, and personal courage. Eventually they would call each other "Harry" and "George." For the "three years before Pearl Harbor, and for at least a year thereafter," wrote Sherwood, "Hopkins was Marshall's principal channel of communication with the White House." In 1947, Marshall told Sherwood that his appointment as chief of staff "was primarily due to Harry Hopkins."[23]

Marshall foresaw one perilous obstacle in his path to the chief of staff appointment that he might not be able to surmount—his health. Scheduled for the week of January 16 was his annual physical examination, the results of which would be read by Malin Craig and President Roosevelt. The problem was his heart. Even a mild defect could doom his ambition to be chief of staff.

Since 1936, Marshall had experienced an irregularity in his pulse—heart arrhythmia. In February 1937, surgeons at the Letterman Hospital in San Francisco removed his swollen thyroid, which was thought to be causing the arrhythmia. Within a few months his pulse was normal, although he was careful to take catnaps during the day. The only person other than Katherine who Marshall told about the operation and his heart condition was Colonel Morrison Stayer, the army doctor whom he had befriended in China and who treated him privately during his years at Fort Benning and thereafter. When Marshall's episodes of arrhythmia began recurring in the fall of 1938, he turned to Stayer, knowing he would soon have to pass a physical.

The two men secretly devised a scheme whereby Marshall was to begin in-gesting an undisclosed medication prescribed by Stayer a week before the physical in order to obscure the pulse irregularity.[24]

Their plan was thrown into a cocked hat by General Malin Craig. After what Marshall described as a "tumultuous" morning with "much emphatic argument"—not great for his arrhythmia—Craig and Marshall were eating a sandwich in Craig's office when the subject of Marshall's physical exam came up.[25] Marshall, who had begun his dosage of Dr. Stayer's medicine only the day before, said his physical was scheduled to take place in a week. Craig re-plied that there would never be time to fit it in during that week. In Marshall's presence, Craig picked up the phone and made an appointment for Marshall for that very afternoon. Marshall had no choice. He had to undergo the phys-ical without benefit of the weeklong drug regimen that Stayer prescribed.

Somehow Marshall received a passing grade, even though an "irregular-ity of pulse" was found, which the attending doctor attributed to smoking. When Marshall admitted that he had stopped smoking, the doctor deftly adjusted his theory of causation and said the arrythymia was probably due to "desk belly" and lack of exercise.[26]

Now that Marshall had been given the green light on his health, a few stumbling blocks remained on his path to chief of staff. One was his flock of overzealous supporters. "My problem," he confided to Rose Page, "is stop-ping the well-wishers who want to intercede for me."[27] He had been in Washington long enough to know that a flood of supportive letters, tele-grams, and telephone calls to the president or members of his administration would be counterproductive. Recipients, most importantly FDR, would suspect Marshall of orchestrating a lobbying campaign, which was the last thing he wanted. Marshall did what he could to discourage well-wishers from voicing their support, making it clear that he wished to be considered for the position strictly on the basis of his record. More than that, however, there was little Marshall could do to restrain headstrong supporters such as the vociferous and overbearing Louis Johnson. He could only hope that the president would see that Johnson's motives, like those of many others, were self-serving—if Marshall received the appointment, Johnson would take credit for making it happen and use it to curry favor with Marshall.

Lynne Olson, in her book *Those Angry Days*, states that Marshall "qui-etly lobbied for the top Army job [chief of staff] for more than a year."[28] A

thorough review of the papers of Pershing, Marshall, and those who surrounded him, as well as press reports during the year prior to the president's
decision, indicates that Marshall actively discouraged anything remotely
resembling a lobbying campaign. Although there are letters showing that
Marshall enlisted Pershing in the mid-1930s to recommend him for his first
star, there is nothing to indicate that he asked Pershing in to advocate on his
behalf for the chief of staff position, nor is there any evidence that Pershing
approached Roosevelt or anyone else in the administration to recommend
that Marshall be named to the top army job. Indeed, Marshall avoided publicity and public appearances that might give the impression he was seeking
the appointment. In a letter to Pershing dated January 16, 1939, Marshall
said that he was "sorry to see" his name mentioned as possible chief of staff
in the New York newspapers. "I suppose this is inevitable," he wrote, "but it
is certainly distasteful to me—and I think not at all helpful."[29] Nor is there
evidence that Marshall discussed, much less advocated, his appointment
with "Harry Hopkins and other key presidential advisers," as Olson asserts.[30]

Another barrier to the chief of staff job was Major General Hugh Drum,
whom many regarded as the clear front-runner. His record was impressive.
At age eighteen he had been the youngest lieutenant in the army. In the
Great War he served as chief of staff of Pershing's First Army during the
Meuse-Argonne offensive. Between the wars Drum achieved notoriety, at
least in army circles, by leading the charge to prevent the U.S. Army Air
Service from being separated from army control and set up as an independent service in the War Department. As a brigadier general in 1930, Drum
had been considered for chief of staff before Douglas MacArthur was eventually selected by President Hoover. In 1931, he was promoted to major general, five years before Marshall received his first star. Notwithstanding
recommendations by Pershing and MacArthur that Drum be made the next
chief of staff, he was passed over again in 1935 when Roosevelt put Malin
Craig in the job. Since that time Drum had served with distinction as commander of the U.S. Army's Hawaiian Department and the Second Corps at
Governors Island.

Since Craig's stint as chief was coming to an end, Drum wanted the job,
but unlike Marshall, he made the mistake of actively lobbying for it. Drum's
papers provide ample evidence of a lively lobbying campaign engineered by
the general beginning in late 1937. For example, a lengthy dossier written by

Drum articulates the reasons why he should be chosen as chief of staff and why the others eligible for consideration should not. This document served as "talking points" for Drum's friends and supporters who were enlisted to advocate his case to key administration officials. The outgoing chief of army chaplains wrote Drum that "following your suggestion" he had called on Secretary Woodring "to put in a good word for you."[31] R. E. Wood, president of Sears, Roebuck, reported to Drum a conversation he had with "Pa" Watson, one of FDR's closest friends who served as his White House adviser on the military. According to Wood, Watson told him that letters recommending Drum were "ill-timed" and "ill-advised" because the decision is the president's prerogative and he needs "no outside advice."[32]

Drum's lobbying was probably enough to turn the president off. However, there was more. General MacArthur, then in the Philippines, was advising Drum by letter on how to conduct his lobbying campaign, telling him, "Watch [out for] George Marshall."[33] In addition, Drum's papers reveal that he and MacArthur were critical of the administration's policies on neutrality and trade and lacked respect for Roosevelt as president. It is fair to say that MacArthur was not one of the president's favorite generals. Since the summer of 1932, after Roosevelt had won the Democratic nomination, FDR had been highly suspicious of MacArthur's loyalty, reportedly labeling him one of the two "most dangerous men" in America, the second being Huey Long, the Louisiana demagogue.[34] He came to regard MacArthur as a potential right-wing political rival. While there is no hard evidence that Roosevelt was aware that Drum was conniving with MacArthur, the president's political antennae were sensitive. He might have picked up signals that Drum was politically aligned with MacArthur. Thus, in addition to the lobbying campaign, Drum's sympathy with MacArthur could have caused the president to turn to Marshall rather than Drum in 1939. Whether or not this figured in his decision, Roosevelt never gave serious consideration to the appointment of Marshall's principal rival.

* * * * *

Meanwhile, a firestorm broke out on Capitol Hill. In a parking lot near the Los Angeles airport, a Douglas bomber, its existence still classified, crash-landed.

Pulled from the wreckage was a seriously injured Frenchman named Paul Chemidlin, a representative of the French air ministry who had been piloting the plane. Was the president involved in selling state-of-the-art army bombers to France in violation of U.S. neutrality laws? Isolationists from both political parties saw an opportunity to embarrass Roosevelt. In a most unusual move, Democratic senator Bennett "Champ" Clark's entire Military Affairs Committee met with FDR in the White House at the end of January to get the whole story. Claiming that the new Douglas bombers were not owned by the army, which was technically true, the president admitted that he had authorized cash sales to the French that were perfectly legal under the letter of the neutrality laws. Then he attempted to draw the senators into his confidence, arguing that Hitler was intent on subjugating other nations in Europe, including France, and contending that if Germany was not stopped she would be a threat to America's national security. "That is why," said FDR, "the safety of the Rhine frontier does interest us."[35] Not surprisingly, a version of the statement was leaked to the press (by some "boob," said FDR). Headlines had the president proclaiming a new foreign policy: "America's frontier is on the Rhine."[36]

The isolationists and noninterventionists in Congress expressed outrage. The public was alarmed, fearing that the president was drawing the nation into another war. Roosevelt, who had called in his January 4 State of the Union address for a relaxation of the neutrality statutes, was forced to back off, assuring reporters that his "foreign policy has not changed and it is not going to change."[37] U.S. diplomat John Cudahy, quoting a European leader, warned Roosevelt that his retreat from what he promised in his State of the Union message "cleared the atmosphere concerning America as far as the dictators are concerned."[38]

Cudahy's warning was prescient. With the United States on the sidelines, the descent into the maelstrom of world war rapidly accelerated. In a fiery speech to the Reichstag, Hitler prophesied "the annihilation of the Jewish race in Europe."[39] At six in the morning on March 15, 1939, German storm troopers marched into and quickly occupied the remainder of Czechoslovakia. Hitler thus thumbed his nose at the Munich agreement and broke his pledge not to seek further territory. That evening, he motored triumphantly through Prague, just as he had done a year earlier in Vienna, the city of his youth, when he annexed Austria. Five days later, on March 20, Hitler's foreign minister, Joachim von Ribbentrop, issued an ultimatum to Lithuania. If that small nation on the Baltic Sea did not immediately cede the

Memel Territory to Germany, including its vital seaport, the Wehrmacht would invade. On March 21, the pattern repeated itself. Ribbentrop demanded that Poland cede Danzig to the Reich, a free city that had been granted to Poland in the aftermath of the Great War. Reacting to this threat to Poland's sovereignty, the British and French abandoned the policy of appeasement and announced that they would guarantee Polish borders with force if necessary. Not to be outdone by his German ally, Benito Mussolini delivered an ultimatum to the Kingdom of Albania on March 25, demanding that it consent to Italian occupation.

The imminence of war in Europe reverberated in the Far East. In China, Japanese armies continued advancing south, capturing the city of Nanchang on March 27. In the South China Sea, Japan's naval forces annexed a necklace of strategically situated islands that lay athwart sea lanes to Singapore and the island of Luzon in the Philippines. As proclaimed by its foreign ministry, the Japanese were pursuing a "New Order"—one that threatened European colonies in Southeast Asia as well as the Philippines. Facing the probability of having to defend their respective homelands in Europe, the British and French navies were not large enough to also protect their resource-rich possessions in Asia against Japanese attack.

On or about March 19, the president received a note through diplomatic back channels from British foreign secretary Lord Halifax suggesting that he should consider moving the U.S. fleet to Hawaii in the event war should break out in Europe. At the time the American fleet was in the Caribbean to project its concerns about hemispheric defense. Responding to Halifax, Roosevelt ordered his main fleet to proceed through the Panama Canal to its bases around San Diego and agreed that the U.S. would participate in secret naval talks with the British aimed at concentrating the fleet at Pearl Harbor in order to deter Japan. As Cambridge historian David Reynolds observed, "the parallelism of policy was clear: as Britain became committed to Europe, America would do more in Asia."[40] For Roosevelt and his beloved navy, the prospect of a two-ocean war was becoming more than a sand table planning exercise.

* * * * *

Not even the prospect of a global war would cause the president to postpone his nine-day Easter trip to Warm Springs, which began on the afternoon of March 29. A day or so before he departed, he asked Secretary Woodring to provide him with the records of the generals eligible for chief of staff so that he could study them while on vacation. Woodring delegated the task to Craig, who took it upon himself to eliminate two of the five eligibles as unsuitable (generals Rowell and DeWitt). Inexplicably, Craig added four more who were junior to Marshall. Perhaps he was having second thoughts about Marshall, or possibly Pa Watson, FDR's military aide, gave him the notion that Roosevelt wanted to see a few younger candidates.

Harry Hopkins accompanied Roosevelt on his visit to Warm Springs. If the subject of the chief of staff appointment came up, and there is no evidence that it did, circumstances suggest that Hopkins would probably have recommended Marshall. But when or how the president reached his decision is unknown.

At half past three on April 23, a quiet Sunday, more than two weeks after FDR had returned from Georgia, Marshall entered the Oval Study on the second floor of the White House. The president had asked him to come over for "an interview." Roosevelt was wearing an old sweater, working on his stamp collection, his massive desk cluttered with medicine bottles, a ship's wheel clock, two packs of Camels, a bronze bust of his wife, Eleanor, and odd knickknacks from past campaigns. Ship models adorned the bookcases. Roosevelt's instinct was to address Marshall as "George" and to begin with banter and small talk, but he knew from the embarrassing encounter the past November that Marshall preferred to keep his distance, avoiding small talk and refusing to be charmed. The president was unusually direct. "General Marshall, I have it in mind to choose you as the next Chief of Staff of the United States Army. What do you think about that?" Instead of expressing his gratitude, Marshall coolly replied, "Nothing, except to remind you that I have the habit of saying exactly what I think . . . Is that all right?" Roosevelt simply said, "Yes," and flashed a genial smile. "You said *yes* pleasantly," rejoined Marshall, pushing his point, "but it may be unpleasant." Marshall stood, ready to leave. "I feel deeply honored, sir, and I will give you the best that I have."[41]

Setting aside Marshall's record, his reputation for speaking truth to power, Pershing's support, and the probable recommendation of Hopkins, the president's decision most likely was based on his judgment, and his alone, that he could *trust* Marshall to remain loyal to his commander in chief, to follow orders once a decision was made, and to be discreet.

Justifying his decision to Sam Rayburn, the powerful Speaker of the House, Roosevelt explained, "When I disapprove his [Marshall's] recommendations, I don't have to look over my shoulder to see whether he is going to the Capitol to lobby against me. I *know* he's going back to the War Department, to give me the most loyal support as chief of staff that any President could wish."[42] While the president seemed to be comfortable with his choice, Marshall was not at all sure of where he stood. He believed that among those eligible the president chose him as "the best of a bad bargain," that he would have to prove himself before FDR "built up confidence" in him.[43] With this in mind, Katherine penned a personal note to the president thanking him for placing his "confidence" in her husband and assuring him that his "loyalty to you and to this trust will be unfailing."[44]

It was agreed that the announcement of Marshall's appointment would be delayed for a few days so that he would be out of town on a West Coast inspection trip and thus not available for interviews, congratulatory phone calls, and other distractions. The news was released on Thursday, April 27. Marshall would become chief of staff when Malin Craig officially retired on August 31; he would take over as acting chief of staff on July 1, at which point Craig would depart on terminal leave.

* * * * *

During the summer of 1939, Marshall lived in a rented house on Wyoming Avenue and worked at his new office in the Munitions Building near the Lincoln Memorial on the National Mall. In a July 17 letter to Pershing, he apologized for being out of touch, saying he had "been intensely busy of late," trying to make some progress toward strengthening national defense.[45] Meanwhile, Katherine spent the summer on Fire Island, never dreaming that it would be her last. "As the summer advanced," she wrote, "George's weekends on the Island ceased."[46]

Parts of the world were already at war that summer; much of the rest was on the brink. Soviet and Japanese armies had begun an undeclared war along the disputed Manchurian-Mongolian border that would eventually involve 100,000 troops. Mussolini, having completed his conquest of Albania, entered into a formal alliance with Germany—the "Pact of Steel"—that bound each country to support the other economically and militarily.[47] Following almost three years of civil war in Spain, Generalissimo Francisco

Franco emerged victorious and joined Hitler and Mussolini as the third fascist dictator in Europe. Hitler ramped up pressure on the Poles to cede the strategic port city of Danzig, using the so-called Danzig crisis as a catalyst to provoke a war with Poland. London and Paris diplomats shuttled to and from Moscow, seeking to enlist the Soviet Union in an agreement to form a common front against Hitler's threat to invade the Polish territory. Stalin toyed with them, having little confidence that the British and French would fight for Poland. In response to Japan's New Order presaging domination of China and Southeast Asia and its aggressive moves against Western settlements in China, President Roosevelt abrogated the commercial treaty between Japan and the U.S., placing Japan on notice that it would be subject to trade sanctions in 1940. In secret talks with the British in Washington, the United States confirmed that in the event of war in Europe it would move its fleet to Pearl Harbor in order to deter further Japanese aggression.

With war in the offing, Roosevelt pleaded with Congress to revise the neutrality laws so the U.S. could supply arms—on a cash-and-carry basis—to the Western powers. Vice President John "Cactus Jack" Garner polled the Senate. "Well, Captain," Garner said to the president, "[y]ou haven't got the votes, and that's all there is to it."[48]

To maintain peace on the domestic front, Marshall dickered with decorators over wallpaper and paint samples that Katherine had selected, and he attended to the installation of a commercial dishwasher at Quarters One, the official residence of the chief of staff at Fort Myer. The Marshalls planned to move in when Katherine returned from Fire Island near the end of August. In order to closely supervise the renovations and the movers before and at the end of his workdays, Marshall bunked at Fort Myer with Colonel George Patton, his friend from the Great War, who was commander of the fort itself as well as the 3rd Cavalry Regiment that was posted there. With pride and exuberance Patton wrote to his wife, Bea, who was summering at their permanent residence in Massachusetts, "I have just consummated a pretty snappy move . . . Gen George C. Marshall . . . and I are batching it. I think that once I can get my natural charm working I won't need any letters from John J. P[ershing] or anyone else. Of course it may cramp my style a little about going out but there are compensations."[49]

Quarters One is a three-story Victorian-style redbrick house that sits at the crest of Arlington Heights with commanding views of the Potomac

River and the city of Washington. The land was once owned and occupied by descendants of Martha Washington, one of whom married Robert E. Lee. After the Civil War, the majestic house where Lee had lived and 200 surrounding acres were designated as the national cemetery. The remainder of the land, above Arlington Cemetery, was taken over by the army and became known as Fort Myer, a cavalry post. The construction of Quarters One was completed in 1899. It consists of twenty-one rooms, including six bedrooms and a second-floor north-facing sunporch that had been added by General MacArthur for his mother. The entryway on the south side of the main floor is girdled by a long white porch.

Fortunately for Marshall, whose principal exercise was riding, there were eight low brick stables, with arched entries, situated behind and to the north of Quarters One that sheltered the horses and caissons of the post's cavalry regiment. A student of Marshall's at Benning, Lieutenant Terry de la Mesa Allen, arranged to send two horses from Fort Riley, Kansas, to Fort Myer for Marshall's personal use.

During the last days of August 1939, when the Marshalls were moving into Quarters One, newspapers began reporting that German troops, artillery, trucks, horses, ammunition trains, and rolling field kitchens were massing in towns close to the Polish border. On August 23, Hitler and Stalin stunned the world by signing a nonaggression pact—they agreed not to fight each other or aid opponents of either, namely the British, French, and even the Japanese. Hitler reportedly banged the table when he heard that Stalin would accept the deal, declaring, "I've got them! I've got them."[50] Stalin signed the agreement because of his belief that the British and French would probably not go to war over Poland and the consequent need to protect his borders. The nonaggression pact would protect his western borders in Europe against his now former enemy, the Nazi fascists, and prevent the Germans from aiding the Japanese in their battles against the Red Army on Stalin's eastern borders in Asia. Plus, under secret protocols Stalin received the go-ahead to seize half of Poland, absorb the Baltic States, and take territory in Finland and Bessarabia (today part of Moldova and Ukraine). Hitler, like Stalin, also thought the British and French would back down. He needed the deal in order to mollify his generals, who weren't so sure and feared a two-front war. Without the Red Army to worry about, the German generals could easily overrun the Polish armed forces and the Führer would gain a large chunk of living space for his people in the east.

The diplomatic consequences of the pact were far-reaching. The Japanese, who had fought the Soviets in Manchuria and were following what they thought was a pro-German foreign policy, were shocked. They had been betrayed by Hitler, deserted by Germany. The prime minister of Japan resigned; his government collapsed. In the words of David Reynolds, Japan was "forced to rethink the fundamentals of its foreign policy."[51] As a further result of the pact, Chiang Kai-shek's Nationalists also rethought their foreign policy and decided they could no longer look to the Soviets as their potential ally against Japan. Instead, they began cultivating the United States.

In Europe, the French and the British, who were counting on an alliance with the Soviets, regarded the pact as a bombshell. In light of Stalin's agreement with Hitler, would they still honor their commitments to go to war over Poland? The world wondered. In Washington, a State Department official said the suspense was like "sitting in a house where somebody is dying upstairs."[52] After visiting Campobello Island—for the last time—Roosevelt cut short his cruise on the USS *Tuscaloosa* along the Nova Scotia coast and returned to the White House on August 24. That evening he sent messages to Hitler, the king of Italy, and the president of Poland urging them to avoid war.

A week later, George and Katherine were having pre-dinner cocktails at the home of Supreme Court associate justice and Mrs. Harlan Fiske Stone. Everyone there knew that Marshall was to be officially sworn in as chief of staff the next day. No doubt the conversation touched on the latest developments in Europe, including reports that this time it appeared that the French and British, and certainly the Poles, were not going to back down. The governments of each nation had mobilized and called up reserves, determined to fight if Hitler actually followed through with his threats to invade Poland. Anticipating war from the air, the British had announced that children were to be evacuated from London. During dinner Marshall was called to the telephone by a duty officer at the War Department and told that Hitler's armies were poised to invade. Marshall returned to the table, certain that war in Europe was about to begin. Neither his words nor his expression revealed the fateful news.

Meanwhile, on the Polish border, the German high command activated

Plan White, and the invasion began. At about 4:45 a.m. on Friday, September 1, two powerful wings of the Wehrmacht, totaling forty-two divisions, including ten armored divisions, stormed across the frontier. Heinkel bombers plus Dorniers and Junkers (Stuka) dive-bombers began pounding airfields, rail junctions, roads, and the city of Warsaw. In the harbor at Danzig the training ship *Schleswig Holstein* started shelling the Polish garrison. The objective was to quickly crush all Polish resistance and capture Warsaw. Hitler needed the campaign to be over early in case the French attacked Germany from the west.

In Washington, President Roosevelt was awakened at 2:50 a.m. by a call from Ambassador William Bullitt Jr. in Paris. Bullitt repeated a message he had received from Anthony Drexel Biddle Jr. in Warsaw that "Germany has invaded Poland," and that several cities were being bombed.[53] "God help us all," responded Roosevelt when told the news.[54] Some minutes after three a.m., Marshall was also woken up by his aide and given a similar message. He went into Katherine's adjoining bedroom, put his hand gently on her shoulder, and waited until she opened her eyes. "Well, it's come," he said. Marshall quickly dressed, made a call to the War Department, and left for the Munitions Building.

Attired in a white Palm Beach suit, standing before an American flag with his right arm raised, Marshall was sworn in as army chief of staff by army adjutant general Emory Adams at 10:30 a.m. on September 1. The brief ceremony took place in Harry Woodring's office in the old State, War, and Navy Building, a few steps from the West Wing of the White House. After thirty-seven years in the army, Marshall had reached his goal. As chief of staff he was entitled to the four stars of a full general; moments before, he had only one. The title and stars weighed heavily on him. Several days later Marshall, tongue in cheek, complimented his predecessor, Malin Craig, for his exquisite sense of timing, which "certainly left me on a hot spot."[55]

A hot spot it was. Two days after he was sworn in, Britain and France declared war against Germany. Marshall had inherited a regular army ranking in size somewhere between the armies of Portugal and Bulgaria. He could cobble together three or perhaps four understrength and poorly equipped infantry divisions. By contrast, the Wehrmacht had roughly one hundred divisions, sixty of which Hitler assigned to the conquest of Poland, leaving the remainder of forty to protect his western border. The Imperial

Japanese Army had about forty divisions, twenty-seven fighting in China and the bulk of the rest in Manchuria. Marshall's job was to transform his tiny, ill-equipped army of 188,000 officers and men into a formidable force capable of defending the Western Hemisphere against attack and, if necessary, bringing the fight to enemies overseas. He had to do this in the face of an American public overwhelmingly opposed to another war, an election-year Congress dominated by isolationists, a noninterventionist secretary of war, and a cautious commander in chief partial to the navy and airpower.

CHAPTER 6

A Time to Plant

On the stone terrace and rolling lawns below Quarters One, the leadership of the American military, a blend of blue, white, and gold braid, mixed easily with the sea of suits and spring party frocks of official Washington. The society editors wrote that "Gen. George C. Marshall and Mrs. Marshall" received more than fifteen hundred guests at their garden party, the "first of the season," on the late afternoon of May 10, 1940.[1] The small army band could barely be heard above the roar of conversation. When the shadows had lengthened, the musicians put down their instruments. An army bugler and a color guard belonging to General Patton's 3rd Cavalry Regiment emerged from the crowd. The first note of "Retreat," the bugle call signifying the end of the day that has been used by the United States Army since the Revolutionary War, brought a hush to the chatter and laughter. The officers turned toward the flag and saluted. Male civilians removed their hats. When the Stars and Stripes were lowered the sunset gun fired, its concussion bouncing off the monuments on the Mall. The band broke army tradition. Instead of "To the Colors," it played "The Star-Spangled Banner."[2]

It was a fitting end to a momentous day. At three a.m. that morning, "by dawn's early light," the German invasion of the Low Countries had begun—in the air and on the ground. Ninety minutes later Hitler arrived at his command post, a hilltop bunker known as Felsennest that afforded views of the Belgian border twenty miles to the west. His Panzer divisions were massing in the Ardennes, poised for a lightning drive to the French coast. "At twilight's last gleaming," Winston Churchill emerged from an audience with King George VI as prime minister of Great Britain with a commission to form a new administration. Everyone at the Marshalls' garden party had been following the breaking news throughout the day. Many began to realize, for the first time, that a Nazi victory in Europe would constitute a grave threat to the security of the United States.

128

Marshall knew that his small army was ill-prepared to deter the threat. All spring he had been appearing before congressional appropriations committees, arguing for increased funding. "If Europe blazes in the late spring or summer," he warned, "we must put our house in order before the sparks reach the Western Hemisphere."[3]

The sparks were beginning to fly. For Marshall the time had come to try to jump-start the army portion of the nation's defense capability. But first he had to persuade the president to get out front on the vital need to prepare. As recently as the morning of the garden party, when Marshall met with the president in the White House, FDR started talking about *cutting* the military budget by $18 million. The chief of staff could hardly contain himself. He was keenly aware that 1940 was a presidential election year and that Roosevelt might be thinking of running for a third term. He also knew that even though public opinion had shifted in favor of increasing military budgets, there were still substantial voting blocs in Congress and in the American heartland that opposed any moves by Roosevelt to beef up the military as unnecessary warmongering. Nevertheless, the latest attacks by the Germans meant that the Nazis would likely control all of Europe and probably the British Isles as well. The next step could be an invasion somewhere in the Western Hemisphere or occupation of islands near the American east coast or perhaps in the Caribbean. As Marshall told a handful of senators during a late-night meeting in April, his job as chief of staff was on the line. "I feel culpable," he confessed.[4]

What was the most effective way to approach and persuade Roosevelt? Marshall, still an outsider, needed advice. Harry Hopkins was out of the loop, having spent much of the spring at the Mayo Clinic or at home recovering from severe malnutrition and intestinal problems following radical surgery for stomach cancer. The next best source for understanding FDR's way of thinking was Treasury Secretary Henry Morgenthau Jr., the president's Dutchess County neighbor and one of his oldest friends. Marshall and Morgenthau arranged to meet at the Treasury Department on Saturday, May 11, the morning after the garden party. Morgenthau bluntly told Marshall that the War Department's approach was all wrong, that "the President [is getting] little pieces and not the whole picture." The overall need, admitted Marshall, was a heart-stopping $50 billion, but in the near term the army must have at least $650 million, enough to achieve a modest increase in defense capability (among many other things, Marshall sought to expand the Regular Army to 280,000 by the end of September). These large numbers "make me dizzy," said Marshall. "It makes me dizzy, if we don't get it," responded Morgenthau.[5] When we "go to see the President," he advised Marshall, "stand right up and tell him what you think . . . There are too few people who do it and he likes it."[6] In Morgenthau, Marshall had found a valuable ally.

On Monday morning, May 13, as Hitler's Panzers poured out of the Ardennes and wheeled north toward the English Channel, Morgenthau and Marshall, along with their advisers, met with Roosevelt in the Oval Office to discuss army appropriations. "It was quite evident," recalled Marshall, that the president "was not desirous of seeing us."[7] Roosevelt as usual began with idle chitchat having little to do with the subject of the meeting. When Morgenthau saw an opening he made his pitch for increased army appropriations. Roosevelt resisted, insisting on cuts. They started arguing. The president grew annoyed. "I am not asking you," he said to Morgenthau, "I am telling you."[8] Marshall assumed FDR was "staging this rather drastic handling" of Morgenthau to convince the chief of staff that there was no point trying to talk him out of his decision to decrease the army's budget.

Morgenthau launched a Hail Mary. "Mr. President, will you hear General Marshall?" Roosevelt shot back, "Well, I know exactly what he would say. There is no necessity for me to hear him at all."[9] The president gestured that the meeting was over. As Marshall recalled later, the moment "was catastrophic in its possibilities and this last cut [in the army's appropriations request] just emphasized the point." Marshall rose from his chair, "walked over and stood looking down at" the wheelchair-bound president. His posture was deliberate, ruthless if not cruel; later, he frankly admitted that he "took advantage, in a sense, of the president's condition."

"Mr. President, may I have three minutes?" Roosevelt's irritable mood seemed to fall away. Graciously and without hesitation, he replied, "Of course, General Marshall." By this time he was not even tempted to call him "George."

Words tumbled out, just as they had twenty-three years earlier when Marshall confronted General Pershing in France. There are no accounts that describe what he said, but he must have provided the president with a passionate overview of the present dangers to national security. And he must have summarized with precision the principal shortages in manpower, infrastructure, and equipment that his requested increases in funding were intended to address. The one shortcoming that Marshall clearly recalled identifying was the president's own penchant for creating bureaucratic havoc by assigning critical military tasks to government departments with no military expertise (as FDR had done in assigning aircraft production to the Treasury Department).

Marshall concluded his "three minute" fusillade with these words: "I don't know quite how to express myself about this to the president of the United States, but I will say this—that you have got to do something and you've got to do it today." Morgenthau was impressed. More important, so was Roosevelt. The president told Marshall that he was prepared to ask Congress in the next few days for most but not all of the $650 million that Marshall requested for the army. However, he assured him that he would seek additional funds to make up the deficiency later in the year. Marshall's three minutes, which stretched to twenty or so, had moved the president to act.

The next day Marshall worked with Roosevelt to refine the president's overall request for defense appropriations—army, army air corps, navy, marines, and production facilities. And he personally prepared a first draft of the president's message of justification to Congress. Roosevelt was still having doubts, worried about how his request would be received on the Hill. Marshall urged him not to back down. "I know you can get them to accept it; they can't evade it."[10] Events in Europe and a well-timed plea from Prime Minister Churchill, however, were much more persuasive. At 7:30 a.m. on the morning of May 15, French premier Paul Reynaud telephoned Churchill. In English he said, "We are beaten. We have lost the battle."[11] German armor had broken through the French lines and would soon reach the English Channel. This was an overly pessimistic, if not defeatist, view of the situation in the field. Reynaud was right that they had lost the initial battle, but it would take another month for the Wehrmacht to defeat the bulk of the French army. Later that day Churchill cabled Roosevelt, his first message to the president since becoming prime minister. Churchill began by noting that "the scene has darkened swiftly . . . the small countries are simply smashed up, one by one, like matchwood." He predicted that "we," meaning Great Britain, "expect to be attacked here ourselves, both from the air and by parachute . . ." Referring obliquely to the French debacle, Churchill assured the president that "if necessary we shall continue the war alone," but he warned that "the weight may be more than we can bear." Appealing to Roosevelt, who at that moment was worried about being too far out in front of Congress and public opinion, Churchill wrote, "I trust you realize, Mr. President, that the voice and force of the United States may count for nothing if they are withheld too long." He concluded with a blunt request for immediate American aid—forty or fifty destroyers, several hundred late-model aircraft, antiaircraft guns, ammunition, and steel and other raw materials—and an appeal to "keep that Japanese dog quiet in the Pacific."[12]

No doubt Churchill's cable strengthened the president's resolve. On May 16, Roosevelt made a dramatic appearance before a joint session of Congress and asked for a supplemental military appropriation of more than $1.1 billion ($546 million to create a "thoroughly-rounded out army"). "These are ominous days," he began, making an obvious reference to the imminent fall of France and the impending Battle of Britain. Almost all of the president's message stressed the need to beef up the U.S. armed forces to defend "the whole American hemisphere" against invasion or domination. However, with respect to his proposal for funds to produce "50,000 military and naval planes," a breathtakingly ambitious goal, FDR made it clear that the planes would not necessarily be used for defense of the Western Hemisphere. Rather, in a single sentence that he added to Marshall's draft message, the president pointedly asked Congress not to "take any action" that would prevent or delay him from selling U.S. planes to "foreign nations."[13] Thus, FDR deftly kept his options open. He satisfied isolationists and noninterventionists in Congress as well as his army and navy war planners, including Marshall, by being able to say he was focused on hemispheric defense. At the same time, he retained discretion to aid other countries, namely Great Britain, by supplying her with the latest American-made warplanes—FDR's own "short of war" strategy. He did this even though he knew Marshall and his other military advisers would likely argue that the planes were needed to defend the homeland, and that it would be a waste to send planes to England because the odds were against her ability to defeat the Germans.

Two weeks later the spigot opened. Influenced by Roosevelt's personal appearance, Marshall's frank testimony before the Senate Appropriations

Committee, and most of all the reports from Europe, Congress voted to appropriate $300 million *more* than the president had requested. By that time, General Heinz Guderian's Panzer divisions had split France in two and reached the English Channel at Abbeville, an accomplishment that General Ludendorff failed to attain during the four-year carnage of the Great War. On May 22, the Germans swept north and pinned the Belgian army, the French First Army, and the British Expeditionary Force against the sea. The Belgians surrendered. Assembling a fleet of warships, ferryboats, tugs, and all manner of privately owned vessels that shuttled across the Channel for eight days, the British evacuated some 225,000 British and 113,000 French soldiers from the beaches of Dunkirk. Churchill cautioned the House of Commons that the so-called miracle of Dunkirk should not be regarded as a victory. "Wars are not won by evacuations."[14] Nevertheless, the mass evacuation spawned Churchill's most magnificent wartime oratory, notably the passage that began "We shall not flag or fail," continued with "We shall fight on the beaches," and ended with Churchill's famous pledge on behalf of his people and to the free world: "We shall never surrender."[15]

Desperate to keep France in the fight, Churchill flew to Tours on June 13, when German units were in sight of the Eiffel Tower, and proposed a merger whereby France and Great Britain would be fused into a single political entity. Vice Premier Philippe Pétain, the hero of Verdun, rejected the idea out of hand. Pétain, by then an octogenarian, was firmly in favor of an armistice, convinced that France was already defeated and that Britain would soon face the same fate. Why "fuse with a corpse," he remarked dismissively to Churchill.[16] Eric Sevareid, a young CBS war correspondent who was covering the fall of France, wrote that he was "the first to announce [to America] that the great French Republic had quit and intended to sue for armistice."[17]

On the morning of June 14, General Bogislav von Studnitz led his 87th Infantry into Paris. Knots of citizens stood silent as his troops, motorcycles, and horse-drawn vehicles moved through the streets. Some Parisians wept; others smiled and waved. Resistance was minimal. Soldiers removed French battle flags from Napoleon's Tomb and draped the Nazi swastika from windows above the avenues. That afternoon, the pilot of General Walter Warlimont's tiny two-seat Storch reconnaissance aircraft circled above the City of Light and landed at the end of the Champs-Élysées.

The formal surrender of France took place on Saturday, June 22, in the same railway carriage in the Forest of Compiègne where the Germans surrendered in November 1918. Hitler himself presided over the carefully choreographed ceremony, which was designed to blot out "once and for all" the "greatest German humiliation of all time."[18] As a symbol of his intent, Hitler ordered the destruction of a granite tablet memorializing the site of the 1918 armistice and the shipment of the historic carriage to Berlin. A famous film clip shows him smiling in triumph outside the railcar, his booted left foot raised as if dancing a jig. Under the armistice terms, roughly three-fifths of France—its north and western parts and the whole Atlantic coast—were to be occupied by Germany, the costs to be paid by France. The remaining two-fifths would be ruled by newly installed prime minister Pétain from his headquarters in a hotel in the spa town of Vichy. Reynaud, the former premier, having already resigned, was imprisoned in Germany. Under the armistice agreement, the government of unoccupied "Vichy France" was afforded the appearance of autonomy, although the elderly Marshal Pétain usually deferred to German wishes.

By the end of June, Congress, reacting to the fall of France and the expected attack on Great Britain, authorized another $1.7 billion in military appropriations. Marshall was no longer in desperate need of money. He finally had enough to at least begin building a modern army and air corps, properly balanced with state-of-the-art equipment, infrastructure, and logistical support. With periodic infusions of additional funding, this process would take at least two years.

Marshall's more immediate problem was how to satisfy the president, who was pressuring the War Department to supply virtually all war matériel on hand to Great Britain, and at the same time preserve enough to protect the nation and the rest of the Western Hemisphere against a possible attack. Marshall appreciated the military benefits of supplying the British, who had lost so much equipment at Dunkirk. If—and for Marshall it was a very big if—the British and its fleet could survive the coming German onslaught, then supplying them with maximum quantities of armaments would be in the national interest of the United States. As long as the British lived to fight and tie down the German armed forces, Hitler would be less likely to attempt an attack on the Western Hemisphere. On the other hand, if Britain could not survive, or if she decided to seek terms with the Nazis, then

Marshall and his colleagues would be regarded as criminally negligent for squandering vital military assets on another nation while leaving America defenseless. Major Beetle Smith, now a member of Marshall's personal staff, put it this way: "If we were required to mobilize after having released guns necessary for this mobilization and were found to be short . . . everyone who was a party to this deal might hope to be hanging from a lamp post."[19]

Fully aware that both he and Roosevelt were gambling on British survival, Marshall for the most part was cooperative with his commander in chief's desire to expedite the sale of everything possible to the British purchasing agency. Under a scheme to avoid neutrality laws that was blessed by the U.S. solicitor general, Marshall certified as "surplus" hundreds of thousands of rifles, machine guns, howitzers, and antiaircraft weapons and millions of rounds of ammunition. Working through Morgenthau's Treasury Department, these munitions were sold to Curtiss-Wright and United States Steel, and then resold to the British at cost on a "cash and carry" basis, meaning the British paid cash for the matériel and were responsible for shipment on their vessels. The transactions were briefly delayed when Secretary of War Woodring refused to sign the necessary contracts. The president had to intervene and order him to execute the documents.

When it came to the sale of U.S. warplanes, however, Marshall, with the backing of air chief Hap Arnold, was much less cooperative, fearing that loss of a hundred planes would "set the pilot-training program in America back at least six months."[20] When FDR and Morgenthau proposed in June to sell twelve of the latest B-17 long-range bombers to Great Britain, Marshall pushed back, arguing in a June 18 memorandum that since the army air corps had a total of only fifty-two B-17s, the loss of twelve would be "seriously prejudicial" to national defense.[21] Though Roosevelt was far more optimistic than Marshall about the odds of British survival, he ultimately withdrew his request. Even he was not willing to risk the loss of almost one-quarter of the army's precious bombers.

Congress made Marshall's job even more difficult at the end of June when it enacted a law providing that war matériel belonging to the army could not be sold or otherwise disposed of unless the army chief of staff first certified that it is "not essential to the national defense."[22] Marshall regarded the law as unconstitutional since it arguably usurped the role of the commander in chief (that was in fact the intent of the bill's sponsor, anti-FDR and anti-British Senator David I. Walsh, a Massachusetts Democrat). Nevertheless, to carry out the wishes of Roosevelt, Marshall certified sales of a broad range of munitions over the next nine months as not essential to defense, admitting later "that it was the only time that I recall that I did something that there was a certain amount of duplicity in it."[23]

* * * * *

Meanwhile, the need for compulsory service—that is, a draft law—began to gain traction. The idea was spearheaded not by Marshall but by a private citizen, fifty-seven-year-old Grenville Clark, an East Coast blueblood and cofounder with Elihu Root Jr. of an elite Manhattan law firm. Called "Grenny" by his friends, Clark was a classmate of Roosevelt's at Harvard. As a young lawyer, Clark had clerked with the future president at the New York firm Carter, Ledyard & Milburn. He had been raised to believe that it was the duty of all citizens to serve their country. When the sinking of the *Lusitania* in 1915 convinced him that America would be drawn into the war in Europe, he and Root, realizing that the nation was woefully unprepared, set up a military training program for college-educated professionals outside Plattsburgh in northern New York. The Plattsburgh model was replicated throughout the United States, and the program's graduates became the officers who trained draftees and led the doughboys in the Great War.

Twenty-five years later, Clark once again led the charge, only this time the goal—a law compelling millions of American boys to train for war when the nation was not at war—seemed impossible. Undaunted, Clark wired Roosevelt in May, but, not surprisingly, FDR brushed him off. It was a presidential election year; even if Roosevelt had not yet decided to run for a third term, he certainly did not want to foreclose that option by getting too far ahead of Congress and the American people on the need for a peacetime draft. Moreover, setting aside election-year politics, Roosevelt was heavily biased in favor of producing warplanes both to defend the homeland and to sell to the British and other allies in order to keep them, not Americans, fighting the Germans. He was resistant to the notion of raising a huge ground army. He did not want to expose millions of Americans to a second bloodbath in Europe.

Having had no luck with the president, Clark next targeted the army chief of staff. On May 31, 1940, Clark and Julius Ochs Adler, general manager of *The New York Times* and nephew of its publisher, flew to Washington and met with Marshall to convince him of the need for a draft and to ask for his immediate backing of draft legislation. They were not aware that six days prior, Marshall had been informed by his old friend General John McAuley Palmer that the president was unwilling to support compulsory military service legislation, and that Marshall "was not free to do so himself."[24] Consequently, Marshall courteously told Clark and Adler that he would not publicly back their group's proposed legislation and was not prepared to recommend it to the president.

Historian Lynne Olson suggests that Marshall was not ready to support the draft because he was "fixated" on defending South American countries and the Panama Canal, and that he was hamstrung by "misguided priorities" and "unwonted caution."[25] This interpretation seems unwarranted. In fact, Marshall privately supported the draft; he had already authorized General Palmer and Major Lewis Hershey to assist Clark and his team in drafting a compulsory service bill. Moreover, ten months into his job as army chief of staff, he was not about to announce his support for the draft against the wishes of his commander in chief. "I very pointedly did not take the lead," Marshall later said, reflecting on the debate over draft legislation. "I wanted it to come from others."[26]

Indeed, a few minutes after Clark and Adler left the chief of staff's office, Marshall met with another visitor, Representative (former senator) James W. Wadsworth Jr., an upstate New York congressman who was a well-known proponent of the draft. Wadsworth was eager to introduce a bill in Congress to conscript manpower for Marshall's army. Within three weeks he and Senate cosponsor Edward Burke of Nebraska, a Democrat, would do so.

Marshall had learned from the nation's master politician. Convinced that overt advocacy would be harmful to the army and to himself, he played the kind of "let others take the lead" politics practiced by Roosevelt. Once Congress stepped forward and his commander in chief signaled he would not object, Marshall would "take up the cudgels" and go all out to advocate conscription.[27]

Having been turned down by both the president and the chief of staff, Clark came up with an innovative strategy for accomplishing his objective: replace the current secretary of war with a person of stature and influence who favors conscription. It is hard to imagine that a private citizen could engineer such a coup. Nevertheless, with persistence and a bit of luck, Clark pulled it off. And in doing so he managed to eliminate not just one but two of the principal obstacles to Marshall's effectiveness—Harry Woodring and Louis Johnson. Clark's efforts set the table for Marshall's vitally important working partnership with the new secretary that would lead to victory in World War II.

Within hours after meeting with Marshall, Clark lunched with Felix Frankfurter, associate justice of the Supreme Court. Clark was well aware that Frankfurter, a trusted adviser to the president, had long urged the removal of Woodring as head of the War Department because his opposition to aid Britain and his ongoing feud with Louis Johnson were hampering the president's efforts to prepare the nation for war. At lunch it didn't take long for Clark and Frankfurter to come to agreement on the ideal candidate to replace Woodring: seventy-two-year-old Henry L. Stimson.

Stimson, a Republican internationalist and leading mandarin of the Eastern Establishment, had built an impressive résumé. He had served with distinction as U.S. Attorney for the Southern District of New York, secretary of war during William Howard Taft's presidency, and secretary of state under Herbert Hoover. He first met Marshall in France during the Great War where he commanded a field artillery battalion. Like Marshall, Stimson had no political ambitions; in 1940, he was nearing retirement in the New York law firm Winthrop, Stimson, Putnam & Roberts, having withdrawn as a partner several years earlier. Though he opposed many of the president's domestic policies, his views on foreign affairs were similar to those of FDR. Among other things, Stimson was a stalwart proponent of supplying armaments to Great Britain and to France before she surrendered.

Clark telephoned Stimson at Highhold, his estate on Long Island, and asked him whether he was willing to take the secretary of war job if offered by the president. At first Stimson thought the idea preposterous. After an hour or so of argument and seduction, Clark extracted a tentative yes. Stimson would accept the post provided he could select his own subordinates (including the assistant secretary) and retain freedom to advocate for immediate compulsory military service legislation. Stimson's position on the need for a draft was exactly what Clark wanted to hear.

The next step was to lobby the president. Having been briefed by Clark that Stimson would accept, Frankfurter met with Roosevelt in the Oval

Study. The justice strongly urged the president to appoint Stimson as soon as possible. Anticipating a question from FDR about Stimson's advanced age and stamina, Frankfurter recommended that Stimson's former law partner, Robert Patterson, a judge on the U.S. Court of Appeals for the Second Circuit, and a much younger man, should be brought in to replace Louis Johnson as Stimson's assistant secretary of war. Roosevelt seemed keen on Frankfurter's proposals but was noncommittal. Meanwhile, Clark, unbeknownst to Stimson, convinced Stimson's family physician (who was also Clark's doctor) to provide him with a report on Stimson's health. Normally the physician would not have released such a document. However, because Stimson's health was excellent, he apparently saw no harm or ethical reason to refuse. Frankfurter sent the doctor's report to the White House.[28]

As far as the president was concerned, Stimson's availability and good health were the inputs he needed in order to make his historic decision to stand for a third term. For several months he had kept his own counsel on the issue, enjoying and even encouraging speculation, but giving no outward indication of whether he was a candidate. As war became more than a possibility Roosevelt began seriously considering the idea of forming a bipartisan coalition war cabinet—something like Churchill's War Cabinet—as a way to promote national unity. He had already lined up Frank Knox, publisher of the *Chicago Daily News,* to replace isolationist Charles Edison as secretary of the navy. Knox was a prominent Republican interventionist who had been Alf Landon's running mate in 1936. The publisher was eager to serve, but he persuaded the president that his so-called War Cabinet would not be truly bipartisan unless a Republican was appointed to head the War Department. Stimson filled the bill.

Grenny Clark's audacious plan was falling into place. All that stood in its way was Secretary Woodring. The president had to find a pretext for firing him. Two weeks passed. Ironically, FDR seized on a memorandum written by Marshall—not by Woodring—as his excuse for relieving his secretary of war. As previously mentioned, Marshall had written a note to Woodring on June 18 objecting to the sale of twelve B-17s to the British. Woodring implicitly endorsed the note by arranging to have it delivered to the White House. Whether feigned or not, the president regarded this as another instance of Woodring's obstructionism. The following morning FDR requested the secretary's resignation, the only time in his thirteen years as president that he actually asked a cabinet member to resign.

Oddly, Roosevelt never directed his displeasure at Marshall, the author of the note; in fact, a few days later he dropped the idea of sending the B-17s to the British.[29] The circumstances suggest that Marshall, perhaps with White House connivance, might have set Woodring up for the firing. After all, Marshall longed for an end to the dysfunction in the War Department. And if the president was so upset with Woodring, why didn't he lay into Marshall, the apparent source of resistance to selling the twelve B-17s? And why did FDR decide not to transfer the planes to the British after conferring with Marshall two weeks later? For the rest of his life Woodring believed Marshall was behind his firing. Years later he wrote that "Marshall would sell out his grandmother for personal advantage."[30]

With Woodring's resignation in hand, Roosevelt telephoned Stimson and offered him the secretaryship. Stimson accepted, again making clear his understanding that he would be free to bring in Judge Patterson to replace Johnson. On June 20, just days before the GOP gathered in Philadelphia for its nominating convention, the president announced that Republicans Stimson and Knox, whom he knew were strong advocates of compulsory military service, would join his cabinet following confirmation. The next day the Burke-Wadsworth draft legislation, titled the Selective Service Training and Service Act, was introduced in Congress.

Clark's plan had succeeded and then some. His immediate objective, persuading the president to appoint a secretary of war who was an aggressive proponent of draft legislation, was a stunning success. In addition, his plan enabled the president to pull off a shrewd political masterstroke—the appointment to his cabinet of two of the most prominent Republican foreign policy voices in the nation, Stimson and Knox. On the eve of the Republican convention, Roosevelt's bipartisan coalition move exposed the isolationist versus interventionist fissures that split the party and set the stage for FDR's decision to stand for an unprecedented third term.

For Marshall, Clark's plan was a godsend. Once Henry Stimson was appointed to succeed Woodring, and once it dawned on Johnson that he would soon be replaced by Judge Patterson, the internal struggle in the War Department came to an end. For the first time Marshall would be working beside a unified civilian leadership team with extraordinary devotion and superb capability. From the outset Stimson was convinced that Marshall was the "right man" for the chief of staff job.[31] Marshall was pleased to have a person of Stimson's accomplishments and reputation for integrity as his new boss. The fact that Stimson's stature strengthened Roosevelt's hand with Congress and the American people in preparing for a possible war made Marshall's job easier. There would be disagreements, but the Stimson-Marshall partnership remained remarkably effective and largely frictionless from the beginning to the end of the Second World War.

* * * * *

Throughout the rush of historic events in late spring and summer of 1940, George and Katherine remained in Washington. The single exception was the wedding of Allen Tupper Brown, Katherine's youngest. In the ten years since he had met the young man, Marshall had formed an unusually close friendship with Allen, coupled with an easy but frank mentor-mentee relationship. As a substitute father and avid football fan, Marshall followed Allen's football and wrestling exploits at Woodberry Forest, delighting in yearbook reports that Allen, "with his fighting heart and determination . . . was a true scrapper from start to finish."[32] Like Marshall in his youth, Allen was a risk-taker, once coming close to expulsion for "borrowing" a car from a school employee during a fall dance. Marshall, perhaps remembering how he risked demotions at VMI in order to spend time with Lily after hours, never lost confidence in his stepson.

Now twenty-four, Allen was temperamentally the opposite of Marshall—intensely impatient, unable to repress his feelings. After less than a year at the University of Virginia, and without a college degree, he worked as a salesman for a radio station in Poughkeepsie, New York. In correspondence shortly before the wedding, George counseled Allen about controlling his "emotions" and maintaining a "continuity of purpose." Allen's fiancée, Margaret Goodman Shedden, called Madge, had graduated from Vassar and was working as a stringer for The New York Times. Marshall surmised that she would be "a splendid stabilizer" of Allen's emotional ups and downs.[33] Indeed, she was a leveling influence, with a gift for capturing the Marshall family dynamics. She later recalled a country drive out to Dodona, the early nineteenth-century colonial manor house near Leesburg, Virginia, that Katherine had recently purchased. With Marshall behind the wheel,

Katherine seated next to him, and their dog named Fleet in her lap, "Fleet threw up all over Mrs. Marshall's skirt," remembered Madge, who was in the backseat with Allen. Without a word, Marshall stopped the car. Katherine got out, took off her dress, "dipped it in a ditch, washed it, and wrung it out." Wearing only her silk slip, she got back into the car. Madge noted that "only an accomplished actress" could have maintained such composure. Allen could not suppress his laughter; General Marshall was "stoic as always."[34]

Madge and Allen were married at St. Mark's Episcopal Church in Mount Kisco, New York, on Saturday, June 22, the day the French surrendered to Hitler. Held up in Washington, Marshall flew in on an army plane and arrived just in time for the ceremony. The reception was at the home of the bride's parents, followed by a dinner in the St. Regis Roof Ballroom in New York City. The guest list included a number of generals who would lead infantry divisions in the coming war, including Courtney Hodges, Sandy Patch, "Lightning Joe" Collins, and Matt Ridgway.

* * * * *

On the Monday following the wedding, newspapers were full of stories about the collapse of France, the convening of the Republican convention, and the astonishing rise of utility executive Wendell Willkie, an internationalist who was a serious contender for the GOP nomination. Marshall decided it was time to test the waters with the president face-to-face. Was FDR ready to endorse immediate enactment of compulsory military service legislation? At about noon, Marshall, Admiral Harold R. "Betty" Stark, chief of naval operations, and Undersecretary of State Sumner Welles met with the president for a half hour in the Oval Office and put that question to him along with eight other defense policy recommendations. According to Marshall's penciled notes, the answer was no. Instead of a military draft, the president breezily outlined at length his idea of requiring a year of government service, not necessarily military service, for all youths at age eighteen or upon graduation from high school.[35] Marshall was no doubt disheartened. Given the immediate need for army manpower and the commander in chief's refusal to support conscription legislation, he had no choice but to press forward with the next best solution—a program to put into effect an all-out voluntary recruitment drive. Two days later Louis Johnson, acting secretary of war, sent a letter to the president asking him to authorize the army's proposed voluntary recruiting program. Instead of signing off, FDR decided to solicit Henry Stimson's views, since he was about to become war secretary and would have to implement the program. Once Stimson saw Johnson's letter, he concluded that if the voluntary program was given a try it would seriously delay if not kill the chances of getting the Burke-Wadsworth bill or any other conscription legislation through Congress. On June 27, Marshall flew up to Stimson's home on Long Island, where the two men "talked until almost midnight."[36] At some point Stimson probably told Marshall that he had recommended (or would recommend) that the president not sign off on the army's voluntary program. Indeed, according to historians J. Garry Clifford and Samuel R. Spencer Jr., the visit to Highhold "produced a meeting of minds on the general desirability of army support for selective service."[37]

At his Senate confirmation hearing, Stimson stressed in his opening statement the "unprecedented peril" facing the nation and the vital "element of time"—the time it was going to take to prepare to "meet the emergency of a possible war." He made it clear that he planned to advocate the "prompt enactment of a statute" establishing a system of compulsory military service, just as he had done two weeks before in a widely publicized speech at Yale University and a radio address the following evening. The president was aware of the speeches and had been fully briefed on Stimson's position. By the time of the Senate hearing FDR had scotched the army program for voluntary recruitment, along with his own ideas for a year of government service. He silently acquiesced to the need for military conscription legislation. Throughout Stimson's hearing, not a single senator questioned or even mentioned his position on the draft. Tempers flared, however, when Republican senator Robert Taft tried to get Stimson to admit that he favored going to war to save England, a style of courtroom cross-examination that Stimson repeatedly labeled as "unfair." Another anti-interventionist Republican, Senator Arthur Vandenberg (who would emerge as an internationalist and side with Marshall after the war), engaged Stimson in a scholarly debate over what constitutes "an act of war," questioning that Stimson later regarded as "courteous" and "fair."[38]

On the eve of the Senate vote, Stimson convened a noon gathering at Woodley, his eighteenth-century Washington estate overlooking the Rock Creek valley, with Marshall among the attendees. It came as no surprise to

Marshall when Stimson announced that it was time for the army to come out in support of the Burke-Wadsworth bill to establish a military draft. Marshall was convinced that Stimson would not have made this statement without the express or implied backing of the president. He therefore felt free to follow Stimson's lead and to begin publicly advocating the need for compulsory conscription. His only concern was whether the officers and men in the Regular Army would be prepared to "manage" the training of a huge influx of draftees.[39]

Having been given the green light, Marshall went into action. Three days after Stimson's nomination was confirmed by a vote of fifty-six to twenty-eight, Marshall testified before the Senate Committee on Military Affairs in favor of the need for draft legislation and for authority to call National Guard units to active duty to train draftees. For the rest of his life Marshall believed that his decision to not take the lead in promoting the draft was politically wise and added to the credibility and persuasiveness of his testimony in the halls of Congress.

* * * * *

Washington, known for its equatorial summers, was especially steamy, pungent, and virtually unlivable in the summer of 1940. During the last half of July the temperature exceeded ninety degrees almost every afternoon. Marshall and Stimson endured several days in sodden linen suits testifying in committee rooms on the Hill and meeting with congressmen in their sweltering offices. The president made no public comment on the compulsory military service issue, though he had become convinced that conscription legislation was necessary. Thousands of anti-draft protestors descended on the Capitol. Millions of telegrams, postcards, and letters poured into congressional offices, mostly expressing opposition to the draft. To appease isolationists and secure votes Marshall had little choice but to accept potentially crippling amendments to the Burke-Wadsworth bill, including provisions to limit inductees' length of service to a single year (unless Congress were to declare a state of national emergency), and to prevent the army from deploying draftees outside the Western Hemisphere. Still, the legislation languished in Senate and House committees. Secretaries Stimson and Knox pressed the president to speak out. At last he did. At a press conference on August 2, he authorized White House reporter Fred Essary of the *Baltimore*

Sun to quote him as favoring "the selective training bill" because it is "essential to adequate national defense."[40] Versions of the bill were reported out of the committees. Fights, including one fistfight, broke out on the floors of the House and Senate. Filibusters and amendments caused further delays. Willkie, in his speech accepting the Republican nomination for president, helped to break the back of the opposition by endorsing "some form of selective service."[41] The president mobilized Democrats by announcing that he "was absolutely opposed" to any further delays.[42]

Katherine tried to think of ways to relieve the strain on her husband when he returned to Quarters One in the evenings. As the "heat grew more intense," she wrote, "riding became more of an endurance test than relaxation." Her solution: "canoeing on the Potomac River" where there "was always a cool breeze." After George changed clothes, they would drive across Key Bridge as the sun was setting and rent a canoe at the foot of 35th Street in Georgetown. On at least one occasion they asked Stimson, who loved to exercise, and his wife to join them. In two canoes, the secretary of war, the army chief of staff, and their spouses paddled upstream between the high cliffs of the Palisades as dusk descended. Just before Little Falls, they lashed the canoes together, lit lanterns, and drifted back in the dark, enjoying a scotch or two and eating a "picnic supper" prepared by Katherine. She recalled that when the four returned to the boathouse, Mabel Stimson said, "This is the nicest evening I have ever had in Washington."[43]

The evening on the Potomac, together with a promise at the outset to keep the door that divided their Munitions Building offices "always open," was the beginning of a personal and professional partnership between Marshall and Stimson that lasted for the next five years. According to scholar Mark Stoler, "their collaboration would be one of the closest and most important in Washington during the war."[44]

Despite the president's call for an end to further delay, the bitter debates in the House and Senate over the Burke-Wadsworth draft legislation continued unabated through all of August and into September. Knowing that he might appear presumptuous and thus strengthen the opposition, Marshall nevertheless called for a second supplemental appropriation of $1.4 billion, with the army portion to be earmarked for equipping and housing 1.2 million draftees and 800,000 National Guard reserves. He told the military subcommittee of the Senate Appropriations Committee that they needed to act before approval of the selective service legislation so that the army would be ready for first call-up of inductees.[45] The subcommittee voted to approve Marshall's request.

While Congress continued to debate, the German Luftwaffe, in an attempt to achieve air supremacy over Great Britain, launched massive daylight attacks on Royal Air Force (RAF) airfields throughout southern England and bombed coastal installations and industrial targets at night. Hitler made preparations for Operation Sealion, a cross-Channel invasion to take place as soon as the RAF had been destroyed or degraded. In the second week of September the Führer's air minister, Hermann Goering, commenced the terror-bombing of London—the so-called Blitz—which continued throughout the fall. Responding to Marshall's blunt warnings and the devastation in England, as broadcast nightly by Edward R. Murrow, the House of Representatives defeated a last-gasp effort to delay the draft legislation until after the election and voted to adopt the Senate version of the selective service bill. On the night Burke-Wadsworth was signed into law, General Marshall spoke to the nation on CBS radio, informing Americans that "for the first time in our history we are beginning in time of peace to prepare against the possibility of war." Using words likely approved if not dictated by Roosevelt or his political advisers, Marshall stressed that an "army of citizen soldiers" was the best way to avoid being drawn into "the tragedy of war," and to preserve "our American way of life."[46] With six weeks until the election Marshall did what he could to protect his commander in chief from charges of warmongering, while at the same time promoting the benefits to western hemispheric defense of a large citizen army. On October 16, 1940, more than sixteen million men between the ages of twenty-one and thirty-five registered for the draft.

Marshall finally had the makings of the army he desperately wanted and needed. Over the next year, at a rate of 50,000 per month, 600,000 men would be inducted into the United States Army. They were to be trained by the half million soldiers already in the Regular Army and 270,000 from the soon to be mobilized National Guard and reserves. By mid-1941, Marshall's army would number 1.4 million men—a remarkable rise from the total 189,839 at the end of 1939.[47] In the words of Forrest Pogue, the Selective Training and Service Act of 1940 "made possible the huge United States Army and Air Force that fought World War II." That said, the Act contained a ticking time bomb. It specified that inductees were required to serve for only twelve months unless Congress voted before their terms expired to declare a national emergency. Thus, as early as October of 1941, the army would begin to melt away unless Congress was moved to revisit the politically charged issue of compulsory military service.

* * * * *

Within days after President Roosevelt signed the Selective Service Act, Marshall was forced to face up to an equally charged issue—how the army should interpret the antidiscrimination provisions that Congress inserted into the legislation. Under the Supreme Court's decision in *Plessy v. Ferguson*, state-sanctioned racial segregation—that is, mass discrimination—was constitutionally permissible so long as African Americans and other minorities were afforded "separate but equal" treatment. By tradition, the army had stretched the "equal" part of the doctrine to the breaking point, consigning virtually all black troops to menial labor or service jobs. Despite strong combat performances by African American soldiers stretching back to the Revolutionary War, there was a conviction, reinforced by General Pershing, that they fought poorly in World War I. The evidence suggests that Marshall was comfortable with army tradition and that he probably shared Pershing's views. Yet he knew firsthand from his experiences with the black troops who functioned as day laborers at Fort Benning that they were in no sense treated equally in comparison to white troops. And he knew from his years associating with Rotary Club members and friends in Columbus, Georgia, of the daily abuses and injustices suffered by African Americans in the Deep South.

More than twenty years had elapsed since the black troops of the 92nd and 93rd Divisions fought in the Great War. Was it time to interpret the antidiscrimination provisions of the new selective service law literally and take at least a few steps toward integrating the army? For Marshall the answer was a firm and unequivocal no. In fact, he seemed to step backward. In a letter to Republican senator Henry Cabot Lodge Jr. that he asked Beetle Smith to draft, Marshall announced that "it is the policy of the War Department not to intermingle colored and white enlisted personnel in the same regimental organization." Since a combat regiment in World War II would consist of approximately 3,000 to 5,000 men, this foreshadowed an unusually wide separation of whites and African Americans. Marshall sought to justify his policy, declaring that "[t]his is not the time for critical experiments which would inevitably have a highly destructive effect on morale—meaning military efficiency."[48]

On September 27, 1940, the same day Marshall sent his letter to Lodge, three prominent black civil rights leaders met with Roosevelt, Navy Secretary Knox, and Assistant War Secretary Patterson in the Oval Office to urge them to integrate not just the army but the navy and marines as well. A recording machine with a hidden microphone picked up the conversation, providing a fascinating glimpse into FDR's breezy executive style. At one point Roosevelt said African Americans would be "put right in, proportionately, into the combat services." This assurance, which seemed to directly contradict Marshall's letter to Lodge, was exactly what the civil rights leaders wanted to hear. Several minutes later, when Walter Francis White, executive secretary of the National Association for the Advancement of Colored People (NAACP), suggested that the army should organize at least one completely integrated regiment, Roosevelt responded, "We've got to work into this . . . you may have a Negro regiment . . . and . . . a white regiment, in the same division . . . After a while, in case of war, those people get shifted from one to the other . . . gradually . . . you may back into what you are talking about." If they had listened closely, Roosevelt was agreeing with Marshall, implying that blacks and whites should be kept in separate combat regiments. The commander in chief was saying that sometime down the road—"gradually"—there might be some mixing of the races within a combat regiment—but not now.

Twelve days later the White House issued a press release purporting to summarize the meeting, which tracked the language of Marshall's letter to Lodge. The civil rights community was outraged. A press release by the NAACP bore the headline: "White House Charged with Trickery in Announcing Jim Crow Policy of Army."[49] With the election set to take place in three weeks, FDR rushed to announce a few palliative measures in an attempt to placate black voters (e.g., promotion of Colonel Benjamin O. Davis Jr. to be the first African American general and appointment of Judge William Hastie Jr., a prominent African American jurist, as an assistant secretary of war), but nothing that would jeopardize his base of white support in the "Solid South." In addition, the president enlisted Marshall in a scheme to assure that state governors did not get the impression on the eve of the election that he favored integration of the army. On October 25, 1940, Marshall reported that he had carried out FDR's order to withhold from state governors the large quotas of African Americans that would be subject to the draft in each of their states "until after November 5th," which happened to be election day.[50]

For the duration of the coming war blacks and whites in the army remained separate and far from equal under the policy set forth in the chief of staff's letter to Senator Lodge. Marshall believed it was "not the task of the Army" to try to solve the perplexing "negro problem" at "the expense of national defense." In a September 1941 memorandum he maintained that the "negro race is amply protected" from brutal treatment by the "civilian heads of the Army."[51] However, in a 1957 interview, Marshall expressed regret that in order to save expenses for heating and shelter he assigned most black troops to train in the South, where they faced harsh treatment by whites, which he said was "utterly beyond our control."[52] Though there is evidence that Marshall believed a movement to investigate "'brutal treatment' of negro army personnel" was backed by Communists, he was never outwardly hostile toward black soldiers.[53] Rather, he was a blend of indifference and condescension, probably driven, as was Roosevelt, by racist beliefs that African Americans were fundamentally inferior to white people. One could try to explain Marshall's attitude toward race by saying he merely reflected society at large, that he was a captive of his times. But Marshall was by no means a conformist. He was capable of rising above army tradition and societal mores. In the case of racial integration, however, he did not rise, convincing himself that war was not the time for engaging in social experimentation.

* * * * *

Since becoming chief of staff in 1939, Marshall had been mainly concerned with the expansion, organization, and training of a much larger army, as well as the production of armaments to equip and support that army. Global strategy in the event of war was not his top priority. In the fall of 1940, however, a confluence of events drew him into the center of a fundamental reassessment of U.S. national security strategy.

To the surprise of the chief of staff and many of his army colleagues, it had become increasingly apparent that the British would survive the

German onslaught. Against heavy odds the RAF had maintained air supremacy, meaning that Hitler would probably not risk a cross-Channel invasion; indeed, he secretly suspended Operation Sealion in late September. Despite the Blitz, morale in England was high. Roosevelt had stepped up his collaboration with Churchill, insisting that the U.S. continue to supply armaments and other aid to Great Britain over the opposition of army and navy strategists who believed they were needed for hemispheric defense.

Hitler had to do something to deter Roosevelt from further intervention on the side of Great Britain. His clever solution: the Tripartite Pact. Under the pact, which was announced on September 27, 1940, Germany, Japan, and Italy (the "Axis powers") agreed that if any party was attacked by a nation not yet in the war—namely, the United States—the others were bound to come to its assistance with "all political, economic, and military means." Thus, if the U.S. were to step up aggression against Germany, it would risk war with Japan and Italy. Likewise, if the U.S. were to take offensive actions against Japan to prevent further incursions into French Indochina (30,000 Japanese troops were already in what is today Vietnam and Cambodia), it would risk war with Germany and Italy. As Mark Stoler observed, the Tripartite Pact "threatened the United States with a multifront war." As a consequence, it became a catalyst that "forced a reassessment of American war plans and priorities."[54]

Taking the lead in drafting the global reassessment was Admiral Harold "Betty" Stark, chief of naval operations. Since his plebe year at the Naval Academy, Stark was nicknamed "Betty," and his friends, including Marshall, called him by that name. Likeable and respected, Stark wore round, rimless glasses and had a thatch of white hair that lent him a scholarly demeanor. He had been a friend of Roosevelt's since the Great War, and had easy access to the White House. In command of the blue-water navy, the only American forces operating outside the U.S., his authority over global strategy was only natural. Over a ten-day period beginning in late October, Stark and his navy planners produced what became known as the "Plan Dog" memorandum (army lingo for plan D). Plan Dog was premised on a statement of of national interests: the preservation of U.S. "territorial, economic, and ideological integrity," which meant freedom from invasion, access to capitalistic trading partners, and a democratic system of governance. In the event of war with the Axis powers, the plan stipulated that the best way to protect and defend these interests was for the United States to ally itself with Great Britain in defeating Germany first, while maintaining a defensive stance against Japan. Plan Dog acknowledged that this would probably involve a full-scale "land offensive" in Europe, a war that Britain could not wage on its own. After the defeat of Germany, the combined forces of the U.S. and Great Britain would take on Japan.[55]

Plan Dog was a sharp departure from previous war plans. For the first time it linked U.S. national security to the survival of Great Britain and her navy as an offset to, or balance against, the totalitarian powers in Europe. By mid-November, when he first reviewed Stark's Plan Dog memorandum, Marshall was in "general agreement" with its statement of national interests and consequent strategy.[56] He had already acknowledged that defense of the Western Hemisphere depended on the survival of Britain, asserting that "if we lose in the Atlantic, we lose everywhere."[57] And he seemed to agree with what an aide called "an outstandingly significant article" by Walter Lippmann, America's leading journalist and commentator, published in *Life* magazine. Lippmann argued that there were only four industrial regions capable of supplying the globe—the United States, Western Europe, Russia, and Japan. If the British Commonwealth fell, only America would remain under a free enterprise system; American manufacturing, he predicted, would not be able to compete with totalitarian states. As a result, Lippmann warned, the American "domestic economy" would "face unprecedented difficulties."[58]

General Marshall weighed in to the debate over grand strategy for the first time on November 29, a little more than a year before the United States entered the war. Reacting to a navy proposal for a buildup in the Pacific, which was at odds with the "defensive" posture set forth in Plan Dog, Marshall pronounced the "Germany first" (or "Europe first") strategic doctrine that he would advocate throughout the war. Writing to Stark, he said that as a first principle the United States must "resist proposals that do not have for their immediate goal the survival of the British Empire and the defeat of Germany." As a critically important corollary, the U.S. must "avoid dispersions that might lessen our power to operate effectively, decisively if possible, in the principal theatre—the Atlantic."[59] In all of Marshall's correspondence this is the clearest but least known exposition of his overall strategy for conducting the Second World War, as well as a precursor of his Cold and

Korean War grand strategy. And its adoption meant that Marshall had moved from hemispheric defense to a global strategy for winning the war.

For the rest of his career, Marshall would strive to adhere to this doctrine. He was not always successful. On more than one occasion he was overruled by his commander in chief. Frequently he gave in, or was forced to give in, to the conflicting demands of navy colleagues, General MacArthur, and British allies. Yet this remained his polestar, even after the war when, as secretary of state and then defense, he consistently advocated a "Europe first" national security worldview.

*　*　*　*　*

During the days leading up to Christmas 1940, Katherine seemed addicted to Bromo-Seltzer, a popular nerve-calming sedative that was eventually withdrawn from the U.S. market due to its toxicity. Her daughter, Molly, was to be married on Christmas Day at Quarters One, and Katherine was frantically attending to all of the details, readying the big house for the wedding. Each morning George gently chided her about her "Bromo" habit, which she said relieved her neck pain. On Christmas Eve the family gathered in the library after the wedding rehearsal. George strode in carrying a present for Katherine wrapped in silver paper. Inside was a "huge bottle of Bromo-Seltzer, a foot high."[60] Amid the laughter she vowed to get even.

The next afternoon Molly descended the stairway into the front hall of Quarters One on the arm of her stepfather. Rose Page, Marshall's friend for more than twenty years, wrote that Molly was "elegant and svelte," but appeared "nervous," her "lips set in a little, fixed half-smile," while "Colonel Marshall" (she always addressed him that way) looked "as pleasant and composed as if he were coming downstairs to greet a few old cronies."[61] They proceeded by candlelight into the large oval dining room, where James Winn Jr., a West Point graduate, and his uniformed groomsmen were waiting in front of a temporary altar. Following a brief ceremony and a reception, the newlyweds left for Panama, one of the most strategically vital points on the globe, where Captain Winn, a field artillery officer, was stationed at Fort Davis.

On New Year's Eve, George's sixtieth birthday, it was payback time for Katherine. She presented him with a leather-bound scrapbook, the first page of which contained a New Yorker cartoon—a drawing of a middle-aged couple. The man was in an easy chair with a large book spread across his lap. His portly wife was almost asleep on a nearby chaise lounge, her eyes barely open. The caption: "I do love you, George, but I just don't feel like talking military tactics with you."[62]

Following his reelection, President Roosevelt had been preoccupied due to a cruise in the Caribbean with Harry Hopkins and the promotion of his arsenal of democracy and lend-lease initiatives as alternatives to war. Versions of Stark's Plan Dog memorandum and Marshall's Germany first policy, along with a joint recommendation that "every effort" be made to avoid war with Japan, found their way to the White House, but almost two months elapsed without any feedback from the commander in chief. Finally, on January 16, 1941, Roosevelt summoned Marshall, Stark, Stimson, Knox, and Secretary of State Cordell Hull to the White House for what they hoped might be an overdue discussion of war plans and strategy. Not surprising, however, the president chose to keep all of his options open. He did not commit to, approve, or even discuss the specifics of the national interests, strategies, and war plans recommended by Stark and Marshall (although he did authorize staff talks on Plan Dog with the British). He avoided any mention of America entering the war. Rather, he continued to adhere to his "short of war" strategy, depending on lend-lease aid and diplomacy to avoid conflict with the Axis powers. According to Marshall's notes of the meeting, FDR "was strongly of the opinion" that in the event of "hostile action" by Germany or Japan, the U.S. "would not curtail the supply of materiel to England," thus underscoring the strategic importance of her survival, a goal stressed by Stark and Marshall. The president's only other instructions were that the U.S. would "stand on the defensive in the Pacific with the fleet based on Hawaii [Pearl Harbor]"; the navy should be "prepared to convoy shipping in the Atlantic to England"; and the army would not be committed to "aggressive action" until it was fully prepared.[63] Both Stark and Marshall must have been frustrated by the president's refusal to commit to their war plans. Even if the arsenal of democracy and lend-lease programs enabled Great Britain to survive and diplomacy with Japan bought more time, the two military chiefs believed that America itself would not be secure, and the millions already enslaved by Germany and Japan could not be liberated, unless the United States eventually became a belligerent.

Four days later Franklin Roosevelt walked bareheaded into the ten-degree wind chill on the arm of his son James, a marine captain, to the front of the white-pillared platform on the East Portico of the Capitol. Whether planned or not, James's blue uniform symbolized the theme of Roosevelt's third inaugural address—a call to Americans to save their democracy "from great perils never before encountered." Before a crowd over-estimated by police to be "a million souls," among them Charlie Chaplin and Mickey Rooney, the president began by reminding his countrymen of pivotal periods in their history when the people rallied to "weld together a nation" under George Washington and rallied again during the Civil War to "preserve that Nation from disruption from within." Today, intoned FDR in his mellifluous tenor voice, "the task of the people is to save that Nation and its institutions from disruption from without," a veiled allusion to the Axis powers. Appealing to the "spirit of America" and the "peril of inaction"— namely, "tyranny and slavery"—Roosevelt tried to move Americans a step closer to the possibility of war and the need to serve their country. His "high-toned" abstractions, however, originally drafted by poet Archibald Mac-Leish and diluted by a committee of four, fell flat upon the shivering multitude. Not once did the president identify the disruptors or explain how they might span oceans to kill democracy and enslave Americans.[64]

The martial theme carried over to the inaugural parade. In addition to the usual procession of civilian dignitaries, marching bands, Boy Scouts, WPA and CCC detachments, West Point cadets, and Annapolis midshipmen, the new armed forces were on conspicuous display. It was the first inaugural parade in which tanks took part. Katherine Marshall described the scene from the heated reviewing stand on Pennsylvania Avenue in front of the White House, where she sat with the president, the first lady, the president's eighty-six-year-old mother, and several of the Roosevelt children and grandchildren. "A dull rumble came up the Avenue," she wrote. "[T]he President, quite near-sighted, groped for his glasses." General Marshall, "on his bay gelding 'King Story'" led a column of soldiers, sailors, and marines who marched smartly in combat uniforms, rather than the traditional parade dress. The president smiled and waved. Marshall saluted, "after which he dismounted and took his post at the side of the President's reviewing stand."[65] The latest armored tanks, trucks carrying antiaircraft guns and pontoon bridges, and armored cars rumbled by. Flights of B-17s and other bombers plus squadrons of fighter aircraft, a total of nearly 300, roared overhead and down the Mall.

While the show of force appeared formidable to the crowd of hundreds of thousands, Marshall knew the ugly truth. The nation was not prepared. Roosevelt told Marshall days earlier that in his judgment there was "one chance out of five" that the U.S. would be suddenly and simultaneously attacked by Germany and Japan any day.[66] If that happened in the next several months he would not have the trained troops, equipment, and shipping to defend the Western Hemisphere, let alone launch an overseas mission. More than anything, Marshall needed time—time to reap that which had been planted.

CHAPTER 7

The Hour to Reap Has Come

In June 1941, George Marshall was about to face the first and arguably his greatest test as a leader on the national stage. Under the selective service law passed nine months earlier, the one-year service obligations of more than 600,000 draftees already in the army, plus the active-duty service terms of hundreds of thousands of National Guardsmen and reservists who had been called up for one year, would begin to expire in October. Unless Congress could be convinced to extend the service terms by declaring "that the national interest is imperiled," as provided in the law, the army would disintegrate. Almost two-thirds of Marshall's enlisted men and three-fourths of his officer corps would have to be released after completing their twelve months of service. Scrawled on the walls of barracks, mess halls, and latrines across America where the draftees were in basic training, the acronym OHIO began appearing. The letters stood for "Over the hill in October."

Stimson and Marshall had been warning the White House all spring to urge Congress to act. Yet the president was reluctant to take the lead. Speaker Sam Rayburn and majority leader John McCormack had told him that the votes in the House weren't there. Facing reelection in 1942, most House members wanted nothing to do with voting to extend the one-year terms of service. Even if the national security was in greater peril than it was in 1940, the American people were likely to view a vote to extend the draft as a breach of a moral commitment that Congress had made to the draftees, yet another step that would move the nation closer to war. What's more, a powerful isolationist/noninterventionist lobby and a growing number of congressmen in both parties were ready to oppose virtually anything that Franklin Roosevelt was for.

Marshall seized the initiative in an unlikely place—the president's bedroom. Roosevelt was still in bed when Marshall and Stimson arrived on the second floor of the White House on June 19 for a 10:30 a.m. meeting.

They were there to discuss ways to expedite delivery of lend-lease aircraft and supplies to the British, but at some point in the conversation either Stimson or Marshall saw an opening. Was Roosevelt willing to issue a statement stressing the need for Congress to act to extend the military terms of service before the army melted away? The president was hesitant, citing the strong opposition in Congress, especially in his own party. He indicated that he might make a public statement about extending the draft sometime in the future, perhaps when he was ready to announce his decision to send U.S. Marines to Iceland for the purpose of relieving the British garrison. Marshall stepped up. He suggested that there would be less opposition if the army, rather than the administration, made the case for the draft extension. Recognizing that Marshall would be regarded as nonpartisan and had already established a reputation in Congress for integrity and honesty, Roosevelt and Stimson approved. Marshall would carry the ball. Stimson would be sidelined, since he was regarded by fellow Republicans on the Hill as something of a traitor for having defected to the Roosevelt administration.

The meeting in the president's bedroom was a pivotal moment for Marshall and for the country. As the chief of staff recalled in an interview, he was "much criticized" for not taking "the lead" on the original selective service legislation.[1] However, by holding back and taking the long view, Marshall instilled confidence in his commander in chief that he was both loyal and committed to the principle of civilian control of the military. The president's trust in Marshall was manifested when he made him the administration's point man on the critically important and highly controversial task of convincing Congress to extend terms of military service beyond one year.

*　*　*　*　*

How should George Marshall approach Congress? What should be his initial move? According to Katherine the solution came to her husband "while horseback riding" along the Potomac. He decided to issue a "biennial report" under his name that would lay out fact-based arguments for extending service terms beyond one year. This would be a "dignified procedure," wrote Katherine, for bringing the "situation and his recommendations to the attention of the Nation."[2] Stimson advised Harry Hopkins that the War

Department would take full responsibility for the report's content and release, in effect informing the White House that its denizens would have no input, no prior review.

Without a press release, an executive summary, or any advance warning to congressional leaders, Marshall's seventeen-page report (exclusive of dozens of pages of charts, maps, and appendices), much of which he wrote himself, was a shocker. Its two recommendations—that Congress act without delay to extend the terms of military service beyond one year and at the same time remove the statutory ban on overseas deployment—attracted a storm of outrage and protest.[3] Newspapers, in a rush to grab headlines, distorted Marshall's report, suggesting that he was asking for authority to create an army of almost three million men to join the war in Europe. House and Senate leaders swamped White House and War Department switchboards, demanding to know why they were being suddenly put on the hot seat. Isolationists and noninterventionists in Congress and throughout the country, as well as a number of editorial writers, believed that Roosevelt the warmonger was behind Marshall's recommendations.

It was not an auspicious beginning. As Marshall himself admitted, it was "clear that the public ha[d] not understood the nature and purposes" of his "recommendations."[4] In part this was because of his lack of experience in dealing with the press and Congress. Further complicating matters was his dense, hard-to-follow prose, and, more important, the fact that his report simply did not explain why the "national interest" was any more "imperiled" in July 1941 than it had been a year earlier. Since this was the legislative trigger that Marshall was tasked with convincing Congress to pull, its omission naturally raised questions.

In fact, the national security of the U.S. was far more imperiled when Marshall's report was released than it was when the selective service law was passed. On June 22, 1941, Hitler had torn up his nonaggression pact with the Soviet Union and launched a massive attack against Russia, deploying 3.6 million Axis troops along a 900-mile front from the Baltic to the Black Sea. Most of the Soviet air force—some 1,800 fighters and bombers—was destroyed by the Luftwaffe on the first morning. Within a few days much of the Red Army's Mechanized Corps was liquidated.

"We have only to kick in the door," Hitler had told his commanders, "and the whole rotten edifice will come crashing down."[5] At the outset,

Marshall and most of his colleagues in the military establishment agreed. They believed the Soviets would surrender or be conquered by Germany within a matter of a few weeks or months. And when that happened, Hitler would be free to turn to the conquest by arms, or threat of arms, of Spain, Portugal, Finland, Sweden, the British Isles, and much of the British Empire. If one counted his previous conquests in Europe (thirteen countries), it was not unreasonable to surmise that he would come to control and enslave upward of a billion people. In Asia, matters appeared just as threatening. A few days before Marshall's report was released, Emperor Hirohito presided over a conference with Japan's military and political leaders. According to Japanese diplomatic messages code-named MAGIC that had been intercepted and decrypted by the U.S. Army, Japan was "preparing for all possible eventualities," including invasion of Siberia to assist Germany in "combatting the Communist menace," or moving south beyond China into French Indochina with the objective of using it as a staging area to seize vital resources in the Dutch East Indies and Malaysia.[6] It was clear that Japan intended to pursue a policy of aggression in order to establish its so-called Greater East Asia Co-Prosperity Sphere.

Marshall, of course, was not about to predict in his report that the Soviet Union was likely to be defeated by Germany. Nor could he disclose information about the meeting with Hirohito that he had learned about from the top secret MAGIC intercepts. Nevertheless, he could have marshalled convincing arguments based on publicly known facts that aggressive moves by Germany and Japan during the past year increased the threat to America's national security. Yet, other than a bare reference to "events of the past few days"—meaning Germany's attack on the Soviet Union—Marshall's report did not attempt to make the case that the national interest was in greater peril. And nowhere in his report was Japan even mentioned.

While the dry sentences in Marshall's Biennial Report were not particularly persuasive, his personal encounters with congressmen in public hearings and off-the-record sessions during the next several days began to change minds. Whether it was an ornate Senate chamber, a private club, or an office somewhere in Washington, when Marshall entered the room politicians from both sides of the aisle believed they were in the presence of a formidable individual in complete command of the facts and situation. Attired in a conservative business suit rather than his uniform, he spoke quietly yet forcefully, projecting an image of cool professionalism. With patience and courtesy, he answered their questions. They treated him with respect, believing him to be devoid of personal ambition, partisanship, or guile.

By mid-July Marshall's recommendations were still tied up in the military affairs committees of the Senate and House. The president had not gone public with his support, but he agreed to convene the committee chairs and leaders of both houses, all Democrats, plus two Republicans (Representative James Wadsworth Jr. and Senator Warren Austin of Vermont), for a secret briefing by Marshall followed by a strategy session. Stimson, vacationing in the Adirondacks, arranged for Marshall to carry the load. There is no record of what Marshall told the legislators at this White House session held on July 14. However, based on a note that Marshall sent Roosevelt the next day it appears that he disclosed in detail how his ability to defend Pearl Harbor and Alaska and to replace marines in Iceland with army troops would be severely curtailed unless Congress acted on his recommendations immediately. Having gone this far he likely revealed additional instances of how "the national interest would be imperiled" if Congress did not act.

With regard to legislative strategy, the experienced congressmen believed that while there might be just enough votes in the House and Senate to extend the terms of service beyond one year, Marshall's other recommendation—to end the ban on deploying troops outside the Western Hemisphere—should be withdrawn. There would never be enough support in favor of this explosive proposition, they advised. To link them together would doom both. The president compromised. He dropped the deployment ban and Marshall reluctantly acceded. The chief of staff, they all enthusiastically agreed, should continue to lead the fight for extension of the draft. He was asked to focus on the Senate first, since only one-third of its members would be up for election in the following year. The much tougher nut would be the House. Roosevelt agreed to deliver a single radio address in an effort to build public support.

In the ensuing days Marshall found his voice, a voice that became dominant in colloquy with the legislators. He spoke the way they thought a leader should speak. To the chair of the Senate's Military Affairs Committee, North Carolina's Robert Reynolds, whom Isaiah Berlin described as "a bitter Isolationist of a disreputable kind," Marshall articulated with unusual eloquence why the nation was in greater peril.[7] "We have watched [Hitler's] time schedule in operation which began with Austria and has now reached Russia. In each case it has been one country at a time . . . After each one the Axis forces are that much more ready for another undertaking . . . and they are getting closer and closer . . . their future plans are so apparent, so conclusive that there is no doubt in my mind that, unless we make very serious and very businesslike preparations, we may find ourselves in a very tragic situation."[8] He was no less direct with the lower chamber. After laying out specific threats to U.S. interests in Alaska, Trinidad, Newfoundland, and Iceland that did not exist the year before, Marshall bluntly challenged skeptical members of Chairman Andrew Jackson May's House Military Affairs Committee: "I am asking you to recognize the fact—the fact that the national interest is imperiled . . . I am not asking you to manufacture a fact."[9]

Marshall, for the first time, was bold enough to draw a contrast between himself and Roosevelt on matters of national defense, characterizing the president as "very conservative," which was intended to protect FDR against charges of warmongering while Marshall shouldered the responsibility and took the heat.[10] To his chagrin, however, Marshall discovered that this contrast instilled in the legislators the idea that he was the stronger and more forthright of the two, that his word was more credible than that of his commander in chief. "Let us remember," Sam Rayburn famously said of Marshall, "that we are in the presence of a man who is telling the truth."[11] He never said that about Franklin Roosevelt.

As July came to a close the votes in the House of Representatives were still not there. Marshall decided he needed to make a more personal appeal. He asked his friend, Congressman James Wadsworth, cosponsor of the original selective service act, to convene a gathering of his fellow Republicans. To put everyone at ease Marshall suggested drinks and dinner at a private club in Washington, a practice he would employ during the war and thereafter. On the designated night, roughly forty GOP congressmen met with Marshall in a private dining room at the Army and Navy Club, a seven-story Italian Renaissance edifice at the corner of 17th and I Streets across from Admiral David Farragut's statue on the square named for him. They began with daiquiris, the Cuban rum cocktail first introduced to the U.S. by club members. When dinner was served, Marshall eased into a discussion of the reasons why he believed the reluctant Republicans should vote to extend military service terms beyond one year. As Marshall recalled later, it was more a "struggle" than a discussion and it went on until "two in the morning." One unnamed congressman said, "You put the case very well, but I'll be damned if I am going to go along with Mr. Roosevelt." With a flash of anger, Marshall countered with a question that challenged the congressman's integrity: "You are going to let plain hatred of the personality dictate to you to do something that you realize is very harmful to the interests of the country?"

Marshall understood that for most of the Republicans in the room it wasn't just Roosevelt's personality that fired their opposition. It was their jobs. If they voted to extend service terms they faced almost certain electoral defeat. Marshall remembered that at one point during the evening he offered to campaign for them in 1942 if they would vote to extend (thus breaking his pledge never to participate in partisan politics). Most said it wouldn't do any good, they would still be defeated. However, "a certain number of them said, 'All right, we'll accept defeat [because this is] essential to the country.'"[12]

The long evening paid off. Whether it was just a few or a certain number or perhaps a dozen—no one knows for sure—Marshall came away with at least some Republican votes favoring extension. His efforts that night might well have made the difference.

*   *   *   *   *

With the existence of his army dependent on floor debates and final votes in Congress that would take place in the next ten days or so, Marshall was suddenly summoned to the White House. The president directed him "to prepare, in utmost secrecy, to leave for a meeting somewhere at sea with British Prime Minister Churchill and his military advisers."[13] He was to tell no one, not even his wife or Secretary Stimson. The lobbying efforts he had planned as well as all other appointments in the coming days would have to be canceled. He hated to leave Washington at this terribly critical moment, but he had no choice.

"He left Ft. Myer . . . without mentioning where he was going," wrote Katherine, but "I felt sure he was to be with the President. His orderly had packed winter clothes, so I knew he was going north, but that was all I knew."[14]

On Sunday, August 3, Marshall flew to LaGuardia Field in New York. There he was taken by barge and then by destroyer out to College Point, where Admiral Ernest King's huge flagship, the Northampton-class heavy cruiser *Augusta*, and a light cruiser, the *Tuscaloosa*, were anchored. Along with Admiral Stark, Marshall boarded the *Augusta*. Hap Arnold, the army air corps chief, who had been told nothing about the trip, was instructed to board the *Tuscaloosa*. The two cruisers, screened by five destroyers against the threat of lurking U-boats, got under way sometime in the middle of the night. The next evening, off Martha's Vineyard, a launch bearing the president and some of his aides approached the *Augusta* (the press had been tricked into believing that FDR was on a fishing trip near Cape Cod aboard the presidential yacht). After the president and his party settled into their quarters, the cruisers and their escorts zigzagged on a northerly heading through light fog. When they entered Canadian waters they were joined by the battleship *Arkansas* and eight more destroyers. On the morning of August 7, the flotilla steamed into broad Placentia Bay on the southeastern coast of Newfoundland. The two cruisers proceeded ahead and dropped anchor in a narrow fjord called Ship Harbour, at the end of which was a small fishing village of the same name.

The Americans were early. It would be another forty-eight hours before Prime Minister Churchill and his military chiefs arrived on the battleship *Prince of Wales*.

Based on what little the president had told him, Marshall assumed that for him and his fellow chiefs the shipboard conference would be nothing more than an ice-breaking get-together, simply an opportunity for them to informally meet their British counterparts with the objective of getting to know them and understanding how they worked. He had no intention of engaging with them in joint war-making plans, nor had he been given time to prepare for such discussions. More important, the fight for the very existence of the U.S. Army was being waged in Washington. He could not make any commitments unless and until Congress acted. If it did not act, and act soon, "[w]e" would be "literally destroyed for the time being," remembered Marshall.[15]

With this in mind, Marshall, Stark, King, Arnold, and a few others gathered in Roosevelt's spacious cabin on the afternoon of August 7 for a briefing. Based on detailed notes taken at the meeting by Hap Arnold, the only source for what the president actually said, FDR informed them that the meetings with Churchill and the British chiefs should focus on U.S. responsibility for defense of convoys, relief of the marines in Iceland, delivery of aircraft to England, Russia, and the Philippines, and the possibility that Japan might invade the Dutch East Indies. Beyond those subjects there is no hint in Arnold's notes that the president instructed Marshall and the others that they were forbidden to discuss operational military cooperation or an alliance in their upcoming talks with the British. With the American army in danger of melting away, everyone on the U.S. side, and most especially Marshall, understood that it would be premature to discuss such matters. Plus, they all knew that until their commander in chief gave the go-ahead these issues were off the table.[16]

On Saturday morning, August 9, Marshall watched as the camouflaged, battle-scarred *Prince of Wales*, preceded by an American destroyer, steamed slowly into Ship Harbour and dropped anchor about three hundred yards from the *Augusta*. The first passenger to motor over to the *Augusta* was Harry Hopkins. Hopkins, perpetually in ill health, had just completed an exhausting and incredibly dangerous flight to besieged Moscow to meet with Joseph Stalin. Upon returning to Scapa Flow off the north coast of Scotland, he sailed with Churchill on the *Prince of Wales*. As soon as Hopkins boarded, Marshall and the other chiefs huddled with the president to hear his firsthand report. Contrary to what Marshall had learned from his intelligence sources, Hopkins expressed optimism about the chances that the Soviets would be able to survive the German onslaught. According to Arnold's notes, Hopkins told the group that "the Russians are confident. Claim 2500 plane output a month without counting 15 training planes a day . . . Stalin claims the Russians have 24,000 tanks . . ."[17] Arnold's notes suggest he was skeptical of Stalin's claims. How much credit Marshall gave to Hopkins's positive report is unknown.

Over the next few days, Marshall spent hours chatting with his British counterpart, Sir John Dill, chief of the imperial general staff. Tall and sinewy, Dill looked every inch the British field marshal with a long-boned face, chiseled chin, and bamboo swagger stick tucked under his arm. Like Marshall, he was reticent, speaking or acting only after due thought, but when he did speak, he was straightforward and often blunt. At the same time, he preserved a wry sense of humor and a charm that appealed to Marshall. From the outset Dill was judged by Marshall to be a man of high moral character. During the emotional apex of the conference, Churchill's carefully choreographed "divine services" on the sunlit quarterdeck of the *Prince of Wales,* photos show Marshall and Dill standing together singing "O God, Our Help in Ages Past" and chatting amiably. The two men were destined to develop a relationship of trust, confidentiality, and intimate friendship that would prove vitally important to the maintenance of the Anglo-American alliance during the war years.[18]

Throughout the four days of what came to be called the Atlantic Conference, American and British military chiefs conferred with one another informally, in small groups, to discuss British needs for convoy protection, airplanes, tanks, and other supplies. The first meeting of all of the joint chiefs was scheduled for the third day, August 11, when the British hoped to secure American agreement to a war strategy document that had been personally approved, if not authored, by Churchill. The day before the meeting the document was distributed to the American chiefs, and after a quick reading, Marshall and Stark were both alarmed.

Back in March, after several weeks of joint American-British staff "conversations" known as the "ABC" talks, the two delegations of second-level military planners had reached consensus on a strategy for defeating the Axis powers that rested upon a joint buildup of forces for an "eventual offensive against Germany." Now the British were trying to renege, intent on persuading the U.S. chiefs and their president to endorse a fundamentally different grand strategy. The British were proposing that Germany be defeated not by a ground offensive but by massive bombing, naval blockade, partisan activities, peripheral raids, and propaganda campaigns. Furthermore, the paper contained a plea for early intervention by the U.S. in the war and held forth on the importance of holding the Middle East and Singapore, points that were not stressed in the earlier ABC talks.[19]

Marshall was appalled. He was convinced that Germany could not be defeated, at least in the near term, without a massive invasion of the European continent by ground troops and armor. Bombing alone, he believed, would not win the war—after all, the British had survived eight months of aerial attacks. Moreover, he was concerned that the British were trying to get the Americans to help protect their empire instead of concentrating on the defeat of Germany.

The next morning, in the Admiral of the Fleet's cabin on the *Prince of Wales,* First Sea Lord Sir Dudley Pound began the meeting of the Anglo-American chiefs of staff with the intention of reviewing the British strategy paper "point by point."[20] Admiral Stark politely interceded. As prearranged with Marshall, Stark spoke from a one-page memorandum of talking points and made clear at the outset that he and Marshall were willing to discuss the strategy paper, but that they were "averse to nullifying any part" of the strategy agreed at the ABC conversations. That said, they would "transmit a formal reply" soon after returning to Washington. Assuming Stark adhered to the talking points, he concluded his opening remarks by declaring that "General Marshall and I are of the opinion that this meeting today is one for discussion, and not a meeting for reaching new agreements or accepting new commitments."[21]

Historians have since suggested that Roosevelt orchestrated the outcome of the chief of staff talks at the Atlantic Conference, guaranteeing that nothing of "lasting importance" would emerge.[22] Yet there is no evidence that FDR had a hand in drafting Stark's talking points, nor that he engineered the stance of Stark and Marshall.[23] Indeed, neither man needed to be told by the president or anyone else to avoid signing on to a strategy they opposed. They did not need to be reminded that it was the commander in chief's responsibility, not theirs, to decide when and how to intervene in the war.

The British were disappointed, privately questioning why they came all this way for more talk and no decisive action. Moreover, they regarded the Americans, particularly Marshall, as lacking global strategic vision. The next afternoon, with flags and pennants flying, the Prince of Wales weighed anchor and steamed slowly out of Ship Harbour as the Royal Marine band played "The Star-Spangled Banner."[24] Marshall, standing on the fantail of the Augusta, could barely make out the figures of Churchill and Dill waving goodbye. As they disappeared into the fog, the chief of staff might have given pleasurable thought for a moment or more to his burgeoning friendship with "Jack" Dill, wondering when and under what circumstances he would see him again. And he might have reflected with some concern on how differently he and Churchill's military chiefs viewed the strategy for winning the war. Would they ever be able to agree?

* * * * *

Throughout the Atlantic Conference, Marshall had been monitoring radio messages from Washington on the debate in Congress over the military service extension resolution. He was heartened to learn on the evening of

August 7 that the Senate by a vote of 54–30 approved a resolution declaring "the national interest to be imperiled" and authorized the president to extend the terms of service of most army personnel by eighteen months.

Marshall knew it would be a different story in the House. On the morning of August 12, as he was having a last meeting with the British chiefs aboard the *Prince of Wales*, Speaker Sam Rayburn called the House of Representatives to order to begin the final debate and vote on the extension resolution. Aside from the working press, the capacity crowd in the gallery above the House floor was mostly opposed to the draft. Members of "Mothers for America," wearing all-black dresses and brandishing tiny American flags, were particularly noticeable, as were the colorful ranks of uniformed servicemen. When the debate began, Rayburn, who had been Speaker for less than a year, knew that he had not yet persuaded anywhere near enough Democrats to assure passage of the extension. He judged that he would need at least twenty Republicans. Joe Martin of Massachusetts, the minority leader, was personally in favor of extension. However, he advised his Republican colleagues that they should feel free to vote their consciences. Michigan congressman Clare Hoffman circulated a letter that morning to his fellow Republicans appealing not so much to their consciences as to their livelihood. He warned them that "if you don't watch your step, your political hide, which is very near and dear to you, will be tanning on the barn door."[25] It was up to Marshall's friend, respected Republican James Wadsworth, to work the floor and cloakroom throughout the day and corral the needed votes. Based on reactions following the Army and Navy Club dinner with Marshall and some forty Republicans in late July, Wadsworth knew who was wavering and who would likely hold the line on the extension resolution.

The speeches, arguments, and points of order droned on all day and into the evening with no breaks for lunch or dinner. This time there were no fisticuffs. From the speaker's rostrum Rayburn deftly beat off several crippling amendments. Outside, a rainstorm subsided as the session moved into its ninth hour. It was time for an up or down vote. Everyone on the House floor expected it to be extremely close, but no one—not even Rayburn, Martin, or Wadsworth—had any idea which way it would go. The Speaker instructed the clerk, Hans Jorgenson, to call the roll. From his list of 432 members, Jorgenson announced each name and recorded the votes and abstentions. Majority leader John McCormack, out on the floor, convinced three Democrats who intended to abstain to switch their votes to yea. The clerk went through his list a second time, calling out the names of those who had not previously responded. He tallied the votes—yeas, nays, and abstentions—on a slip of paper and finally handed it up to Rayburn. Before the Speaker could proclaim the results, Andrew Somers, a New York Democrat, rose and announced that he was changing his vote from yea to nay, a move permitted under House rules, since the final result had not been announced. With the switch, Rayburn could see that the vote for extension of the draft stood at 203 for and 202 against, a one-vote margin of victory.

Rayburn paused. Hands went up. Shouts for recognition broke out in the chamber. Inexplicably, Rayburn recognized Dewey Jackson Short, the Republican deputy whip from Galena, Missouri, a well-known opponent of the extension resolution and a card-carrying member of the Committee to Keep America Out of the War. It could have been one of the Speaker's greatest mistakes, an error that almost certainly would have doomed Marshall's fledgling army and changed the course of history.

Providence, dumb luck, or a dab of chicanery intervened. Short, a highly educated college professor and ordained Methodist pastor, either didn't know the rules of the House or perhaps misspoke. Instead of calling for a "reconsideration," which would permit members to change their votes—his obvious intent—Short requested a "recapitulation," or at least that's what the wily Speaker chose to hear. A recapitulation is a routine process to ensure that each member's vote or abstention has been properly recorded by the clerk.

Rayburn, a student of the rules, realized at once that his blunder, calling on opposition leader Dewey Short, was correctible. He quickly read the result of the vote. "On this roll call, 203 members have voted aye and 202 nay, and the bill is passed." Once these words were spoken the vote was frozen, subject only to recapitulation. Thereupon the clerk conducted the recapitulation pursuant to which the members were required to repeat but not change their original votes. At the conclusion, the one-vote margin of victory held. Rayburn declared, "No correction to the vote. The vote stands and the bill is passed."[26]

The sharp blows of Rayburn's gavel were drowned out by the uproar in the House chamber. Supporters of the extension resolution cheered, clapped, and whistled. Mothers in the gallery wept and booed. Servicemen jeered. Opponents, mainly Republicans, charged into the well of the House hollering foul and demanding a reconsideration. According to *The New York Times*, Rayburn declared "in positive tones that the chair does not permit to have its word questioned."[27]

Years later, Speaker Rayburn credited James Wadsworth for changing "the *result* of the vote."[28] With the critical assistance of Marshall, particularly his performance at the Army and Navy Club, Wadsworth was largely responsible for persuading many of the twenty-one Republicans to cross over and vote for extension, thus providing the razor-thin margin of victory. Four months later, when Pearl Harbor was attacked and war declared, the chief of staff at least had the makings of an army, though it was pitifully small, about 1.5 million men, compared to the armies he would soon face in Europe and the Pacific.

*   *   *   *   *

Having been given a pale green light by Congress to train and hopefully to increase the size of his forces, Marshall could hardly catch his breath upon returning from the Atlantic Conference before he was caught up in yet another existential threat to the army. This time the source was not Congress but his commander in chief. On Monday, September 22, 1941, Marshall, along with Secretary Stimson, was invited to the White House to discuss a proposal by Roosevelt to "*reduce* the size of the Army," as well as the "materiel being used by the Army."[29] The chief of staff was not all that surprised. He knew what was behind the president's thinking. Based on the firsthand report by Harry Hopkins and the prescient views of Joseph Davies, former ambassador to the Soviet Union, FDR had become convinced that American national security was dependent on providing massive amounts of war matériel to the Soviet Union even if it meant, as it surely would, reducing the strength of the U.S. Army. In the words of historian Waldo Heinrichs, Roosevelt had come to believe that "survival of the Soviet Union was essential for the defeat of Germany and that the defeat of Germany was essential for American security."[30] In light of reports of the ferocious resistance in recent weeks by the Red Army, Marshall and his army war planners were in partial agreement. They had initially thought that the Soviets would be defeated in only a few weeks or months. By early September, they had begun to come around, no doubt prodded by the president. With aid, the Soviets might be able to hold off Hitler and survive, at least for a year or more. Indeed, the army and navy planners' "Victory Program," which would shortly be delivered to the White House, stressed that aid to the Soviet Union "was one of the most important moves that could be made by" the U.S. and Great Britain.[31]

The chief of staff, however, strongly disagreed with a key premise underlying the president's proposals—that with enough aid from America (plus naval and air support), the Red Army, along with the British, could actually "defeat" Hitler's 300 to 400 divisions, as opposed to holding them off or slowing them down. Marshall's war planners estimated that additional ground forces—up to a total of 215 American army divisions—would eventually be required.

Face-to-face with the president at noon on September 22, Marshall was blunt. Talking from a "Ground Forces" memo that he had provided the White House in advance, he told FDR that "Germany cannot be defeated by supply of munitions to friendly powers [meaning Britain and the Soviets], and air and naval operations alone. Large ground forces will be required." Rather than decrease the size and strength of the American army, asserted Marshall, "we must come to grips with and annihilate the German military machine."[32] This means, urged the chief of staff, that the size of the American army should continue to be rapidly expanded and trained so that, in accordance with the Victory Program of his war planners, it will be prepared to launch a large-scale land offensive by "1 July 1943 . . . the target date."[33] A great deal of "time [will be] required" to prepare, he stressed. "We are already late."[34]

Marshall emerged from the sixty-five-minute meeting with one depressingly small but nevertheless important victory. At least "there would not be any reduction in the military forces," wrote Marshall to one of his planners later that day. Rather, the president seemed to be intent on "looking everywhere to find ways and means to find materiel for Russia."[35]

Three days later, during a session with Stimson to review the army and navy Victory Program, the president made it clear that Marshall had failed to persuade him of the need to vastly expand the size of the army and that the strategy and policy recommendations in the program were neither welcome nor politically prudent. Roosevelt was particularly displeased over the recommendation by Marshall and his planners that "we must invade and crush Germany."[36] Given the recent one-vote decision of Congress to extend the draft and the public aversion to sending another American expeditionary force to fight in Europe, Roosevelt was convinced, or more likely hoped, that by supplying munitions to the Soviets and the British he could keep America out of the war even if it meant short-changing the army. As a consequence, he would not move to expand the army until early 1942.

While Marshall and Roosevelt were at odds over the need for a large land army to invade Europe and defeat Germany, they remained committed to the "Germany first" global strategy. But what about Japan and the Far East? There had been an implicit understanding with the president that the army and navy would endeavor to remain on the defensive in the Pacific and that America's outpost in the Philippines was indefensible. By July 1941, however, when it became known through MAGIC decrypts and other intelligence that Japanese warships and troops were definitely moving into southern Indochina, first Marshall and then Roosevelt began to see the Philippines as a potentially important strategic asset. As explained by Marshall in a memorandum to Hap Arnold, the islands of the Philippines "constitute a Naval and Air Base upon the immediate flank of the Japanese southern movement."[37] Properly reinforced by new B-17 long-range bombers and pursuit planes, along with coastal guns, torpedo boats, and a complement of trained army troops, Marshall and his strategists were starting to convince themselves that the Philippines could be defended and that American airpower based there could serve to deter or at least delay further Japanese aggression, namely attacks on the Dutch East Indies, Malaya, and Singapore. Moreover, the Philippines were an American possession. If the United States were to abdicate responsibility for defending the Philippines, they would have difficulty persuading other nations to join them as allies in fighting the Germans and the Japanese, or so the thinking went.

Who better to command America's strategic redoubt in the Pacific than sixty-one-year-old Douglas MacArthur? The decorated Great War hero and former army chief of staff—the youngest ever—was already in the Philippines, living rent-free with his new wife and three-year-old son in a seven-room, air-conditioned penthouse apartment atop the Manila Hotel. Having retired with full pension from the U.S. Army at the end of 1937, he was now serving as field marshal in the Filipino army and military adviser to President Manuel Quezon, at a salary of $18,000 per year with an annual personal allowance of $15,000, paid by the Philippine government. Aware of the

Japanese threat to American interests in the Pacific, MacArthur had been lobbying Marshall and the president through his press secretary since February of 1941 for a Far East command, contending with characteristic optimism that he could "provide an adequate defense [of Luzon] at the beach against a landing operation of 100,000."[38] Marshall had informed Stimson as early as May 21 that he intended to recall MacArthur and place him in command of the army and army air corps in the Philippines if a "Far Eastern crisis arose."[39]

The crisis was now at hand. According to MAGIC intercepts, Marshal Pétain, leader of the Vichy French, had acquiesced to Tokyo's demands for permission to establish a major military presence in southern French Indochina, including eight airfields in-country and naval bases at Saigon and Cam Ranh Bay. From these positions Japanese bombers could interdict overland supply routes to China and its warships and air force could threaten the Dutch East Indies, Malaya, and the Philippines. On July 24, thousands of Japanese troops landed in Saigon. At a cabinet meeting in the White House on the same day, the president's proposed executive order freezing Japanese assets in the United States was approved. Under the order, which was issued on Friday, July 26, all future trade with Japan, including sales of crude oil and petroleum products, could be conducted only pursuant to licenses granted by agencies of the U.S. government for each shipment. Since Japan's economy and military power depended on American oil, the Japanese quickly realized that Roosevelt had his hands firmly around their neck. He could start squeezing whenever it suited his purposes.

Marshall understood that the president was playing a dangerous game. If he allowed licenses for oil to be granted piecemeal, it might deter Japan from further aggression southward, yet at the same time it could encourage Japan to assist Germany by attacking Russian Siberia from the northeast. On the other hand, if he squeezed too hard, the Japanese would be forced to either back down or seize oil fields and other vital resources in the Dutch East Indies, which would likely lead to a Pacific war. FDR's stranglehold was fraught with risk. Yet whether he squeezed, relaxed, or did nothing, the strategic importance of the Philippine archipelago was enhanced.

Pursuant to Marshall's recommendation, Roosevelt nationalized the Filipino army on July 26. On the same day—also the day the president's freeze order was issued—the chief of staff recalled MacArthur to active duty and designated him "Commanding General, United States Army Forces, Far East," while Roosevelt bestowed on him the temporary rank of lieutenant general. Four days later, in a meeting with Marshall and Stark, FDR approved a remarkable reversal of military strategy. Henceforth, announced Marshall to his staff the next day, it will be "the policy of the United States to defend the Philippines."[40] Supplemented by American airpower, the islands were to be used as a base both to defend against an invasion and to deter further Japanese aggression.

For the past twenty years it had been army doctrine that the Philippine archipelago could not be defended and that airpower was no substitute for land and naval forces. Why then the dramatic shift? Most likely it was due to an excess of confidence in General MacArthur and misplaced trust in reports concerning the range and firepower of the new B-17 Flying Fortresses that for the first time were rolling off Boeing's assembly lines in substantial numbers. It might also have been due in part to the natural resistance to giving up American territory without a fight. In the absence of a written record there is no better explanation for why the policy was altered or who among the three—Marshall, Stark, or the president—was most responsible for the fateful change.

Marshall had enormous confidence in and respect for MacArthur's ability and intelligence as a military strategist, tactician, and combat commander. Six Silver Stars awarded during World War I were a testament to his almost suicidal bravery under fire. Marshall still deferred to MacArthur as his senior, a living legend even though he was chief of staff. Contrary to tales of ancient quarrels and snubs, Marshall harbored no perceptible hostility toward MacArthur at the time, nor did he begrudge him for assigning him to the National Guard in Chicago in 1933, one of the reasons his first star was delayed. Their personalities, of course, were vastly different—MacArthur flamboyant, Marshall reserved. And Marshall was well aware that MacArthur could be "very, very difficult at times," especially in matters involving army politics.[41] Yet in some important ways, the two men were alike. Both were fiercely loyal to the army, possessed of extraordinary self-confidence, and adept at acquiring and projecting power.

Given his charge to defend and deter, the forces MacArthur acquired when he assumed command in the Philippines were anything but potent. All that he could count on to protect the 7,100 islands and 10,850 miles of coastline in the Philippines were a Regular Army regiment of 10,000 officers and men; 12,000 U.S.-trained Philippine Scouts; 12 untrained, under-strength, and poorly equipped Philippine infantry regiments; and about 165 obsolete aircraft. Though MacArthur had made wildly implausible claims that he could fend off an invasion with these meager forces, even he could not make the case that they were capable of deterring the Japanese from attacking elsewhere.

Just as Marshall had been challenged with the job of extending the peacetime draft to build and train an army strong enough to take on the Wehrmacht in the west, a process that would take at least two years, now he was confronted with the task of providing MacArthur, as quickly as possible, with forces able to defend at least part of the archipelago and to deter aggression against American interests and possessions in East Asia. Several companies of infantry and perhaps a regiment, along with a tank battalion, could be shipped to the region in the coming weeks, but they, alongside MacArthur's existing assets, would not be enough to repel a landing in force on the beaches of Luzon, much less deter other aggressive moves by the Japanese in the Pacific. The best and indeed the only other way to rapidly reinforce MacArthur, reasoned Marshall, was to rush bombers and pursuit planes out to the Philippines. He was stymied, however, by conflicting orders of the president and pressures from the State Department to allocate planes to the Soviet Union, Britain, China, and Brazil. Plus, he needed to retain planes in the U.S. to work with ground troops in large-scale army maneuvers and to be used in training pilots and crews. There were simply not enough warplanes to go around.

To resolve his dilemma Marshall needed an in-person meeting with Roosevelt, an opportunity to provide him with a complete picture. According to Hap Arnold's notes the session took place aboard the *Augusta* on the afternoon of August 7, two days before the British arrived for the Atlantic Conference. When the gathering in the president's stateroom reached the subject of aircraft, Marshall laid out the conflicting demands and his recommendations concerning priorities. Then, as previously agreed with Arnold, he asked FDR to order an air force buildup in the Philippines consisting of "1 group B-17s," meaning thirty-six of the four-engine heavy bombers in four squadrons, and "1 group P-40s," ninety single-engine fighters in five squadrons. The president agreed. Not only that, he also approved the shipment of

an unspecified number of tanks and antiaircraft guns to the Philippines.[42]
A few days later in a conversation with Jack Dill, his British counterpart,
Marshall claimed that the decision to reinforce the Philippines with Boeing
B-17 Flying Fortresses and Curtiss-Wright P-40 Warhawks would act as a
"serious deterrent" to Japan.[43]

Backed by the president, egged on by Arnold, and willingly seduced by
MacArthur's boundless confidence, Marshall was beginning to believe that
squadrons of warplanes could be the solution to the problem of defending
the Philippines and deterring the Japanese. During the third week of August
he and Stimson visited the Boeing plant in Seattle, to personally inspect
B-17C models that were currently in use and the brand-new longer and
more heavily armed B-17Es that were just coming off assembly lines. Boeing's chief executive, Philip G. Johnson, and its engineers and marketing
representatives subjected their very important government customers to two
days of "discussions" (i.e., lobbying) concerning ranges and capabilities of
Boeing's B-17s, emphasizing that each model could bomb targets as far as
Formosa and Okinawa and that the model E could even strike Kyushu,
Japan's southern home island.

Secretary Stimson was sold. In his diary he wrote that with enough B-17s
the Philippines could become "a self-sustaining fortress capable of blockad-
ing the China Sea by air power." To the president and his cabinet he went
even further—some would say over the top—claiming that Boeing's B-17s
and other air assets would enable the United States to accomplish a "reversal" of its global war strategy, whatever that meant.[44] Marshall, normally
cautious and restrained, was almost equally effusive. In a recorded telephone
conversation with Admiral Stark he said that with "those planes," meaning
B-17s, "we can cover the whole area of possible Japanese operations," even
to the extent of basing American airpower in Vladivostok, as a means to
deter Japan from invading the Soviet Union from the east. With regard to
Japanese moves south to Malaysia, Marshall confidently asserted, "We can
certainly stop them."[45]

In retrospect, the newfound faith by the chief of staff and the secretary
of war in the capability of airpower in the Pacific bordered on the delusional.
It was particularly remarkable, not to mention inconsistent, because Marshall and Stimson maintained throughout the war that airpower would
never be a substitute for land armies in the West.

The first flight of nine B-17s arrived safely at Clark Field near Manila on September 12. Two additional groups of thirty-six each were scheduled by Marshall to depart, the first group in October and the second in December. The rushed buildup of airpower was broadened and accelerated in September with orders to send a second group of P-40 fighters, fifty-four dive bombers, and various supporting units out to the Philippines.

The buildup would take time, but time was running out. At some point, probably not until September, Marshall and Stark learned that Roosevelt or someone in his administration had squeezed too hard. Instead of continuing to grant at least some export licenses to the Japanese so that they could purchase and ship low-grade oil from the U.S., which was Roosevelt's plan before he departed for the Atlantic Conference, a flat-out total embargo on *all* trade with Japan, including its ability to purchase oil, had been put into effect. The individual who actually pulled the trigger on the Japanese was Dean Acheson, assistant secretary of state, the dominant figure on a three-person interagency committee responsible for granting licenses to withdraw funds for purchases. As Acheson later explained, he "discovered" a technique through inaction, obfuscation, and bureaucratic red tape to completely cut off Japan's oil lifeline.[46] Though Acheson did not lack self-confidence and was known to favor a "bullet proof" freeze on all oil shipments to Japan because he did not think it would provoke war, he probably did not act entirely on his own. More likely his actions were sanctioned by Undersecretary of State Sumner Welles, who in turn may have received signals from Roosevelt and Secretary of State Cordell Hull.

On behalf of the navy, Stark warned the administration against continuation of the embargo. With his fleet stretched in the Atlantic, the last thing he needed was war in the Pacific. For a time, Marshall's war planners actually supported the embargo, believing it was more important to prevent Japan from attacking Siberia than trying to deter it from moving south. In any event, Roosevelt and Hull did nothing to reverse Acheson's action, "in effect ratifyi[ng] the unplanned embargo."[47]

*   *   *   *   *

Once it became apparent to planners in Japan's imperial military headquarters that the complete trade embargo was not going to be relaxed, they knew that oil to fuel their fleet and warplanes, along with rubber, rice, and other

vital reserves, would soon run out (Japan's oil reserves would last for no longer than eighteen months). By the end of 1941 at the latest, Japan would
need to seize new supply sources in the oil-rich Dutch East Indies, which
the United States would surely oppose. And to protect its long exposed flank
as it moved south, the Japanese navy would have to deliver a knockout
punch to U.S. naval and airpower in the Pacific.

Plans for the decisive blow—simultaneous surprise attacks on the American fleet at Pearl Harbor and against the forces of MacArthur in the Philippines and the British in Singapore—were well under way. Months before the
embargo was put into effect, Admiral Yamamoto Isoruku had come to believe that war with the United States and also Great Britain was inevitable.
On January 7, 1941, in his cabin aboard the battleship *Nagato* anchored in
Hiroshima Bay, Yamamoto, commander of Japan's Combined Fleet, outlined in his own brushstrokes the key elements of the plan, predicting that if
implemented it would destroy American morale and decide the fate of the
war in the Pacific on the first day.

As a young ensign, Yamamoto had been seriously wounded by shrapnel
while aboard a cruiser during the Battle of Tsushima Strait, but now, in his
fifties, he still looked youthful, even boyish. His years at Harvard and then
the Japanese Embassy in Washington lent him an air of confidence and charisma. Having come to understand the United States, he was opposed to war
with America, believing the chances of success were slim and that the U.S.
would not give up easily. Yet at the same time his reputation as an innovative
operational planner and a brilliant gambler enabled him to convince Japan's
political and military leaders that if they decided on war, his Pearl Harbor/
Philippines/Singapore strategy afforded the best odds of achieving their
objective—breaking through the real or imagined encirclement by its three
international rivals, the United States, Great Britain, and the Soviet Union.
The ultimate goal was economic survival: establishment of a Greater East
Asia Co-Prosperity Sphere.

During the summer and fall of 1941, Yamamoto's grand strategy de-
volved into detailed operational plans. The principal technical obstacle to
destroying the U.S. fleet in Hawaii was the feasibility of low-level attacks by
Japanese torpedo planes over Pearl Harbor's unusually shallow waters. Part
of this problem was addressed by adding stabilizing fins to the torpedoes.
The rest was solved by intensive pilot training at Kinko Bay in Kagoshima,

which resembled the geography and depths of Pearl Harbor. The pilots had no clue why they were being driven so hard, but by October they were able to release their new torpedoes at extremely low levels, so low that they would sink no more than ten meters into the water before thrusting forward.

The problem with the second part of Yamamoto's overall plan—destruction of MacArthur's air capability in the Philippines, followed by amphibious landings—was lack of adequate fighter cover. Japanese long-range bombers, which had to operate from airfields in Formosa, needed fighter protection in order to accomplish their missions. The Japanese Zero was not capable of carrying enough high-octane aviation fuel to provide cover for the entire run to and from bombing targets in the Manila area, some 500 miles from Formosa. To succeed, Tsukahara Nishizo, the admiral responsible for wiping out U.S. airpower in the Philippines and supporting the landings, desperately needed carrier-based fighter support. The issue was confronted and resolved at a commanders' summit at Kanoya in late September. Vice Admiral Nagumo Chuichi, chief of the First Air Fleet responsible for attacking Pearl Harbor, agreed to cede Zeros, seaplanes, and other carrier-based aircraft to Tsukahara's Philippine mission.

By the end of October 1941, Yamamoto's risky war plans, still a closely guarded secret, had been approved by Japan's Naval General Staff, though the ultimate decision rested with the government. Snippets of intelligence began arriving in Washington suggesting that Japanese political leaders were preparing to implement some sort of an alternative in the event that peace negotiations with the State Department, which had been ongoing since August, should fail. In his long telegram dated November 3, Joseph Grew, U.S. ambassador in Tokyo, counseled that "Japanese sanity cannot be measured by American standards of logic." He warned ominously that "armed conflict with the United States may come with dangerous and dramatic suddenness."[48] MAGIC intercepts conveyed a sense that negotiations were coming to a head. Japan's chief diplomat in Washington, Nomura Kichisaburo, was informed on November 2 that forthcoming peace proposals to be made to Secretary of State Cordell Hull were a "last effort," and that without a "quick accord," negotiations would "certainly be ruptured."[49]

Marshall was obviously concerned. His all-out efforts to reinforce the Philippines were far from complete. He joined Admiral Stark in sending a message to Roosevelt on November 5 that his reinforcements would not be adequate to pose a "threat to any Japanese operations south of Formosa" until "the middle of December, 1941."[50] By the 10th, he expected thirty-five more B-17s to arrive "which would double the number of heavy bombers in the Philippines, along with 145 P-40 interceptors and 54 dive bombers."[51] (Neither Marshall, Stark, or any other U.S. leader suggested the possibility of an air attack at Pearl Harbor.) Marshall and Stark pleaded with Roosevelt and Hull's State Department to buy more time, at least ninety days, by engaging in "clever diplomacy" and making "minor concessions," such as relaxing the oil embargo.[52] American airpower in the Philippines would not reach full strength, they said, until February or March 1942.

In Tokyo during the first week of November the political and military leaders of Japan, each professing not to want war, collectively made war inevitable. The operational details of Yamamoto's war plans, together with a definite attack date, were presented to forty-year-old Emperor Hirohito Showa on the afternoon of November 2. Like his subjects, Hirohito expressed a preference for a diplomatic solution, as he had in the past, but he resigned himself to the very real prospect of war. Two days later the emperor was present at a meeting of the Supreme War Council. Recently installed prime minister Tojo Hideki, formerly minister of war, had pledged to support diplomatic efforts, but because of compromises he had to make to gain the backing of hard-line militarists in his administration, he believed there was little chance that talks would result in a peaceful settlement and that war was a virtual certainty. Addressing the council and his emperor, Tojo's foreign minister was equally pessimistic about the ongoing negotiations. "If we just stand by with our arms folded and allow our country to revert to the 'little Japan' that we once were, we would be tainting its twenty-six-hundred year history."[53] This was a call for war. There was no talk of the endgame or an exit strategy. The next day, November 5, an imperial conference was convened in the First Eastern Hall of the Meiji Palace. It was largely ceremonial, a quasi-religious ritual. The grave fate of Japan had already been decided. Almost everyone in the room believed the odds were against a Japanese victory over the United States. No one, however, wanted to take responsibility for the devastating consequences of defeat.

On Friday, November 7, Admiral Yamamoto issued his first combined fleet operational order, a 100-page long-range strategic war plan that included attacks on Pearl Harbor, the Philippines, Singapore, and a number of other simultaneous actions in the Pacific. Operation Hawaii began as follows: "The Task Force will launch a surprise attack at the outset of war upon the US Pacific Fleet supposed to be in Hawaiian waters, and destroy it . . . The date of starting the operation is tentatively set forth as December 8, 1941."[54]

Marshall, of course, knew nothing of Tokyo's plans. He did know, however, that Secretary Hull was making little progress on the diplomatic front. Meanwhile, the Japanese press was clamoring for the U.S. to end its trade embargo and its demands for Japanese troop withdrawals in China; if America did not back off, it would "face conflict," screamed headlines.[55]

It was clear that the U.S. was edging ever closer to war in the Pacific. Marshall needed more time to reinforce the Philippines. What could he do to prolong the peace negotiations? Someone in the White House or State Department, perhaps Marshall himself, came up with an idea that in hindsight would seem to be the longest of longshots and in today's world would be a nonstarter.

The idea was to quietly leak to Japan's peace negotiators in Washington that a large fleet of long-range B-17s capable of bombing the Japanese homeland was already in the Philippines. The hope was that this threat would cause the negotiators to urge their superiors in Tokyo to slow down or perhaps even stop the march toward war. To pull this off, Marshall convened an off-the-record meeting of the top Washington military and foreign affairs correspondents to persuade them not to report anything in the near future that might undermine the success of the plan. Taking the reporters into his confidence, he informed them of the proposed leak and told them that by mid-December there would be fifty-five B-17s in the Philippines capable of bombing Japanese cities and landing safely at airfields being built in Vladivostok. He made it clear to them that the existence and capability of the B-17s should not be reported to the Japanese public because the fanatics there "would demand war immediately." Invoking national security, Marshall intended to put a lid on the press and to temporarily influence its reporting on the game-changing power and range of the new B-17s.[56]

Even if the leak to the Japanese negotiators took place and even if the press was compliant, it is doubtful that the fanciful scheme that Marshall attempted to engineer bought a single additional hour to prepare for war. Yet his secret press conference and the fact that the reporters seemed to trust his word were an indication of Marshall's power and capacity to reach beyond the War Department and work the multiple levers that shape U.S. foreign policy. More significantly, it revealed how misguided Marshall was at the time about the effective combat range of B-17s and the prospect of establishing U.S. airfields in the Soviet Union. He actually boasted to the reporters that American land-based B-17s and B-24s could degrade Japanese naval strength throughout the Pacific and bomb their cities at will.

Following the press conference Marshall caught up on correspondence and then returned to Quarters One to look in on Katherine. Three weeks earlier she had suffered a nasty fall, slipping on a rug and striking her back against the sharp corner of a table. She broke four ribs, bruised a nerve in her back, and spent ten painful days at Walter Reed Hospital before returning home with a nurse, who stayed with her throughout daylight hours. During that period George made a special effort to get back to Quarters One for lunch with Katherine, and to be home in the evenings when the nurse left. By the afternoon of November 15, Katherine was "well on the way to a comfortable recovery," wrote George to his stepdaughter, Molly, "and felt much stronger."[57] The following day the couple flew in the chief of staff's army plane to Fort Lauderdale and drove to Pompano Beach, where Ed Stettinius, former chairman of U.S. Steel and future secretary of state, owned "a luxurious dune cottage" on the ocean.[58] Stettinius had offered his cottage to the Marshalls for as long as they wanted to stay, but George didn't linger for long. The next morning he left Katherine and flew up to Charlotte to observe the "Carolina" army maneuvers along the Pee Dee River, where he critiqued a mock battle between a traditional infantry-oriented army of eight divisions and six antitank groups and a more mobile force consisting of two armored, one motorized, and two infantry divisions. By the 18th, he was back in Washington to testify before the House Appropriations Committee in support of the War Department's $6.7 billion supplemental appropriations request, part of which was to be used to mobilize, train, and maintain the Philippine Commonwealth Army. The next day he flew back to Pompano Beach to spend Thanksgiving Day and a long weekend with Katherine. It was to be Marshall's last peacetime vacation.

Among papers marked "urgent" on Marshall's desk when he returned to the Munitions Building on Monday, November 24, was a decrypted MAGIC message from Tokyo's foreign office and a draft warning that

Admiral Stark wanted to send to navy commanders at Pearl Harbor and Manila as soon as possible. The message from Tokyo was addressed to the two Japanese peace negotiators in Washington (a second diplomat, Admiral Kurusu Saburo, arrived in the capital on the 17th). It instructed them that if they could not finalize a peace agreement with the Americans by November 29 (the 28th in Washington), "things are automatically going to happen."[59] The significance was obvious. Marshall read Stark's draft warning, telephoned the admiral, and told him he concurred. He asked that Stark's message also be sent to army commanders at Pearl and Manila. The warning that Stark sent stated as follows:

> Chances of favorable outcome of negotiations with Japan very doubtful. This situation coupled with statements of [Japanese] government and movements of their naval and military forces indicate in our opinion that a surprise aggressive movement in any direction including attack on Philippines or Guam is a possibility. Chief of staff has seen this dispatch, concurs and requests action addressees to inform senior army officers their areas [meaning Generals Short and MacArthur, among others]. Utmost secrecy necessary in order not to complicate an already tense situation or precipitate Japanese action.[60]

This warning should have alerted Admiral Husband Kimmel and General Walter Short, the commanders responsible for defending the fleet at Pearl Harbor, to be ready for an attack. Kimmel received the message, but it is arguable that the specific mention of the Philippines and Guam diminished its impact on him. Marshall's army commander at Pearl, General Short, testified later that he never saw it. Even if true, he should have been prepared. As far back as February 1941, when Short took over command at Pearl, he was warned by Marshall in an extraordinary three-page letter about the capabilities of Japanese carrier-based aircraft and that his mission, his first responsibility, was to provide the "fullest protection for the Fleet."[61]

Roosevelt's War Cabinet—Hull, Stimson, Knox, Marshall, and Stark—gathered the next day, November 25, at noon in the White House. Secretary Hull provided his assessment of the state of negotiations and the likelihood of an attack by the Japanese. Turning to Marshall and Stark, he said, "These fellows mean to fight; you will have to be prepared."[62] According to

Stimson's diary, the president surmised that an attack could come as early as Monday, December 1, "for the Japanese are notorious for making an attack without warning. The question is how we should maneuver them into the position of firing the first shot without allowing too much danger to ourselves."[63] That afternoon, back in his office, Marshall learned from one of his intelligence officers that a large Japanese convoy, including troopships, had departed Shanghai and was slowly steaming south, destination unknown. "The first Japanese attack was going to be directly south," Marshall understandably predicted. "That would be the main campaign, and the Philippines of course would be involved in it."[64]

*   *   *   *   *

Dusted by a light snowfall, the ships of the Kido Butai—Admiral Nagumo's powerful First Air Fleet—left Hittokappu Bay in the Kuril Islands in strict secrecy and put out to sea in the little-traveled North Pacific. The First Air Fleet consisted of two battleships, six aircraft carriers (carrying a total of 378 airplanes), three cruisers, nine destroyers, three submarines, and seven oil tankers. Having been lulled into believing that the Japanese would strike south, Marshall had no idea, no inkling whatsoever, that they would begin their war against the United States thousands of miles to the east.

Once Roosevelt and Secretary Hull learned from army intelligence that a large Japanese convoy with troopships was heading south—an unmistakable sign of "bad faith" in the middle of peace negotiations—they decided, without consulting Marshall or Admiral Stark, to effectively end the negotiations.[65] On November 26, Hull presented the Japanese with a new "ten-point plan," demanding among other things that they withdraw from China. He knew it would be dead on arrival.

The same day, a group of Japanese officers conferred aboard the *Ashigara*, Admiral Takahashi Ibou's flagship, to finalize plans and orders for the invasion of the Philippines. Following air attacks to destroy MacArthur's air force, General Homma Masaharu was given sixty days to launch a series of amphibious landings and conquer the islands.

Stimson called Hull first thing on the morning of November 27 to find out whether the negotiations were in fact over. "I have washed my hands of it," Hull replied, "and it is now in the hands of you and Knox, the Army and the Navy."[66] Marshall, out of town observing phase two of the Carolina maneuvers, had left Stimson a draft of a "hostile action" warning that he had prepared the day before in case it was needed. Between interruptions, Stimson and General Leonard "Gee" Gerow, Marshall's chief of war plans, worked on revisions to the draft, and that afternoon the War Department sent the modified draft to all army commanders in the Pacific, including MacArthur in the Philippines and Short at Pearl. In essence, it warned that "hostile action" by the Japanese was "possible at any moment," and that if hostilities could not be avoided, "the U.S desires that Japan commit the first overt act." However, the radiograms that were sent to General Short at Pearl and to the commanders at the Presidio and Panama contained an addition to one of Marshall's sentences that turned out to be a source of confusion, at least as far as General Short was concerned. The sentence originally drafted by Marshall was straightforward: "Prior to hostile Japanese action you are directed to take such reconnaissance and other measures as you deem necessary," which meant that Short should conduct reconnaissance to protect the fleet via his radar and short-range army aircraft. Yet someone, probably Stimson or Gerow, added onto Marshall's directive: "but these measures should be carried out so as not, repeat not, to alarm civil population or disclose intent."[67] In interpreting the amended sentence, General Short seized upon the thing he was instructed *not* to do—alarm the local population, much of which was of Japanese ancestry, or otherwise signal an aggressive intent—instead of what he was affirmatively expected *to* do. As a result, Short ordered Alert No. 1, defense against sabotage, the option least likely to alarm the local population. This meant that Short's warplanes were to be parked wing to wing on the ground so they could be closely guarded and his antiaircraft ammunition stowed in storage when the Japanese finally attacked. Short's excuse was that if Marshall was concerned that there was going to be an all-out air attack by the Japanese at Pearl "he would have said so."[68]

In later testimony, Stimson and Marshall expressed astonishment that Short could misinterpret their "hostile action" warning. Short, however, regarded the warning as ambiguous, a set of "do-don't" instructions that gave him license to focus on sabotage instead of an air or sea attack. Similarly, when Short received two more warnings on the same day, one a "war warning" from Stark and Kimmel, and the other an advisory from army intelligence that "subversive activities may be expected," Short chose to focus on protecting against sabotage rather than taking precautions against an attack from the air or sea. As far as Marshall was concerned, a "war warning" could not have been clearer and more alarming.[69]

Responses from the four Pacific commanders to the warnings were waiting for Marshall when he returned to Washington the next day. Short's differed from the other three. He reported that his army and air corps assets at Pearl Harbor had been put on alert to "prevent sabotage," that is, Alert No. 1.[70] Whether Marshall actually read Short's response is not known; he "assumed" he read it, but it does not bear his initials. What is known is that neither Marshall, Stimson, nor anyone else in the War Department realized that Short had misinterpreted the warnings. As a consequence, no one told him that the warning sent out under Marshall's name the day before meant that he should have gone on an advanced alert, including activation of round-the-clock radar and lookout stations and readiness of his air assets to defend the fleet.

Marshall had no doubt that Short had been properly warned and simply failed to carry out measures necessary to prevent an attack. Nevertheless, four years later an army board investigating the causes of the Pearl Harbor debacle censured both Marshall and Gerow (but not Stimson) for failing to realize that Short had not properly responded to their instructions by going on full alert.[71] Gerow attempted to take the blame, since he helped write the clause that may have confused Short. Yet Marshall assumed full responsibility, saying, "[t]hat was my opportunity to intervene and I did not do it."[72]

Later, Marshall sought a measure of indulgence for his oversight. "I am not a bookkeeping machine," he explained, "and it is extremely difficult . . . for me to take each thing in its turn and give it exactly the attention it had merited."[73] One can sympathize with the "too much on my plate" defense, but that should not exonerate Marshall or any other chief executive. His failure to step in when it was obvious that Short was confused or mistaken and there was still plenty of time to make a real difference in the defense of Pearl Harbor means that Marshall rightfully shares some degree of responsibility for the disaster that ensued.

* * * * *

Only one man could avert the death and destruction that awaited the army and navy at Pearl Harbor, one man who could change history: Emperor Hirohito. On November 30, Hirohito confessed to his brother his fear that

Japan would eventually be defeated, yet the government and the military had already made the decision to go to war. He was not sure he could exercise an effective veto at this late stage. "If I did not approve of war Tojo would resign," he said, "then a big coup d'état would erupt, and this would in turn give rise to absurd arguments for war."[74]

The next day Hirohito convened an imperial conference. The deadline for finalizing negotiations had passed. Bowing to the emperor, Prime Minister Tojo took charge of the proceedings. "Matters have now reached the point where Japan, in order to preserve her empire, must open hostilities against the United States, Great Britain and the Netherlands," he said.[75] Hirohito apparently said nothing. Eventually, everyone approved Tojo's recommendation. The emperor nodded, signaling his acceptance of their decision and acknowledging their bows. On December 2, coded messages were sent from Tokyo to naval task forces headed for, among other places, the Gulf of Siam, the Malay Peninsula, the Dutch East Indies, the Philippines, and Pearl Harbor.

A few hours later Admiral Yamamoto radioed a prearranged coded message to the *Akagi*, flagship of the First Air Fleet, that was about 940 miles north of Midway Island. Admiral Nagumo read the message. "Climb Mount Niitaka, 1208."[76] His mission was a "go." The attack on Pearl Harbor would take place on December 8—December 7 in Hawaii and the U.S. Japan was going to war.

In Washington, there were reports of Japanese interest in ship traffic at Pearl Harbor as well as several other places in the Pacific, but almost no specific, credible intelligence indicating an attack on Pearl. The MAGIC team had broken the diplomatic exchanges to and from Tokyo, but had not yet penetrated the Imperial Navy's secure codes. Colonel Rufus Bratton, head of army intelligence, Far East Section, told his staff that "something is going to blow in the Far East soon," but no one knew where or when.[77] During the next four days, Marshall became even more convinced that the first blow would fall on the Philippines. On December 3, he received reports that a lone Japanese plane was conducting reconnaissance over Clark Field and Manila. In light of this evidence, he was angered the next day when he learned that a flight of thirteen B-17s bound for Manila had been held up on the West Coast due to headwinds. He sent Hap Arnold to Hamilton Field in California to get the big bombers moving. During the morning of

December 6, Marshall read a report from British intelligence saying that three Japanese convoys, including forty-six troop transports, had rounded Cambodia Point and were steaming slowly west toward the Kra Isthmus north of Singapore. He estimated that they would arrive there in fourteen hours, sometime before dawn in the Far East. Again, the signs pointed to a flank attack to neutralize MacArthur's forces in the Philippines. Marshall pressured Arnold to break the logjam at Hamilton Field.

* * * * *

Meanwhile, Nagumo's First Air Fleet was roughly 600 miles northwest of Pearl Harbor, refueling for the last time before the attack. For the Japanese, these were the most dangerous moments because the First Air Fleet was within the range of U.S. Navy reconnaissance aircraft but beyond the range of their targets in and around Pearl Harbor. Nagumo and his commanders were not aware, but all three aircraft carriers in the U.S Pacific Fleet had left Pearl Harbor. They too could stumble upon the First Air Fleet. However, the seas remained calm and the refueling was accomplished according to plan.

On Saturday afternoon, December 6, when Marshall was still at the Pentagon, Colonel Bratton delivered to the chief of staff's office a copy of the so-called pilot message, a MAGIC intercept informing the two Japanese negotiators in Washington that a coded communication in fourteen parts—a response to Secretary Hull's ten-point proposal—was about to be sent to them. They were to keep the long communication secret until presenting it to Hull the next day under conditions to be relayed later. The situation "is extremely delicate," the Japanese negotiators were advised.[78] Critics of Marshall claim that upon reading the pilot message he should have immediately picked up a scrambler phone and warned General Short that an attack was imminent. If he had done that, they say, Short might have upgraded to full-alert status. In testimony during one of the several Pearl Harbor investigations, Marshall said that he never saw the pilot message, and that if he did, he would not have regarded it as anything significant enough to warrant a call to Short. Besides, he believed that Short had understood his earlier warnings and instructions and was fully prepared for an attack at any time.

Navy cryptanalysts, working with army intelligence, began decoding and translating the first thirteen parts of the top secret message from Foreign

Minister Togo to the Japanese diplomats in Washington at around 2:45 p.m. on Saturday afternoon. Sometime between nine and ten p.m., Navy commander Lester Schulz entered the Oval Study on the second floor of the White House and handed the translated pages to the president. While Harry Hopkins paced the floor, Roosevelt carefully read through the thirteen parts. In an argumentative but not overly hostile tone the document misstated Japan's intentions, characterizing its moves into French Indochina as defensive and blaming the U.S. for obstructing peace between Japan and China. The final page stated that the "attitude of the American Government . . . shatters the very basis of the present negotiations" between the two nations.[79] Then it ended as if in midair. The fourteenth and final part would be radioed from Tokyo to Nomura on Sunday morning.

The president handed the sheaf of papers to Hopkins. According to Commander Schulz, who remained in the Oval Study, the president waited until Hopkins finished reading. He looked over at Hopkins and declared, "This means war."[80]

Later that evening Roosevelt reached Admiral Stark at his residence at the Naval Observatory. They discussed the message and decided nothing in it required action. Commanders in the Pacific had already been warned that the Japanese were "likely to attack at any time in any direction." The message simply confirmed what was already known and conveyed. Perhaps for that reason the president did not place a call to Marshall or Stimson that night.

Colonel Bratton was supposed to deliver copies of the message that evening to those on the army list. His later testimony is confusing, but it appears that General Sherman Miles, head of army intelligence, was the only one on that list who received a copy. Miles and Bratton agreed that the document "had little military significance," so they "decided there was no reason to bother the chief of staff."[81] They too apparently believed that Short and the other Pacific commanders had been adequately alerted to a possible attack. Miles later took full responsibility for failing to contact Marshall that evening.

Historians and conspiracy enthusiasts have questioned Marshall's whereabouts that night, suggesting that Miles and Bratton were providing "cover" for his absence and speculating that if Marshall had been reachable he would have called Short and warned him. Anything is possible, of course, but there is no evidence to support the "cover" theory; Marshall later testified that he was home with Katherine that night.[82] Moreover, it is likely that even if Marshall had received the message that night he, like Stark, would have concluded that nothing in it "required action."

That said, if Marshall had read the communication on Saturday night, he probably would have reacted much more quickly than he did on Sunday morning. As it was, he made no change in his usual Sunday routine. After breakfast at around eight o'clock, later than usual, he called the stables for his mount and set out on his leisurely ride—usually about fifty minutes—along the Virginia side of the Potomac to the government experimental farm, where construction crews were digging the foundation of what would become the Pentagon. His dog, Fleet, raced happily alongside.

At about nine a.m., Bratton was in the Munitions Building reading the freshly translated fourteenth part of the instructions to the Japanese Embassy when a short decrypt from Tokyo was placed in front of him. It instructed Nomura to deliver the entire message to Secretary of State Hull precisely at "1 p.m. on the 7th, your time," and to destroy the embassy's cipher machines, codes, and sensitive documents. The specificity set off an instant alarm. The Japanese were going to attack the United States, most likely on or just after one p.m. Washington time.

Bratton had no authority to order an alert. He called Quarters One. An orderly answered. Bratton asked him to find the general and have him call back as soon as possible on a "vitally important" matter. Perhaps because Marshall was always involved in "vitally important matters," or possibly because Katherine told the orderly not to disturb Marshall on his Sunday ride—the reasons are unknown—Marshall did not return Bratton's call until 10:30. Rather than discussing the matter over the phone, Marshall insisted on coming in to the office.

Later accounts conflict, but it appears that he arrived around eleven a.m. Through his cheap dime-store glasses, Marshall proceeded to slowly read the entire fourteen-part document. As he concentrated, Bratton was barely able to restrain himself, wanting the general to skip to the end to see the one p.m. deadline. When Marshall finally finished, he looked up and asked Bratton and General Miles, who were hovering over him, what they thought it meant. They agreed with him that the one o'clock deadline had "some definite significance."[83] At one p.m. in Washington, it would be dawn in the Pacific.

Approximately 230 miles northwest of Oahu, the First Air Fleet was on the rim of the launching sector. Deck crews on the carriers had armed their planes' torpedoes and topped off gas tanks. Reconnaissance seaplanes were scouting the anchorages at Pearl and Lahaina. As airmen prepared to enter their cockpits, the six carriers turned into the wind and increased their speed to twenty-four knots.

At 11:30 a.m., 6:00 a.m. in Hawaii, Marshall called Stark and asked him what he thought about sending a warning to all Pacific commanders. Stark wasn't sure—another warning might confuse them. Despite the admiral's hedging, Marshall decided to proceed. In pencil he scrawled out an order to all Pacific commanders, advising them that the Japanese were presenting an "ultimatum" at one p.m. Eastern Standard Time and that they were under orders to destroy their code machines. "Just what significance the hour set may have we do not know, but be on the alert accordingly," he wrote.[84] Moments after he finished, Stark telephoned. He had reconsidered. Marshall added another sentence to his alert, telling the army commanders to notify their navy counterparts. He handed the message to Bratton at about 11:50 a.m., just as the first attack wave of more than 180 torpedo planes, bombers, dive-bombers, and fighters gathered above the carriers and began heading south toward their targets: dozens of American warships arrayed in rows in Pearl Harbor and hundreds of fighter planes packed together on tarmacs at Hickam and Wheeler Fields and Kaneohe Air Station. When Bratton was leaving for the signals room with Marshall's message in hand, General Gerow called out, "If there is any question of priority, give the Philippines first priority."[85] Marshall's warning to MacArthur was successfully transmitted at 12:06 p.m. The message to General Short's headquarters in Hawaii, however, hit a snag.

The tangled tale of how and why Marshall's alert to Short could not be sent through army radio communications that morning due to atmospheric conditions, and instead was transmitted to Honolulu via Western Union and RCA, has been told many times. It need not be repeated here. Rose Page recalled that Marshall summed it up best during a horseback ride with her in February 1942: "You will find this hard to believe, but a Western Union boy was riding his bike to deliver my alert to General Short when the Jap bombs hit."[86]

Marshall's leisurely morning canter on December 7 and the time that elapsed before he wrote out an alert has been the subject of myth and criticism, not to mention a web of conspiracy theories, ever since that fateful Sunday morning. His latest biographers damn the chief of staff for failure to "cancel" his horseback ride, but there is no indication that anyone ran him down on the trail to tell him about Bratton's call. And because no one contacted him the night before about the thirteen-part message, there was no reason to check with his office early in the morning before he went off on his ride. If he is to be faulted for any "complacency" it was his failure to respond more quickly when Bratton reached him at about ten a.m., taking his time driving into the office, plodding slowly through the fourteen-part message, and dispatching his warning via army communications instead of using the scrambler phone.[87]

But why should he shoulder the criticism for the delay? Admiral Stark, responsible for the fleet at Pearl Harbor, was in his office before ten a.m. Stimson, Knox, Hull, and the two intelligence chiefs and chiefs of war plans of both services, as well as Stark, had seen the one p.m. deadline message and the complete message to the embassy at least a half hour if not more before Marshall arrived at the War Department. The president had concluded the night before that the first thirteen parts meant war, yet he and Stark conferred near midnight and decided that it "was of no military significance." Why didn't one of them get out an earlier alert to the Pacific commanders? Stark provided the answer when Marshall called him around 11:30 a.m. Another warning might confuse the commanders, he said.

Assured that his alerts were on the way to the Pacific, Marshall packed his old leather briefcase—the briefcase that he had carried since leaving for France in 1917—with papers he would need for a previously scheduled three p.m. conference at the White House and drove across Memorial Bridge to Quarters One for a quick lunch. Shortly after 1:30, he received a call from Colonel John R. Deane, secretary to the General Staff, the only officer on duty in Marshall's office at the War Department. "Pearl Harbor attacked. This is no drill."

The hour had come. With George Marshall at point, America would lift up her sword.

CHAPTER 8

Germany First

Ten minutes after learning of the Pearl Harbor attack Marshall was back in the Munitions Building on the Mall. After reviewing incoming damage reports, making a few calls, and issuing orders, he telephoned the president. Since the one-sided battle was still in progress, his report was vastly understated. All he knew was that at least one battleship was lost, fifty Japanese bombers were involved, and that two of the army airfields were in flames. Before leaving for the White House, he dictated a message to MacArthur, advising him that hostilities between the United States and Japan had commenced as a result of the attack at Pearl. He authorized MacArthur to initiate air raids against Japanese forces in the region while continuing to carry out his primary mission: defense of the Philippines. Marshall's message was received at MacArthur's headquarters at 5:35 a.m., seven hours before Japanese bombers would attack airfields north of Manila with devastating results.[1]

Roosevelt was on the phone when Marshall and the rest of the War Cabinet took their seats in the Oval Study. The president was "deadly calm" as he was told that eight battleships were sinking or severely damaged in Pearl Harbor, three-quarters of General Short's air force had been destroyed on the ground, and casualties were in the thousands.[2] When he put down the receiver he did not look back and cast blame. Instead, he was concerned about where Japan would strike next and what needed to be done. Asked by FDR about troop deployments, Marshall suppressed his anger and coolly responded at some length. He assured the president that the Panama Canal was on alert, that he had issued orders to MacArthur, and that guards would be placed at defense plants. As the discussion wore on, Marshall was anxious to get back to his office, his mind racing with all of the details that needed his attention. Just before leaving, a call from Prime Minister Churchill was put through to Roosevelt. "What's this about Japan?" Churchill asked. "They have attacked us at Pearl Harbor. We are all in the same boat now," replied the president. "That certainly simplifies things," said Churchill. "God be with you."

With one bold and foolhardy stroke, Japan both answered Churchill's prayers and solved Roosevelt's political problem. Convinced that Germany would take advantage of Japan's attack in the Pacific by declaring war against the United States, the prime minister "slept the sleep of the saved and thankful" that night, knowing that the U.S. would at last be allied on his side and would rescue his beloved island from defeat or onerous terms at the hands of the Nazis.[3] Moreover, because the sneak attack promised to unite the American people as never before, political opposition to war would surely vanish. On December 8, Congress voted with but a single dissent to support Roosevelt in declaring war on Japan. When Germany elected to declare war on the U.S., as Churchill and Roosevelt (due to MAGIC intercepts) believed it would, Congress would have no choice but to respond with a counter-declaration.

Adolf Hitler reacted as expected. When he heard the news that Japan was at war with the U.S., he slapped his thighs with delight, telling his generals that "it is impossible for us to lose the war; we now have an ally that has never been vanquished in three thousand years."[4] On December 11, Hitler delivered a ninety-minute harangue in the Reichstag. Though he was not obligated under the terms of the original Tripartite Pact, he proclaimed at the end of his speech that a state of war existed between the United States and Germany (Italy quickly followed suit). It was Hitler's greatest miscalculation. His action silenced the voices of the isolationists in America. Later the same day, Roosevelt delivered a message asking Congress to "recognize a state of war between the United States and Germany," as well as "between the United States and Italy."[5] The votes in both houses were unanimous. America was committed to fighting a multifront global war.

By this time, Marshall had learned the full extent of the damage to MacArthur's command in the Philippines. Eighteen of his thirty-five precious B-17s, along with fifty-six fighters—more than half of his air force— were destroyed while parked on runways at Clark and Iba airfields, leaving the Philippine garrison almost defenseless against amphibious invasion. Marshall found it inexplicable that seven hours after being warned of a likely attack, most of MacArthur's air force was caught out in the open on the ground. When MacArthur called to explain, something which he rarely felt compelled to do, Marshall must have been furious. There is no record of what was said. All that is known is that Marshall chose not to relieve MacArthur of command, possibly because MacArthur cast blame on his air commander or perhaps because there was no one in Marshall's "black book" with the experience and leadership ability who could replace him. Whatever Marshall's reasons, the tectonic plates of the relationship between MacArthur and the chief of staff shifted that day. Marshall would remain deferential toward MacArthur, yet he was no longer the underling. He was the judge of who in the army would command and who would be relieved in all theaters of the coming war.

Since MacArthur's forces were vulnerable to imminent invasion and thus in grave danger, Marshall chose to call upon fifty-five-year-old Brigadier General Dwight Eisenhower, who had served under MacArthur in the Philippines for three years and knew better than any other officer whether and if so how the garrison could be reinforced and supplied. Marshall had met Eisenhower briefly in 1930 when the two of them were asked by Pershing to help him write his World War I memoir. Since then, Marshall had followed Eisenhower's career, noting that he received high marks at the Army War College and stellar fitness reports at every subsequent posting, most recently for planning the Third Army's successful assault in the Louisiana maneuvers. Along the way his intelligence and attractive personality impressed a number of respected generals, including Fox Conner, Walter Krueger, Gee Gerow, Mark Clark, and of course, Douglas MacArthur.

On December 12, Eisenhower, who was stationed at Fort Sam Houston near San Antonio, received a call from one of Marshall's aides. "The chief says for you to hop a plane and get up here right away."[6] He was to be assigned to the War Plans Division in Washington. Two days later, the Sunday after the Pearl Harbor attack, Eisenhower was led into Marshall's office. The chief of staff barely looked up. There was no small talk. "Within ten seconds," Eisenhower recalled, Marshall "was telling me the problem he wanted me to attack." In clipped sentences Marshall summarized the dire situation in the Far East, emphasizing the significance of the losses in naval strength at Pearl Harbor and airpower in the Philippines. Reinforcement of the Hawaiian Islands would have to take priority over the Philippines, he explained, and the three U.S. carriers that escaped the attack at Pearl were needed to protect Hawaii and the West Coast. Even if a task force could be organized and supplied in the near future, it was questionable whether it could get through to the Philippines without being destroyed by the Japanese navy. "Your problem," he concluded, is "what should be our general line of action?"[7] By that he meant, "Where do we draw the line and fight? And do we abandon our men in the Philippines?"[8]

Eisenhower hesitated for a moment. "Give me a few hours."[9] He was back that afternoon with his thoughts set forth in a three-page typewritten paper, which he kept in his pocket because he had been told Marshall expected briefings to be conducted without notes. In essence, Eisenhower asserted that the line should be drawn along the air and sea lanes from the West Coast of the U.S. to Australia, which should serve as the launching pad for the future counteroffensive against Japan. As to the Philippines, it would be a long time before reinforcements could get through, predicted Eisenhower, longer than MacArthur's garrison could hold out. Nevertheless, he told Marshall that because millions of people under the grip of the Japanese will be watching, we must do what we can. "They may excuse failure but they will not excuse abandonment."[10] Marshall agreed. "Do your best to save them." As Eisenhower turned to leave, Marshall said, "Eisenhower, the Department is filled with men who analyze their problems well but feel compelled always to bring them to me for final solution. I must have assistants who will solve their own problems and tell me later what they have done. The Philippines are your responsibility." Eisenhower remembered that when Marshall said this he had an "eye that seemed to me awfully cold."[11]

Thus began a partnership that led to the greatest victory in American history since the Revolutionary War.

* * * * *

In London, Prime Minister Churchill feared that the Japanese attack might cause Roosevelt and his military advisers to concentrate the bulk of U.S. forces on Japan instead of trying to defeat "Germany first," the grand strategy that had been previously agreed upon. To head off this possibility, he cabled the president and proposed coming to Washington "by warship . . . with necessary staffs."[12] On Monday evening, December 22, Churchill and his entourage, carrying their distinctive red leather dispatch cases, arrived. The forthcoming conference with Churchill and his top military advisers would be code-named Arcadia. Though Marshall had mixed feelings about debating strategy with Churchill and his experienced British counterparts

so soon, it was during the three weeks of Arcadia deliberations that he came
into his own.

Churchill, who took up residence in the Rose Suite on the second floor
of the White House, had no reason to fear a turn to the Pacific. As he and
his British military chiefs learned during the first few days of the conference,
Roosevelt, Marshall, and the rest of the U.S. team were solidly behind the
idea that Germany was the prime enemy and that her defeat was the key to
victory. As it developed, the debate during Arcadia focused on initial military
operations to be undertaken and the establishment of "Anglo-American coordinating machinery" for fighting a multitheater war.[13]

During the first meeting with the British military chiefs, Marshall felt that
they were patronizing, regarding the Americans as naïve and not very smart,
and that his own colleagues were overly suspicious of British motives, suspecting them of proposing military operations aimed more at protecting their
empire than defeating Germany and Japan. In an effort to allay these feelings, he and Katherine hosted an early afternoon dinner at Quarters One on
Christmas Day. The guests included Field Marshal Dill, soon to head the
Washington-based British Joint Staff Mission; Admiral of the Fleet Sir Dudley Pound, who was afflicted by an undiagnosed brain tumor that caused him
to doze during meetings; Air Chief Marshal Sir Charles Portal, the youngest
at age forty-seven, regarded as the brightest of the British chiefs of staff; and
Marshall's navy counterpart, Admiral Ernest "Ernie" King, commander in
chief of the U.S. Fleet, a self-proclaimed son of a bitch, and his wife, Mattie.[14]
Since King was on best behavior, it was a relaxed and convivial affair. After
dinner, Marshall rose and proposed a toast to Dill, since he knew it was his
birthday. A plain white cake decorated with candles shaped like "red-coated
soldiers" and "two silk flags, one British and one American," was brought into
the dining room. Sir John was "deeply moved," wrote Katherine, and "said it
was his first birthday cake since he was a small boy." When he reached to cut
the cake he removed one of the flags and read aloud the small print on the
staff: "Made in Japan."[15] The room erupted in laughter.

An hour later Marshall and his guests, with the exception of Mattie
King, regrouped in the new Federal Reserve Building on Constitution Avenue across from the Munitions Building. They were joined there by Admiral
Stark and Generals Arnold and Eisenhower. After a few preliminaries, Marshall took the floor. He had been thinking, he told the group, about his

experiences with the French in the Great War. There he had learned that agreements on military strategy—on *how* to win the war—cannot succeed without first establishing principles for achieving cooperation. "I am convinced," declared Marshall, "that there must be one man in charge of [each] entire theater—air, ground and ships . . . operating under a controlled directive from here." The "controlled directive," he proposed, would emanate from a small Anglo-American chief of staff organization located "here," presumably in Washington. Marshall's idea—the concept of "unity of command"—was simple: achieve cooperation by eliminating rivalry between services and allies in all the various theaters of the global war. Yet his strategy to achieve such unity was radical, unprecedented in coalition warfare involving separate navies, air armadas, and ground troops. Beyond military doctrine, it implicated matters of politics and diplomacy. To those in the room, it was shocking. "If we make a plan for unified command now," Marshall concluded, "it will solve nine-tenths of our troubles."[16] The British chiefs were opposed. Stark and King were noncommittal.

After they adjourned Marshall asked Eisenhower to draft a letter of instruction that would govern a prospective theater commander for a vast area in the Far East that encompassed Burma, the Netherlands East Indies, Australia, New Guinea, and the Philippines. Since American, British, Dutch, and Australian navy, army, and air forces were (or would be) engaged against the Japanese in this part of the world, Eisenhower named the theater ABDA and the command was called ABDACOM. Two days later Marshall aggressively pushed for and succeeded in obtaining the backing of the president and the support of Stimson, Knox, Stark, and King to his plan for unitary command. In an effort to gain the favor of Churchill and the British chiefs the U.S. Navy agreed with Marshall that a British ground commander, General Sir Archibald Percival Wavell, was the logical choice to be designated supreme commander of all Allied forces fighting in the ABDA theater. On December 27, Marshall held forth to the British chiefs of staff who, according to Stimson, "kicked like bay steers."[17] Throughout its storied history, the British Royal Navy had never been subjected to direction and control by an army ground commander. Marshall pressed his case, arguing that the powerful Japanese naval, air, and ground forces in the Pacific operated pursuant to an efficient unified command structure. To his surprise, the objections of the British chiefs melted away.

The chief of staff had one more person to persuade: the formidable prime minister. Late on the morning of December 27, Marshall was ushered into the Rose Suite across the hall from the Lincoln Bedroom, where Harry Hopkins resided. Marshall found Winston Churchill in a paper-strewn bed, propped up by pillows, wearing his crimson Chinese-dragon dressing gown. The room reeked of cigar smoke. A tumbler of scotch and soda sat next to an overflowing ashtray on the night table. Marshall, now accustomed to bed-room meetings in the Roosevelt White House, looked down at Churchill and launched into his pitch for unitary command, pacing back and forth as he talked. Churchill interrupted, growling that an army general like Wavell would not know anything about "handling a ship." Marshall barked back, "[W]hat the devil does a naval officer know about handling a tank?"[18] Ex-pertise in the handling of ships or tanks was not the point, he stressed. "I told him," Marshall recalled, "that I was interested in having a united front against Japan, an enemy which was fighting furiously. I said if we didn't do something right away we were finished in the war."[19]

Churchill broke off the argument, saying he needed to take his bath be-fore lunch. He thought it over as he splashed in the tub. He worried that if he approved the unitary concept, American theater commanders would even-tually outnumber those of the British because the U.S. would surpass them in numbers of troops, ships, and quantities of arms. On the other hand, he realized that Marshall had emerged as the dominant and most influential figure of the Allied war commanders. As Lord Moran (Charles Wilson), the prime minister's personal physician wrote of that moment, Churchill under-stood that Marshall was "the key to the situation." Since the attack on Pearl Harbor, the American public was clamoring for the U.S. to concentrate on Japan rather than Germany. If he, Churchill, became too obstinate, Mar-shall could relax his commitment to "Germany first," or he might even re-sign. "Neither the PM nor the President can contemplate going ahead without Marshall," wrote Moran.[20]

The prime minister decided to side with Marshall. "It was evident," he later wrote, "that we must meet the American view."[21] Later that day Mar-shall learned that he had succeeded in persuading Churchill. When Stim-son found out he was delighted, writing in his diary that the support of Churchill, as well as the president and the Anglo-American chiefs, for unitary command in the huge area of the Pacific known as ABDA was "due

largely—almost wholly—to Marshall's initiative and vigor." He thought
that if the principle could be followed in other theaters, they could "avoid a
year of disaster which . . . attended the Allies in the last war arising out of
disunity."[22]

Once unity of command was agreed upon, a related issue—the structure
and composition of the organization that would issue "directives" to theater
commanders around the world—needed to be addressed. A solution fell into
place rather quickly. At the suggestion of the British, who were supported by
Marshall and King, a single organization called the Combined Chiefs of
Staff, or CCS, consisting of the army, navy, and air chiefs of each nation,
would be established. The CCS, of course, would be accountable to the
president and the prime minister. However, at Marshall's insistence, it would
be responsible for formulating and communicating strategy, allocating resources, setting production goals, and controlling shipping. To parallel the
British, who already had a four-person chief of staff organization called the
Imperial General Staff, the Americans would create their own body, to be
called the Joint Chiefs of Staff, or JCS, and Marshall would effectively ele-
vate Hap Arnold, his subordinate, so that he would have coequal status with
Marshall, Stark, and King on both the CCS and the JCS.

What about other allies, like the Australians, the Dutch, the Chinese,
and the Free French? Would their military chiefs sit on the CCS? The answer, in the words of Admiral King, was a "hard-boiled" no. "It is bound to
cause friction and unhappiness among the smaller nations," said King, "but
it is the only way to function effectively." King was right. The war could not
be conducted by a multinational committee.[23]

The situs of the CCS was much more controversial. From the outset
Roosevelt, Marshall, and the other American chiefs insisted that the CCS
should be located in Washington, since the U.S. would be producing most
of the war matériel and Washington was safely centered between the European and Pacific theaters. The British, who had been running the war from
London for more than two years, were understandably resistant. After much
argument, the British gave in to the logic of the American view and agreed
that the CCS and its administrative machinery would be located in Washington. Since the British members of the CCS would be in London for day-
to-day running of the war for much of the time, they agreed to delegate
senior officers who would individually represent them at CCS meetings in

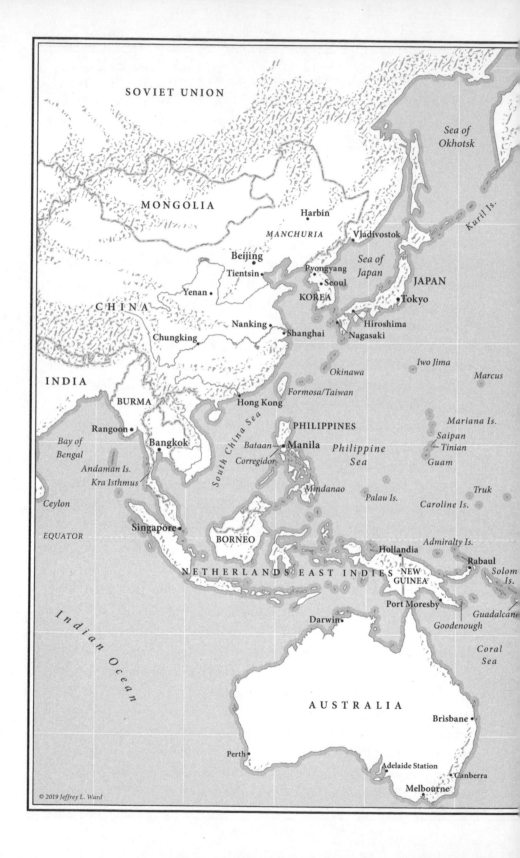

SOVIET UNION

Sea of
Okhotsk

MONGOLIA

Harbin

MANCHURIA

Kuril Is.

Vladivostok

Beijing

Sea of
Japan

JAPAN

Tientsin

Pyongyang

Yenan

Seoul

KOREA

Tokyo

CHINA

Hiroshima

Nanking

Nagasaki

Chungking

Shanghai

Iwo Jima

Marcus

Okinawa

INDIA

Formosa/Taiwan

BURMA

Hong Kong

Mariana Is.

Rangoon

PHILIPPINES

Saipan

Bay of
Bengal

Bangkok

Bataan

Manila

Tinian

Philippine
Sea

Guam

Corregidor

Andaman Is.

Kra Isthmus

South China Sea

Mindanao

Truk

Ceylon

Palau Is.

Caroline Is.

EQUATOR

Singapore

Admiralty Is.

BORNEO

Hollandia

Rabaul

NETHERLANDS EAST INDIES

NEW
GUINEA

Solom
Is.

Port Moresby

Guadalcan

Darwin

Goodenough

Indian Ocean

Coral
Sea

AUSTRALIA

Brisbane

Perth

Adelaide Station

Canberra

Melbourne

© 2019 Jeffrey L. Ward

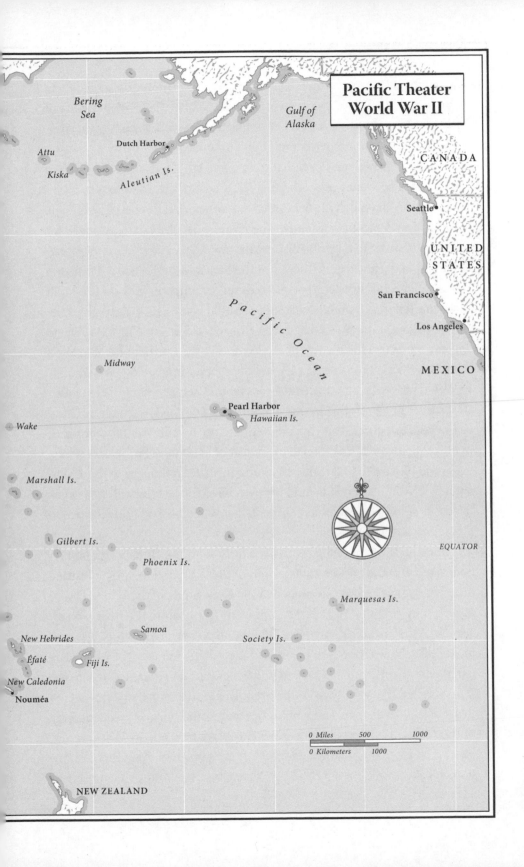

Pacific Theater World War II

Bering Sea

Gulf of Alaska

CANADA

Attu

Dutch Harbor

Kiska

Aleutian Is.

Seattle

UNITED STATES

San Francisco

Pacific Ocean

Los Angeles

Midway

MEXICO

Wake

Pearl Harbor

Hawaiian Is.

Marshall Is.

Gilbert Is.

EQUATOR

Phoenix Is.

Marquesas Is.

Samoa

New Hebrides

Society Is.

Éfaté

Fiji Is.

New Caledonia

Nouméa

| 0 Miles | 500 | 1000 |
| 0 Kilometers | 1000 | |

NEW ZEALAND

Washington. At the same time, they would be collectively represented there by Sir John Dill, named chief of what would be called the British Joint Staff Mission. Dill and his new wife, Nancy, who became dear friends of the Marshalls, would live at Fort Myer until Dill's untimely death in 1944.

Having observed and personally experienced Marshall's leadership in establishing the framework of the Anglo-American wartime alliance, Churchill judged Marshall as the one American, other than Roosevelt, whom he needed to woo most persistently. Therefore, when Marshall arranged for the prime minster to take a break from the Arcadia conference in Washington and spend a few days in the sun at the Stettinius residence at Pompano Beach, Churchill insisted that the general accompany him on the flight down to Florida. (Churchill had suffered a mild heart attack one night at the White House and his personal doctor insisted he get some rest.) While no account exists of what the two discussed during the five-hour flight to West Palm Beach, it is probable that Churchill probed Marshall on how strongly he would resist pressures to divert forces to the Pacific to fight the Japanese. As a matter of grand strategy and of course his own national interest Churchill was concerned that his new American partner remain steadfast in devoting most of his efforts to the defeat of Germany. As he later wrote, "[n]o one had more to do with obtaining this cardinal decision than Marshall."[24] Given his schedule and his own need for rest, as well as a break from Churchill's torrent of talk, Marshall dropped him off and returned to Washington.

Marshall thought he had won his battles with the British over unitary command and the powers and location of the CCS. However, he learned otherwise when he was summoned to the Oval Study in the White House at 5:30 p.m. on January 14, 1942, a few minutes before the final plenary session of the Arcadia conference. There the president and Hopkins, who looked like he was about to collapse from exhaustion, sought Marshall's agreement to a Churchill-inspired written proposal to create a civilian authority called the Munitions Assignment Board that would be empowered to allocate all armaments and munitions and would operate independently of the CCS. The board would have two branches: one in Washington, headed by Hopkins, who would report to the president, the other in London, led by production czar Max Beaverbrook, who would report to

Churchill. Both Churchill and Roosevelt had already agreed to the creation of the board, subject to Marshall's approval.

Marshall immediately saw this as the prime minister's last-ditch effort to influence CCS-directed military operations and undermine unitary command by retaining power to allocate war matériel and other supplies among the various war theaters and the forces fighting in them. He objected vehemently, explaining that allocation of supplies was an integral part of CCS strategic directives to theater commanders and must be subordinated to and controlled by that body. According to Robert Sherwood, Marshall then informed the president that unless the Munitions Assignment Board was placed under the authority of the CCS, "he could not continue to accept the responsibilities of Chief of Staff."[25] Marshall's words sucked the air out of the room. There was no doubt what he meant. Roosevelt was shaken. His experience with Marshall thus far was that he did not make idle threats. The president looked to Hopkins for support. Hopkins, who had been slumped back in his chair, his eyes barely open, gathered himself and sat upright. Marshall assumed that Hopkins would support the Munitions Board proposal since he had apparently participated in its formulation. Instead, to the surprise of Marshall as well as Roosevelt, the president's closest adviser changed his mind. Not only did Hopkins support Marshall vociferously, he also said that if the Munitions Board was not subordinate to the CCS he too could not assume any responsibility for it. Hopkins's supple mind had quickly assessed the merits of Marshall's arguments and weighed the alternatives. He regarded Marshall as far too important to the war effort and to the presidency to risk his resignation.

Minutes later the final session of the Arcadia conference began. Without the backing of Marshall and Hopkins, Roosevelt felt he had no choice. He had to renege on a solemn agreement that he had made with Churchill earlier that day. With what Marshall called his "cigarette-holder gesture," the president disguised his embarrassment and blithely informed Churchill, Beaverbrook, and the British chiefs that due to Marshall's objections the Munitions Board would have to be subordinate to the CCS, in effect a subcommittee.[26] The British must have been stunned. Even more forcefully than before Marshall explained his reasoning. Hopkins and Stimson added their rock-solid support. Churchill and his countrymen protested heatedly, sometimes with acrimony, threatening to end the Arcadia conference in a deadlock. The president stood firm. As Sherwood observed, it was as if notice had been served that "Roosevelt was the boss and Washington the headquarters of the joint war effort."[27] Finally, Churchill made a face-saving proposal that the system proposed by Marshall "be set up and tried for one month." Roosevelt was visibly relieved. "We shall call it a preliminary agreement," he happily said, "and try it out that way."[28] The debate was over. The one month tryout of the Munitions Board lasted for the duration of the war, functioning efficiently as a subcommittee of the CCS with Hopkins at the helm, except when he was hospitalized or otherwise incapacitated.

When the three-week Arcadia conference ended it was apparent that George Marshall had emerged as the commanding military figure. It was Marshall who shaped the design of the "coordinating machinery" for the joint conduct of the war.[29] And it was Marshall who was chiefly responsible for persuading the military and civilian leadership of the Anglo-American alliance to put it into operation. This in itself was a major achievement, a testament to Marshall's growing power and influence. However, whether and the extent to which Marshall's "machinery" would actually be used in formulating and implementing war strategy would be dependent on the whims, schemes, and desires of Roosevelt and Churchill, the crafty and resourceful politicians who in the end were in ultimate command.

* * * * *

For the time being, plans for defeating "Germany first" had to be shelved. The unfolding disaster in the Pacific during the first few months of 1942 grabbed the attention of the American public and tested the mettle of Marshall and his president just as George Washington and his frozen troops had been tested at Valley Forge. With the destruction of much of the U.S. fleet and air forces at Pearl Harbor, both Hawaii and the West Coast appeared vulnerable to attack. Marshall had "sweated blood" to rush planes to the Philippines, yet more than half of them were obliterated while "still on the ground," despite receiving warnings several hours before Japan attacked.[30] MacArthur's plans to stop the Japanese invasion forces at the Luzon beaches were quickly abandoned. He declared Manila an open city, concentrated his forces in a defensive line at the base of the Bataan Peninsula, and established his headquarters in the Malinta Tunnel on the fortified island of Corregidor.

Ignoring lessons taught by Marshall and his White Force in 1914, MacArthur left most of his supplies behind on the plain around Manila, only to have them captured by the Japanese. With the Philippines neutralized, additional Japanese troops separately landed in Malaysia (on the Kra Isthmus), Borneo, and islands in the Netherlands East Indies. Singapore, the Gibraltar of the East, fell on February 15, 1942, thus opening the way for the Japanese to invade Burma and possibly even India and Australia. If the Germans achieved victory in Russia and North Africa, they could link up with Japanese forces somewhere in the Middle East, possibly the Persian Gulf, a frightening possibility.

The pressures on the chief of staff during this period were "unimaginable," wrote Katherine Marshall. It was "difficult to comprehend how one man could" bear them alone. Yet to colleagues and others at the War Department and White House who dealt with him daily Marshall showed no signs that he was shaken, no loss of confidence or self-doubt, and very little emotion except a cold, steely resolve to confront each problem head-on. He remembered General Pershing's admonition that the slightest expression, gesture, or comment by a commander could convey discouragement. On twilit winter walks before dinner Katherine had the feeling that her husband "lived outside" of his own body, constantly disciplining himself as if he were his own subordinate. "I cannot allow myself to get angry," he would say to her, meaning this was not the time for blame or recriminations. General MacArthur and his beleaguered garrison needed to be given hope and encouragement, not anger for their past failures. Or he would blurt out, "I cannot afford the luxury of sentiment, mine must be cold logic."[31] He was probably referring to the fact that he had to say no to yet another relief proposal by MacArthur, possibly the one where MacArthur begged him to risk sending one of the three remaining U.S. aircraft carriers through the Japanese naval blockade to provide planes and supplies to the Philippines.

Cold logic informed Marshall that MacArthur's forces on Bataan were almost certainly doomed and that the entire archipelago would soon be occupied by General Homma's Japanese invaders. Nevertheless, with the backing of the president, as well as Stimson and Eisenhower (who had replaced General Gerow as head of the War Plans Division), Marshall tried everything possible to get armaments, food, and supplies through to MacArthur, including hiring commercial ships in Australia to try to run the

Japanese blockade. The motive was not only humanitarian, it was political. The Philippine islands were much more than an ally. In 1898, they were ceded by Spain to the United States for $20 million and governed as an American territory for more than thirty-five years. The Philippine Commonwealth was established in 1935 with a ten-year period of transition leading to full independence. The transitional government was headed by popularly elected president Manuel Quezon. Given this political history, not to mention the chief of staff's own emotional ties due to his years of service in the islands, Marshall believed it was his duty to do whatever he could to prevent the Philippines from falling into Japanese hands. Moreover, the American media, aided by General MacArthur's own colorful press releases, had built MacArthur into a national hero who was seen as almost single-handedly holding off "the Japs" in the Pacific. Marshall understood that if he was not perceived as devoting maximum effort to getting aid through to MacArthur and his starving troops, or if MacArthur himself was captured by the Japanese and paraded through the streets of Manila, the Roosevelt administration would pay a huge political price.

President Quezon, holed up with MacArthur in the 1,400-foot-long tunnel dug into Malinta Hill on Corregidor, had his own political problems. By early February General Homma, whose troops controlled most of Luzon, had installed a puppet government in Manila headed by Quezon's former secretary and some of the members of the Philippine legislature. Homma and his Philippine collaborators issued vague promises of an early independence from American imperialists ("shake off the yoke of white domination").[32] Calls for Filipino soldiers to lay down their arms and for MacArthur himself to surrender began reaching Corregidor. Quezon, dying of tuberculosis, had come to the conclusion that his countrymen were being abandoned by the American military, that it was futile to continue to resist the Japanese onslaught. On February 8, the Philippine president cabled a proposal to Roosevelt that he thought might save his country and his political life. Quezon asked FDR to grant immediate independence to the Philippines, after which he as president would declare neutrality and disband the Filipino army. As a neutral, Quezon would call on the U.S. and Japan to withdraw their troops from the Philippines. He knew this was a long shot, but he claimed it was the only way to "save my country from further devastation as the battleground of two great powers."[33]

Along with Quezon's cable MacArthur forwarded his own cover letter to Marshall. There, he asserted that from a military point of view the question was whether "the plan of President Quezon might offer the best possible solution to what is about to be a disastrous debacle." By not indicating any disagreement or even any doubts about Quezon's proposal, MacArthur suggested by implication that he thought it was the best solution.[34]

Roosevelt scanned Quezon's cable and looked up at Stimson and Marshall, his eyes blazing. "We can't do this at all," he raged.[35] There will be no declaration of neutrality, no political deal with Japan, and no withdrawal of U.S. troops, he said. The Filipino soldiers can leave the field if necessary; however, MacArthur and his army regulars will have to fight to the finish. In a reply drafted by Marshall and Eisenhower, the president ordered MacArthur to "keep our flag flying in the Philippines so long as there remains any possibility of resistance."[36]

This was a critical moment in George Marshall's relationship with Franklin Roosevelt. Up to then he privately doubted whether the president, who was prone to avoid taking firm stands, was up to the job of making the kind of ruthless life-or-death decisions that would have to be made in the course of waging a world war. "I immediately discarded everything I had held in my mind to his discredit," he later told Forrest Pogue. "I decided he was a great man."[37]

Similarly, Roosevelt's opinion of Marshall had grown exponentially since he appointed him chief of staff in 1939. Even though Marshall was always all-business, avoiding small talk and social intimacy, Roosevelt was not put off. He had come to realize that Marshall was a man of integrity, utter selflessness, and iron will. The president had confidence that his chief of staff could be counted on to tell him the truth as he saw it, that he was the right man for the job.

As it became more and more apparent that General MacArthur's "battling bastards of Bataan" would have to surrender or die, Marshall pondered the consequences of MacArthur and his family suffering the same fate.[38] If MacArthur's wife and young son, or even MacArthur himself, were captured alive and tortured or humiliated, or if their bodies were photographed and shown to the world, the propaganda value to the Japanese would be enormous. The effect on American public opinion would be devastating. In Washington, former presidential candidate Wendell Willkie and several congressmen were pressuring the administration to recall MacArthur from the Philippines to assume supreme command of all U.S. troops or at least for duty commanding Allied forces elsewhere in the Pacific. Marshall did not have to be told that four-star general MacArthur was the only active American general with extensive experience leading large bodies of troops in combat and that he was the best-informed American officer in the Far East. With General Wavell's command of all Allied forces in the ABDA theater disintegrating, the chief of staff cabled a hint to MacArthur that he might be ordered to leave Corregidor for some other point in the Far East.

While Marshall conferred with Eisenhower, Stimson, and the president about a possible new command for MacArthur, President Quezon, having been assured by Roosevelt that "whatever happens to the present American garrison," U.S. forces will "return to the Philippines," made plans to be evacuated from Corregidor.[39] He would proceed to Australia and then to America, where he would set up a government in exile. Before leaving, however, he made good on a contract that he had entered into with MacArthur in the fall of 1935, when the general withdrew from active duty with the U.S. Army and agreed to organize and train a first-class Filipino army. Pursuant to the contract, which had been approved by the president and the secretary of war long before Marshall arrived in Washington, MacArthur was to receive, in addition to his generous salary, expense allowance, and other perks, a percentage of the ten-year Philippine defense budget, assuming, of course, that he actually did deliver a first-rate army (which by all accounts he did not). On February 15, the same day Singapore fell, MacArthur wired Chase National Bank in New York, instructing the bank to transfer funds from accounts of the Philippine government to himself and three of his closest aides, as follows: $500,000 to MacArthur (about $8 million in 2018 dollars); $75,000 to Major General Richard Sutherland; and an additional $65,000, roughly two-thirds earmarked for General Richard Marshall and the remainder to Colonel Sidney Huff. The total actually exceeded what was due under the terms of the contract. Whether President Quezon conditioned these payments on promises by MacArthur to arrange for Quezon's safe evacuation via submarine from Corregidor, or to organize a speedy return by American forces to the Philippines, is not known. Nor is it known whether MacArthur's relentless pursuit of a "Pacific first" strategy throughout the war and his insistence on approaching Japan via the Philippines was influenced by Quezon's payments.

MacArthur's wire transfer request was held up for four days, during which time a copy was "shown to the President of the United States and to the Secretary of War" and they were "informed of the action taken."[40] On February 19, Chase National Bank transferred the funds to MacArthur and his three aides. The next day Quezon and his entourage were evacuated from Corregidor on the U.S. submarine *Swordfish*.

Was Marshall consulted on the propriety of the funds transfer? It is possible, of course, but if he was in the loop he did not leave any written tracks. Consequently, Marshall's complicity in approving or advising on the funds transfer cannot be determined with any certainty.[41]

Whether or not Marshall was involved, the large payments to U.S. Army officers raised obvious questions of legality and ethics that could not have escaped the attention of Stimson and Roosevelt. So why did the president and the secretary of war give the go-ahead for the funds transfer? Most likely because they knew that if they signaled disapproval, MacArthur might not be willing to cooperate with their plans to save him from surrender and capture in the Philippines so that he could fight another day. In the end the president probably made the decision, willing to take the risk that the payments would remain a secret from the American public until long after the war.

Through Stimson and others in the War Department who reviewed the transfer instructions, it is probable that Marshall became aware of the payments at some point after they were made and that Eisenhower was a likely source. In June 1942, when Quezon arrived in Washington to set up his government in exile, he offered Eisenhower a payment of $60,000 for his years as an aide to MacArthur working for the Philippine government. Marshall advised his protégé to "stay clear" of Quezon's offer "lest it destroy him" and Eisenhower declined Quezon's offer.[42]

*   *   *   *   *

Just after sunset on March 11, 1942, MacArthur, his family, his son's Cantonese nanny, and a few aides boarded PT-41 at Corregidor's North Dock. Marshall had drafted orders, signed by Roosevelt, directing MacArthur to leave for Australia, where he would assume a yet-to-be-identified command.

Taking a last look at Corregidor, "the black mass of destruction," wrote MacArthur in his typical dramatic style, "I raised my cap in farewell salute."[43]

MacArthur's boat rendezvoused with three other PT boats and roared out to sea, heading south to Mindanao, where they would be flown in B-17s to Darwin on the north coast of Australia. While MacArthur was en route, Marshall, with the skill of a veteran diplomat, arranged through the CCS and various allied representatives for MacArthur to be named supreme commander of all air, ground, and naval forces in a newly created Southwest Pacific theater. Carved out of the western part of Wavell's shattered ABDA command, MacArthur's theater would span the Netherlands East Indies, Australia, New Guinea, and the Philippines.

From Adelaide railway station MacArthur released his inspiring but controversial statement. "The President of the United States ordered me to break through the Japanese lines for the purpose, as I understand it, of organizing the American offensive against Japan, a primary object of which is the relief of the Philippines. I came through and I shall return."[44] It was controversial, especially at the War Department, because it was all about "me" and "I" and it suggested a departure from the "Germany first" strategy. At the same time it gave hope to the Filipinos and reassured the Australians. Most of all, it boosted the morale of the American public by promising that MacArthur would avenge Pearl Harbor. Roosevelt loved it, provided MacArthur remained in the Far East, far from Washington. MacArthur's words would soften the blow on the home front when his successor, General Jonathan "Skinny" Wainwright, and the last of thousands of American and Filipino soldiers were compelled to surrender to the Japanese.

On the evening of March 26, during a lavish state dinner to honor General MacArthur in Canberra, Australia's capital, an idea that Marshall had been mulling over since the end of January came to fruition. Nelson Johnson, the American ambassador to Australia, rose and announced that MacArthur had just been awarded the Medal of Honor. MacArthur was stunned. The guests stood and applauded. The citation, written by Marshall himself, said that MacArthur was receiving America's highest military honor "for conspicuous leadership in preparing the Philippine islands to resist conquest . . . gallantry and intrepidity beyond the call of duty . . . utter disregard of personal danger under heavy fire . . . calm judgment in each crisis . . ."[45] Marshall was aware that there was no specific act of bravery by

MacArthur in the Philippines that would justify the medal. However, the final words of the citation—that MacArthur's performance "confirmed the faith of the American people in their armed forces"—revealed Marshall's principal objective in recommending the award. He knew that once the Japanese, German, and Italian press learned that MacArthur was in Australia, they would accuse him of cowardice for abandoning the Philippines and would sneer at the weakness of the Roosevelt administration for not even trying to come to the aid of his forces. In pressing Stimson and the president to confer the medal, Marshall aimed to counteract Axis propaganda, transforming MacArthur's flight to Australia and the fall of the Philippines into acts of heroic sacrifice.

Marshall likely had a secondary purpose for seeing that the prestigious award was bestowed. Judging from MacArthur's tempest of pleas and complaints while still on Corregidor, Marshall could not help but know that the general was bitter, blaming him personally for making false promises of reinforcements in order to keep the "battling bastards" fighting, starving, and dying in a futile cause. And Marshall knew that MacArthur resented the fact that Pershing's "Chaumont crowd" had deprived him of the Medal of Honor for specific acts of bravery and courage in the Great War, the award his father had won at Missionary Ridge in the Civil War. Perhaps the medal would blunt some of the hard feelings. Marshall still admired MacArthur, regarding him as one of America's finest combat leaders, despite his monumental ego, his prickly and manipulative personality, and the debacle at Clark and Iba airfields on the day the war began. Marshall saw MacArthur as a management challenge. If he was going to be able to manage MacArthur as the army's principal commander in the Pacific, he needed to improve their relationship.

Minutes after the applause subsided at the Canberra dinner, MacArthur stood and delivered an emotional speech, words that made manifest one of the most difficult management problems that Marshall would face. "We shall win or we shall die," said MacArthur, referring to the war in the Pacific. "[A]nd to this end I pledge the full resources of all the power of my mighty country and all the blood of my countrymen."[46] This was a direct challenge to Marshall's "Germany first" grand strategy, a pledge that MacArthur had no authority to make.

* * * * *

Halfway around the world Marshall was intent on convincing the president to pledge America's resources and blood to attack Germany first, through an Allied troop and air force buildup in the British Isles for the rest of 1942, coupled with raids and air strikes, and a cross-Channel invasion into northwest France in the spring of 1943. A plan had been drawn up by Eisenhower, premised on the conviction that Germany, not Japan and certainly not Italy, posed the greater threat to the security of the U.S., and that only a large land army could defeat the Nazis. The idea behind the plan was to use Great Britain as a staging area for Allied air and ground forces. The island was akin to a huge stationary aircraft carrier and troopship. The Dover cliffs were scarcely more than twenty miles across the English Channel from the French coast, the gateway to Germany. Of all the war theaters, the flow of supplies, manpower, and communications from the U.S. to Britain to sustain an assault into France would have to travel the shortest distance, provided the North Atlantic lifeline was kept open by Allied navies. The buildup in Great Britain and of course the invasion itself would threaten Germany, causing it to divert troops away from its battles against the Red Army in the east, thus assuring that the Soviets would remain in the fight. Marshall was fully committed to this plan. By agreeing to open a second front in Western Europe in 1943, dispersion of American resources and forces to other theaters could be effectively resisted.

On March 25, Marshall strode into the Cabinet Room in the White House, along with King, Arnold, Stimson, and Knox. Hopkins and Roosevelt were already there, the president seated at the head of the long table. Marshall's task was to explain the plan and gain the president's agreement. He had barely begun when FDR interrupted, tossing out his own ideas about engaging the Germans in the Mediterranean and the Middle East. After he finished, Marshall launched into his own presentation, stressing the fact that the mere buildup of troops and equipment in Great Britain would divert German troops from the east to the west and take some pressure off the Soviets. Everyone in the room knew that the Germans had regained the initiative in Russia and were driving south toward Stalingrad and the oil fields in the Caucusus. If the Soviets collapsed, the German armies in the

Caucusus and Rommel's Afrika Corps in North Africa could join forces in the Middle East and link up with the Japanese, who were already threatening to move through India. This was a nightmare scenario that could not be permitted to take place. After an hour or so the president came around, "favorably impressed," wrote Stimson, and keenly interested in Marshall's plan for invading France in 1943. FDR directed Marshall to finalize the plan and bring it back for review before presenting it to Churchill and his military chiefs in London.

During the last days of March, lights blazed throughout the night in the Munitions Building as Eisenhower, Arnold, and their teams of war planners perfected the "Germany first" cross-Channel invasion plan.

On the afternoon of April 1, Marshall presented the president with the three main phases of the plan. Relying on what became known as the Marshall Memorandum, he began by assuring Roosevelt that the plan contemplated active operations against the Germans in the summer of 1942, namely massive bombing and continuous "raids or forays all along the [French] coasts" held by the Germans, which would not only help the Soviets and satisfy public demand for taking the fight to the Nazis, but would also provide critically important opportunities "for intensive and specialized training," under combat conditions, for amphibious landings on fortified beaches, and for air and ground forces. The initial phase of the plan, which included the aforesaid bombing and continuous raids, entailed a buildup in the British Isles of 48 infantry divisions (30 U.S. and 18 British); 9 armored divisions (6 U.S. and 3 British); 7,000 landing craft; and 5,800 combat airplanes. This preparatory phase was code-named Operation BOLERO. It would commence when the plan was adopted by the British, presumably within the next week or two, and continue through the spring of 1943.

The second phase, code-named Operation ROUNDUP—the cross-Channel seizure of permanent beachheads between Le Havre and Boulogne in northwest France—would be launched a month or two after April 1943, when the necessary buildup in Britain was estimated to be accomplished. This phase contemplated Anglo-American air superiority and sufficient landing craft to land an infantry and armored force of at least six divisions in the first wave of the assault. Parachute and glider-landed troops would assist in seizing key points behind the beachheads. The initial wave of the invasion would be backed by landings of "a weekly increment initially of at least 100,000 troops," and "a continuous flow of reinforcements from the United States."

The third and final phase envisioned the consolidation and expansion of the beachheads and the beginning of a general advance. This would entail a push by armor to break through German resistance along the coast and a drive toward Antwerp.

As events unfolded, it turned out that the most controversial part of the cross-Channel plan was buried in paragraph 12 of the Marshall Memorandum. Code-named Operation SLEDGEHAMMER, it called for a "sacrifice" invasion by British and American troops in the fall of 1942 but *if and only if* a Soviet collapse was imminent. SLEDGEHAMMER was conceived as a contingency operation, to be undertaken only in the most desperate of circumstances. In the next few months, it would take on a life of its own, destined to become the focus of a heated strategic debate with the British.[47]

Near the end of the discussion with FDR, Hopkins, probably for the benefit of Marshall and Stimson, cornered Admiral King with a pointed question. "Do you see any reason why this [plan] cannot be carried out?" The crusty admiral responded, "No. I do not." Hopkins knew that King had reason to waver on moving forward with the "Germany first" strategy while the issue in the Pacific was still in doubt.[48] He wanted to make sure that King, in the presence of everyone in the room, reiterated his commitment to the Marshall Memorandum. With that, the president approved the plan and adjourned the meeting. In his diary Stimson applauded the president's decision, writing that it "would mark this day as a memorable one in the war."[49]

Later the same day Roosevelt cabled Churchill. Referring to his agreement with the Marshall Memorandum, Roosevelt wrote that he had reached "conclusions of such vital importance that I want the whole picture to be presented to you and to ask for your approval thereon." He advised the prime minister that Hopkins and Marshall were on their way to London to present the "salient points" and gain the "complete co-operation of our two countries."[50] Two days later he penned a "Dear Winston" personal letter that he asked Hopkins and Marshall to hand-carry to the prime minister. "What Harry and Geo. Marshall will tell you about has my heart and *mind* in it.

Your people and mine demand the establishment of a second front to draw off pressure from the Russians [who] . . . are today killing more Germans and destroying more equipment than you and I put together. Even if full success is not attained, the *big* objective [relieving pressure on the Soviets] will be."[51]

*   *   *   *   *

The trip across the Atlantic took four days, thanks to a mechanical failure that resulted in an Easter Sunday layover in Bermuda. Marshall occupied his time by reading a scathing critique of Britain's Gallipoli campaign, the disastrous operation championed by Churchill during the Great War that led to his downfall as First Lord of the Admiralty. The chief of staff anticipated that the prime minister might advocate one or more similar diversionary schemes as alternatives to the American plan for a buildup and cross-Channel invasion in 1943. He needed to be fully prepared. This would be Marshall's first encounter with the British leadership where he, without the presence of the president, would take the lead in advocating a strategy that had profound military, diplomatic, and political consequences. His greatest concern was that Churchill would try to convince his countrymen to violate what Marshall and most military strategists at the time regarded as an essential condition of success in war—concentration of effort on the decisive front.

By the time Marshall, Hopkins, and their aides were driven through the bomb-cratered streets of London and checked into Claridge's, the nightmare scenario that they feared had already started to unfold. On April 6, seventy-five carrier-based Japanese planes bombed wharves and port facilities in Colombo, the capital of Ceylon (today Sri Lanka), a few miles off the southern tip of India, an attack "viewed in many quarters . . . as the beginning of Japanese concentration on the Asiatic subcontinent."[52] Japanese bombers sank two British cruisers and the carrier *Hermes* in the Bay of Bengal near Ceylon. Admiral Nagumo's powerful carrier strike force, Kido Butai, was already far west of the Malay Barrier, wreaking havoc across the Indian Ocean. When augmented by troopships, Nagumo was capable of providing air cover and firepower to land ground forces in India and points west all the way to the Persian Gulf.

Marshall's presence at No. 10 Downing Street during the second week of April was not a secret. A headline in the *Daily Herald* read: "Tough Guy

to Murmansk, 350 miles

eningrad

• Moscow

Volga

SOVIET UNION

Don R.

• Kursk

Kiev

Stalingrad •

Volga

Yalta

Black Sea

Caspian Sea

TURKEY

SYRIA

• Tehran

AFGHANISTAN

PALESTINE (BR.)

IRAQ

IRAN

TRANS-JORDAN

iro

KUWAIT

Indus

INDIA

Nile

GYPT ITISH)

Red Sea

Persian Gulf

ARABIA

Arabian Sea

European and Mediterranean Theaters World War II

0 Miles	250	500	750
0 Kilometers	500	750	

[meaning Marshall] Drops In. Attack! And start the attack soon."⁵³ Another was typical: "General Marshall in London to Plan Allied Offensive Against the Axis."⁵⁴ Nor was the Marshall Memorandum a surprise to Churchill and his warlords. Four days earlier, a member of the British Joint Staff Mission somehow caught a glimpse of the document and promptly cabled the British War Cabinet. When Marshall presented his case during the initial sessions to Churchill, Field Marshal Sir Alan Brooke, and several other British chiefs, they had already had plenty of time to digest the key elements of the Marshall Memorandum and to formulate their responses.

The British response was nuanced, some would say disingenuous, reflecting the difficult position they were in. Churchill and most of his military experts were of the view that a cross-Channel invasion in 1943 would be premature and could never succeed until Germany had been significantly weakened by an intensive bombing campaign, losses inflicted by the Red Army in the east, and peripheral operations by Anglo-American land forces in the Mediterranean basin, the Middle East, or perhaps Norway. Yet because the British desperately needed BOLERO, the American buildup in the British Isles, to forestall an invasion by the Germans should the Soviets collapse or sue for peace, they could not afford to reject the Marshall Memorandum no matter how flawed they thought it to be. If they did so, Marshall might abandon the "Germany first" strategy and convince Roosevelt to turn to the Pacific, pulled as they already were in that direction by MacArthur, public opinion, and the Japanese threat to invade India. Two weeks earlier Eisenhower had advised Marshall that if the British did not firmly commit to confronting Germany first, "the United States should turn its back on the Atlantic area and go full out against Japan."⁵⁵

As a consequence, in dealing with Marshall, the strategy of Churchill and Brooke was to agree in principle with the plan described in his memorandum, particularly BOLERO, but to continue to politely identify defects in aspects of the 1942 contingency plan (SLEDGEHAMMER) and to suggest reasonable-sounding conditions that should be met before actually launching the cross-Channel invasion in 1943. To put it another way, they hedged but did not oppose. Their strategy seemed to work. According to Hopkins's notes, Marshall came away from his initial encounters with Churchill and Brooke "expecting far more resistance than he got," though Brooke managed to get "into it enough to indicate that he had a great many misgivings about our proposal."

"I liked what I saw of Marshall," wrote Brooke in his diary the night after meeting with his American counterpart, "a pleasant and easy man to get on with, rather over-filled with his own importance. But I should not put him down as a great man."[56] Marshall's initial impression of Brooke, the man who had recently and rather abruptly replaced his new friend Jack Dill as the British army chief of staff, was likewise pointedly conditional. "[H]e may be a good fighting man," Marshall reportedly confided to Hopkins, "but he hasn't got Dill's brains."[57]

Their first impressions, as they often are, were incomplete and misleading. Brooke later wrote that Marshall was indeed "a great man," though "definitely not a strategist."[58] Nor would it take long for Marshall to realize that beneath Brooke's rude and condescending manner was a first-rate mind. He spoke rapidly but precisely, with an off-putting habit of darting his tongue about his lips. Moreover, Brooke could not disguise his impatience with those whose brains could not keep up with his. The irritation he fostered in others was not helped by the fact that he was physically unimpressive, thin, slope-shouldered, and delicately boned, like the birds he had the lifelong hobby of watching. Yet the longer Marshall was around Brooke, the more he appreciated his intelligence.

Unlike Marshall, Field Marshal Brooke was a descendant of warriors, the Anglo-Irish "Fighting Brookes," and had led troops in battle, namely the bulk of the British Expeditionary Force in Belgium and France in 1940. Still, they had a good deal in common. Both suffered the tragic loss of their first wives, Brooke's from an automobile accident in 1925 when he was at the wheel of his Bentley, leaving him shrouded in grief and blaming himself. Each of them were naturally reserved but had to struggle to control their explosive tempers. They were selfless, preferring quiet country pleasures (gardening and horses for Marshall, nature and bird-watching for Brooke) to showy pomp and ceremony.

Three days into the conference Hopkins reported to the president that the talks with Churchill and the British chiefs of staff concerning the Marshall Memorandum "were progressing very satisfactorily."[59] Though Brooke had taken issue with some of the details of ROUNDUP (the cross-Channel invasion to be launched in the summer of 1943), no one on the British side proposed that it be deferred beyond 1943, mothballed, or canceled. Furthermore, while the British questioned the feasibility of mounting SLEDGE-HAMMER in the fall of 1942, they conceded that Anglo-American forces might nevertheless be compelled to undertake "some action on the Continent this year" to prevent the collapse of the Soviets in the east.[60]

Throughout the conference Marshall emphasized the importance of more and bigger cross-Channel raids so that American ground troops and their leaders could gain valuable combat experience. Along with a major air offensive and naval support, such raids could divert German troops away from the Eastern Front and relieve at least some of the pressure on the Red Army. Marshall did not come out and expressly propose this as an alternative to SLEDGEHAMMER, but it was certainly implied.

Marshall made a point of seeking out Vice Admiral Lord Louis Mountbatten, who had recently been made chief of British Combined Operations Headquarters (COHQ), popularly known as the Commandos. Mountbatten was by far the most colorful of the British chiefs—young (age forty-three), Cary Grant handsome, a cousin of the King, and one of Churchill's favorites. Mountbatten's task was to recruit and train interservice special forces units for cross-Channel hit-and-run raids, akin to today's Navy SEALs and Army Special Forces. Although Mountbatten was resented by the older chiefs, Marshall took a liking to him at once. He recalled with a smile the night Mountbatten arrived for dinner at Claridge's standing in a miniature tank that he wanted to show Marshall.[61] A day or so later, the chief of staff visited COHQ for a briefing by Mountbatten and his commando leaders. Summoning the same enthusiasm he had for revolutionary tactics at Fort Benning, Marshall saw the potential for creating American commando units that could take the fight to the Germans and provide badly needed combat and amphibious landing experience, sooner rather than later. When Mountbatten invited Marshall to send American officers of captain and major rank from the three services to work with his staff, he accepted with enthusiasm. Asked what was most needed to "get ahead with planning and training," Mountbatten responded to Marshall, "Double every British order for landing ships and landing craft" and build a landing ship big enough to hold "around 230 to 240 men," capable of making "a trip across the Atlantic under their [sic] own steam."[62]

Early on Sunday morning, April 12, ubiquitous Colonel Louis Johnson, who played bit parts in a series of events that marked Marshall's career from World War I to Korea, made another appearance. As the chief of staff was probably aware, the president had appointed Johnson to be his personal representative and sent him to India in April to negotiate a political settlement with the British government and the Indian congress that would incentivize the Indian armed forces to aggressively defend the British possession against invasion attempts by the Japanese. On April 8, Johnson worked out a deal in New Delhi, called "the Johnson formula," with Sir Stafford Cripps, Churchill's representative, whereby Britain would cede a measure of control over its Defense Ministry in Delhi to nominees of India's political leaders. After the Johnson formula was rejected by Churchill's War Cabinet, Johnson prevailed upon Roosevelt to send a cable to Churchill criticizing him and his cabinet for being unwilling to "concede the right of self-government" to the Indian people.[63] The cable was delivered to Hopkins at Chequers, the prime minister's country residence, at three a.m., while he was still sipping brandy with Churchill. Hopkins handed the cable to the prime minister immediately. Churchill was outraged by the tone and substance of Roosevelt's message, deeply resentful that the American president was interfering in imperial affairs. Churchill informed Hopkins that if the president and Johnson persisted he would resign and "retire to private life."[64] Hopkins knew that he had to act, and act fast, to head off this potentially disastrous situation.

At this juncture, accounts differ. According to Robert Sherwood, Hopkins immediately telephoned FDR from Chequers and persuaded him to back off, arguing that nothing further could be done, "since Cripps had left India the day before, and explanations had been issued by both the British and Indian authorities."[65] In *Mantle of Command*, historian Nigel Hamilton offers an alternative version of how Hopkins defused the situation. As a stratagem to persuade Roosevelt to "back off"—that is, cease his and Johnson's insistence that India be granted a measure of self-government—Hamilton asserts that Hopkins convinced Churchill to ditch his draft resignation letter, ignore the "President's plea regarding India," and instead promise Britain's cooperation in carrying out the plan set forth in the Marshall Memorandum.[66] Consequently, claims Hamilton, Churchill prematurely informed Roosevelt that he would support the Marshall Memorandum, not because he was wholly committed to it, but because he needed Roosevelt's help in preserving complete military control over the jewel of the British empire.

There is a certain plausibility to Hamilton's version, though he cites not a single source. On Sunday afternoon, April 12, two days before his War Cabinet Defense Committee made it official, Churchill cabled Roosevelt. "I have read with earnest attention your masterly document," meaning the Marshall Memorandum, "about future of the war and the great operations proposed. I am in entire agreement in principle with all you propose, and so are the Chiefs of Staff."[67] By using the phrase "all you propose," he included the contingent operations in SLEDGEHAMMER. The same afternoon, Marshall, who had spent the weekend at Chequers, telephoned General Joseph McNarney in Washington and informed him that Churchill had "indicated that he had virtually accepted in toto the proposals I submitted to him, and that the Defense Cabinet Committee would undoubtedly approve. I regard this as acquiescence in principle."[68]

Churchill's hasty action—pledging his wholehearted support for the Marshall Memorandum *before* his War Cabinet Defense Committee had even met—suggests that his motive for endorsing the Marshall Memorandum had more to do with control over India than with his view of its merits. If that was not his motive, why wouldn't the prime minister have waited a couple of days until he, his British chiefs, and the Cabinet Defense Committee considered the wisdom of the Marshall Memorandum? And why did he decline to provide an immediate response to Roosevelt's meddling three a.m. cable?

Whether it was Hopkins's phone call to Roosevelt or the "stratagem" he sold to Churchill, it is apparent that Hopkins caused FDR to "back off." As a result the prime minister did not carry through on his threat to resign. And Churchill gave Marshall every indication that he agreed with the Marshall Memorandum.

At ten p.m. on the night of April 14, the Defense Committee convened at No. 10 Downing Street to hear the official response of the British government to the Marshall Memorandum. Hopkins and Marshall were present. Churchill opened the meeting, stating that he "had no hesitation in cordially adopting the plan," which he characterized as a "momentous proposal." His "one broad reservation," however, was the need for American support in maintaining "the defence of India and the Middle East" without which the main object of the Marshall Memorandum "would be fatally compromised."[69] This emphasis on the importance of defending India that he and his colleagues repeated throughout the meeting provides additional support for Hamilton's version of what happened at three a.m. on April 12 and why Churchill assured Roosevelt before the Defense Committee had even met that he accepted the Marshall Memorandum in toto.

The Defense Committee meeting concluded well after midnight. Summarizing, the prime minister said that while details of the Marshall Memorandum needed to be worked out, it was clear that there was "complete unanimity on [its] framework."[70] He promised Marshall "that nothing would be left undone on the part of the British Government and people which could contribute to the success of this great enterprise on which they were about to embark."[71] No one on the British side expressed disagreement with Churchill's concluding remarks. The following day, April 15, Marshall radioed Secretary Stimson that "our proposal," the Marshall Memorandum, "was formally accepted," and that the "PM in impressive pronouncement declared a complete agreement." He added, "Their pressing worry is over naval situation in Indian Ocean."[72]

When Roosevelt got word that the British had accepted the Marshall Memorandum he cabled Churchill that he was "delighted" at the "unanimity of opinion." While acknowledging "future difficulties," he concluded by saying, "I feel better about this war than at any time in the past two years."[73]

In his memoir, Churchill admitted that he was not forthcoming with "his cherished Ally" in April 1942. His objective all along, he wrote, was to "work by influence and diplomacy" to convince the Americans to join the British in invading French North Africa or northern Norway in 1942. Since it would take time to secure their "agreed and harmonious action," he wrote, "I did not therefore open any of these alternatives at our meeting on the 14th [of April]."[74] Given his assurances to Roosevelt and Marshall at the time, this was a breathtaking confession.

Lieutenant-General Sir Hastings "Pug" Ismay, military secretary to the War Cabinet, who was present at the midnight meeting, later said that "we could have come clean, much cleaner than we did," citing a fear of sustaining a repeat of the horrific losses suffered by British troops in the Great War.[75] "Our American friends," wrote Ismay, "went happily homeward under the mistaken impression that we have committed ourselves to both ROUNDUP and SLEDGEHAMMER."[76]

What about Marshall? Did he have doubts about the British commitments? What little evidence there is suggests that Marshall was reasonably confident that the British sincerely intended to pursue BOLERO—the buildup. As to ROUNDUP, the cross-Channel invasion in the summer of 1943, Marshall probably harbored some doubt, due to British focus on the seriousness of the Japanese threat to India and the Middle East and the obvious fact that the summer of 1943 was a long way off. Based on comments by Brooke and others, Marshall must have had serious doubts regarding the British commitment to SLEDGEHAMMER if a Soviet collapse was deemed imminent. He too was not at all convinced of the wisdom of a cross-Channel bridgehead in the fall of 1942. Nor was he persuaded that it would prevent the defeat of the Red Army. However, he believed it was vitally important to proceed with the planning of such an emergency operation because it would guarantee continued concentration of resources and training in Great Britain, thus avoiding dispersion to other fronts. Marshall was intent on doing everything possible to ensure that the main show, the cross-Channel invasion in the summer of 1943, would actually go forward. Concentration on the "decisive front"—Germany first—was his mantra.

Marshall and Hopkins, joined by Averell Harriman (lend-lease expediter in the UK), flew from Hendon aerodrome to Northern Ireland on April 17. At a base in Ballymena, Marshall was to inspect recently arrived American troops, soldiers who were the vanguard of the million-man army that he expected would be training in the British Isles for the cross-Channel invasion. Along with Hopkins and Harriman, the chief of staff was billeted at the country house of a retired British officer who Hopkins quickly discovered was an admirer of Adolf Hitler. By this time Marshall and Hopkins were far more than colleagues who happened to both work for Roosevelt. They had established an easy friendship, often even addressing each other in private by first names, an intimacy that Marshall would not abide with the president. Rather than deal directly with Roosevelt, Marshall would often present his proposals and suggestions informally to Hopkins, relying on him as an alter ego and trusting the presidential aide to honestly and frankly reflect FDR's reactions and thought processes. Early on their first morning in the officer's rather small house, Marshall's orderly brought him a note from Hopkins written in pencil on a pink radiogram form. "Mr. Hopkins expresses the hope," the note read, "that the Chief of Staff slept well and is in reasonable good humor." Hopkins knew that Marshall was hungry and miserable, as was he. At dinner the previous evening they were exposed to the serious deprivations of wartime rationing in the countryside, though the wine was excellent and the dining room elegant. Hopkins's note continued. "He begs to inquire whether the General would be disposed to have some pork and beans for breakfast and porridge (oatmeal) to you." Marshall chuckled and penciled a reply on his own radiogram form. "The Chief of Staff suggests that instead of a crude meal of pork and beans Mr. Hopkins would be better off with a small circle of liverwurst, the ragged edge of a piece of lettuce and the false hope of more to come." Except for the finger-size bread strips, this was a fair description of what they had been served the night before. "I'll be along presently," concluded Marshall.[77]

* * * * *

On the flight home Marshall thought about who should head the group of officers that he would shortly be sending to London to be schooled by Mountbatten's Combined Operations. He needed a rising star, a youngish colonel who had punched all the right tickets at the service schools and had received superior efficiency reports as an innovative leader, trainer, and organizer. Whether Marshall's famous "black book" resided in his back pocket or his memory, he leafed through the pages that contained the names of promising officers. His top choice was Colonel Lucian Truscott Jr., destined to become one of the war's most outstanding combat generals, who was then commanding a regiment of the 1st Cavalry Division. Truscott had distinguished himself in the Louisiana maneuvers in 1941, but he was too young to have seen combat in the Great War. Marshall knew that Eisenhower, under whom Truscott served at Fort Lewis in the northwest, had a high opinion of the man. Noted for his raspy voice, dog face, and huge hands, Texas-born Truscott was "brusque and profane, capable of hocking tobacco with the most unlettered private in the Army."[78] Marshall believed Truscott fit the bill for the officer who could succeed in organizing and training American raiders to conduct cross-Channel operations against the Germans along the French coast.

Colonel Truscott arrived at the 20th Street entrance to the Munitions Building in Washington in late April 1942. "[O]fficers of every branch and rank," he wrote, were streaming through the halls under the watchful eyes of "strategically placed guards" with a "sense of urgency, of hurry, as if time were pressing."[79] Truscott was ushered into Marshall's office, where he met Marshall for the first time. He had been briefed by Eisenhower, so he knew he was going to command a group of American officers who would be sent to London to work with Mountbatten's Combined Operations. His job would be to organize and train small U.S. assault units for the kind of hit-and-run raids on the French and Norwegian coasts that British commandos, under Mountbatten, were conducting. The purpose was to provide actual combat experience against German troops so that these men could then be distributed throughout the infantry divisions that would constitute the first wave of the main cross-Channel invasion in 1943 (or perhaps an emergency operation in the fall of 1942).

According to Truscott, Marshall leaned back in his chair and gazed steadily at him. Marshall spoke slowly and deliberately, his first words disarming. "You are an older man than I wanted for this assignment. I looked you up. You are forty-seven, Mountbatten is forty-three. Most of his staff are younger. All of them are battle-experienced. They are even now planning and conducting raids against the Germans."

Truscott said nothing. Marshall continued. "But some of your friends assure me that you are younger than your years, and that your experience especially fits you for this assignment."[80] The colonel started to explain his lack of qualifications, namely that he had never been in combat, but Marshall brushed him off. He went on to express his concern that unlike World War I, where the doughboys were "blooded" at relatively quiet sectors of the Western Front before being committed to all-out battle, the nature and timing of the proposed plan for invading France precluded the attainment of combat experience on a large scale for the divisions that would be crossing the English Channel. Consequently, Truscott's job was to impart combat experience through small-unit commando raids and then to make sure the "blooded" men were assigned to each new assault unit so that the green troops would have the benefit of combat veterans. Marshall's concept was to increase participation as rapidly as possible by launching larger and larger raids until the main event in the summer of 1943.

The interview with Marshall, wrote Truscott, "removed in my mind any confusion as to what was expected of me. For the rest, it was up to me—and I could not fail."[81] After arriving in Scotland and familiarizing himself with

Mountbatten's Combined Operations, Truscott established the U.S. Army's First Ranger Battalion. To distinguish his special forces from the British "commandos," Truscott came up with "rangers," a uniquely American name, borrowed from "Rogers' Rangers," a band of irregulars that fought in the French and Indian War and were celebrated in the 1937 novel *Northwest Passage*. Major William Darby, a thirty-three-year-old charismatic West Pointer, with training in amphibious landings and assaults, was selected to command the battalion. "Darby's Rangers" became one of the most acclaimed fighting units in the Second World War.

* * * * *

Marshall returned from London having every reason to believe that resources needed for BOLERO, the buildup in Britain for a cross-Channel invasion in 1943 while conducting air strikes and raids in 1942, would clearly have priority over those allocated to the Pacific. His equally ranked navy counterpart, foul-tempered Admiral Ernest King, as well as the president himself, seemed to have other ideas. A collision with the chief of staff was inevitable. Things came to a head in early May 1942.

The clash involved an urgent request by King for 215 army combat planes to be sent to the Southwest Pacific. "The mounting of BOLERO," he wrote, "must not be permitted to interfere with our vital needs in the Pacific."[82] At the same time the president requested that Australia be immediately reinforced with 1,000 combat aircraft and 100,000 army ground troops. Together, these requests challenged the "Germany first" policy and the actions described in the Marshall Memorandum.

Marshall asked his commander in chief to make a stark choice: Which will it be, "The Pacific Theatre" or "Bolero"? In his supporting memorandum Marshall pointed out that allocation of the requested aircraft to the Pacific would delay the "initiation of an American air offensive in Western Europe" in 1942 by "more than two months." And that the diversion of ground forces to Australia would mean that the U.S. could not participate in any "landing operation" in France in the fall, assuming that became necessary. Marshall concluded by asserting that if "Bolero" is not "the primary objective of the United States," then it should be abandoned and the British should be "formally advised that the recent London agreement must be cancelled."[83]

Much as he would have liked to, this was a decision that Roosevelt could not duck or delay. To his credit, he promptly replied in writing, emphatically asserting, "I do not want BOLERO slowed down."[84] He claimed that his request that planes and troops be sent to Australia was only a suggestion, not a directive. In a separate, much longer memorandum to Stimson, Knox, Hopkins, and the three chiefs of staff, the president wrote that it was "essential that active operations be conducted in 1942 [in Western Europe]," ostensibly for the purpose of drawing off German air and ground forces from the east and assisting the Soviet Union. As examples of "active operations," FDR suggested that once air supremacy was achieved, Anglo-American forces might conduct small commando raids or larger "super commando raids" in 1942, or perhaps secure and reinforce a permanent bridgehead in France and hold it until 1943 when the main cross-Channel invasion was launched.[85] Thus, the scale of the operations that would satisfy the president's demand for active operations against the Germans in 1942 was by no means clear.

Most likely, Roosevelt was vague because, as a self-described "juggler," he preferred to keep all of his options open. By the first week of May the fate of the Red Army was still in the balance. Since the expected spring offensive by the Wehrmacht was delayed, the president and his advisers were in no position to predict that a Soviet collapse was imminent, the condition that would trigger the perilous five- or six-division emergency amphibious attack contemplated by SLEDGEHAMMER. FDR expected Foreign Minister Vyacheslav Molotov to arrive in Washington in a few weeks, when he would probably demand a "second front." Roosevelt could offer to meet Molotov's demand, but it would be he who would define the size, scope, and timing of the so-called second front. It would be he who would determine whether the American effort would be a mere token or a major undertaking to draw enough German troops away from the Eastern Front to significantly assist the Red Army. Moreover, if it turned out that Molotov preferred a maximum flow of lend-lease supplies by convoy to Murmansk as an alternative to a second front (he couldn't have both), Roosevelt could still satisfy public demand for action against the Nazis by ordering spectacular and well-publicized raids and bombing attacks, thereby minimizing the risk of a large and bloody defeat at the hands of the Germans.

For the time being, General Marshall was not concerned about Roosevelt's lack of clarity. As long as the president ordered that BOLERO not be "slowed down" and demanded "active operations" against the Germans, Marshall was satisfied that America's military was on the right track. In his commencement speech to the West Point cadets on May 29, the same day Molotov arrived in Washington, Marshall, speaking without notes, confidently assured the audience that American soldiers "will land in France."[86] The front page of *The New York Times* reported that when the corps heard that line, they stood and cheered. It was to be Germany first. The question left hanging was when.

CHAPTER 9

Hardest Fought Debate

By June of 1942, the plan set forth in the Marshall Memorandum was in complete disarray. Against the chief of staff's advice, Roosevelt had unilaterally moved up the timetable by informing Joseph Stalin through Foreign Minister Molotov that the United States intended to open a "Second Front" in Europe in 1942. Marshall was dismayed, to say the least. Why the president did this and whether or not he intended to carry through will never be known for certain. Perhaps he suspected that Hitler was about to cut a deal with Stalin or that the Red Army was on the cusp of defeat. Or maybe he felt he had to give in to the "second front now" demands by the Soviets and a growing slice of the American public. With midterm elections looming, a boost to homefront morale was probably on FDR's mind.

Whatever motivated the president, he believed it to be of paramount importance that Allied troops take the fight to the Germans before the year was out. Continuous air attacks and commando raids would not be enough; the Anglo-American alliance must establish some kind of a front in Western Europe in 1942. Since the buildup for the main invasion would take too long, SLEDGEHAMMER, the emergency cross-Channel invasion, would have to be launched by September, even though there were no clear signs that a Soviet collapse was imminent.

It was this decision by the commander in chief that set the table for what military historian John Keegan called "the hardest-fought strategic debate in the war."[1]

* * * * *

Informed of Roosevelt's decision by Molotov, Churchill confided to Field Marshal Brooke that Roosevelt had gone "off the rails and some good talks as regards western front were required."[2] On June 19, Churchill and Brooke arrived at Anacostia naval air station in Washington. From there the prime minister flew alone up to Hyde Park, where Roosevelt planned to spend the weekend. During their private talks in the president's stifling library, Churchill handed FDR a note saying that the British government and its military were of the view that a cross-Channel attack in September was "certain to lead to disaster" and would therefore not help the Soviets. Since the British, who would have to supply the bulk of the troops, were opposed, and the Americans did not have enough trained troops to launch such an operation on their own, Churchill was in the driver's seat. He posed two related questions to Roosevelt: "Can we afford to stand idle in the Atlantic theatre during the whole of 1942?" Should we not revisit Operation GYMNAST, the invasion of French North Africa that we had shelved a few months ago?[3]

The next day an answer to the prime minister's questions presented itself. The president had cut short his weekend at Hyde Park and returned to Washington with Churchill and Hopkins in his private railcar. In Roosevelt's Oval Study Churchill read aloud a pink-tinted message handed to him by Marshall. "Tobruk has surrendered, with 25,000 men taken prisoner." The numerically superior British Eighth Army had suffered a humiliating defeat in the Libyan desert at the hands of General Erwin Rommel's Afrika Korps. "Defeat is one thing, disgrace is another," Churchill wrote later.[4] What was left of the British army was retreating east toward the Egyptian border. No one suggested it at the moment, but this debacle provided a convenient answer to Churchill's two questions. Instead of remaining "idle" for the rest of 1942, American troops could take the fight to Rommel's Germans in North Africa. GYMNAST was back on the table.

That afternoon and into the evening Churchill, with his usual eloquence, presented his views on the strategic advantages of GYMNAST, sidestepping those that would accrue to the Eighth Army. He predicted that once the Germans were driven out of North Africa, Italy almost certainly would collapse, a point that must have made Marshall suspect that Churchill would eventually push for a further diversion into Italy. The prime minister stressed that GYMNAST would reopen the Mediterranean to Allied shipping, thus providing a warm-water route to supply the Soviets via the Persian Gulf. And he saw the operation as both an opportunity to transform America's raw green troops into combat veterans and a testing ground for general officers. In his diary that night Secretary Stimson wrote that by arguing for the revival of GYMNAST, Churchill "knew well, I am sure, that it was the president's great, secret baby."[5] Stimson was recalling how intrigued FDR was with GYMNAST before it had to be postponed indefinitely in March because of expected Vichy French opposition and lack of shipping.

At the conclusion of what became known as the Second Washington Conference, shaky compromises were worked out that foreshadowed the demise of the Marshall Memorandum. According to General Ismay's notes, if a "sound and sensible plan" for a cross-Channel operation in 1942 cannot be "contrived," the next "best alternative" was GYMNAST, an invasion of French North Africa.[6] Left unstated was its immediate aim: attack Rommel's forces from the west. This would relieve pressure on the British Eighth Army, allowing it to regroup and launch a counterattack against Rommel from the east. It was thus becoming apparent that Roosevelt's insistence on an emergency cross-Channel operation in 1942 to keep the Soviets in the war and satisfy the home front was being converted by Churchill into an effort to rescue his beleaguered Eighth Army.

*   *   *   *   *

General Marshall was implacably opposed to GYMNAST. A June 9 British intelligence estimate that had been forwarded to him concluded that the situation on the Eastern Front was "touch and go"—either the Germans or more likely the Soviets could collapse "with startling rapidity." The trained Anglo-American forces assigned to SLEDGEHAMMER constituted a kind of "strategic reserve," able to react quickly to either one of those possibilities.[7] To remove these critically important assets and ship them along with others to fight in North Africa would be dangerous and foolhardy, argued Marshall. Moreover, an Allied operation thousands of miles south into North Africa, as opposed to France, would not be of much help to the Soviets. It would not pose the kind of threat to the fatherland that would cause the Germans to withdraw divisions from the Eastern Front.

As Marshall saw it, GYMNAST was also fraught with tactical risk. The Germans, with an assist from Franco's Spain, could capture Gibraltar and block the western entrance to, or exit from, the Mediterranean. U-boats in the Atlantic Ocean would menace Allied troopships that would have to traverse the vast, far less protected distances from the U.S. and Great Britain to get to the coasts of North Africa. Allied troops landing in Morocco and

Algeria would likely have to fight French ground and naval forces answerable to the Vichy government before encountering any German units.

Marshall's greatest concern, however, was that the North Africa operation was an unnecessary 2,500-mile diversion that would slow down the buildup in Great Britain and delay the cross-Channel invasion into Western Europe well beyond 1943. While the Allies were being sucked into the Mediterranean theater, the Soviets might collapse or negotiate an armistice with Hitler, making victory over Germany impossible. Fresh dispatches to Marshall by his Military Intelligence Service indicated that the German summer offensives on the Eastern Front were "continuing with undiminished power" and that large elements of the Red Army were "in desperate straits."[8] Based on these reports Marshall believed that an "emergency requiring heroic measures" by Anglo-American forces was "rapidly developing."[9] He was convinced that a commitment to GYMNAST at a time when the survival of the Soviet Union hung in the balance posed an unacceptable strategic gamble, a toss of the dice that could lose the war.

On July 8, Marshall's concern turned to a moment of rage when Dill brought him the news that Churchill and his War Cabinet had decided against SLEDGEHAMMER and in favor of GYMNAST, which meant that a cross-Channel invasion would be delayed until at least 1944 or perhaps indefinitely. Churchill had convinced his cabinet that the North Africa operation "offered considerable attractions" because it would pose "a threat to Rommel's rear," a rationale that Marshall suspected, but was not disclosed to him by Dill. Churchill also promoted GYMNAST to his cabinet on the ground that "the President had always expressed the keenest desire to carry it out."[10] It is true that FDR gave Churchill this impression from time to time, but once he signed on to the Marshall Memorandum at the end of March he did not convey such a desire to his chief of staff.

Marshall had reason to be incensed. Since early April he had spent countless hours—precious time—arguing, cajoling, and eventually forging what he was led to believe were British commitments to a decisive cross-Channel invasion of northwest France in 1943, the only way to win the war. "Three times the British had seemingly agreed," wrote one of Marshall's biographers.[11] Each time they backed off by misstating conditions and employing slippery language, notably saying they agreed "in principle" or were committed to the "framework" of a cross-Channel invasion. Marshall was

fed up with British duplicity. He could not, however, allow himself to prolong his anger. As he had remarked to Katherine during a winter walk at the
outset of the war, "that would be fatal." [12]

Two days later, his anger under control, Marshall posed two questions at
a meeting of the Joint Chiefs of Staff. Should the United States agree to go
forward with GYMNAST? The answer was a unanimous no. Are the British serious when they say they remain committed to BOLERO and
ROUNDUP—the buildup and main cross-Channel invasion in 1943?
Again, the answer had to be no. It was clear to everyone in the room,
and it must have been obvious to Churchill and Brooke, that once Anglo-
American divisions were diverted to North Africa in the fall of 1942, it would
be virtually impossible to launch a major invasion of northwest France in
the spring of 1943. Indeed, until they had been silenced in recent days
by Churchill, the British chiefs themselves opposed GYMNAST, ostensibly
because the operation would preclude the main cross-Channel invasion
in 1943.

Since it was also obvious that neither SLEDGEHAMMER nor
ROUNDUP could succeed "without full and whole-hearted British support," what should the United States do? Marshall had an answer. Out of
desperation, he proposed a radical shift in grand strategy. If the British per-
sist in delaying decisive action against Germany, the United States should
"turn to the Pacific for decisive action against Japan." [13] Marshall's proposal
was immediately seconded by Admiral King, who had always believed the
British were reluctant to go along with America's cross-Channel invasion
plans. Backed by Stimson, King, and Arnold, a memorandum prepared by
Marshall was delivered to the president at Hyde Park on Saturday morning,
July 11. In a cover message, the chief of staff urged Roosevelt to put the
Pacific-first proposition to Churchill and the British "on a very definite basis"
immediately. "My object," wrote Marshall, "is to force the British into acceptance of a concentrated effort against Germany, and if this proves impossible, to turn immediately to the Pacific with strong forces and drive for a
decision against Japan." [14] To put it another way, Marshall recommended
that FDR present the threat of "Pacific first" as an ultimatum, making it
clear that he and his military chiefs were serious, that this was not a bluff. If
the British persisted, the United States really would turn all of its efforts toward the defeat of Japan.

Was it a bluff? Fourteen years later Marshall declared in an interview that for him "it was a bluff," but that King was dead serious about the Pacific alternative.[15] The president suspected a split among his military advisers, but he couldn't be sure. He asked the joint chiefs to provide him with a detailed outline of a plan for "your Pacific Ocean alternative."[16] The next day Marshall and the other chiefs had to admit that there was as yet no such detailed plan. In addition, they conceded that a shift to the Pacific might "adversely affect" the fortunes of the Soviets on the Eastern Front. However, they offset that concession by pointing out that such a shift would favor the Soviets by precluding the likelihood of a Japanese attack on their rear in Siberia, a plausible scenario as warned in recent intelligence reports.[17] The president smelled bluff. How could he convince Churchill that he was serious if his own chiefs had not yet thought out the details of a strategically sound plan for turning to the Pacific?

Marshall's proposal, which had the support of the other joint chiefs, their deputies, and the entire civilian leadership of the War and Navy Departments, confronted Roosevelt with a ticklish situation. On the one hand, he completely understood how exasperated Marshall, Stimson, and their navy counterparts felt as a result of the shabby treatment by the British and why they were so emotionally committed to using the Pacific threat as leverage. He couldn't afford to further damage their morale or, worse yet, have one or more of them resign in protest or disgust. On the other hand, the very idea of presenting an ultimatum to Churchill on such a profound change in grand strategy was anathema to Roosevelt. As FDR famously remarked to Stimson, a threat to abandon the British in these dark days would be an act of childish petulance, like "taking up your dishes and going away."[18] Marshall should have known that the president was not about to threaten to abandon the prime minister, who was already suffering political pressures at home due to the Tobruk debacle and other British defeats in the field. Churchill's continuance as prime minister was of vital importance to the United States and the entire war effort.[19]

Roosevelt remained at Hyde Park, pondering what to do, alone and in long talks with Hopkins. On Tuesday, July 14, he telegraphed Marshall. "I have definitely decided to send you, King and Harry to London immediately." He added, "I want you to know that I do not approve the Pacific proposal."[20] A separate message to Marshall, signed "Roosevelt C-in-C," contained a stinging rebuke: a turn to the Pacific "is exactly what Germany hoped the United States would do following Pearl Harbor."[21]

The next day, having rushed back to Washington on his private train, FDR met with Marshall and softened the blow. Based on a three-page letter that set forth the president's final instructions for the London trip, Roosevelt told Marshall that he wanted plans and preparations for ROUNDUP, the main cross-Channel invasion in 1943, to move forward. The president advised Marshall to push for SLEDGEHAMMER "with utmost vigor." It must be "executed [in the fall of 1942] whether or not Russian collapse becomes imminent." However, if such a collapse appears "probable," instructed the president, then the SLEDGEHAMMER operation should be regarded as "imperative." In the event the British cannot be persuaded to participate in SLEDGEHAMMER, then Marshall must consider sending ground forces to either the Middle East (i.e., Syria, Egypt, Persian Gulf) or to French North Africa in 1942. He described the latter option, GYMNAST, as a "[n]ew operation in Morocco and Algiers intended to drive in against the backdoor of Rommel's armies," obviously to assist the British Eighth Army. At the same time he cautioned that the issue of whether French troops might contest Allied landings in North Africa "is still in doubt." The president made it clear that whether it is the northwest France bridgehead (his stated preference), the Middle East, or North Africa, "it is of the highest importance that U.S. ground troops be brought into action" against Germany in 1942.[22]

Knowing that he would have a tough time convincing the British to agree to participate in SLEDGEHAMMER, Marshall could have recommended during his July 15 meeting with FDR that the best way to get U.S. ground troops "into action" against the Germans in 1942 would be to conduct larger and larger hit-and-run raids against German troops stationed along the French coast and farther inland, as Colonel Truscott was already charged with organizing. This option would avoid a massive dispersion of American forces to North Africa or the Middle East and the postponement of the main invasion beyond 1943. It would also provide the troops and their officers with plenty of amphibious landing and combat experience while pinning down German divisions in France, thus preventing them from being moved to fight the Soviets in the east. However, there is no indication in any of the accounts of Marshall's meetings with Roosevelt that he suggested repeated raids, combined with a major air offensive, as alternatives to SLEDGEHAMMER or to the diversions into North Africa or the Middle East. Nor is there evidence that Marshall questioned Roosevelt on exactly why he had become so insistent on a major U.S. ground action against the Germans in the fall of 1942, and why he couldn't wait until the spring of 1943, when they would be better prepared. All that historians really know about what Marshall actually said to the president that day comes from the secretary of war's contemporaneous diary entries. According to his diary, Marshall told Stimson he had a "thumping argument" with Roosevelt and "thought he had knocked out the President's lingering affections for first Gymnast and then Middle East" alternatives.[23] This suggests that FDR left Marshall with the impression that he strongly favored SLEDGEHAMMER—the fall 1942 cross-Channel bridgehead in northwest France—and that the other two options were perhaps off the table. Whether the president meant to convey this impression and, if so, whether he was sincere in doing so, are open questions. Likewise, the issue of whether Marshall simply heard what he wanted to hear, as so often happened with those dealing with the president, cannot be resolved with any certainty.

With a sure green light from the president to push hard for SLEDGE-HAMMER, Marshall sent a "radio" message on July 16 to General Eisenhower, who was already in London. In mid-June Marshall had appointed him to take command of the newly designated European Theater of Operations (ETO), headquartered in a converted apartment building at 20 Grosvenor Square. Marshall requested Eisenhower to prepare a "searching analysis" of SLEDGEHAMMER and to have it ready when he arrived in London with Hopkins and King, probably on the 17th or 18th of July. Reflecting the impression the president apparently gave him at their last meeting, Marshall told Eisenhower that GYMNAST "was completely out of the question" because it would require the diversion from the Pacific of vitally important naval assets, including at least one aircraft carrier, and that an operation against the Germans in the Middle East would be feasible only if a "turn is made to the Pacific."[24] These conclusions, of course, were at odds with his written instructions from the president.

According to the final line of Roosevelt's instruction letter, Marshall, King, and Hopkins were to reach "total agreement" with Churchill and the

British "within one week" of their arrival in London. Marshall was well aware of the reason for this tight deadline. Harry Hopkins, a widower, had to be back in Washington before July 30 in time for his White House wedding to Louise Macy, former Paris editor of *Harper's Bazaar*. Before departing for London, Marshall had taken time to write a letter to the future Mrs. Hopkins. "To be very frank," he began, "I am intensely interested in Harry's health and happiness, and therefore in your impending marriage." Her betrothed, he wrote, "is of great importance to our National interests . . . and he is one of the most imprudent people regarding his health that I have ever known . . . I express the hope that you will find it possible to curb his indiscretions and see that he takes the necessary rest."[25] Marshall's words conveyed not only his affection for Hopkins but also how much he relied on him as a medium of communication with the president and an interpreter of FDR's thoughts and moods. "Whenever I had a tough knot," recalled Marshall to his interviewer, "I would call [Hopkins] and he would either arrange the meeting with the president for me, or he and I together would see the president . . . So he was quite invaluable to me and he was very courageous."[26] In the coming days Marshall and Hopkins would remain close friends. Hopkins, however, would serve the president's interests, which were not always aligned with those of the chief of staff.

*   *   *   *   *

Marshall's olive-drab TWA Stratoliner landed in Prestwick, Scotland, late Friday afternoon, July 17. In addition to Hopkins and King, the party included Steve Early, FDR's press secretary; Colonel Frank McCarthy, aide to the chief of staff; Brigadier General Beetle Smith; and Hopkins's doctor. Heavy fog delayed their connecting flight to London. Advised of the delay, Churchill sent his private train to take Marshall, King, and Hopkins to Chequers so that he could work his persuasive powers on them before their views on the feasibility of a cross-Channel bridgehead were informed by Eisenhower, Truscott, and others in the capital. Churchill was most anxious to see them. Dill had already advised the prime minister by telegram that unless he could persuade Marshall in the next few days "of his unswerving devotion" to a cross-Channel invasion of France, "everything points to a complete reversal of our present agreed strategy and the withdrawal of

America to a war of her own in the Pacific, leaving us with limited American assistance to make out as best we can against Germany."[27]

Time was limited. Marshall was not about to spend the weekend listening to Churchill. Though the train engineer had been instructed to take the senior Americans to Chequers, Marshall ordered him to rush the entire party straight to London. Hopkins, indulging one of his milder "indiscretions," stayed up most of the night chain-smoking Luckies and playing low-stakes gin rummy with Steve Early as the train raced toward dawn. They were met at Euston rail station at 7:50 a.m. by Brooke, Eisenhower, and John Winant, American ambassador to the Court of St. James's. It was "a queer party," wrote Brooke in his diary. "Hopkins is for operating in Africa. Marshall wants to operate in Europe, and King is determined to stick to the Pacific."[28]

Once again Marshall and his party checked into Claridge's, only this time their presence was kept as secret as possible. Sixteen rooms on the fourth floor were quickly and efficiently converted into a quasi-military headquarters, luxurious bunkhouse, and communications hub, with sentries posted at doors along the halls and access closely guarded. It didn't take long for Hopkins to be summoned to the telephone. Calling from Chequers, the prime minister, outraged that Marshall had bypassed him and gone on to London, demanded an explanation. Hopkins did his best to calm him down, claiming that Marshall and King were under orders from the president to meet with Eisenhower as soon as they arrived and that no rudeness or disrespect was intended. Unable to dissipate Churchill's wrath and concerned about the forthcoming talks, Hopkins drove to Chequers to spend the rest of the weekend with the prime minister. There is no record of what the two of them talked about, except Hopkins's brief report to FDR that by Sunday evening "everything was cleared up" and that Churchill was "in the best of spirits."[29] However, piecing this weekend together with later events, it is likely that Hopkins soothed Churchill by giving him, in strict confidence, a sense of the president's instructions to Marshall's team and perhaps even suggested that Roosevelt had not lost sight of GYMNAST. In fact, all Hopkins had to do was signal Churchill that the "turn to the Pacific" proposal was off the table and Churchill would know that he and his military chiefs could safely oppose whatever plan Marshall came up with for a cross-Channel bridgehead in the fall of 1942. Without British participation the Americans did not have enough troops and landing craft to pull it off on their own.[30]

Meanwhile, Marshall summoned King; Eisenhower; General Mark Clark, commander of II Corps; General Carl "Tooey" Spaatz, head of the Eighth Air Force; and Admiral Stark, commander of U.S. naval forces (ETO) to his suite to review and critique the state of plans for SLEDGE-HAMMER. At this early point in the week, Saturday, July 18, the best they came up with was a plan to land with air cover and naval support two U.S. and four British divisions near Le Havre on or about September 15, 1942. Eisenhower estimated that there was only about a 20 percent chance of successfully establishing a six-division beachhead at Le Havre, "[b]ut we should not forget that the prize we seek is to keep 8,000,000 Russians in the war." If we do nothing and allow the Red Army to collapse, argued Eisenhower, we would be "guilty of one of the grossest military blunders of all history."[31]

Marshall thought that the British would almost certainly balk at the risks, especially because they would be supplying two-thirds of the troops. He needed a different plan, one that posed less risk. Marshall decided to reach out to Colonel Truscott, who he knew had been working closely with the British planners in Admiral Mountbatten's Combined Operations Headquarters (COHQ). Late Saturday afternoon when Truscott returned to his office a message from the chief of staff was waiting for him. When Truscott entered Marshall's suite at Claridge's an hour or so later a voice from the bathroom called out, "[s]it down. I am dressing. I will be with you in a few minutes." Marshall soon came out, continued dressing, and engaged Truscott in casual conversation about his job. Within minutes the colonel found himself having a scotch and soda with the general followed by "a delicious dinner." All the while he was "being subjected to the most thorough examination and in the most charming manner that one can imagine," wrote Truscott.

Before long Marshall asked Truscott what the British officers at COHQ thought about the risks of launching SLEDGEHAMMER in 1942. As Truscott recalled, he told Marshall that the "younger planners" believed that an amphibious landing to seize and hold the lightly defended "Cherbourg peninsula," rather than Le Havre as proposed by Eisenhower, was "practicable," within "our means," and "a desirable operation to undertake during the fall in preparation for ROUNDUP the following spring." He hastened to add, however, that the next higher level in COHQ disagreed with the

Cherbourg operation. Nevertheless, Marshall was "keenly interested" in the details of the plan, wrote Truscott, and "gave me a searching investigation of the young planners' ideas."[32] Later that evening, Eisenhower, Clark, and King arrived and engaged Truscott and Marshall in a lengthy discussion concerning the feasibility of seizing and holding the Cherbourg Peninsula in the fall of 1942. Well after midnight they adjourned. Truscott agreed to convene the planners the next morning and provide Marshall and his colleagues with an outline of their Cherbourg operation. With the open-mindedness and enthusiasm that he had exhibited since his days orchestrating the Benning revolution, Marshall held out hope that they might yet come up with a plan that stood at least a better than even chance of success, a plan convincing enough to stop the British from forcing a dispersion to North Africa or the Middle East.

The next morning, Sunday, July 19, Truscott delivered copies of the British planners' proposed Cherbourg operation, including their written responses to the objections of the COHQ higher-ups, to Eisenhower's headquarters.[33] For the rest of the day and deep into the night, Eisenhower's staff thrashed out the details and put the plan into a form that Marshall could use in his forthcoming discussions with the British chiefs of staff.

* * * * *

The "Cherbourg operation" was the term used by the British to describe a proposed invasion and occupation of a peninsula in Normandy that juts northwestward into the English Channel toward the southern coast of Great Britain. The peninsula is known as both the "Cotentin" and the "Cherbourg" Peninsula. Its principal town is Cherbourg on the north coast, a major cross-Channel port, ninety miles from southern England. The Cherbourg Peninsula is roughly sixteen miles wide along its northern tip and only about sixty-five miles wide at its southern base. Because of its relatively narrow base, much of which is marshy and could be intentionally flooded by an invasion force, Mountbatten and many of his planners had recommended since March of 1942 that the Cherbourg Peninsula, with its deepwater port, was the ideal place along the entire French coast for Anglo-American forces to establish, hold, and defend a bridgehead.

By Monday morning both Eisenhower and Marshall approved a draft plan for invading the Cherbourg Peninsula, the essential elements of which were derived from the plan drawn up by the British planners. They were convinced that their plan, though obviously risky, offered the best odds of successfully achieving and sustaining a bridgehead on the French coast in the fall of 1942 that could be held through the winter and into the following spring. Armed with the Cherbourg plan, Marshall, with the support of Arnold, Spaatz, King, Eisenhower, and Truscott prepared to debate its merits with the British chiefs of staff.

Virtually all World War II historians agree that an attempt by Anglo-American forces to establish and hold through the winter a bridgehead on the Cherbourg Peninsula or anywhere else on the French coast in 1942 would have ended in disaster. Many have questioned the wisdom of

Marshall's decision to advocate the Cherbourg operation and have lauded the two civilian leaders, Churchill and Roosevelt, for rejecting his plan. Yet none of them have closely examined the plan, which resides today in the British National Archives, and the actual state of German defenses at the time. Once the details of the plan and facts concerning German strength and capabilities are presented, as they are in the ensuing pages, Marshall's judgment can be better understood. The point here is not to argue that Marshall was necessarily right to press so hard for the Cherbourg operation or that it would have succeeded. Rather, the object is to provide essential context for evaluating the "hardest-fought debate" in which Marshall, arguing in the affirmative for Cherbourg, led the fight and lost.

In July 1942, the 200 miles of coastline of the Cherbourg Peninsula were defended by a single low-quality German division, the 320th, known through British intelligence to have had little training, no combat experience, no tanks, and very little motor transport. It was equipped with pre-WWI artillery.[34] The Cherbourg operation envisioned simultaneous landings in mid-October on gently sloping Madeleine Beach (Utah Beach two years later) and two other lightly defended beaches located along the east coast of the peninsula. Based on records of weather conditions during the previous ten years, the odds of gale-force winds in the Channel in October were very low. During that month there were on average more than two periods of four consecutive days when conditions were favorable for landing operations. The beaches on the east side of the peninsula where the landings were to take place were completely sheltered from prevailing winds, which typically blew from the west in the fall. Since Hitler had not yet ordered construction of the Atlantic Wall, there were no beach obstacles and no concrete- and steel-reinforced bunkers and gun emplacements, as there were in 1944. A single company of the 17th Machine Gun Battalion, barely 150 men, was responsible for the eastern coastal sector and most of them were to the north of the proposed landing beaches. There was not a single German unit larger than a company within fifteen miles of Madeleine Beach.[35] Most units of the 320th were deployed in and around Cherbourg.

According to initial versions of the Cherbourg plan, 7,000 commandos, rangers, and specially trained infantry would begin the assault two hours before nautical twilight. They were to take out the coastal guns and secure the beaches. By dawn of the second day a total of 19,000 Allied troops, together with equipment and vehicles, were to be landed. Two columns would march north and attack the port of Cherbourg. The port featured an anchorage inside the breakwater, which the plan said would be difficult for the Germans to immobilize and block. With a capacity to unload at least 3,000 tons of supplies daily, capture of the port was crucially important to maintenance of the Allied occupation force through the winter. Elements of the northern force were also assigned to capture a German aerodrome to the east of Cherbourg in case weather precluded paratroops from doing the job. A third column was to move south and establish a defensive line from the town of Carentan southwest to the town of Lessay, blow up the locks, and flood the marshes at the base of the peninsula. Meanwhile, landings on the east coast beaches would continue. By day seven a total of three divisions were to have been landed, a force that the plan said could easily overwhelm the 320th and occupy the entire peninsula. In all, nine divisions (six British, three American) were dedicated to the operation. The U.S. pledged to add even more divisions by late November or December, when they were projected to begin arriving in Britain at the rate of two per month.[36] The Allied ground forces were to fight a defensive war along a line at the base of the peninsula through the winter and into the spring. To break through, the Germans would need almost twice as many divisions.

Intelligence sources indicated that a total of twenty-two to twenty-seven German divisions were in France and Belgium during the period of July–October of 1942.[37] In addition to the 320th, seventeen of those divisions were spread along the 1,780 miles of coastline from Belgium to Brest. All of the infantry divisions were poorly equipped, low-quality "static" divisions with limited mobility, fit only for occupation duties.[38] The division closest to the Cherbourg Peninsula, the 716th, stationed to the east in the Calvados near Caen, was one of the weakest, only lightly armed with captured French or other non-German weapons and vehicles.[39] Farther inland, the remaining infantry divisions were being refitted and readied to send back to the Eastern Front. Of the three Panzer divisions, the 7th to the south did not have enough fuel to redeploy and the 6th was about to be sent east. The 10th Panzer Division, though short of men and vehicles, was the best-equipped German division in the West.[40]

The Cherbourg plan adopted by Marshall assumed that the Germans would bring in reinforcements at the rate of one and a half divisions per day, up to a total of nine divisions, possibly including the 10th Panzer Division, then situated in the Laon-Soissons area.[41] Marshall and his planners did not know it at the time, but the Germans were reluctant to deploy their armored forces in the *bocage*—the hedgerow country of the Cherbourg Peninsula and much of the rest of Normandy.

Recognizing that a roughly even matchup of ground forces (nine German vs. ten Allied by December) meant little without consideration of airpower, the Cherbourg plan conceded that unless the Allies could either capture and use the two to three German aerodromes on the peninsula, or prevent the Luftwaffe from using air bases within range of the peninsula, there would be periods after day ten when Allied ground forces would be subject to heavy bombing.[42] The Allies allotted 1,120 fighter aircraft (62 squadrons) based in southern England to protect the troops and port in the Cherbourg Peninsula against an estimated 235 German bombers. If forced to guzzle aviation fuel from the English coast to Cherbourg and back, Allied fighters could remain over the peninsula for only ten minutes, not enough time to provide continuous coverage and chase off or shoot down enough German bombers. Similarly, if available German fighters (estimated at 352) were permitted to fly from bases in or close to the peninsula, they would have a better chance of protecting their bombers. The Cherbourg plan stressed the need for the Allies to quickly capture and make use of German aerodromes on the peninsula and to deny the use of in-range aerodromes to Luftwaffe fighters and bombers. However, it made no predictions that such efforts would succeed, and if so, when. It was this aspect of the Cherbourg operation—the adequacy of air cover—that the British chiefs targeted for criticism. For without adequate air cover the Allies and the Cherbourg port could be bombed to pieces by the Luftwaffe throughout the winter and into the spring.

* * * * *

For three exhausting days, Marshall wrangled with the British chiefs of staff over the feasibility of his Cherbourg plan. According to Field Marshal Brooke's diary entry on Monday, July 20, he did his best that day "to convince" Marshall and his colleagues that there was "no hope of such a bridgehead surviving the winter." He and his colleagues claimed there were not enough landing craft, though that argument was later overcome. Brooke also belittled the intelligence of Marshall and King, writing that "they failed to realize that such an action could only lead to the loss of some 6 divisions without achieving any results!"[43] On Tuesday Brooke tried to persuade Marshall that the weather in October would make the operation "practically impossible." Besides, he wrote, after September "the Russians might be past requiring assistance."[44] To Marshall's argument that an invasion of the Cherbourg Peninsula "would allow us to operate in France against the weakest force we can ever hope to find there," Churchill responded on Wednesday afternoon that the Germans had sufficient strength in France to "deal with anything we could do on the Continent."[45]

Accepting that Churchill, Brooke, and the rest of the British chiefs would not likely change their minds, Marshall made a statement for the record on Wednesday, saying he realized that the Cherbourg plan was "filled with hazards and not at all the operation that one would deliberately choose, if choice had been possible . . . However, there was no choice in the matter. Time was tragically against us."[46] Marshall wanted the world to know and remember that in the face of grave risks the Americans were prepared to do everything possible to prevent a Soviet collapse.

Marshall stole a few minutes that day to write a note in his own hand to Katherine on Claridge's stationery, the only known letter that he wrote to her during that crucial week. "I have been terribly, pressingly busy. The first few days I never left my rooms—was at it from 9am to 1am. Still intensely occupied. Time of return uncertain, but I hope by the end of the week . . ." He wrote of the flight, the train ride from Scotland, and lunch with Clementine Churchill and "their cute daughter." He closed with what was for him unusual tenderness. "I love you very much. I hope you are in Leesburg [Dodona] and wish I were."[47]

At 5:30 p.m. on July 22, Churchill convened a session of his War Cabinet. Marshall and King were not invited to sit in.[48] The official minutes provide the only account of this critically important meeting. At the outset Brooke said that Marshall's proposed Cherbourg operation presented two issues for consideration: whether the Allied forces could successfully land on the peninsula in October; and if so, whether the bridgehead could be maintained through the winter. As to the first, Brooke reportedly said that the landing would be "a difficult operation," but it nevertheless "held out some prospect of success in certain conditions." Coming from Brooke, this was a grudging concession that the amphibious landings on the east coast of the peninsula had a good chance of succeeding. He offered no comment about possible adverse weather conditions in October, adequacy of landing craft, the need to neutralize the nearby Channel islands, or any of the other obvious hazards.[49]

According to the minutes, Brooke informed the War Cabinet that the Germans had "about 27 divisions in France of which about 15 were in the coastal areas from Belgium to Brest." These bare facts were at least close to being correct. However, he did not disclose other key facts (known to him through reliable intelligence), namely that most of those German divisions were understrength, poorly equipped, and largely immobile. He then told the Cabinet that "a force of 6 to 10 [German] divisions could be quickly built up and brought to bear against our invading force." This prediction was consistent with the nine German divisions assumed in the Cherbourg plan. However, once again Brooke did not disclose the weaknesses and strengths of those divisions, nor did he account for the fact that under the Cherbourg plan the Allies were charged with flooding much of the base of the peninsula and establishing a defensive line well before the German divisions could be "built up and brought to bear" on the Allies. As Brooke knew, the six to eight Allied divisions that would likely defend the flood-shortened baseline, their flanks protected by the sea, would have a significant advantage over the attacking forces.

Aside from this misleading overview of enemy ground forces, the presentations of Brooke and Air Chief Portal boiled down to a single argument: that the Allied bridgehead could not be maintained through the winter because of inadequate air cover. As noted in the minutes, they each told the War Cabinet that unless the Allies could seize and make use of two or more aerodromes on the peninsula, their fighter planes based in southern England could not provide enough cover to prevent the Luftwaffe, with some 230 to 240 serviceable long-range bombers, from eventually destroying the Cherbourg port facilities ("within six months," Portal reportedly said, "the port would be a heap of ruins").[50] Keeping the port open, the two British chiefs argued, was essential to the buildup and maintenance of the ten Allied divisions and the supply of antiaircraft protection that they claimed would be needed to defend and hold the bridgehead through the winter.

Brooke and Portal, of course, were correct to stress the importance of defending the port. However, they failed to mention that by far the largest concentration of airpower anywhere in the world in 1942 was in southern England. In October the Allies were capable of sending up to 700 heavy and medium bombers to bomb the aerodromes in France where the German bomber forces were located (Brooke told the War Cabinet there were "four" such aerodromes) and to destroy rail lines and roads leading to the peninsula.[51] Apparently, no serious consideration was given to the possibility that the Allies might be able to diminish German bomber strength, thereby preventing or lessening destruction of the port.

Portal suggested that the Allies might actually succeed in capturing aerodromes on the peninsula and Channel islands from which to base and maintain fighter squadrons. In the next breath, however, he advised the War Cabinet that this would only "add to the maintenance problem" because it would require shipment to the peninsula, presumably through the main port, of six hundred antiaircraft guns together with ammunition.[52] Taking into account the myriad items that would have to be shipped into the peninsula during the bridgehead, it is hard to understand why this particular shipment was the kind of additional "maintenance problem" that would justify canceling the entire operation. If Marshall or King had been at the meeting they might have been able to address this and other arguments advanced by Portal and Brooke.

Perhaps unwittingly, Portal's final argument offered a rationale for opposing and at the same time supporting the Cherbourg operation. He told the War Cabinet that under the assumptions that the Soviets were holding on the Volga, that Rommel had been driven back in Libya, and that Germany was not engaged in major operations elsewhere, the Luftwaffe could build up a force against the Cherbourg invasion of "700 bombers and 930 fighters."[53] If true, this would be a persuasive reason to oppose the Cherbourg plan. However, as Portal knew (or should have known), his own War Office on July 15 expressed serious doubt that the Soviets would be able to hold out.[54] In addition, he vastly overstated the power of the Luftwaffe. At the time there were only about 1,500 fighters and 1,300 serviceable bombers in the entire Luftwaffe, two-thirds of which were fighting against the Red Army in Russia.[55] It is difficult to believe that the Germans would have been able to withdraw that many air assets from Russia and its other theaters to concentrate on the Cherbourg Peninsula. On the other hand, even if half true, the withdrawal of a proportionate number of bombers and fighters from the Eastern Front would be an enormous boost to the fortunes of the Red Army and could have even prevented it from collapsing. Moreover, it would present the Allied powers with an unprecedented opportunity to hurl their entire air fleet into the heart of the Luftwaffe, a chance to deal a crippling blow.

When the British chiefs concluded their presentations, Churchill was pleased. It seemed that everyone in the room opposed the Cherbourg operation. Before the prime minister had a chance to ask his War Cabinet for a formal expression of views, Clement Attlee, the Labour Party leader, asked a question. "Have the Americans worked out a definite plan?" Admiral Mountbatten, who thus far had said nothing, felt compelled to speak up, knowing that he would irritate Churchill. As recorded in the minutes, he declared that "the assault of the Cherbourg peninsula would be feasible." He went on to say that for several months he had held "the view that this was the one area of the coast on which we could stage a successful assault this year."[56] The minutes do not indicate Churchill's reaction, but he must have been upset that Mountbatten had broken ranks with the other British chiefs.

Why was Churchill so opposed to the Cherbourg plan, or, for that matter, any other cross-Channel invasion plan? Marshall later recalled that he once put that question to his "great friend," Lord Moran, the prime minister's personal physician, who replied, "'You are fighting the dead on the Somme,'" a reference to a World War I battle in which a million men were killed or wounded. Churchill had a "horror of bodies floating in the Channel," Moran claimed, and was "haunted" by the slaughter that wiped out a generation of Englishmen during the Great War.[57]

Notwithstanding Mountbatten's dissent, the War Cabinet meeting ended with a unanimous decision by its members to oppose the Cherbourg operation. Though the members also expressed unanimous support for an invasion of French North Africa in 1942, Churchill directed that Marshall be told only that the British government could not reach agreement on Cherbourg or any other plan to invade France in 1942. When he was informed that evening, Marshall was disappointed but not surprised. Eisenhower was despondent. He told his aide Harry Butcher that July 22, 1942, could go down as "the blackest day in history" if Russia was defeated by the German offensive "so alarmingly under way" and the West had done nothing to save her.[58] Both Eisenhower and Marshall were almost certain that once Allied forces were diverted to North Africa or some other place thousands of miles from France, it would not be possible to mount ROUNDUP, the main cross-Channel invasion, until 1944 at the earliest. Churchill and Brooke continued to give lip service to ROUNDUP in 1943, but they and the other British chiefs must have known that it was unlikely to come about.

* * * * *

Marshall, King, and Hopkins cabled Roosevelt, advising him of the deadlock and asking for instructions. That evening, while they awaited Roosevelt's response, the British chiefs hosted their American counterparts at a dinner at Claridge's. It could have been strained, perhaps unpleasant, since the Americans had just suffered a potentially fatal blow to their "Germany first" strategy, a diversion they thought could have disastrous consequences. Marshall, however, was warm and friendly, regarded by Brooke, his arch-antagonist, as a great gentleman.[59]

In the morning the president's response arrived. He too was not surprised by the British rejection of the Cherbourg plan. With northwest France off the table, FDR repeated his directive: American ground forces must go on the offensive in 1942 at places that would not "require [a] very long sea trip." He listed five locations in order of priority as having "the best chance of success combined with political and military usefulness." All except Norway involved extremely long sea voyages. Nevertheless, the president's first choice was "Algiers and/or Morocco" in French North Africa, thousands of miles by sea from the U.S. and Great Britain. He ordered Marshall to reach a consensus with the British. "Tell our friends we must have speed in a decision."[60]

Marshall went to his room and started writing. Hours later he emerged with a cleverly written draft agreement to be presented to the British. Marshall's proposed agreement purported to comply with Roosevelt's orders, yet at the same time it preserved a go/no go decision on what was always Marshall's primary objective: ROUNDUP, the massive 1943 cross-Channel invasion. Part 1 of the agreement required that preparations for ROUNDUP should continue. Part 2 called for landings in French North Africa in 1942, *provided* the parties understood and agreed that ROUNDUP in 1943 would be "impracticable" and that they would "definitely" assume a "defensive, encircling" posture in Europe. Part 3 stipulated that a final decision to either proceed with ROUNDUP in 1943 or invade North Africa in 1942 would be deferred until September 15 and would depend on "the situation on the Russian front."[61]

Marshall hoped that the proviso in Part 2 might cause Brooke and his British colleagues to reconsider their rejection of the Cherbourg operation, since acceptance would mean an admission, indeed an agreement, that there would be no Allied ground action in Europe until 1944 at the earliest. Equally important, acceptance by the British of a "defensive, encircling" strategy for defeating Germany could be interpreted as giving Marshall and the Americans permission to turn to the Pacific in the interim (in fact, Marshall's draft provided for the transfer of an infantry division and about 800 planes to the Pacific, which proved critical to victory on Guadalcanal). If they agreed to the language of the proviso in Part 2, the British would be on record as conceding that North Africa in 1942 would preclude ROUNDUP in 1943 and also accepting at least a temporary departure from the "Germany first" strategy, stances that Marshall knew they would be reluctant, for national security and political reasons, to take.

Surprisingly, Brooke and the other British chiefs did not hesitate to accept Marshall's proposal for going forward. They had no problem agreeing that a North Africa invasion in 1942 would preclude ROUNDUP in 1943. In fact, they were probably relieved to be free of having to pretend that ROUNDUP would not have to be postponed. Nor did they regard "defensive, encircling" as a proxy for departure from "Germany first." The War Cabinet, however, focused on this language (they aptly called it "poisonous") and initially balked.[62] Brooke said he "perspired heavily," but eventually pulled "things straight" and brought them into line.[63] By the end of the day—Friday, July 24—Brooke and the War Cabinet had approved and agreed to Marshall's plan, designated CCS 94. In his diary Brooke wrote, "We have got just what we wanted out of the USA Chiefs."[64] As far as Marshall was concerned, CCS 94 allowed him to salvage two things that he wanted. First, a final decision to either proceed with ROUNDUP in 1943 or invade North Africa in 1942 would not have to be made until September 15. Perhaps events on the Eastern Front would cause minds to change. Second, a decision to invade North Africa in 1942, once made, meant the Allies would be committed to a "defensive, encircling" European strategy, thus affording Marshall license to allocate more forces to the Pacific. Having been forbidden by his commander in chief from threatening the British with a turn to the Pacific, this time Marshall employed artful draftsmanship rather than a threat.

Harry Hopkins was not fully on board. He feared that Part 3 of CCS 94, which postponed the final go/no go decision on North Africa until September 15, would result in "procrastination and delay." Without informing Marshall and King, Hopkins circumvented normal channels and sent a message to Roosevelt through the British Embassy in Washington "very strongly" recommending that the president set a firm date for the North African invasion to be launched "not later than October 30th, 1942," because of the "dangerous situation in Russia."[65] Since Hopkins had been told that the North Africa landings would draw few if any German troops away from the Eastern Front, his stated rationale for selecting this precise date does not ring true. Indeed, it is difficult to explain this deadline other than on the basis of domestic politics: October 30 was four days before the midterm elections.

Roosevelt responded quickly. In a July 25 cable to Hopkins, Marshall, and King, FDR wrote that it was his "opinion" (he didn't say "order") that the North Africa landings should take place no later than October 30. The president asked Hopkins to tell Churchill that he was "delighted" that a final decision had been made and that it was "full speed ahead."[66] Though it was an opinion, not an order, it appeared that the president intended to unilaterally excise the go/no go date of September 15 from CCS 94. A few minutes later Roosevelt read his cable to Generals McNarney and Arnold, who happened to be in his office. McNarney almost immediately radioed a message to Marshall informing him that the September 15 deadline in CCS 94 had apparently been countermanded by the president. In the same message, McNarney also notified Marshall that the president told him he "could see no reason why" going forward with the North Africa invasion in the fall of 1942 would prevent the launch of ROUNDUP from taking place in the spring or summer of 1943.[67] Thus, the president appeared ready to override a second key provision in CCS 94 that the British and American military chiefs had all agreed to.

As noted earlier, the last line of the instructions the president gave Marshall before he left for London ordered him to reach "total agreement" with the British. Marshall carried out FDR's orders to the letter. He was about to fly back to Washington with an agreement in hand. Yet Roosevelt, probably without even reading CCS 94, was already expressing opinions and suggesting fundamental changes at odds with the agreement that the chief of staff had worked so tirelessly to nail down. Though there is no contemporary account of Marshall's reaction, he probably was at best frustrated and at worst furious. Once again his commander in chief was questioning if not ignoring his judgment, perhaps for reasons of partisan politics. Marshall understood, of course, that it was Roosevelt's prerogative to second-guess and make changes to CCS 94. He just wished that the president would be up front with him before disclosing his amendments to others.

* * * * *

"The three musketeers," the term used by Roosevelt to describe Hopkins, Marshall, and King, "arrived safely this afternoon and the wedding is still scheduled."[68] This was the president's response to a cable from Churchill saying success in London could not have been achieved without "Harry's invaluable aid," no doubt referring to Hopkins's backdoor role in establishing the October 30 deadline for the North Africa invasion.[69] The wedding of Hopkins and Louise Macy—a second marriage for her, the third for him— took place upstairs in the White House in the flower-bedecked Oval Study at noon on Thursday, July 30. Hopkins's best man was the president, who was wheeled in wearing a white linen suit and white shoes. Marshall and King, in dress uniform, were among the few guests. They excused themselves from the wedding luncheon featuring jellied salmon to attend a 2:30 meeting of the Washington branch of the CCS, the first to be presided over by Admiral William Leahy, former ambassador to Vichy France. Acting on Marshall's recommendation, Leahy had recently been appointed by the president to be his representative at meetings of the CCS and the Joint Chiefs of Staff.

Admiral Leahy opened the meeting, stating that it was "his impression" that Roosevelt and Churchill "firmly believe that the decision has already been reached" to "undertake TORCH," the optimistic new name for the invasion of French North Africa, "at the earliest possible date."[70] Sir John Dill, the British representative, concurred. Marshall did not. He patiently pointed out that as stipulated in the proviso in Part 2 of CCS 94 a decision to mount TORCH in 1942 was in effect a decision to abandon ROUNDUP in 1943. Until the president and the prime minister face up to and accept this critically important proposition and its national security implications, they cannot be deemed to have reached a final decision, he said. King supported Marshall, adding the additional point that Roosevelt and Churchill should focus on how abandonment of ROUNDUP in favor of TORCH might affect the defense of Great Britain against invasion. Both Marshall and King agreed that because of "logistic considerations" a decision to choose either TORCH or ROUNDUP should not be postponed until September 15. It should be "made almost immediately."[71]

Leahy must have been astonished that there could be a disagreement at this late date over whether such a momentous decision had or had not been made. He had no choice but to notify Roosevelt of the impasse. According to the CCS minutes Leahy said he would "tell the President that a definite decision was yet to be made."[72] Roosevelt wasted no time. At 8:30 that same evening he summoned Leahy, General Walter Bedell Smith, secretary of the Washington CCS, General Arnold, and Captain John McCrea to the Oval Study (Arnold and McCrea represented Marshall and King). Smith transcribed almost verbatim FDR's unequivocal words. "The President stated very definitely that he, as Commander-in-Chief, had made the decision that TORCH would be undertaken at the earliest possible date." TORCH was "now our principal objective," Roosevelt reportedly said, and it would "take precedence" over BOLERO-ROUNDUP. "[W]e are now, as far as the record in [sic] concerned, committed to the provisions of C.C.S. 94 . . ."[73]

The president could not have been clearer. With glacial reluctance, Marshall conceded that FDR's decision to mount TORCH had been made. Yet during most of August his letters and memos indicated that he held out hope that Roosevelt's decision could be reversed as a consequence of the "vicissitudes of war."[74] By this, he presumably meant the emergence of new hazards that would compel the North Africa operation to be canceled as too risky or developments in Europe that would render the Cherbourg operation necessary. Marshall did not directly approach the president in August and try to change his mind. Nor is there evidence that he was responsible for rumors in the press of his and King's disagreements with Roosevelt.

Sir John Dill sensed that the chief of staff and his subordinates were not devoting their "whole-hearted" support to TORCH. In a letter responding to Dill's tactful criticism, Marshall tried to cover his tracks, stating that he and the planners in the War Department "enthusiastically and effectively support" the decision made by the "Commander-in-Chief."[75] Nevertheless, it was apparent that Marshall was engaged in a form of passive resistance to Roosevelt's decision throughout the first three weeks of August.

Historian Kenneth Davis wrote that Marshall's "conduct [was] the most questionable in the whole of his great service to the nation," behavior that came very close to subverting the president's constitutional role as commander in chief of the army and navy.[76] Nigel Hamilton judged Marshall's resistance as "disgraceful," and speculated that Roosevelt had "real concerns about his loyalty and willingness to subordinate himself to civilian leadership."[77]

Did Marshall cross the line? Normally, when a president clearly states his political objective in waging war and selects a military option to meet that objective, the senior military officer is duty-bound either to loyally execute the option or resign. However, this principle of American civil-military relations, the academic godfather for which was Harvard Professor Samuel Huntington, often does not work in the real world.[78] Here, Roosevelt, without revealing his political objective, asked Marshall to present him with options to achieve a military goal—fight the Germans somewhere in 1942. The real-world problem was that the president found it difficult, or simply chose not to articulate, his political objective. If Roosevelt's purpose in advocating military action was to preserve the alliance with Great Britain, to engage American public opinion in the fight in the Atlantic as opposed to the Pacific theater, or simply to increase his party's majority in the November elections, or a combination of all three, the military option presented would most likely be North Africa. On the other hand, if his objective was to keep the Soviets in the war by drawing German forces away from the Eastern Front, to save European Jews and others from extermination, or to end the war earlier, the military options would have been a Cherbourg bridgehead or larger and larger raids and air attacks in France while continuing the buildup for the main invasion in 1943.

Roosevelt was notorious for hiding his political motives deep within his "heavily forested interior."[79] Instead of trying to draw him out, Marshall took it upon himself to judge what the president's objectives should have been, not what they apparently were. His mistake was to try to substitute his own view of the political objective that should have dictated the decision—keeping the Soviets in the war—for that of the president's. Since the president's decision to invade North Africa would do nothing to prevent a Soviet collapse—the event most likely to lose the war—Marshall sincerely believed that it posed a threat to national security and that he owed a duty to the country to resist in some fashion. For the next three weeks he came dangerously close to crossing the line.

An August 17 report from Generals Eisenhower, Patton, and Clark (the men who would command the North Africa invasion) concerning the risks and prospects of success provides perspective on why Marshall was less than enthusiastic about TORCH. Their "frank" estimate was that the "chances of overall success, including the capture of Tunis before it [could] be reinforced by the Axis, [was] considerably less than fifty percent." They predicted that the landings would encounter "considerable resistance from certain sections of [Vichy] French forces," and that success was dependent on Spain staying "absolutely neutral." Marshall requested that this gloomy assessment, together with an earlier report indicating that the Germans had already made "plans to meet a US invasion of Northwest Africa," be formally considered at a meeting of the JCS on the following day.[80] It is likely that Marshall expected Admiral Leahy to share these pessimistic reports with the president in the hope that he would change his mind about TORCH. However, whether Leahy delivered these reports to or discussed them with FDR is not known. What is known is that these reports were never formally considered by the JCS. After August 17, Marshall's resistance wound down.

On August 28, the president invited Marshall to join Hopkins and himself for lunch in the Oval Study to discuss the status of plans for TORCH, his first face-to-face meeting with his chief of staff since early August. By this time it was apparent that Marshall had abandoned his resistance, passive or otherwise, and was fully committed to carrying out the mission. Roosevelt listened without interruption as Marshall argued that in order to make TORCH a success one of the two all-American landings in French North Africa must take place outside the Mediterranean along the Atlantic coast of Morocco in the Casablanca area. This was necessary, Marshall explained, to protect against the very real possibility that Spain might become a belligerent and try to block, or allow the Germans to block, the narrow passage into and out of the Mediterranean by seizing Gibraltar. If Spain were to make such a move it would trap Allied troops inside the Mediterranean. Amphibious landings on Atlantic beaches near Casablanca would enable the establishment of land-based lines of supply and communications east along the North Africa littoral. The president agreed with and supported Marshall's reasoning. Marshall also pointed out that American troops would need additional amphibious training, which meant that the landings probably could not take place until early in November. It was probably at this point that Roosevelt clasped his hands in mock prayer and said, "Please make it before Election Day."[81]

If there was any lingering doubt, Marshall made it clear five days later that he was "all in." Consulted beforehand, he agreed to Roosevelt's proposed compromise with Churchill and his British military chiefs: in addition to all-American landings outside the Mediterranean at Casablanca and inside at Oran, there would be a third landing, this one a U.S.-British landing inside the Med at Algiers. On September 5, Churchill signed off. Roosevelt responded, "Hurrah." Churchill replied with his version of an American expression, "Okay full blast."[82] The TORCH was lit.

For Marshall the hardest-fought debate was over. But he could never forget. Remembering his advocacy of the Cherbourg plan, Marshall told his interviewers in 1949 that there was "at least a good chance of seizing and holding [the] beachhead which could have been exploited later even though [it] would probably have suffered severe attack."[83] Given his perception of the precarious situation on the Eastern Front, Marshall went to his grave believing his judgment was correct.

For Second World War historians the debate will probably never end. Some invoke the ill-fated cross-Channel raid on Dieppe in August 1942 as "proof" that the Cherbourg operation would likewise have failed and that Marshall was foolish to fight so hard for it. Others point to the temporary setback at Kasserine Pass in February 1943 as "evidence" that the inexperienced Allies would have been driven into the sea had they attempted the Cherbourg bridgehead in the fall of 1942. The Dieppe reconnaissance in force, however, proves only that a frontal assault with no bombing and bombardment prep on a heavily defended port town flanked by overlooking bluffs was likely to be repulsed (especially the case since the Dieppe assault forces were discovered by the Germans in the Channel more than an hour before they hit the beaches). Similarly, the Kasserine debacle, a war of mobility in the Tunisian mountains hundreds of miles from the landing sites, bears little resemblance to a static defense in the *bocage* along the narrow base of the Cherbourg Peninsula. The Kasserine setback was mostly due to piecemeal deployment, which destroyed unit cohesion, lengthy supply lines that left troops at the front short of essential resources, and intelligence failures. Kasserine is not evidence that the proposed Cherbourg beachhead was doomed to failure.

* * * * *

When arguing for the cross-Channel strategy Marshall used to say that if the Allies only had the "will," they would succeed.[84] As the weeks slipped by in the fall of 1942, the will of two great English-speaking nations coalesced and focused as one on mounting TORCH, the largest amphibious operation in the history of warfare. Three hundred warships, including the new battleship *Massachusetts* and four other battleships, an aircraft carrier (*Ranger*), and four escort carriers, fourteen cruisers, and almost 400 transports and cargo vessels gathered in British and American ports or prepared to sortie at sea. They were to land and support 106,000 troops and 430 tanks at nine sites along 600 miles of the coast of French North Africa. Three-quarters of the soldiers, including six divisions that had never seen combat, were Americans. The rest were British.

U.S. Navy Task Force 34 was scheduled to depart Hampton Roads, Virginia, on October 23–24 with 34,000 troops for its 4,500-mile voyage east to the Atlantic shores of Morocco. The other armada would leave the Firth of Clyde for its 2,800-mile trip south and then east through the Strait of Gibraltar into the Mediterranean, where it would deposit some 72,000 American and British troops at landing sites along the coast in and near the cities of Oran and Algiers.

Since U.S. troops would be preponderant, Churchill proposed that an American command TORCH. He nominated Marshall. However, Roosevelt was persuaded that Eisenhower, who was already in London planning the North Africa operation, should be named commander in chief of TORCH and that Marshall should remain in Washington because he was indispensable to the smooth functioning of the JCS. To command the three American divisions that would land near Casablanca in Morocco, likely to be opposed by naval forces and a number of French divisions under the command of the Vichy government, Marshall and Eisenhower selected Major General George Patton. On October 21, the day before he headed off for Hampton Roads, Patton stopped by Marshall's office in the Munitions Building. Marshall knew that Patton's brusque, overly aggressive personality offended Admiral Kent Hewitt, the commander of Task Force 34. Patton feared that Hewitt would delay or cancel the invasion because of weather, tides, or some other unexpected hazard. Marshall counseled his old friend "to influence Hewitt but not to scare him."[85] This was not the first nor would it be the last time that Marshall would try to rein in his fighting general.

An hour or so later Patton and Hewitt were at the door to the Oval Office. Roosevelt called out, "Come in, skipper and old cavalryman, and give me the good news."[86] Patton was surprised when Hewitt introduced him to the president. It turned out that Hewitt and Roosevelt were old friends, the admiral having captained the ill-fated *Indianapolis* after the election in 1936 when Roosevelt journeyed aboard her to South America. Hewitt began by outlining the TORCH operation, suggesting that they expected little opposition from French Vichy forces and expressing the hope that the Allies would win the long race to Tunisia before the Germans could send in reinforcements. Patton picked a spot to interject. In his surprisingly high, squeaky voice, he said, "Sir, all I want to tell you is this—I will leave the beaches either a conqueror or a corpse."[87] Roosevelt beamed with delight.

At about the time Hewitt's Task Force 34 was putting out to sea, a principal rationale for the invasion of North Africa—rescuing the British Eighth Army—was about to be rendered unnecessary. On the night of October 23–24, General Bernard Montgomery, having assumed command of the Eighth Army, attacked the far-outnumbered Afrika Korps at the second battle of El Alamein with a fleet of a thousand tanks, half supplied by the U.S. Over the next two weeks, his 195,000 troops sustained heavy casualties, but they inflicted a decisive defeat on Rommel's army, driving it from the field (Rommel himself was on sick leave when the offensive began). By November 4, the Afrika Korps began a 240-mile retreat west along the Libyan coast toward Tunisia.

As the two huge armadas were converging on Gibraltar, Marshall was planning a morning of duck hunting on the Potomac with General Omar Bradley. At eleven the night before, Katherine heard the War Department scrambler phone ring in her husband's bedroom. When Marshall finished the call she asked him if plans were still on for his outing with Bradley. "This matter is very important," Marshall replied. "I can't go." "Oh! Every little thing is important but you!" she erupted, and slammed the door.[88] The "matter" that Marshall could not reveal was a last-minute plea to delay the invasion. The caller had repeated a message received from Robert D. Murphy, the State Department's diplomat in Algiers. French General Henri Giraud, who was believed to be sympathetic to the Allies, had warned Murphy that if the invasion was not delayed by two weeks, French forces would oppose the landings. Giraud predicted that if the invasion "went ahead it would end in a disaster." Marshall made a quick but crucial decision—he told the caller that the invasion would proceed as planned. He explained later that he had to cancel his hunting trip in order to "see the president and tell him what I had done."[89]

A few nights later, on November 8, Katherine attended a Washington Redskins–Chicago Cardinals game at Griffith Stadium. Marshall begged off, saying he needed to stay in touch with his office. The crowd cheered when General Hap Arnold arrived with his wife, Eleanor, both joining Katherine in her box seats. While the game was in progress, an announcer stopped play and silenced the crowd. "The President of the United States of America announces the successful landing on the African Coast of an American Expeditionary Force." If Joseph Stalin had been in the audience, the next sentence would have provoked a derisive guffaw from him: "This is our Second Front."[90]

Back at Quarters One, Marshall was pleased, but he must have reflected on the fact that only three weeks after the date set for the Cherbourg operation the Allies had managed to transport and land six American divisions and 25,000 British fighters consisting of two infantry brigades and two commando units in, of all places, North Africa, thousands of miles south of Normandy. If they could accomplish such an ambitious undertaking by the first week in November, Marshall wondered, why couldn't they have mounted the Cherbourg beachhead in mid-October? Better yet, why couldn't they have waited another six months to launch the main cross-Channel invasion, all the while building up forces in England instead of dispersing troops to North Africa and the Pacific?

Late in life, Marshall blamed himself, albeit with a tinge of sarcasm. "We failed to see," he said, "that the leader in a democracy must keep the people entertained. That may sound like the wrong word but it conveys the thought ... People demand action." For this reason, Marshall lamented, the president would not permit us to wait until we were "completely ready to mount the cross-Channel invasion in 1943 ... But I could see why [Roosevelt] had to have something" in 1942.[91]

"Had to have something"—generous words for a decision that would cost the lives of tens of thousands, including one so dear to George and Katherine Marshall.

CHAPTER 10

He Ruleth His Spirit

They had come to say farewell. The Marshall family gathered under the old oaks at Dodona Manor, the antebellum hilltop house overlooking the town of Leesburg that Katherine had bought as a weekend retreat. It was Sunday afternoon, July 18, 1943. Allen, Katherine's youngest, would leave in the morning, bound for North Africa to join "Old Ironsides," the 1st Armored Division, his hopes set on commanding a tank platoon.

Allen was to be the first of the family to go off to war. He had just graduated from Fort Knox with the bars of a second lieutenant. As the boys sprawled on the lawn, bantering about which branch of the army was most important, Allen bragged that he was a tanker and that "tanks lead the fight." His older brother, Clifton, an antiaircraft gunnery officer stationed in Richmond, scoffed at Allen. "Where would the tanks be without the Antiaircraft?" The third young man on the grass, Major Jim Winn, an artillery officer married to Katherine's daughter, Molly, spoke up. "Who clears the way for the tanks?" He answered his own question—"the Field Artillery." Molly and Allen's wife, Madge, a Vassar-educated stringer for *Life* magazine, joined the jolly debate. George, sitting nearby sipping a drink, was asked to settle the argument. "I am only a lowly foot soldier," he said with a wink, "but I would say—when the fighting is at its fiercest, it is invariably the Infantry that carries the ball over for the touchdown."[1]

At dinner, Katherine served the dishes that Allen liked most. With much ceremony, Marshall opened a bottle of fine champagne that he'd brought back from the conference at Casablanca with Roosevelt and Churchill in January. The bottle, he said, came with a story—it had been stolen from the French by the Nazis, and then in turn seized by the British, who presented it to him. According to Katherine, George delivered a "truly wonderful toast" to Allen's health and success, ever his "friend indeed." After dinner, Katherine asked the clan to bring their glasses and assemble outside in front of the garage, where she handed Allen an old horseshoe that she had dug up in the garden. As they drank again to Allen's safe return he stood on a ladder in the twilight and hammered a nail into the wood facing of the garage, hanging the horseshoe points down. Someone protested that "points down" augured bad luck. With the help of Madge, Allen rehung the horseshoe with two nails, this time with points up.[2]

Katherine and Madge had both hoped that Allen, as stepson of the army chief of staff, would receive special treatment, perhaps with an assignment stateside, out of harm's way. In fact, he was afforded special treatment, but it certainly was not what they had envisioned. Allen had told his stepfather that he wanted to get into combat as soon as possible, and Marshall was happy to oblige. Though he had carefully crafted a reputation of never showing favoritism, particularly to a relative or friend, he issued a highly unusual secret order that resulted in Allen's immediate assignment to join the veterans of the 1st Armored who had survived Kasserine Pass, defeated the Germans in Tunisia, and were refitting for further action in Sicily or Italy. In a June 29 letter to Allen, Marshall confided that he had asked his aide Frank McCarthy to "change your assignment" in an "unobtrusive way." Marshall rationalized this act, telling his stepson that he felt "OK when intervening to help in a move to the front rather than the opposite."[3]

When Allen's wife and mother learned of the intervention they directed their anger at Marshall. "She [Katherine], and Madge also I believe," he wrote to Allen later, "feel *very strongly* about your going overseas at present and *resent* my offering you the opportunity. This not to be repeated. GCM."[4]

* * * * *

One of Marshall's most important but little-known achievements of the entire war came to fruition about two weeks prior to the farewell gathering for Allen at Dodona. Since the Pearl Harbor attack the chief of staff and his planners had wrestled with the problem of determining the size and shape of the army that would be needed to defeat Germany, Italy, and Japan. In mid-June 1943, a year before the invasion of France, Marshall made a chancy decision, approved by Stimson and eventually the president. He decided that a total of ninety U.S. divisions, all but two already activated, would be the "cutting edge" needed to win the global war against the Axis powers.[5] At the same time he approved completion of a previously authorized program to train and activate 273 army air force combat groups. The number of men (and some women) that would serve in these divisions and air groups, plus service and support personnel, was set at a ceiling of 7.7 million. (U.S. Army divisions during WWII consisted of roughly 15,000 men each; an air combat unit comprised three or four flying squadrons, together with ground support elements.) Marshall disclosed his decisions to the press on an "off the record" basis. They were quietly circulated throughout the War Department on July 1.[6]

The idea of limiting the number of ground troop units while doubling the army's commitment to airpower was a bold departure from the mobilization plans that existed prior to the decision to invade North Africa. Moreover, it was extremely risky. In the summer of 1943, when the army was just beginning to engage the enemy, who could possibly know what it would take to defeat Germany, Italy, and Japan?

The story of how Marshall arrived at the ninety-division cap begins in the fall of 1941. It was then that Major Albert Wedemeyer finished his part of what became known as the Victory Program, an estimate of the strength and composition of American armed forces needed to defeat Germany. Portions of Wedemeyer's report, which were leaked to Robert McCormick's *Chicago Tribune* and his cousin Cissy Patterson's *Washington Times-Herald* two days before the Pearl Harbor attack, contended that it would take 215 U.S. Army divisions to defeat the Wehrmacht. His estimate was premised on the widely accepted assumption that the Soviets would collapse and that the United States and Great Britain would be left on their own to engage upward of 300 German divisions in a land battle in Europe (German divisions consisted of roughly 10,000 troops, less than U.S. divisions). In the weeks after Pearl Harbor and throughout the first seven months of 1942, estimates varied, largely dependent on the fortunes of the Red Army, but in general U.S. mobilization planners believed it would be necessary to organize, train, and activate around 200 divisions and 115 air combat groups to defeat the three Axis powers. When the decision to invade North Africa was made at the end of July, Marshall was convinced that a cross-Channel invasion of Europe would be delayed until 1944 and that American forces would be dispersed into the Mediterranean and Pacific. For the chief of staff and his mobilization planners, it was a turning point.

Between August 1942 and the summer of 1943 a number of key events caused Marshall and his mobilization staffers to double the number of planned air combat groups and then to scale back their estimates of ground troop needs by more than 50 percent—a stunning realignment of forces. The first event took place on August 17, 1942, when a dozen B-17s in the U.S. Army Eighth Air Force bombed railroad yards near Rouen, the first attack by American bombers on Nazi-occupied Europe. This modest success fueled the hopes and ambitions of airpower advocates. By mid-September, Marshall signed off on a recommendation to expand the number of army air groups from 115 to 273, an aspirational goal that prevailed for the rest of the war.[7] Meanwhile, economists working under Simon Kuznets and Robert R. Nathan at the War Production Board circulated a 140-page report, claiming that it was not feasible for the American economy to expand fast enough to supply an army of more than 100 divisions by the end of 1943 and at the same time meet the needs of the navy, the army air force, the civilian workforce, and the British and Soviet allies who were relying on lend-lease aid. The American economy was strong but not that strong, they concluded. Kuznets, a Russian immigrant, went on to win a Nobel Prize in economics for his insights into the processes of economic growth. Nathan was an expert on industrial mobilization who founded a highly successful economic consulting firm after the war. As Marshall and his planners were digesting the implications of this report, the strategic picture brightened. With the Soviet victory at Stalingrad and the earlier defeat of Japan's navy in the Battle of Midway, it appeared by early 1943 that the Red Army had the ability to stop the German advances in Russia and the Japanese could no longer threaten India and the Middle East. In addition, the American air force was gaining air superiority over Western Europe.

Throughout the opening months of 1943, Marshall and the War Department fought battles of numbers and growth economics. The numbers of divisions and soldiers that it would take to win the war needed to be matched by the capacity of the U.S. economy to equip and transport them to the battlefields. A dizzying array of Washington agencies, boards, commissions, and committees weighed in. Six separate investigations were conducted by the Senate and House. A newspaper cartoonist depicted a frustrated Marshall running through the halls of Congress saying, "And I thought they only wanted one front." Katherine wrote that George was subjected to "endless grilling" by Congress, which she characterized as a "bitter, exhausting fight."[8] The Farm Bloc, strengthened by a resurgence of Republicans in the 78th Congress, succeeded in exempting two million agricultural workers from the draft. Almost everyone argued that the army could get by with less. However, no one wanted to risk committing to a number. "They will talk, but they won't act," quipped the War Department's director of public relations.[9]

Near the end of Trident, the Anglo-American conference that took place in Washington in the second half of May, Marshall authorized the appointment of a special committee of three army colonels to conduct an in-depth study of the number of divisions and troops needed to defeat the Axis powers. Taking into account the conclusions of the economists, the improved strategic situation, and the decision made at the Trident conference to launch Operation OVERLORD* in May 1944, the committee called for a reduction in authorized army troop strength (including service personnel) for 1943 from 8.2 million to 7.7 million. In addition, it recommended that the number of divisions remain for the time being at eighty-eight, the number already activated. The committee expressed a belief that if the Red Army in the east and the Allied bombing offensive in the west continued to be successful, twelve more divisions would probably need to be activated in order to win the war. Marshall approved the committee's recommendations. A few months later he authorized activation of two light divisions, bringing the total to ninety. However, he never activated another division and he stabilized troop strength at 7.7 million for 1944. The president took his time, but he signed off on the troop strength numbers for both 1943 and 1944.[10]

With huge land battles ahead of him in Western Europe and possibly mainland Japan, Marshall knew it was dicey to accept a ninety-division cap on his ground forces. Yet he embraced the risk, believing he could rely on air superiority (i.e., the 273 air groups), the numerical strength and resilience of the Red Army, and the quality of American arms, training, and personnel. On the eve of OVERLORD and again during the Battle of the Bulge his ninety-division gamble would be tested and criticized.

* * * * *

During the first week of August 1943, Marshall prepared for a second major showdown with the British. Prime Minister Churchill and his military chiefs were scheduled to arrive at Quebec City for the Quadrant conference with

---

* Operation ROUNDUP, the code name for the cross-Channel invasion, was renamed Operation OVERLORD about the time of the Trident conference.

their American counterparts in a few days. They had planned to meet in September, but battlefield successes and political challenges made it necessary to convene earlier. Following landings on July 10, American and British invasion forces in Sicily had advanced more quickly than anticipated and were on the verge of encircling the entire island. In Rome, Benito Mussolini was deposed and arrested on July 25, opening up the prospect of a complete capitulation by Italy, including the surrender of its armed forces and its fleet.

Once again, the British were known to be wavering on their commitment to a cross-Channel invasion of France, the "concentration of force" strategy that they had originally signed on to fifteen months earlier. At the May 1943 Trident conference, Marshall had reason to believe that he had at last brought them around. In exchange for a concession by the Americans to mount operations in the Mediterranean "best calculated to eliminate Italy from the war," the prime minister and his chiefs agreed that OVERLORD would be launched with a "target date of May 1, 1944 to secure a lodgment on the Continent from which offensive operations can be carried out." As an integral part of the agreement Marshall insisted that seven of the twenty-seven to twenty-nine divisions needed for OVERLORD would be transferred in the fall of 1943 from the Mediterranean to staging areas in Britain.[11]

In late July, Marshall learned from Secretary Stimson (who was meeting in London with Churchill), and probably from other sources as well, that the prime minster was considering covert operations in the Balkans and in other Nazi-occupied territories with the hope of fomenting a political revolt or economic collapse that would weaken the Reich. After the war Marshall told interviewers that he and the other U.S. "Joint Chiefs were ever apprehensive of further British proposals along such lines."[12] Marshall knew from experience that Churchill's Balkans strategy, like so many other schemes since TORCH, would divert manpower and resources away from what should be the Allies' top priority—the cross-Channel invasion. Churchill continued to say he supported OVERLORD. However, his heart was not in the operation.

The last time Marshall led a showdown with the British, back in July 1942, he failed. This time he was intent on succeeding. His first move, persuading the president to back him completely, was critically important. A week before the conference in Quebec was to begin, Marshall circulated a memorandum to the president and each officer who would attend the

conference. Without implicating one side or the other, the memo bluntly
asserted that since April 1942 the Allies had failed on at least three occasions
to stick to agreed decisions to "concentrate their forces" and mount a cross-
Channel invasion against the European Axis. As a result, the paper argued,
men and resources had been diverted "bit by bit" and "day by day" farther
into the Mediterranean, a secondary theater; there had been a "net decrease" in the buildup of forces and supplies in the UK for the "main and
decisive effort"; and the sheer quantity of waste from constant changes of
plans had been "terribly destructive" and "will certainly postpone victory."[13]

In fact, as the president and his joint chiefs were aware, the number of
U.S. army and air force personnel in the Mediterranean theater had exploded from a landing force of 80,000 in November 1942 to more than
700,000, reaching a peak of nine divisions and about thirty-five air groups
by September 1943. As a result, the buildup of forces in the British Isles for
the cross-Channel invasion was anemic. As late as July 31, the 29th Infantry
Division was the only major U.S. ground force in the UK. At the same time
Marshall had to meet the demands of MacArthur and others for army troops
to battle the Japanese in the Far East, where the number of divisions exceeded those deployed in the West.

Marshall went out of his way to credit the president for his decision to
mount TORCH, claiming in his memo that it "was successful and brought
about great results." Among other things, it opened the Mediterranean to
shipping, it would enable the Allies to establish air bases "far enough north
in Italy to bomb southern Germany," and it would likely result in removing
Italy from the war. Having said that, he asserted that decisive military action against Germany cannot come from the Mediterranean. It must be
launched from the UK, the only "base capable of unleashing a mass explosive air, sea and land attack directly against the German army." The Allies
had reached a "crossroads," the memo concluded. A firm decision to mount
OVERLORD in May 1944 and a determination to stick to the decision "is
now a must."[14]

Marshall's arguments were persuasive. Two days later, at a meeting in
the Oval Study with Marshall and the other joint chiefs, "the president went
the whole hog" on the subject of OVERLORD, wrote Stimson in his diary.
He "was more clear and definite than I have ever seen him since I have been
in this war." The joint chiefs were "astonished and delighted."[15]

The August 10 session had been called by Roosevelt to determine the position they would be taking at the forthcoming conference in Quebec with their British counterparts. In the dry language of the official minutes, the president directed that henceforth the "buildup and carrying out" of OVERLORD would be "the main effort," and that he was "opposed to operations into the Balkans." He confirmed that seven divisions would be withdrawn from the Mediterranean in the fall and sent to England, as previously agreed, and that they would not be replaced by an equal number of divisions sent from the U.S. More than once the president reportedly said there needed to be a "preponderance" of American forces available for OVERLORD so that he could justify and thus insist that an American as opposed to an Englishman command the cross-Channel invasion.[16]

Most of those in the room that day guessed that Marshall would be the commander. Stimson was certain. An hour or so before the president's meeting with the joint chiefs, Stimson and Roosevelt had lunch together, just the two of them. Stimson brought with him a letter to the president that he had dictated that morning in which he strongly recommended that Marshall rather than Field Marshall Brooke be placed in command of OVERLORD. After it had been typed and signed, Stimson showed it to Marshall, "in case he had any objections to it." Marshall expressed no objection, but he told Stimson not to tell the president or anyone else that he had seen the letter. During lunch the Secretary handed his letter to Roosevelt, which, according to Stimson, he read "through with very apparent interest."[17] The first point in his letter set the stage. "We cannot now rationally hope to be able to cross the Channel and come to grips with our German enemy under a British commander . . . The shadows of Passchendaele and Dunkerque still hang too heavily over the imagination" of Churchill and Brooke. "Though they have rendered lip service to the operation their hearts are not in it." Our difference with them, wrote Stimson, is a "vital difference of faith." Arguing that the U.S. "pledged" to Stalin that the Allies would open "a real second front" and warning that a breach of America's promise could result in "postwar problems," Stimson concluded with a fervent plea. "I believe the time has come when we must put our most commanding soldier in charge of this critical operation at this critical time." That soldier, of course, was General Marshall, "the man who most surely can now by his character and skill furnish the military leadership . . . in this great operation. No one knows better than I the loss in the problems of organization and world-wide strategy centered in Washington which such a solution would cause, but I see no other alternative . . ."[18]

In his diary Stimson wrote that when Roosevelt finished reading the letter he said that he too had reached the same "conclusions."[19] Did this mean that the president actually planned to appoint Marshall supreme commander of OVERLORD? Or was it simply a general endorsement of Stimson's letter? Whatever Roosevelt said or meant, Stimson was convinced that Marshall would get the command.

* * * * *

Due to heavy, overcast skies and rain, Marshall's plane from Washington to Quebec City on August 13 was forced to land in Montreal. Marshall and Admiral Leahy were driven to the old French city by limousine and checked into the Château Frontenac, a magnificent hotel perched on a bluff high above the Saint Lawrence River. All but one of the hotel's six hundred rooms had been set aside for the American and British conferees. An elderly woman in ill health who was expected to die was allowed to remain in her suite (she was still alive a year later, living in the same room, when the second Quebec conference was again held at the hotel). Marshall, Leahy, and the other American officers were assigned rooms on the top floor, the sixteenth, and every even-numbered floor down to the lobby. The British, who had already arrived via the Queen Mary and two Canadian National Railway trains from Nova Scotia to the city, were billeted on the odd-numbered floors. The Combined Chiefs of Staff would hold their meetings in the Salon Rose on the second floor, a pale pink room with a sweeping view of the Saint Lawrence. Press conferences would be held in the coffee shop.

Churchill and Roosevelt had spent a couple of days together at Hyde Park. When they arrived at Quebec City, they and a few of their aides were invited to reside in the Citadel, the Canadian governor-general's summer residence. The Citadel is an eighteenth-century military stronghold on the crest of Cape Diamond overlooking the river and the Plains of Abraham where the British defeated the French in 1789 and won Canada.

On Sunday, August 15, Churchill asked Brooke to meet with him at the Citadel a quarter hour before lunch. "I remember it as if it were yesterday," wrote Brooke years later. The two of them walked outside on the terrace, looking down on "the fateful scene of Wolfe's battle for the heights of Quebec. As Winston spoke all that scenery was swamped by a dark cloud of despair." Churchill coldly informed Brooke that when he was at Hyde Park, Hopkins, on behalf of Roosevelt, pressed hard for the appointment of Marshall as supreme commander of OVERLORD. "As far as I can gather," Brooke confided to his diary, "Winston gave in, in spite of having previously promised me the job!!" Brooke was shattered. Other than the death of his wife, Janey, it was the worst day of his life. Churchill went on to tell him that Eisenhower would replace Marshall in Washington, that British General Sir Harold Alexander would take over for Eisenhower in the Mediterranean, and that the president agreed that Mountbatten should be appointed supreme commander in southeast Asia. To Brooke it sounded like Churchill had bargained away command of OVERLORD in exchange for the appointment of British commanders in Italy and the Far East. "Not for one moment did [Churchill] realize what this meant to me," wrote Brooke. "He offered no sympathy, no regrets at having to change his mind, and dealt with the matter as if it were one of minor importance!"[20]

With little time to calm his emotions, Brooke had to chair a meeting of the Combined Chiefs of Staff that afternoon, "a most painful meeting and we settled nothing," wrote Brooke in his diary (when CCS meetings were held on British or non-U.S. soil Brooke served as chair; in Washington, Leahy was chair).[21] Marshall argued that OVERLORD should have "overriding priority" over the Italian theater and all other operations.[22] Brooke disagreed. He contended that the Italian and cross-Channel operations were interrelated, with the former intended to draw off German forces from the latter. "It is quite impossible to argue with him," wrote Brooke, "as he does not even begin to understand a strategic problem!" They were at loggerheads.[23]

At this point Field Marshall Sir John Dill stepped in, convening first with Marshall and then with Brooke in an effort to form a bridge across which they could meet. The problem, he surmised, was the term "overriding priority." Did it mean, for example, that all seven divisions would have to be withdrawn from Italy and sent to England in the fall, notwithstanding significant changes in the strategic situation that might warrant keeping some in Italy to prevent a disaster or to exploit an opportunity? Dill huddled with

Marshall. Didn't the British deserve some kind of qualifying clause to cover a change in circumstances? Dill's point secured a purchase with Marshall. Trusting Dill, the chief of staff admitted to a degree of flexibility, but he needed assurance that the British chiefs were sincere about OVERLORD and would not take advantage of slippery language. Dill went to Brooke's room after dinner on the evening of August 15. "[T]ill midnight," he "concentrated on Brooke," claiming, as mediators do, that he had just met with Marshall and found him "most unmanageable and irreconcilable."[24] Dill counseled Brooke that he needed to come to grips with the fact that the Americans simply did not trust the British and to confront that issue head-on. The next morning at breakfast Dill let it be known that the British chiefs were prepared to break the deadlock. That afternoon, August 16, Brooke cleared the Rose Salon of "all secretaries and planners"—everyone except the eight British and American chiefs—and went into closed session. According to Brooke's diary, he opened with uncharacteristic candor, "by telling them that the root of the matter was that we were not trusting each other." The Americans, he said, doubted that the British had their "full hearts" in the "cross-Channel operation next spring." The British feared that if "changed strategic conditions" caused them to insist on actions that in any way could be interpreted as lessening the priority accorded to the cross-Channel operation, they would be accused by the Americans of duplicity.[25]

Brooke's approach, brokered by Dill, eventually cleared the air. At a closed session of the CCS the next day, again with only the chiefs of staff attending, the principals agreed on compromise language that ended the deadlock.[26] Instead of stipulating that the cross-Channel operation would have "overriding priority," the chiefs agreed that as between OVERLORD and the Mediterranean, "resources will be distributed and employed with *the main object* of insuring the success of OVERLORD."[27] Referring later to this breakthrough, Brooke wrote, "I do not know what I would have done without [Dill]. He knew Marshall so well that he was able to explain to me the working of his brain. And as both Marshall and I trusted him implicitly he was the most excellent intermediary, and repeatedly brought us together again when we were at loggerheads."[28]

Marshall was aware, of course, that by agreeing to the compromise language he had given away some of his leverage. However, Brooke's willingness to frankly address the need for mutual trust—for appreciating the other side's point of view—got through to Marshall. It provided him with a measure of assurance, or perhaps just enough assurance, that the British chiefs were sincere about prioritizing OVERLORD.

Brooke's observation in his diary that night was correct. Both he and Marshall trusted Dill when he told them that they need not fear compromise. As a consequence, they came together, deciding to place renewed trust in each other. Churchill, however, who never had any personal empathy for Dill (his nickname for him was "Dilly Dally"), was not within the circle of trust.

When the meeting in the Rose Salon on the afternoon of August 17 was breaking up, "Dickie" Mountbatten (Brooke referred to him simply as "Dickie") rushed up and prevailed upon Brooke and Marshall to let him demonstrate to the chiefs his outlandish plan, backed by Churchill, for building 2,000-foot-long self-propelled floating aircraft bases out of a frozen mixture of ice and wood pulp. It was hoped that these unsinkable airfields could be motored across the Channel and used by fighter squadrons during OVERLORD. To illustrate the indestructibility of the ice-pulp mixture, known as "pykrete" after its eccentric inventor, Geoffrey Pyke, either Mountbatten or one of his assistants "pulled a revolver out of his pocket" and fired at an ordinary block of ice, which instantly shattered. He then fired a round at the unbreakable pykrete. The bullet ricocheted "like an angry bee" around the room between the legs of the chiefs.[29] "The damn fool!" Admiral King complained later. The shot "passed to nearby one of my own shins."[30] Outside the salon, one of the officers who had been excluded from the closed session, believing that it had become particularly heated, shouted, "Good heavens, they've started shooting now!!"[31]

As the Quebec portion of the Quadrant conference wound down, Marshall had reasons to be pleased. For the first time the U.S. chiefs, firmly backed by their president, had entered strategic negotiations fully prepared and with a united army-navy front. Marshall's primary goal was achieved. Aided by Dill's skillful mediation, it was agreed that the "main object" of the Anglo-American war effort would be operation OVERLORD, targeted to commence on May 1, 1944. Thus, in terms of strategic priorities, OVERLORD, aimed at the heart of Germany, was ranked first; the Far East/Pacific was second, and the Mediterranean theater was relegated to third place.

Given the preponderance of U.S. forces in the Allied coalition,

Churchill had little choice but to concede that an American should command OVERLORD, provided operations in the Med be headed by a British commander. According to Robert Sherwood, it was Churchill who strongly recommended to Roosevelt that Marshall should command the cross-Channel invasion, "because of his enormous prestige with the British Cabinet and the British people."[32] By all accounts, Roosevelt agreed. In an interview in 1956, Marshall said that a "conclusive" decision to appoint him commander was apparently made by the president at Quebec, though FDR never made any such promise directly to him.[33] Someone, however, must have told him, most likely Stimson or Hopkins, because it is clear that by the conclusion of the Quebec meetings Marshall believed he would receive the command. So did Katherine. As she wrote in her memoir, at the end of the summer or in the early fall she "bought an old second-hand trailer," and began "surreptitiously" moving furnishings from Fort Myer out Route 7 to Leesburg. By mid-September "they were all but moved out of Quarters Number One."[34] While her husband was overseas commanding the cross-Channel invasion of Europe she planned to live at Dodona.

The army chief's spirits were also boosted by battlefield successes. On August 16, while Marshall was still in Quebec, Brigadier General Lucian Truscott's 3rd Infantry Division overcame the last German resistance in Sicily, although 40,000 German and 70,000 Italian troops managed to escape across the narrow Strait of Messina to the toe of southern Italy. On the windy heights west of Messina, Truscott accepted "submission" of the city by civilian bureaucrats, but he delayed entering its gates below until his superior, General Patton, commander of the Seventh Army, arrived for the formal surrender ceremony. Patton was intent on winning his race against British General Bernard Montgomery to take Messina. When Patton arrived on the heights the next day he greeted Truscott with typical bluster. "What in the hell are you all standing around for?" Truscott responded with a grin. "We were waiting for you, General."[35] Patton's command car, at the vanguard of several vehicles, including an armored car, raced through mountain switchbacks leading to Messina. A Ranger battalion was already there with orders to keep the British from capturing the city ahead of the Americans. Patton was given a hero's welcome by citizens lining the streets of Messina. The surrender ceremony took place in the city hall piazza, interrupted by shell fire lobbed by Truscott's "Long Toms" across the straits at the retreating German and Italian troops.

* * * * *

Based on sketchy reports from army intelligence, Marshall was aware that a cataclysmic battle had been raging in Russia since early July. Known as the Battle of the Kursk Salient, it ranged over an area the size of Great Britain. Two million men, 4,000 aircraft, and 6,000 tanks fought for fifty days. It was the largest land battle in the history of warfare. German losses were appalling: 300,000 killed; 200,000 wounded, missing, or taken prisoner. By the third week of August, the Red Army seized the initiative, regained Kharkov, and crossed the Donets. The Germans fell back to the Dnieper River. There was no possibility that they could again threaten Moscow. Marshall probably could not have appreciated its significance at the time, but the Soviet victory at Kursk was decisive. Stalingrad might have marked a turning point. After Kursk, however, the "*Wehrmacht's* offensive capability" was "extinguished."[36] Most German officers on the Eastern Front believed that Germany could not win the war militarily.

In the Pacific the only battlefield successes in August 1943 that heartened Marshall were those that took place in Papua New Guinea and along the Solomon Island chain, an area vitally important to the defense of Australia–New Zealand and the maintenance of shipping lanes to the United States. In New Guinea, American and Australian forces led by MacArthur stopped a Japanese threat to nearby Australia at Milne Bay and crushed enemy ground troops in the Lae and Salamaua area. From August 6–7, Admiral William "Bull" Halsey Jr. engaged elements of the Japanese fleet and scored the navy's first night victory of the war. By the end of the month Halsey's forces controlled New Georgia and several other islands in the Solomons. As a result, the Japanese army bastion at Rabaul on the island of New Britain, home to 100,000 ground troops, was bracketed by Halsey's aircraft carriers to the east and MacArthur's ground-based bombers to the west.

Fortunately for the lives of thousands of American soldiers and airmen in the Southwest Pacific, Marshall and the other chiefs made a bold and brilliant decision at the Quadrant conference in Quebec. Since the Rabaul stronghold was about to be surrounded by superior U.S. airpower they concluded that there was no need for a bloody invasion. It could simply be bypassed—reduced, isolated, and starved by an unremitting bombing campaign. As William Manchester wrote in *American Caesar*, MacArthur took credit for the decision by the Combined Chiefs to neutralize Rabaul—indeed, for the whole idea of "island hopping" or "leapfrogging" over enemy strongpoints in the Pacific that captured the imagination of the American public. In fact, it was George Marshall, "MacArthur's strongest supporter at the [Quebec] conference," said Manchester, who pressed the strategy of bypassing Rabaul as a way to conserve manpower and resources.[37] He did this to overcome objections by the British chiefs who wanted to shut down MacArthur's Southwest Pacific

Marshall's Meeting with MacArthur in late 1943 and MacArthur's Approach to the Philippines in 1944

© 2019 Jeffrey L. Ward

command and release forces for the campaign against Germany. Due to Marshall's influence with the CCS and the president, MacArthur was allowed to continue to maintain his separate command of army and naval forces in the Southwest Pacific. His mission in the near term was to skirt Rabaul and seize the Admiralty Islands and the Bismarck Archipelago to the north, bringing him ever closer to the Philippines. Whether and when he would return were questions left hanging in the air.

* * * * *

Allen was excited, aching to get into combat. Six weeks after the farewell dinner at Dodona, he was training with veterans of the 1st Armored Division somewhere near Oran in North Africa. In an early September letter to his mother Allen wrote that he "was very lucky." He had just been assigned to I Company, an outfit decorated for its three hours of glory when it took Hill 609, "the linchpin of Axis defenses" in northern Tunisia, and drove General Jürgen von Arnim's German troops from its summit. With evident pride Allen's letter informed his mother that the leader of the assault "had 3 tanks shot out from under him" and received the Silver Star for his bravery.[38] Katherine must have wondered whether the soldiers of I Company would bring the same luck to her beloved Allen, whom she often called Beau.

At the Pentagon, General Marshall was completing his second biennial report. Much of it was written by Marshall himself on long flights and during weekends. Laced with maps and charts, the report spelled out the improvement of the Allies' strategic position in mid-1943 compared with that of a year earlier. Marshall noted in particular the rapid growth of the U.S. Army from 1.4 million men on July 1, 1941, to 7 million two years later, while signaling that it would soon level off. He praised the contributions of the 182,000 officers and nearly 2 million enlisted men in the army air forces, especially "how they have carried the war, in its most devastating form, to the enemy" in such a short time. Having built an army and air force Marshall suggested that the remaining task of the nation should be to concentrate on developing new weaponry and improving existing armaments in "preparation for great battles to come." He concluded with a blend of caution and optimism: "The end is not yet clearly in sight but victory is certain."[39]

Before releasing the report to the public, the chief of staff sent a draft to Harry Hopkins, seeking his opinion as to whether Roosevelt might object.

To justify widespread dissemination of the biennial report Marshall stated in his cover memo to Hopkins that he and his staff felt it important to "wipe from the slate" all "rumors and conjectures" about "what we did and why we did it." Once the American public has an opportunity to read the report, argued Marshall, it will be "prepared to view the great battles to come with a better understanding of all that is involved."[40]

Hearing no objection, Marshall released his report to the press in the early hours of September 8. To boost home-front morale and maximize its impact he timed the release to coincide with the Allied landings at Salerno, some 200 miles up the Italian west coast, as well as the launch of a British operation aimed at securing the Italian boot. By coincidence, General Eisenhower announced the surrender of the Italian armed forces on the same day, leaving the Germans to fight the Allies in Italy for the rest of the war.

Marshall's second biennial report, the first authoritative history of America's involvement in the war, was an instant best seller. Its reception by the media, politicians on both sides of the aisle, and the general public burnished Marshall's reputation as the most revered and trusted figure in Washington.

*   *   *   *   *

Far from the Strait of Messina and the terrible bloodshed that would follow, boatloads of unarmed Republican politicians were being ferried across the choppy straits of Mackinac in Michigan on the same long weekend—Labor Day 1943. The party that helped scuttle U.S. participation in the League of Nations after the Great War was intent on having a strong voice in shaping America's role in the postwar world, a message of international engagement that would appeal to the millions of returning veterans and the next generation of voters. If they could not take back the White House in 1944, Republicans wanted to diminish the dominance of Democrats in Congress. To achieve these goals, party unity needed to be restored by reconciling the views of prewar isolationists with those of the staunch internationalists led by Tom Dewey, governor of New York.

The gathering at the Grand Hotel on Mackinac Island that weekend marked a turning point for the Republican Party and for Michigan senator Arthur Vandenberg, who managed to bridge the divide. Grand Rapids–born Vandenberg, a hard-core anti-Roosevelt isolationist before Pearl Harbor, was perceived as moving gradually toward postwar international cooperation. For that reason, and also because he was a member of the Senate Foreign Relations Committee, the Michigan senator was picked to head the foreign policy arm of the party's Post-War Advisory Council. Perhaps he could find a middle ground and bring the party together.

Out on the long porch facing the straits, in the Terrace bar, and behind closed doors, the Republicans debated America's role in the postwar world. Should the United States participate with other nations in a global peacekeeping organization? Wouldn't this once again draw the country into foreign wars and impinge upon America's sovereignty? Vandenberg gathered the key players on each side of the argument into a small room. After sandwiches and a midafternoon request by freshman senator Bob Taft (R-OH) for a couple of bottles of bourbon and scotch, they hammered out compromise language that was turned into a document known as the Mackinac Declaration. Henceforth, the Republican Party with one voice would call for "responsible participation by the United States in [a] postwar cooperative organization among sovereign nations to prevent military aggression and to attain permanent peace with organized justice in a free world."[41] Preservation of U.S. sovereignty was essential to the compromise. With temperatures near freezing and a storm blowing in from Lake Michigan, Vandenberg and the rest of the conferees departed the island on September 9, the day General Mark Clark's Fifth Army stormed ashore at Salerno.

Back in Washington, Democrats in the Senate, who had not taken a position on postwar security, were stirred into action by the Mackinac Declaration. Chairman of the Foreign Relations Committee Tom Connally (D-TX) introduced a resolution modeled along the lines of the Mackinac charter. It ran into opposition on the floor because, among other things, it did not provide the peacekeeping organization with an enforcement mechanism. Connally reached across the aisle to Vandenberg for help. The two of them worked out language that broke the stalemate. On November 5, 1943, the resolution passed the Senate with only five dissenting votes.

Almost no one recognized it at the time, but the Mackinac Declaration and the Senate resolution midwifed by Vandenberg were the birth pangs of a new era of bipartisan foreign policy. Roosevelt was the immediate beneficiary. With the voices of the isolationists silenced, he was free to move forward with his idea of engineering a pledge by the "four powers"—the United States, Britain, the Soviet Union, and China—to establish an international peacekeeping organization. He would lay the groundwork for the United Nations at the forthcoming conferences in Cairo, Tehran, and Yalta.

As will be seen, the careers of Vandenberg and Marshall would intersect in 1947–48, the two of them forming a partnership that led to the most consequential foreign policy achievements of the postwar era.

*   *   *   *   *

On the cold, rainy morning of November 11, 1943, a quarter century since the end of the Great War, Marshall's driver dropped him off in front of Pier 1 of the Washington Navy Yard on the Anacostia River. There he joined Admiral King, Hap Arnold, and sixteen other senior generals and admirals. Sailors hauled their luggage up the gangway of King's flagship (aka "houseboat"), the 258-foot steam yacht *Dauntless*. Except for watch officers and brief stays by a few aides, King lived alone on the converted pleasure yacht, spending Sundays with his wife and two daughters, who resided at the Naval Observatory.

A few minutes after eight a.m., King gave the signal. Marshall and the others on the pier were piped aboard *Dauntless*. They were about to embark on the first leg of a wartime journey that would take them through U-boat-infested waters to North Africa and eventually to an historic meeting in Tehran with Soviet premier Joseph Stalin. *Dauntless* was striped for war with the green, blue, and gray hues of camouflage paint.

Since midsummer the president had been trying to arrange military and diplomatic meetings with Stalin and Generalissimo Chiang Kai-shek. With the success of the Soviets at Stalingrad and Kursk, the fall of Italy, and the progress of MacArthur, Halsey, and Admiral Chester Nimitz in the Pacific, the time had come to nail down once and for all the grand strategy for defeating Germany and Japan and to set the stage for a postwar peacekeeping organization. After weeks of cable traffic it was finally agreed that Roosevelt, Churchill, and their military chiefs would meet with Chiang and Madame Chiang in Cairo during the third week of November and with Stalin in Tehran for three days at the end of that month. "The whole world is watching for this meeting between the three of us," wrote Roosevelt to Stalin.[42]

Marshall knew there would be trouble in Cairo. As he suspected, Churchill was not in the circle of trust that Dill had brokered in the Rose Salon. Several days earlier the prime minister sent a worrisome cable to Roosevelt, stating that the decisions made at Quadrant "were open to very grave defects" and arguing for a complete reexamination of whether OVERLORD should go forward as planned in May 1944. With the agreed date for withdrawing seven divisions from Italy for the cross-Channel invasion looming, the British wanted to renege. The prime minister begged Roosevelt to set aside time at the Cairo conference so he could make the case for postponing OVERLORD and allocating more forces and landing craft to "Mediterranean operations." Using his prodigious powers of persuasion, Churchill hoped he could change Roosevelt's mind before they left Cairo to meet Stalin in Tehran.[43]

In broad daylight, guns manned, *Dauntless* steamed slowly down the Potomac with her priceless human cargo, the cream of the American military. Marshall was glad to leave the "hullabaloo" (his term) in Washington behind.[44] Since September, when word leaked out that he was to be sent to London to command the cross-Channel invasion, rumors began circulating that unnamed "powerful influences" were trying to "kick Marshall upstairs" and replace him with a more malleable chief of staff.[45] From Walter Reed Hospital, General Pershing wrote FDR that the transfer of Marshall "to a tactical command in England" would be a "grave error."[46] Journalists and prominent Republicans, encouraged by Admiral King, launched a campaign to persuade Roosevelt that Marshall was needed in Washington, that he was indispensable to the management of the global war effort. Marshall broke silence only once. After receiving a report of a Nazi broadcast from Paris saying he had been "dismissed" as chief of staff and replaced by Roosevelt, Marshall sent the report and the following handwritten note on War Department stationery to Hopkins: "Dear Harry: Are you responsible for pulling this fast one on me? G.C.M." Hopkins showed it to the president, who then wrote in pencil at the bottom of Marshall's note: "Dear George— Only true in part—I am now Chief of Staff *but* you are President. F.D.R."[47] Through his dry humor, "George" had edged a bit closer to the inner sanctum of "Harry" and "F.D.R."

At the mouth of the Potomac, the captain of *Dauntless* spotted the superstructure of the battleship *Iowa* riding at anchor some five miles distant out in Chesapeake Bay. By four p.m., *Dauntless* was alongside the massive warship. At the top of the battleship's accommodation ladder, Marshall and the other officers were greeted by Captain John McCrea, the president's former naval aide and curator of the White House map room. The 58,000-ton *Iowa*, bristling with 157 guns (including 9 sixteen-inchers), was brand-new, having been commissioned in late February. In addition to cabins, mess locations, and deck promenade spaces, Marshall and each of the other officers were assigned battle stations, since they would be traveling into a war zone. At 8:45 the next morning, the white presidential yacht *Potomac*, a converted Coast Guard cutter, approached *Iowa*. Using a "special brow [gangway] which was rigged from the after sun deck of the *Potomac* to the main deck of the *Iowa*," the partially paralyzed president was comfortably lifted on board.

Escorted by a screen of destroyers and a pair of "baby flattops" (small aircraft carriers), the *Iowa*, with her precious cargo, zigzagged eastward across the Atlantic at a cruising speed of twenty-five knots. On the second afternoon at sea, just after lunch, the president and his party, including King and Marshall, were on deck to witness an antiaircraft firing demonstration. Suddenly the great dreadnought lurched and changed course. An alarm bell rang, followed by the excited voice of a sailor who shouted over the ship's loudspeaker, "Torpedo defense! This is not a drill!" A number of guns from the *Iowa* and nearby destroyers fired at the wake of a torpedo six hundred yards away. A muffled underwater explosion hammered the hull of the *Iowa*. King bolted for the bridge. Captain McCrea shouted that the source of the torpedo was not a German U-boat but the U.S. destroyer *William D. Porter*, which was supposed to be protecting the huge battleship. As part of a simulated attack, two crew members on the star-crossed destroyer—thereafter nicknamed the "Willie Dee"—had accidentally fired an armed torpedo directly at the *Iowa*. Had officers on the Willie Dee not broken radio silence and warned *Iowa* in time for her to take evasive action, the battleship, with the entire wartime leadership aboard, would have taken a direct hit. King was furious. He threatened to put the captain and entire crew of the destroyer under arrest.[48] Hopkins thought it was hilarious. "Can you imagine," he wrote later, "our own escort torpedoing an American battleship—our newest and biggest—with the President of the United States aboard—along with the Chief of Staff of the Army and the Chief of Naval Operations [?] . . . I doubt if the Navy will ever hear the last of it."[49] King saw no humor in the incident. Marshall's reaction was not recorded.

Without further incident, the *Iowa* safely crossed the Atlantic, passed through the Strait of Gibraltar, and anchored at Mers el-Kébir, the great harbor six miles west of Oran, Algeria. From La Sénia airfield, about fifty miles from Oran, the president and his party, including Marshall, King, and General Eisenhower, who greeted them in Oran, flew in Douglas C-54 Skymaster transports along the North Africa coast to Tunis, where they planned to spend the night before flying on to Cairo. Having loaned "Casa Blanca," his spacious villa, to the president, Eisenhower asked Marshall and King to bunk with him in his temporary cottage at La Mersa near Carthage. That evening, Eisenhower and his young British driver, Kay Summersby, were invited to dine with the president and his sons, Elliott and Franklin Jr., who met FDR when he landed at Oran (Summersby was decorously listed as Franklin Jr.'s dinner guest, though she was seated one place from the smitten president).

Before leaving for dinner, Eisenhower sat down for a few minutes with Marshall and King for a tumbler of whiskey and water. It was anything but relaxing. With his singular lack of emotional intelligence King abruptly brought up the subject of the OVERLORD command. As if Marshall was not there, King claimed that while the president had apparently decided to give the command to Marshall, he and the other chiefs of staff wanted him to remain in Washington. Marshall "seemed embarrassed" that the touchy subject was being discussed, recalled Eisenhower.[50] Ike was likewise embarrassed, and also disappointed to be informed by King that he "would soon be giving up field command to return to Washington."[51] Marshall had had enough. "I don't see why any of us are worrying about this. President Roosevelt will have to decide on his own, and all of us will obey."[52] This was a revealing remark. It meant that Marshall had come to believe that the president still had not made up his mind and that it was no use speculating or trying to persuade him one way or the other. In effect, Marshall was saying that they should all "back off." The president would have to make the decision on his own. And under the Constitution, everyone in the military, from the top on down, *must* obey.

The next evening the sensitive subject of the OVERLORD command came up again, only this time it took place in the backseat of Eisenhower's olive-drab staff Cadillac, moments before the president boarded the "Sacred Cow," the nickname of his C-54, for Cairo. Roosevelt had spent the entire afternoon getting to know Eisenhower while they toured some of the recent battlefields near Tunis as well as those of ancient Carthage. "FDR and Ike were both engaging extroverts," wrote biographer Jean Edward Smith, "and they hit it off from the beginning." The briefing by Eisenhower about the battles and the picnic lunch in "a rare eucalyptus grove" turned into a "love-fest" between the president and the general, said Smith.[53]

There are conflicting accounts of what was said during the backseat conversation. According to Robert Sherwood, Roosevelt turned to Eisenhower and said in "his casual, seemingly offhand manner," that he wanted "'George to have the big Command'" because "'he is entitled to establish his place in history as a Great General,'" just as "'Grant, of course, and Lee, and Jackson,'" and others established theirs. "'I hate to think that 50 years from now practically nobody will know who George Marshall was.'"[54] Sherwood put quote marks around Roosevelt's words, yet he neither cited nor referred to a source. The other version of the conversation comes from Eisenhower himself. In *Crusade in Europe*, released in 1948, the same year Sherwood's book was published, Eisenhower wrote that FDR told him that "'it was dangerous to monkey with a winning team,'" meaning that he was inclined toward giving him the OVERLORD command and retaining Marshall as chief of staff in Washington.[55] Eisenhower's account appears to be more authoritative because he was there; Sherwood, who probably based his account on what Hopkins told him, was not.

It is entirely possible that while Marshall was still on the tarmac Eisenhower, ever loyal to his mentor, told him in confidence what the president had said a few minutes before in the backseat, especially the part about not disturbing "a winning team." Or perhaps Marshall had come to his own conclusion that the president was leaning toward giving Eisenhower the command of OVERLORD. Whatever Marshall's impression, late that night or the next morning he wrote a secret note to Colonel Bill Sexton, secretary to the general staff at the Pentagon: "For your eyes only, I am giving superficial consideration to the possibility of continuing on around the world instead of returning by the Atlantic . . . Have the returning courier bring me a summer cap and my khaki kepi, also a waist belt . . ."[56] Marshall was thinking about making a long overdue trip to the South Pacific tropics to see MacArthur. His note suggests that he suspected FDR was on the verge of giving the command to Eisenhower. Marshall wouldn't have written a note like this if he thought he would be going to London to assume command of OVERLORD.

Since Eisenhower did not have enough fighters under his command to escort the Sacred Cow and the other C-54s from Tunis to Cairo during daylight hours, the president and his delegation flew all night to Cairo, landing at Cairo West airfield on the morning of November 22. Roosevelt hoped that the relatively brief meetings in Cairo would be dominated by diplomatic and military matters involving China, leaving little time for Churchill to meet alone with him. In fact, he had planned it that way. China was vitally important to the war effort. Chiang's nationalist army, never an offensive threat, had managed to hold down roughly half of Japan's fighting strength since 1937 when it invaded China's vast territory. FDR's aim at Cairo was to provide Chiang with plenty of reasons to not only stay in the fight but also help the Allies retake Burma, which would reopen the overland supply route from India to China (the "Burma Road").

The president opened his diplomatic offensive by hosting a three-hour dinner for Madame and Generalissimo Chiang at Ambassador Alexander "Buffy" Kirk's elegantly appointed villa, during which he made expansive promises to keep Chiang's troops in the war and to ensure a long postwar friendship between China and the United States. Among other things, FDR assured Chiang that China would be a permanent member of the "Big Four" in what would become the Security Council of the United Nations after the war. He promised that Chinese territories seized by the Japanese would be restored, that he would support China at the talks in Tehran against Soviet territorial claims (provided the Communists would have a voice in Chiang's government), and that U.S. economic and military aid to China after the war would be given "close and practical consideration."[57] For his part, Chiang backed off of an earlier agreement to a joint Soviet-Chinese-American trusteeship for Korea because he feared a Soviet foothold in the peninsula. Instead, he advocated independence for Korea. Roosevelt agreed.

It did not take long for Marshall to be apprised of these commitments. They would have profound implications for the future. The implied assurance of economic and military aid would hamstring Marshall two years later when President Truman sent him to China as his special envoy to negotiate an end to the civil war between Chiang's Nationalists and Mao Zedong's Communists.

In private discussions at the Mena House hotel, most likely at the Chiang-Marshall luncheon on November 24, Chiang told Marshall that he would commit his troops to assist the Allies in opening the Burma Road, provided they agreed to simultaneously conduct a naval and amphibious operation in the Bay of Bengal that would draw the Japanese away from the land action in Burma and provide the Allies with a naval base to interdict Japan's supply lines to Burma. Specifically, Chiang insisted that the Allies capture the Andaman Islands off the Burma coast near Rangoon. During tea with Madame and the Generalissimo on Thanksgiving afternoon at Kirk's villa, Roosevelt promised them that the Andaman operation would be launched within the next few months, as demanded by Chiang. Unwittingly, the commander in chief's promise, dutifully backed by Marshall and King, threatened to unravel Marshall's "Germany first" global strategy for winning the war.

The next day, when the British chiefs were informed by Marshall that for political and other reasons FDR's promise "could not be interfered with," Brooke and Marshall had what Brooke described in his diary as "the father and mother of a row!"[58] It began when Brooke bluntly informed Marshall that if the Americans regarded the Andaman amphibious landings as essential, then OVERLORD must be postponed. Based on a detailed analysis, Brooke argued that there were simply not enough landing craft to mount the Andaman operation, keep OVERLORD on schedule, and at the same time capture Rhodes in the Aegean Sea (a mostly British operation that Leahy tentatively approved pending discussions with Stalin at Tehran and that Marshall opposed). Marshall hated to admit it, but Brooke was right. If the Andaman and Rhodes operations went forward, OVERLORD would have to be postponed. Brooke was not content to extract this painful admission from Marshall. He pushed further. Instead of putting off the Rhodes operation, Brooke recommended that the Andaman landings be canceled. The capture of Rhodes and other islands in the eastern Mediterranean, he and his colleagues argued, would open the way for the Soviets through the Dardanelles and "allow the full weight" of Allied resources "to be brought to bear on Germany, thus bringing the war to an end at the earliest possible date."[59] Marshall recognized at once that Brooke was a stalking horse for Churchill's Balkans strategy. As far as he was concerned, the capture of Rhodes would be only the beginning of a major shift in strategy orchestrated by Churchill that would inevitably draw the full weight of Allied forces into the mountainous Balkan states, further delaying OVERLORD and the ultimate defeat of Germany.

Marshall lost his patience, if not his temper. Recalling that moment years later, Marshall said he was "furious when [Brooke as Churchill's proxy] tried to push us further in the Mediterranean."[60] Brooke cleared the room of aides. The Combined Chiefs went into closed session. Minutes were not kept. In his diary that night Brooke wrote that the British chiefs made more progress and in the end "secured most of the points we were after."[61] In fact, other than an agreement that all operations in the Mediterranean should be under a separate command, nothing of consequence was actually decided. Backed by their commander in chief, Marshall and King refused to abandon the Andaman operation. Brooke and the other British chiefs, with the support of Churchill, put forth proposals for several operations in the eastern Mediterranean, including Rhodes, which would "necessitate a delay in the target date for OVERLORD." Everyone paid lip service to the need to build up forces in the United Kingdom for an eventual cross-Channel invasion to be launched when "there is a good prospect of success."[62]

Further discussions were suspended. They had to leave Cairo early the next morning for the flight to Tehran. With Roosevelt, Churchill, and their respective military chiefs at loggerheads, Premier Joseph Stalin held the trump card on strategy for ending the war. Would it be Marshall's version of "Germany first," the cross-Channel invasion that he had been advocating since April 1942, and if so, when? Or would Stalin insist that the Allies force their way up through the Balkans to take pressure off the left (or southern) flank of the Red Army in Romania and Poland?

Midst the days and nights of tension-filled meetings and sidebars in Cairo, Marshall managed to keep an eye on Second Lieutenant Allen Brown, who had arrived in liberated Naples with elements of the 1st Armored in early November after the Salerno landings. Marshall sent his close aide Frank McCarthy to the city to deliver to Allen a sleeping bag, letters, and candy. Marshall knew that Allen would need the sleeping bag, though he never got to Italy to visit with him that winter. According to charts of troop deployments that the chief of staff received daily, elements of Mark Clark's Fifth Army, including units in the 1st Armored Division, were moving up in late November to prepare for an attack near San Pietro Infine, the key to the Fifth Army's northward advance along Route 6 toward Cassino and then Rome.

The night before leaving Cairo for Tehran, Marshall penned a short note to Katherine. Without disclosing his location or where he was going, Marshall closed by writing, "I can give you no date for return. Trust you have no sprains, broken bones, infected scratches, etc. Goodbye my dearest. All my love, GCM."[63]

Marshall's "date for return" was dependent on the president's decision. If FDR appointed him to command OVERLORD, he would probably go directly to London and not return to Washington until after the invasion. If Roosevelt appointed Eisenhower, Marshall would fly the rest of the way around the world, stopping in the Pacific to meet with MacArthur, and would be back in Washington by Christmas.

* * * * *

Cairo West airport was shrouded in light fog when the American and British delegations began arriving around six a.m. on Saturday morning, November 27. The large crowd of travelers waited for the fog to lift. A few minutes after seven, Roosevelt's Sacred Cow and Churchill's Avro York rolled down the runway. Marshall and the rest of the entourage followed, bound for Iran and their historic meeting with Stalin.

While Marshall's plane was winging east over the deserts of Syria and the valleys of the Tigris and Euphrates rivers, Allen was slogging in the mud, rain, and sleet through the Campanian Apennines toward the village of San Pietro at the base of Monte Sammucro. To Madge he wrote that he was "optimistic" about getting home. "I wouldn't be surprised if [the war] isn't all over by early summer."[64] Had he shared that thought with "George," he would have been sternly told that it was far from over.

The Sacred Cow and the other transports began landing at Ghale Morghe Airport, a Russian army airfield near Tehran, at around three p.m. on Saturday afternoon. Mike Reilly, the burly head of the president's secret service detail, recalled that the field "was covered with American-made aircraft, recently painted with the huge red star of Russia."[65] The president and his party were driven to the American Legation on the outskirts of the city, about four miles from the center of Tehran where the Soviet Embassy and the British Legation were located. Tehran, a city of 700,000 situated in a large valley at the foot of the Alborz Mountains, was a treacherous place, home to thousands of war refugees and hundreds of Germans, some of whom were intelligence agents. Recently deposed Reza Shah Pahlavi was regarded by the Allies as a Nazi sympathizer. Marshall and the other military chiefs were driven about two miles outside the city to sprawling Camp Amirabad, headquarters of the U.S. Army's Persian Gulf Command, where they would be billeted in the bachelor officer quarters during the conference. By late 1943, there were 30,000 army personnel and upward of 60,000 U.S. civilians in Iran and Iraq building and managing port facilities, railroads, highways and aircraft, truck, and barge assembly plants to expedite the delivery of lend-lease war matériel to the Soviet Union. Marshall helped set up what became the Persian Gulf Command, which was little known but critically important to the war effort because access to Soviet ports in the North Atlantic was often cut off by U-boats and German bombers based in Norway and the transport of cargo from the U.S. West Coast to Vladivostok presented too many diplomatic and military obstacles to make it practical.

Stalin had arrived the day before. Escorted by twenty-seven fighter aircraft, the Soviet leader flew in from Baku in an SI-47, the first time he had ever flown, and the last—he was terrified of flying. Among those in his comparatively small entourage was Lavrentiy Beria and his son Sergio, who was believed to be responsible for bugging Roosevelt's quarters; Foreign Minister Molotov; Marshall Kliment Voroshilov, the only ranking military officer in the Soviet party; and Stalin's personal bodyguard of twelve imposing, heavily armed Georgians.

When Marshall, along with King and Arnold, arrived at the American Legation on Sunday morning for a meeting with the president and joint chiefs, everyone was talking about a change in plans. The night before, Stalin had sent word through Molotov that due to information concerning a possible assassination attempt by "German agents," Roosevelt and his party should relocate to safer quarters inside the walled compound of the Soviet Embassy, where the talks were to be held, rather than risk navigating the city streets each day.[66] Some of FDR's aides questioned Stalin's motives, believing the threat was a pretext—that Stalin wanted the president to be quartered inside the Soviet compound so that Sergio Beria could eavesdrop on their private conversations. Others, most important Secret Service agent Mike Reilly, felt there could be some truth to Stalin's warning; in fact, Reilly had been informed by his Soviet counterpart that six Germans who had parachuted into the area were on the loose "with a radio transmitter," though he was not told whether they were saboteurs or assassins.[67] Roosevelt was urged to avoid the risk and take shelter in the Soviet compound. He was happy to oblige, "delighted" to have an excuse to move, because his strategy all along was to build a personal relationship with Stalin. Logistics delayed their departure, however, until mid-afternoon.[68]

Near the end of a late-morning discussion with the president to strategize over the upcoming session with Stalin, Roosevelt told Marshall and the other chiefs that no more meetings involving them were planned for the rest of the day. With a free afternoon, Marshall and Arnold departed at once for the mountains to the north, which rose to a height of 14,000 feet and were partially covered with snow. High above Tehran the two men discovered the ancient water system that carried fresh water for miles through craters, shafts, and underground tunnels down to ditches and streams that ran through the streets of the city.

While Marshall and Arnold were hiking along a mountain slope, fascinated by Persian plumbing, Roosevelt and Stalin were meeting privately for the first time in a sitting room "decorated with Tsarist gilt and Communist red stars" at Roosevelt's yellow stone villa, shielded by the walls of the Soviet Embassy compound.[69] On the spur of the moment they decided to call Churchill and convene a formal meeting of the "Big Three." Staffers were dispatched to notify the military chiefs of the three nations that the first plenary session of the Tehran conference would take place at four o'clock in the embassy's spacious hall. An army messenger, riding up the steep roads in a jeep, could not locate Marshall and Arnold until after four. Since they were almost sixty miles from Tehran they missed the entire meeting. King, Leahy, and the others made it on time.

Marshall was chagrined to have missed the meeting, concerned that he may have lost opportunities to weigh in and make a difference. That evening, after listening to Admiral King's summary, he was relieved and deeply gratified. According to King, Stalin questioned the wisdom of dispersing Allied forces into the Adriatic and the Balkans, as proposed by Churchill. Instead, after listening patiently to the prime minister, he forcefully pronounced that OVERLORD should be the "basis for all 1944 operations." The president agreed that OVERLORD should not be delayed in order to permit secondary operations in the eastern Mediterranean. He also went along with Stalin's suggestion that to assist OVERLORD the Allies should launch a diversionary attack in southern France, preferably in advance of the landings in the north.[70]

Marshall felt vindicated. The Soviet leader finally tipped the scales two-to-one in favor of Marshall's version of "Germany first." There was an added bonus. Without any prompting, Stalin also pledged that after Germany was defeated the Soviets would send reinforcements to Siberia and join the U.S. and Britain in a common front against Japan. King was surprised that Stalin even brought up the subject of Japan, since the peace treaty between Japan and the Soviet Union was still in effect. Marshall was not only surprised. He was convinced, possibly for the first time, that the United States and its allies would win the global war.

The next afternoon Marshall and Arnold made sure they were on time for the staged ceremony at the Soviet Embassy. Together, they stood and watched as Churchill, in full voice, solemnly presented Stalin with the Sword of Stalingrad, "a gift from King George VI as a token of the homage of the British people." In his memoir Arnold described Stalin that day as "not tall, about 5' 4", handsome, a fine looking soldier," notwithstanding his "pockmarked face and tobacco-stained teeth."[71] Clad in a plain mustard-colored tunic and red-striped trousers with the Order of Lenin suspended by a ribbon on his chest, Stalin accepted the scarlet and gold scabbard and raised it to his lips.

A few minutes before four p.m., Marshall and Arnold reentered the great hall of the embassy where the Big Three were gathering for the second plenary session. The windows were curtained and the walls were covered with heavy tapestries. Soviet secret police were stationed along the perimeter of the hall. Marshall was directed to a chair to the right of the president. The session had hardly begun when Stalin interjected with the question few dared to ask aloud. "Who will command OVERLORD?" Roosevelt, taken aback, replied that "it had not yet been decided." With a dismissive gesture, Stalin declared, "nothing [will] come out of the operation unless one man [is] made responsible not only for the preparation but for the execution of the operation."[72] He returned to his doodling, taking a long drag on one of his Litakia cigarettes. Roosevelt leaned to his left. Leahy remembers that he whispered, "That old Bolshevik is trying to force me to give him the name of the supreme commander. I can't just tell him because I have not made up my mind."[73] Whether or not Marshall heard that remark, his expression did not change.

Marshall was the only American military officer who spoke at the second plenary session. Unlike Brooke, who carried on about several possible operations in the eastern Mediterranean and Italy, Marshall's remarks focused on OVERLORD. Marshall made it clear to Stalin that the buildup in England for OVERLORD was on "schedule as regards ground troops, air force and equipment." He added that transfers of divisions from the Mediterranean to the United Kingdom for the buildup "had virtually been completed."[74] Stalin was impressed. He had heard about Marshall's longtime advocacy of a cross-Channel invasion and he knew that he was a serious contender—perhaps the only contender—for the post of supreme commander of OVERLORD. As Marshall recalled, Stalin "pressed for me" to be given the appointment "all the time and made it quite a point" at Tehran. In what Marshall called a "sort of semi-affectionate gesture," the Soviet leader would often "stand with his hand on my shoulder" while arguing for OVERLORD and "turning the hose on Churchill."[75]

For Marshall and the other military chiefs the Tehran conference ended around midnight on November 30 in the elegant dining room of the British Legation, the crystal and silver sparkling in the candlelight. They were about to end an alcohol-fueled dinner in honor of Churchill's sixty-ninth birthday, "the high-water mark of Anglo-American-Soviet collaboration during the war," wrote Charles "Chip" Bohlen, the young American interpreter and note-taker.[76] After Stalin offered a stirring tribute to American "machines," without which "the war would have been lost," the president raised his glass for the concluding toast. "We have proved here at Teheran [sic] that . . . our nations can come together . . . for the common good . . . So as we leave this historic gathering, we can see in the sky, for the first time, that traditional symbol of hope, the rainbow."[77] He was referring to commitments made earlier that day when the CCS and the Big Three came together. It was decided that OVERLORD would be "launched during the month of May, 1944," and that it would be supported by an invasion of southern France. Stalin pledged that a large-scale offensive by the Red Army would be mounted simultaneously in the east to prevent the Germans from transferring troops to the west. And Roosevelt promised that he would appoint a commander of OVERLORD within "three or four days."[78]

While the Big Three remained in Tehran to conclude political discussions, the Combined Chiefs returned to Cairo on the morning of December 1 to figure out how they could cobble together enough LSTs (landing ships that carried tanks) and landing craft (for troops and equipment) to support three separate amphibious operations—OVERLORD and southern France plus the Andaman Islands, which had been promised to Chiang the week before. After three days of wrangling, it became apparent to the British and American chiefs, except King, that the Andaman invasion would have to be canceled or postponed. There were simply not enough LSTs and landing craft to support that operation and still meet the May 1944 deadline for OVERLORD and the landings in southern France. Marshall agreed, though he presciently warned of the military, political, and diplomatic consequences of canceling Andaman in light of Roosevelt's promise to Chiang.[79] On December 5, the president, after returning to Cairo from Tehran and having participated in the latter stages of the Combined Chiefs' debate, reluctantly decided he had to renege on his promise to Chiang. He sent a telegram to the Generalissimo informing him of the reversal and asking him whether he would still go ahead with the land campaign to help open the Burma Road. Chiang's response was to ask for a $1 billion loan.

As Barbara Tuchman wrote in *Stilwell and the American Experience in China*, Roosevelt's decision to cancel Andaman "marked a turning point, though not then recognized, in relations with China." The president had begun his trip determined to forge a successful relationship with China. At the end, she wrote, "he sacrificed Chiang Kai-shek to Stalin. He had found a new partner at the dance."[80] As Marshall would learn during his 1946 mission to China, Chiang never forgot nor forgave FDR's broken promise. If the Americans could so easily renege on this commitment, were they ever worthy of his complete trust?

Still in Cairo, ensconced in Kirk's sumptuous villa, Roosevelt had one more decision to make before he returned to Washington. He had promised Stalin that he would appoint the commander of OVERLORD in "three or four days." Near the end of the fourth day, he made his opening move. He sent Harry Hopkins over to Marshall's quarters. Hopkins's mission was to find out which way Marshall was leaning so the president could calibrate his approach to the chief of staff.

Did Marshall want the command or was he content to remain in Washington as chief of staff? If he really wanted it, the president would likely give it to him. According to Marshall's version of his encounter with the president's aide, Hopkins tipped him off, saying at the outset that the president was "in some concern of mind" over the appointment.[81] As Marshall suspected, Roosevelt was still having second thoughts, troubled by the intense lobbying of politicians and others back home, including General Pershing and Admirals King and Leahy, who claimed that relieving Marshall of his chief of staff duties and sending him to London to command OVERLORD would be seen as a demotion and would deprive the country of his vital role in the waging of global war. Marshall understood that if he wanted the command, he would need to ask for it. Or at least express an opinion. This he declined to do. Hopkins returned to Kirk's villa that night empty-handed.

The next day, December 5, Roosevelt asked Marshall to stop by his villa at midday. "After a great deal of beating around the bush," recalled Marshall, the president asked me "just what I wanted to do. Evidently it was left up to me." Marshall did not take the bait. He declined to discuss his capabilities or the pros and cons of the issue. And he did not "express any desire one way or the other." Instead, Marshall told the president, just as he did the night before to Hopkins, that he should "feel free to act in whatever way he felt was to the best interests of the country . . . and not in any way to consider my feelings." With that, the president "concluded the affair," remembered Marshall, "because he said, 'Well, I didn't feel that I could sleep at ease if you were out of Washington.'"[82] This was Roosevelt's typically oblique way of saying Marshall would remain chief of staff. Eisenhower would command OVERLORD.

There is reason to question Roosevelt's "I could not sleep at ease" rationale for denying Marshall the command. According to Churchill, while touring the pyramids together in Cairo, Roosevelt had told him that because he and the British war cabinet adamantly refused to allow Marshall to have supreme command of both OVERLORD and the Mediterranean (including Italy), "he would prefer to keep [Marshall] in Washington."[83] In other words, if Marshall had been permitted to have a sufficiently big job, his absence from Washington could have been justified politically and the president, therefore, would have found a way to soundly sleep at night. Assuming Churchill's recollection is correct, the decision by Roosevelt hinged not on Marshall's vital role in Washington but on the size and scope of his command of Allied forces overseas.

The afternoon after learning that Eisenhower would command OVERLORD, Marshall drafted in his own hand, and the next day the president signed (after inserting the word "immediate"), the following handwritten message to Stalin: "The immediate appointment of General Eisenhower to command of OVERLORD operation has been decided upon." With his customary thoughtfulness Marshall had the original retrieved from the message center. At the bottom he wrote: "Dear Eisenhower: I thought you might like to have this as a memento. It was written very hurriedly by me as the final meeting broke up yesterday, the president signing it immediately. G.C.M."[84] The note is emblematic of Marshall's magnanimous style of leadership. Eisenhower later called it "one of my most cherished mementos of World War II."[85]

Whether Marshall was crushed, merely disappointed, or relieved when the president informed him that he would not command OVERLORD will never be known for sure. No doubt he disclosed his true feelings to Katherine and possibly to Jack Dill. But neither of them chose to talk or write publicly about his emotions in the wake of the president's decision. And, of course, Marshall himself said not a word.

Stimson was among the few who suggested that Marshall must have been profoundly disappointed. In a conversation with FDR in the White House several days after the command decision was made, Stimson claimed that he had finally wrung out of Marshall an admission that he desired "above all things" to command OVERLORD. If this is accurate, and it probably is, then it required extraordinary moral discipline—strength of character—for Marshall to refrain from asking FDR for the command when he knew it would be granted. At bottom, if he truly wanted the command his refusal to ask was an act of humility, an awareness by him that his ambition to command OVERLORD, what Stimson called his "secret desire," was a selfish weakness. During the same White House conversation Roosevelt said he thought Marshall "perhaps really preferred to remain as Chief of Staff."[86] The president may have said this to justify his decision or salve his conscience. But even if Marshall, viewing the situation objectively, had come to the conclusion that he could better serve the country by staying in Washington as chief of staff, why did he remain silent instead of expressing his preference when the president asked him in Cairo? Again, it was humility, the virtue that undergirded Marshall's character. Just as it would be selfish to yield to his ambitious "secret desire" and affirmatively seek the OVERLORD command, it would be immodest and presumptuous for him to suggest that his role as chief of staff was more important than a field command. This was the code he lived by.

In that moment, the quintessential moment after the president asked him just what he wanted to do, Marshall was utterly selfless. It was Stimson, the lifelong Presbyterian, who found an apt proverb. "He that ruleth his spirit is better than he that taketh a city."[87]

CHAPTER 11

The Road to Rome

A fter the meetings in Cairo adjourned, most of the Allied leadership flew west toward their respective homes in London and Washington. Not Marshall. Twice before he had to put off trips to the Far East. With the OVERLORD command going to Eisenhower, Marshall was free to make the 10,000-mile flight east to the Pacific theater, where he planned to personally assure Douglas MacArthur that he was not forgotten and to assess for himself the situation in the general's Southwest Pacific command. Fortunately, General Richard Sutherland, MacArthur's chief of staff and alter ego, was headed in the same direction. As MacArthur's representative, Sutherland had made a presentation in Cairo to the Combined Chiefs asking them to prioritize MacArthur's drive to recapture the Philippines and to downgrade Admiral Nimitz's central Pacific offensive. He was unsuccessful, largely due to the objections of Admiral King. The chiefs continued to endorse a two-pronged island-hopping approach to the defeat of Japan.

The night before leaving Cairo, George wrote a brief note to Katherine. He would fly east in the morning, he wrote, land in Australia around December 15th, and be home by New Year's. "I have had a very hard time here—work," he continued, but he did not elaborate. Quite possibly this was in reference to how he felt about FDR's command decision. George thanked Katherine for her latest letter, especially the part about "Fleet's induction into the army," a running story the couple shared about the exploits of their hapless Dalmatian.[1] She had written that Fleet had been banished from Dodona for killing chickens and sent to Front Royal to train for a slot in the K-9 Army. The witless dog "turned out to be the worst coward," she wrote, "the dunce of the school" and "disgraced the name of Marshall."[2]

The following morning, December 8, 1943, Marshall, along with Lieutenant Colonel Frank McCarthy, his executive secretary, and General Thomas Handy, hitched a ride on Sutherland's C-54. They were joined by Admiral Charles "Savvy" Cooke, King's chief planner, and four other general officers. Shortly after they took off from Cairo, Sutherland's veteran pilot, Weldon "Dusty" Rhoades, wrote in his diary, "I have aboard more brass than I've ever hauled on one trip before." Over the Persian Gulf, Rhoades encountered turbulence. His copilot was taken ill and had to leave the cockpit. Rhoades asked Sutherland to sit in the copilot's seat. Either Sutherland or Rhoades misread the old French map they were using that expressed elevations in meters rather than feet. As a result, somewhere east of the Gulf, Rhoades narrowly avoided slamming the plane directly into a mountain, saved only by a flash of lightning that illuminated its face for a second or two. "It was the nearest I have ever come to killing myself in an airplane," he later wrote.[3] For Marshall, it was the closest he ever came to perishing in the war.

Throughout the seven-day trip, Marshall said nothing about the president's decision to confer the command of OVERLORD on Eisenhower, and his demeanor betrayed no hint of disappointment. "If he would have shown emotion to anybody except his wife, I think he would have shown it to me," recalled McCarthy, who sat with Marshall during those days and nights. "He was really a stolid man . . . a duty-bound man."[4]

The last leg of the flight was the most dangerous—more than 3,400 miles over Japanese-held territory. Thanks to the skill of Captain Rhoades, however, Marshall and his party were safely landed at Port Moresby, MacArthur's forward headquarters in Papua New Guinea. The general, however, was not there to greet them. MacArthur had flown the day before to Goodenough Island off the eastern tip of New Guinea to oversee amphibious landings by elements of General Walter Krueger's Alamo Forces on the nearby island of New Britain. Biographer Ed Cray wrote that MacArthur deliberately snubbed the chief of staff, leaving him to waste a day at Port Moresby "shelling at the beach" and chasing "kangaroos" before "impatiently" flying some 200 miles out to the island to meet with his theater commander.[5] There is no truth to these characterizations. Marshall actually spent the better part of the day on a highly informative flying tour of the New Guinea front hosted by MacArthur's air force chief, General George Kenney. Furthermore, MacArthur was not in Port Moresby to greet Marshall because he had a previous commitment to meet with Krueger on Goodenough Island to discuss his battle plans. Krueger's troops were landing the next day at Arawe and were scheduled to land at Cape Gloucester on December 26.

Perhaps because it makes for a more engaging narrative, Cray, like many other writers, suggests that there was more antipathy between MacArthur and Marshall than actually existed. In fact, there had been moments of friction, but the history of their relationship since the Great War was generally one of mutual respect. MacArthur did not regard Marshall as part of the "Chaumont crowd" who was out to get him (as MacArthur realized, if Marshall wanted to get rid of him he could have easily done so, with justification, when the heart of MacArthur's air force was destroyed on the ground at Clark and Iba airfields). For his part, Marshall insisted that all that had been written about him being "hostile" to MacArthur was "damn nonsense. I did everything in the world I could for him."[6] Since the debacle in the Philippines, Marshall had a growing regard for MacArthur's skill as a theater commander and his symbolic value to morale on the home front. He was impressed with what he observed at Port Moresby and the progress MacArthur's army forces had made against veteran Japanese troops in the "green war" up the east coast jungles of New Guinea.

On the afternoon of the 15th, Marshall and MacArthur met on Goodenough Island, the first time the two of them had seen each other since 1935, when MacArthur retired as army chief of staff. Those who were there recalled that there was no evidence of conflict or "any particular strain." The two generals were relatively "formal and restrained," showing little warmth or intimacy, although they occasionally addressed each other as "Douglas" and "George."[7] Marshall left no record of his impressions, but MacArthur in his memoir wrote that the two of them "had a long and frank discussion." As to the relative "paucity of men and material" that the Southwest Pacific command was receiving, Marshall admitted, according to MacArthur, that "he realized the imbalance and regretted it, but could do little to alter the low priority accorded the area." This reads like something close to what Marshall might say. However, in the next few sentences of his memoir MacArthur claimed that Marshall blamed it all—that is, the shortages—on Admiral King. Marshall supposedly told MacArthur that King "resented" MacArthur for the "prominent" part he had in the Pacific war, that King was "vehement in his personal criticism" of MacArthur, and that his enmity toward MacArthur influenced navy secretary Frank Knox, Admiral Leahy, the president, and even Hap Arnold.[8] These words and characterizations attributed to Marshall are so indiscreet and out of character that they could not possibly have been uttered or even suggested by him. Instead, they reflect MacArthur's well-known self-aggrandizement and paranoia.

The myth that hostility pervaded Marshall's meeting with MacArthur on Goodenough Island appears to have been spawned by William Manchester in *American Caesar*. Manchester wrote that "during their Goodenough lunch," when MacArthur "began a sentence, 'My staff—'" Marshall angrily interrupted, declaring, "You don't have a staff, General. You have a court."[9] Manchester cited Forrest Pogue's biography of Marshall as his source. The problem, however, is that Pogue's biography does not contain this quote or anything similar. And when the Manchester quote was brought to Pogue's attention, he wrote that Marshall would never have said such a thing to MacArthur.[10] Manchester's immaculate conception has been picked up and requoted by several historians and biographers, thereby perpetuating the myth.

The following morning, MacArthur accompanied Marshall back to Port Moresby, and the two men spent much of the afternoon together before Marshall departed at midnight, bound for Guadalcanal, 900 miles to the east. MacArthur had to have been pleased. The chief of staff's globe-circling odyssey to meet MacArthur and his commanders was the ultimate demonstration of personal support. As soon as Marshall returned to the Pentagon he cabled MacArthur, praising him for "the admirable organization and fighting force you have under development" in the Southwest Pacific. "I was greatly impressed by all that I saw."[11] In his memoir MacArthur wrote that Washington became "more generous" after Marshall's visit.[12] By the end of the year, Marshall promised to send MacArthur fifty P-38 pursuit planes and to increase his reserve by 20 percent. Within two months three new bombardment groups and the 1st Cavalry Division were transported to Australia for MacArthur's Southwest command.

*   *   *   *   *

While Marshall was at Guadalcanal's Henderson Field inspecting army troops and conferring with their operational commander, on the other side of the globe Allen Brown was angry, frustrated, and suffering from back spasms. Expecting to see action in the Italian Winter Line campaign near San Pietro, he found that his unit was held in reserve while three companies of the 753rd

Tank Battalion participated in a coordinated attack with infantry, the objective of which was to push beyond the village and open a corridor along Highway 6 toward Cassino. In letters to his wife, Madge, Allen complained bitterly that he was at a loss to understand why he was suddenly transferred to a company in the 13th Armored Regiment where he would have to "start all over" gaining the confidence of his men and learning to operate and maintain light tanks (he had trained for four months with medium tanks). In addition, he lamented that there were many more second lieutenants with combat experience ahead of him on the promotion lists than there were in his old regiment.[13] He desperately wanted to become a platoon leader.

It was fortunate that Allen was held in reserve. To put it mildly, the mountainous terrain around San Pietro was unsuitable for tanks. The unit that saw the most action sent fifteen medium tanks into battle, only to have them picked off by shell fire or mines, or roll over due to the treacherous topography. Only four returned. General Mark Clark's Fifth Army at San Pietro sustained 16,000 casualties before the Germans withdrew during the night of December 17 under cover of a deadly counterattack.

By the time Hollywood director John Huston and his crew arrived at San Pietro to film a reenactment of the ten-day battle and the plight of the villagers, Allen and his company had moved out. Due to its scenes of dead Allied soldiers wrapped in mattress covers and its perceived emphasis on the terrible cost of the Italian campaign, Huston's film of the battle was at first deemed unreleasable. Yet "the picture was saved" when Marshall viewed it, sometime in the summer or fall of 1944. According to historian Mark Harris, Marshall believed the film would have value if it was reshaped and used as a GI training film, its gritty realism and depiction of death an inspiration for soldiers to take their training more seriously. This was hardly an endorsement, but, as Harris wrote, Marshall's opinions were enough to cause Huston to completely recut the film.[14] Praised by movie critics, *The Battle of San Pietro* was released to theaters throughout the United States in July 1945.

On the way back to the United States, Hollywood was on Marshall's mind. Frank McCarthy remembered that when they reached Honolulu Marshall told him that since the "motion picture industry had done a great deal for the Army . . . he would like to stop in Los Angeles long enough to express his appreciation."[15] In fact, film industry leaders had reason to thank Marshall for envisioning the critical role that moviemaking could play in helping to win the war. Within days after the Pearl Harbor attack, the industry had signaled its eagerness to help, but it needed direction. Marshall intervened. In February 1942, he met with Frank Capra, three-time Academy Award winner, former head of the Academy of Motion Picture Arts and Sciences, and Hollywood's most successful director. Marshall told Capra he wanted him to make a series of short films that "would show our boys in the Army *why* we are fighting, and the *principles* for which we are fighting," movies that would be exciting enough to motivate and inspire young draftees who would have to fight the war.[16] Without compensation Capra produced a series of seven films called *Why We Fight* that were initially shown to millions of soldiers during training and later viewed in theaters by the American public. Mark Harris wrote that these movies were "the single most important filmed propaganda of the war."[17]

To show his gratitude to Capra, George Stevens, Darryl Zanuck, and other leaders of the movie industry who had donated their "finest talents . . . production and output to the troops," Marshall hosted a lunch in Los Angeles on December 21, 1943, the day after he and McCarthy landed.[18] According to Zanuck, president of Twentieth Century Fox, Marshall encouraged the moguls to begin thinking about movies to address the emotional problems and rough adjustments of the millions of veterans who would be returning home after the war to resume civilian life.[19] The industry responded to Marshall's suggestions with movies like *The Best Years of Our Lives.*

That evening Louis B. Mayer, head of Metro-Goldwyn-Mayer and at the time the highest-paid executive in the United States, organized a dinner party for Marshall involving about one hundred guests, including Katharine Hepburn, Hedy Lamarr, Greer Garson, and many other movie stars, studio executives, directors, and writers. McCarthy recalled that when dinner was announced, Mayer "invited General Marshall to select the lady of his choice" and escort her into the dining room. "The General . . . walked straight across the room to Margaret O'Brien," the seven-year-old child star, "and gallantly offered his arm. She took it and with him led the march to the dining room."[20]

* * * * *

With a planeload of wounded soldiers, Marshall landed in Washington in time for Christmas at Dodona. Over the holidays he cabled Eisenhower, suggesting that he fly back to the States to take a break, see his family, and consult with the War Department before going on to London to assume command of OVERLORD. From Algiers, where he had paused to meet with Charles de Gaulle on his way to England, Eisenhower responded that coming home in the near term was an "impossibility."[21] There was too much organizing and planning to do in London. By return cable, Marshall insisted: "It is of vast importance that you be fresh mentally and you certainly will not be if you go straight from one great problem to another. Now come on home and see your wife and trust somebody else for 20 minutes in England."[22] Eisenhower realized that this was tantamount to an order.

On the afternoon of the last day of December 1943, Marshall's sixty-third birthday, Kay Summersby drove Eisenhower to the airport in Algiers. According to her memoir published in 1976, words of mutual affection were exchanged in the car.[23] Upon parting at the airport, Ike slipped a note to Kay. "Think of me," he had written. "You know what I will be thinking."[24]

It was after one in the morning on January 2 when Eisenhower and his naval aide Harry Butcher knocked on Mamie Eisenhower's door at the Wardman Park apartments in northwest Washington. Under tight security and in strict secrecy, they had arrived in an unmarked car and rode up to her apartment in the freight elevator. Ike had been away for eighteen months. As is true of any married couple who have been separated by war for so long, the homecoming was awkward. Mamie was overjoyed to see her husband. However, she sensed within the first hours how time and the stresses of high command had changed him. He had gained weight and smoked incessantly. He seemed tense and abrupt.

Eisenhower had returned to America at a time when it seemed that the eyes of the world were locked on George Marshall. The "Man of the Year" issue of *Time* magazine, the most-read publication in the nation, had just hit the newsstands. The austere face on the cover, thinner and handsomer than it actually was, belonged to George Catlett Marshall. Beneath the portrait the caption read: "He Armed the Republic." In the background the artist had painted a likeness of the American flag with its horizontal stripes aimed at the coastline of Western Europe. The symbolism was obvious. Somewhere between Norway and Spain the American armed forces would attack from the Atlantic. It was to be Germany first. To keep the Germans guessing, Marshall wanted them to believe that the invasion of Western Europe could come at any moment. The president had already announced to the world on Christmas Eve that Eisenhower would command the invasion of Europe from England. Marshall did not want to dispel rumors that Eisenhower was in London, about to give the order to attack. For this reason, elaborate steps were taken to assure that Eisenhower's presence in Washington was not discovered by spies or leaked to the press. Wearing a civilian fedora and a plain overcoat that covered the stars on his shoulders, Eisenhower entered the Pentagon through a private entrance. Rather than meeting in Marshall's office, he was escorted to Secretary Stimson's suite, where Marshall and a few senior officers were waiting.

As Marshall and the others settled into a series of briefings for and by Eisenhower, there were not-so-subtle signs that the mentor-mentee relationship between the chief of staff and the newly appointed supreme commander of OVERLORD was beginning to shift. Subordinate in rank and seniority, Eisenhower remained deferential toward Marshall, but he was no longer awestruck. He acted, spoke, and carried himself with greater confidence and gravitas, no doubt due to his experiences wrestling with the wide range of military, political, and personnel issues that he was forced to confront in North Africa, Sicily, and Italy since leaving his desk in Washington. As *Time* wrote, George Marshall was the "closest thing to the 'indispensable man,'" in Washington.[25] In the field, however, Eisenhower was Marshall's managing partner, commanding a growing share of the voting power and almost equal equity.

In private discussions during the next few days Marshall provided Eisenhower with insights about the capabilities of commanders for the various stages of OVERLORD, but in almost every respect he accepted the judgment of the younger man, typically saying it's "your affair." Until Eisenhower had a chance to spend time in London reviewing and revising the invasion plans with General Sir Bernard Montgomery, who had left Italy to lead the Allied ground troops in OVERLORD, it was premature to finalize more than a few command decisions. Nevertheless, it was decided (or reconfirmed) that Omar Bradley, one of "Marshall's men" from the Fort Benning days, would be the senior U.S. Army group commander; Tooey Spaatz would command the strategic air force; and modest but competent Courtney Hodges, whom Marshall befriended in the Philippines, would be sent to England to "live by Bradley's side," with the thought that he would probably command an army group after the initial invasion (Marshall commented that Hodges was the

"same class of man as Bradley . . . great hunter, quiet, self-effacing . . . [t]hor-
ough understanding of ground fighting"). Based on Marshall's remark that
Lesley McNair "has a serious disability of deafness," Eisenhower decided he
should remain in Washington in command of Army Service Forces.[26]

The question of what to do about George Patton, a hot topic in Washington, undoubtedly came up. In August, the temperamental general had
slapped and publicly berated shell-shocked GIs on two separate occasions
while inspecting field hospitals in Sicily. Eisenhower had managed to keep a
lid on the incidents, at least until investigative journalist Drew Pearson, already both famous and reviled for revealing MacArthur's affair with Isabel
Rosario Cooper during the 1930s, broke the story in his Sunday evening
NBC radio program in November, reporting that Patton was reprimanded by
Eisenhower and would never have another battle command. In his report of
the incidents to Marshall, Eisenhower said that he had reprimanded Patton,
instructed him to apologize to his troops, and told him that any repetition
would result in his immediate relief. It was clear, however, that Eisenhower
believed that Patton, notwithstanding his hot temper and eccentricities, was
too valuable as an offensive-minded battle commander to keep him out of the
big show in France. Biographer Ed Cray wrote that Marshall disagreed with
Eisenhower, preferring that Patton not be given a command.[27] This is incor-
rect. On December 7, during a visit with Patton at Castelvetrano, his headquarters in Sicily, John J. McCloy, assistant secretary of war, repeated what
Marshall had told him about Patton's role in OVERLORD: "He [Patton]
will have an Army."[28] The next day the president landed in Sicily near Patton's headquarters following the second Cairo conference. According to
Mark Clark, who was there along with Marshall, Hap Arnold, and Eisenhower, the commander in chief grasped Patton's hand in the receiving line
and said to him, "General Patton, you will have an army command in the
great Normandy operation."[29] Patton, who thought he had been banished
forever, was so overwhelmed that he found a secluded spot, "looked around
to make certain he was not being watched, and then burst out sobbing."[30]

When they met in the Pentagon in early January 1944, Marshall and
Eisenhower were of one mind concerning Patton. Absent another embarrassing indiscretion, he would lead an army in OVERLORD. Eisenhower
stressed, however, that he did not intend to "advance" Patton beyond an
"army command."[31]

On Monday evening, January 3, Marshall hosted a "coming-out" dinner for Eisenhower at the Alibi Club, which was located in a narrow, rather shabby-looking three-story brick townhouse at 1806 I ("Eye") Street NW, just a few blocks from the White House.[32] Except for the green front door, the Italianate residence, built in 1869, is unobtrusive. In 1944, there was no sign indicating that the building housed a men's social club.

The Alibi Club was founded in 1884 by seven members of the nearby Metropolitan Club for the purpose, according to its first president, of relieving "what some call the monotony of domestic life and the toll of business."[33] Its name derived from a requirement that the doorkeeper provide a plausible "alibi" whenever the whereabouts of a member were questioned by the member's wife or family. Over the years, its members, limited to fifty, consisted of business and congressional leaders, Supreme Court justices, diplomats, and at least one president, George H. W. Bush. During the war, retired diplomat Robert Woods Bliss, a club member who owned Dumbarton Oaks in Georgetown and served as a consultant to Secretary of State Hull, sponsored Marshall's membership and encouraged him to use the club for entertaining small groups.

On that memorable night Marshall was the solicitous father figure, proudly introducing Eisenhower, his loyal protégé with the luminous smile, to the guests, many of whom met the new OVERLORD commander for the first time. Among those who tramped in from the snow and sleet outside were the leaders of the War Department (Stimson and two of his assistant secretaries, McCloy, and Robert Patterson), James Byrnes (head of the Office of War Mobilization, future secretary of state), Bernard Baruch (unofficial adviser on mobilization), two senators (including an influential member of the Foreign Relations Committee), three representatives (including the chair of the Military Affairs Committee), Admiral Stark (recently returned from London), and Generals Kenney and J. Lawton "Lightning Joe" Collins (just in from the Pacific). They all gathered for drinks in the small front parlor, warmed by the blaze in the fireplace. As Marshall explained later, one of his purposes was to build up Eisenhower's "position" with the men in the room, especially the "leaders of Congress . . . so that he could resist any attacks that would come with any misfortune."[34]

By the time dinner was announced everyone except Marshall was addressing Eisenhower as "Ike." Once the meal was served—on pewter plates—Marshall acted as master of ceremonies, proposing that tough, wiry Joe Collins begin by describing how his 25th Division ("Tropic Lightning") ended Japanese resistance on Guadalcanal and won the battle for Munda on New Georgia, where he earned the nickname "Lightning Joe." Collins was followed by Admiral Stark, who explained that once the U-boat peril was eliminated in May 1943 by British code-breaking and American long-range aircraft, the Battle of the Atlantic was effectively won. Marshall called on Eisenhower last, asking him to review the latest developments in Italy and the Mediterranean. According to Harry Butcher, Eisenhower held forth impressively for roughly twenty-five minutes.[35] Since he had not yet studied the plans for the cross-Channel invasion, Ike mentioned but provided no particulars on OVERLORD. Marshall ended the evening with a toast to the health of the president, who was in bed with a "touch of the flu" (or so he said).[36] They all raised their glasses to the success of General Eisenhower in the forthcoming invasion of Western Europe.

* * * * *

Amid the ruins at Carthage, Prime Minister Winston Churchill was suffering a "fever which ripened into pneumonia." Using the sobriquet "Naval Person," he cabled the president on Christmas Day 1943 with what appeared to be an innocuous request. Fifty-six LSTs scheduled to be transferred from the Mediterranean to England and refitted for OVERLORD were needed for an amphibious landing at Anzio (Italy) on or about January 20. Would it be okay, he asked, to delay the transfer for three weeks? Surely, he argued, such a brief delay would not jeopardize the sacrosanct May 1 date for the launch of OVERLORD.[37]

With the consent of Marshall, Roosevelt promptly agreed, provided the delay would not "hazard the success" of OVERLORD and the companion landings in southern France, code-named Operation ANVIL, that they had promised Stalin at Tehran; and provided further, that any operations in "Rhodes and the Aegean must be sidetracked."[38] (Marshall drafted this cable for the president.) From Morocco, where he was convalescing, Churchill wired his response to Roosevelt. "I thank God for this fine decision. I propose to stay here in the sunshine until I am quite strong again."[39]

As far as Churchill was concerned, this was a particularly "fine decision." The fifty-six LSTs would enable him to revive the proposed Anzio operation that Eisenhower had shelved as too risky shortly before leaving the Mediterranean to assume command of OVERLORD. With Eisenhower out of the picture, Churchill and his all-British team were in control of Allied operations in Italy and the rest of the Mediterranean. Field Marshal Henry Maitland "Jumbo" Wilson replaced Eisenhower as supreme commander of the Mediterranean theater. General Sir Harold Alexander was in charge of the Italian ground campaign (Mark Clark's Fifth Army was under Alexander's command). As Eisenhower wryly observed, Churchill himself "had practically taken tactical command" over operations in Italy and the Mediterranean.[40]

The Anzio invasion was a daring plan to leapfrog up the coast of Italy and land the Fifth Army's VI Corps under the command of U.S. General John Lucas on shingled beaches less than forty miles southwest of Rome. Churchill and his malleable British commanders were of the view that because this surprise move would threaten the right flank of General Albert "Smiling Al" Kesselring's German forces who were fiercely holding down Allied armies in the mountains of central and eastern Italy, Kesselring would be forced to withdraw to the north. As a result, so they believed, the stalemate in the mountains could be broken and the Allies should be able to trap the retreating Germans and quickly capture Rome, the "title deeds" to Italy, said Churchill.[41]

On the morning of January 22, the assault troops of Lucas's VI Corps, 47,000 men and 5,500 vehicles on the first day, landed unopposed, but instead of striking boldly inland and taking the high ground northeast of Anzio (the Alban Hills), Lucas hunkered down. He spent the next three days securing the beachhead. While Lucas's troops dug in, his LSTs, including the fifty-six that Churchill promised to send back to England, shuttled from ships to shore, off-loading thousands of additional troops and tons of supplies. Meanwhile, Kesselring did not react as expected. Instead of withdrawing, "Smiling Al" chose to fight for every inch of Italian territory. By the third day, portions of eight German divisions arrived from the north, their artillery raining shells down onto Lucas's exposed troops and equipment on the beaches.

As January passed into February, it became increasingly apparent that VI Corps at the Anzio beachead was hopelessly hemmed in by Kesselring. Elements of Clark's Fifth Army to the southeast were stalled around

Cassino, unable to link up with Lucas's besieged troops at Anzio. There would be no quick breakout, no dash through the Alban Hills to Rome.

A number of the LSTs ticketed for England were at the bottom of the Tyrrhenian Sea or disabled by mines and Luftwaffe bombs. Most of the rest were desperately needed to ferry replacements and supplies to the Anzio beaches and to evacuate the wounded and the dead. The remaining LSTs and other landing craft in the Mediterranean theater were being held by General Alexander for future operations in Italy. Without these landing craft Eisenhower could not possibly train the necessary numbers of assault troops and then launch OVERLORD as well as ANVIL by early May. Eisenhower and Montgomery had agreed that the OVERLORD assault waves needed to be increased to seven divisions and that ANVIL in southern France required a minimum of two. To lift this many divisions, something had to give.

The British had a ready solution. Instead of offering to provide the LSTs that they were holding in reserve in the Mediterranean, they pressed Eisenhower to cancel ANVIL. All along, Churchill and Brooke believed that it was strategically more advantageous to deploy Allied troops in Italy than in southern France. From the Pentagon, Marshall registered a strong protest. In his view, the OVERLORD and ANVIL operations were linked—the success of OVERLORD in northwest France was dependent on ANVIL, an invasion of France from the south, because it would protect Eisenhower's right flank and draw off German forces as his armies drove toward the Reich. Marshall believed that the British were trying to scuttle ANVIL in order to preserve troops and resources, including LSTs, for the Italian campaign and an eventual advance from the Adriatic Sea up into the Balkans. Furthermore, since he regarded OVERLORD and ANVIL as interdependent—a single combined operation—he suspected the British push to cancel ANVIL was their way of delaying OVERLORD, perhaps permanently.

Setting aside Marshall's suspicions, the final decision as to whether the ANVIL invasion would be mounted at the same time as OVERLORD was dictated by battlefield setbacks in Italy, not by debates with the British. By mid-March, VI Corps still had not broken out of the Anzio beachhead, even though Lucas had been relieved and replaced by General Truscott. Fifty miles to the southeast, the rest of Clark's Fifth Army was bogged down along the Gustav Line, which stretched across the waist of Italy. General Bernard "Spadger" Freyberg's 2nd New Zealand Division was about to launch another attack—the third by the Allies in the last two months—to break through the line at Cassino. Even if Freyberg succeeded, there was no chance that Clark's other forces could link up with Truscott at the Anzio beachhead until April at the very earliest. Given this reality, it became obvious that LSTs and "fresh and effective troops" could not be safely withdrawn from Italy in time to train for and launch ANVIL in late May or early June along with OVERLORD.[42] As Marshall radioed Eisenhower on March 16, "the basis for a final decision appears no better than a month ago. The only clear-cut decision [is] to cancel the ANVIL operation."[43] In fact, it was postponed, with July 10 as the target date.

* * * * *

Preserving OVERLORD was Marshall's paramount professional concern, yet he had a deep personal interest in the fighting at Cassino—his stepson Allen Brown was there. He knew Allen had temporarily joined "a New Zealand outfit" and guessed that he was taking part in General Freyberg's attack on the town of Cassino.[44] It would be weeks later before he learned what Allen had gone through while there.

Freyberg's plan was to attack the town with tanks and infantry, kill or capture German defenders, and clear a path along Highway 6 west into the Liri Valley, the route through Valmontone to Rome. Second Lieutenant Brown and the five men from the 1st Armored under his command were temporarily attached to Freyberg's division. With the aid of a T2 armored recovery vehicle—a medium Grant tank equipped with a boom and winch—Allen was to retrieve and repair disabled tanks with the aim of keeping as many in the battle as possible. Allen's wife, Madge, later recalled that she was amazed that her husband had been assigned this job because "he was an absolutely hopeless mechanic."[45]

Allen and his men were ordered to the front lines in late February, but the opening air attack on the ancient town was delayed by weather. For more than two weeks Allen endured intermittent artillery fire and played cards with a young New Zealander from Auckland, Captain Geoff Wiles, who he and his men would work with when the battle began. By the morning of March 15, the weather cleared. For three and a half hours, hundreds of

Allied aircraft pulverized Cassino with more than 2,000 bombs. That afternoon the tanks and the infantry attacked, but progress was impeded by craters and debris that blocked the narrow streets. A surprising number of German defenders survived the bombing and fought the Kiwis with skill and ferocity. At dusk, Allen and his men, along with Captain Wiles, ventured into the town to rescue and repair tanks that had thrown a track or were otherwise disabled. After dark, Allen and Wiles had to guide the T2 tank retriever through the rubble on foot, exposing themselves to sniper, mortar, and artillery fire. The tank and infantry assault on the town persisted for eight days. Allen and his crew caught a few hours of sleep during daylight hours and crept into the town each night. In his letters to Madge, Allen described a number of "miraculous escapes," including being "blown over" on his "side like a pin in a bowling alley" by the blast of a nearby artillery shell. On the fifth night at about two a.m., shrapnel from a shell injured Wiles "plus nine Maori infantrymen."[46]

In a "V-letter" scrawled on two tissue-thin squares of paper, Allen wrote his mother Katherine that "after 28 days at the front my men and I were relieved . . . we were lucky and got by." Referring to the farewell gathering at Dodona in the summer of 1943 when they were last together, Allen wrote, "Your horseshoe has been a real charm, just how much I am glad you will never know. Tell George to hurry up and end this thing."[47]

Allen was not only feeling lucky to be alive, he was proud of his performance. In a "Dear George" letter dated a few days after the Cassino operation, he wrote that he felt great satisfaction in knowing that he was able to "stand up" to his "first experience under fire." He also noted that he recommended a medal for two of his crew members in recognition of their courage.[48] Allen was hoping to receive a sign of his stepfather's approval. However, if Marshall sent a letter praising Allen for his bravery and leadership it no longer exists. There are two surviving letters that Marshall wrote to Allen touching on his actions at Cassino. One compliments him for sending interesting accounts of his "situation and experiences." The other comments on how difficult it must have been to operate tanks in the mud and mountains "of the Cassino region."[49] Neither contains a hint of praise or even a suggestion of gratitude that Allen emerged intact from his ordeal.

Allen received plenty of praise from his New Zealand brethren. Their official historian wrote that Allen and his crew did "magnificent work in getting vehicles back on their tracks and keeping all the tanks in the town in fighting trim." Nevertheless, "the Gustav Line held and the road to Rome was still closed."[50] The town of Cassino and the ruined abbey high above were not captured and secured by the Allies until the morning of May 18.

* * * * *

Amid the artillery rounds and indiscriminate bombing that pounded the Italian countryside in 1943–44, tens of thousands of citizens were driven out of their homes, desperate for food, shelter, and medical aid. A refugee crisis was at hand. In Washington, Marshall's office received an urgent appeal from the World Jewish Congress that would not only add to the refugee problems, but confront Marshall and the other joint chiefs with the moral question of when the military should engage in operations to rescue Jews who were fleeing from the Nazis or starving in concentration camps and ghettos. By late 1942, Marshall and virtually everyone else in the Roosevelt administration had known that the Nazis were engaged in a campaign to exterminate all Jews in Europe on an industrial scale. They were not, however, aware that upward of three million Jews had already been shot, gassed, or worked to death.

In response to the World Jewish Congress, a message was sent to Eisenhower at his headquarters in North Africa on November 22, 1943, the day Marshall landed in Cairo to meet with Chiang, Churchill, and FDR. This message, which was drafted in the Pentagon and signed "Marshall" by the head of Army Civil Affairs, stated that 4,000 refugees, mostly Jews, had been freed by Yugoslav partisans from Nazi concentration camps and shipped to the island of Rab off the Dalmatian coast in the northern Adriatic Sea. Because the island was likely to be recaptured by the Germans, "Marshall" asked Eisenhower whether the refugees could be either evacuated by military transport ship to Italy's southeast coast or at least furnished with funds so they could make their own arrangements to get to Italy.[51] Eisenhower responded on December 6 that southern Italy was already overloaded with "displaced persons." An operation to rescue those trapped on Rab by military transport or the provision of funds, he wrote, "might create a precedent, which would lead to other demands and the influx of large numbers of additional refugees."[52] Contrary to some accounts, Eisenhower did not claim lack of shipping or some other military concern as a reason for refusing to rescue the Jews. Instead, by asserting that the Rab rescue operation should be scrubbed because it might encourage others and lead to major refugee management problems, it appears that Eisenhower's bloodless recommendation, if adopted as army policy, would stray beyond the civil-military boundary.

Preoccupied with meetings in Cairo and Tehran, Marshall did not personally respond to Eisenhower's recommendation. Instead, by letter dated December 15, 1943, the joint chiefs (presumably including Marshall's designee) stated that after consulting with Eisenhower they "determined that the *military situation* does not permit the military authorities to render any direct assistance to these refugees at this time."[53] By adding "military situation" to their reasons for refusing assistance, the joint chiefs sought to step back from Eisenhower's incursion into the province of civilian authority. Nevertheless, their failure to define or limit the breadth of the term provided them with a convenient way to deflect—that is, to deny—any and all future requests to rescue Jews.

As of late December, when Marshall finally returned to Washington, the joint chiefs appeared to have adopted a practice of citing "military situation" or a similar phrase as a reason for denying requests to participate or assist in rescue operations. If the chief of staff was inclined to modify this practice, he could have weighed in shortly after January 22, 1944, when the president created the War Refugee Board. On that day Roosevelt issued an executive order declaring that the State, Treasury, and War Departments henceforth had a "duty" to assist the new board in rescuing "with all possible speed…the victims of enemy oppression."[54] The principle "victims," as everyone knew, were Jews. The idea of a government rescue agency had been promoted since the previous July. However, it was Secretary Henry Morgenthau and three courageous lawyers in Morgenthau's Treasury Department (Josiah Dubois, Randolph Paul, and John Pehle) who moved the ailing president to establish the War Refugee Board. In a seminal meeting with FDR, Morgenthau presented a report prepared by the three lawyers proving without a doubt that for at least the past two years the State Department had deliberately and willfully procrastinated and prevented the "rescue of the Jews" through bureaucratic restrictions and subterfuges.[55] Roosevelt was convinced. He "glanced at the proposed Executive Order" and suggested that Secretary of War Stimson should serve as a member of the board along with Morgenthau and Hull.[56] In doing so the commander in chief underscored his intention that the U.S. military should participate in rescuing the Jews.

Six days after the War Refugee Board was created, the office of the chief of staff, and probably Marshall himself, was presented with what some would characterize as a humanitarian opportunity. Others would call it a diversion from the war effort. Acting at the request of Morgenthau, Assistant Secretary of War John J. McCloy asked General Joe McNarney, one of Marshall's deputies, if the office of the chief of staff would be willing to instruct "theater commanders" to cooperate with the new board in "doing everything possible, *consistent with the successful prosecution of the war,*" to help rescue the Jews of Europe.[57] Marshall could have stepped in and responded in the affirmative, saying he would take it up with the Combined Chiefs of Staff, the only body with authority to instruct theater commanders. He did not. Instead, McNarney, most likely with Marshall's concurrence, responded in the negative, stating his "concern" over the military's involvement in rescue operations while the war was still on.[58] He said he would submit the matter to the Combined Chiefs. There is no evidence that he ever did.

The record is not clear, but at some point in early February of 1944, Marshall, the other joint chiefs, and representatives of the War Department either met secretly or conferred by telephone and adopted the following policy: since speedy defeat of the Axis is the best way to save the Jews, the U.S. military will not use "combat units" (including air and sea forces) in rescue operations "unless the rescues are the direct result of military operations."[59] Even though this policy was far more restrictive than that set forth in the president's executive order, it was accepted by Morgenthau, Hull, and John Pehle, acting director of the War Refugee Board. The president, who was ill for much of the winter and spring, did not push back.

In late February Marshall was once again drawn into a question of whether military concerns should trump Jewish lives. This time it involved a Senate resolution sponsored by Senators Wagner and Taft that called upon the U.S. to support the "free entry of Jews" into Palestine and reconstitute Palestine as a "Jewish commonwealth." The chief of staff was asked to present his views to the Senate Foreign Relations Committee in a closed hearing (it was not transcribed). Relying on a memo prepared by McCloy, Marshall objected to the resolution because it advocated establishment of a

Jewish state and promoted unlimited immigration (though he probably did not object to temporary camps in Palestine for Jewish refugees). According to Marshall's report of his testimony, he told the senators that passage of the resolution would likely cause the Arabs in the region to engage in hostilities against Jews already settled in Palestine and against American civilian and military citizens in the area. This would mean that Allied forces needed in other theaters would have to be garrisoned in Palestine. In addition, he claimed that U.S. policy favoring a Jewish state would probably cause the Arabs to cease providing vital logistical and military support for Allied operations in the Mediterranean. Senator Vandenberg probed Marshall on whether his concerns were hypothetical or real. Marshall responded that there was a "serious probability" of an adverse reaction from the Arabs if the resolution was passed. That satisfied Vandenberg. The rest of the senators on the Foreign Relations Committee "said they had heard enough and would vote against the resolution."[60]

Given Marshall's position as chief of staff in the midst of global war and his forty years in the army, it is perhaps understandable that military concerns would override his sympathies for the plight of the Jews in Europe. Moreover, since early 1942, he was convinced that the fastest and only way to win the global war was to launch a risky cross-Channel invasion aimed at the heart of Germany—"Germany first." Everything else, even the rescue of the Jews, was regarded by him as secondary, a diversion from the war effort. Yet when pressed by Churchill, Roosevelt, and the joint chiefs in the past, there were occasions when Marshall had shown a willingness to compromise, to deviate from his singular objective. In the case of the doomed Jews he surely could have called upon noncombat personnel or a slice of the seemingly unlimited army appropriations to support and fund rescue operations.

Was there something else lurking beneath Marshall's impenetrable reserve that was contributing to his negative attitude? It's possible, though there are few clues. In his book subtitled *Anti-Semitic Politics of the U.S. Army*, Joseph Bendersky wrote that a number of those at the "top of the military hierarchy" before and during World War II "harbored negative views on Jews" that may have influenced Marshall. However, Bendersky hastened to add that the chief of staff's "real thoughts" and "perspectives" left "those around him wondering."[61] Certainly Marshall shared some of the same prejudices and attitudes toward Jews that were held by the generation of army officers and civilians who were his friends and associates for decades. Yet he was not in the least hostile toward Jews, nor was he invested with the nativist sentiments that many of his colleagues embraced in the 1920s. In Marshall's fifty-plus years of correspondence his only mention of Jewish heritage was made around the time he was being asked to participate in rescuing the Jews. It appeared in a chatty letter to Katherine dated December 29, 1943. In the midst of a sentence about holiday gifts, Marshall wrote, "a turkey is due New Years from a Jew hunting friend of mine."[62] The reference was not meant to be pejorative. It was almost certainly a humorous and affectionate reference to Bernard Baruch, a wealthy financier who usually sent Marshall a freshly killed bird during the holidays, and the only Jew whom Marshall is known to have befriended. He later called Baruch "a dear friend," a term he used sparingly.[63]

Marshall's friendship with Baruch was not established until he was almost sixty years old. Very few Jews lived in Uniontown when Marshall was growing up, and there is no evidence that Marshall or his family associated with any of them. The first synagogue, Tree of Life, was not founded until February 1902. At VMI, Jewish cadets were rare (the first and most famous, Moses Jacob Ezekiel, fought with the cadets at the Battle of New Market in the Civil War). In the army Marshall must have encountered enlisted men who were Jews, especially in the Great War, but Jewish officers were few in number (Mark Clark, whose mother was a Romanian Jew, was one of the few, though Clark was baptized an Episcopalian at West Point's chapel when he was a cadet). Harry Truman's religious and racial tolerance as president famously took root in World War I when he formed a lifelong friendship with Sergeant Eddie Jacobson. As a young man Marshall never had a similar experience.

Friendship engenders empathy. Had Marshall associated with and become close friends with Jews earlier in life, the latent prejudices that he probably had toward them might have faded or even disappeared. He might have been more open to devising ways for the army to assist in rescue initiatives without interfering with his principal goal—winning the war.

The bottom line is that Marshall and the other chiefs did not act to provide material assistance to the War Refugee Board in its efforts to rescue the Jews in Europe. Marshall's civilian boss, Secretary of War Stimson, agreed

to cooperate with the board as long as it did not impinge upon military operations and resources. Stimson's designated liaison to the board, Assistant
Secretary McCloy, penned a note to Marshall's office saying, "I am very
chary of getting the Army involved in [rescue operations] while the war is
on."[64] McCloy's biographer, Kai Bird, wrote that McCloy's attitude toward
the board from its inception was one of "benign obstruction."[65] In late
March, a few days before cardiologist Dr. Howard Bruenn concluded that
FDR was suffering from congestive heart failure, the president released a
statement originally drafted by the board that called on the free peoples of
Europe and Asia to open their frontiers temporarily to refugees. As regards
the U.S., election year politics caused Roosevelt to permit just a token opening in the iron doors of American immigration policy. Only 982 refugees,
mostly Jews from southern Italy, were admitted in August and housed at a
camp in upstate New York. After that, the doors were closed.

Nevertheless, through bribery, forgery, diplomatic prodding, public pressure campaigns, and other actions, the War Refugee Board managed to
rescue an estimated 200,000 Jews. This was an impressive number for an
agency that was underfunded and short-staffed. But as board director John
Pehle said later when the scope and enormity of the Holocaust was revealed,
"What we did was little enough. It was late . . . Late and little, I would say."[66]

* * * * *

The president's health continued to decline. During the last week of March
1944, his temperature spiked to a dangerous 104 degrees. He was in bed
much of the time, too exhausted to focus on decisions involving the military.
On April 8, he secretly departed Washington near midnight for a one-
month attempt to recuperate at Bernard Baruch's estate in South Carolina.
The public was told that he was recovering from a "persistent mild bronchial
condition" following an attack of influenza.[67] As a consequence, matters of
global war strategy that FDR would typically weigh in on were effectively
left in the hands of General Marshall.

For the first time Churchill could not go over or around Marshall and
work his rhetorical magic on the president. The chief of staff had insisted
that infantry divisions and a number of landing craft be withdrawn from Italy so that ANVIL, the invasion of southern France, could be launched by
July 10, the new target date. As if this was not enough to upset Churchill, he

could not understand why Marshall had expressed the view that the AN-VIL operation was strategically more important than the taking of Rome. From the standpoint of strategy and psychology, Churchill believed that "All turned on the capture of Rome."[68] Cables flew back and forth. The British chiefs lined up with Churchill. Finally, the deadlock was broken on April 19 after General Alexander, the supreme commander in Italy, reorganized the Allied armies and announced a plan to launch an all-out offensive in May to break through the Gustav Line at Cassino and link up with the forces besieged at the Anzio beachhead. Persuaded that this would provide the greatest assistance to OVERLORD by containing the maximum number of German divisions in the Mediterranean, Marshall agreed to yet another delay of ANVIL while continuing to insist on that operation or, alternatively, an equally advantageous support operation in Italy.

During April there was a lull in the fighting in Italy. It took almost the entire month for General Alexander to shift the British Eighth Army from the Adriatic coast to take over the front at Cassino while units of the U.S. Fifth Army under Mark Clark withdrew from Cassino and moved west to mass along the Italian coast for the linkup to the Anzio bridgehead. In his postwar memoir Clark wrote that Marshall instructed him to return to Washington for "consultation" before renewal of the Allied offensive.[69] In fact, it was Clark who asked Marshall (via General Jacob Devers) for permission to return to the States for a visit of "approximately two weeks." He had been away for almost two years. Marshall approved Clark's request, though he said it "comes at a most inopportune moment," because he and the other joint chiefs were pressing Alexander to resume the offensive earlier than his target date of May 10.[70] The longer the lull in Italy, reasoned Marshall, the greater chance the Germans would move more divisions to France, thus threatening the success of OVERLORD.

When Clark's plane landed in Washington at three a.m. on April 11, he was met by Frank McCarthy, who handed him a letter from Marshall. The letter outlined the special arrangements Marshall had made for Clark's visit, including a week with his wife, Maurine ("Renie"), in a cottage at the Greenbrier Hotel in West Virginia that had been taken over by the army. The principal purpose of the letter, however, was to stress the need for strict secrecy. Marshall had reason to be concerned. Clark was known to be a compulsive self-promoter who had already "drawn sharp rebukes from

Marshall and Eisenhower."[71] Marshall was well aware that Renie traveled the country, touting Clark's accomplishments at war bond drives and in appearances before women's groups, causing an outbreak of titters and sarcasm in army circles. She made the mistake of sending a note to Marshall to assure him that her husband was "trying" his best in Italy, along with a boastful letter from Clark to her.[72] Marshall abhorred self-promotion. He chastised Katherine in January for being photographed by the *New York World-Telegram* while eating doughnuts with Renie following a war bond talk.[73]

In a note to the president advising him that Clark had arrived home, Marshall underscored his concern about secrecy. If the Germans learned that Clark was in the U.S., he wrote, "it would be a definite indication" either of Clark's "relief" or that "no offensive operations" in Italy by the Allies would take place in the near term.[74] On April 18, Clark flew to meet with FDR in South Carolina. Based on notes by Admiral Leahy, who was there, Clark expressed hope that the offensive planned for mid-May would succeed "in driving back the German troops." He told the president that a major problem was coordination of the multiple nationalities that comprised the Allied forces, "many of them of inferior quality compared with the Germans" and "having their own ideas as to how the campaign should be conducted." Leahy gave no indication that FDR encouraged or ordered Clark to be the first to enter Rome. Indeed, his notes do not even mention the capture of Rome.[75] Clark later claimed in his memoir that he "explained *our* plans for reaching Rome."[76] It is not clear from the word "our" whether Clark meant his own Fifth Army plans or the plans for the combined Allied forces dictated by British General Alexander, the supreme commander for Italy. Given Clark's controversial mid-battle decision to ignore General Alexander's order, this ambiguity may have been intentional.

Near the end of Clark's ten-day furlough, Marshall risked a breach of security. Just as he had done for Eisenhower, he arranged an evening at the Alibi Club for Clark to meet with key politicians. This time Marshall assembled an even more impressive guest list that included Speaker Sam Rayburn, Vice President Henry Wallace, and a carefully selected bipartisan group of five senators and eight representatives who virtually controlled the legislative branch of the government.[77] While there is no known contemporaneous report of what Clark actually said, Clark later wrote in his memoir that at Marshall's request to "tell everything," he explained to the congressmen "exactly how *we* were going to capture Rome."[78] His words imply that Clark openly expressed his intention to capture Rome and that Marshall was fully on board.

Under orders not to go outside, Clark spent his last two nights with his wife and her mother at Renie's Kennedy-Warren apartment before departing for Italy. He carried with him letters and packages for Marshall's stepsons, Allen and Clifton (also in Italy, serving with an antiaircraft unit).

* * * * *

With OVERLORD less than a month away, the wisdom of Marshall's risky decision to cap the nation's ground forces at ninety divisions was put to the test. On May 10, Stimson presented Marshall with a compelling case for lifting the cap. In a memo titled "Our Military Reserves," the secretary of war argued that after OVERLORD was mounted in early June the U.S. would not be able to match the fifty-six German divisions estimated to be available in France until the end of the summer at the earliest.[79] And when all of the divisions earmarked for OVERLORD departed American shores, the nation would be left with only fourteen uncommitted divisions, a reserve that barely exceeded that of the Germans. The Soviets were a long way from the German frontier, wrote Stimson. They could decide to halt when they regained their lost territories. As happened in Italy, a stalemate could develop in France in November when winter weather would begin to neutralize U.S. air strength and degrade the maneuverability of Allied ground troops. Wouldn't it be prudent, inquired Stimson, to seek legislation from Congress to fund and activate additional army divisions?

In discussions with Stimson that ensued, Marshall treated the secretary's request with the seriousness and depth of analysis it surely deserved. Millions of lives, perhaps the outcome of the war and the peace that followed, depended on the chief of staff's decision. On May 16, Marshall informed Stimson in writing that he was adhering to his ninety-division cap, a decision based on facts and faith that historian Maurice Matloff called "one of the boldest calculations of the war."[80] Marshall explained that he was sticking with his ninety-division plan primarily because of Allied airpower, the fact that Stalin assured Ambassador Harriman that the Soviets would not halt until Germany was defeated, and his judgment concerning the qualitative as opposed to quantitative superiority of U.S. ground combat units. Regarding the latter factor, Marshall stressed the advantages of his system of sending trained replacements to the front to keep combat divisions in the line at full strength, the high standard of infantry training, and the quality and preponderance of American equipment, especially artillery.

Another factor must have influenced Marshall's decision, though it was not mentioned in his written explanation to Stimson. The army's manpower needs had to be balanced against the huge workforce required to maintain America's role as the arsenal of democracy for coalition warfare. As Matloff noted, there "were limits to [the army's] slice of the manpower pie."[81]

Stimson backed down. However, he continued to believe the ninety-division cap was dangerous. His anxiety was rekindled in December 1944 during the Battle of the Bulge when the Germans broke through the Ardennes and threatened the enormous supply dump at Liège and the harbor at Antwerp. To meet this challenge, the strategic reserve of infantry divisions in the U.S. was almost wiped out. Marshall stood firm. By the time Japan surrendered in August 1945, all of the eighty-nine active divisions were deployed abroad (the 2nd Cavalry Division had already been inactivated).

The question of whether Marshall's ninety-division gamble was the product of wisdom, luck, or a happy combination of the two can never be answered. In May of 1944, when he doubled down on the cap, there were so many unknowns. He could not be certain that OVERLORD would succeed or that the Soviets would follow through with promises to defeat Germany and then declare war against Japan. He had no way of knowing whether the Manhattan Project would produce any functioning atomic bombs, much less two. Yet after carefully weighing the knowns and the unknowns he had the self-confidence to make the fateful decision. His judgment was vindicated.

* * * * *

Second Lieutenant Allen Brown finally got what he wanted. After his steady performance under fire with the Kiwis at Cassino he was returned to the 1st Armored Division and placed in command of a platoon of five tanks. By early May Allen's unit became part of Lucian Truscott's VI Corps at the Anzio beachhead. "My luck has run out in poker," wrote Allen to Madge. "I am living in a dugout with my tank gunner about four feet underground . . .

shelter-halfs lined around the walls keep the dirt from falling on the beds when shells hit . . . Sixty sand bags around the top . . . Pretty comfortable."[82]

Allen and everyone at Anzio knew that a major attempt to break out was imminent. On May 18, the British Eighth Army finally smashed through the Gustav Line at Cassino and was moving north on Route 6 up the valley of the Liri River. Along the west coast of Italy, General Geoffrey Keyes's II Corps fought its way from the south and was close to linking up with Truscott at the beachhead, thus uniting both corps of Mark Clark's Fifth Army.

The time had come for VI Corps to end the four-month siege at Anzio and play its part in the overall strategy for the Italian campaign. Like Marshall, British General Sir Harold Alexander, the supreme commander in Italy, did not regard Rome as the main strategic goal in Italy. Instead, he believed the primary objective should be to compel the Germans to draw divisions away from France and into Italy, thereby assisting OVERLORD. Accordingly, Alexander ordered that after breaking out of the beachhead VI Corps should drive to the northeast to block the enemy's path of retreat up Highway 6 at the town of Valmontone. By trapping and threatening annihilation of Kesselring's army, reasoned Alexander, the German high command would be forced to divert troops from France or perhaps the Eastern Front, either of which would hasten the defeat of Germany.

Clark assured Alexander that VI Corps of his Fifth Army would strike northeast as ordered. However, in his memoir, Truscott, who commanded VI Corps, wrote that Clark remarked to him privately that "'the capture of Rome is the only important objective.'" Truscott further wrote that Clark was "fearful that the British were laying devious plans to be first in Rome," and ordered him to be prepared to "fight" either toward the northeast, as dictated by Alexander, or northwest through Campoleone, "the quickest way into Rome."[83] Thus, Clark laid the groundwork for ignoring a direct order by Alexander, his superior commander.

On May 22, the night before VI Corps' Anzio breakout, CBS reporter Eric Sevareid and several other correspondents were ushered into an illuminated cave. With a "dramatic flourish," wrote Sevareid, a "beefy" officer bellowed "Ten-shun!" and Clark strode in, acting as if "embarrassed by his colonel's unjustified command." Clark told the reporters that the attack in

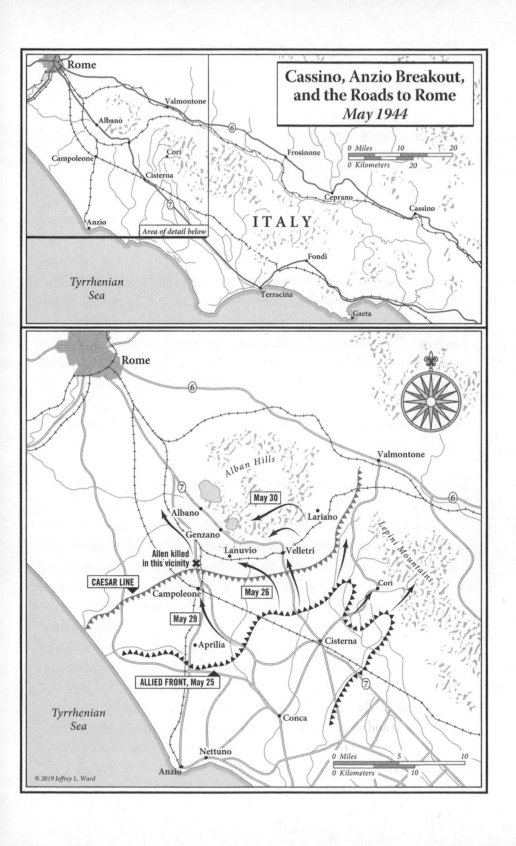

Cassino, Anzio Breakout,
and the Roads to Rome
May 1944

Rome

Valmontone

Albano

Cori

Campoleone

Cisterna

Anzio

Area of detail below

Frosinone

Ceprano

Cassino

ITALY

Fondi

Terracina

Gaeta

*Tyrrhenian
Sea*

0 Miles   10   20
0 Kilometers   20

Rome

Valmontone

Alban Hills

May 30

Albano

Lariano

Genzano

Lepini Mountains

Allen killed
in this vicinity

Lanuvio

Velletri

CAESAR LINE

May 26

Cori

Campoleone

May 29

Cisterna

Aprilia

ALLIED FRONT, May 25

Conca

*Tyrrhenian
Sea*

Nettuno

Anzio

0 Miles   5   10
0 Kilometers   10

© 2019 Jeffrey L. Ward

the morning would be aimed northeast to "cut Highway Six at Valmontone" and "bottle up the main body of the German army from the Cassino front." Parroting Alexander, Clark said the strategy was to "aid the second front" in France. He added that "Rome could be taken almost at leisure," suggesting that it was of no military significance.

On a rise near a field aid station at Anzio, Sevareid watched the next day as tank columns of the 1st Armored Division clanked up the road. Fog partly obscured the German-occupied hills to the north. Allen Brown's platoon, part of a large tank and infantry task force, crossed Highway 7, the most direct route to Rome, and continued for two days to drive northeast across a handsome valley dotted with olive orchards between the Alban Hills to the west and the Lepini Mountains to the east. By evening of the third day, Allen's platoon was almost halfway to Route 6, where it intended to engage the retreating German army in a fierce firefight. Leading elements of the 1st Armored, far ahead of Allen's platoon, expected to be "astride the German Line of withdrawal" on Highway 6 within a matter of hours.[84]

Truscott's pleasure at the progress of VI Corps in reaching Alexander's objective was short-lived. On the afternoon of May 25, he was ordered by Clark via his operations officer to pivot the bulk of his corps, including Allen's platoon and task force, more than 90 degrees to the left. Truscott wrote that he was "dumfounded [sic]." He protested that this was not the time to reverse direction. Clark's order would put most of the VI Corps west of the Alban Hills on the shortest path to Rome, but the way would be blocked by the I Parachute Corps, a battle-tested German unit that was defending the fortified Caesar Line. This was the moment, Truscott argued, for "maximum power" to be poured into the area around Highway 6 at Valmontone to "insure the destruction of the German army."[85] (The operations report for the 1st Armored Division agreed, saying it "was a definite mistake" not to focus all resources there.)[86] Clark's operations officer would not budge. Clark himself could not be reached by radio. Consequently, Truscott complied with the order.

Eric Sevareid included a line in his broadcast script that questioned the wisdom of abruptly turning to Rome instead of cutting the escape roads and destroying the enemy. "The censors" of the Fifth Army "cut this line out," he wrote. Sevareid and the other correspondents wondered "[w]hat had happened that we must now rush straight for Rome?"[87]

Clark's decision to violate Alexander's order remains "among the most controversial episodes in World War II," wrote Rick Atkinson.[88] Clark made no apology. He did not even notify Alexander of his decision until twenty-four hours after it was made. In his memoir Clark wrote that "nothing," presumably not even a direct order by a superior, "was going to stop us on our push toward the Italian capital."[89]

Given the restricted road net and congestion, Clark's decision to wheel most of VI Corps to the left was complicated and time-consuming. On the morning of May 26, Truscott, as ordered by Clark, opened his first sustained attack on the Caesar Line west of Highway 7. The attack stalled two miles south of Campoleone Station, the 1st Armored having lost eighteen tanks.

At dawn on Monday, May 29, Truscott renewed the attack. This time Allen's 1st platoon and two others led the way. Supported by artillery and the guns of a Free French cruiser in the Tyrrhenian Sea, they trundled north on the Albano road toward Campoleone Station. It was poor tank country. Ravines, gullies, and dry creekbeds—called *wadis* in this part of the world—bisected the road. The *wadis* not only had to be bridged or otherwise circumvented, they provided cover for flanking fire by the veteran German defenders. The American tanks soon outran the infantry. Three and a half hours after jumping off, the three platoons encountered a large *wadi*. Allen directed his tanks forward and "found a crossing of the wadi." As he neared the crest of a hill on the other side, "he saw a machine gun firing." A German soldier "waved a white rag." Allen ordered his driver to move up to the rim of the machine-gun emplacement. As he rose from the turret, a machine pistol fired at him from his right. Hand grenades were thrown his way. Allen was killed instantly. A medic later said that Allen died "from hand grenade wounds in his head and neck."[90]

At Quarters One that same morning Katherine and George received a letter written weeks earlier from Allen. "The horseshoe has held my luck," he wrote. "I shall take it down this Christmas and keep it for the rest of my life."[91] Later in the day Katherine wrote to Allen's wife Madge. ". . . in the night I wake up praying that all will be well with my boy. I can see [Allen] at the head of the long stairway on Calvert St. [Baltimore] with his flaxen hair calling . . . come get me."[92]

The following morning, May 30, not long after Marshall arrived at the Pentagon, he was handed a message that had been sent by General Clark. With deep condolences, Clark informed him that Allen had been killed in action near Campoleone. The chief of staff emerged, ashen-faced, and called for his driver. Marshall quietly entered Katherine's bedroom at Quarters One and closed the door. In her memoir Katherine wrote, "A blessed numbness comes to one at a time like this. I could not comprehend George's words."[93] Later that day, Marshall dictated a brief telegram to Madge, informing her of Allen's death. "Katherine is leaving here by plane at ten o'clock for New York and will go direct to your apartment," he wrote. "This is a distressing message to send and you have my deepest sympathy."[94]

In Italy, Clark arranged for Clifton Brown to temporarily leave his antiaircraft unit to attend his brother's funeral at the American cemetery at Anzio. Eric Sevareid happened to be at the cemetery on the day of Allen's burial, probably because it was Memorial Day. As the echoes of battle reverberated from another attack a few miles north, Sevareid wrote that groups of mourners huddled amid the "white crosses . . . shimmering in the hot morning sun . . . Thick smoke from our concealment screen drifted across one edge of the field, and one could hear the sound of our guns and the motors of the ambulance planes which lifted away toward Naples every few minutes bearing the injured . . . The unfilled graves were so neatly aligned, and there were so many of them, waiting."[95] Clifton wrote that he "took Allen's flag covered remains to the grave and there [the chaplain] said a few prayers and we buried him there with some of his comrades in arms."[96]

Two days later, Katherine's brother, Brigadier General Tristram Tupper, flew from North Africa to visit Allen's grave. In a letter to Marshall he recalled that in his last talk with his nephew, "it was evident that he was delighted and proud of his new command." Then, in words that he must have thought would be of some comfort, he wrote that Allen "died as he had lived, fearlessly, and surely there is no more glorious death in battle than leading troops."[97]

Katherine had little interest in a paean to her son's death. Her last letter to Allen said it all. "Dearest Beau," she began. "Darling, come and have lunch with me under the apple tree. I am alone today. G at the Chief of

Staffs meeting. I will give you turkey salad—and cornbread and cranberry jelly . . . and listen to every word that you say of this great world crisis . . . Most of all! I will love you . . . and you will be my baby son once more. Mother."

Her letter was returned, "Deceased" stamped across the front of the envelope.[98]

Chapter 12

Keep the Main Thing

Weather conditions over the English Channel were abysmal. Force 6 westerly gales whipped up waves eight feet or higher. The skies were completely overcast with a ceiling of gray clouds as low as five hundred feet blanketing the roiling waters from southern England to Normandy.

In the high-ceilinged library of Southwick House at Portsmouth near the Channel, Eisenhower and the high command for Operation OVERLORD gathered again. It was 9:30 on Sunday night, June 4, 1944. Nerves were raw. D-Day, the date for the invasion of Normandy, had already been postponed once due to weather. Assault troops were entombed belowdecks, most of the invasion fleet having returned to ports along the southwest coast of England. RAF Group Captain James Martin Stagg, a dour Scotsman who headed the Meteorological Committee, finally had news that penetrated the gloom. "There have been some rapid and unexpected developments," he reported. "I am quite confident that a fair interval will follow tonight's front."[1] With the usual caveats he predicted that winds would moderate over the Normandy beaches for a period of thirty-six hours and that cloud conditions would permit bombing and airborne operations beginning Monday night. Landings could proceed at dawn on Tuesday, June 6. The weather was expected to be tolerable but far from ideal.

Eisenhower and his chief of staff, General Beetle Smith, were inclined to give the order to go. Because of moonlight and tidal conditions, another postponement would mean they could not try again until June 19. General Bernard Montgomery agreed with Eisenhower and Smith. Others expressed skepticism or hedged their recommendations. Eisenhower brought the meeting to a close, saying: "I don't like it, but there it is . . . I don't see how we can possibly do anything else."[2] Since there was still time before a final go/no go decision had to be made, Ike asked the group to reconvene at 4:15 the next morning.

After a few hours of either fitful sleep or fruitless attempts to fall asleep,

Eisenhower arose in his spare personal quarters, a small trailer parked on the lawn near Southwick House. Before his feet hit the floor, he lit the first of more than sixty Camels that he would smoke that day. The trailer shook, buffeted by blasts of gale-force wind and pelted by rain. When the weatherman walked into Southwick House, Beetle Smith detected "the ghost of a smile on Stagg's tired face."[3] There were a few changes in his forecast, but they were all "in the direction of optimism."[4] With little discussion, everyone agreed that the invasion should proceed. Eisenhower paused for a moment, then said, "O.K. Let's go."[5] As the room cleared, he instructed an aide to notify General Marshall as follows: "HALCYON 5 finally and definitely confirmed."[6] Decoded, this meant that D-Day for the landing phase of OVERLORD, originally set for June 1, would begin at dawn on June 6.

More than six thousand ships and landing craft, fifty-nine darkened convoys carrying 130,000 soldiers, disembarked and began steaming toward "Piccadilly Circus," the assembly area out in the Channel. At last the cross-Channel invasion of France and ensuing drive to the heart of Germany that Marshall had envisioned since early 1942 was about to take place. There is no record of Marshall's reaction when he received Ike's message that the invasion was finally on. Stimson's diary entry, however, captured the gravity and historic significance of the moment, calling it "perhaps the greatest and sharpest crisis that the world has ever had, and it has all focused together on tonight."[7]

As 13,000 paratroopers were nearing their drop zones in France, the chief of staff arrived at the Soviet Embassy, a four-story Beaux Arts mansion on 16th Street three blocks from the White House. Marshall was there to receive the Order of Suvarov, the highest Soviet decoration awarded to a foreign military commander. The award was bestowed by Andrei Gromyko, the recently appointed Soviet ambassador to the United States who at the time was just thirty-two years old. Accepting the medal, Marshall foreshadowed the cross-Channel invasion when he said, "the final action in this European war is *now* focused on a single battle . . . a battle to the death for the Nazis."[8]

The publicity surrounding Marshall's attendance at the embassy the night before D-Day was designed in part to convince the German high command that nothing unusual was afoot. "No one could tell from Marshall's calm demeanor," wrote Chip Bohlen, a Soviet expert with the State

Department, "that the greatest military action in the history of the world was at that moment underway." Marshall departed for Quarters One as soon as protocol and courtesy allowed. Bohlen later asked him whether he had further communications that night concerning the invasion. "Well, there was nothing I could do about it anymore," he responded. "It was much better to get a good night's sleep and be ready for whatever the morning might bring."[9]

As Marshall was returning to Fort Myer, the president was in the Diplomatic Reception Room at the White House delivering one of his "fireside chats," this one on the fall of Rome. If Mark Clark heard the speech he would have been disappointed. He and his Fifth Army were not singled out for praise. Instead, Clark's name was mentioned only once during Roosevelt's speech, and even then it was lumped in among the names of seven other Allied commanders. Furthermore, the president downgraded "the military importance of the capture of Rome," and said a "greater effort and fiercer fighting" would be required for the "push" into Germany via a "strike into western Europe." This was a thinly disguised reference to the forthcoming cross-Channel invasion.

Throughout Roosevelt's forty-minute "chat" he suggested that the goal of the Allied liberation of Rome, "the great symbol of Christianity," was to free the pope, the Vatican, the Catholic Church, the Italian people, and even Christianity itself from enslavement by the Nazis. In doing so, FDR was quite obviously appealing to large segments of the American electorate.[10] It would be another five weeks before the president let it be known that he was willing to be renominated for a fourth term. However, based on the content and tone of this speech it appears that he had already decided to run.

Accounts differ as to whether Marshall actually slept through the night. Chip Bohlen claimed that the Marshalls spent the night out at Leesburg (unlikely) and that Katherine refused to waken her husband when she was presented with a message from Eisenhower that "Allied troops were landing in Normandy."[11] On the other hand, Doris Kearns Goodwin wrote that General Marshall telephoned the White House at "3 a.m. Washington time" on June 6 to tell the president that "troops were making their way onto the beaches and up the hills."[12] Marshall may have had a reason to call the White House, but at that time he had no information that troops were on the Normandy beaches, much less that they were moving up the bluffs. Eisenhower's first message to Marshall that morning, which arrived at the War

Department at around three a.m., said that there was "as yet no information concerning the actual landings nor of our progress moving through the beach obstacles."[13]

The strange fact is that until late afternoon of D-Day, Eisenhower himself received only the "barest of information" about the battles on the Normandy beaches. The switchboard and clerks at Eisenhower's headquarters on the morning of June 6 were completely swamped by incoming messages. The decoders and their machines were overwhelmed. It took hours for messages from offshore and the beaches to be transcribed and delivered.[14]

Given the dearth of information, Marshall spent much of the morning in his Pentagon office responding to letters of condolence concerning Allen's death. He worked alone at his antique mahogany desk, one of six that had been donated by General Philip Sheridan to the government in the 1880s. Behind him hung a portrait of General Pershing. A huge oil painting of the Meuse-Argonne battle on loan from the Smithsonian was mounted on the opposite wall. If Marshall was ever asked about how he felt during these nerve-racking hours on this momentous day his answer was not recorded.

In Washington at around 11:30 a.m., Marshall joined Arnold and King in the Oval Study to brief the president. The news from Normandy was fragmentary. By early afternoon encouraging reports began trickling in. At the eastern landing zones, two British assault divisions and one Canadian division fought through moderate resistance. By nightfall they linked up with airborne troops on the Orne River. To the west, the U.S. 4th Division under the command of "Lightning Joe" Collins was swept south of its landing zones at Utah Beach on the lee (east) side of the Cherbourg Peninsula. Among the very first to splash ashore was Brigadier General Theodore Roosevelt Jr., who had been gassed at Cantigny during the Great War. At the request of Eleanor Roosevelt, Marshall had reluctantly approved Ted Roosevelt's petition to be assigned a combat billet in the 4th Division. Weak-eyed, bandy-legged Roosevelt rallied the arriving assault troops at the waterline, roaring, "It's a great day for hunting."[15] Utah Beach turned out to be relatively benign with few obstacles and fortifications. Infantry and tanks quickly overwhelmed the weak German 709th Infantry Division in the low dunes and joined up with airborne troops inland. (The 4th, which had never been in combat, suffered only 197 casualties out of a total of 23,000 troops that landed at Utah, the same beach that Marshall argued would be the easiest to seize in 1942.)

No reliable reports reached Washington concerning the crisis at Omaha Beach. Even Eisenhower, who spent "most of the day in his trailer drinking endless cups of coffee," was in the dark.[16] For several hours General Omar Bradley, overall commander of the U.S. landings, had no idea what was going on at Omaha. Bradley was stuck offshore on his command ship, the *Augusta*, and his communications with the troops assaulting Omaha Beach were almost nonexistent. At about eleven a.m., more than four hours after men of the 1st and 29th divisions reached the beach, Major Chester Hansen returned to the *Augusta* with a firsthand report. He told Bradley that the "second, third, and fourth assault waves were stacked up behind the first."[17] The beach was a scene of total disorganization, he said. Troops that had not drowned at sea were being slaughtered by the hundreds at the waterline. Survivors were pinned down on the beach under plunging enemy fire from the 352nd Infantry Division, a first-class German unit that had moved into the area without detection by Allied intelligence. Hansen reported no significant progress scaling the exit pathways up the bluffs. At noon the situation at Omaha was "still critical."[18] Bradley considered evacuating the beachhead and diverting what was left of the 29th Division east to another beach. Fortunately, he did not. To coincide with the second high tide of the day he decided to order the remainder of the 29th Division and units of the Big Red One—a total of 25,000 men and 4,400 vehicles—to land at Omaha. Twelve navy destroyers, venturing so close to the beach that their keels scraped bottom, provided close-in fire support. At 1:30 p.m., Bradley received the first good news of the day from V Corps commander General Gee Gerow. "Troops formerly pinned down on beaches . . . advancing up heights behind beaches."[19] Gradually, the attackers fought their way up the draws that led through the cliffs to the plateau above. By the end of the afternoon the Americans had established a foothold on the heights and secured the exit paths from the rear.

By the evening of June 6, Marshall knew that the Allies had breached the Atlantic Wall and that elements of ten Allied divisions occupied disconnected slivers of the Normandy coast. Casualties were anyone's guess. From sketchy reports it appeared that the Allies had achieved a measure of tactical surprise and that the Germans had not reacted as forcefully in the air and on the ground as they might have. But Marshall knew that with General Erwin Rommel in command they would soon be on the move.

Throughout the night of the 6th and all day of the 7th, Marshall heard nothing from Eisenhower. He assumed, correctly, that Ike had his hands full, making tactical adjustments that entailed linking up the five beacheads to make a solid line and expediting the buildup of troops and supplies. This was no time to bother Eisenhower with questions and recommendations. Marshall would see him soon enough. A few days earlier the Combined Chiefs of Staff had agreed to meet in England shortly after D-Day. There, they could make quick decisions to exploit success or to address a possible failure of OVERLORD, whichever the case might be, and plan future operations in southern France or the Mediterranean that would best assure the success of OVERLORD. Marshall and the American chiefs hoped that if, as it turned out, the Allied landings were successful they would have an opportunity to cross the Channel and confer with Eisenhower, Montgomery, and Bradley on French soil.

On Thursday, June 8, Marshall was on his way to England, having packed a sack of grapefruits for Eisenhower. King and Arnold were on his plane. Before landing for a fuel stop in Newfoundland, George wrote a note to Katherine, who was having a terrible time dealing with Allen's death. "I hated to go off and leave you, particularly as you were feeling so weak and pathetic . . . Be careful, dearest and get back your strength . . . I love you, GCM."[20] He knew that Katherine was intent on returning to her cottage on Fire Island for the first time since the summer of 1939, the scene of her happiest times with Allen.

* * * * *

The morning after they arrived in London, June 10, Marshall, King, and Arnold, along with their British counterparts, were escorted through a sandbagged guardpost at 2 Great George Street near Storey's Gate and into the War Cabinet offices. They crossed a small lobby and then descended beneath St. James's Park to Churchill's command post. While the Combined Chiefs were discussing proposed operations in the Pacific, Burma, and China in a tiny conference room, Joan Bright, who ran the Special Information Centre out of a single office elsewhere in the Cabinet War Rooms, knocked at the door. She had in her hand an ULTRA intercept from Bletchley Park that had been received and decoded during the previous night. According to the message, the precarious Normandy beachhead would not be the target of a massive German counterattack because "Hitler had cancelled Case Three." Cancellation of "Case Three" meant that General Gerd von Rundstedt's five Panzer divisions of armored reserve and the nineteen divisions of the German Fifteenth Army would not be moved 120 miles from the Pas-de-Calais to Normandy to push the Allies back into the sea. Marshall and Brooke were extremely pleased once they appreciated the implications of the ULTRA message. An elaborate Allied deception plan—involving the postioning of George Patton's fictitious First Army in the Dover area—had worked. Hitler continued to believe that Normandy was only a diversion and that the main attack, to be led by Patton, was about to be aimed at the Pas-de-Calais.

The news that Case Three had been suspended meant that the Combined Chiefs could safely visit the beachhead (this is consistent with General Montgomery's statement on June 10 that the beachhead "was secure").[21] To maintain the secrecy of ULTRA and the existence of the underground bunker, Brooke's diary entry for June 10 did not mention the message that Miss Bright showed to the Combined Chiefs nor did he disclose the place where they met. Instead, he wrote only that the CCS convened for ninety minutes that day and that he was told by Churchill that they would travel "by destroyer" to the Normandy coast on June 12.[22]

Marshall was eager to inspect firsthand the armies that he had been organizing, equipping, and training for the cross-Channel mission since the outbreak of the war. First, however, he needed to take up once again Operation ANVIL, the proposed invasion of southern France that had been postponed in April. After the brief meeting in the bunker, Marshall spent the evening with Churchill out at Chequers. Presumably they talked about the pros and cons of ANVIL and operations in Italy and the Adriatic, though there is no account of their discussion. Sunday at noon the American chiefs hosted lunch for their British counterparts at Stanwell Place, an estate near Staines, Surrey, where they were billeted. For the rest of the afternoon the CCS debated their next move in the Mediterranean, focusing on the best way to divert German troops away from northwest France. Marshall clearly favored ANVIL, but he was amicable and unusually open to alternatives. They concluded at 5:30 p.m. in order to make Churchill's private train to Portsmouth for the trip to Normandy. It was agreed that amphibious operations with a three-division lift would be planned for southern France, the Bay of Biscay, and the Istrian Peninsula in the northern Adriatic. A final place for an actual landing would be decided later.

In the morning Marshall, King, and Arnold were greeted by a grinning Eisenhower at the Portsmouth naval base. Under skies filled with friendly aircraft, the American chiefs crossed the placid but crowded Channel in the U.S. destroyer *Thompson*. For the first time since 1917, Marshall approached the coast of France, the land where he had made his reputation planning the battles at Cantigny, Saint-Mihiel, and Meuse-Argonne. As the barrage balloons came into view above the Normandy bluffs, Eisenhower, who had missed the Great War, assumed the role of host and tour director. This was Ike's show—he, not Marshall, was commander of the largest amphibious invasion in the history of warfare. Marshall must have been pleased to witness his mentee's newfound confidence and growing stature.

At about 11:15, *Thompson* docked at Mulberry "A," one of two large artificial harbors, the steel components of which had been dragged across the Channel by fleets of oceangoing tugs. As supplies and vehicles were being off-loaded onto a causeway leading to Omaha Beach, Marshall and the other VIPs puttered along the edge in a DUKW, an amphibious vehicle that could both swim and operate on land. At the crest of the bluffs in an apple orchard behind Pointe du Hoc, Marshall, Eisenhower, and the other American chiefs joined generals Bradley, Gerow, Collins, and Courtney Hodges for a lunch in the open of C rations and hardtack biscuits. Bradley's briefing was balanced, expressing satisfaction at the rapid buildup and complete Allied air superiority while pointing out shortcomings, mainly the lack of depth everywhere in the bridgehead. German artillery was still harassing Omaha and the Mulberry offshore. As the visiting brass returned to the beach below in a cavalcade of jeeps, the troops recognized Eisenhower. "There's Ike," they shouted, "the old man himself."[23] Marshall was either unrecognized or ignored.

On the trip back to Portsmouth, Harry Butcher overheard Marshall talking to Eisenhower about his prediction that Ike would succeed him as chief of staff after the war. When Eisenhower expressed skepticism, Marshall said, "Why do you think we have been pushing you? When the war is

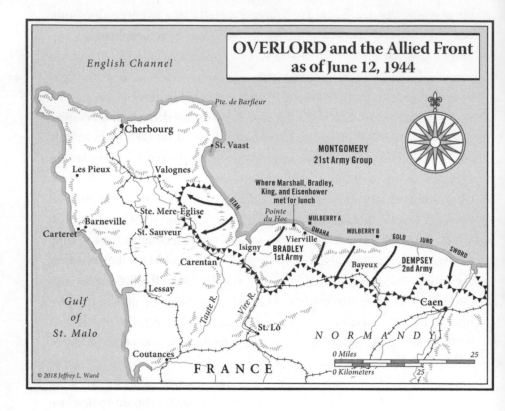

over I expect you will have ten years of hard work ahead of you." Eisenhower replied, "General, I hope then to have a long rest."[24] Destined for the presidency, Ike would enjoy little rest after his postwar stint as chief of staff. Marshall too was in for little relaxation. It would be years before he retired from government service.

Aside from Patton's fictitious army, another reason for Hitler's belief that the main attack of the Allies would be at Calais was that many of the launching sites of his new secret weapon, the V-1 pilotless bombs, called "buzz bombs," were located there. On June 13, the day Marshall returned to London, the first twenty-seven V-1s, powered by crude pulse-jet engines and carrying 1,875-pound high-explosive warheads, began to fall on or near London. V stood for "vengeance." The buzz bombs, which made an alarming screech as they fell to the ground, were designed to terrorize the populace. On the 15th of June, two hundred V-1s targeted on Tower Bridge were launched across the narrow straits of Dover. One of them dropped from the sky and exploded a mile and a half from Stanwell Place, twenty miles south-east of London, where Marshall, King, and Arnold were sleeping.

* * * * *

Marshall decided to fly to Italy, not for fear of buzz bombs but because he was getting nowhere with the CCS. Churchill and his British chiefs continued to oppose ANVIL. Instead, they pressed for further advances in Italy beyond the Pisa-Rimini Line, conjoined with an Allied drive in the northeastern Adriatic up through the Ljubljana Gap and into the Balkans, Hungary, and Austria. Having just witnessed in Normandy the importance of controlling established ports instead of deploying artificial harbors to offload armor, artillery, and mechanized ground troops, Marshall was more than ever convinced that seizing the Mediterranean ports of Marseilles and Toulon, as proposed in Operation ANVIL, was the most effective way to support OVERLORD and defeat Germany. By assessing the Italian front for himself and meeting face-to-face with General Clark and the two British theater commanders, Marshall believed he might be able to either break the deadlock or force the issue.

During three days in Italy Marshall honed his arguments for ANVIL, but he did not break the deadlock. General Alexander, the supreme commander in Italy, held firm. "He wanted to go up in the Balkans," recalled Marshall, "where he would be in command."[25] Field Marshal Wilson, the Mediterranean theater commander, was personally convinced by Marshall's "masterly manner" that seizure of ports in southern France was vitally important to the success of Eisenhower's campaign against Germany. He conceded that "strategically [ANVIL] was the only way."[26] However, out of loyalty to Alexander and in deference to the views of Churchill, Wilson informed the CCS in writing that "the best chance of really decisive results in this theatre is to exploit the present success in Italy through the Pisa/Rimini Line across the Po River and then to advance toward southern Hungary through the Ljubljana Gap."[27] Even Mark Clark favored pressing on in Italy and then into the Balkans. However, as Marshall recalled later, once he stressed to Clark the importance of seizing ports in southern France, the Fifth Army commander "never said a word [publicly] at the time. He was a very good soldier and very loyal."[28] The British commanders, who were probably aware of Clark's real position, were equally loyal to the views of their prime minister. The issue would have to be forced. A showdown with Churchill was in the offing.

While in Italy, Marshall set aside time for a personal mission. Accompanied by Katherine's brother, Tristram, he journeyed to Anzio and paid a solemn visit to Allen's grave, marked with a plain white cross among rows and rows of some seven thousand others. A panel in the marble chapel begins with a line from Simonides's poem "The Greek Dead at Thermopylae": "Nobly they ended, high their destination." Later that day, Marshall flew north to Clark's headquarters, where he met tankers who had fought alongside Allen when he was fatally shot. They "spoke in very high terms of Allen," Marshall wrote in a letter to Madge. A lieutenant gave him Allen's battle map, "a much rumpled paper with the various lines and objectives noted in crayon."[29] The next day, with the help of the map, Marshall identified the place where Allen was killed while flying low up the Albano road in a small reconnaissance plane.

During the same week, Katherine returned to her cottage at Fire Island. The ferry captain, who had known Allen since he was a toddler, left the pilot house on the trip across Great South Bay and sat in silence next to Katherine for a spell. "He was a man of few words and he spoke none," wrote Katherine. "This was his tribute to Allen." When the postmistress at Ocean Beach spotted Katherine, "tears filled her eyes." Inside the cottage Allen's black letter sweater from Woodberry with the "big block 'W' in yellow" was hanging in Katherine's closet. "A kind of panic seized me," she wrote, "and I left the house for the beach." After a day or two she returned to Dodona and remained in bed for more than a week. "By the time George returned," she was "up once more and ready to carry on."[30]

* * * * *

When Marshall got back to the Pentagon it was even more important to force through a decision to launch ANVIL. By mid-June Allied progress was stalled in Normandy by stubborn German resistance, aided by the natural barriers of the Norman hedgerows. As Marshall later complained, army intelligence did not warn him about the *bocage* "until it was so late we had to pay in blood."[31] Beginning on June 19, the worst Channel storm in forty years raged for four days and destroyed the Mulberry harbor at Omaha Beach. Three days later, as General Collins's troops were mounting their final assault against Cherbourg, it became apparent that German engineers, with months to prepare, had done a masterful job of completely demolishing the huge deepwater port. It would be the end of September before it could be reopened. Backed by Roosevelt, Marshall pressed for a date to launch ANVIL, arguing that unless major ports in the south of France could be seized in the near future, the planned advances by Eisenhower's armies in France would literally and figuratively run out of gas.

The British chiefs of staff resisted. It is "unacceptable," they said, to withdraw troops from the Italian campaign in order to capture ports in southern France.[32] Instead, Eisenhower should develop port facilities along the west coast of France. The U.S. chiefs shot back a tit-for-tat reply, using blunt language that was likely drafted by Marshall. "The British proposal to abandon ANVIL and commit everything to Italy is unacceptable . . . There is no reason for discussing further except to delay a decision which must be made."[33]

Churchill entered the fray. His "row with the Americans over Anvil," wrote David Reynolds, "was his most passionate of the war." The debate was "complex and important, impinging not just on Anglo-American relations but on the postwar balance."[34] On June 28, the prime minister sent a 2,000-word cable to Roosevelt, one of the longest he ever sent to the president. The essence of his argument was that ANVIL, by siphoning troops and resources from Italy to southern France, would prevent "an attack eastward across the Adriatic or/and around its shores," and "ruin all hopes of a major victory in Italy . . ."[35] Marshall and his aides drafted two responses for the president, the first, a brief message that was dispatched to Churchill on the day his lengthy cable was received, and the second, much longer, that was cabled to him the next day. The president added words and sentences to each of the drafts, but Marshall's original intent remained untouched—the refusal of Churchill and his British chiefs to go along with ANVIL was "not acceptable" to the president. The final sentences in the second message were vintage Roosevelt. "Now that we are fully involved in our major blow, history will never forgive us if we lost precious time and lives in indecision and debate. My dear friend, I beg you to let us go ahead with our plan." He ended with a pointed reference to his run for a fourth term. "Finally, for purely political considerations over here, I should never survive even a slight setback in 'Overlord' if it were known that fairly large forces had been diverted to the Balkans."[36]

As far as Marshall was concerned, the ANVIL debate was over. Churchill, however, was far from being ready to give up. Twice he hectored Eisenhower and tried to change his mind, "using phrases that only he can use," wrote Butcher.[37] He continued his campaign even after the CCS ordered General Wilson, on July 12, to launch the invasion of southern France at the earliest possible date. During the first week of August, when the code name of the invasion was changed from ANVIL to DRAGOON for security reasons and the landings were set to commence on August 15, the prime minister still persisted. He sent cables to Roosevelt and Hopkins begging them to switch the landings to Brittany on the west coast of France. On August 9, less than a week before the invasion, he staged one last stand with Eisenhower, threatening that if DRAGOON went forward as planned he might have to go to the King and "lay down the mantle of my high office."[38]

The Americans were unmoved. Though he registered a "solemn protest," Churchill had no choice but to capitulate.[39] This was the moment when the prime minister's peripheral strategy for winning the Second World War was laid to rest. The strategy that Marshall had envisioned and fought for since the beginning—a massive ground war in France aimed at the heart of Germany—prevailed. Later, Churchill told Lord Moran, "Up to July 1944 England had a considerable say in things; after that I was conscious that it was America who made the big decisions."[40]

Churchill's spirits revived when he arrived in Italy on August 11 for a working holiday. Weeks earlier he had been dissuaded by the King from witnessing the invasion of Normandy. He was not about to miss an opportunity to participate in DRAGOON, possibly the last major amphibious operation in the European war. On August 15, the morning of the invasion, the prime minister, clad in his zippered siren suit, boarded the British destroyer *Kimberley* for a five-hour trip to the Bay of Saint-Tropez, thirty miles east of Toulon. *Kimberley*'s skipper ventured within seven thousand yards of the beaches, but no closer due to the presence of mines. At that distance Churchill could see little of the actual landings; the shoreline was obscured by haze and smoke. Three experienced American divisions, followed by seven Free French divisions, a total of 151,000 troops, actually landed on D-Day. The American troops, most of them veterans of North Africa, Sicily, or Italy, were led by General Truscott, his third invasion of the war. With the

Germans offering little resistance, casualties during the landings were light. Churchill was "in a querulous mood," probably because the captain refused to get him closer to the action. He left the bridge to read *Grand Hotel* alone in his cabin. On the inside cover of the novel he wrote, "This is a lot more exciting than the invasion of Southern France."[41]

For the most part DRAGOON was a success, though the cost of the entire operation was between 2,000 and 3,000 Americans killed or missing and 4,300 wounded. Once captured and made operational, the ports of Marseilles and Toulon provided over one-third of Allied supply needs in northern France. Within a month French armored units that had landed in southern France advanced hundreds of miles north to a point above Dijon, where they linked up with elements of General Patton's Third Army that were driving east toward the Rhine River. Thus, two of the three tactical objectives of the operation—access to deepwater ports and protection of the Allied right (or southern) flank—were achieved. The third objective— diversion of German troops away from Normandy—was not met because DRAGOON, which was originally scheduled to coincide with D-Day in Normandy, was launched much too late.

In less than five weeks of fighting, the U.S. and French divisions in southern France killed or captured 158,000 German soldiers, but 130,000 survived and retreated to the edge of the rugged Vosges Mountains, where they established an east-west defensive line, "still able to fight although much weakened."[42] With the onset of freezing autumn rains and the enemy holding the high ground, veteran GIs were reminded of the winter they endured in Italy. To his wife, Truscott wrote, "I dread the approaching wet and cold and tedious mountain work. The skies weep continuously now."[43]

After the war Churchill and Clark publicly claimed that even if DRA-GOON's goals were achieved, the operation was nevertheless a military and a political mistake because, as Churchill wrote, it deprived the Allied armies in Italy from reaching "Vienna before the Russians, with all that might have followed therefrom."[44] Marshall thought this was nonsense, not to mention the idea of trying to send a military force across the Julian Alps by way of the Ljubljana Gap. In a 1956 interview he said that "[if] we had accepted the Balkan thing, it would have scattered our shots. They [meaning Churchill and Clark] are letting political considerations after the fact dominate the whole concept. My idea was that we should defeat the German army ... *Keep the main thing.*"[45]

*   *   *   *   *

After two and a half years of the war Washington was still abuzz with rumors about who on the U.S. side should be held responsible for the Pearl Harbor attack. An initial investigation, hastily completed in January 1942, had publicly condemned General Walter Short and Admiral Husband Kimmel, the two commanders in Hawaii, for dereliction of duty, and Roosevelt promptly relieved them of command. None of the higher-ups, namely Marshall, Stark, and the president himself, were held accountable for failure to provide adequate advance warnings. The report of the investigation, a mere twenty-one censored pages, was released to the public, but two thousand pages of testimony and exhibits were withheld. Supporters of Short and Kimmel and enemies of the Roosevelt administration suspected a whitewash. They spun theories that Marshall and the others had notice well before the morning of December 7 that the Japanese fleet would attack and failed to warn the commanders in Hawaii.

Insatiable curiosity about who was really responsible for the Pearl Harbor debacle eventually collided with partisan politics. In May 1944, freshman senator Homer Ferguson (R-MI) introduced legislation designed to force a court-martial of Kimmel and Short before the November presidential election. His hope was that once the full story of Pearl Harbor was made public, voters would fault Roosevelt and his administration. Ferguson's proposed legislation failed to pass, but he managed to persuade the Senate to enact a joint resolution requiring the army and navy to convene separate in camera reinvestigations of the Pearl Harbor attack. In early August, after the Republicans nominated New York governor Thomas Dewey and the Democrats rubber-stamped Roosevelt's desire to run for a fourth term, the army board of inquiry met with Marshall at his office in the Pentagon. At the outset, the chief of staff asked that his office be cleared of everyone but the three presiding officers, at which point he briefed them on the importance to national security of maintaining the secrecy of MAGIC—that is, the ability of the U.S. to decode certain Japanese messages. He explained that the Japanese had not changed two of their diplomatic codes. As a result, said Marshall, the War Department was still able to decode communications between

The Marshall children, circa 1884. After his older brother made derogatory remarks about Marshall's first wife and "attempted to run my life," Marshall cut him off and had little to do with him for the rest of his life. *Left to right:* Marie, Stuart, and George.

Sixteen-year-old George, nicknamed "Flicker," stands outside the family house on the Old National Pike several months before he left home for the Virginia Military Institute. Marshall would never forget overhearing Stuart telling their mother that his feckless younger brother should not be allowed to attend VMI because he "would disgrace the family."

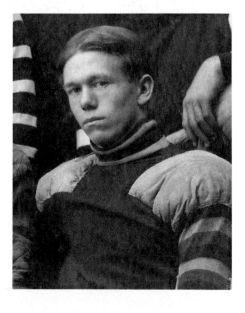

Marshall in his VMI football uniform. A 150-pound tackle, he ran fifty yards for a touchdown in a game against Washington and Lee University on November 17, 1900, the fall of his senior year. *Courtesy the Virginia Military Institute Archives.*

All photographs courtesy the George C. Marshall Research Library unless otherwise noted.

Cadet staff of the Virginia Military Institute, in dress uniforms, 1901. First Captain George Marshall is seated third from the left.

The Marshall-Coles wedding party on the front porch of the Coles home, February 11, 1902. *Left to right:* Marie, Lily Coles, George, Stuart, Laura Bradford Marshall (George's mother), George C. Marshall Sr., and Elizabeth Coles (Lily's mother).

Lieutenants Marshall (*right*) and Bruce Palmer take a break during engineering class at Fort Leavenworth, Kansas, in the spring of 1907. Marshall spent four years at Leavenworth, excelling as a student and instructor.

For six gloomy months during World War I, Major Marshall was billeted in a tiny house near Gondrecourt, France, with a family headed by Madame Jouatte, with whom he formed a close and lasting friendship. *Standing left to right:* Marshall, Colonel Alvin C. Voris, Lieutenant Jean Hugo (son of Victor Hugo, the famous French writer), and Major James A. Drain. *Seated left to right:* Jouette, and a couple described only as "cunning little girl" named Nannette and her mother, a French refugee whose husband was in the French army.

Major General Robert Lee Bullard and the staff of the 1st Infantry Division at Gondrecourt, January 17, 1918. Marshall is third and Bullard is fourth from the left in the first row.

General John J. Pershing addresses the 1st Division on April 16, 1918, the day before the division moved out to the front. Standing behind Pershing (*left to right*) are General George Duncan, Colonel George Marshall (*partially obscured*), and division commander Bullard (*in fur coat*).

Heavily laden doughboys of the 28th Infantry Regiment, accompanied by Schneider tanks, cross no-man's-land and assault heavily defended Cantigny May 28, 1918.

Marshall laughs with his fellow officers on General Bullard's staff, the men with whom he had been "so intimately associated for over a year in France."

A traffic jam on one of the few roads from Saint-Mihiel to the Meuse-Argonne, September 1918. Marshall planned and supervised the enormously complicated sixty-mile nighttime movement of American troops from one battlefield to another.

General Pershing, commander of the
American Expeditionary Force, and his aide-de-
camp, Colonel George C. Marshall, during a tour
of French battlefields, 1919. Marshall served as
Pershing's aide for six years.

After World War I, when Marshall and his wife
were living in Washington, Rose Page, a precocious
eight-year-old, initiated a friendship with the colonel.
For almost forty years Marshall was Rose's loyal friend,
confidant, mentor, and godfather to her children.
Courtesy J. Page Wilson, son of Rose Page Wilson.

Lily Marshall at a railroad station in Tientsin, China,
September 20, 1926. She and her mother lived with
Marshall during his three-year tour of duty as executive
officer of the 15th Infantry. A year later, Lily died.

The assistant commandants and department heads of the Fort Benning Infantry School, 1930-1931. *Front row, left to right:* Morrison C. Stayer, Jr., Joseph W. Stilwell, George C. Marshall, William F. Freehoff, Edwin F. Harding. *Second row:* Howard J. Liston, Omar M. Bradley, Emil W. Leard, Fremont B. Hodson.

Katherine Boyce as Rosalind in Shakespeare's *As You Like It* onstage somewhere in England. To avoid embarrassing her father, who disapproved of her ambition for a career in theater, she had dropped her surname, Tupper, and substituted her middle name. Katherine became Marshall's second wife in 1930.

After her return to America, Katherine Tupper married Clifton Brown, a prominent Baltimore attorney. In 1928 her husband was murdered outside his law office by an insane client. *Courtesy Enoch Pratt Free Library.*

Marshall surf-casts in front of Katherine's cottage on Fire Island, 1939.
Courtesy Thomas D. McAvoy, Life Pictures Collection / Getty.

Cooking on Fire Island, the last summer before the war. *Left to right:* Allen Brown, Molly Brown, Clifton Brown, and George Marshall.
Courtesy Thomas D. McAvoy, Life Pictures Collection / Getty.

General Marshall is sworn in as chief of staff of the United States Army on September 1, 1939, the day the Germans invaded Poland and World War II in Europe began. *Left to right:* Secretary of War Harry H. Woodring, Marshall, and the Adjutant General, Major General Emory S. Adams.

The appointment of Republican Henry Stimson as secretary of war was one of the shrewdest and best appointments President Roosevelt ever made. The close collaborative relationship between Stimson and Marshall was profoundly important to the winning of the war. Stimson's handwritten note below the photo says it all.

"The door that was never closed"
Henry L Stimson

The chief of staff on a morning ride along a path above the Potomac River, which led to the Pentagon construction site, 1941. As usual, he is chased by Fleet, his hapless Dalmatian.

Marshall and Vice Admiral Lord Louis Mountbatten, chief of British Combined Operations, observe an amphibious landing exercise at Fort Bragg, June 11, 1942. Mountbatten was the only senior British commander who supported Marshall's plan to establish and hold through the winter a beachhead on the Cherbourg Peninsula.

The U.S. Joint Chiefs of Staff discuss plans for TORCH during a lunch meeting, October 1942. *Left to right:* Admiral Ernest J. King, Marshall, Admiral William D. Leahy, and Lieutenant General Henry A. "Hap" Arnold. The wall map to the right appears to be of Tunisia.

Pressed by Winston Churchill, General Dwight Eisenhower and Marshall discuss a proposed invasion of Italy at a meeting in Algiers on June 3, 1943. Marshall was reluctant to commit to the operation, concerned that it might jeopardize the buildup in Great Britain for the cross-Channel invasion of France in May 1944.

On the terrace at the Citadel overlooking the Saint Lawrence River and the Plains of Abraham, the principals at the Quebec conference in August 1943 pose for a photograph. *Front row, left to right:* Canadian Prime Minister Mackenzie King, President Franklin Roosevelt, and British Prime Minister Winston Churchill. *Back row, left to right:* General Arnold, Air Chief Marshal Sir Charles Portal, General Sir Alan Brooke, Admiral King, Field Marshal Sir John Dill, General Marshall, Admiral of the Fleet Sir Dudley Pound, and Admiral Leahy. Note that Dill and Marshall, by then good friends, are the only ones engaged in conversation.

Following the conferences at Cairo and Tehran, Marshall returned to the U.S. via the Southwest Pacific, a ten-thousand-mile trip to assure General Douglas MacArthur that he was not forgotten and to assess for himself the situation in the general's Southwest Pacific command. After landing on Goodenough Island on December 15, 1943, he is greeted by (*left to right*) General George C. Kenney, commander of Allied Air Forces in the Southwest Pacific; General Stephen J. Chamberlin, MacArthur's operations officer; General Walter Krueger, commander of the U.S. Sixth Army; and MacArthur himself (*far right*).

Having just arrived at Omaha Beach on June 12, 1944, General Marshall looks up at Admiral King, chief of naval operations, who is about to disembark from a DUKW amphibious landing craft. General Eisenhower, OVERLORD commander, is in front of Marshall, and General Arnold, head of the air force, is behind him, his face partially obscured.

General Lucian Truscott, commander of the Fifth Army in Italy, leads Marshall and General Mark Clark, commander of the Fifteenth Army Group, along a snowy mountain path. After the Yalta conference, Marshall had flown to Italy to meet with the senior commanders and talk to the American troops who were in pursuit of General "Smiling Al" Kesselring's German forces.

President Harry Truman congratulates Marshall on his retirement as chief of staff at a ceremony in the courtyard of the Pentagon, November 26, 1945. The next day at Dodona, the Marshalls' house in Leesburg, Virginia, the general received a phone call from Truman: "General, I want you to go to China for me." Marshall reportedly said, "Yes, Mr. President," and hung up abruptly.

Madame Chiang and her husband, Chiang Kai-shek, toast Marshall's sixty-fifth birthday at a dinner in the Generalissimo's residence in Nanking shortly after Marshall arrived in China, December 1945.

Along with Mao Zedong (*far left*) and his military chief Chu Teh (*far right*), the Committee of Three—Chou En-lai, Marshall, and Nationalist General Chang Chih-Chung—inspect Communist Party honor guard in Yenan, March 4, 1946.

Marshall has final talk with Mao before departing Communist headquarters in Yenan on March 5, 1946. Captain E. K. H. Eng (*left*) is the interpreter.

Secretary of State Marshall marches in the procession with honorary degree recipients at Harvard University commencement exercises, June 5, 1947. Later that day, Marshall delivered the speech that launched the European Recovery Program, commonly known as the Marshall Plan.

Secretary of State Marshall and Undersecretary Robert Lovett testify before Congress in support of interim aid for European recovery, November 11, 1947.
Courtesy International News.

Secretary of State Marshall addresses the UN General Assembly in Flushing Meadows, New York, about the U.S. position on the partition of Palestine, September 17, 1947.

Secretary Marshall meets with Republican Senator Arthur Vandenberg (*left*), Chairman of the Senate Foreign Relations Committee, and the ranking member, Senator Tom Connally, to discuss the European Recovery Program, February 14, 1948.

As part of Secretary Marshall's effort to sell the $13 billion European Recovery Program to Congress and the American people, he and his public relations staff staged a press event featuring seven Cub Scouts who had taken it upon themselves to raise money to feed a group of European children for a year. The messaging was obvious: if a few Cub Scouts could assist in the recovery of Europe, so could the most powerful nation in the world. February 10, 1948.

Marshall accepts the medal awarding him the 1953 Nobel Peace Prize in Oslo's Festival Hall. The next day, Marshall delivered his Nobel lecture, acknowledging at the outset that his speech "lacked the magic and artistry" of Churchill's oratory.
Courtesy Valldal / NTB scanpix / Sipa USA.

Berlin and Tokyo that were critically important to the war effort in Europe as well as Japan and had saved thousands of lives. Marshall went on to testify that as far as he was concerned Short was adequately warned prior to December 7 about a possible Japanese attack and that he, Marshall, was not made aware of advance information from MAGIC or any other source that the attack was targeted at Pearl Harbor.

On September 11, 1944, Indiana Republican Forest Harness, an anti-Roosevelt and ultra-reactionary member of the House Military Affairs Committee, announced on the House floor that he had abundant evidence that Marshall and others failed to adequately warn Short and Kimmel of the forthcoming attack. He asserted that the Roosevelt administration was in possession of "inside information" and "does not want the truth of Pearl Harbor to become known." Citing a source believed to be "thoroughly reliable and trustworthy," Harness claimed that Marshall "had learned very confidentially" about a Japanese "ultimatum" to the U.S. government and instructions to destroy code machines in Washington "about 6 hours before the attack." According to Harness's undisclosed leaker, the chief of staff's warning to Short was inexplicably sent by "commercial radio instead of the usual more rapid direct military means."[46] As a result, this extremely significant message did not reach Short until hours after the attack.

Harness's allegation that Marshall "learned very confidentially" about the ultimatum suggested that the U.S. had broken Japan's diplomatic code before the attack, though he had no way of knowing that the Japanese continued to use the same code and that the the military was still able, in effect, to listen in on communications between Berlin and Tokyo. Harness didn't realize it at the time, but he came close to revealing America's most closely guarded operational secret: if the congressman's claim was read by the Japanese when it was eventually published in the *Congressional Record* they might change their codes.

Three days later James Forrestal, who had been appointed secretary of the navy after Knox's death, sent a note to the White House warning that Dewey's campaign staff had been told by an army officer that the administration knew in advance that Pearl Harbor would be attacked. Ominously, Forrestal added, "[i]nformation has come to me that Dewey's first major speech will deal with Pearl Harbor."[47] Someone, possibly Forrestal or Hopkins, notified Marshall that Dewey, in order to disparage Roosevelt and win the election, was on the verge of revealing that the United States had broken Japanese codes and knew beforehand of the Japanese attack.

Marshall believed he had a duty to prevent this disclosure from being made. "[I]t was of tremendous importance to us to keep this code business quiet," he said, "because if we lost it, we lost the most valuable thing we could possibly have gotten regarding the Japanese operations. It was the same code that they had at the time of Pearl Harbor."[48] Knowing he was taking an enormous risk, Marshall decided that the only way to preserve the secrecy of MAGIC was to orchestrate a direct approach to candidate Dewey, thereby inserting himself into an increasingly bitter presidential campaign. For an army chief of staff, much less anyone in the military, it was a bold and unprecedented move.

Scarcely five weeks before election day, Marshall sent Colonel Carter Clarke, head of cryptography in the War Department, to Tulsa, Oklahoma, where Governor Dewey was campaigning. Dressed in civilian clothes to deflect press attention, Clarke handed Dewey, the forty-two-year-old former prosecutor with his trademark "bottle brush" mustache, a sealed envelope and explained that it contained a letter for his eyes only written by Marshall. They were alone in the governor's hotel suite. Dewey opened the envelope and began reading. In the second sentence, Marshall wrote that before reading further Dewey had to agree not to communicate the substance of the letter to anyone because it revealed a top secret matter regarding Pearl Harbor. Furthermore, he would not be permitted to keep a copy of the letter. Dewey glanced farther down the page and saw the word "cryptograph."[49] At that point he stopped reading. He sensed a trap. According to Clarke's memo of the meeting, the governor put aside the letter and said he "did not want his lips sealed on things that he already knew about Pearl Harbor, about facts already in his possession . . ."

Dewey was astonished that Marshall would approach him this way in the midst of the campaign. "Marshall does not do things like that," he said to Clarke. "I am confident that Franklin Roosevelt is behind this whole thing." The governor did not end it there. He suggested to Clarke that he knew the U.S. had broken Japanese codes, "and Franklin Roosevelt knows about it too. He knew what was happening before Pearl Harbor, and instead of being re-elected he ought to be impeached."[50] Dewey returned the letter to Clarke. Before the colonel departed, the governor left the door open to a further meeting. Aware of Marshall's reputation as a straight shooter he told Clarke that he would be willing to meet with Marshall or his designee after he returned to Albany. Perhaps Marshall really did know something important that he did not know.

Two days later Clarke was shown into a reception room at the executive mansion in Albany. Governor Dewey was there along with Elliott Bell, his trusted campaign strategist and speechwriter. The letter from Marshall that Clarke presented was substantively the same, but it contained an assurance by Marshall at the beginning that "neither the Secretary of War nor the President" has any knowledge of the letter or that its substance was being communicated or discussed with Dewey.[51] Before reading beyond the beginning the governor had two demands. He insisted that Bell be permitted to read the letter in its entirety and they must be permitted to retain a copy. Clarke did not have authority to accept these conditions. After some back-and-forth, Dewey spoke with Marshall by telephone. Marshall agreed to Dewey's demands. Dewey, however, was still hesitant to dip into the letter. He and Bell jousted with Clarke. If Marshall's letter is about maintaining the secrecy of Japanese codes, they argued, it doesn't make sense because everyone in Washington knows that the codes have been broken. "I'll be damned," said Dewey, "if I believe the Japs are still using" the pre–Pearl Harbor codes. "Why in hell haven't they changed [them], especially after what happened at Midway and the Coral Sea?"[52] Clarke explained the variety of codes used by the Japanese and insisted that they had not changed two of their prewar codes, as unlikely as that might seem. He must have been persuasive because Dewey finally began digesting the substantive part of the letter.

Marshall's letter to Dewey explained that success of the Allies in both Europe and the Pacific was dependent in part on the ability of the U.S. to continue to decrypt Japanese codes, including two diplomatic codes that had not been changed since the beginning of the war (the most important was Berlin/Tokyo, which revealed war plans of Hitler). Referencing Congressman Harness's statements on the House floor, he warned of "tragic consequences if the present political debates regarding Pearl Harbor," meaning the presidential campaign, "disclose to the enemy, German or Jap, any suspicion of the vital sources of information we possess." Marshall made it clear that nothing less than "American lives" and "the early termination of the war" were at stake. As to advance notice of Japan's plan to attack Pearl Harbor, Marshall wrote that the United States possessed no information concerning Japan's "intentions toward Hawaii."[53] Overall, Marshall's letter was a plea to the Republican candidate to "keep this code business quiet."

With Marshall's letter in hand, Dewey and Bell stepped out of the room to confer in private. They were gone for more than twenty minutes. When they returned Dewey was visibly angry. However, he simply told Clarke that he had no more questions. The meeting was over. Later, Dewey and Bell debated what to do with Herbert Brownell, a prominent Republican lawyer who would eventually serve as attorney general in the Eisenhower administration. Dewey was convinced that Roosevelt was a "traitor," but Marshall had him in a box. As Brownell pointed out, if Dewey released Marshall's letter or otherwise referred to the code business, the administration would fight back. They would accuse him of aiding the enemy, even treason.[54] Given Marshall's reputation, they had to accept his word even if they did not believe him.

Marshall hoped that Dewey would put the national interest in winning the war ahead of his desire to win the presidency, but he had no way of knowing what he would do in the final days of the campaign. In late October, before election day, Marshall informed Harry Hopkins about his letters to Dewey. Hopkins promptly told the president. Roosevelt's reaction was "that Governor Dewey would not, for political purposes, give secret and vital information to the enemy."[55] He was right. On election night, November 7, Roosevelt, as he had done three times before, sat in the dining room at his Hyde Park residence with a pencil and long tally sheets as results came in by news ticker tapes, radio, and calls from campaign headquarters. By ten p.m., he said to Admiral Leahy, "It's all over, Bill. What's the use of putting down the figures."[56] The Roosevelt-Truman ticket carried thirty-six states and 432 electoral votes. The Democrats retained comfortable majorities in both the Senate and House.

The chief of staff had managed to keep a lid on the "code business." However, he did not escape censure by the army board appointed at the instance of Senator Ferguson to reinvestigate the Pearl Harbor attack. Four days after the election the final report of the army's inquiry was released to the War Department. The criticism aimed at Marshall was far greater than that directed at General Short. Among other shortcomings, the chief of staff was faulted for his delays in sending important information to Short on December 6 and 7 and his "admitted lack of knowledge" of the actual state of readiness of Short's Hawaiian command in November and December 1941. With some justification, Marshall was criticized for failing to question Short's "defense against sabotage" (Alert No. 1) response to his November 27, 1941, "war warning" message. However, there was no suggestion in the army board's report that Marshall knew in advance that the attack would target Pearl Harbor.[57] At lunch in the White House on November 21, Secretary Stimson handed the report to the president. When FDR came to the section criticizing Marshall, he said, "Why this is wicked. This is wicked."[58] The army board report and that of the navy were ordered by Roosevelt to be kept under seal until after the war.

Both candidate Dewey and the army board of inquiry accepted Marshall's word when he assured them that he had no information whatsoever prior to the attack regarding Japanese "intentions towards Hawaii" (the phrase Marshall used in his letter to Dewey). As it turns out, however, he did. A damning sixteen-line MAGIC intercept came across Marshall's desk in October 1941. The intercept, message "#83," disclosed that Japanese intelligence officials in Tokyo, who had previously focused only on U.S. fleet movements, were carefully mapping the exact location of each moored warship at Pearl Harbor in five specified sectors.[59] If Dewey or the army board had known about and followed up on this particular intercept, the election of 1944 might have turned out differently. Certainly those who read this message in the fall of 1941 would have come in for much greater criticism by the army board than they did.

For unknown reasons message #83, the MAGIC intercept that revealed or at least strongly suggested Japanese "intentions toward Hawaii," did not surface until hearings by a joint congressional committee (known as the Pearl Harbor Committee) to investigate the Pearl Harbor attack commenced after the war in late November 1945. The committee consisted of six Democrats and four Republicans (five senators and five representatives). At these hearings Colonel Rufus Bratton, the army intelligence officer at the Pentagon who monitored incoming MAGIC messages, testified that when he saw the intercept in October 1941 he recognized at once that it could be an indication that the Japanese were setting up a grid system for an air attack on Pearl Harbor. He alerted his boss, General Miles. Bratton discussed it with colleagues in navy intelligence. However, he had no authority to warn Short and Kimmel in Hawaii. All he could do was route the intercept to Marshall, Stimson, and General Gerow, chief of the War Plans Division, which he did.[60] No one showed any interest. Marshall testified that he "had no recollection" of reading the intercept.[61]

The final reports of the Pearl Harbor Committee were released in July 1946. Notwithstanding MAGIC intercept #83 and Short's Alert No. 1 (defense against sabotage), each of which were sent to the chief of staff, the majority report absolved Marshall of any blame or responsibility for failure to warn General Short, the army's commander in Hawaii. Committee member Senator Ferguson, joined by fellow Republican senator Owen Brewster, issued a minority report. Not surprisingly, their report charged Marshall and others in Washington (including Stimson, Gerow, and Roosevelt) with "failure to perform the responsibilities indispensably essential to the defense of Pearl Harbor."[62] With that, the last of the eight separate investigations of the Pearl Harbor attack was concluded.

In the end, blame for the Pearl Harbor tragedy can never be fairly allocated. Its causes transcend the actions and omissions of dozens of individuals. They reside somewhere inside a haystack of assumptions and complacency. As army chief of staff, Marshall willingly accepted responsibility. But that gesture would never satisfy the thirst of the American public, especially its politicians, to conjure conspiracies and pinpoint fault. Marshall was probably correct when he said the joint congressional investigation "was intended to crucify Roosevelt, not to get me."[63]

* * * * *

The day of Roosevelt's fourth inaugural "was bitterly cold," recalled Katherine. Since weather and frail health caused the president to shift the traditional ceremony from the Capitol to the White House, the Marshalls were swathed in coats and scarves on the south portico along with the cabinet, Supreme Court members, and congressional leaders. Looking "pale and drawn," his hands trembling, FDR gave a brief but prophetic speech, a mere 573 words.[64] The "fearful cost" of the war, he said, had taught Americans that they "cannot live alone," that henceforth their "well-being will be dependent on the well-being of other nations far away." Total victory is at hand, he suggested, and Americans should be ready to "perform a service of historic importance that men and women will honor throughout all time."[65] These were the first public utterances by FDR that consigned isolationism to the past and portended America's influence in the postwar world. Before long Marshall would be one of those citizens called to serve.

* * * * *

The previous three months were a reminder to Marshall that the fighting was far from over. In the Far East Marshall's hopes that General Joseph Stilwell, as Chiang Kai-shek's chief of staff, could mold Chiang's army into an effective fighting force against the Japanese in China had been thwarted. The Generalissimo was happy to have American armaments and supplies, but he wanted to preserve his army to fight Mao Zedong's Communists for domination of postwar China. He was not about to allow his ground troops to be controlled by Stilwell, especially since he knew the U.S. general held him in contempt. In his diary and reports to Washington, Stilwell referred to Chiang as "the Peanut."

As Vinegar Joe predicted, during 1944, Japanese troops overran Chinese bases that were to be used by the U.S. to stage air strikes against Formosa and the Japanese homeland. In a telegram to Chiang drafted by Marshall, Roosevelt threatened to cut off supplies unless Chiang put Stilwell in full charge of his troops. Chiang at first appeared to accede to FDR's threat, but only a few days later he demanded Stilwell's recall. Roosevelt backed down in October and ordered Marshall to recall Stilwell.

The problems with Chiang had played a key role in the decision by Marshall and the JCS to order the invasion of the Philippine island of Luzon instead of Formosa and to drive north to Iwo Jima and Okinawa, where American forces could establish bases to bomb and invade Japan. By the time of Roosevelt's inauguration, General MacArthur had already landed several army divisions on Leyte and was in the process of landing fifteen divisions on Luzon, the largest deployment of ground forces in the Pacific war. His battles in the Philippines were so vast that Marshall had to reprimand him for monopolizing cargo vessels to the detriment of his own "future operations and those in other theatres."[66] MacArthur hoped to take Manila by January 26, his sixty-fifth birthday, but the Japanese, with twenty thousand sailors and soldiers, vowed to fight to the death in Old Manila. Still, MacArthur had made good on his pledge to the Filipino people when he left Corregidor in 1942. After splashing ashore at Leyte, he broadcast his staged arrival via a portable transmitter set up on the beach. "People of the Philippines. I have returned. By the Grace of Almighty God, our forces stand again on Philippine soil. Rally to me. Let the indomitable spirit of Bataan and Corregidor lead on."[67]

Marshall intended to be at Washington National Airport when General Stilwell, having been recalled from China, landed on November 3. Instead, he found himself at Walter Reed Hospital, sadly saying farewell to his closest wartime friend, Sir John Dill, head of the British Joint Staff Mission. Dill had lapsed into a coma and died the next day of aplastic anemia. His funeral was held at the National Cathedral the day after the election. Visibly moved, Marshall stood in the pulpit and read the lesson, a verse from Paul's letter to the Romans: "For as many as are led by the Spirit of God, they are the sons of God."[68] For George it was a "cruel blow," wrote Katherine.[69] Other than Allen, Sir John's death affected Marshall more deeply than anyone else. As Marshall recalled later, they had a "very intimate understanding of each other."[70] Like Marshall, Dill was reticent but straightforward. Though he represented British interests he had a capacity to address both sides of an issue, which appealed to Marshall. During their three years of friendship Dill routinely shared with Marshall confidential communications between Churchill and Roosevelt so that Marshall could understand "why they were doing as they did."[71] Marshall felt comfortable passing along his frank views and opinions to Dill, knowing that his friend would be discreet. They trusted each other. In Marshall's judgment Dill was essential to the preservation of the wartime alliance between the United States and Great Britain. "Few will ever realize," wrote Marshall to Churchill, "the debt our countries owe [Dill] for his unique and profound influence toward the cooperation of our forces."[72] Marshall made sure that Dill would be remembered in America although "his acclaim ... was by no means echoed in Britain."[73] He not only arranged for his friend to be interred at Arlington Cemetery, he also worked with Robert Woods Bliss to commission an equestrian statue of Dill near the entrance to Arlington that was dedicated by President Truman in 1950.

*　*　*　*　*

In Europe, victory was by no means at hand. On December 16, 1944—the day Marshall became the first army officer to receive the newly created five-star rank—Hitler gave the order for a quarter-million men and more than a thousand tanks and assault guns to attack the Americans along their eighty-five-mile front in the Ardennes forest. His goal was to split the American and British armies and force a stalemate, perhaps cause the Allies to sue for peace, by seizing the huge fuel and supply dumps at Liège and capturing the port of Antwerp. A breathtakingly ambitious and desperate gamble, the offensive became known as the Battle of the Bulge, the largest battle fought by the U.S. Army in Europe. Eisenhower and Bradley had been caught by surprise, and Marshall, with no choice but to endure a nerve-splitting two weeks, had to resist the temptation to interfere.

The Germans planned to break through the Allied line in the first twenty-four hours, but the American northern shoulder held, forcing the attackers to sideslip to the southwest. Eisenhower assumed control of the front and moved quickly to narrow and slow the German onslaught. By December 19, he had committed his last reserves—the 82nd and 101st airborne divisions—to block the German advance at the towns of Saint-Vith and Bastogne. That day, in a meeting at Verdun, he ordered General Patton, whose Third Army was about one hundred miles south of the bulge, to pivot three divisions ninety degrees to the left and drive north into the flank of the German forces outside Bastogne. Patton electrified the meeting when he said he would be ready to attack on the morning of the 22nd. Meanwhile, the German advance continued. On December 20, Eisenhower temporarily shifted command of the U.S. First and Ninth Armies from Bradley to Field Marshal Montgomery. He did this because Bradley's headquarters in Luxembourg was not in close contact with these two armies that were deployed north of the breakthrough and also because Montgomery needed the additional firepower to halt the German Panzers before they reached the Meuse River.

With poor weather precluding air support and the outcome of the Battle of the Bulge in doubt, Marshall broke silence just once to assure Eisenhower that he had "complete confidence" in his handling of his forces and to offer to send replacement officers in case they were needed. Otherwise, no one in Washington was to bother Eisenhower.[74] By Christmas Day the weather cleared. The Allies were finally able to provide close air support to troops on the ground. On the afternoon of December 26, units of the 4th Armored Division in Patton's Third Army joined up with the 101st Airborne at Bastogne. In the north, Montgomery turned tactical control of the American forces over to Joe Collins. His VII Corps counterattacked. Less than three miles from the Meuse the German Panzers ran out of fuel. They were anni-hilated by Collins's troops from the 2nd Armored Division. The crisis in the Ardennes was over, but the fighting would go on for weeks.

Montgomery took advantage of Eisenhower's temporary assignment of U.S. armies to his command by dropping hints to the British press that the change was due to the incompetence of Bradley and Eisenhower in manag-ing Allied forces, and that he was the general who turned the tide toward victory in the Battle of the Bulge. Editorial writers in London, as well as Brooke and Churchill, began pressuring Eisenhower to appoint Montgom-ery as overall ground commander. In Washington Marshall was monitoring these developments, concerned that Ike might give in, and on December 30 he cabled his protégé. Noting press reports in London proposing appoint-ment of a commander for all ground forces, Marshall wrote, "My feeling is this: under no circumstances make any concession of any kind whatsoever. You not only have our complete confidence but there would be a terrific resentment in this country following such action." To strengthen his men-tee's resolve, he added a compliment, which he knew Ike would cherish, and a wish for the New Year. "You are doing a grand job and go on and give them hell."[75]

With Marshall's complete support, Eisenhower was ready for a confron-tation with Montgomery. On the afternoon of December 30, Montgomery's chief of staff informed Eisenhower that his boss would not, as he previously promised, mount an attack on the base of the Maas salient on January 1, leaving Patton to fight alone in the south. Eisenhower was furious. He showed Monty's chief of staff the cable from Marshall and a draft ultimatum he was prepared to send to Marshall for immediate delivery to the Com-bined Chiefs of Staff. In essence, the ultimatum said the CCS must choose between Eisenhower and Montgomery. "One of the two of us has to go."[76] Montgomery backed down. He dispatched a "Dear Ike" note of apology signed, "Your very devoted subordinate, Monty."[77]

Hard fighting would continue for another four months, but Hitler's de-feat in the Battle of the Bulge meant that the Wehrmacht was no longer capable of offensive action. The Germans lost between 80,000 and 100,000 men. Most of their armored reserves were destroyed. Casualties incurred by the American armies, which did almost all of the fighting in the battle,

totaled 80,987 killed, wounded, captured, or missing. The Battle of the
Bulge was the costliest for Americans since Grant's Overland Campaign in
Virginia in 1864.

* * * * *

As 1944 drew to a close, Henry Stimson was alarmed about whether the
U.S. was capable of replacing these huge losses given the casualties he knew
the army would suffer when Eisenhower's armies entered Germany and
MacArthur's forces advanced toward the Japanese home islands. Moreover,
he was worried that the Soviets might renege on their promise to keep advancing from the east through Poland into Germany. Since August the Red
Army had halted on the east bank of the Vistula River outside Warsaw, supposedly because they exhausted their supplies and outran their lines of communication. In fact, they paused at the Vistula to allow the Nazis to crush an
uprising by the anti-Communist Polish Home Army in Warsaw. In a message to Roosevelt on December 27, Stalin accused the U.S. and its Western
allies of supporting the uprising in Warsaw, calling the Polish army a "criminal terrorist network."[78] In view of the Red Army halt and Stalin's accusations, Stimson "became convinced," according to Marshall, that the Soviets
"were going back on us," meaning they intended to stand still on the Vistula
in the east while the U.S. suffered even more casualties taking on the full
brunt of the Wehrmacht in the west.[79]

Stimson asked Marshall to revisit the manpower problem. Was it time to
raise the ninety-division cap? Marshall responded that by spring Eisenhower
would command fifty-nine U.S. and at least twenty Allied divisions in Europe outside of Italy. Stimson was not reassured. The last of the eighty-nine
activated army divisions were scheduled to leave the States for Europe in the
spring. Eisenhower should have enough manpower under his command,
but what if the Soviets remained at the Vistula? What if the Japanese continued to resist and the U.S. had to invade the Japanese home islands?
Should the nation go along with Marshall's ninety-division gamble? At a
meeting in early January Stimson told Marshall that he had "an uneasy feeling that we ought to make some more divisions and begin to do it now and
have them ready by next summer or next autumn . . ."[80] He recommended
that ten new divisions be activated, organized, and trained. Marshall

resisted, as he had before, arguing that American air superiority and his replacement system for keeping all existing divisions at full strength were enough to win the war. He did not believe the Soviets would remain idle at the Vistula for long. Stimson was still not persuaded. He brought in Jack McCloy to strengthen his case. Marshall "was very stormy," wrote Stimson in his diary.[81] This was an understatement. In fact, as Marshall recalled later, he bluntly told Stimson that he opposed the activation of ten new divisions "to the point of resigning, and asked him to tell the president this." He conceded that his threat to resign "wasn't a nice thing for an army officer" to do in wartime, but he was convinced that Stimson's recommendation would rob the existing divisions of their officers and he knew it would take "almost twenty-two months to get a division to go overseas."

Stimson believed Marshall would eventually reconsider, while at the same time Marshall assumed the matter was dropped.[82] Fortunately, as Marshall recalled, "the Russians showed up." The Soviets "did not turn us down on the plans they were committed to."[83] On January 12, 1945, they not only crossed the Vistula as Marshall predicted, they kicked off a massive 200-division offensive all along the front from the Baltic Sea in the north to the Carpathian Mountains in the south against some seventy understrength and war-weary German divisions. As a consequence, the U.S. adhered to Marshall's ninety-division ceiling.

*   *   *   *   *

With the inauguration out of the way and the end of the war in Europe in sight, it was time for the Big Three and their military advisers to meet. Marshall left Washington in late January, the plans for finishing off Germany and a strategy for defeating Japan foremost on his mind. In Europe, seven Allied field armies, about four million men, were gathering on the west bank of the Rhine, preparing to cross after March 1. In the Pacific, American air, sea, and ground forces were drawing closer to Japan. Intelligence sources revealed that upward of three million Japanese soldiers would defend the home islands and fight to the death to protect their emperor. Assuming no help from the Soviets, U.S. planners estimated that casualties could reach as high as 350,000 if American troops had to invade Kyushu, Honshu, and the Tokyo Plain. In a memo by General Leslie Groves, Marshall, Stimson, and the president had been previously advised that a single uranium "gun type bomb" with an estimated yield of 10,000 tons of TNT—enough to destroy a large city—"should be ready by about 1 August 1945," though there was no assurance that it would actually explode.[84]

Marshall's ultimate destination, the Crimean resort town of Yalta on the tideless Black Sea, was top secret. He could not tell Katherine where he was going or when he would return. After conferring with Eisenhower near Marseilles and Churchill in Malta, Marshall arrived at Livadia Palace, the summer home of Czar Nicholas II, on the evening of February 3, 1945, where he was billeted along with Roosevelt, Hopkins, and the other U.S. military chiefs. Within a few days, the secret was out. "Since the press has come out with the news of our meeting on the Black Sea," wrote Marshall to Katherine, "I can tell you that I have been occupying the bedroom of the Tsarina or Csarina, the wife of poor old Nicholas who was killed with her in the cellar of Katerinenberg in 1919 . . . I am overloaded with fish eggs, sour cream, and good wines and champagne as desired . . ."[85]

The Yalta conference, code-named Argonaut, lasted for a week. Contrary to allegations in the early 1950s by Senator Joseph McCarthy (and others), Marshall was not at "Roosevelt's elbow" throughout the Yalta meetings, "urging the grim necessity of *bribing* Stalin to get into the war [against Japan]."[86] There is no question that in order to limit American casualties Marshall's main objective at Yalta was to nail down a date when Stalin would join the war against Japan, and that he forcefully made it clear to his Soviet counterpart, General of the Army Aleksei Antonov, that a joint U.S.-Soviet planning group must be set up in Moscow. However, Marshall was not consulted and had no say in the territorial concessions that Roosevelt secretly extended to Stalin at Yalta to ensure Soviet entry into the war against Japan. These so-called political conditions were hammered out during a meeting at Livadia Palace between Roosevelt and Stalin that began at 3:30 p.m. on the afternoon of February 8.[87] Biographer Ed Cray wrote that Marshall "apparently briefed" Roosevelt on Soviet intentions a few minutes before he sat down with Stalin, suggesting that the chief of staff may have provided advice on territorial concessions.[88] Yet the record shows that this was impossible. At that time, Marshall was six miles away at Yusupov Palace, headquarters of the Soviet delegation, meeting with Antonov and the Soviet air and navy chiefs.[89] Moreover, as Marshall said later in an interview, "I did not talk to the president about the need of making concessions to Russia in order to get help against Japan."[90]

In fact, Marshall had little contact with Roosevelt and his political advisers throughout the Yalta conference. Aside from the opening plenary session on February 4, where he held forth on Eisenhower's plans to cross the Rhine, Marshall did not even attend, much less participate, in the meetings and elaborate dinners involving the Big Three. For the most part the formal and informal discussions among Roosevelt, Churchill, and Stalin at Livadia Palace dealt with political questions—dismemberment of Germany, reparations, war criminals, United Nations, Polish government, and the future of postwar Europe. Marshall spent most of his days at Yusupov Palace, conferring with his fellow military chiefs and their Soviet and British counterparts on coordination of offensives in Germany, mapping bombing areas, mutual use of air bases, and Pacific operations.

On February 11, the last day of the Yalta conference, the Big Three signed a "top secret" agreement. In exchange for Stalin's pledge to enter the war against Japan within ninety days after Germany surrendered, it was agreed that designated islands near Japan and the east coast of the Soviet Union would be ceded to the Soviets and that they would have rights to railroads and ports in Manchuria (subject to the concurrence of Chiang Kai-shek, which FDR was bound to obtain). Most important, as far as Marshall was concerned, Stalin agreed to use the Red Army to liberate "China from the Japanese yoke," by tying down the million-man Japanese army in China.[91] Before departing Yalta, Ed Stettinius, the newly appointed secretary of state, approached Marshall outside Livadia Palace and reportedly said, "General, I assume you are very eager to get back to your desk." Marshall smiled and responded, "Ed, for what we have got here I would have stayed a month."[92] He was referring, of course, to Stalin's promise to help the U.S. defeat the Japanese.

* * * * *

While Marshall was out of the country Katherine was at Lipscombe Lodge in Pinehurst, North Carolina, a small one-floor house surrounded by pines and magnolia trees that she had purchased and was refurbishing as a winter home. After Marshall returned to Washington in the third week of February, his habit was to fly down to Pinehurst for weekends, where he would take walks with Katherine "through the sandhills" and work on his "pouch of official mail" on Sundays.[93] By late March Marshall's pouch was bulging with pages of complaints from the British chiefs and Churchill himself concerning Eisenhower's revised plan for the defeat of Germany.

The original plan called for the Allies to cross the Rhine on a wide front. Since Field Marshal Bernard Montgomery's 21st Army Group in the north, augmented by the U.S. Ninth Army, had the preponderance of men and matériel, it was assumed that he would push on to Berlin once the Ruhr pocket—the industrial heart of Germany—had been taken. Omar Bradley's 12th Army Group, directly to the south of Montgomery, was to launch a secondary effort. In the third week of March developments on the battlefield caused Eisenhower to take a fresh look at his plan. Leading elements of one of Bradley's armored divisions had forced a crossing of the Rhine over a stone railroad bridge at Remagen on March 7, much earlier than expected. Before long, nine divisions of Bradley's group had crossed and occupied a ten-mile salient in the Rhineland on the east side of the river, well ahead of Montgomery. German resistance was crumbling. Eisenhower began exploiting these developments by increasing the strength of the assault into Germany on Bradley's front. On March 27, he and Bradley worked out a new plan. In effect they decided to rotate the axis of the Allied advance from Montgomery's group in the north to Bradley's forces in the center. According to the revised plan, command of General William Simpson's U.S. Ninth Army was to be transferred from Montgomery back to Bradley. After liquidating the Ruhr pocket, Bradley would then drive east along a line toward Leipzig and Dresden and link up with the Red Army at the Elbe River. Farther to the south General Jacob Devers's 6th Army Group would block the Wehrmacht from establishing a redoubt in the Bavarian Alps. Montgomery (less the Ninth Army) was to protect Bradley's flank and march to the northeast toward Hamburg and Lübeck on the North Sea. Eisenhower's revised plan prevented Montgomery from even trying to take Berlin.

Eisenhower's decision to destroy the German army in the center and south instead of allowing Montgomery to drive toward Berlin in the north was militarily sound. Marshal Georgy Zhukov's First Belorussian Army Group, almost a million men, had crossed the Oder River and was just thirty miles east of Berlin. Another Red Army group was moving on Berlin from the south. Montgomery could not possibly beat the Red Army in a race to Berlin, a city of obvious political significance but of little or no military value.

Besides, it was about a hundred miles inside the Soviet zone of occupation that had been approved by the Big Three at Yalta. It would make little sense to incur enormous casualties getting into Berlin, only to withdraw after Germany surrendered.

At the Pentagon Marshall was monitoring developments, heartened by the news that Patton had crossed the Rhine seventy miles south of Remagen. On the afternoon of March 27, before Eisenhower informed Montgomery of his revised plan, Marshall cabled Eisenhower, suggesting that he take "steps . . . without delay" to coordinate a link-up of U.S. forces with the Red Army along the Elbe in Germany.[94] Ike did not delay. Without advising the CCS or Montgomery, he sent an "unprecedented 'personal' message to Marshal Stalin," advising him of his revised plan for crushing the German army in the center and south, proposing a link-up with Soviet forces, and notifying the Soviets that Montgomery had been relegated to providing flank support for Bradley, thus letting them know that the Allies would not be advancing toward Berlin.[95]

When they received copies of Eisenhower's message to Stalin, the British chiefs in London were outraged. They called on the CCS to condemn Eisenhower for communicating directly with Stalin and to order Montgomery's 21st Army Group to march on Berlin. Guided by the dominant voice of Marshall, the U.S. chiefs disagreed. The "primary object," they wrote, was to "destroy the German armies." This was not the time to "disperse" and "turn to the region," namely the heavily defended, marshy approaches to Berlin, where "German resistance" would be "most successful."[96]

In other words, "keep the main thing."

Knowing that Eisenhower's battlefield decision, backed by Marshall, was likely to prevail, Churchill radioed Roosevelt on Easter Sunday, one of the last times he would communicate with the president. Churchill was tactful, but his plea was unmistakable. "[F]rom a political standpoint," he argued, Montgomery's 21st Army Group should "march as far east into Germany as possible," and "should Berlin be in our grasp we should certainly take it."[97] Roosevelt was at Warm Springs, accompanied by his traveling secretary, Bill Hassett, and his cardiologist, Dr. Howard Bruenn, among others. Lucy Rutherfurd, the woman whom FDR had had an affair with during the Great War, had not yet arrived. To Bruenn, who knew how ill the sixty-three-year-old president was, Hassett remarked, "He is slipping away from us and no earthly power can keep him here . . ."[98]

Marshall received a copy of Churchill's message either in his pouch at Lipscombe Lodge or when he returned to the Pentagon at the beginning of the week. By this time the president had turned over all matters concerning the conduct of the war to Marshall, even those that ventured into the political realm. Marshall prepared a response and read the text to the president over the scrambler telephone. Instead of responding to Churchill's point about the political importance of taking Berlin, Marshall's draft was essentially a three-page defense of Eisenhower's revised plan to "destroy in detail the separated parts of the Nazi army." It echoed what Marshall had been advocating since early 1942. The president orally approved Marshall's draft. It was finalized and dispatched from the White House Map Room to Churchill on April 4, 1945.[99]

Churchill responded with grace. "I regard the matter as closed," he wrote. And to "prove my sincerity I will use one of my very few Latin quotations, 'Amantium irae amoris integratio est.'" Someone penned the translation at the bottom of the prime minister's cable. "Lovers' quarrels always go with true love."[100]

*   *   *   *   *

On the afternoon of April 12, a message was delivered to the Pentagon for transmission overseas: "Darlings. Pa slipped away this afternoon. He did his job to the end as he would want you to do. Bless you. All our love. Mother."[101] This was Eleanor Roosevelt's way of notifying her four sons in uniform that their father had passed. Marshall had left his office early and was on the porch at Quarters One when Frank McCarthy gave him the news that the president was dead. George and Katherine rushed to the White House and spent a few minutes with Mrs. Roosevelt in the family quarters before she left for Warm Springs. She asked Marshall to take responsibility for transporting the president's body back to Washington, arranging a funeral service at the White House, and attending to the internment at Hyde Park. While Marshall was in the Cabinet Room with Harry Truman, who had just been sworn in as president, a reporter in the crowded hall asked Katherine to describe Marshall's reaction when he heard the news. She replied, "I am sorry but I can't answer that. If you wish to know you will have to ask General Marshall."[102]

Perhaps someone asked Marshall then or later how he felt about the death of the president. If that happened, there is no known record of the question being asked or of Marshall's response. Merrill Pasco, a member of Marshall's staff, recalled to an interviewer more than forty years later that Marshall "seemed impassive and showed no outward emotion."[103] There is no basis for questioning Pasco's recollection. For the past six years Marshall had made a point of intentionally maintaining an emotional distance from the president, refusing to laugh at his jokes or to spend leisure time with him at Hyde Park, at Warm Springs, or in the White House during "children's hour." Surely Marshall felt that the death of the president was a profound loss for the nation, especially in wartime. Setting aside FDR's maddening tendencies to shift positions and meander off on tangents, by the end of 1943 Marshall came to believe that Roosevelt was a great wartime leader. But he was not greatly moved by his passing as he was when he learned of the deaths of Allen, Dill, and of course Lily.

The next day, hundreds of thousands of Americans gathered alongside railway tracks and in adjacent fields as the long train bearing Roosevelt's 760-pound casket slowly made its way north. Reporters wrote that it must have been like this eighty years earlier when Abraham Lincoln's procession crept by rail across New York State before turning west toward Illinois. Both presidents had been struck down just days before the wars they fought had ended.

At noon in Washington Marshall and the rest of the military high command briefed President Truman on the probable collapse of the Third Reich by early May and the challenges that lay ahead in the Pacific. The atomic bomb was not mentioned, although Truman had learned the night before from Stimson of "an immense project" that was developing "a new explosive of almost unbelievable power."[104] On the drive back to the Pentagon with Stimson, Marshall, who knew and respected Truman as a senator, withheld his judgment of how the new president would perform as commander in chief. "We shall not know what he is really like until the pressure really begins to be felt."[105]

On April 23, when the Red Army was on the outskirts of Berlin, Truman summoned Marshall, Stimson, Leahy, Forrestal, Stettinius, and Harriman to a meeting in the Oval Office for advice on how he should respond to Stalin's apparent violation of agreements at Yalta guaranteeing free elections for the government of Poland. Should he take a hard line? Everyone except Stimson and Marshall said yes. Stimson suggested that the Soviets had a "quite different" conception of free elections and that their concerns about security were legitimate. Marshall held back, and then finally spoke up. He was concerned that if Truman drew a line in the sand, the Soviets would back off their commitment to join the war against Japan. "The Russians had it within their power," he said, "to delay entry into the Far Eastern war until we had done all of the dirty work."[106] Notwithstanding Marshall's views, Truman chose, at least initially, to take a hard line with the Soviets. Later he came around, agreeing with Marshall that "if we were to win the peace after winning the war, we had to have Russian help."[107]

In Germany the end was near. During the last days of April, advance patrols from the U.S. 69th Infantry Division spotted what appeared to be Russian soldiers on the east bank of the corpse-strewn Elbe near the small town of Strahle. The Americans commandeered a small boat and paddled across. There they shook hands and spoke in hand gestures with soldiers in the 175th Rifle Regiment of the First Ukrainian Army. The linkup of the armies was emblematic of the emergence of the United States and the Soviet Union as the two most powerful nations in the world. Five days later, Hitler committed suicide by a gunshot to his head in a bunker beneath the Reich chancellery. At two a.m. on Monday, May 7, General Alfred Jodl and Admiral Hans-Georg von Friedeburg were escorted into a room on the second floor of a redbrick school building in Reims, the "war room" of Eisenhower's headquarters. In the presence of Beetle Smith, a Soviet general, other allied officers, and seventeen reporters and photographers, Jodl and Friedeburg signed the surrender documents. The ceremony lasted ten minutes. Jodl was led into Eisenhower's office. By this time Eisenhower had personally toured Ohrdruf, a recently liberated Nazi death camp, where he was sickened when he viewed more than "3,000 naked, emaciated bodies" that had been flung into shallow graves or lay in streets where they had fallen.[108] Eisenhower, seated at his desk, looked up at Jodl. "Do you understand the terms of the document of surrender you have just signed?" Jodl answered, "Ja. Ja." Eisenhower added a warning. "You will be personally held responsible if the terms of the surrender are violated. That is all." A few minutes later Ike cabled his last war report to Marshall. "The mission of this Allied Force was fulfilled at 0241, local time, May 7, 1945."[109] Jodl was placed under arrest as a prisoner of war, tried at Nuremberg, and hanged for war crimes in October 1946.

On V-E (Victory in Europe) Day, May 8, the doors to Marshall's office at the Pentagon were wide open. Well-wishers stopped by. Congratulatory telegrams poured in. At noon Stimson asked Marshall to come to his office. When he arrived he found fourteen generals and high officials seated around the secretary's desk. Stimson beckoned Marshall to a chair in the center of the room. Glancing at his prepared remarks he thanked the chief of staff on behalf of the nation and commended him for his selflessness. "I have seen a great many soldiers in my time," said Stimson, who was born two years after the end of the Civil War, "and you, Sir, are the finest soldier I have ever known. It is fortunate for this country that we have you in this position because this war cuts deeper into the eternal verities than any other."[110] As Katherine wrote, "when George returned home that evening he was strangely silent . . . His feelings were too deep for words."[111]

*   *   *   *   *

Forty-eight hours after V-E Day a propaganda film directed by Frank Capra and starring General George Marshall was released to theaters across America. It opened with an animated sequence depicting ugly caricatures of Hitler, Mussolini, and General Tojo Hideki, the symbol of imperial Japan. Red X's were superimposed slowly across the faces of the two dictators, leaving a scary visage of Tojo, his slanted eyes staring out at the audience through oversized spectacles. The Technicolor film cut to General Marshall, who was seated at his desk with a huge portrait of General Pershing looming behind him. Marshall's chest was covered with rows of ribbons. The point of the movie was to prepare the American public for the bloody invasion of Japan and to explain the army's complicated point-based rotation system that would determine who among the millions of servicemen in Europe would be shipped to the Pacific to fight and possibly die in the war against Japan; and who would be among the lucky few allowed to return home safely from Europe. The number one priority for the nation, intoned Marshall, "was to beat the Jap." The film was titled *Two Down and One to Go.*

With the defeat of Italy and Germany behind him, Marshall focused on the main thing—a swift end to the war with Japan. On paper, Japan had already lost the war. Her navy, air force, and industrial capacity were virtually destroyed. American B-29s had bombed and fire-stormed her cities at will. As an island nation Japan was isolated, her access to oil and other raw materials eliminated. Yet the Japanese continued to mount a savage resistance, using kamikazes to cripple or sink U.S. naval vessels and fighting almost to the last man from caves, tunnels, and bunkers. As American troops neared the home islands, their combat units incurred higher and higher percentages of casualties. At Iwo Jima the marines suffered 26,000 casualties, including 6,000 killed. Of the 20,000 Japanese defenders, only 218 were taken prisoner.

Two key questions had to be faced by Marshall and his advisers. How could the Japanese militarists and their emperor be compelled to surrender? And what would be the cost in American blood? U.S. Navy and Air Force planners, led by King and Arnold, were claiming that a tight naval blockade of the home islands, combined with stepped-up bombing, including incendiaries, would result in surrender with relatively few casualties. Marshall maintained that this would take too long and in the end would not be enough. Based on suicidal resistance at Iwo Jima and Okinawa and the existence of pockets of Japanese fighters still holding out on several so-called conquered islands (e.g., Guam, Tinian, Saipan, Luzon), he believed that blockade and bombing would not force the 2.6 million-man Japanese army garrisoned in the home islands to lay down arms and surrender their emperor to the enemy. Rather, to bring the war to a close Marshall reluctantly concluded that full-scale invasions of the two main home islands, backed by overwhelming air and naval power, were necessary. American troops would have to pay a heavy price, an estimated 193,500 casualties according to Marshall's Joint Staff planners. And if Truman pushed too hard on the issue of free elections in Poland, causing Stalin to postpone or ignore his agreement to enter the war and tie down Japanese troops in China, U.S. casualties could be much higher.

What about the bomb? Could it end the war? By late May 1945, Marshall had come to believe that the use of the atomic bomb, if it actually worked, could shorten the war and reduce U.S. casualties, though he wasn't sure that it alone would force the Japanese to surrender. He knew that Stimson had briefed Truman in April on the fact that a uranium bomb capable of destroying an entire city would be ready by August 1 and that a plutonium bomb would be tested in July. Marshall was also aware that Truman had appointed a blue-ribbon Interim Committee of civilians, including Stimson as chairman, to advise the president on, among other things, whether and how to use the bomb against Japan. In late May, two days before the Interim Committee was to meet, Marshall sat down with Stimson and McCloy to discuss his views on the bomb and other weapons to hasten the end of the war. Perhaps because he was influenced by physicists working on the Manhattan Project, Marshall drew a new moral and ethical line on the use of the atomic bomb, a line he chose not to draw when he sanctioned (or did not oppose) the fire-bombings of Dresden and Tokyo that caused tens of thousands of civilians to be burned alive. To Marshall, the ability to release city-destroying energy by splitting a tiny atom represented the dawn of a new and profoundly unsettling relationship between man and the universe, with effects that involved "primordial considerations."[112] He warned Stimson that the use of a nuclear bomb to destroy an entire Japanese city and all of its non-military inhabitants would subject America and its leaders to moral opprobrium for generations. To avoid censure and protect the president, he proposed alternatives. The bomb should be used first on a "straight military" target, "such as a large naval installation," argued Marshall. If that does not move the Japanese government toward surrender, then the president should designate a number of "large manufacturing areas [cities] from which the people would be *warned* to leave," and then destroy just one of these areas.[113]

Of the four U.S. joint chiefs, Marshall was the only one who, before the bomb was used in August to kill more than 100,000 Japanese civilians, advocated a way to avoid the use of atomic bombs on Japanese cities or to provide an advance warning so that noncombatants could safely evacuate. As Stanford historian Barton Bernstein has pointed out, after the war Leahy, Arnold, and King each criticized the use of the bomb, suggesting that there were other ways of ending the war, but none expressed an opinion beforehand to Truman or any other government official that it should not be used against innocent civilians.[114] Marshall took the opposite approach. He offered ways to avoid massive civilian casualties. However, once Truman decided to use the bomb on Hiroshima and Nagasaki, Marshall strongly defended the president, saying the decision was "quite necessary in order to shorten the war."[115] He never told his postwar interviewers about his advice to Stimson.

If Stimson was inclined to agree with Marshall on ways to use the bomb without killing and burning huge numbers of Japanese noncombatants, he was talked out of them during the meeting of the Interim Committee at the end of May. James Byrnes, soon to be Truman's secretary of state, was an influential member of the committee. He scotched Marshall's advance warning proposal, arguing that the Japanese would bring American POWs to the cities designated for destruction, although if enough cities were designated and only one was destroyed, it is difficult to understand why this was such a winning argument. Robert Oppenheimer and James Conant, president of Harvard, argued against a purely military target, stressing the need for the "brilliant luminescence" of the atomic explosion to make a visual and psychological impression on as many people as possible. Although Marshall was not a member of the committee, he was an invited participant. He could have defended his proposals, yet he remained silent. Apparently, he felt he had made his case to Stimson, his civilian boss, and it was not his place as a military invitee to argue with or go around him. At the conclusion of the discussion, Stimson, as chair, made it clear that there would be no advance warning and that a military installation alone would not be targeted. Instead, the preferred target would be a "war plant employing a large number of workers" that was "closely surrounded by workers' houses." Under this formula, any Japanese city with a "war plant"—that is, virtually every city—was fair game.[116] From the May 31 meeting, until the order to deploy the atomic bombs was issued on July 29 in his name, there is no evidence that Marshall ever repeated his ethical concerns to Stimson, the president, or anyone else.

Because no one knew for sure whether the bomb would work and if it did what effect it would have on Japanese resistance, Marshall still needed the president to approve his plan to invade the southern home island of Kyushu. At a meeting at the White House on June 18, he described the Kyushu operation as essential to "tightening our strangle hold" over Japan and preparing the way for the final step, the invasion of Honshu and the Tokyo Plain that would force the government and the emperor to surrender. With regard to numbers of casualties, it appears that Marshall deliberately suppressed estimates by MacArthur, his Joint Staff planners, and others of expected casualties in excess of 100,000, most likely because he did not believe they would reach such magnitudes. Instead of providing unambiguous assessments, he told Truman that because experience with casualties in the various Pacific operations was "so diverse . . . [it] would be wrong to give any estimate in numbers" for the Kyushu invasion. He stressed the importance of "Russian participation," suggesting that it could lead to an earlier capitulation and therefore fewer American casualties. King, Arnold, and General Ira Eaker (representing Arnold) supported Marshall's strategy and did not offer their own casualty estimates. Leahy said that U.S. casualties likely to be suffered could be as high as "35 percent," based on the Okinawa experience. He pressed for a relaxation of Roosevelt's unconditional-surrender policy, which he thought might lead to a settlement that would preserve the emperor, reduce American casualties, and eliminate the need for Soviet participation. Truman responded that in the absence of congressional action to change the unconditional-surrender policy he did not have the backing of "public opinion" to make this change on his own. Without insisting that Marshall provide him with estimates of expected casualties, the president approved the chief of staff's Kyushu plan, targeted for November 1, and authorized the joint chiefs to "go ahead with it." The final operation, the invasion of Honshu in March 1946, would be considered later.[117]

* * * * *

For Marshall, the final act of the Second World War played out while he was in Potsdam, a relatively unscathed suburb of Berlin on narrow Lake Griebnitzsee in the Soviet zone. The Potsdam Conference, code-named Terminal, was Churchill's idea. He was "profoundly concerned" about the potential domination of Europe by the Soviet Union and the spread of Communism. In a May 1945 letter to Truman urging the need for a meeting of the Big Three, he complained that an "iron curtain" had descended across Europe, "and we don't know what is going on behind."[118] The Potsdam Conference was largely political, a meeting of Churchill, Stalin, Truman, and their delegations of advisers to try to shape postwar Europe. Marshall and the other joint chiefs were there, mainly to plan with their counterparts the entry of the Red Army into the war in Manchuria against Japan and the integration of British naval and air forces into the Pacific theater.

Marshall arrived at his quarters in Babelsberg near Potsdam on July 16, the day before the conference was to begin. That afternoon the JCS met briefly with the president. Truman approved Marshall's proposal to appoint

General Douglas MacArthur as commander of all Allied ground, sea, and air forces in the Pacific. That meant that MacArthur would command Operation DOWNFALL, the invasions of the Japanese home islands. At 7:30 p.m., a top secret cable to Stimson arrived at the army message center, which he took directly to Truman after it was decoded. "Operated on this morning," it read. "Diagnosis not yet complete but results seem satisfactory and already exceed expectations."[119] It meant that the plutonium bomb, the implosion bomb that needed to be tested first in the New Mexico desert to know whether it would actually explode, did in fact explode. Indeed, the first nuclear explosion in history was a spectacular success. The test was crucial. In the time they had, engineers and scientists in the Manhattan Project were able to refine only enough plutonium for two bombs, and to process enough uranium for a single bomb. After the test there were two remaining atomic bombs that could be used against Japan, the unexploded plutonium bomb ("Fat Man") and the uranium gun-type bomb ("Little Boy"), that the engineers knew would work and did not therefore need to be tested. To convince the Japanese government to surrender, the explosion of at least two nuclear bombs was essential. The first bomb would demonstrate its destructive power, the ability to destroy a large city and most of its inhabitants. The second would prove that there was more than one and at least suggest that the U.S. had produced and could explode many more. Two bombs would convince the Japanese that their situation was completely hopeless and they would surrender unconditionally, or so the strategists predicted.

Truman was delighted with the news. At noon on the 17th, he showed Churchill the cables that had come in concerning the successful test and indicated that Stalin ought to be informed. Churchill agreed, but said he should be told none of "the particulars."[120] At about the same time Stimson briefed Marshall and Arnold on the test. Along with McCloy they discussed the timing for deploying the bombs and the list of cities from which the targets would be selected by the air force commander in the Pacific.

That evening Churchill invited Marshall to dine with him alone at 23 Ringstrasse, the prime minister's pink Tuscan-syle villa. Marshall described the evening in a letter to Katherine. They sat "at a tiny table on the terrace looking out over the lake . . . Churchill was intimate and very flattering . . . He proposed dignifying me as 'the noblest Roman of them all,' as he put it in conceiving the campaigns, building the great army and fighting through to the end for a proper employment of the forces."[121] At another dinner later in the conference Stalin was equally complimentary, in his own inimitable way. "That is a man I admire," he said, pointing to Marshall across the table. "He is a good general. We have good generals in the Soviet Army, but so have you and the Americans. Only ours still lack breeding, and their manners are bad."[122]

There was no singular moment when Truman finally decided that he would authorize a nuclear bomb to be exploded over a Japanese city. In fact, he never issued a presidential order. However, by all accounts Truman made up his mind on Tuesday, July 24, 1945. By that time he had signed off on the final draft of the Potsdam Declaration, a thirteen-point statement calling on Japan to surrender. The declaration was scheduled to be announced to Japan and the world two days later. Although it demanded "unconditional surrender," it also suggested that under certain conditions the American occupation would be temporary and that Japanese sovereignty over the home islands would be restored. However, despite Stimson's last-minute plea, the declaration did not preserve the emperor's position. Nor did it warn or even hint at the existence of new weapons of mass destruction possessed by the United States. The most it said was that if the Japanese government refused to surrender, the only "alternative for Japan is prompt and utter destruction."[123] At 11:30 a.m. on the morning of July 24, the Combined Chiefs of Staff met with Truman and Churchill at Truman's villa, 2 Kaiserstrasse, to finalize their report on the Potsdam Conference. It was the one time when the president, the prime minister, and all of their top military advisers were together behind closed doors. It was not a timid group. If anyone had an objection or something to say about dropping atomic bombs on Japanese cities, this was the time. No one spoke up. Truman had the support of all of the military chiefs.[124] Absent something unforeseen, at least one of the two bombs would be detonated over Japan within a few weeks.

Late that same afternoon as a heated meeting with the Soviets was breaking up, Truman walked over to Stalin and his interpreter, Vladimir Pavlov. "I casually mentioned to Stalin that we had a new weapon of unusual destructive force," recalled Truman. "All he said was that he was glad to hear it and hoped that we would make good use of it against the Japanese."[125] Stalin feigned indifference. Through master spy Klaus Fuchs and others he already knew a great deal about the Manhattan Project.

According to Marshal Zhukov, when Stalin returned to his quarters he instructed Molotov to "tell Kurchatov [chief of Soviet nuclear research] to hurry up the work."[126]

The actual order to detonate nuclear bombs over one or more Japanese cities was drafted and redrafted in Washington by General Leslie Groves, head of the Manhattan Project. The final draft, for approval by Marshall and Stimson, arrived at Potsdam early on the morning of July 25. The first bomb was to be dropped as soon after August 3 as weather would permit. A message signifying approval in the name of the chief of staff and secretary of war was dispatched from Berlin to Washington at 9:45 a.m. Berlin time, at about the same time Stimson and then Marshall were conferring with Truman at Potsdam.[127] The potential targets, approved by Truman, were the cities of Hiroshima, Nagasaki, Kokura, and Niigata. The next day the Potsdam surrender ultimatum was released.

While Marshall was flying from Berlin back to Washington, Japan's prime minister, Suzuki Kantaro, responded to the Potsdam Declaration. "The government does not think that it has serious value. We can ignore [*mokusatsu*] it. We will do our utmost to complete the war to the bitter end." The word *mokusatsu* was reported to the White House as meaning "ignore." Depending on context, it could be translated as meaning something like "wait in silence until we can speak with wisdom."[128]

Clouds were sparse over Hiroshima. Airmen in the *Enola Gay* donned their polarized glasses. At 8:15 a.m. (Tinian time) the nine-thousand-pound Little Boy fell from the bomb bay and the B-29 lurched upward. Minutes later a flash of blinding light illuminated the cabin. On the return flight an encoded message was sent back to Tinian. "Results clear cut. Successful in all respects. Visible effects greater than New Mexico tests."[129]

It was almost midnight on Sunday, August 5, when Frank McCarthy called Quarters One and gave Marshall the news. By seven the next morning the chief of staff was at the Pentagon reading a two-page report prepared by General Groves during the night. According to the messages from the crew of the *Enola Gay* the entire city of Hiroshima was covered by a three-mile "dark grey dust layer" with "flashes of fire visible in the dust." A mushroom cloud rose to 40,000 feet.[130] Later in the day Truman issued a statement promising a "rain of ruin from the air" unless the Japanese surrendered.[131]

Nothing was heard from the Japanese government. On August 8,

Marshall was having lunch with Helen Rogers Reid, president of the *New York Herald Tribune*, when he received word that the Soviet Union would declare war on Japan at midnight. The following morning he learned that Fat Man, the plutonium bomb, had been exploded over Nagasaki and that more than a million Soviet troops were pouring across the 2,700-mile-long border with China, attacking from several directions into Manchuria and the Korean Peninsula. In Tokyo, the government believed that the U.S. had more atomic bombs and that Tokyo and Kyoto would be wiped out. At two a.m. on August 10 (Japan time), Emperor Hirohito decided to "swallow" his "tears" and directed his government to accept the Potsdam terms, provided, however, that they would not "prejudice the perogatives" of the emperor as sovereign.[132]

The next morning Truman, Stimson, Byrnes, Forrestal, and Leahy debated whether to depart from FDR's 1942 "unconditional surrender" policy and preserve the emperor's status. Byrnes argued that departure was a political risk that could lead to the "crucifixion of the President" by the American people, while Stimson and the others sought a compromise.[133] At noon Stimson returned to the Pentagon to consult with Marshall. The chief of staff agreed with Stimson that as far as he was concerned the emperor could be retained so long as he remained under MacArthur's control. Marshall believed that the lives of tens of thousands of American troops need not be sacrificed on the beaches of the Japanese home islands over this issue. At a cabinet meeting in the afternoon, Truman agreed to compromise language: "From the moment of surrender the authority of the Emperor and the Japanese Government to rule the state shall be subject to the Supreme Commander of the Allied Powers," namely General MacArthur.[134] The Allied governments were notified and asked to agree. The Australians were initially opposed and Stalin delayed, but they all eventually fell into line. A formal response was sent to Tokyo via the Swiss Political Affairs Department on August 12.

In Washington the wait began. Marshall took it upon himself to order the temporary suspension of bombing of Japan and notified the president. Truman called Marshall to approve his action and ordered him to keep the suspension in effect while they awaited the Japanese response. On Monday the 13th, having heard nothing, the president ordered a resumption of conventional bombing and also authorized a B-29 mission to drop millions of leaflets on Japanese cities containing the text of the Japanese conditional acceptance of surrender and the U.S. reply. Based on a report by his chief intelligence officer indicating that the entire nation of Japan was preparing to mount a fanatical death wish resistance effort, Marshall asked his assistant chief of staff to reserve all additional atomic bomb production for tactical deployment in the event an invasion became necessary.

Meanwhile, in Tokyo, Major Hatanaka Kenji and his young army co-conspirators attempted a coup d'état to prevent the government from agreeing to the U.S. surrender terms. When they learned that the Emperor had recorded a capitulation speech to the Japanese people, they surrounded and stormed the Imperial Palace on the night of August 14 in an effort to seize the recording. By dawn the next day the coup collapsed when senior army generals refused to go along. Hatanaka and his fellow plotters committed suicide in front of the Imperial Palace.

At noon (Tokyo time) on August 15, Japanese soldiers and citizens listened by radio to the voice of their Emperor for the first time. He spoke in an archaic Japanese that was used only in official court circles. The people could scarcely comprehend what he was saying, but they understood the gist. Their war was over. A large weeping crowd gathered outside the Imperial Palace. Somewhere outside Nagasaki, enraged army officers hacked sixteen American POWs to death with swords.[135]

The exact total of Japanese civilian and military deaths caused by the nuclear explosions over Hiroshima and Nagasaki will never be known for certain. According to Richard Frank's exhaustive research, the "best approximation is that the number is huge and falls between 100,000 and 200,000."[136]

A crowd began to gather in Lafayette Square across from the White House shortly after the first word came from the Japanese government a few minutes after four p.m. on Tuesday, August 14. Japan had finally agreed to the revised terms of surrender. Two hours later, about the time the official notification was delivered by the Swiss chargé d'affaires to the State Department, a mob of several thousand was blocking traffic on Pennsylvania Avenue in the ninety-degree-plus heat, cheering and calling for Truman to appear. Uniformed sailors climbed on top of streetcars to get a glimpse of Truman. A conga line formed and snaked through the park. Automobile horns blared as one.

There is no record of where Marshall was at this moment, but given the hour he was probably at Quarters One. If George and Katherine were out on the porch that overlooked the river and the Mall, they would have heard faint sounds of the celebration rising from the humid streets of Washington.

Marshall had no second thoughts, no what-ifs, no doubts. Years later, he said that more than anything else the "shock" effect of the two bombs ended the war. "In retrospect . . . We had to save American lives . . . The bomb stopped the war."[137]

CHAPTER 13

Great Hope of China

Marshall's letter of resignation as chief of staff was submitted to the president two weeks before General MacArthur formally accepted the Japanese surrender aboard the battleship *Missouri* in Tokyo Bay. It would not be acted upon until Marshall's successor, General Eisenhower, returned from Germany in November. During the fall Katherine sorted and packed their possessions, the accumulation of her own things plus forty years of George's army uniforms, riding outfits, hunting and fishing equipment, boxes of papers and books, trophies, and hundreds of souvenirs, even a "canteen with water from Bataan still in it." She and George spent evenings talking about the next phase of their lives. After moving their belongings to Dodona and preparing the place for the winter, they planned to drive to Pinehurst, where George would hunt quail. Then, a few months on the west coast of Florida, fishing in the Gulf and reading, before returning for spring gardening in Leesburg. Katherine wrote that "mentally and physically," her husband "was a very weary man."[1]

Marshall delivered his farewell remarks at a ceremony attended by the president in the center courtyard of the Pentagon on November 26, 1945. Premised on what he called "the genius of America" and "the strength of a free people," Marshall marked a sharp departure from prewar isolationism and glimpsed a new world order. "I am certain," he said, that the United States "desires to take the lead in the measures necessary to avoid another world catastrophe . . . And the world of suffering people looks to us for such leadership." His closing lines charged the next generation of Americans with a duty and a responsibility. "It is to you men and women of this great citizen-army who carried this nation to victory, that we must look for leadership in the critical years ahead. You are young and vigorous and your services as informed citizens will be necessary to the peace and prosperity of the world."[2]

The next day George and Katherine left Quarters One for the last time, leaving the chickens and the henhouse in their yard to Dwight and Mamie Eisenhower. With Marshall at the wheel of their prewar Plymouth they drove out Route 7 to Leesburg, "full of our own thoughts and plans," wrote Katherine. From a gas station just outside the entrance to Dodona Katherine heard a jukebox blaring out a 1920s popular song that her children and their friends used to dance to at Fire Island. She "began to hum the refrain," but stumbled over the words. "Sing hallelujah, hallelujah / And you'll shoo the blues away..."[3] When they entered the gate, Katherine recalled, "George looked at me and smiled."[4]

After a few hours of emptying the car and unpacking with the help of George and her daughter, Molly Winn, who had been staying at Dodona, Katherine announced that she was going to take a nap before dinner. Halfway up the front stairs she heard the phone ring. Out of earshot, Marshall answered it in his downstairs office. The White House operator announced that the president wished to speak with him. Truman's post-presidency memoir purports to report the entire conversation. "Without any preparation," wrote Truman, "I told him: 'General, I want you to go to China for me.' Marshall said only, 'Yes, Mr. President,' and hung up abruptly."[5]

Marshall must have been forewarned about the background of the president's request and what it would mean for him. Otherwise, Truman's recounting of the extremely brief conversation is unbelievable, coming as it did on the day after Marshall retired. Suspecting that Molly knew that Truman had called, Marshall told her that he would shortly be going to China and asked her to keep it to herself for the time being. He wanted to pick the time and place to tell his wife about his new assignment. Later, Katherine came down from her nap. By happenstance, the radio was turned on then or during dinner. Katherine heard the breaking news: "Mr. Hurley resigns. President Truman has appointed General of the Army George C. Marshall as his Special Ambassadorial Envoy to China. He will leave immediately." Katherine was shocked, "rooted to the floor," she wrote. Marshall put his arm around her. "That phone call," he said, that came in as she was going upstairs, "was from the President. I could not bear to tell you until you had had your rest."[6] Two days later when Truman asked Marshall about Katherine's reaction, he said, "There was the devil to pay."[7]

Marshall in fact did have an idea of why the president suddenly called him and asked him to go to China. As chief of staff he had received pessimistic reports throughout the fall from General Wedemeyer, commander of U.S. forces in the China theater, warning that civil war between the Nationalist army of Chiang Kai-shek and Mao Zedong's Communist forces in pockets of north and central China had intensified and that the Soviet Union, with the Red Army still occupying parts of Manchuria, was providing arms and other assistance to the Communists. The United States faced the possibility of being drawn into the Chinese civil war and conceivably an armed confrontation with the Soviets, who were vying with the U.S. for postwar influence, if not dominance, in East Asia. Efforts by American diplomats to negotiate a cease-fire and unification of China by peaceful methods had failed. Consequently, Marshall knew that a military and diplomatic crisis in China was in the offing. However, unless he had been tipped off by Secretary of State James Byrnes, he was probably not aware of what had transpired in Washington behind closed doors in the thirty hours or so before Truman phoned him at Dodona.

* * * * *

Sometime before three p.m. on Monday, November 26, while Marshall was at the Pentagon for his retirement ceremony, the U.S. ambassador to China, Patrick J. Hurley, who was in Washington for consultations, informed Byrnes that he did not want to return to China and was thinking of resigning. The secretary urged him to stay on and told him the country needed him. Byrnes came away from the conversation thinking he had persuaded Hurley to return to China. He should have known better. Hurley, born in the Choctaw Nation in Oklahoma, was a real estate and oil and gas millionaire, a staunch Republican who had served as President Hoover's secretary of war. He was appointed ambassador to China by Roosevelt in 1944, but he had proven to be increasingly erratic, reckless, and unreliable, famously having greeted Mao and others on more than one occasion with the Choctaw war cry "Yahoo!" He was prone to drunken rants, and quarreled with Wedemeyer so often that the general sent cables to Washington questioning Hurley's sanity. Hurley's colleagues at the embassy in Chungking urged the State Department to fire him for incompetence. Dean Acheson's characterization of Hurley was apt: "Trouble moved with him like a cloud of flies around a steer."[8]

Though there is no supporting record, Truman claimed in his memoir that he met with Hurley in the White House at 11:30 a.m. the next day about the "seriousness of the situation" in China and that Hurley assured him that he would "wind up a few personal matters and then return to China."[9] Later, during his weekly cabinet luncheon, an aide handed the president a scrap of yellow news copy that had been torn off the White House ticker tape machine. According to Secretary of Commerce Henry Wallace, Truman glanced at the news flash, held it up, and angrily said, "See what a son-of-a-bitch did to me?"[10] Without informing the president, Hurley had released to the press a scathing letter of resignation, dated the day before, claiming that "career men" in the State Department continuously undermined his efforts to support the Nationalist government of Chiang Kai-shek by siding with "the Chinese Communist armed party" and "the imperialist bloc of nations" whose policy it was to keep China divided against herself. He warned that "[t]here is a third world war in the making."[11] Hurley's allegations of unnamed Communist sympathizers in Truman's State Department were explosive. He was among the first to plant the seeds of McCarthyism and Red-baiting that consumed U.S. politics in the 1950s.

"To me," wrote Truman, the letter "was an utterly inexplicable about face, and what had caused it I cannot imagine . . ."[12] Worried about the political damage that Hurley's allegations would cause, Truman polled his cabinet. All concurred that Hurley would have to go. Clinton Anderson, secretary of agriculture, recommended that the president immediately appoint General Marshall as new special ambassador to China, a move that would steal the headlines from Hurley. Two or three hours later Truman called Marshall at Dodona. On the following day, Hurley gave a press conference at the National Press Club at which time he named names. By that time the news that Marshall was his successor was out.

It was understood that Marshall could not depart for China until he finished his testimony before the Joint Committee that was investigating the Pearl Harbor attack. While he was busy testifying he asked Secretary Byrnes to prepare specific written instructions to govern his mission. Byrnes had already articulated his overall view: Marshall should use U.S. economic and military aid as leverage to "force" Chiang to negotiate a cease-fire and form a coalition government with Mao's Communists.[13] Byrnes delegated the task of drafting detailed instructions to Undersecretary of State Acheson and John Carter Vincent, the State Department's expert on China policy (one of Hurley's "superiors" that he complained about in his letter of resignation). Marshall rejected their initial draft, saying it lacked clarity and would not be understood by the American public. He insisted on revising it with the help of a few trusted army officers. During periods when Marshall was not testifying, Acheson worked with Marshall for hours to talk through and hammer out language acceptable to the State Department and Marshall. Acheson had encountered Marshall's way of thinking during the war, but he had never been exposed so intimately to what he called in his memoir "the art—of judgment in its highest form. Not merely military judgment, but judgment in great affairs of state, which requires both mastery of precise information and apprehension of imponderables."[14]

On December 14, Marshall and acting Secretary of State Acheson (Byrnes was on his way to Moscow) met with Truman to finalize the documents that governed Marshall's mission. They consisted of a statement of United States policy with respect to China, a memorandum for General Wedemeyer, and a press release. The policy document made it clear that the U.S. would not intervene militarily to influence "Chinese internal strife."[15] A cover letter, which Truman signed in their presence, summarized Marshall's charge, as follows: broker a cease-fire; persuade Chiang to convene a national conference to bring about the unification of China under a coalition government that included the Chinese Communist Party; complete the evacuation of Japanese troops from China; and withdraw American armed forces (i.e., 50,000 U.S. Marines) from China.[16] It was a challenging assignment, to say the least. As an incentive, Marshall was authorized under the policy document to offer U.S. economic and military assistance to the Nationalist government as "China moves toward peace and unity."[17] The power to grant or deny aid to the Nationalists was the only real leverage Marshall could use to influence the behavior of the two parties.

There were two provisos, not mentioned in the cover letter, that undermined Marshall's status as an impartial mediator. The first was contained in "notes" of a conversation between Truman and Marshall in which it was understood that if the mission should fail, the Truman administration would "continue to back" Chiang's government.[18] The second, buried in the China policy document, stated that since Chiang's Nationalist government was the only "legal government in China," it was "the proper instrument"—that is, the *only* instrument—"to achieve the objective of a unified China."[19] The latter proviso meant that the Communists would be at best a minority voice in a unified China ruled by Chiang. The former, which Chiang became aware of via a leak in Washington, was akin to a guarantee.[20] No matter how unreasonable or obstructionist in negotiations, Chiang could fall back on the support of the U.S. government.

The next day, Katherine and John Carter Vincent accompanied Marshall to National Airport. As Marshall's plane taxied out onto the runway Vincent turned to his ten-year-old boy and said, "Son, there goes the bravest man in the world. He's going to try and unify China."[21] Katherine had a different reaction. In a letter to Frank McCarthy, she wrote, "When I saw his plane take off without anyone to be close to him . . . I felt I could not stand it . . . I give a sickly smile when people say how the country loves and admires my husband . . . I know just how he felt too, but neither of us could speak of it because it was too close to our hearts . . . This sounds bitter. Well, I am bitter. The President should never have asked this of him and in such a way that he could not refuse . . . and now my daily prayer is that he can bring some sort of unity out of chaos somehow."[22]

*   *   *   *   *

It took Marshall's C-54 almost six days and five refueling stops to hop across the Pacific to Shanghai. On his last layover before reaching China's east coast, Marshall spent an evening with MacArthur at the embassy in Tokyo. In *Reminiscences*, MacArthur wrote that the general, about to reach the age of sixty-five, "had aged immeasurably" since they were last together in Papua New Guinea at the end of 1943. "The war had apparently worn him down into a shadow of his former self."[23] As usual, MacArthur was given to dramatic overstatement.

During the flight Marshall's aides, James Shepley, a correspondent for Henry Luce's *Time* magazine, and Colonel Henry Byroade (nicknamed "Side Street"), a West Pointer who had spent forty months in China, provided him with a "preliminary estimate of the political situation in China." It was hopeful. According to their report, Chou En-lai, the Communist's chief negotiator, had just returned to Chungking, the temporary wartime capital of China, where Chiang and the Kuomintang (KMT)—literally translated as the National People's Party—were headquartered. The KMT and its armed forces, led by Chiang, often called the Nationalists, controlled the rich and heavily populated provinces in the south. The other main political party, Mao Zedong's Chinese Communist Party (CCP), was based

more than 500 miles to the north in the old walled city of Yenan. As Marshall's aides reported, the fact that Chou En-lai and his delegation were in Chungking was a positive sign because they had come to begin deliberations of the Political Consultative Council, an organization sanctioned by Chiang that would bring together the KMT, the CCP, and the other political factions in China. The council's lofty goals were to stop the fratricidal warfare, end one-party rule by the KMT, decide on a framework for constitutional government, and convene a national assembly. Shepley and Byroade advised Marshall that the council was proceeding "in a more conciliatory manner" and "in a better atmosphere than has existed heretofore." They suggested that this was due to Marshall's appointment and "Truman's public statement" announcing the Marshall mission.[24]

Marshall was skeptical. During the war he had been on the receiving end of a blizzard of caustic complaints about Chiang from General Stilwell, the chief of staff of Chiang's nationalist armed forces. Typical was a memo that Vinegar Joe wrote to Marshall in 1944. "The only thing that keeps" China "split" is Chiang's "fear of losing control. He hates the Reds and will not take any chance on giving them a toehold in government."[25] As for the attitude of Mao and the CCP concerning unification, Marshall was similarly pessimistic. Shortly before leaving for China he wrote a note to Admiral Leahy saying he expected "the Communist group [to] block all progress in negotiations as far as they can, as the delay is to their advantage."[26]

Marshall's doubts were reinforced by his experiences in China in the 1920s and his knowledge of events since the 1911 revolution inspired by Dr. Sun Yat-sen, namely Chiang's Northern Expedition and purge of the Communists in 1926–28; the Long March to Yenan in the mid-1930s led by Mao Zedong; the cessation of hostilities between the Nationalists and the CCP when the Japanese invaded; and the resumption of fighting after it became clear that Japan would lose the war. As a young army officer in Tientsin, when Chiang was securing nominal allegiances with warlords in the north, Marshall had expressed prophetic views on the future of U.S. relations with China. "How [foreign] Powers should deal with China, is a question almost impossible to answer," he wrote General Pershing.[27] Staring out the window on the long flight across the Pacific in December 1945, Marshall, as one of the "Powers" he referred to so long ago, must have realized the enormity of the challenges that lay ahead.

*　*　*　*　*

"Everybody scurries around here not doing much of anything, but with the impression of great accomplishment, and all scared to death over the impending arrival of the great man himself." John Melby, a young American foreign service officer, scribbled this note of anticipation in his diary the day before five-star General Marshall landed in Shanghai.[28] Like many of his colleagues at the embassy, Melby believed expectations were unrealistically high. When Marshall stepped off his plane at Shanghai's Ganzhou Airport on December 20, he and his small staff were greeted by General Wedemeyer, commander of American forces in China, and two lines of uniformed Chinese and American honor guards. After reviewing the soldiers, Wedemeyer and Marshall climbed into the backseat of a black Buick sedan and sped downtown to the famous Cathay Hotel on the Bund, the eleven-story art deco masterpiece built by Sir Ellice Victor Sassoon, who led the real estate boom that transformed Shanghai into the Paris of the Far East.

By 1945, the Cathay had lost a bit of its luster, having been tarnished by bombing attacks and years of Japanese occupation. After settling into rooms in the tower section, Marshall summoned Wedemeyer and Walter S. Robertson, the American embassy's chargé d'affaires, to explain his mission and to be briefed on the military and political situation. Years later, Wedemeyer and Robertson separately recalled their meeting with Marshall that began in his rooms and continued through dinner downstairs. While each remembered telling Marshall that it was "not possible" for him to achieve the main goals of his mission—a coalition between the Nationalists and the Chinese Communists and an end to the civil war—their recollections of Marshall's reaction to their negative assessments were starkly different. Robertson, a Richmond investment banker turned diplomat, recalled that Marshall "listened very carefully to what we had to say," and "asked questions," but he did not reveal how "he evaluated" their disheartening views.[29] By contrast, Wedemeyer wrote in his 1958 book, *Wedemeyer Reports!*, that "Marshall reacted angrily and said: 'I am going to accomplish my mission and you are going to help me.'" To Wedemeyer, it appeared that Marshall did not want to hear the truth. Wedemeyer further wrote that during dinner Marshall "continued to show his displeasure." He attributed Marshall's foul mood and resistance to expert advice to his belief that fatigue and the "heavy toll of the war" must have worn down Marshall's "physical condition and his nerves."[30]

It is possible, of course, that Wedemeyer's memory was accurate and Robertson's was not. However, it is more likely that Wedemeyer mischaracterized Marshall's reaction and mental state in order to align them with one of the main themes of his book—the failure of Marshall to "understand the nature and aims of Communism in general and of the Chinese Communists in particular." By the end of the 1950s when he wrote his book, Wedemeyer was a card-carrying member of the "China Lobby," part of the crowd that blamed Acheson, Truman, Marshall, and the so-called communist sympathizers in the State Department for "losing China."[31] Marshall told his interviewer in 1956 that Wedemeyer "had developed an obsession" and was not acting rationally on the subject of Communism. "Got into politics," he said with evident derision. Coming from Marshall, it was the ultimate sin that an army officer could commit.[32]

The next day Marshall, Wedemeyer, and Robertson flew to Nanking to meet with Chiang, often referred to as the Generalissimo, and Madame

Chiang Kai-shek. It was a short trip, about 168 miles by air. Nanking sits on the floodplain of the Yangtze River, surrounded by an ancient wall bearing the "chop" of the Ming dynasty. Large sections of the wall were in disrepair in late 1945 due to Japanese bombs and artillery shells. In 1937, Nanking was Chiang's capital city, with a population of 1.5 million. It was then and there that the infamous "rape of Nanking" took place. Over a two-month period, some fifty thousand Japanese soldiers bayoneted, hacked, burned, disemboweled, raped, machine-gunned, buried alive, and otherwise murdered tens of thousands of residents, some say as many as 300,000. By the end of 1945, the population was half of what it had been. However, visitors were "impressed by the amount of building" going on in the city as residents who had fled the Japanese began returning.[33] People in the surrounding area and an increasing number of tourists once again flocked to Nanking's most prominent building, the mausoleum of Sun Yat-sen, which remained intact outside the city wall on the slopes of Purple Mountain. The Lincolnesque memorial to the founder of modern China looked almost the same as it did in 1929 when it opened.

Marshall and his party were met at the airport in Nanking by the Generalissimo and Madame Chiang. Marshall had not seen the couple since the Cairo conference in late 1943. At age fifty-nine Chiang's mustache and eyebrows had begun to turn gray. Otherwise, he did not seem to have aged. There were few lines on his ascetic face. His dark eyes were alert and piercing. His clean-shaven skull gleamed. As always, he was slim, modestly attired in an army uniform bereft of ribbons and medals. In important ways Chiang and Marshall shared similar attributes. Both were introspective, reserved, and personally incorruptible. They valued duty, honor, and love of country. As young army officers they practiced self-control and discipline. (One of Chiang's teachers at the Dragon River Academy recalled Chiang's morning ritual. Upon rising in the morning he would stand outside his bedroom for thirty minutes, "lips tightly pressed," and concentrate "on his goals for the day and in life."[34]) They each rose to the top by cultivating career-altering mentors—Chiang to Sun Yat-sen and Marshall to Pershing—yet they were not afraid to passionately disagree with them. The Generalissimo and the American General were charismatic leaders of men.

Soong Mayling, known to Marshall as Madame Chiang Kai-shek, was unique, one of the most influential women of the twentieth century. Unlike

Marshall and her husband, Madame Chiang was outgoing and garrulous, born to extraordinary wealth. Eleven years younger than Chiang, she was attractive and sexy, almost always wearing makeup and a traditional *qi pao* dress that was slit to the knee and sometimes above. Soong Mayling was a Christian, a devout Methodist, who had been educated in America, first at Wesleyan College in Macon, Georgia, then at Wellesley in Massachusetts so she could be close to her brother, T. V. Soong, who was at Harvard. She spoke perfect English with a Georgia accent. Mayling and Kai-shek were known throughout the world as symbols of Chinese bravery and dignity. She spent the last fourteen months of the war living on the Long Island estate of H. H. Kung, supposedly a direct descendant of Confucius, who was married to her sister Ai-ling (her other sister, Ching-ling, was the widow of Sun Yat-sen). During that time Madame and the ten lobbying firms on retainer by the Nationalist government worked to create and build a pro-Chiang, anti-Communist movement in the United States—part of the China Lobby.

Marshall's trust in and regard for Chiang when he landed in Nanking to begin his mission to China are difficult to assess. He swore to his interviewer that he always was "fond" of Chiang and that his views toward him were not influenced by Stilwell. Marshall said he believed Chiang was not "personally corrupt," but "there were many corrupt people around him" and his advisers "constantly sold [him] down the river." Yet in the same interview, he claimed that Chiang "betrayed me down the river several times during the war." It was "Madame," he made clear, who during the war "was always for me against the generalissimo."[35] This comment surely referred, at least in part, to the fact that Madame, as well as her two sisters, supported Marshall in 1944 by pressing Chiang to retain Stilwell as his chief of staff. It is safe to say that by the end of 1945, Marshall had no objection to spending a good deal of time with Chiang, but he was not sure the Generalissimo could be trusted, especially when Madame was absent.

On the evening of December 21, Marshall arrived at a small two-story brick house in the compound of the Nationalist army headquarters to meet with the Generalissimo and Madame Chiang, his first as a diplomat. Chiang was probably nervous, mindful of Stilwell's contempt for him and aware of Marshall's close relationship with Stilwell. Chiang need not have worried. The name "Stilwell" was never uttered or even implied. Marshall was remarkably humble and deferential. He stressed throughout the two-and-a-quarter-hour session that he was there to listen and that he had much to learn. As to substance, he said U.S. assistance for the "rehabilitation of China" would be dependent on concessions made by each party that would lead to a peaceful settlement. However, he tilted toward Chiang and the Nationalists by saying that the solution lay with the Communists, who needed to "relinquish autonomy" over their army in order to earn "sympathy in the United States." This was what Chiang and Madame wanted to hear. Chiang's response to Marshall's remarks focused more on the importance of eliminating the Communist army as an autonomous force than on the details of forming a coalition government. In addition, while warning Marshall that the Communists would try to "play [him] for time" so they could strengthen their military position, a stratagem that Marshall was keenly aware of, Chiang hinted that he had a similar aim. Through Mayling as translator, Chiang told Marshall that he planned to move additional troops into "North China," so as to compel Mao's CCP to "resort to political means" to reach a settlement. In other words, he too intended to use Marshall's mediation process to strengthen his position on the battlefield, thereby increasing his ability to wield the upper hand in negotiations leading to a so-called coalition government. When Chiang tried to persuade Marshall that the Soviets, despite appearances and a treaty with the Nationalists, were actively frustrating his generals' efforts to move their forces into North China, Marshall demurred, saying he wasn't ready to impugn Soviet actions and motives. He ended the meeting by assuring Chiang that, on the basis of his previous "personal dealings" with Stalin, he could get the straight story from the Soviet leader himself.[36]

For Kai-shek and Mayling it was an auspicious beginning, an evening that ended with dinner and a toast to Marshall's forthcoming birthday.

* * * * *

The next morning, Marshall, the Generalissimo, and Madame Chiang flew together to Chungking, the wartime capital located in southwest China, to meet with Chou En-lai and other top CCP officials who were there to help set up the Political Consultative Council (PCC) with the KMT. When they touched down at about noon they could see that large delegations of CCP and KMT party members were waiting to greet them. John Melby, the advance man from the U.S. embassy who was on the tarmac, wrote that because of harassment by the Nationalist police, "the mood" among the

Communists "was anything but joyous." As Marshall and Chiang emerged from the plane into the windy and raw cold, they were each "grim and un-smiling," wrote Melby, and Marshall looked "tired."[37] Marshall spoke briefly to Chou En-lai, but was unable to understand the interpreter because his ears were blocked due to the landing. He departed without delivering re-marks to the crowd, leaving it to Shepley to handle press questions. Chiang stayed behind to chat with members of the KMT and to stiffly acknowledge the presence of Chou and his CCP comrades.

To mark Marshall's arrival in Chungking for the American press, Ma-dame Chiang offered a positive, though not particularly optimistic, com-ment. "I wish him every success. He is an able and forthright man."[38]

Chungking was a city in transition. Its heroic legend, earned through years of relentless bombing of its defenseless residents, was fading. Thou-sands of government workers were scheduled to move to Nanking in the spring, leaving in their wake the stench of corruption, profiteering, the rav-ages of inflation, and hundreds of alcohol-fueled lend-lease buses. Yet Chungking was blessed by natural beauty. Situated on a promontory above the junction of two major rivers, the city is encircled by soaring mountains. During the war the population had doubled, growing to more than a million. The mayor and planning commission were anticipating substantial growth, with plans on the drawing boards in early 1946 for two major bridges, tun-nels, funicular railways, roads, factories, and office buildings to replace the jerry-built government shacks.[39]

From the airport Marshall was driven to his temporary headquarters, a cramped two-story building, sarcastically called "Happiness Gardens," where he and his staff were to reside and conduct business. The living room on the first floor had been converted into a conference room. A desk for Marshall was placed in the hall and his bedroom was in one of two small rooms at the rear. The second floor was set aside for the staff. Marshall set-tled in and prepared for his meeting the next afternoon with Chou En-lai and two of his CCP colleagues.

Marshall had been briefed. He knew that Chou was the official "face" of Mao's Communist Party in Chungking, having lived in the capital city off and on during much of the war. And he was relieved to know that Chou spoke excellent English (Marshall's ability to understand the conversational Chinese that he learned when he was stationed at Tientsin had long since atrophied due to lack of practice). Chou had been born into an upper-class family of scholars in 1898. He was worldly, sophisticated, and socially adept. He attended elite schools in China, studied Marxism, and traveled throughout Europe in the early 1920s, spending the most time in Paris, where he joined the Communist Party. In Chungking during much of the war, Chou cultivated American diplomats and journalists, persuading many of them that the Chinese Communists were enlightened reformers and that right-wing elements of the KMT party were corrupt and treacherous. What Marshall was not told was that Chou was ruthless, with a hidden history of murder and revenge. In the late 1920s and early 1930s, Chou controlled Teke, the CCP's intelligence agency and its "Red Squad" that tortured and assassinated KMT intelligence agents and those in the CCP suspected of disloyalty. Theodore White, prominent correspondent for *Time* who lived in Chungking from 1941 to 1945, was one of the journalists originally seduced by Chou. Much later he wrote that Chou was a man "as brilliant and ruthless as any the Communist movement has thrown up in this century."[40]

In his first meeting with Marshall, Chou proved for the most part to be a deft negotiator. At the outset, Marshall stressed the "urgency of an early agreement" for a unified government and the need to end the "existence of two armies in China." Relaxed and engaging, Chou responded with an offer that seemed on its face to be more than reasonable. He said he was prepared to "guarantee" that his side would "cease firing." If the Nationalists reciprocated, "the war can be stopped." The optics of Chou's opening move were good. However, Marshall knew that it was in the interests of the Communists to stop the fighting because they were losing on the battlefield and needed a substantial pause to recruit fresh troops and replenish supplies. Chou might be playing him and the Nationalists for time. As for the integration of the two armies into one, Chou said that effort would, of course, have to await the formation of a "coalition government." Once formed, the new government would unify not only "the political administration of China, but also its troops"—that is, its two armies. To sweeten his proposals Chou agreed that Chiang should remain as sovereign and the KMT "would be in first place" in the new government.

Chou's proposals must have struck Marshall as reasonable starting points. While they could be nothing more than stalling tactics, Chou had adroitly shifted the burden to Chiang. With Marshall pressing for an early settlement, Chiang would have to respond with something other than a flat refusal to negotiate. Marshall was encouraged, but he voiced no opinion.

Chou should have stopped when he was ahead. Instead, in a transparent attempt to ingratiate himself with Marshall, he closed the meeting by claiming that the CCP desired an "American style" democracy. He suggested that the new China would emulate the spirit of "independence" of George Washington, a government by and for the people preached by Lincoln, and the "four freedoms" proclaimed by FDR. Chou misread his man. After listening to this paean, Marshall must have questioned Chou's sincerity or his judgment, or both. Nevertheless, he was gracious. Marshall proposed a modest toast: "To a generous understanding."[41]

Chiang and his advisers wrestled for a week on how to respond to Chou's proposals. Their initial draft, presented to Marshall on the night of December 30, was anything but generous. "For the first time," wrote Marshall, he weighed in with his own opinion. The next afternoon, Marshall's sixty-fifth birthday, Chiang's foreign minister, Dr. Wang Shih-chieh, drove out to Chiang's cottage in the country where Marshall was staying. As a result of Marshall's suggestions the night before, the Nationalist government decided to respond to Chou by proposing: (a) an immediate cease-fire; (b) appointment of a "Committee of Three," consisting of Marshall, Chou, and Chiang's designee, to oversee enforcement of the cease-fire and disarmament of Japanese troops; and (c) a commission to visit disputed areas in the north in order to "determine facts and make recommendations."[42] Marshall was pleased with their proposals. He started planning for the establishment of an executive agency to administer the proposed truce.

As Marshall knew, the cessation of hostilities was the easy part. Both sides could agree to an armistice, at least for a limited time, while unification was pursued. The hard part was to negotiate an agreement to deal with troop movements *after* the fighting stopped. Parties needed to be prevented from using the truce to gain an advantage, which they could exploit when the cease-fire ended either by its terms or by breach. To solve this problem, the Nationalists and Communists agreed that in most provinces of China their combat units would remain in the positions they were in as of the effective date of the cease-fire. However, the three northeastern provinces of China, a region known as Manchuria, were a major stumbling block. In late 1945, long after the Japanese surrender, many of the main cities and towns of

Manchuria were still occupied by the Red Army. The Nationalists, as the recognized and legitimate government of all of China, were entitled to establish sovereignty in Manchuria by moving their troops and administrators into the cities and towns in the region. Moreover, by the terms of a Sino-Soviet treaty, the Soviets agreed that as they withdrew their forces from Manchuria they would help the Nationalist government move in. The problem was that the CCP was strongest in rural areas of Manchuria. CCP troops and organizers had already infiltrated parts of the region and had taken possession of arms surrendered by the Japanese. Chou could have refused to allow the Nationalists to move, thus jeopardizing the overall cease-fire agreement. Surprisingly, he gave in. In the case of Manchuria, the CCP agreed to create an exception to the general rule of nonmovement that prevailed throughout the rest of China. Pursuant to the "Manchuria exception," the Nationalists would be permitted to move their forces into and within the region to establish sovereignty and prevent a vacuum as the Soviets withdrew. CCP troops already situated in the three provinces comprising Manchuria would not move. They would stay where they were, mainly in the rural areas. For the Communists it was a remarkable compromise.

The details of the truce were falling into place. The plan was to announce its signing on January 10 so that it would coincide with the long-anticipated opening of the PCC, the body of thirty-eight delegates representing all of China's political parties who were poised to begin hashing out the terms of unification. However, on January 9, the cease-fire negotiations conducted by the Committee of Three—Chou, General Chang Chung (representing Chiang), and Marshall as the mediator—ground to a halt. They had reached an impasse over the issue of Nationalist troop movements into two towns situated athwart rail junctions north and northeast of Beijing in what were then Jehol and Chahar Provinces. The towns, which offered a route into Manchuria from Yenan, were held by the CCP. "It would be a tragedy," pronounced Marshall, "to have this conference fail at the last moment."[43] For Marshall and the prospect of a unified China, it was a critical moment. Unless the cease-fire agreement was signed, the PCC would almost certainly collapse. With neither side giving ground, the meeting adjourned.

Late that evening, the night before the PCC was to meet for the first time, Marshall went alone to Chiang's residence. Arguing that Chiang had little to lose and everything to gain by postponing negotiations over the issue of troop movements into the two towns until a later date, Marshall prevailed upon him to concede. Marshall "suggested and [the] Generalissimo agreed" to announce the cease-fire agreement at the opening of the PCC meeting the next morning.[44]

The cease-fire announcement electrified the PCC delegates. Chiang's opening address to their convention added to the momentum and raised expectations. To the dismay of the conservative wing of the KMT, Chiang advocated that the new unified China should adopt Western democratic principles, including freedom of speech and assembly, popular elections, equal status for all political parties, and release of political prisoners. Most Communists were euphoric. Their party newspaper, the *Liberation Daily*, proclaimed that the "rejoicing with which the Chinese people" received the cease-fire announcement "marks the beginning of peaceful development, peaceful reform, and peaceful reconstruction unique in the modern history of China."[45]

To supervise the terms of the truce, Marshall directed that an Executive Headquarters be set up at Peking Union Medical College. Walter Robertson was appointed high commissioner and Colonel Byroade his chief of staff. Two other commissioners were appointed, one Nationalist and the other Communist. A cohort of 125 U.S. officers and 350 men, equipped with jeeps, trucks, planes, and radios, was assigned to conduct inspections and write up reports. As Byroade and the others began arriving at the college, the CCP was already accusing the KMT of cease-fire violations, and vice versa. "It appears that both sides are greatly exaggerating their claims," wrote Byroade to Marshall. "Our teams will strive to obtain factual evidence to disprove claims if they are false."[46] Within days the truce machinery was in high gear. "The fighting did stop," recalled Byroade. "A lot of sieges were lifted. It looked like progress was being made, and then both sides, but particularly the Communist side, started violating the agreement." Byroade believed there would never be peace until the CCP army was integrated into Chiang's Nationalist army.[47]

Marshall regarded the truce violations as inconsequential. On February 4 he reported to Truman that the PCC was "doing their job well," and likened their deliberations to an American-style "Constitutional Convention." With evident pride he told the president that even though he had no official role, he provided the PCC with the details of a draft "interim constitution" and that the PCC incorporated his draft into its plan for a "democratic coalition government."[48] Chiang did not share Marshall's optimism. Privately, he confided to his diary that Marshall was naïve, that he was being taken in by the Communists and did not understand their deceptive nature.[49]

Even if Chiang was right, Marshall had reason to continue to pursue his mission with optimism. Thus far, he had already brokered a cease-fire. Unofficially, he had helped the PCC set the stage for a national assembly and a coalition government. Wedemeyer, Byroade, Melby, and many others had doubted these goals could be achieved. The third piece of his mission—integration and reorganization of the two armies—would be the most difficult. It was also the most important. Without true integration of the two armies, the political and economic basis for a coalition government could not be sustained.

By early February Marshall and his staff had drafted a plan for a "complete reorganization of Chinese military forces" and received authority from the Nationalists to discuss it with Chou En-lai.[50] Explaining his plan to Chou, Marshall made it abundantly clear that commanders in the reorganized army must have no position in the civil government, a change fundamentally at odds with Chinese custom and practice. A few days later Chou reported that he and General Chang (on behalf of the Nationalists) had agreed that eventually the two armies would be reorganized and integrated into a total of sixty divisions—fifty KMT and ten CCP. Under the plan, a total of some 250 KMT and CCP divisions would have to be demobilized. That evening Marshall reported to Truman that "prospects are favorable for a solution to this most difficult of all problems."[51]

After a series of marathon sessions, Marshall, Chou, and Chang concluded and signed an agreement to reorganize and integrate the CCP forces into the Nationalist army over an eighteen-month period. For the first time the two armies were to be combined under the control of a single government, not a political party. KMT troops would outnumber those of the CCP five to one. Even more notably, the Communists agreed to reduce their forces in Manchuria to a fraction of what they had been when Marshall first introduced his integration proposal. The meetings were surprisingly devoid of rancor. With humor and affection, Chou and Chiang began referring to Marshall as "the Professor." Since Marshall as special U.S. envoy was not a party to the agreement, he expressed reluctance to be a signator. Both sides pressed him to sign as "Advisor." Marshall gave in, saying, "If we are going to be hung, I will hang with you."[52]

To the waiting press correspondents, General Chang and Chou En-lai proclaimed an end to eighteen years of hostilities and a new era of peaceful reconstruction of China. They heaped praise on Marshall, the "midwife" of unification. Marshall concluded the proceedings with a speech consisting of two sentences, the first aspirational, the second a warning. "This agreement . . . represents the great hope of China. I can only trust that its pages will not be soiled by a small group of irreconcilables who for a selfish purpose would defeat the Chinese people in their overwhelming desire for peace and prosperity."[53] To Marshall, the "irreconcilables" referred to the right wing of the KMT, members of a clique headed by the influential brothers Chen Li-fu and Chen Kuo-fu, who were implacably opposed to unification with the Communists.

While Marshall anticipated a threat from the right, he was not yet aware of an even larger threat from the left. Twelve days earlier, Mao had advised his politburo in Yenan that "the United States and Chiang Kai-shek intend to eliminate us by way of nationwide military unification . . . In principle, we have to advocate national military unification; but, how we shall go about it should be decided according to the circumstances of the time."[54] To put it another way, Mao was reserving judgment on whether the CCP would actually comply with the letter of the military integration agreement. As far as he was concerned, it was a scrap of paper that could be ignored at any time.

A few days after the military integration agreement was signed, the Committee of Three—Marshall, Chou En-lai, and General Chang Chi-Chung (who replaced General Chang Chun)—departed on a 3,500-mile tour of more than a dozen cities and towns, mainly in "troubled areas" in northern China, to explain the terms of the cease-fire and integration agreements to the principal army commanders on both sides and at the same time demonstrate by their presence the "appearance of cooperation" that the three of them represented.[55] Marshall was treated as a conquering hero, signs in towns and cities calling him "Most Fairly Friend of China" and "First Lord of the Warlords." At some point during the journey Chou left his personal notebook on Marshall's C-54. Instead of having it examined or photocopied, Marshall turned it over to Chou unread and intact, thus earning a measure of trust that Chou could hardly forget. The notebook contained information identifying CCP's secret agents, one of whom was a mole embedded in the KMT.[56]

The stop to visit with Chairman Mao at CCP headquarters in Yenan was the highlight of the trip. Yenan lies on the arid Loess Plateau in northwest China almost 500 miles south of the Great Wall, its highly friable and fertile "loess" soil deposited on the plateau by windstorms over the centuries. Mao and his CCP followers lived and worked there in hundreds of tiered one- or two-room caves carved into the sides of steep hills and valleys.

When the Committee of Three landed, thousands of Chinese citizens stormed the rocky airstrip in hopes of catching a glimpse of the world-renowned General Marshall. Round-faced Mao, dressed in blue peasant clothes with a China Red Army cap over his shaggy black hair, greeted Marshall and the others. In contrast to what he had told his politburo, the fifty-three-year-old Chairman "assured" Marshall during their first meeting that "the Chinese Communist Party would abide wholeheartedly by the terms" of the army integration and cease-fire agreements and the resolutions of the PCC. Though Marshall later told Truman he spoke frankly to Mao, in fact he was too diplomatic. During their talks Marshall began by telling Mao that he was "embarrassed" by a CCP press statement "to the effect that Manchuria was not within the scope" of the cease-fire agreement. As Mao knew, the Nationalists' right to establish sovereignty in Manchuria was clearly covered by that agreement. The CCP statement was a deliberate fabrication. Instead of putting Mao on the spot by insisting that he come up with an explanation or denial, Marshall said that he did not wish him to respond.[57] In retrospect, it was probably a mistake to allow Mao to save face. This was the time for Marshall to make clear that he would hold the Chairman responsible for mischaracterizing or otherwise trying to undermine the agreements. Marshall ended the day being entertained by folk dancers and skits in an "icy auditorium" and watching a film with Mao while lying beneath thick rugs to ward off the cold.[58]

Marshall wasn't sure what to make of Chairman Mao. As he confessed later, Mao "remained a mystery."[59] Nevertheless, in his overly optimistic trip report to Truman, Marshall claimed that all "difficulties" were "straightened out" and that Mao as well as his field commanders pledged complete "cooperation." His reception "everywhere was enthusiastic and in cities tumultuous."[60] This was an opportune time, Marshall wrote, to return to Washington. It was necessary to persuade Congress and various federal agencies to extend financial and other assistance to the KMT and the CCP, provided substantial progress was made toward the formation of a coalition government and an integrated army. Truman responded, ordering him home for consultation. He added that Winston Churchill was in the U.S. and "desires to see you."[61] Accompanied by Truman, the former wartime prime minister had just delivered his "iron curtain" speech at Westminister College in Fulton, Missouri, the same day Marshall met face-to-face with Chairman Mao in Yenan. Most of Churchill's speech focused on the "front of the iron curtain which lies across Europe." But, in an often overlooked line, Churchill warned that "[t]he outlook is also anxious in the Far East and especially in Manchuria."[62] No wonder he wanted to speak with Marshall.

* * * * *

The outlook in Manchuria was beyond anxious. It was dire. While Marshall was flying to Washington, the first large-scale cease-fire violation took place in and around Mukden, the old Manchu capital and the largest city in Manchuria. Marshall had firsthand knowledge of the terrain in and around Mukden, having inspected it on horseback in 1914.[63] After looting Mukden of everything of conceivable value right down to the light switches, the Red Army, without any notice to the Nationalists, finally withdrew. Fifty thousand CCP troops led by General Lin Bao began to move in right behind them, planning to occupy and govern the city. However, the Nationalist New First Army, under General Sun Liren, a VMI graduate, raced up the rail line from the port of Ching Wang Tao to block their entry. In fierce street fighting Sun and his forces drove the Communists ten miles out of the city. The Nationalists entered Mukden on March 13. Under the "Manchuria exception" explicitly set forth in the cease-fire agreement, they were entitled to establish sovereignty. But CCP troops remained in the area and could counterattack at any time. Due to a marked shift in Soviet policy away from a peace settlement in China and in favor of supporting the CCP, Mao had no intention of honoring the Manchuria exception. Soviet policy had changed because Stalin felt threatened by Marshall's initial success, worried not only about too much American influence near his border in Manchuria but also the political survival of the CCP. As a consequence, Mao and his party leaders decided in late March to "use maximum strength to control" key cities in Manchuria.[64]

When Marshall landed in Washington he knew that fighting could break out again in Manchuria. At his first press conference his optimism was muted. "I am not quite as certain," he said, whether the Chinese political leaders understand the "vital importance" to peace in the Pacific of "their efforts toward unity and economic stability."[65] Concerned that the cease-fire agreement could disintegrate, Marshall radioed General Alvan Gillem, who was substituting for him in China while he was away. Marshall urged Gillem to travel to Mukden as quickly as possible to stop the fighting and the struggle for favorable position. "Further delay may be fatal," he said.[66]

Relying on Gillem to hold things together until he returned, Marshall characterized the next four weeks as "the busiest, most closely engaged period of [his] experience, not even excepting wartime."[67] With his insider's knowledge of the people and agencies that run Washington and the assistance of Dean Acheson, Marshall managed to cobble together an impressive aid package under the assumption that a coalition government would be formed. Among other items, he secured a commitment from the Export-Import Bank to extend a credit for $500 million (roughly $6 billion in today's dollars), a new lend-lease program to be funded by Congress, $30 million in cotton credits, and the transfer of surplus coastal vessels and other such properties to China. "All in all," he wrote Wedemeyer, "I think I have sold China."[68]

Marshall thought he would have to "sell" Katherine on returning with him to China. In a letter to Frank McCarthy he confided that he "hope[d] to bring Mrs. M. back with me for the remaining months of my stay—until about August or September."[69] Research reveals, however, that Madame Chiang, probably at Marshall's suggestion, began a campaign in February to convince Katherine to join her husband in China. Katherine recalled that Mayling sent her two letters claiming that she, Madame Chiang, "made" George "promise he'd bring me back with him."[70] A surviving letter that Katherine sent to McCarthy on February 19, 1946, confirms her memory. In that missive she wrote that "a letter from Mm Chiang came this A.M. asking me to come over. She says George needs me in the wonderful work he is doing for her country."[71] Whether it was Mayling's or George's idea, by the time Marshall landed in Washington Katherine was sold on going to China. She spent at least a week out at Leesburg, packing and getting "all those injections" from doctors to ward off diseases she might be exposed to in the Far East.

One weekend afternoon while George was relaxing at Dodona,

Katherine handed him a typed manuscript and asked him to read it while she took a walk. She had just finished the last chapter of a memoir about their life together that she had been secretly writing for months. Katherine walked for what seemed to her like hours. When she returned George was still reading. Eventually, he laid it down and said, "Well, I think it's time for us to go to bed." So they went upstairs. "He didn't say a word—not a word," she recalled. In the breakfast room the next morning, she asked him what he thought of the manuscript and whether it should be sent to the publisher. He replied, "If you feel that way about me, yes, but on condition that you don't sell it on my name."[72] With a few revisions by Marshall, the memoir, titled *Together: Annals of an Army Wife,* was published later that year by Katherine's brother, Tristram Tupper. It became a Book of the Month Club selection and a best seller.

* * * * *

Since the cease-fire, particularly in Manchuria, was crumbling, Marshall was pressured to return to China sooner than planned. On April 2, Madame Chiang wrote, "I hate to say 'I told you so' but even the short time you have been absent proves what I have repeatedly said to you—that China needs you."[73] Apparently, Madame had begged Marshall not to leave China in the first place. A few days later, a radio message to Marshall from Walter Robertson was more emphatic. "[T]he situation is so serious and is deteriorating so rapidly that your immediate return to China is necessary."[74]

Despite the urgency, George and Katherine did not leave Washington until April 12, and their flight back to China was leisurely. They arrived in Chungking on April 18, almost six weeks after Marshall had left. While they were in the air, Soviet general Fedor Karlov notified detachments of the Communists' Eighth Route Army that he and his Red Army troops intended to withdraw from Changchun, a city of 750,000 that had been the capital of Manchukuo, the Japanese puppet state that included all of Manchuria and Inner Mongolia. Changchun was almost 300 miles north of Mukden on the main railway that ran up through the middle of Manchuria to Harbin, the northernmost big city. At the time, the Nationalists had 4,000 poorly equipped regular army troops in Changchun, plus a few thousand local conscripts and Japanese soldiers. As General Karlov boarded his special train for Harbin and the remainder of his Soviet forces were still

departing the city, 20,000 CCP troops, armed with Japanese weapons, captured the surrounding airfields and attacked the Nationalist forces. American correspondents who were there reported that gunfire was constant for
three days and nights. The fighting in the streets was savage and casualties
were heavy. On the fourth day, what was left of the Nationalist garrison set
up a defensive perimeter with sandbags and barbed wire around the five-
story Central Bank Building and put up "an Alamo-type defense." Out-
gunned and outnumbered, they were forced to surrender or be wiped out. It
ended when Japanese (and possibly Soviet) artillery and tanks manned by
the Communists turned the bank building into what Henry Lieberman of
The New York Times called an "inferno" and the Nationalist commander fell
wounded after rushing into the plaza from the burning bank.[75]

The capture of Changchun, coming as it did on the day Marshall returned to Chungking, was by far the most significant military success by the
CCP against Chiang's Nationalists. The State Department's white paper
on the fall of China, published in 1949, called it a "flagrant violation of the
cease-fire agreement which was to have serious consequences." For two reasons, it may have doomed Marshall's mission. First, the Changchun conquest instilled confidence in Mao and his generals in Manchuria that they
could eventually defeat the Nationalists on the battlefield, thus making
them "less amenable to compromise." And second, "it greatly strengthened
the hand of the ultra-reactionary groups" in the KMT government, providing them with solid reasons for claiming that the CCP "never intended to
carry out" the agreements leading to unification.[76]

*   *   *   *   *

"The dust heat s[t]ench are beyond description," wrote Katherine.[77] Her
mood during her first week living in Chungking matched the grave situation
that confronted her husband. As it turned out, the Nationalists had also violated the truce agreement, which provided the Communists with a handful
of convenient excuses to justify their bold attack on the city of Changchun.
Though each side, therefore, shared blame, Marshall's initial approach as a
mediator was to fault the Generalissimo's "advisors" for gifting the Communists with credible accusations that the Nationalists were the first of the two
sides to breach the cease-fire.[78] His objective was to move the Nationalists
toward restoring the truce. Chiang resisted, vowing to continue fighting

until his KMT troops recaptured Changchun and controlled the rest of Manchuria. With Chairman Mao's blessing, Chou, on behalf of the CCP, was willing to enter into another cease-fire pact, provided the Communists occupied Changchun while the agreement was being negotiated. Marshall met day and night separately with each side. By April 29, Chiang offered the Communists what Marshall characterized as a "great concession." If the CCP agreed to evacuate Changchun, Chiang was willing to establish a cease-fire line north of the city, suggesting that the Communists might be left with de facto control of all of northern Manchuria. Casting blame on the Communists for their attack on Changchun, Marshall talked tough to Chou. He implored him to accept Chiang's proposal, saying he "had exhausted his means." If the CCP would not go along with Chiang's offer, Marshall implied that his mediation efforts were over. "Moved by Marshall's efforts," Chou said he would wire Yenan "in hope for an early reply."[79]

Chou may have been moved, but his boss, Mao, would not budge. His generals believed they were in a strong strategic position in Manchuria. The Soviets had just turned Harbin over to the CCP. The Red Army formally withdrew from Manchuria and pulled back into the Soviet Union. The Communists were not about to give up Changchun without a fight, or so they said at that time. Marshall was discouraged. On May 6, he wrote Truman that he was at an "impasse" and that "[t]he outlook is not promising." In Marshall's view, there was so much distrust and fear that each side preferred to take its chances on using force rather than pursuing a genuine coalition government through peaceful negotiations. Nevertheless, he told the president that he would keep trying "to resolve the difficulties . . . in a manner that will keep the skirts of the U.S. Government clear and leave charges of errors of judgement to my account."[80]

At the beginning of May, Chiang moved his government down the Yangtze to the old capital in Nanking. Katherine was "glad to have seen Chungking but once is enough." The Marshalls were billeted in a fine house and grounds on Ning Hai Road that had formerly belonged to the German ambassador. The place was large enough to accommodate offices, the mission staff, and a large conference/recreation room, where movies were shown in the evenings. Katherine and George lived in a wing on the second floor with two bedrooms and a porch overlooking the garden and lawn. Katherine wrote that their quarters "had an electric fan which is a godsend here for the heavy dark curtains must stay drawn all day—to keep out heat & dust."[81] John Hart Caughey, who lived in another upstairs room, wrote his wife that although servants wait on Mrs. Marshall "hand and foot," she is "none too happy" because she doesn't have much to do and says she "feels like a kept woman. The general makes a big point of it because he thinks it is so funny."[82]

On May 9, a beautiful spring day, Dwight Eisenhower, who succeeded Marshall as chief of staff, arrived at the Marshalls' new home. He was on a lengthy inspection tour of army installations in the Far East. Ostensibly, he stopped in Nanking to assess the readiness of troops still stationed in the area. His real mission, however, was to deliver a top secret message to Marshall from the president. After lunch with Madame and the Generalissimo, the two old friends retired to the privacy of Marshall's office. Eisenhower explained that Secretary of State Byrnes would be resigning due to "stomach trouble."[83] (In fact, Truman had long been disenchanted with Byrnes because he was too cozy with the Soviets and failed to show proper deference to the presidency.) The president wanted to know if Marshall would take the job. Years later, Eisenhower recalled Marshall's response: "Great goodness, Eisenhower, I would take any job in the world to get out of this place. I'd even enlist in the Army."[84] Marshall's serious answer was a conditional yes. He would accept the position if offered, but he could not leave China until September, by which time he hoped that the parties would agree to a new truce and a path toward unification. Upon his return to the U.S., Eisenhower explained Marshall's position to the president. In a letter to Marshall dated May 28, Eisenhower wrote that Truman "expressed great satisfaction, saying 'This gives me a wonderful ace in the hole because I have been terribly worried.'"[85]

Since informing the president that his efforts to restore the cease-fire were at an "impasse," Marshall spent the rest of the month talking with each side separately. However, both were beginning to privately question his judgment and impartiality. The Nationalists held Marshall responsible for persuading them to trust the CCP, which in their view led to the loss of Changchun. Chou and the CCP were critical of Marshall for previously allowing U.S. naval vessels and American flag shipping to transport Nationalist troops and supplies to ports in North China.

Meanwhile, developments in the field trumped negotiation. On May 19, American-trained Nationalist divisions, under the command of General Du Yuming, having moved north from Mukden along the railroad route, inflicted what some said was a decisive defeat on General Lin Bao's Communist armies in the Second Battle of Siping. The battle lasted for more than a month. Lin's troops suffered heavy casualties and desertions while trying to defend the small railway city. However, his main force, though battered and weakened, managed to withdraw from Siping and limp to the north. For the Communists, the defeat at Siping was a turning point because it forced them to temporarily abandon conventional tactics and return to a strategy of guerrilla and smaller-scale mobile warfare while they recruited, trained, and strengthened their armies. With Mao's approval, Lin elected not to try to defend Changchun and he continued his withdrawal north through Changchun all the way to the Sungari River, only sixty miles south of Harbin. Du's Nationalist troops, wearing American-style uniforms and carrying U.S.-made rifles, marched unopposed through the gates of Changchun on May 24.

Well aware that the Nationalists had recaptured Changchun, Marshall wired Chiang that his advances into Manchuria were making Marshall's efforts to broker a cease-fire "increasingly difficult" and compromising his "integrity."[86] By that time Chiang was already weighing the pros and cons of a cease-fire. The closer his troops got to the border of the Soviet Union, the greater his concern that the Soviets would intervene on the side of the CCP. Marshall was also worried about how the Soviets would react. In light of the difficulties the Truman administration was having with Stalin in Europe he could not afford to get mixed up in a confrontation with Soviet forces in Asia.

Chiang met with Marshall on the morning of June 4. Curiously, there are no minutes or other contemporaneous records of this critical "three hour conference" that Marshall referred to in his letter to Truman.[87] Precisely what was said, or what threats were made or not made during this long meeting, will never be known. What is known for sure is that by the end, Chiang agreed to a cease-fire in Manchuria, a decision that he told Marshall was "his final effort at doing business with the Communists" and later called "a most grievous mistake."[88] Looking back through fogged glasses, Chiang claimed years later that he frittered away the best chance the Nationalists would ever have to defeat the Communists on the battlefield.[89]

At noon on June 6, the Generalissimo and the CCP issued orders to their respective generals for a fifteen-day truce (later extended to the end of June) to end the fighting in Manchuria, during which the parties were to reach agreements on the details for a permanent cease-fire and implementation of the previous agreement of February 25 for the reorganization and integration of the two armies. With a show of optimism, Marshall wrote Colonel Marshall Carter, who was the liaison between the Pentagon and the State Department, that he was faced with "a hell of a problem but we will lick it yet, pessimists to the contrary notwithstanding."[90] The shaky cease-fire held, aided by the fact that Colonel Byroade dispatched eight truce teams to Manchuria and North China, but as June drew to a close Nationalist generals were preparing to attack CCP forces for violating the truce. On the 30th, with the extended cease-fire in Manchuria about to expire, Marshall met with the Generalissimo. According to John Robinson Beal, an American adviser to the KMT, Marshall argued that if Chiang's military leaders were to break the truce and attack, they would be "decreeing war against the will of the people," similar to what happened in Japan. "[A]nd look at Japan today," Marshall reportedly said to Chiang. Since the Generalissimo regarded himself as the George Washington of China, the savior of his people, he "quoted the Bible" and "almost wept" in response. Marshall told Beal that his argument had a "tremendous effect" on Chiang, and it did.[91] By the end of the five-hour session, the Generalissimo made up his mind. He did not want to end the truce with an attack on Lin Bao's main forces in Manchuria. He ordered that no "aggressive offensive action" should be taken by Nationalist generals and their forces.[92]

*   *   *   *   *

From June through October, there was almost no fighting in Manchuria, yet in the south limited offensives and counteroffensives were launched by both sides. While Chiang seemed confident that his troops were pushing back the People's Liberation Army—the new name for Mao's armed forces—Marshall was worried that the sporadic fighting would lead to all-out civil war. He tried to find a solution, but his meetings with Chiang and Chou were, in his words, "unproductive."[93] In mid-July the Generalissimo and Madame, with Katherine as their guest, left for Kuling, their summer residence high in the mountains 250 miles southwest of Nanking. "Marshall was plainly annoyed," wrote Beal in his diary. Chiang's "departure stopped the negotiations cold," and Marshall interpreted it as an effort "to force the Communists into coming to terms."[94]

Shortly before Chiang and his entourage departed for Kuling, Dr. John Leighton Stuart, the newly confirmed U.S. ambassador to China, arrived on the scene to assist Marshall, who realized he was in desperate need of political expertise. Except for Stuart's age—he was seventy—he appeared to be the ideal choice. Stuart was born in China, son of missionaries, but educated in America, where he was ordained as a Presbyterian minister. He spent most of his adult life in China, serving for years as president of the prestigious church-affiliated Yenching University near Beijing. Stuart knew almost all of the Chinese political leaders. As one of the most highly respected foreigners living in China, he was liked and trusted by the liberal, conservative, and moderate wings of the CCP, the KMT, and other political parties. Marshall believed Stuart could help him "raise the present negotiations from the level of military disputes to the higher political level for securing a genuine start towards a democratic government."[95]

Though Chiang had decided to spend the summer up at Kuling, Marshall could not afford to allow his mission of unification to stall. Thus, he had little choice but to journey by plane, boat, and jeep to the base of Lushan Mountain, where he would be carried by "coolies" in a sedan chair over six miles of trails to the top of the mountain. Each weekend from July 18 until the last week of September, the general, frequently accompanied by Stuart, would make the trip, patiently meeting for hours with Chiang and his aides in an effort to continue negotiations toward peace and a coalition government. It was not all business. During his visits to China's summer capital, where the air was fresh and cool, he would spend private time with Katherine in her European-style stone cottage that overlooked a swimming pool and the mountains beyond.

Despite their efforts, Marshall and Stuart made little if any progress during the exhausting summer of 1946. The Nationalists, whose armies seemed to be winning battles for towns in the south, insisted on extracting political concessions from the CCP before they would agree to another truce. The Communists, who were rebuilding in the north, demanded a cease-fire before they would enter into serious political negotiations with the KMT. "For the moment," wrote Marshall to Truman, "Dr. Stuart and I are stymied."[96]

By the time the Generalissimo was carried down from the mountain in late September Stuart and Marshall were not only "stymied." In Marshall's words, Chiang had made "stooges" of them.[97] That remark was triggered right after the KMT Central News Agency announced on September 30

that Nationalist forces had begun a three-pronged offensive to capture Kalgan, the largest and most important city in the hands of the Communists
south of the Great Wall. Marshall was thoroughly fed up, convinced that
Chiang was using negotiations as cover while his Nationalist forces moved
on Kalgan, blocking the Communists' gateway to Manchuria. The next day
Marshall threatened Chiang with an ultimatum, telling him that he was going to recommend to Truman that his mission be terminated.[98] Though
Marshall was probably bluffing, Chiang could not risk losing face (and vital
support) by having the U.S. president shut down Marshall's mission. He hurriedly summoned Stuart and told him that he was amenable to halting his
advance on Kalgan and agreed to a short truce.

The details of Chiang's standstill and ten-day cease-fire offer were sent
to Chou, who was in Shanghai. It was proposed that during the truce a
group under Stuart would establish a formula to determine the number of
CCP delegates allowed to participate in the National Assembly for formation of a coalition government and that Marshall's Committee of Three
would implement the February agreement to reorganize and integrate the
two armies. For a few hours Marshall and Stuart allowed themselves to
dream that a deal might still be possible.

In Shanghai, Chou greeted the proposal with suspicion. He believed the
latest cease-fire proposal was just another scam by Chiang to obtain a
breathing spell while falsely professing a desire for peace. He rejected
Chiang's offer. The odds were against him, but Marshall was not ready to let
hope die. Since Chou was unwilling to sit down with him in Nanking, Marshall cooked up a ruse with General Gillem, who was posted in Shanghai,
to confront him there. Marshall phoned Gillem. "I've got to see Chou En-lai
once more . . . gonna make one final move here [to] see if he won't assist me
in breaking this thing up." Early on the morning of October 9, Marshall
secretly flew to Shanghai and concealed himself behind a screen in the living room of Gillem's house. Chou entered the house with Gillem, under the
impression that he and Gillem were going to have a quiet lunch. When Marshall appeared from behind the screen, Chou was caught off guard and
"damn near died," recalled Gillem.[99] Having ambushed Chou, Marshall
immediately went to work, gambling that a face-to-face appeal, heightened
by the element of surprise, might persuade Chou to agree to a truce and take
steps leading to a coalition government.

As soon as Marshall gave Chou a chance to speak, he could tell that his gambit had failed. Chou did not mince words. He was outraged over the attack on Kalgan, claiming the Generalissimo was "driving headlong into a nation-wide split." Chou said he would consider a truce only if it was permanent and only if the Nationalists moved their troops back to the positions they held in China proper and Manchuria when the earlier cease-fire agreements were signed. He impugned Marshall's integrity, suggesting that Marshall and Stuart were helping Chiang "find time for moving troops and munitions" into place for a renewed attack on the Communists defending Kalgan.

This was too much for Marshall. He had spent weeks trying to persuade Chiang to stop the fighting and start the peace process. Barely concealing his anger, he responded to Chou with what must have been a chilling tone. "I told you some time ago that if the Communist Party felt that they could not trust my impartiality, they merely had to say so and I would withdraw. You have now said so." He paused for effect. "I am leaving immediately for Nanking."[100]

Despite the implication of his words, Marshall was still unwilling to let hope die. Rather than withdraw, he agreed to a plan hatched by Ambassador Stuart and two left-leaning political parties that succeeded in persuading Chou to return to Nanking without losing face.[101] However, while Marshall planned to salvage negotiations leading to an end to the fighting, Chiang had different ideas. On the day after Marshall and Chou clashed at Gillem's house, the Generalissimo addressed the nation. It was Chinese National Day, the anniversary of Sun Yat-sen's 1911 revolution. Chiang announced that a national assembly would convene in a month to fashion a constitution and he would continue to seek a settlement through mediation with the CCP. His message of conciliation was drowned out by news that Kalgan fell that day to the Nationalists. The Communists lost roughly 100,000 men. Those who survived retreated into the northern provinces. CCP forces in Yenan were cut off from Manchuria. Fifteen days later, Chiang ordered his troops to attack the city of Antung on the Chinese side of the Yalu River border with Korea. It was obvious that Chiang's strategy was to use force rather than compromise to compel Chou to return to the bargaining table.

After capturing Antung, the first major city in Manchuria to fall to the Nationalists since the June cease-fire agreement, Chiang announced that it was time for another truce. In his diary John Melby wrote that Marshall told him, "I can't go through it again. I am just too old and too tired for that."[102]

Marshall may have said what he felt at the moment, but the stakes were too high to throw in the towel. Once again he spent hours meeting with Chiang, trying to shape cease-fire terms that might be acceptable to the CCP. Asked by Marshall to discuss terms in a meeting of the Committee of Three, Chou replied, "I will make another try."[103] Notwithstanding Marshall's efforts, it soon became apparent that there would be no agreement. Chou made a seemingly reasonable request. He asked that Chiang postpone the convening of the National Assembly until decisions were made via negotiation as to how many Communists would be allowed to become voting members of the assembly and thus have a voice in formulating the new constitution. Chiang agreed to a three-day postponement, but the delay yielded nothing. The National Assembly convened on November 15 even though not a single Communist had been selected as a delegate. The plan for a cease-fire collapsed.

The next day, Chou told Marshall that Chiang and the KMT had "sealed the door of negotiations." Accordingly, he was going to return to Yenan to confer with Mao and "analyze the overall situation." Chou assured Marshall that he still had "high respect for [him] personally," but "the Chinese problem was too complicated and the changes are tremendous." Before they departed, Marshall asked Chou to determine whether the authorities in Yenan wanted him to continue in his "present position" and to provide him with an honest answer without regard to whether he might lose face.[104] Knowing the Chinese Communists, he doubted he would get a straight answer. As they said their goodbyes Marshall wasn't sure he would ever see Chou again.

This was one of the few times in his career that Marshall faced failure. His closest aides sensed his despair. "I know," wrote John Melby, that "Marshall now believes he made a mistake in ever thinking coalition was desirable or useful or possible."[105] In a rare outburst Marshall complained bitterly to John Robinson Beal, his adviser to the KMT (the National People's Party), that the Generalissimo was pressuring him for more loans while the Nationalist generals "were draining 80 to 90 percent of the [government's] budget." Inflation was rampant. The economy would soon collapse. Marshall raged, "[I]f you think the US taxpayer is going to step into the vacuum this creates, you can go to hell."[106]

* * * * *

It is likely that Chiang's attacks on Communist-held cities and his intransigence in negotiations during the fall of 1946 were influenced, in part, by the rising Red scare in America, the growing unpopularity of Truman, and the sweeping victory of Republicans in the midterm elections. For the first time since before the Depression, Republicans would control both the Senate and the House. Throughout the fall campaign, Republicans, supported by the well-funded China Lobby, claimed that Truman and the Democrats were appeasing Communists abroad and harboring them at home. Now that they would control the legislature, and with Senator Arthur Vandenberg about to become chairman of the Foreign Relations Committee, Chiang could expect an even greater tilt in U.S. foreign policy toward the Nationalists.

For a handful of days in late November, Marshall's spirits were lifted. Katherine's daughter, Molly Winn, along with her two children, visited the Marshalls in Nanking. They had been flown from the States in Chiang's newly purchased four-engine Douglas C-54 Skymaster. After visiting the Marshalls they planned to take commercial flights to India, where husband and father Lieutenant Colonel James Winn was stationed. At the conclusion of a letter referencing Molly's visit, Katherine wrote, "No definite news of our return but probably will be some soon."[107] This was the first hint from a reliable source that Marshall's mission to China had likely failed and that he would soon return to Washington.

Marshall's last substantive discussion with Chiang took place at the Generalissimo's residence. In his diary Melby wrote that the session was "endless," qualifying both men for the "Order of Saint Simeon Stylites," named after the fifth-century Syrian ascetic who lived for years atop a pillar near Aleppo.[108] Marshall began by saying that "the only hope" of bringing the Communists back to the table would be the adoption by the KMT-dominated National Assembly of a constitution permitting proportionate CCP representation and the cessation of all offensive military operations by the Nationalists. Knowing that Chiang was emboldened, preferring force over serious compromise, Marshall pointed out that because of the size and geographic dispersal of the CCP's military and civil manpower, the Nationalist armies could never completely defeat them. Instead, they would melt into the countryside, attack Nationalist supply lines, and engage in guerrilla war indefinitely. Conquering cities, Marshall advised, was not the same as establishing control. In addition, he stressed that Chiang's economy could not come close to sustaining the military expenditures required to bring the Communists to their knees.

For more than an hour Chiang argued that he could "destroy the Communist military forces" in "eight to ten months," that by "showing a strong hand" the Soviets would not intervene, and that his economy, "largely based on the agrarian population," was not in danger of collapse. Chiang was convinced that the Communists "never intended to cooperate." As far as he was concerned, a coalition government would not work. Integration of the two armies was out of the question. The U.S., he said, should face up to this reality and "redefine its policy toward China," meaning it should throw its full support behind the cause of the Nationalists.

At some point, Marshall abandoned diplomatic niceties. Addressing Madame Chiang, who was acting as interpreter, he said in English, "I will tell you something, but it is so strong, you may not want to translate it. Don't translate it if it goes too far." He then turned to Chiang: "You have broken agreements, you have gone counter to plans. People have said you are a modern George Washington, but after these things they will never say it again." Madame nodded affirmatively. "I want him to hear it."[109] Chiang sat expressionless, listening as she translated, but his emotions were revealed by his habit of jiggling his foot when upset. Recounting the moment later to Beal, Marshall said, "[h]is old foot went round and round and almost hit the ceiling."[110]

* * * * *

Once Truman read Marshall's report of his meeting with Chiang, the president gave Marshall permission to end the mission and come home. All he had to do was let Truman know how "he wanted the matter handled and it would be done that way."[111] Marshall could have ended it in early December. However, he felt he should stay for a few more weeks to keep close watch on the National Assembly as it struggled against right-wing KMT opposition to adopt a constitution. Since the CCP and most other political parties were excluded or chose to be excluded from the assembly, a new constitution would be at most a primitive step forward toward democracy and possible reform. Marshall decided he had an obligation to the future of China and the United States to work with Ambassador Stuart and do whatever he could to see the process through to its completion.

Meanwhile, Katherine had developed a serious sinus condition and was getting ready to leave. During the weeks she spent with Mayling and the Generalissimo up at Kuling, the three had become close friends. Her letters were full of references to picnics in the mountains, luncheons on the lawn with Madame Chiang, and Chinese checkers in the evenings with the Generalissimo. Near the end of September when they returned to Nanking, the three plus George continued to spend leisure time together, including celebrations of birthdays and holidays. In early December, Chiang offered to have Katherine, along with a Shanghai-born maid and cook, flown in his new C-54 from Nanking to Guam, where they would pick up a navy transport for Honolulu. The idea was that Katherine would spend the winter months in Honolulu until, as she wrote, "Gen. M comes through and picks me up on the way home."[112]

John Caughey, Marshall's executive officer who lived with the Marshalls in Nanking, wrote his wife that "the house seems awfully empty with Mrs. M gone." Caughey, who had become particularly close to Katherine, was a keen observer of the domestic interactions between the General and Mrs. Marshall. With Katherine away in Hawaii, Caughey wrote that he was worried about who Marshall would use as the "butt of some of his jokes," even though half the time he was the loser in the couple's "verbal battle." According to Caughey, Katherine showed flashes of anger when her powerful husband tried to intimidate or control her. One evening the general, who had a habit of "sticking his chin out" when he was "ready for real battle," aimed his chin at her. Katherine shot back, "Don't you do that to me." Afterward, when Caughey was alone with Katherine, she laughed about her outburst and told him of another habit her husband had. In crowds, he would "put his hand on the small of her back" and "propel her forward" so they wouldn't be detained by strangers and autograph seekers. One evening he did it at the theater and Katherine, in a loud voice, said, "Don't you push me out of here." After that incident George never did it again. Mrs. Marshall knew how to say "the right thing at the right time," concluded Caughey.[113]

On Christmas Eve, the night before the National Assembly approved the constitution, Marshall and his aides, along with several American military officers, attended a Christmas party hosted by the Generalissimo and Madame. With a Christmas tree in the corner and a phonograph playing Christmas carols, the guests gathered for old-fashioneds and martinis. Madame, clad in a black silk gown with green and gold brocade, mixed some of the drinks herself. Chiang wore his black mandarin outfit. The highlight of the evening was the appearance of H. L. Huang, a large man dressed in a red

Santa suit with a sack of presents on his back. Huang, a graduate of Vanderbilt who spoke excellent English, fancied himself as sort of a Chinese Bob
Hope. One of his lines, directed at Marshall and the army crowd, "went
something like this," wrote Caughey: "You know when I came past Honolulu, I saw Katherine and she said be sure to say hello to George for her."[114]
The American guests roared, especially at his use of first-name familiarity.
It is probable that Madame or perhaps the Generalissmo himself fed Huang
the lines.

* * * * *

With the constitution in place Marshall decided that the time had come to
return home. In a lengthy report to the president, he wrote that while the constitution as written was sound, it would mean little unless Chiang took steps to
establish a new liberal party and welcome participation by the Communists.
"[T]here is no real place for me" in these maneuvers, wrote Marshall. "It is
now going to be necessary for the Chinese, themselves, to do the things I en-
deavored to lead them into ..." Marshall was of the view that he could do more
at home to bring a "liberal element" into Chiang's government and combat the
"vicious propaganda" of the Communists than he could by staying in China.
He told the president that the Generalissimo repeatedly urged him to remain
in China as his special adviser and that Chiang was doing this in order to increase "American support and to indicate the US Government's heavy backing of the Kuomintang Government." Marshall refused to be used for these
purposes. "I think I should be recalled," he wrote.[115]

Truman agreed. On January 3, 1947, the State Department radioed
Marshall that the president wanted Marshall to "return for consultation on
China and other matters."[116] Three days later Ambassador Stuart and Marshall formally advised Chiang that the general had been recalled to Washington and would leave Nanking on Wednesday morning the 8th. Marshall
did not mention the fact that he intended to release a "personal statement"
explaining why he was unable to accomplish his mission and that a day or
two thereafter Truman would announce the nomination of himself to replace Byrnes as secretary of state. On the evening of January 7, Mayling,
Kai-shek, and George, just the three of them, had what Marshall described
as a "family dinner" at the Generalissimo's residence, featuring the North
China cuisine he favored.[117] The two generals toasted each other with

expressions of friendship and respect, and Marshall told Chiang that he admired his "thoughtfulness, . . . endurance, and sincerity." As to his impressions of their last evening together, Chiang wrote that while he was unsure whether Marshall would support him when he returned to the U.S., "it will be a success for me if he leaves without holding any grudges against me."[118]

Frank Rounds, a reporter for *U.S. News & World Report*, was at Marshall's residence in Nanking early on the cold and clear morning of January 8. "Members of his staff were running up and downstairs with suitcases and swords and mementos of many kinds," he remembered. "Some were still being crated and rushed into cars to go out to the airfield."[119] A couple of hours later Marshall, in trench coat and peaked cap, was standing on the gravel runway, surrounded by Stuart, T. V. Soong (Madame's Harvard-educated brother who was serving as Chiang's finance minister), and several other Chinese officials saying their goodbyes. Marshall's well-traveled C-54, which had been used by Churchill during the war, was warming up, its silver tail painted with a circle of five blue stars. The Generalissimo and Madame drove up in a bulletproof Cadillac, bundled in fur coats against the cold. With Marshall they climbed the boarding steps for a few private moments in the warmth of the plush aircraft cabin. A correspondent for *Time* wrote that Mayling urged Marshall to "Come back . . . come back soon."[120] Ten minutes later Marshall and his entourage were gone.

About three hours into the flight when they were directly over Okinawa, Colonel Homer Munson, Marshall's pilot, came back from the cockpit and "congratulated Mr. Secretary Marshall."[121] Munson had just heard a news report from the States. Byrnes resigned and the president nominated Marshall to succeed him as secretary of state. John Caughey "broke open" a bottle of scotch.[122] Marshall was not pleased with the timing of Truman's press release. He had carefully worked out a plan with the president whereby Truman agreed not to announce Marshall's nomination until after the general released his personal statement containing his views on the China mission. Truman later expressed his regret at having to jump the gun, but he had no choice. There had been a leak. *The New York Times* received information that Truman was about to nominate Marshall. Truman called in Charlie Ross and Bill Hassett. They quickly "cooked up" a press statement and released it to the world, three days earlier than planned.[123]

When Marshall's plane was far out over the Pacific, but well short of

GEORGE MARSHALL

Hawaii, the State Department released the general's statement, a four-page document that he had been working on since mid-December. It addressed two different audiences—first, the American people, and second, the political and military adversaries in China. As to the first, Marshall presented a compelling case to Americans for why his mission to forge a coalition government in China failed. In essence, he wrote that the two warring parties— the KMT and the CCP—continued to view each other with "overwhelming suspicion" and that the suspicions were warranted because each party evidenced an implacable intent to destroy the other through "military force" or by "wreck[ing] the economy."[124] Marshall explained that he tried for a full year to bring the parties together, but in the end he was powerless to solve China's problem peacefully through mediation, or so his argument went. (Left unsaid was the fact that the president had previously announced that the U.S. would not intervene militarily on one side or the other in the "internal affairs of China."[125]) The American press characterized Marshall's statement as "a blistering plague on both your houses."[126]

With regard to Marshall's appeal to the second audience, the Nationalists and Communists, his statement denounced the "extremists" in each of the two parties for standing in the way of a coalition government and argued that salvation lay in diminishing the influence of both the "reactionaries" in the KMT and the "irreconcilables" in the CCP. Marshall wrote that he believed there was a "liberal group" in the CCP as well as a "splendid group of men" in the KMT who currently lack political power, but who could, through "successful action on their part," achieve unity under the leadership of Chiang Kai-shek.[127] This was wishful thinking, not a solution. Political parties in China, like those in the U.S., were big tents that housed several factions. If Marshall thought his advice from afar would exert pressure on the two parties to purge themselves of hard-liners, he was mistaken. Chou En-lai made light of this proposed path to salvation, claiming that Marshall "did not point out that Chiang Kai-shek himself is the leader of the reactionary group" in the KMT.[128] The far-right KMT clique heaped scorn on Marshall's so-called solution, saying he lacked an understanding of Communist tactics, while Chiang, whom Marshall held blameless, said Marshall's statement was "friendly and constructive."[129]

Ironically, Marshall, one of the most experienced military strategists in the world, could not afford to disclose a critically important military insight in his statement. After his year in China he was convinced that Chiang's Nationalists could never win the civil war against Mao's Communists unless the U.S. were to intervene—and that was not going to happen. He had repeatedly stressed this point in private talks with Chiang. Events in the following two years would prove that he was dead right. However, if he even hinted at this truth in his public statement, it would only encourage the Communists to stand their ground and fight. It would also bring the wrath of the China Lobby down on the Truman administration.

* * * * *

After a "32 hour straight through flight with 2 three-quarter hour stops," wrote Caughey, Marshall's plane landed at Hickam Field on Oahu on the same day it left Nanking ("that confusing Date Line again," Caughey explained).[130] Along with a gaggle of reporters, Katherine was there to meet her husband. A *Newsweek* reporter asked Marshall if he would consider the presidency in 1948. He responded, "I am an army officer and presumably will be secretary of state. And I am an Episcopalian."[131] Without further comment he steered Katherine through the crowd. Marshall should have answered the question with a firm no. As he departed Hickam, a State Department wireless bulletin was handed to him. Earlier that day the Senate Foreign Relations Committee, under the leadership of its new chairman, Arthur Vandenberg, dispensed with a hearing and approved without opposition Truman's nomination of Marshall to become the next secretary of state. The bulletin stated that Vandenberg urged the Republican-controlled Senate to "act quickly 'to notify the world that unity still prevails' in US foreign policy." Minutes later, the Senate voted to waive its one-day "lie over" rule. There was no debate. General George C. Marshall was unanimously confirmed.[132] From start to finish the process lasted less than an hour.

For the next several days George vacationed with Katherine at Waikiki Beach. The army had requisitioned a roomy cottage with an ocean view on the grounds of Fort DeRussy, an army base with a shore battery of big guns to protect Pearl Harbor and Honolulu. With an orderly to attend to their needs, and a chauffeur to take them shopping or out to dinner, George and Katherine were well situated. A posed photo in the *Honolulu Star-Advertiser* showed the couple strolling along a breakwater on the day after they arrived, looking relaxed but hardly ready to hit the beach. George, though tieless, was wearing pressed slacks and a dark sport coat. Katherine was clad in a checked suit, her silver hair freshly coiffed. In a letter to Rose Page, Marshall wrote that he was "loafing on the beach most of the day." Yet the demands of his new position were not far from his mind. "I have a pretty heavy daily radio business," he told Rose, "about thirty messages a day, some of two or three hundred words."[133]

Rested and ready, the Marshalls departed Honolulu on the 18th of January, planning to spend a day with Frank McCarthy in Hollywood before flying on to Washington. When the war was ending, Marshall had helped thirty-three-year-old Colonel McCarthy secure an appointment from Truman as assistant secretary in the State Department, the youngest to hold such a position in U.S. history. Oddly, McCarthy resigned in October 1945, after only six weeks on the job. He claimed that he left because of health—anemia, low blood pressure, and bursitis.[134] Presumably, he could have gone on sick leave or asked for a leave of absence, but he did not. Circumstantial evidence suggests that McCarthy was asked or forced to resign because he was thought to be a homosexual. From 1945 through the 1950s, the State Department, due to rampant homophobia and pressure from Congress (notably, Senator Kenneth Wherry of Nebraska), "purged" dozens of homosexuals on grounds that they could be security risks or, even worse, Communists.[135] The period of ugly persecution and blatant discrimination was called the "pervert purge" and the "lavender scare." McCarthy left Washington and secured a position in Hollywood as assistant to the president of the Motion Picture Association of America, which is where he worked when George and Katherine visited him in early 1947. If McCarthy was gay, Marshall had no clue. Writing from China, he had chided McCarthy for being a "confirmed bachelor" who might never marry, and advised him that "a wife is a very necessary part of the balance of life in a man."[136]

After their reunion with McCarthy, George and Katherine flew out of Burbank, bound for Washington. Because weather forced them to land in Chicago, they arrived by train at Washington's Union Station at seven a.m. on January 21, and were met on the platform by Colonel Marshall Carter, the general's liaison to the State Department. Carter handed Marshall an "eyes only" telegram. It was a warning from James Shepley, the journalist with *Time* magazine who Marshall had worked with in China. Although Marshall had been confirmed unanimously, two key senators had serious issues that needed to be addressed. According to Shepley, Senator Vandenberg had confided to a reliable source that he was "not so damned crazy about [Marshall]," who the senator thought might be a closet Roosevelt Democrat. Senator Tom Connally, the ranking Democrat on the Foreign Relations Committee, believed Marshall's appointment would contribute to the impression that "the military is taking over our foreign policy," and that he might compete with Truman for the 1948 nomination.[137] Their concerns were heightened by the fact that under an 1886 law governing presidential succession, Marshall was next in the line, since there was no vice president (the law was changed in July 1947 to make the Speaker of the House next in line after the VP). Marshall understood at once that the answer he gave to the reporters in Hawaii about his presidential ambitions—that he was an "army officer" and "Episcopalian"—was too glib. He asked the State Department's press officer to arrange a press conference. At nine a.m., still at Union Station, Marshall opened by answering several questions from reporters. Then he read a statement that he had worked over with Carter and the press officer from State. "I am assuming that the office of Secretary of State is nonpolitical," he declared. Therefore, "I am going to govern myself accordingly." After that, "I cannot be considered" nor can I "be drafted for any political office." He concluded by saying, "I am being explicit and emphatic in order to terminate once and for all any discussion of my name with regard to political office."[138]

David Lawrence, the conservative publisher of *U.S. News & World Report*, wrote that Marshall's Shermanesque announcement would disappoint many "because he is just the kind of man who should be President—he is one of the great statesmen of our time." Nevertheless, his Union Station disclaimers "surrounded him with a prestige both inside and outside this country which no man in public office, not even President Truman, can command."[139]

When the press conference was over, Marshall—the so-called great statesman—turned to Colonel Carter and asked, "Do you know how the State Department operates?"[140]

* * * * *

During the two years that Marshall served as secretary of state, 1947–48, Chairman Mao's Communist forces, as Marshall had predicted, gathered strength and drove Chiang's armies out of Manchuria even though the

Nationalists had "a decided superiority over Communist troops in terms of arms and military equipment."[141] The Communist victories were attributed to superior morale and the caliber of their leadership. Marshall once told John Melby that Mao "was one of the great guerilla strategists of all time," and that his generals "would have been an ornament on any general staff in the history of warfare."[142] Shortly after Truman was inaugurated to begin his first full term as president, all of China north of the Yangtze was in the hands of the Communists. Aided by Soviet weapons and assistance, they swarmed across the great river in the spring and captured Nanking. On October 1, 1949, with the rest of the mainland under his rule, Mao proclaimed the establishment of the People's Republic of China. By then, the Generalissimo and his dispirited armies had fled to the island of Formosa to regroup and lay plans to retake the mainland.

The emergence of China as a Communist nation, thought to be closely allied with the Soviet Union and intent upon promoting revolutions throughout Asia, was regarded as a blow to American prestige. *Time* reported that "the Red tide has risen mightily in Asia and now threatens to engulf half the world's people."[143] The influential China Lobby and the voices of the China bloc in Congress heaped criticism on the Truman administration. They blamed the president's China policy, individuals in the State Department, and the failed Marshall mission for "losing" China. To respond to these accusations the State Department published a 1,054-page volume of documents later known as *The China White Paper*.[144] John Melby, who compiled much of the material in the *White Paper*, said its purpose was to "call the dogs off from the China Lobby."[145] In a controversial preface, Dean Acheson, having succeeded Marshall as secretary of state in 1949, summarized the case for the administration, arguing that mainland China was lost by Chiang Kai-shek's corrupt, demoralized, and unpopular government, despite massive economic and military aid provided by the United States.

The "dogs" were not satisfied. The *White Paper* and Acheson's defense failed to blunt a revival of the charges made by Patrick Hurley when he abruptly resigned—that pro-Communist experts inside Truman's State Department sabotaged his efforts to forge a pro-American coalition government in China. A few weeks after the *White Paper* was published, the Soviet Union detonated its first nuclear bomb. Conservatives and right-wing demagogues, including first-term Republican Senator Joseph McCarthy, quickly added the fall of China and Soviet possession of atomic secrets to their on-going narrative that Communists had infiltrated the United States government, posing an existential threat to the republic.

Forty-two-year-old Senator McCarthy burst onto the national scene in February 1950, not with allegations against Marshall himself—those would begin in April—but with a speech to a Republican women's club in Wheeling, West Virginia. There he claimed that the "swiftness of Communist victories"—a veiled reference that included the fall of China—was due to "traitorous actions" of those who have had the benefit of the "finest jobs in government we can give." Then, as if he were sharing a secret but with full knowledge that one or more reporters were in the audience, he waved a piece of paper and said, "I have in my hand a list of 205 cases of individuals [whose names] were made known to the Secretary of State [Acheson] as being members of the Communist Party and who nevertheless are still working on and shaping the policy in the State Department."[146] Shortly thereafter he made the same claim in two other speeches, although his numbers were different. McCarthy's "list" of Communists in the government was a strategic bombshell that he knew would make headlines, a modern-day Trump tweet. When asked to produce the list or the names, he bluffed, demurred, and refused. Truman issued a statement that there was no truth to McCarthy's allegations. The senator, with characteristic audacity, responded that the president "should refresh his memory."[147]

A Senate subcommittee, chaired by Millard Tydings (D-MD), was appointed to investigate McCarthy's charges. McCarthy fought back in the press, accusing "egg-sucking phony liberals" of holding "sacrosanct those Communists and queers" who sold China into "atheistic slavery."[148] This would not be the first time, nor the last, when McCarthy would conflate Communism and sexual preference. In April he took aim at Marshall by name, calling him "completely unfit" and suggesting that he lost China because he studied the writings of Owen Lattimore, director of the Johns Hopkins School of International Relations, a target of the China Lobby who McCarthy accused of being a "top Russian spy" or at least a concealed Communist.[149]

A year later beneath a packed gallery McCarthy stood almost alone on the Senate floor. For three hours he read, apparently for the first time, from a 60,000-word savage diatribe against Marshall that had been ghostwritten for him by his wife, Jean Kerr, his staff, and Forrest Davis, a newspaperman known for his strong anti-Communist views who was a speechwriter for Senator Robert Taft. McCarthy began his speech by linking Marshall to "the highest circles" of "a conspiracy of infamy so black that, when it is finally exposed, its principals shall be forever deserving of the maledictions of honest men." The objective of the "great conspiracy," as to which Marshall was an alleged principal, was to "diminish the United States in world affairs," to weaken it militarily, and to cause "talk of surrender in the Far East." With regard to China in particular, McCarthy charged that Marshall and Acheson, acting on orders from Moscow, were the "executioners" of Chiang Kai-shek's "Republic of China," a loyal friend of the U.S. "It was Marshall," McCarthy declaimed, who engaged in the "criminal folly" of the "disastrous Marshall mission" that destroyed Nationalist China and "robbed us of a great and friendly ally."[150] Needless to say, no supporting evidence was provided. The speech was published as a book titled *America's Retreat from Victory*, with Senator McCarthy listed as its author. It was distributed nationwide.

McCarthy alleged in his speech that the general committed several other traitorous acts, beginning with his insistence in the summer of 1942 that the Allies establish a beachhead in France rather than invade North Africa. However, McCarthy's 1951 harangue was by far the most vitriolic and bombastic "he lost China" speech ever leveled at Marshall. His lengthy screed attracted wide media attention, more for its over-the-top outrageousness than anything else. Marshall declined to respond, telling columnist Clayton Fritchey that "if I have to explain at this point that I am not a traitor to the United States, I hardly think it's worth it."[151]

* * * * *

Stepping back, is there any truth to the charges by McCarthy and others that Marshall "lost" China? Put that way, the question cannot be answered because China was not something that Marshall or the United States was in a position to lose. Indeed, it is presumptuous even to suggest that China was "ours" to win or lose. The relevant question is whether Marshall, during the course of his yearlong mission in 1946, could have prevented the eventual defeat and expulsion of Chiang's Nationalist government from mainland China by Mao's CCP.

To address this question it must be understood that from the outset Marshall's authority, indeed his ability, to influence the behavior of the two sides was severely circumscribed. Pursuant to his instructions, his mission was to persuade Chiang's one-party Nationalist government to open up and allow Mao's smaller Communist party, as well as other political parties, to have a significant voice, albeit a minority voice, in a reformed coalition government that would have a single civilian-controlled army. Other than his stature and prestige, the only real leverage Marshall had to stop the fighting and move the parties toward a coalition government was his power to grant or deny economic and military aid to Chiang's government, since it was the "proper instrument" recognized by the U.S. His authority to grant aid to the Nationalists gave him power to pressure the Communists, while he could use the threat to deny aid to exert pressure on the Nationalists. His leverage was limited by two factors. First, Marshall was prohibited from intervening militarily—that is, from deploying U.S. forces to tip the scales in favor of one side or the other. The Second World War had just ended. America was war-weary. Perhaps later, but in 1946 Truman was not about to involve the U.S. in another war, especially a war near the Soviet border. Second, if negotiations broke down, the influence of the China Lobby, the China bloc, the Red scare, and the new Republican congressional majority in America virtually guaranteed that the U.S. would still back the Nationalists. This second factor undermined Marshall's impartiality and the balance of power in the negotiations. Since Chiang was confident that the U.S. would not in the end withhold support, he could refuse to compromise with impunity. Similarly, Mao and the Communists probably knew enough about American politics and foreign affairs to realize that the U.S. would not abandon the Nationalists. Therefore, they had good reason to question the fairness of the process and Marshall's impartiality. Why should either party bargain in good faith if they knew or suspected that Marshall and the U.S. would side with the Nationalists?

Notwithstanding Marshall's limited leverage and the perception that he was biased in favor of the Nationalists, there was one plausible move that might have led to the success of his mission, albeit short term, or at least could have delayed its failure. In March 1946, when the parties were the closest they would ever be to forming a coalition government, a case can be made that Marshall should not have decided to leave China. Or, if he really had to be in Washington to arrange for an aid package at that particular time, he should have returned to China much earlier when he first learned from General Gillem that the cease-fire agreement was being violated by both parties. "[H]is absence was critical," concluded Forrest Pogue, because during the six weeks he was away from China the Communists, citing violations by the Nationalists as a pretext, attacked and captured the capital city of Changchun in Manchuria.[152] This conquest was a turning point, because it strengthened the confidence of Mao and his generals that they could eventually defeat Chiang's forces and it stiffened the opposition of the KMT's conservative wing to the formation of a coalition government with the Communists. It is counterfactual, of course, but if Marshall had been on the scene he might have prevented the cease-fire violations and the consequent fall of Changchun to the Communists. The final steps leading to a coalition government could have been taken. Perhaps so, but would such a coalition, with the CCP in the minority, have lasted? Highly unlikely. Even with massive aid, military force, and covert action, the history of the U.S. experience in Vietnam and other civil wars indicates that an eventual Communist victory in the Chinese civil war could not have been prevented.[153]

With characteristic humility Marshall blamed himself for the failure of his mission. "I tried to please everyone," he later told French foreign minister Georges Bidault. "The result was that by the time I left, nobody trusted me."[154] He was right about the trust factor, but it wasn't his fault. The erosion of trust was inevitable, beyond his control. Aware of the anti-Communist climate that pervaded the executive and legislative branches of government in Washington, the warring parties in China could not view Marshall, the American mediator, as impartial. As Barbara Tuchman and others have argued, the U.S. lost its "last chance" to gain the trust of the CCP in early 1945, when Roosevelt spurned a secret offer by Mao and Chou to come to Washington and establish a working relationship with the U.S.[155] By 1946 and thereafter, "China was a problem," she wrote, "for which there was no American solution."[156]

Marshall's year in China was an education in the art of diplomacy and the limits of American power. It was an introductory course in Communist ideology and leadership. The failure of his mission was difficult for him to accept. However, what he learned had a lasting effect on his performance as secretary of state, shaping the Marshall Plan in Europe, and containing the spread of Communism throughout the world. Never again would Marshall advocate or attempt to negotiate a power-sharing arrangement with a Communist party or regime.

Years later, Henry Byroade recalled being with Marshall during the final days of the mission. "I felt sorry for him. Marshall was a winner . . . he had never really known defeat . . . a stream of elderly Chinese people would beg him not to leave, that he was the only hope China had . . . [t]hat's what kept Marshall there really too long."[157]

CHAPTER 14

Vision of a New Europe

P resident Truman stood at his desk in the Oval Office, a tight smile on his face. Arrayed behind him were members of his cabinet, grouped shoulder to shoulder before a phalanx of news photographers. In the middle of the room sixty-six-year-old George Marshall, dressed in a dark pin-striped suit, laid his left hand on a Bible and raised his right. Facing him was Supreme Court Chief Justice Fred Vinson, Truman's affable poker pal and confidant, who guided the general through the oath of office. It was noon, January 21, 1947, when Marshall became the nation's fiftieth secretary of state.

Harry Truman admired and respected Marshall more than any other public figure. "The more I see and talk to him," he wrote, "the more certain I am that he's the great one of the age."[1] Marshall's mere presence was reassuring. It boosted the president's confidence and elevated his spirits. Plus, his popularity edged back up to 48 percent in the polls. Speaking of Marshall, Truman remarked, "[h]e was a man you could count on to be truthful in every way, and when you find somebody like that you have to hang on to them [*sic*]."[2] Hang on to him he did. With bipartisan support the two of them would launch the most significant American foreign policy initiatives since the Monroe Doctrine.

After lunch in the soon to be renovated White House, Marshall walked with Undersecretary of State Dean Acheson across to the old State, War, and Navy Building. Knowing that Acheson expected to return to his law practice, Marshall asked, "Will you stay?" Acheson answered, "Certainly, as long as you need me, though before too long I ought to get back to my profession if I'm to have one." They agreed that he would stay on for another six months. Acheson asked Marshall what role he expected him to fulfill as undersecretary. Marshall responded that he wanted Acheson to function as chief of staff and that the undersecretary would be the one and only channel for matters that needed to be decided or acted upon by the secretary. Acheson smiled, saying he would try to implement such a system. He joked that if the chiefs of the many fiefdoms at State could not get to Marshall except through him, "the incidence of heart attacks in the Department was due for a sharp increase." As to the nature of their professional relationship, Marshall said he expected "complete and even brutal candor" from Acheson. And that "he had no feelings . . . 'except those which I reserve for Mrs. Marshall.'"[3]

Within the first day or two as secretary of state Marshall discovered right off that the department had "no planning agency at all." He blamed this deficiency on the fact that Byrnes, his predecessor, was a lawyer and that "lawyers are not organizers at all."[4] As Marshall learned when he was chief of staff of the army, the operations officers of almost any large organization need a separate group that stays out of the day-to-day crises and is able to step back and think about policy, direction of effort, and reappraisal of what is being done. He asked Acheson to create a new section within the State Department to be called the Policy Planning Staff. According to Acheson, Marshall conceived that the function of the group would be to "look far enough ahead to see the emerging form of things to come and outline what should be done to meet or anticipate them."[5]

Marshall's first choice to become head of the new Policy Planning Staff was forty-three-year-old George Frost Kennan. He was aware that Kennan was regarded as America's foremost expert on the Soviet Union. When Marshall was in China, he read several of Kennan's dispatches from the American Embassy in Moscow, including the "long telegram," probably the most influential analysis of Soviet postwar intentions that has ever been written. Kennan dictated the 5,540-word telegram from his upstairs bedroom at the embassy, while suffering from "cold, fever, sinus and tooth trouble."[6] The telegram was wired to the State Department and circulated to Kennan's superiors at State, the Pentagon, and the White House. Navy Secretary James Forrestal, a fellow Princetonian, became Kennan's Washington evangelist, distributing copies throughout the capital and assuring that Kennan's message was read. The long telegram found its way to Marshall.

According to Kennan's telegram, the Kremlin's "neurotic" worldview was motivated not by Communism but by a "traditional and instinctive Russian sense of insecurity," and a fear that total control of the state would crumble if the Russian people learned the truth about the outside world. Like the czars before them, Kennan wrote, Soviet autocrats hold paranoid beliefs that surrounding nations are perpetually hostile. For them, expansion into neighboring territories is a "strategic necessity." Marxist dogma, Kennan argued, was no more than an ideological "fig leaf" that Russian rulers use as a vehicle to guarantee the survival of their "internally weak regimes." Kennan explained that the Soviet regime operates on two levels, one visible that consists of its official actions, and the other invisible—"subterranean"—for which the rulers accept no responsibility. Foreshadowing the twenty-first-century electoral hacking allegations, Kennan noted that Russia's invisible operatives seek to undermine Western powers by disrupting "national self confidence," increasing "social unrest," and stimulating "all forms of disunity." To cope with Soviet intentions "is undoubtedly the greatest task our diplomacy has ever faced," he wrote. However, it "is within our power to solve"—and without recourse to war. The proper policy, he counseled, is vigilance, a show of force without risking a showdown, a healthy economy, and the provision of a protective umbrella of security to European nations emerging from the devastation of the war.[7] In essence it was a policy of "containment," though Kennan would not use that word until more than a year later when he drafted an eloquent restatement of the long telegram that was published anonymously under the name "X" in *Foreign Affairs*.[8]

Marshall had the 1946 long telegram in mind when he decided during his first few days as secretary of state that Kennan was his first choice to lead the Policy Planning Staff. Marshall's decision was bolstered by the strong recommendations of James Forrestal and Beetle Smith, who had taken over from Averell Harriman as the U.S. ambassador to the Soviet Union. From Moscow, Smith sent a letter to Marshall saying that he "knew all of the Russian experts, here and in Washington, and they are all good, but Kennan is head and shoulders above the lot . . ."[9] On January 24, Acheson, at the request of Marshall, asked Kennan whether he would be willing to lead the new Policy Planning Staff at State. Kennan, who had been recalled to Washington to teach at the National War College, accepted the offer, but due to commitments at the War College he could not report for duty until the spring.

Thus, only three days after he was sworn in, Marshall established a policy organization and he hired a brilliant expert on the Soviet Union to run it. These moves—a management change and a personnel choice—proved to be two of the most important decisions he would make as secretary of state.

* * * * *

During his first few days as secretary, Marshall made another move, this one of little importance except to dozens of tradition-bound State Department employees who had worked for years in the Victorian pile of marble next to the White House. Marshall's "move" was to literally move. Yielding to the president's need for space due to his growing executive staff, Marshall agreed to move the Washington offices of the State Department to a building in Foggy Bottom at 21st and Virginia Avenue that had been built in 1940 to house the War Department before it decamped for the Pentagon. The building lacked the high ceilings and elegance of Old State, but it had more than 600 offices. Best of all, it was air-conditioned.

On Friday, February 21, as staffers were packing up files and preparing for the weekend move to Foggy Bottom, Acheson received word from the British Embassy that the ambassador, Archibald Kerr (Lord Inverchapel), wished to deliver to Marshall "a blue piece of paper," diplomat-speak for an important message. The ambassador told Acheson that the message concerned British aid to Greece. Acheson sensed that Marshall's first crisis was in the making. Since protocol dictated that a message of this nature must be delivered personally by the ambassador to the secretary of state and Marshall was already at Columbia University in New York City and would travel to Princeton and Pinehurst over the weekend, Acheson prevailed upon his friend the ambassador to provide him with a carbon copy of the message. He and his staff needed time to work the issue and be ready to provide Marshall with recommendations when he returned on Monday.

It was bad news, but not wholly unexpected. In two separate notes (called *aide-mémoires*) the ambassador's "blue piece of paper" announced that due to Great Britain's own dire financial situation His Majesty's Government would no longer be able to provide financial aid and military equipment to Greece and also Turkey after the end of March. The British notes explained what Acheson already knew. Without financial assistance Greece was in grave danger of being taken over by Communist insurgents and forces of Soviet puppet governments along Greek borders. Likewise, Turkey was in desperate need of financial aid, although for different reasons. Soviet demands for revisions to the Dardanelles treaty and other threats to Turkish sovereignty had kept its army continuously mobilized, thus putting a drain on the economy and endangering its financial viability. The British expressed the hope that the U.S. would be willing to assume the burden, which they estimated at a quarter of a million dollars for Greece for the remainder of the year, a smaller but equally significant sum for Turkey, and additional sums for both countries in 1948. The stakes were high, they maintained. The entire Middle East was in danger of coming under Soviet domination.[10]

Over the weekend Acheson and his staff prepared position papers arguing that the U.S. should step in and provide the necessary aid to Greece and Turkey. Early Monday morning, when Acheson arrived on the fifth floor of State's new quarters, Marshall was already there. He had finished reading the British notes and Acheson's position papers. Acheson told Marshall he was facing one of the most important decisions since the Second World War.[11] After firing off a number of questions, Marshall said he was inclined to agree with Acheson's recommendation. He authorized his undersecretary to take principal responsibility for moving forward with the plan to provide aid, explaining that he had to spend much of his time in the coming days preparing for the Moscow foreign minister's meeting. Acheson brought the War and Navy secretaries on board. On Wednesday, he and Marshall convinced Truman of the need for immediate action. The final hurdle was Congress. It would not be easy. Controlled by the Republicans, Congress was more interested in cutting foreign aid, defense spending, and taxes than rushing in once again to help fund the obligations of the British to preserve their crumbling empire.

At ten a.m. on Thursday, February 27, the Senate and House leaders on both sides of the aisle and the ranking majority and minority members of the two foreign relations/affairs committees gathered in the White House to meet with Truman, Marshall, and Acheson. The purpose, as Truman recounted in his memoir, was "to advise them of the gravity of the situation and the nature of the decision I had to make."[12] The unstated goal was to get a sense of whether Congress would support the administration's proposed Greek-Turkish aid package. Marshall carried with him a written statement, almost certainly reviewed if not written by Acheson, that he intended to read to the congressmen.

Accounts differ as to what was said at this momentous meeting, arguably the beginning of the Cold War, and who was most influential. In his memoir, published in 1956, Truman wrote that he began by explaining the serious "crisis we were suddenly facing," and the reasons for his decision to "extend aid to Greece and Turkey." According to Truman, Marshall followed with the details of the situation, making it "quite plain that our choice was either to act or lose by default." (These were quotes from the three-page prepared statement that Marshall read.) There is no mention or suggestion in Truman's memoir that Acheson, Senator Arthur Vandenberg, or anyone else spoke up in support. The president concluded his account of the meeting by writing that "the congressional leaders appeared deeply impressed," and there was "no voice of dissent."[13]

A memoir published in 1955 by Joseph Jones, a State Department public affairs assistant who did not attend the White House meeting, states that Marshall's presentation "did not go down well" with congressional leaders.[14] Without citation Jones quoted dissenting remarks by unnamed congressmen. Acheson's memoir, *Present at the Creation*, published after Marshall's death in 1969, says that Marshall "flubbed his opening statement," and that he, Acheson, intervened and saved the day by abandoning "measured appraisal," and arguing that unless aid was given to Greece and Turkey, the Soviet "infection" would spread to "Iran and all to the east," to "Africa through Asia Minor and Egypt," and "to Europe through Italy and France." (In later years, cascading "dominoes" would replace the spread of an "infection" as the metaphor for early intervention.) Acheson recalled that after he finished, a long silence followed. Then Arthur Vandenberg, Republican chairman of the Foreign Relations Committee, said solemnly, "Mr. President, if you will say that to the Congress and the country, I will support you and I believe that most of its members will do the same."[15]

There is no diary entry or other known contemporaneous record that substantiates Acheson's memory twenty-two years after the fact, particularly his quoted recall of Vandenberg's reaction. In Thomas Jones's memoir, he wrote only that Vandenberg was "impressed" by what Acheson reportedly said and that the senator did not signify his support for Greek-Turkish aid. Indeed, Jones pointed out that "Vandenberg wrote some time later that no commitments were made" at the White House meeting and "none had been asked."[16]

Senator Vandenberg's papers were collected, edited, and published by his son and top aide, Arthur Jr., in 1952, a year after his death. Quoting a line from Marshall's statement—"the choice is between acting with energy or losing by default"—the editor commented that this argument "struck a responsive note" with Vandenberg. There is no mention in the senator's papers or diaries that Acheson spoke at the White House meeting, that Marshall's statement was less than well received, or that Vandenberg reacted to the presentations by Truman and Marshall other than by saying he was "impressed."[17]

Acheson's entertaining version of how he turned the tide with Vandenberg and the other congressmen after Marshall "flubbed" has been relied on by most historians and Marshall biographers since 1969. Only Forrest Pogue, Marshall's official biographer, appears to have taken issue, and he buried his doubts about the veracity of the Acheson and Jones accounts in a footnote. Most likely the truth lies somewhere in the middle. Acheson probably did intervene, adding energy and color to Marshall's understated delivery. On the other hand, the words that came out of Marshall's mouth, as documented in his written statement, were roughly the same as those attributed to Acheson first by Jones and later by the undersecretary himself. Rather than a "flub," Marshall's statement probably came off as too dry and matter-of-fact. The quote that does not ring true at all is that of Vandenberg where Acheson has him declaring after a long silence that he will "support" the president and that most members of Congress "will do the same." Given Vandenberg's history of needing to be courted and taking his time before favoring foreign policy initiatives proposed by the Truman administration, it is doubtful that he expressed his support and that of the rest of Congress at this meeting.

Notwithstanding whether Vandenberg or any of the other congressional leaders expressed support, the president came away from the February 27 meeting convinced that he would ask Congress to enact legislation to protect Greece and Turkey from Soviet-backed aggression. He understood, as did most everyone else in the room, that it would mark a grave turning point in postwar foreign policy because the problems in Greece and Turkey were symbolic of a broader clash between Communism and democracy. Since Marshall would be immersed in preparing for and then attending the foreign ministers' gathering in Moscow, he delegated to Acheson and his aides the tasks of drafting the legislation and the message to Congress that would place the issue in a broader context and explain the need for immediate aid. His only advice to Acheson was that he should feel free to shape the Greek-Turkish relief program for the president without regard to how it might influence the Soviet attitude toward him and the U.S. at the Moscow conference.

* * * * *

On the eve of Marshall's departure for Moscow, he wrote a gloomy letter to his widowed sister, Marie Singer. "There is very little of my life left to me now which is my own," he lamented. Referring to the job of getting up to speed on the shifting positions of Britain, France, the USSR, and the U.S. on German reparations, self-government, and economic revival, he wrote that "the past three weeks have been the worst I have ever experienced because of the tremendous amount of work I have had to absorb mentally…"[18]

While Marshall was en route to Europe, Acheson's speechwriters in the State Department, Joseph Jones and Carl Humelsine, began churning out drafts of a proposed speech by Truman that not only made the case for aid to Greece and Turkey but articulated a much broader U.S. policy of providing economic and financial aid to "free peoples" anywhere who were trying to resist "subjugation by armed minorities or outside forces," a veiled reference to the Soviet Union and Soviet-sponsored Communists.[19] More than anyone else, the author of the expanded policy was Acheson who, as historian John Acacia wrote, "instantly recognized the opportunity to seize the initiative and the threat if it did not."[20]

When George Kennan, still with the War College, was shown a draft of the speech, his reaction was extremely negative. He favored aid to Greece because it was involved in a civil war with Communist insurgents, but not to Turkey. More important, he could not understand why the Greek crisis should cause the president to announce an open-ended commitment by the United States to help "free peoples" resist oppression everywhere. The next day, when Marshall landed in Paris on his way to Moscow, he received a draft of Truman's speech. Chip Bohlen, the State Department's Soviet expert, wrote that Marshall objected to the tone of the proposed address to Congress, believing there was "too much flamboyant anti-Communism in the speech."[21] Except for technical word changes, the comments by Kennan and Marshall were not reflected in the State Department draft that was reviewed by Clark Clifford, counsel to the president, and George Elsey, his assistant. They were satisfied with the content, but they thought the draft did not sound like Truman and lacked memorable phrases that the newspapers would likely quote. It was Elsey who came up with the solution. He broke up the key paragraph—two very long and unwieldy sentences that proclaimed a new policy of the United States—into three declarative, dramatic statements. He set each apart as a separate paragraph for emphasis. Each began with the words "I believe that…" Clifford and Elsey called these sentences "The Credo."[22]

On Capitol Hill word leaked that Truman was about to ask Congress for $250 million to help Greece and $150 million to aid Turkey. Opposition was growing. Vandenberg convened a meeting of Republican lawmakers and made a plea for bipartisan support. "This is a matter which transcends politics," he told them. "There is nothing partisan about it. It is national politics at the highest degree [*sic*]."[23]

At one p.m. on March 12, two days after the foreign minister's conference in Moscow began, Truman delivered his historic twenty-one-minute speech before a joint session of Congress. Speaking more slowly than usual, he intoned Elsey's three sentences:

> "I believe that it must be the policy of the United States to support free peoples who are resisting subjugation by armed minorities or by outside pressures.
>
> I believe that we must assist free peoples to work out their own destinies in their own way.
>
> I believe that our help should be primarily through economic and financial aid which is essential to economic stability and orderly political processes."[24]

The reaction from those in the well of the House as he finished was restrained. Some said that the congressmen were stunned. "Applause interrupted the speech only three times, and not at the most critical passages," wrote Clifford, who was in the gallery with his wife, Marny, and Mrs. Truman.[25] *The New York Times* picked up on its significance immediately, calling it a "radical change" in American foreign policy.[26] Within a few days the credo that the president proclaimed became known as the Truman Doctrine. Congressmen were bewildered, not knowing whether to take the president literally. Acheson and others in the administration immediately started spreading the word that Truman's new policy did not mean he intended to offer assistance to every government that felt threatened by an insurgency from the left. But they did nothing to discourage the idea that the president was the steward of a coherent strategy for altering the power balance with the Soviets and safeguarding the free people of Europe and the eastern Mediterranean. Congressman Walter Judd of Minnesota, a former missionary and member of the China bloc, asked Acheson why financial assistance was thought necessary to rescue Greece and Turkey but not to save Chiang's Nationalists. For Acheson this was a softball question. China was a completely different situation, he said. Hundreds of millions of dollars had already been furnished to Chiang's government and was still being provided. Yet his military was engaged in the same self-defeating practices and China's preindustrial economy remained stagnant. Judd and his allies were not persuaded. They thought the Nationalists should get more aid.

Acheson and his colleagues cajoled and wooed individual congressmen, especially Vandenberg. Fear of Communism moved American public opinion. The "Act to Provide for Assistance to Greece and Turkey," formalized as the Greek-Turkish Aid Act, was approved by the House and the Senate with decisive Republican majorities in early May. The president signed the bill into law in a Kansas City hotel on May 22, 1947. Truman later said that it was his "All-Out Speech" that caused Congress to act.

* * * * *

Three days before the Truman Doctrine was announced to the world, Marshall's big C-54 landed at Moscow Central Airport "in the frosty wind and clear sunlight of a Russian early spring day."[27] His flight across Europe with stops in Paris and Berlin was sobering. The winter of 1946–47 was the coldest since 1880. Coal shortages in the UK and throughout the Continent resulted in unheated homes, frozen pipes, and deaths from exposure. People were starving, especially in the cities, due to abysmal harvests and bottlenecks in rail and motor transportation. Mountains of rubble still blocked the streets. The bombed-out shells of millions of homes, factories, bridges, and churches from St. Columba's in Knightsbridge to the gates of Moscow could be seen from the air. Nothing had been rebuilt.

During a layover in Paris, John Foster Dulles joined Marshall's delegation. Before leaving Washington Marshall had invited Senator Vandenberg to accompany him to the Council of Foreign Ministers conference in Moscow because he valued Vandenberg's counsel and he wanted the American delegation to be viewed as nonpartisan. Vandenberg declined due to the press of Senate business. However, he recommended Dulles, a conservative Wall Street lawyer experienced in international affairs. Dulles had functioned as a kind of shadow secretary of state for the Republican Party during the 1930s and '40s when the GOP was in the minority. He would be an influential voice at the forthcoming conference.

In Berlin, Marshall added two U.S. Army generals to his delegation:

Lucius Clay and Mark Clark, military governors, respectively, of the U.S. occupation zones in war-ravaged Germany and Austria. Since the purpose of the Moscow conference was to negotiate German and Austrian peace settlements, the presence of Clay and Clark was necessary.

Ambassador Beetle Smith, Eisenhower's cantankerous chief of staff during the war, was on hand to greet Marshall and his entourage at the airport. "Marshall looked very fit," wrote Smith, "and his quiet dignity made an immediate impression" as Smith introduced him to Russian officials and foreign ambassadors. Marshall was not used to seeing Smith in the uniform of a diplomat. The expression on his face let Smith know that the "bowler" hat he had recently purchased in Paris made him look rather ridiculous.[28]

As Smith and Marshall were driven through the grim streets of Moscow to Spaso House, the ambassador's residence, they downplayed the prospects of success. Marshall had already told reporters in Paris that it was "extremely doubtful" that the terms of a treaty for Germany would be finalized in Moscow.[29] The most he could hope for was to lay the groundwork for a German settlement and perhaps edge close to a pact for Austria. Smith's view was that the conference would be "tedious and prolonged," and that Marshall must be "prepared to match patience with patience, no matter how trying this might be."[30] Remembering his seemingly endless year in China, Marshall knew how hard it was to practice patience. Though the odds of a breakthrough in Moscow were against him, as they were when he went to China, he had to remain optimistic. He was not going to give up in advance.

Throughout the six-week conference Marshall, Chip Bohlen, and Marshall Carter lived with Ambassador Smith at Spaso House, the pre–World War I mansion that served as the U.S. Embassy residence after the United States recognized the Soviet Union. Most of the rest of the American delegation resided at the Moskva Hotel, which had been renovated for the conference. A few days after Marshall's arrival, Smith could be heard spewing a torrent of regular army profanity in his bedroom. A fastidious man, he had just had his hair cut by a Russian barber. When the barber asked Smith whether he wanted hair tonic, something was lost in translation. Smith said yes and received a healthy dose of henna-toned hair dye. According to Bohlen, "Smith's hair had a definite pink tinge" for weeks.[31]

The first of what would turn out to be forty-three meetings of the fourth Council of Foreign Ministers began at four p.m. on March 10 in a large, ornate hall in the Aviation Industry House. In Tsarist times, the handsome Aviation building was the site of the expensive Yar restaurant that only the nobility could afford ("Sweetheart, don't go to the Yar, don't throw your money away," began an old Russian ballad). According to a sketch drawn by Marshall's aide, Colonel Carter, there were twenty-four chairs around the big round conference table. Marshall always sat at the four o'clock position near the entrance. Seated to his right was Ben Cohen, counselor to the State Department, and Foster Dulles. On Marshall's left sat forty-two-year-old Chip Bohlen, who served as Russian expert and interpreter. Next to him was a chair for Lucius Clay or Mark Clark, depending on whether Germany or Austria was the subject of discussion, and lastly a seat for Ambassador Smith. The other three ministers—Vyacheslav Molotov, Ernest Bevin of the UK, and Georges Bidault of France—were arrayed around the table, each flanked by five assistants.

It was apparent from the outset that, as between Germany and Austria, an agreement concerning the future of Germany was far more important to the four powers than that of Austria. With its productive capacity and geographic proximity, Germany was seen by the Soviets as both a potential threat and a nation to be brought under its influence. The U.S. viewed a resurgent German economy—especially its capacity to produce coal, steel, and machinery—as the key to Europe's recovery, an end to its suffering, and a market for American products. A peace treaty with Austria was certainly desirable. However, progress toward a peace deal for Germany was the top priority.

There were several issues, some interrelated, that stood in the way of a German peace treaty. The principal stumbling block, however, was Molotov's demand for $10 billion of reparations to be exacted from Germany. Though the Soviets had already moved entire industrial plants and huge quantities of machinery and other capital assets from Germany to Russia and refused to document their valuations, Molotov insisted that the Soviets were still entitled, under the Yalta accords, to receive goods produced from Germany's *current* production until the $10 billion of in-kind reparations was paid in full.[32] Marshall was flatly opposed to reparations from current production. The U.S. was pouring funds into Germany so that the German economy would be self-supporting in three years. If Marshall and his counterparts in the UK and France were to accept the Soviet position on reparations as the price for a unified Germany, the German economy would not be able to recover without continued subsidization by American taxpayers. In a report to Truman and Acheson, Marshall said he told Molotov that "[we] cannot accept a unified Germany under a procedure which would mean in effect that the American people would pay reparations to an ally," that is, the Soviet Union.[33] Marshall was beginning to believe that Molotov's insistence on extracting reparations from current production was deliberately designed to consign Germany to remaining a "congested slum or an economic poorhouse in the center of Europe."[34]

As a corollary to a strategy of using reparations to weaken Germany's economic revival and forestall the recovery of Western Europe, Molotov was rigid in his opposition to any form of German government, wrote Smith, "except one that provided for . . . complete centralized control," with little or no real power residing in the states. From Molotov's experience with Eastern European countries, he knew that highly centralized governments were, as Smith put it, "vulnerable to penetration" and takeover by Communist minority parties.[35] If and to the extent that Soviet-leaning Communists were able to have a voice in the central government of a politically unified Germany, they could participate in control of the Ruhr, Germany's most important industrial region, or so the thinking went.

Marshall objected to a highly centralized government in Germany. History had shown, he said, that it could "be readily converted into an autocratic government."[36] He proposed the establishment of a provisional government that conferred a significant degree of sovereignty on the several German states (*Länder*), an idea that Molotov argued would "federalize Germany."[37] Marshall and Molotov had reached another impasse. When the secretary moved that the council proceed to the next agenda item, Molotov inexplicably opposed the motion. UK foreign minister Earnest Bevin couldn't contain himself. With disgust, he said he "had been in Moscow for four weeks and done nothing so he didn't care what the Council discussed next."[38]

By the fifth week of the conference Marshall decided that it was time to meet with Stalin himself. Progress toward reaching agreements on any of the main issues concerning Germany and Austria had reached a standstill. Molotov's strategy, probably dictated by Stalin, was to string out the discussions as long as possible, thus facilitating the economic and political disintegration of Western Europe. Perhaps a direct appeal to Stalin could break the stalemate. At ten p.m. on April 15, Marshall, Smith, and Bohlen entered the paneled conference room adjoining Stalin's private office in the Kremlin. According to Bohlen, who took notes of the late-night meeting, Stalin had aged, "much grayer, careworn, and fatigued" than he appeared when he last saw him in December 1945.[39] Stalin reportedly greeted Marshall with a disarming comment. "You look just the same as when I saw you the last time," he said, "but I am just an old man."[40]

Bohlen, the note taker and interpreter, wrote that Marshall began by telling Stalin that he was "very concerned and somewhat depressed" by the "misunderstandings and differences" with the Soviet Union over reparations from current production and the structure of the German government that had been revealed at this conference.[41] Beetle Smith wrote that Marshall stressed the urgency of reaching agreements on those and the other remaining issues because the "security" and "prosperity of all Europe" was at stake.[42] It was time, said Marshall, to end the economic deterioration of Germany and work to restore the economies of Europe. The consequences of delay and inaction would be tragic, he argued.

Stalin "listened impassively" while inhaling a "long Russian cigarette, or doodl[ing] with a blue pencil on notepaper before him," wrote Smith. When Marshall was finished, Stalin replied in a "quiet and friendly tone" that the situation was not so tragic.[43] He said, according to Bohlen's notes, that it was "possible that no great success would be achieved" at this conference, "but that should not cause anyone to be desperate." This was only the first of many skirmishes. Be patient, he counseled Marshall. There is no reason to be "depressed."[44] These last remarks must have infuriated Marshall. He had been patient for five weeks while Molotov lived up to his nickname— "stoneass"—and the people of Europe continued to suffer.

Stalin's "seeming indifference" made a "deep impression on Marshall." It became painfully clear to him that Stalin believed "the best way to advance Soviet interests was to let matters drift."[45] The strategy of drift and delay stood in marked contrast to Stalin's push for quick decisions at the Tehran and Yalta conferences, causing Marshall to conclude that Molotov's stalling was dictated by Stalin and it was in fact deliberate. The cynical goal of the Soviets, Marshall had reluctantly come to believe, was to allow Germany and the rest of Western Europe to slide further toward economic ruin and political and social chaos, thus rendering the region ripe for Soviet influence if not domination.

Pravda and other Soviet newspapers took the position that it was Marshall who was unfairly blocking progress in Moscow by flouting the provisions for reparations set forth in the Yalta and Potsdam agreements. In one of the few surviving letters that George wrote to Katherine during the conference, he made light of the propaganda. "I see the Communist writers are now accusing me of sabotaging the Conference," he wrote. "If you believe all you will read about me in the next two months you will divorce me as an imbecile and scoundrel and at the same time lose a good houseman and gardener." The letter, dated April 17, two days after the revealing meeting with Stalin, suggested that Marshall would be coming home soon. He warned Katherine to expect that there will be a good deal of "entertaining" and "tea calls from diplomats, etc.," and that Dodona would not be off limits—"officials will insist on calling on us there."[46]

The conference went on for another week. Little progress was made. Nothing of substance was decided. At the forty-third and final meeting, pending matters were referred to various entities for further study. The council agreed that its next regular meeting would be held in London in November. That evening Stalin hosted a dinner for the heads of the four delegations and their principal assistants in the hall of Catherine the Great (in the Kremlin). After the members of the foreign delegations, the entire Politburo, and several bemedaled marshals of the Soviet Union were assembled in an anteroom, Stalin and Molotov made their entrance and greeted each of the guests. Stalin, wearing the mustard-colored tunic and striped pants that he had worn at Tehran and Yalta, led them all into dinner in the great hall. Smith wrote that it was a "well-served banquet," but "no more ostentatious than the average American formal dinner." Marshall sat on Stalin's right. There were only five toasts. Stalin began by toasting Secretary Marshall and President Truman. Like the other two western ministers, Marshall's toast expressed disappointment at the lack of progress, but added his "hope for the future," wrote Smith. Understandably, the atmosphere was somber. After dinner a Russian fantasy film, *The Stone Flower*, that was devoid of propaganda or a moral was shown in a theater downstairs. The guests were home by midnight. Smith speculated that many of those present must have wondered "if this would not be the last conference of Foreign Ministers."[47]

Marshall departed Moscow the next morning, bound for Washington via Berlin, Iceland, and Newfoundland. "I thought [the Soviets] could be negotiated with," he recalled later. "I decided finally at Moscow ... that they could not be."[48] Marshall had come to the conclusion that the recovery of Germany was both the stumbling block and the solution. Stalin's fear of a German resurgence was the cause of Soviet intransigence. Yet the recovery of Europe was largely dependent on the revival of Germany's productive capacity. Bohlen, who was on the flight with Marshall, wrote that "all the way back to Washington, Marshall talked "of the importance of finding some initiative to prevent the complete breakdown of Western Europe."[49] The initiative, said Marshall in 1952, became the so-called Marshall Plan, "an outgrowth of the disillusionment over the Moscow Conference, which proved conclusively that the Soviet Union was not negotiating in good faith and could not be induced to cooperate in achieving European recovery."[50]

* * * * *

After a night with Katherine at Lipscombe Lodge in Pinehurst, Marshall addressed the nation by radio. He conceded that efforts at the Moscow Conference to reach a pact to administer and demilitarize Germany and a peace treaty for Austria had largely failed. "The recovery of Europe has been far slower than expected," he observed. "Disintegrating forces are becoming evident." Borrowing a medical metaphor, the secretary concluded with a call for immediate action that presaged his Marshall Plan speech at Harvard. "The patient is sinking while the doctors deliberate. Action ... must be taken without delay."[51]

The next morning, April 29, Marshall met with George Kennan, their first one-on-one conversation. Kennan was tall, slight, and balding. His eyes were his most impressive feature—clear blue, intense, wide-set. The subject was development of a plan for the recovery of the European economy. Something must be done, Marshall told Kennan, and the United States is the only nation capable of taking the lead. He gave Kennan and his yet to be assembled Policy Planning Staff two weeks to come back to him with a set of recommendations that they each knew would involve an unspecified but obviously large infusion of American dollars and in-kind assistance. Marshall's idea from the outset was that a recovery plan would have to be announced in the near future "with explosive force," so that premature political debate in Congress and adverse reactions from isolationist pockets in the Midwest would not "dissipate the chances of U.S. acceptance."[52] He cautioned Kennan to keep his deliberations in strict confidence. Did the general have any further instructions, asked Kennan? Marshall's legendary response: "Avoid trivia."[53] "[W]ith this instruction," wrote Kennan in his memoir, "and with the weight of the world on my shoulders, I went to work."[54]

So did Undersecretary Acheson. In a stump speech to a group of Mississippi farmers and businessmen at Delta State Teachers College, Acheson picked up at the point where Marshall had left off in his nationwide radio address. With his coat off and sleeves rolled up in the college's sweltering gymnasium, Acheson called it his "reveille" speech, his wake-up call.[55] Unless America intervened, he told the gathering, the economies of the free nations of Europe would continue to disintegrate. Eventually they would be dominated by totalitarian regimes. Without specifying dollar amounts, Acheson suggested that a very large recovery effort, financed by the United States, was needed in order to help the stricken countries of Europe become self-supporting. "There is no charity involved in this," he said. "It is not a matter of relief, but an issue of national security," he argued. "It is necessary if we are to preserve our own freedoms and our own institutions."[56] At a press conference in Washington afterward, James "Scotty" Reston of *The New York Times* asked Acheson whether he was announcing a new policy, or "just a bit of private kite flying." Acheson responded, "You know this town better than I do. Foreign policy is made at the White House." Reston asked the president if Acheson spoke for him. Truman said, "Yes, it certainly was Administration policy."[57]

Bow-tied, ample-bellied Arthur Vandenberg needed some stroking. Marshall either heard or sensed that the Republican chairman of the Senate Foreign Relations Committee was irate when he read about Acheson's Delta State speech and the prospect of pushing through Congress a huge foreign aid package. He knew that Vandenberg did not like surprises. According to Acheson, Marshall invited the Michigan senator, as well as himself, to the seclusion of the Blair House at the edge of Lafayette Park for a "long and useful talk." At first, Vandenberg fulminated about "opening the Treasury to every country in the world." Marshall let him run on for a time. He "visibly relaxed," wrote Acheson, when Marshall told him that he would be consulted at every step of the way and that the administration had no intention of asking for the bulk of the funding in the current session (though they might have to ask for a small amount before the end of the year). The security of the United States was imperiled, the two of them explained to Vandenberg. "Now as never before national unity depended upon a purely nonpartisan policy," especially because the heavy lifting in Congress would take place in 1948, a presidential election year. Vandenberg relished the idea of leading a high-stakes legislative challenge. "At the end of the meeting conversion had been accomplished and a search for the Vandenberg brand had begun." Both Acheson and Marshall knew that before Vandenberg would fully support a legislative initiative, he needed to stamp it with an amendment or proviso uniquely his own—the "Vandenberg brand."[58]

It took three weeks, not two, for Kennan to complete the initial draft of his plan—really an outline of a plan—for European recovery (with linkage to the economic plight of the UK). The objective, he wrote, was not to combat and defeat Communism but to restore the "economic health and vigor of European society." To achieve this goal the U.S. would furnish financial and other assistance, provided the European recipients agreed to abide by two fundamental principles: first, the initiative for assistance "must come from Europe, the program must be evolved in Europe, and the Europeans must bear the basic responsibility for it"; and second, the request for U.S. support must "come as a joint request . . . not as a series of isolated and individual appeals."[59] This requirement for joint action was a small but critically important first step toward the integration of Western European economies.

The objective and the two guiding principles of Kennan's outline, known as PPS-1, formed key underpinnings of what emerged as the Marshall Plan. However, it was the written and personal advocacy of six-foot-six, big-boned Will Clayton, undersecretary of state for economic affairs, who had just returned from an inspection trip in Europe, that infused in Marshall an enhanced sense of urgency. Clayton, a few months younger than Marshall, was a self-made multimillionaire, founder of Anderson, Clayton and Company, the largest cotton-trading firm in the world. In 1940, when Anderson, Clayton controlled 15 percent of the world's cotton, he joined the government to help procure strategic materials for the U.S. and to deny them to the Nazis. The opening sentences of a memorandum Clayton presented to Marshall were arresting. "It is now obvious that we grossly underestimated the destruction of the European economy by the war . . . Europe is steadily deteriorating." As an initial move, he proposed that the U.S. provide "as a grant 6 or 7 billion dollars worth of goods for three years," based on a request worked out by a "federation" of European nations headed by the UK, France, and Italy. Other nations should provide goods as well. However, he emphasized that *the United States must run this show.*"[60] Clayton's approach was blunt and anything but altruistic. "Let us admit right off," said Clayton, "that our objective has as its background the needs and interests of the people of the United States. We need markets—big markets—in which to buy and sell."[61]

There was no time to lose. Washington was already alive with rumors that the Truman administration was working on a plan to rehabilitate Europe. Relying on unnamed sources in the State Department, *The New York Times* published a front-page editorial by Scotty Reston indicating that a four-year $16 billion aid program was being considered. The article was titled "Beyond the Truman Doctrine."[62] Reston later wrote that Senator Vandenberg called him after reading the article and told him he must have been misinformed. "Congress," he insisted, "would never appropriate that amount of money to save anybody."[63] Marshall received word that Vandenberg was upset. He immediately met with the senator, briefed him on his proposal for European recovery, and solicited his views. If Marshall knew who on his team leaked the story to Reston—it might well have been Acheson, who was close to Reston—there would have been hell to pay.

On the morning of May 28, Kennan, Clayton, Acheson, Bohlen, and three or four other State Department officials who were working on the plan for European recovery trooped into Marshall's office. Everyone in the room had read Kennan's PPS-1 and Clayton's memo. As was his custom in meetings of this sort, Marshall said little as the participants debated aspects of the proposals outlined by Kennan and Clayton. He preferred to direct the flow and ask pointed questions. Historians John Agnew and Nicholas Entrikin wrote that this discussion "might have been one of the most brilliant political strategy sessions of all time" because it laid out a "simple yet effective plan" for European recovery and provided a "vision of a 'new' Europe to serve as a basis for more specific American military and economic policies toward the region."[64] It became apparent from Marshall's questions that his principal concern was whether the offer of U.S. assistance should be confined to Western Europe and the UK or made available to all of Europe, including Soviet Russia and its satellites. Except for Marshall, who expressed no opinion, they agreed that the offer should be extended to all of Europe. "The

United States should not assume the responsibility of dividing Europe," declared Acheson.[65] Yes, interjected Marshall, but what if the Soviets accept our offer and then try to obstruct and undermine the overall plan for recovery through endless negotiations? Kennan responded as only he could. Stalin will never accept the U.S. plan, he reportedly said, because a condition of participation entails cooperation with the other European nations and exposure of the Russian economy to Western inspection. Plus, the Soviets are bound to be deeply suspicious of our motives and implacably opposed to a resurgence of a unified Germany. "Play it straight," he counseled.[66] Make our plan available to all of Europe and the UK. If satellite nations are tempted, said Kennan, Stalin will probably block them from accepting because he needs them as border buffers and trading partners. Let the Soviet Union take responsibility for dividing Europe, not us. Chip Bohlen said later that "it was a hell of a big gamble."[67]

With a stern admonition against any more leaks, Marshall adjourned the meeting. As usual he did not tip his hand. Marshall may have discussed his next move with the president, but those in the room, with the possible exception of Acheson, had no clue as to how he planned to proceed. Later that day he made up his mind. For the past few weeks Marshall had been thinking about giving a short speech that would jump-start a campaign to persuade Congress and the American people of the urgent need to rehabilitate the European economy. Originally, he considered speaking at the University of Wisconsin in the conservative heartland of the Midwest, where he most needed to attract support. But Wisconsin's graduation weekend was too early. His next choice was Amherst College, where he was scheduled to receive an honorary degree on June 15. That date, however, was too late. The Clayton memo, the fear of more leaks, and the Soviet takeover of Hungary caused Marshall to turn to Harvard University. Harvard's commencement exercises were set for June 5. Late on the afternoon of May 28, Marshall's office contacted James Conant, president of Harvard, and informed him that the secretary would accept a long-standing invitation to receive an honorary degree and "would be pleased to make a few remarks and perhaps 'a little more' at the alumni meeting." The "little more," as Forrest Pogue wrote, "was to have global reverberations."[68]

The next day Marshall asked Acheson whether a brief speech to Harvard alumni in early June during commencement weekend would be the right time and occasion to outline the European recovery plan (he did not tell Acheson that he had already made arrangements to speak at Harvard). Acheson was okay with the timing, but advised against it on the ground that it would not receive the widest press coverage. Marshall was undeterred. He did not want his remarks to be overplayed. As Acheson later commented, "Maybe Marshall was smarter than I was: let this come out gradually and take hold rather than have a big build-up."[69]

Like many great state documents, the seven double-spaced typewritten pages that became famous as "the Marshall Plan speech" had more than one father—in this case, at least three. On May 30, Marshall wrote a memo to his personal assistant, General Marshall Carter. He asked Carter to "have someone . . . prepare a draft for a less than ten-minute talk by me" to Harvard alumni concerning the "proper policy" to address the serious situation in Europe.[70] Forrest Pogue wrote that Carter selected Chip Bohlen to do the drafting because "Marshall liked Bohlen's views and his style."[71] In his 1973 memoir, Bohlen says it was Secretary Marshall, not Carter, who asked him to draft the speech and that Marshall provided him with Kennan's PPS-1 and the Clayton memo to be used as guides in preparing the speech.[72]

Most historians have credited Bohlen with preparing the first draft, the "structure" of which and much of the "phrasing," according to Bohlen, was "picked up" in the final version. Marshall had a much different memory of the provenance of his Harvard talk. In his February 1953 letter to Kennan, less than six years after the speech and twenty years before Bohlen's memoir, Marshall wrote, "I called on Chip Bohlen and you [Kennan] to prepare, independent of each other, a definite recommendation on the subject. Also, I grew restless and dictated one of my own, and that the end result was very much a combination of all three."[73] Similarly, in a 1956 interview, Marshall, commenting on how his speech "was built," said that he "cut out part of Kennan's speech and part of Bohlen's speech and part of my speech and put the three together and that was the beginning of the talk."[74] At some point Acheson and Clayton reviewed one of the drafts and provided their comments. Apparently, the speech was never shown to the president in advance of its delivery.

Since General Omar Bradley, head of the Veterans Administration, was also scheduled to receive an honorary degree at Harvard, George and Katherine joined Omar and his wife, Kitty, for the June 4 afternoon flight to

Boston. During the trip Marshall continued to edit his speech. That evening they dined and spent the night at President Conant's historic residence on the Harvard campus.

Meanwhile, in Washington three British journalists, including Leonard Miall of the BBC, invited Acheson to lunch at the United Nations Club near Dupont Circle. Acheson, admittedly suffering from a "bad hangover," talked at length about the significance of his Delta State address. Contrary to what he wrote later in his memoir, Acheson did not tip them off that day about Marshall's forthcoming speech at Harvard, nor did he urge one of them to call Ernest Bevin in London and read him the text. However, Acheson made sure the three journalists understood that the administration was seriously considering a substantial aid package, provided the Europeans were prepared to quickly seize the initiative.[75]

Harvard's 286th Commencement Day, Thursday, June 5, dawned clear and cool. After making a few more changes to his speech, Marshall left the president's house to lead the procession of honorary degree recipients. When the crowd glimpsed Marshall, who was dressed in a three-piece gray suit and blue polka-dot tie, with Panama hat in hand, they stood and offered a prolonged ovation. Marshall's speech was to be given not on the steps of Memorial Church where the commencement addresses were delivered, but later that day before the alumni in Harvard Yard.

According to *The Harvard Crimson*, a "crowd of 15,000 showed up in the Yard not so much in expectation of seeing history made, as simply in awe of the man." Marshall began with customary humility, noting his inability to live up to the words comparing him to George Washington that President Conant used in conferring his honorary degree. Peering through one of his many pairs of "dime-store" reading glasses, Marshall put his head down and moved quickly to the subject of his talk: the urgent need to rehabilitate the European economy. While his tone was flat and understated, revealing little if any passion, his words were powerful. Without help from America, he declared, Europe faced "economic, social and political deterioration" that would have adverse consequences on the American economy and her national security. It follows, he said, "that the United States should do whatever it is able to do to assist in the return of normal economic health in the world, without which there can be no political stability and no assured peace." Marshall made it apparent that he was talking about a massive infusion of economic assistance when he said it "should provide a cure rather than a mere palliative." He was convinced that it "must not be on a piece-meal basis as various crises develop."

Following Kennan's advice, Marshall's much-quoted statement of who in Europe would be entitled to assistance and who would not was accomplished without ever mentioning the Soviet Union or Communism by name. "Our policy," proclaimed Marshall, "is directed not against any country or doctrine [he crossed out "Communism" in Bohlen's draft] but against hunger, poverty, desperation and chaos." Its aim is to revive working economies where "free institutions can exist" and to be made available to any government that is willing to assist in recovery efforts. On the other hand, "governments, political parties or groups that seek to perpetuate human misery in order to profit therefrom politically" will be opposed by the U.S. These lines attracted sustained applause. Everyone in the audience or who read the speech later knew who Marshall was talking about when he referred to certain "governments" and "political parties."

Although the secretary's words were largely his own, the meat of his short speech incorporated Kennan's two guiding principles. "It would be neither fitting nor efficacious," he said, "for our Government to draw up unilaterally a program to place Europe on its feet economically. This is the business of the Europeans." The initiative must come from them. Second, Marshall made clear that "there must be some agreement among the countries of Europe" as to the nature and amount of assistance they require. "The program should be a joint one, agreed to by a number, if not all European nations."

When Marshall reached the end of his prepared speech and some in the crowd rose to applaud, he removed "his glasses, leaned forward on the lectern, and reached into his [breast] pocket."[76] He drew out a piece of paper that contained a few scribbled closing remarks. It was a final plea, for him a heartfelt request that his countrymen set aside the passions and prejudices that lead to selfish nationalism, and face up to the "real significance of the situation." The "whole world of the future," he concluded, "hangs on a proper judgment" by the American people. It is they who must decide, "What is needed? What can best be done? What must be done?" He paused, and then ended with "Thank you very much."[77]

Marshall had told General Carter that he wanted a speech of less than ten minutes. It actually took twelve minutes and ten seconds to deliver.

Reaction to the speech in the U.S. was muted. James Conant, who spent most of the day with Marshall, wrote that he "had not understood" the meaning of the talk when he heard it.[78] Columnist Joe Alsop, who was on the dais that afternoon, wrote that he did not pick up on the significance of Marshall's speech—perhaps due to the previous night's raucous drinking with friends at the Porcellian Club: "I confess that the wording of the speech was so vague and its delivery so lacking in vigor that I had not the dimmest notion of what the secretary of state was saying, let alone that he was making a proposal that would change the world."[79] The *Washington Post* and *The New York Times* ran front-page reports of the speech, but neither acknowledged the potential historic significance of Marshall's call for the United States to do whatever was necessary to assist in the recovery of Europe. Senator Taft's strong attacks on the administration and the Soviet coup in Hungary, among other news items, were competing for headlines in the U.S.

By contrast, Ernest Bevin, the British foreign secretary, understood at once the implications of Marshall's speech. On the evening of June 5, Bevin was at his home in London. At nine p.m. UK time, not long after Marshall had finished his talk at Harvard, Bevin turned on the radio next to his bed and began listening to a prerecorded BBC broadcast from Washington of *American Commentary*, a regular Thursday night program. This was a program about U.S. foreign affairs that officials in the British Foreign Office typically listened to. Bevin had no idea that Marshall or anyone else in America would be making a major policy address that day. The voice that Bevin heard on his radio was that of Leonard Miall, who had obtained an advance copy of Marshall's speech from the State Department. Miall was a talented newsman, an excellent raconteur with a gentle smile and a non-Oxford accent. When he pieced together the substance of the advance copy of Marshall's speech along with what Acheson had told him at the lunch a few days before, Miall suddenly realized that he was in possession of highly significant breaking news that his government and the nations of continental Europe would find of vital interest. Since Miall was told that there would be no network broadcast of Marshall's actual speech, he decided that the most effective way to convey the news would be to read key excerpts of the advance copy, interspersing his own analysis with these verbatim readings.[80] In his broadcast, Miall characterized Marshall's remarks as "an exceptionally important speech" in which he "propounded a totally new continental approach to the problem of

Europe's economic crisis," similar to the "grandeur of the original concept of Lend-Lease."[81] To Bevin's ears, Marshall's words and Miall's analysis were exhilarating. "It was like a life-line to sinking men," he later told the National Press Club in Washington. "It seemed to bring hope where there was none. The generosity of it was beyond our belief."[82]

The next morning, Bevin burst into the Foreign Office. "Get me Marshall's speech," he demanded. Those who heard him had no idea what he was talking about. Later Bevin rang up Georges Bidault and Vyacheslav Molotov, the foreign ministers of France and the Soviet Union. The three of them agreed to meet in Paris on June 27 to "discuss how Europeans might devise a European recovery plan, its requirements, and the parts they would play in it."[83]

* * * * *

Borrowing the famous line from Ralph Waldo Emerson's "Concord Hymn," Senator Vandenberg called General Marshall's Harvard speech "a shot heard round the world."[84] It was surely revolutionary, marking a sharp departure from America's retreat into isolationism after the Great War. And it ran against the long-standing policy of Marshall's army predecessor, General George Washington, who warned in 1796 that the fledgling republic should "steer clear" of "permanent alliances with any portion of the foreign world." Seen by many as an act of incredible generosity by a nation that had already given more than $13 billion in postwar aid, the offer of assistance announced by Marshall ushered in a new postwar grand strategy, inspired by economic self-interest, national security, and a dose of New Deal state-sponsored altruism. For the first time American policy makers, with Marshall as their spokesperson, offered to help rehabilitate European enemies and allies alike, but only on condition that the recipient nations agreed to a measure of integration for purposes of trade and production. If the Soviets and their satellites refused to participate, so be it. In effect, Marshall's speech laid the groundwork for a new order in Europe, arguably a new world order. Henceforth, the United States would export its brand of organized capitalism and its values in order to protect and sustain itself at home.

It would take months before the broad strokes articulated in Marshall's speech became a fully developed plan. Yet, within a few weeks journalists and virtually everyone else began referring to it as the Marshall Plan. Clark Clifford claimed in his memoir that he "watched as the speech took shape," and suggested to his boss that it be called "the Truman Concept" or "the Truman Plan." He recommended that Truman, not Marshall, should be the one to give the speech. Acutely aware that 1948 would be an election year and that Congress would be asked to enact the plan into law, Truman responded, "We have a Republican majority in both Houses. Anything going up there with my name will quiver a couple of times, go belly up, and die. Let me think about it a little." A day or so later, he told Clifford, "I've decided to give the whole thing to General Marshall. The worst Republican on the Hill can vote for it if we name it after the General."[85]

Truman was right. The association of Marshall's name with the plan, together with his efforts to sell it to Congress and the American people in the ensuing months, would prove to be a game-changing political asset.

CHAPTER 15

Hope for Those Who Need It

L ooking back, Marshall remembered that simply announcing the "idea of the so-called Marshall Plan" was the easy part. The "heavy task," he observed, was "the execution"—how he and his fellow proponents overcame opposition in America, especially in the Midwest, and moved it through Congress.[1] It would take from June 1947 until the following April for the idea to become law and two more months to secure the funding.

* * * * *

During the week after the June 5 speech at Harvard, Marshall met alone at Blair House with Arthur Vandenberg, Republican chairman of the Senate Foreign Relations Committee, to nail down his support and to discuss the heavy task ahead. He succeeded in getting his support, albeit provisionally. At the end of that week, Vandenberg issued a statement endorsing the need for a program to rehabilitate Europe. However, in an effort to quell the opposition at home, he cautioned that the U.S. should not "rush into imprudent or inadequately seasoned plans . . ." In the next breath he proposed the creation of a high-level "bipartisan advisory council" that would assess the ability of the nation's economy to meet Europe's needs. And he let it be known that he would not touch the Marshall Plan unless this was done.[2] Once again, he imprinted the Vandenberg brand on an administration-backed foreign policy initiative.

Marshall was pleased to have the Michigan senator's endorsement, conditioned as it was. The president, after hearing Marshall's explanation of what happened at Blair House, agreed with the secretary that Vandenberg's call for a bipartisan council "was really a good thing coming at the time it did and from him."[3] Acheson too thought it was a positive step, but he believed it was of great importance that Truman move quickly to appoint council members of his own choosing. With Marshall's approval, Acheson and William Foster, undersecretary of commerce, assembled a blue ribbon eighteen-member council consisting of several prominent industrialists (e.g., CEOs of General Electric, Procter & Gamble, B. F. Goodrich, Studebaker), labor leaders (e.g., George Meany of the AFL, James Carey of the CIO), academics/think tanks (e.g., Cornell, Harvard, Brookings, Duke, Colorado School of Mines, University of California), and public officials (e.g., Chester Davis of the Federal Reserve). Acheson recommended that Averell Harriman, his former Groton schoolmate and Yale rowing coach who was then serving as Truman's commerce secretary, be designated chairman.

Armed with the list of council nominees and a press release, Truman summoned Marshall, Vandenberg, Senate majority leader Wallace White of Maine, two Democratic senators, and selected members of his cabinet to his upstairs study. After making sure that Vandenberg received full credit for the idea, Truman read the list of nominees and their qualifications. At Vandenberg's suggestion, former Republican senator Robert La Follette Jr. of Wisconsin was added to the list. Without objection, all of the nominees were approved. The council, known as the Harriman Committee, was officially charged with finding facts and providing a report on the "limits within which" the U.S. can "safely and wisely plan to extend" economic assistance to the Europeans.[4] The president also ordered that two additional reports be prepared: one by the Council of Economic Advisers, headed by Edwin Nourse, on how the foreign aid proposed to be extended would affect domestic production, consumption, and prices; and the other by Secretary of the Interior Julius Krug, on whether U.S. resources and physical capabilities could adequately support a large new foreign aid program.

The next move was up to the Europeans. Could they come together and make a joint request for assistance, as indicated in Marshall's speech? Would the Soviet Union and its Eastern European satellites participate? From Washington, Marshall could only watch and wait.

It didn't take long for the east-west fault lines to appear. During the initial three-party discussions between the foreign ministers of Britain, France, and the Soviet Union that began at the Quai d'Orsay (French Ministry of Foreign Affairs) in Paris, Molotov expressed "serious doubts" about the plan for moving forward proposed by the French and supported by the British.[5] By the 2nd of July it became clear that the Soviet position was fundamentally at odds with that of the British and French. In accordance with

Marshall's speech, the Anglo-French foreign ministers (Bevin and Bidault) insisted on setting up a multinational steering committee that would examine, validate, and coordinate the aid requests of all participating states. On the other hand, Molotov wanted to simply aggregate the amounts requested in each nation's self-determined aid request and forward the total to Washington. He regarded involvement in a European coordinating body—with authority to inquire into each nation's resources—as an infringement of sovereignty that would expose the Soviet economy and that of its satellites to invasive outside scrutiny.

Molotov also demanded assurances that German participation in the Marshall Plan would not jeopardize Soviet claims for reparations taken out of current production in each of Germany's four occupation zones. As to the question of reparations from production in the British and French zones, Bevin and Bidault waffled, ignoring promises made at Yalta and Potsdam. By contrast, the U.S. position on reparations was firm. Pursuant to a directive by the JCS, which made creation of a self-supporting Germany a principal objective of American occupation policy, all prior agreements to pay reparations to the Soviet Union from production in the U.S. zone were to be suspended as of July 7.

The Soviet foreign minister could have dragged things on for weeks, as he was wont to do. However, during his fifth and final meeting with Bevin and Bidault, Molotov decided to stalk out of the conference room, having been given discretion by Stalin, approved by the Politburo, to obstruct and prevent the Marshall Plan from being implemented in the Soviet occupation zone in Germany and the rest of Eastern Europe. A few days earlier, Stalin had been persuaded by a Soviet intelligence report that the multinational body demanded by the Anglo-French and backed by the U.S. would lead to American interference in the economic and political affairs of the Eastern European buffer states in the Soviet sphere of influence. Stalin's overriding concern—his first priority—was maintenance of control over his satellites because they provided him with border security, vital resources, and trade advantages. "Stalin considered the Soviet zone of influence," wrote Russian historian Mikhail Narinsky, "to be the most important legacy of World War II."[6]

Molotov's staged walkout was treated as good news by Kennan and Marshall. In a note to Bevin and Bidault, Marshall wrote that "at least the Soviet attitude . . . has been clarified" and will not continue to hinder the "working out of a recovery program for the other countries."[7] Averell Harriman later commented that if Molotov had not withdrawn, he "could have killed the Marshall Plan."[8]

In Molotov's closing speech on July 3, he accused the Western powers of dividing Europe. Bevin muttered to an aide, "this really is the birth of the Western bloc," and he blamed the Soviets for creating the split.[9] The next day Bevin and Bidault invited all twenty-two European countries (excluding Russia and Spain and including Turkey) to participate in a conference to create a program for the economic rehabilitation of Europe. The gathering was to be held in Paris, beginning on July 12. Once acceptances were in hand, the world would know the depth of the division or, to put it another way, the components of the Western bloc.

In Moscow, Stalin and the Soviet leadership vacillated. At first they cabled their representatives in Eastern European capitals that they should attend the conference, but object to the U.S. offer of assistance and then walk out, taking as many other countries with them as possible. A day later they had second thoughts. Some of their satellites might give in to the temptation of receiving American economic aid. The Marshall Plan, they concluded, was the beginning of a Western offensive against the Soviet Union—a hostile encirclement. On the night of July 7, arguably "the birthdate of the Cold War," Soviet envoys in Poland, Czechoslovakia, Hungary, Yugoslavia, Romania, Bulgaria, and Finland received messages instructing them to refuse to participate in the Paris conference.[10] All complied except for Czechoslovakia. The majority of the Czech ministers, including non-Communist Foreign Minister Jan Masaryk, favored participation in the Marshall Plan. Klement Gottwald, the prime minister of Czechoslovakia and leader of its Communist Party, cabled Moscow that it was impossible to change his government's decision to attend.

Stalin was furious. He ordered Gottwald and his delegation, who were on the way to Moscow for trade talks, to meet with him. The evidence suggests that Gottwald initially met alone with Stalin in the Kremlin at which time he agreed to rescind his government's decision to attend the conference in Paris.[11] Heavy-handed pressure was no doubt applied. Gottwald said later that he had never seen Stalin so angry.

The official meeting of Gottwald and his delegation with Stalin took place at midnight on July 9. The Soviet leader acknowledged to them that he had changed his mind. He said he was convinced that "the Great Powers," using the pretext of offering U.S. economic assistance, "are attempting to form a Western bloc and isolate the Soviet Union."[12] This statement, recorded verbatim in the minutes of the meeting by a member of the Czech delegation, is probably the best evidence of what Stalin actually thought about the Marshall Plan.

Since Prime Minister Gottwald had already given in, Stalin appealed to the rest of the delegation, many of whom were not communists. He made it clear that they had no choice. Two days later the Czech government unanimously canceled its decision to attend the Paris conference. Jan Masaryk reportedly said, "I went to Moscow as the Foreign Minister of an independent sovereign state; I returned as a lackey of the Soviet government."[13]

Once Czechoslovakia's decision, forced upon it by Stalin, was radioed to Washington, the states comprising the East and West blocs were known and the depth of the east-west division was settled. Ambassador Beetle Smith cabled Marshall from Moscow. The "Czechoslovak reversal," wrote Smith, "is nothing less than a declaration of war by the Soviet Union" concerning the control of Europe.[14] It was not exactly a war, but it did represent a shift in Soviet grand strategy, a strategy that in Stalin's mind was driven by the Marshall Plan. In his view the plan was a hostile act. Cooperation was no longer possible. As Smith wrote, "the lines [were] drawn."[15]

* * * * *

On Saturday, July 12, at eleven a.m., representatives of the sixteen nations in the so-called Western bloc took their seats under the gold and blue ceiling cove in the main dining room of the Quai d'Orsay. In response to George Marshall's Harvard speech, states of all sizes, economies, and cultures gathered together to agree on a common program for the economic rehabilitation of Western Europe. The "sixteen power" conference had no precedent in the history of Europe.[16]

Without the presence of Molotov, the parties smoothly and unanimously agreed to an organizational structure and an agenda for moving forward. Ernest Bevin, Great Britain's exuberant foreign secretary who looked like "a cross between Santa Claus and a Welsh coalman," was appointed chairman of the conference.[17] A steering committee called the Committee of European Economic Cooperation, or CEEC, and four technical committees, along with subcommittees, were established and staffed. Their tasks were to study the resources and needs of the states and to devise a four-year program for collective rehabilitation. There was a palpable sense of urgency. The delegates set themselves an ambitious deadline of September 1—just six weeks for the CEEC to devise a program acceptable to the American administrators of the Marshall Plan and the U.S. Congress. Within four days the machinery was set up, the conference disbanded, and the committees and subcommittees got down to business. "It is the quickest conference I have ever presided over," remarked Bevin.[18]

Back in Washington there had been a changing of the guard at Marshall's State Department. The six months of service that Acheson promised Marshall expired at the end of June. He returned to his law practice after several years on a government pay scale. His replacement as undersecretary, Texas-born Robert Abercrombie ("Bob") Lovett, took over the day-to-day running of the State Department on July 1, 1947. In the coming months, with Marshall scheduled to be attending conferences abroad, fifty-one-year-old Bob Lovett was destined to play a vital role in the shaping and selling of the Marshall Plan.

Lovett, a member of Skull and Bones in Yale's class of 1918, left college before graduating to serve as a pilot with the British Royal Air Service in the Great War. He logged numerous combat hours flying Handley Page bombers over German troop concentrations, artillery, and ammunition trains. For the rest of his life Lovett was a student and advocate of airpower. During World War II, he earned Marshall's esteem and friendship when, as assistant secretary for air in the War Department, he was responsible for procurement of aircraft for the huge army air force.

Knowing that Acheson would be with him for only six months, Marshall had his eye on Lovett since the day he was sworn in as secretary of state. In February he enlisted the president to help persuade Lovett to again leave his lucrative partnership with Brown Brothers Harriman, a prestigious investment banking firm in Manhattan (Lovett had left the partnership earlier, during the war, to work with Marshall in the War Department). One morning the White House operator telephoned Lovett at his home in Locust Valley. Truman was on the line. He told Lovett that General Marshall was insistent that his "old copilot" return to Washington to replace Acheson as his undersecretary of state. Lovett asked for time to think it over. It would be almost impossible to refuse both Marshall and the president, but he was concerned about withdrawing from the firm for a second time. Averell Harriman, his former partner and fellow Bonesman, told him he would be a "damn fool" to turn down the job. Acheson, Lovett's friend since their days at Yale, urged him to take the post. Lovett called Truman back. He accepted on condition that he could take two months in Florida to recover from another operation on his "glass insides" (meaning his gallbladder) and a month of on-the-job training with Acheson before "flying solo."[19]

While the force of Acheson's personality was essential to the emergence of the Marshall Plan, Lovett's temperament was suited to the heavy task of transforming the ideas undergirding Marshall's speech into a program acceptable to both the Europeans and Congress. Like Acheson, Lovett had a sharp and worldly intellect. However, he had more self-awareness, a keener sense of how he was perceived by others. In contrast to Acheson, who could be brusque and acerbic and did not suffer fools, Lovett was tactful, genial, and soothing, qualities that were particularly important when dealing with American and European politicians. Moreover, he had an unusually attractive sense of humor. In *Driven Patriot*, Townsend Hoopes and coauthor Douglas Brinkley wrote that Lovett's "'sophisticated witticisms' and 'rueful humors'" made him "one of the funniest men of his generation."[20]

Lovett must have laughed at the first line of Kennan's July 21 memo concerning the Marshall Plan. "We have no plan," it began. The next sentences, however, explained what he meant. It was the Europeans who were responsible for coming up with a plan, he wrote. The U.S. would consider their plan, but only if it did "the whole job," and enabled the "principal European countries to exist without outside charity."[21]

By early August, with the September 1 deadline at hand, the efforts of the Europeans to agree on a plan, let alone one that would do the whole job, had stalled. The problem was Germany. Britain and the Benelux countries were convinced that rehabilitation of the economy in Germany's three western occupation zones (which included the Ruhr Valley) was essential to the recovery of Western Europe. France was adamantly opposed. The wounds inflicted by Germany were fresh. The French feared a German resurgence and believed that their economy should be the main engine of recovery for Western Europe. Marshall decided it was time for the Americans to step in and provide "friendly aid" in the drafting of an acceptable plan, as he had promised in his Harvard speech. Accordingly, he directed Will Clayton and General Lucius Clay, military governor of the U.S. zone in Western Germany and Berlin, to break the deadlock. On August 14, the French agreed to a compromise. With the hope, not yet a promise, of security guarantees, France agreed to join the UK, the Benelux countries, and the U.S. in internationalizing the production of coal, coke, and steel in the Ruhr, a forerunner of the European Coal and Steel Community and the Common Market. As a consequence, Germany was vaulted from "the periphery" of the Marshall Plan "into its core."[22]

In the third week of August, Lovett wired a blunt message to Marshall, who was attending the Inter-American Conference for the Maintenance of Continental Peace and Security at Petrópolis, Brazil's imperial city, to finalize a Latin America mutual defense pact. Progress of the CEEC in Paris, he reported, was "disappointing." All they have come up with is "sixteen shopping lists" totaling $28 billion, Lovett wrote, and "even these huge sums" would not result in "rehabilitation over a four-year period." Lovett recommended that the CEEC promptly be told that its present plan is not acceptable, that George Kennan be sent to Paris to offer realistic proposals, and that the deadline be extended to mid-September. Marshall agreed, stressing that those on his team need to be firm and emphatic.[23]

With Marshall's backing, and the dogged persistence of Lucius Clay, Lovett pushed the European delegates to reduce their collective $28 billion aid request by taking advantage of opportunities for "self-help" and "mutual help."[24] They made it clear that the economies in the three western zones of Germany must operate as one. In Paris, Kennan assisted Clayton in fashioning guidelines to the CEEC that emphasized production (especially production of coal and food), financial and monetary reforms, and liberalization of trade barriers throughout Western Europe. Meanwhile, time was running out. The economic situation was deteriorating so rapidly, reported Kennan, that the U.S. had no alternative but to provide "interim aid" so that the Europeans could survive the winter.[25]

Whether planned or not, Lovett and Marshall embarked on a "good cop, bad cop" maneuver. On September 7, Lovett pressed the CEEC harder than ever. He gave the Paris delegates another two weeks to hammer out a final program that addressed the deficiencies and reforms identified by Kennan and Clayton and substantially reduced the amount of aid requested.

The French and British representatives stubbornly resisted, claiming that the Americans risked "wrecking the whole conference in its final critical stages."[26] Bevin was angry.

It was at this moment—a critical juncture in the implementation of the Marshall Plan—that Marshall chose to step forward and defuse the situation. On September 10, he issued a press release that had been cleared by Truman. Citing the accelerated need of some of the European countries for aid in reducing hunger and cold in the coming winter, Marshall announced that the administration would support a bill in Congress to provide "interim assistance."[27] The next day he offered to soften several of the changes that the U.S. was insisting be made to the proposed plan of the CEEC and he suggested that its report to the State Department be framed as a first report—"a basis for further discussion."[28]

Marshall's intervention was the right touch at the right time. On September 12, Jefferson Caffrey, the distinguished American ambassador to France who served under eight presidents from Taft to Eisenhower, cabled Marshall that the Paris delegates "were prepared to proceed along the lines suggested by the U.S."[29] Nine days later, the CEEC released its historic two-volume *General Report* to the public, which hailed "the advent of a new stage in European economic cooperation" and the inclusion of Western Germany in the program for European recovery.[30] The total request was reduced to $17 billion, a significant improvement, but still more than the State Department wanted. Five signed originals of the report, encased in green manila folders and bound with shocking pink ribbons, were personally delivered by Walter Kirkwood, His Majesty's messenger, to the United States. "It is now for the American people and the American Congress," Bevin reportedly said, "to decide whether this program, undertaken at Secretary Marshall's initiative, should be fulfilled and whether Europe by this means can contribute to the peace and prosperity of the world."[31]

*   *   *   *   *

The selling of the Marshall Plan was going to require a heavy lift. Near the end of September, the president convened a meeting of key leaders of Congress plus Marshall, Lovett, and Harriman for a strategy session. According to Truman's memoir, he began by summarizing the report of the CEEC. He said the Europeans would require an appropriation of $580 million of emergency aid to take care of immediate needs until March 31, 1948—the earliest date by which comprehensive legislation providing for recovery (to be delivered to Congress in December) could be enacted.[32] This meant that Congress would need to adopt a two-part legislative strategy—enact emergency relief by Christmas 1947 followed by hearings and passage of the main recovery plan in the spring of 1948. House majority leader Charles Halleck, a conservative Indiana Republican, spoke up. "Mr. President, you must realize there is growing resistance to these programs. I've been out on the hustings and I know. The people don't like it."[33] Halleck's pessimism was shared by others in the room. Nevertheless, Truman dispatched letters to the House and Senate committees on foreign affairs and appropriations. Citing the "steady deterioration" of the French and Italian economies, the president asked that their committees meet as soon as possible to consider his request for interim aid.[34] In late October he called for a special session of Congress to convene on November 17.

Truman's two-stage proposal meant that political resistance to the first stage—a request for almost $600 million of interim relief—could be just as fierce as the opposition to the $17 billion European recovery plan. Opponents in Congress were likely to claim that a vote for emergency funds would be tantamount to a vote for the entire Marshall Plan. Passage of interim relief arguably would let the horses out of the barn.

The opposition was led by "Mr. Republican," Senator Robert Taft of Ohio. A week before hearings began on interim aid he declared in an address to the Ohio Society that the Marshall Plan was inflationary and would require huge tax increases. Taft complained, yet in the same breath admitted, that he and his colleagues had been out-organized: "We have seen in the past three months the development of carefully planned propaganda for the Marshall Plan, stimulated by the State Department, by widespread publicity, and by secret meetings of influential people in Washington."[35]

Taft was right about meetings of influential people, but the most consequential meetings were not exactly secret. And they were not in Washington. Instead, they took place at the second home of a wealthy Brazilian in the mountains northeast of Rio de Janeiro. Over a period of eighteen days in August 1947, it was there that George Marshall, Arthur Vandenberg, and their respective spouses became close friends. The Vandenbergs were part of the delegation that Marshall brought to the Inter-American conference at

Petrópolis, Brazil's summer capital. In her diary, Hazel Vandenberg wrote about a day during the conference when she found Katherine and George Marshall on the porch of their villa "playing Chinese checkers ... completely congenial and a simply grand pair." Before long the couples spent evenings together, relaxing with cocktails before dinner and playing bridge and other games into the evenings. "There is nothing stuffy at all about [Marshall]," wrote Hazel, "in fact, he is a lot of fun and so human."[36] As a mark of friendship, the general began addressing the senator as "Arthur" and "Van."

Arthur Vandenberg Jr., who edited the *The Private Papers of Senator Vandenberg*, wrote that it was because of the conference in Brazil that Marshall and Vandenberg were able to establish a "new and close working relationship" and an "abiding friendship . . . based on mutual respect and affection." He concluded that the bond between the two of them was largely responsible for the bipartisanship in foreign policy that was to prevail in the coming months.[37] Indeed, in the late 1940s, Vandenberg was regarded as chief advocate of the idea that "politics stops at the water's edge," though a version of the adage was coined as early as 1812 by Daniel Webster.

After returning to Washington in September, the senator became a full partner of the general in "the adventure" (Marshall's term) of trying to persuade Congress to vote for interim aid and to pass the main plan for European recovery. "Van was my right-hand man and at times I was his right-hand man," recalled Marshall. To avoid media attention, their practice was to meet twice a week, on average, at Blair House through the autumn and winter. "We couldn't have gotten much closer together," joked Marshall, "unless I sat in Van's lap or he sat in mine."[38]

Senator Taft's admission that propaganda for the Marshall Plan was "carefully planned" was spot-on. A week before Taft's speech to the Ohio Society, the bipartisan Harriman Committee, originally suggested by Vandenberg, released its unanimous endorsement of aid for Western Europe, making the case that the U.S. could afford a four-year program, that America had a moral duty to help, and that U.S. assistance would halt the spread of Communism in Europe. The conclusions of the Harriman Committee were widely publicized. Similarly, reports issued in October by Julius Krug, secretary of the interior, and Edwin Nourse, chairman of the Council of Economic Advisers, concluded that a recovery plan costing between

$12 and $17 billion would not endanger America's national security and vital resources nor was it likely to cause inflation or necessitate a tax increase.

Support for the Marshall Plan came from an unlikely but highly influential source. Newly appointed Secretary of Defense Forrestal began promoting the plan to key members of Congress as an alternative to an expensive military buildup, a form of asymmetrical warfare. Since Forrestal was the administration's chief spokesman for the military, his endorsement of an economic strategy for defeating the spread of communism constituted a radical departure from conventional military thinking.

From his law firm, Dean Acheson helped set up a first-class lobbying organization in the summer of 1947 called the Committee for the Marshall Plan. Its three hundred bipartisan members were a who's who of the American elite in industry, religion, media, academia, agriculture, and labor. Henry Stimson served as its honorary president. Acheson and former secretary of war Robert Patterson assumed operational responsibility. The committee raised $150,000, hired a staff in Washington, and retained a news bureau to create and publicize editorials and articles favoring the Marshall Plan. To influence public opinion the committee organized hundreds of radio and in-person speaking events. Acheson himself debated the pros and cons of the Marshall Plan in New York City, gave speeches in San Francisco and the Northwest, and teamed up with Hubert Horatio Humphrey, mayor of Minneapolis, to promote the Marshall Plan in the Twin Cities and Duluth.

In July Congressman Christian Herter of Massachusetts, destined to become secretary of state under Eisenhower, pushed through a House resolution providing for the appointment of a select committee to undertake a broad study to determine the relief and rehabilitation requirements of war-torn nations in Europe as well as Asia. Among those chosen to become one of the nineteen bipartisan members of the Herter Committee was freshman congressman Richard Nixon (R-CA), the youngest and the only westerner. Except for a small Asia contingent, the group departed New York near the end of August on the *Queen Mary*. After a six-week fact-finding trip to almost all countries in the Western bloc (Nixon was assigned to Italy), the group returned to Washington in October, burdened with seventeen trunks of facts and figures. Senator Taft and fellow opponents of the Marshall Plan were not happy with the Herter Committee's findings and conclusions.

Almost every single Herter delegate, including Nixon, supported interim relief and a plan for recovery of Western Europe, deeply convinced of the "peril of Communist expansion" and the "necessity for American leadership and aid."[39]

By mid-November it was finally time for the first test of the effectiveness of the blue ribbon fact-finding committees, the lobbying campaigns, and the secret meetings excoriated by Senator Taft. On the 17th, a special session of Congress, the first since 1939 when the war in Europe broke out, was convened to debate and vote on the precursor to the Marshall Plan—an emergency aid package primarily for France, Italy, and Austria—$6.2 billion in today's money. President Truman opened the session with a note of urgency. "The future of free nations in Europe hangs in the balance," he proclaimed.[40]

Since Marshall was about to leave for the Council of Foreign Ministers meetings in London, he was not on hand for the debates. A week earlier he made his final appeal in separate appearances before the Senate and House foreign relations committees. This time, having been advised by Vandenberg to fight for the interim funds on "an anti-Communist line," Marshall invoked iron curtain imagery and fear of alien forces to the east.[41] Once again he was grilled on why emergency aid should be given to three European nations but not China. Calling upon his yearlong ordeal in China, he patiently explained, as he had done previously, that unlike those countries China was not faced with an inability to grow or purchase food for its citizens. Moreover, there was no realistic basis, he said, "on which to act for [the] rehabilitation" of China.[42]

With Marshall off to London, it was up to his trusted friend and "full partner," Arthur Vandenberg, to deliver the votes in the Senate. Except for Senator Tom Connally, the previous head of the Foreign Relations Committee who was jealous of the new chair, Vandenberg had little trouble with the Democrats. His problem was Bob Taft and a dozen or so other dissenting Republicans. In a New York Times piece Scotty Reston observed that the Democrats were only too happy to step back and let Vandenberg twist the arms of members of his own party.[43] To parry arguments by Republican opponents that a vote for interim aid presages a vote for the Marshall Plan, he announced that it carries no such obligation. "The only question here, and there are no other implications, is interim, emergency aid for France, Italy, and Austria . . ."[44]

The final vote in the Senate was 83 for interim aid and only 6 opposed. Even Senator Taft voted "aye." The amount authorized for France, Italy, and Austria was almost $540 million, less than requested by the administration, but nevertheless probably enough for the next three months. It was a remarkable achievement for Vandenberg.

The House was another story. Six days of debate yielded evidence that the Marshall Plan itself was in jeopardy. Lovett wired Marshall in London, reporting that the bill sent to the floor by the House Committee on Foreign Affairs slashed the amount of interim aid that had already been passed by the Senate and it was still under heavy attack. Of forty-seven floor amendments proposed by House members, sixteen passed, many with additional debilitating provisions. Marshall sent a message to Republican Speaker Joe Martin with a copy to Vandenberg, conveying his "grave concern" and stating his preference for the Senate bill. Lovett reported to Marshall that the outlook for the long-term recovery plan was grim. Secretary of Defense James Forrestal wrote in his diary that Vandenberg "was very gloomy" about its prospects.[45]

On December 11, the House bill for interim relief passed. Despite Marshall's letter to Speaker Martin, it provided for a disappointing authorization of only $509 million, $60 million of which was earmarked for China. For the next twelve days the legislation threaded its way through a maze of House-Senate conferences and appropriations committees. In the end, the amount actually appropriated was $522 million for France, Italy, and Austria and $18 million for China.

In a letter to Hazel, who was at home in Michigan, Arthur Vandenberg reflected on the way forward. If the fierce resistance to a "little short-range European relief bill . . . is any criterion," he wrote, "our friend Marshall is certainly going to have a helluva time down here on the Hill when he gets around to his long-range plan . . . Politics is heavy in the air."[46]

* * * * *

The main subject at the London Council of Foreign Ministers (November 25–December 15, 1947) was the future of Germany; that is, whether it could be reunited and its economy restored. Because neither the U.S. nor the Soviet Union would permit a unified Germany to be the ally of the other, the conference ended with a bitter exchange. Molotov charged that U.S. policy, meaning the Marshall Plan, was intended to "enslave"

Germany through economic aid and to develop Germany into a "strategic base" aimed against the Eastern bloc and the Soviet Union. In an icy tone Marshall responded, "Mr. Molotov must recognize" that such "propaganda" makes it "difficult to inspire respect for the dignity of the Soviet government."[47] Molotov winced. Two days later all of the delegates except Molotov approved Marshall's motion to adjourn sine die. Germany would remain divided. For Marshall the Cold War had begun.

After an all-night flight from London, Secretary Marshall landed in Washington on December 19, the same day that the White House delivered a rough draft of the European Recovery Program legislative package, commonly known as the Marshall Plan, to Congress. He was met at National Airport by the president himself and taken to the White House for a cabinet meeting, followed by lunch at Blair House with Kennan, Lovett, and Bohlen. At ten p.m. that evening Marshall addressed the nation from the State Department auditorium by radio and television. It was the television premiere for the State Department and up to that time the largest live coverage ever accorded a secretary of state. The purpose of his talk was to report to the American people on the disappointing outcome of the London conference and to make the case for preserving "western European civilization with its freedoms." As usual, Marshall was frank. Get used to it, he said. Germany was going to remain divided for the forseeable future. He blamed officials of the Soviet Union for their opposition and hostility to the reunification of Germany and the rehabilitation of Western Europe. They were doing this, he said, because they and their fellow communists sought to fill the "political vacuum" created by the war. Marshall didn't use the term "Cold War," but for the first time he indicated publicly that the success of the administration's European Recovery Program was the key to winning the struggle against "governmental tyranny" posed by the Soviet Union and leaders of the Communist parties.[48]

With Marshall that evening was Madge Brown, widow of Allen Brown, the general's stepson who was killed in Italy. In the fall of 1947, Madge and her six-year-old son, Tupper, had moved to a narrow two-story row house on Volta Place, just off Wisconsin Avenue in Washington's Georgetown neighborhood. Madge had left her job as a journalist with *Life* magazine in New York City to work for *Reporter*, a newly formed newsmagazine in Washington, and was supporting herself and Tupper. For the remainder of the two years Marshall served as secretary of state he spent weeknights with Madge and Tupper when he was in Washington. On typical evenings, recalled Madge, they would have drinks before dinner and Marshall would reminisce about his early days in China, the friends he made at VMI, and his love for Lily. One evening when they were playing Chinese checkers, Marshall told her about how he taught Chiang Kai-shek to play the game and allowed him to win every so often. The fact that the secretary of state was staying at Madge's tiny house "was a huge secret," she remembered. "Nobody knew about it. And it worked very well."[49]

Following his televised speech Marshall returned with Madge to Volta Place. He left the next morning to spend Christmas at Pinehurst with Katherine. "I had a fine rest," he wrote to one of his VMI roommates, "the first of more than five days since June '39 and I feel ready for the battle of Washington."[50] After Christmas, George and Katherine drove down to Hobcaw, Bernard Baruch's plantation in South Carolina, for a few days of wing shooting. To Molly Winn, his stepdaughter, Marshall proudly wrote that he "got seven or eight quail each day." He bragged in a birthday letter to Eisenhower that "I have not yet lost my shooting eye."[51]

Senator Vandenberg did not rest. Rather than returning to Grand Rapids, he remained in Washington, thinking about how best to present to Congress the administration's legislation for the Marshall Plan, conferring with key Republicans, and anticipating objections likely to be raised. By the end of the year, Marshall's sixty-seventh birthday, Vandenberg was convinced that it would be a huge mistake to ask Congress to commit to spend $17 billion, the whopping price tag for the entire four-year European Recovery Program set forth in the administration's legislative package. In a letter to Marshall, he argued that while Congress should enact a multiyear program for recovery, it would be much more palatable if the amounts to be spent were presented and considered by the Senate and House annually, or at least not all at once. Bob Lovett, Marshall's undersecretary who had remained at his desk over the holidays, agreed. Since the Eightieth Congress could not bind the next on spending, there was nothing to be gained and a great deal to be lost by asking it to authorize the entire $17 billion. On January 2, 1948, after consulting with the president, others in the State Department, and presumably Marshall, Lovett advised Vandenberg that the administration backed his change.

During the holiday recess Vandenberg acted to remove stumbling blocks to the legislation and to improve his position as its most influential advocate in Congress. First, he asked Harold Moulton, president of the Brookings Institution, Washington's preeminent think tank, to task a team of its scholars to prepare an analysis of the European Recovery Program and to provide advice on whether it should be administered by the State Department or an independent agency, an issue that Vandenberg saw as the "biggest single conundrum." There is no source other than Brookings, he wrote Moulton, "which could be of greater value or command more general respect."[52] Second, since Vandenberg was being talked about as a leading candidate for the presidency in 1948, he did what he could to suppress the speculation. On New Year's Day he called Michigan governor Kim Sigler and wrote Republican leaders in the state, asking that they refrain from nominating him at the party convention in Philadelphia and that they put a stop to the talk. Vandenberg did not want opponents of the European recovery plan to be able to question his motives or tactics on the ground that he was running for president. By setting aside his own presidential aspirations, Vandenberg aimed to be free to work with the Democrats in a bipartisan effort to get the Marshall Plan through Congress.

* * * * *

Marshall returned to Washington on the first Monday of January, mentally refreshed and ready for the battle to persuade Congress to pass the program popularly named after him. The latest issue of *Time* had once again proclaimed him its "Man of the Year." The cover depicted the hooked beak, fierce eye, and curved talons of an American eagle behind a full-color likeness of Marshall. The artist had chiseled Marshall's nose, chin, and jawline to resemble the sharp features of the eagle. Marshall's riveting blue eyes and compressed lips conveyed grim determination. The caption below read "Hope for Those Who Need It," an obvious reference to the Marshall Plan. Describing 1947 as the year Americans "took upon their shoulders the leadership of the world," *Time* declared that "one man symbolized U.S. action. He was Secretary of State Marshall . . . a man of stubborn, unswerving honesty—a good man."[53]

As perhaps the most respected public figure in America—the good man whose name would forever be associated with the European Recovery

Program—Marshall was scheduled to be the leadoff witness before the Senate Foreign Relations Committee, the first of dozens of congressional hearings on the so-called Marshall Plan that would continue into the early spring. Marshall would later say that he "took pride" in his own performance during that period. Yet he also stressed that credit for the "actual movement" of the Marshall Plan through Congress would always belong to Senator Vandenberg. "[H]e was just the whole show," remembered Marshall.[54]

Vandenberg was the Senate concert master. It was he who orchestrated the legislative strategy, a carefully planned series of hearings involving some ninety-five witnesses that led to a consensus by the thirteen members of his committee. And it was he and his staff who turned the administration's rough draft into Senate Bill 2022, a well-crafted piece of legislation that was eventually sent to the floor and passed by the Senate.

At ten a.m. on January 8, Marshall made his way past a crowd at the head of the stairway in the original Senate Office Building and into the marble Caucus Room, featuring twelve Corinthian columns along opposite walls and an elaborately embellished high ceiling from which hung two enormous crystal chandeliers. He was immediately bombarded by the popping of camera flashbulbs, blinding klieg lights, and senators pressing forward to shake his hand. Scotty Reston wrote that despite the cacophony, Marshall looked "even more relaxed and self-possessed" than when he had returned from China a year earlier, still emanating his trademark "quality of moral grandeur."[55]

The secretary chose to begin by reading his entire 5,500-word written statement, copies of which were already in the hands of the press and the senators on the dais. His delivery, wrote Reston, was almost deliberately dull. Dull or not, Marshall's opening words were arresting. Referring to the European Recovery Program, he declared, "This program will cost our country billions of dollars. It will impose a burden on the American taxpayer and [i]t will require sacrifices . . ." Those who read or listened that day to these politically incendiary words knew at once that this was no ordinary sales pitch.

Marshall read on, aggressively making the case that if Congress did not act and act soon, "the vacuum which the war created in Western Europe will be filled by the forces of which war is made." As a result, he feared, "our national security will be seriously threatened." (The "forces of which war is made" was a patently obvious reference to the tyranny of the Soviet Union and the spread of Communism, though he never identified those forces by name.) Despite Vandenberg's misgivings, Marshall did not mince words with the Senate Foreign Relations Committee about the huge cost to America's taxpayers of the administration's proposed recovery program. For the first fifteen months, he said, the cost would be $6.8 billion, while the total would range between $15.1 and $17.8 billion over the four-year period. Marshall made a point of saying that the $6.8 billion number had been carefully computed and thus was "not an asking figure." He challenged the senators to refrain from cutting back on the dollars. "Either undertake to meet the requirements of the problem or don't undertake it at all," he bluntly said. He was adamant that it be all or nothing. Near the end of his statement, Marshall posed a rhetorical question: If Congress were to enact the requested program for the recovery of Western Europe, will it succeed? His candid answer: "It is a calculated risk." However, he believed there was no viable alternative. "The way of life that we have known is literally in the balance."[56]

For the most part Marshall remained "patient and courteous," wrote Reston, while calmly fielding questions following his prepared remarks, "yet he acted like a man determined to get substantially the Marshall plan he wanted or as already rumored in the capital, retire at last to Leesburg."[57] Marshall was interrogated during the four-hour question period about the structure and control of the executive agency that would administer the European Recovery Plan. Premised on the theory that there could be only one secretary of state, Marshall was of the view that on matters of foreign relations the new agency and its administrator should be controlled by the secretary of state. Several senators, including Vandenberg, disagreed. To attract the best results-oriented and pragmatic businesspeople to run the agency, they believed it should have complete autonomy, subject to a provision requiring State and the new agency to establish effective working relations and to try to avoid conflict in matters involving foreign policy. They also thought that to the extent the State Department maintained a measure of control it would be more difficult for Congress to exercise direct oversight of the agency.

Near the end of his Senate testimony Marshall was asked whether the Western European states would continue to cooperate with one another and become more closely integrated in future years following expiration of the Marshall Plan. The questioner feared that after recovery they would revert to their historic pattern of erecting trade barriers and fighting with one another. Marshall's response was both wise and prescient. Promotion of further European integration by the U.S., he warned, will present "delicate" management problems—the need to "keep the process going toward further cooperation" while taking care not "to awaken hostilities because of national pride." However, he expressed confidence that the advantages of integration would become self-evident as a consequence of the success of the European Recovery Program. "You might say it fulminates the charge. It will begin to break the bottlenecks."[58] Marshall could not have realized it at the time, but his words presaged the Common Market and the European Union.

Marshall's testimony before the twenty-five members of the House Foreign Affairs Committee went on much longer—three sessions—and at a leisurely pace. Contrary to Reston's prediction, the questions were not "more serious and fundamental" than those posed by the senators.[59] They were largely the same in substance. The only difference was that several congressmen, including Democrat Mike Mansfield of Montana, sensed a reluctance on Marshall's part to explicitly blame the Soviet Union and the Communist Party for exploiting the economic chaos in Europe, or to at least come out and identify them by name instead of using euphemisms like "police state" and "tyranny" and "totalitarian state" in his prepared statements. They were right. With an eye on Berlin, a divided Germany, and a powerful Red Army, Marshall had no interest in ramping up tensions with the Soviets. Nor did he want to give Stalin reasons for clamping down further on wavering satellites like Czechoslovakia. Nevertheless, when Mansfield asked who would gain if Congress failed to pass the European Recovery Plan, Marshall responded: the leadership of the Soviet Union, "which is antagonistic to all that we find moral and desirable."[60]

* * * * *

In mid-January Marshall took to the road to rally support for the program that bore his name. Though he was not a good public speaker, the administration believed that his honesty, nonpolitical stature, and gravitas would be more than enough to persuade groups of doubting Americans to support the European Recovery Program. "Oh Lord I traveled all over the country," he remembered. "I worked on that as hard as though I was running for the Senate or the presidency. That's what I'm proud of, that part of it, because I had foreigners, I had tobacco people, cotton people, New York, eastern industrialists, Pittsburgh people, the whole West Coast ... It was just a struggle from start to finish."[61]

The first several days were anything but auspicious. In Pittsburgh, where Marshall had many friends due to its proximity to Uniontown, the Chamber of Commerce businessmen he spoke to listened politely, but in his view they were not persuaded that the European Recovery Program was necessary. He spent the night at the Hotel William Penn and returned to the State Department in the morning to conduct business and prepare for another session with the House Committee on Foreign Affairs. During the following week, after an exhausting day of questioning by the House, Marshall was rushed to Walter Reed, probably due to a kidney infection or passing of a stone (five months later he was diagnosed with an enlarged kidney). While hospitalized, he was given injections of penicillin, the new wonder drug, which caused him to suffer painful side effects, probably hives or a rash that broke out on his back. Instead of canceling his scheduled speech to the Cotton Council, Marshall flew to Atlanta, where he struggled through his talk, unable to mask his pain and discomfort. The press corps, who were used to seeing him speak, knew something was terribly wrong. Still, Marshall believed that this time his message got through, mainly because his speechwriters focused on the facts and economics of the cotton export business and its critical role in European recovery. A few days later, reflecting on his first two forays outside Washington to sell the recovery plan—his failure in Pittsburgh and his struggle in Atlanta—Marshall confessed to the press, who had kept his health situation under wraps, "That was the worst two weeks I ever had in my life."[62]

Over the next couple of months Marshall's schedule was packed with day trips and one-nighters along the East Coast, flights to the Midwest where Bert McCormick's isolationist *Chicago Tribune* was leading the opposition to the recovery plan, a long speaking tour in California and the Northwest, and talks to associations and labor organizations holding their annual conferences in DC. After speaking to the New York–based National Garden Institute in early February, he added women's groups to his schedule. Women, he learned, were effective activists. When they heard him speak, the women "went back home and they scared Congress to death in the next twenty four hours ... It was electric what happened, just electric."

On the other hand, he said, "the men will agree with me, but they don't do a darn thing."[63]

Marshall's swing through the Midwest heartland marked a turning point in his rhetoric. His initial speech, which incorporated suggestions by former Senator La Follette (then serving as a foreign-aid adviser in the Truman administration), was to be delivered to the five thousand members of the National Farm Institute who were having their annual meeting in Des Moines, Iowa.[64] En route, Marshall's plane encountered a dangerous winter storm. "I almost lost my life in that," recalled Marshall, because "I got forced down in the only airport that was available."[65] His plane landed in Knoxville, Tennessee. Since gale winds made it impossible to continue to Des Moines, Marshall's speech was broadcast via a radio hookup. Either at La Follette's urging or on his own, for the first time Marshall invoked by name the Soviet Union and the Communist Party as enemies of the United States and the Western democracies. Scarcely four paragraphs into his address, he warned that "the Soviet Union and their Communist allies have been seeking to exploit the crisis so as to gain a controlling influence over all of Europe."[66] Never before had Marshall publicly laid blame for the economic and political crises in Europe so squarely on Soviet leadership.

On his West Coast tour, Marshall went even further. He not only named the Soviets as enemies of America, he compared their regime to that of Hitler's Nazi Germany. At the University of California at Berkeley he spoke of how Soviet "absolute control of the press, domination of the people, [and] the conduct of a skillful campaign of propaganda" were similar to the Nazis.[67] The next day at the University of California in Los Angeles, Marshall made the same comparisons and declared that the responsibility to put a stop to the Soviet takeover of Europe "is now clearly ours."[68]

* * * * *

While Marshall was barnstorming, Senator Vandenberg was busy negotiating changes in the European recovery bill to strengthen its chances for unanimous approval by his committee and to assure a majority vote of the Senate as a whole when it reached the floor. Many of the changes he regarded as window dressing. A handful were critically important. Fortunately for Vandenberg and the success of his bill, the report of the Brookings

Institution helped him push through a significant change that Marshall initially opposed. One of Brookings' principal recommendations was that a separate executive branch agency, headed by a single administrator of cabinet rank, should be established to administer the Marshall Plan. The Brookings report made clear that the administrator must have "direct access"—and "be responsible only"—to the president.[69] In the judgment of its experts, who aligned with the views of Vandenberg and a large bloc of senators, the State Department should not have any control or direction over the administration of the recovery program. If serious disputes regarding the conduct of foreign policy should arise, they were to be resolved by an appeal to the president. Brookings' rationale for the complete separation was based on the idea that the agency administering the vast new recovery program needed to be run according to sound business practices, not influenced by political concerns that sometimes undergird positions of the State Department. Its reasoning was also based on the notion that separation would enhance the ability to recruit outstanding personnel to lead the agency. With the backing of the Brookings report, Vandenberg persuaded Marshall and Lovett to support the change. In the Senate bill, the new independent agency was to be called the Economic Cooperation Administration (ECA). At the insistence of Vandenberg, Truman would appoint Paul Hoffman, CEO of Studebaker, an experienced and nationally known businessman, as administrator of the ECA.

Other important changes in the Senate bill, concurred by Marshall, included a reduction in the initial authorization of funds from $6.8 billion for the first fifteen months to $5.3 billion for the initial twelve months (roughly the same amount per month); a provision requiring the administrator of the ECA to terminate aid if a recipient did not adhere to its commitments to the U.S. or to its other partners in Europe; and a clever requirement that if U.S. raw materials and goods were provided in kind, which would comprise the bulk of the aid provided, the European recipient would deposit payments in local currency into an escrow account maintained by its central bank to be used to finance its national recovery, while the U.S. would pay the providers of goods in dollars. The latter requirement was designed to ease the "dollar shortage," a balance of payments crisis caused by the fact that the Europeans did not have dollars to pay for the products needed to stimulate their economies. The escrowed local currency payments, not convertible into foreign exchange, were known as "counterpart funds." To prevent corruption, Vandenberg made sure that the ECA had authority to veto the use of counterpart funds for purposes other than recovery.

By the second week of February Vandenberg arrived at what he hoped would be a legislative sweet spot, a series of changes and compromises designed to enable all sides of the debate over the Marshall Plan to claim some share of victory. After five days of closed-door deliberations, the Senate Foreign Relations Committee voted 13–0 to approve the European Recovery bill as amended and it was cleared for prompt floor action.

Marshall thanked Vandenberg profusely for his legislative skill. Indeed, he went a bit over the top, proclaiming in a letter to the Michigan senator that he was "a truly great statesman with wisdom and integrity as [his] cardinal virtues."[70] Vandenberg had reason to reciprocate. Just two days before his Foreign Relations Committee voted out the bill, the *Washington Post* published a page-one story, orchestrated by Marshall and the State Department public relations staff, that made an emotional case for why Americans should back the Marshall Plan. Together with a staged photograph, the tongue-in-cheek story was about "an extemporaneous speech on the state of the world" by Secretary of State Marshall to seven awestruck Cub Scouts, aged nine to eleven, who were seated around a table in Marshall's office. The scouts had been invited into the secretary's inner sanctum, wrote the reporter, so that they could tell "the author of the European Recovery Plan . . . about their own little Marshall plan, a project to raise funds to feed eight hungry European boys for a year." Marshall listened respectfully and complimented the cubs on their plan. He spoke at length about his own boyhood and how little he knew about the world. Then the *Post* reporter picked up the words that Marshall wanted to convey to Congress and the American public. "In the short period of my lifetime, we are now recognized everywhere as being the most powerful Nation in the world and being the acknowledged leader in the world." Therefore, he reportedly told the wide-eyed boys, "what you are trying to do . . . for the children of Europe . . . is of great international importance in establishing relations of friendship and good will and trust that are so important to our Government, and to our people and to the world and to peace."[71] A photo accompanying the article showed the scrubbed faces of the young scouts closely surrounding, almost hugging, father-figure Marshall as he sat at his desk. The messaging was obvious. If seven Cub Scouts could raise money to assist in the recovery of Europe, so could the leaders of the most powerful nation in the world.

Marshall's Cub Scout gambit might have swayed public opinion or possibly moved a few congressmen closer to "yes" on the Marshall Plan. However, it was a Soviet-backed communist coup in Czechoslovakia that galvanized Washington and gave rise to a new sense of urgency to pass the European recovery legislation. On February 20, twelve non-communist cabinet members, a minority of the coalition government in Czechoslovakia, submitted letters of resignation. They did so to protest the refusal of the communist minister of the interior to reinstate a number of non-communist senior police officers, despite a cabinet vote ordering reinstatement. Those who resigned assumed and were subsequently assured by Czech president Edvard Beneš that he would not accept their resignations. They were led to believe that Beneš would keep them in a caretaker government and take steps to force favorable changes in the composition of the cabinet or oust Klement Gottwald, the communist premier. It was a tragic miscalculation. Over the next five days the nation was thrown into turmoil and crisis. Gottwald used his party's control of the media to characterize the resignations as treasonous. He took control of the police and government ministries. Students fought with the police. A work stoppage was threatened. President Beneš, who had recently suffered a stroke, proved weak and powerless. Fearing civil war and Soviet intervention, he capitulated and allowed Gottwald to form a new communist-dominated government.

Though Marshall had predicted the previous November that the Soviets would "clamp down" on the Czechs as a "purely defensive move," Americans were outraged and frightened.[72] They remembered that only a decade earlier it was Hitler's invasion of Czechoslovakia that triggered the Second World War in Europe. From Prague, Laurence Steinhardt, ambassador to Czechoslovakia, wired Marshall that the Communists, with Stalin's approval, if not his orders, "have wiped out every vestige of true representative government . . . They have browbeaten and exercised a degree of duress on Beneš strikingly similar to methods employed by Hitler in dealing with heads of states. In short, they have employed identical methods to achieve a successful *putsch* which were first employed by the Nazis and subsequently by the Communists in other satellite states."[73]

Two other ominous events in Europe heightened alarm in the U.S. and spurred the passage of the Marshall Plan. On February 27, Stalin delivered a letter to the president of Finland urging (demanding?) that it sign a mutual assistance pact with the Soviet Union. Eleven days later Jan Masaryk, the American-educated foreign minister of Czechoslovakia, was found dead, dressed in pajamas, forty-seven and one-half feet below his bathroom window in the courtyard of the Czernin Palace (the Foreign Ministry). Masaryk, the son of Czechoslovakia's first president, was the most prominent non-communist in the new government that was formed following the coup. The cause of his death, officially investigated four times over the years, remains in dispute. The initial investigation concluded that he committed suicide by leaping from his window. Some of his close associates, including his private secretary and his former wife, agreed. Many others were convinced that he was murdered—pushed or thrown out of the window to his death—calling it the Third Defenestration of Prague (the fourth and last investigation was completed in 2001). There was a sarcastic joke told by those who discounted the suicide story: "Jan Mastaryk was a very tidy man. He was such a tidy man that when he jumped he shut the window after himself."

* * * * *

On Monday, March 1, 1948, the Senate gallery was jammed to capacity with reporters and spectators. Down on the floor almost every senator was present. House members who had come from the other side of the Capitol stood against the walls of the chamber. After four months of hearings, sixty-three-year-old Senator Arthur Vandenberg advanced to the lectern to open and frame the debate on the Marshall Plan, officially titled the European Cooperation Act of 1948. The plan's namesake was not there.

Over the course of several nights in his Wardman Park apartment, Vandenberg had written and rewritten his speech, pecking out seven drafts on his portable typewriter. For the proponents and the undecideds, some of the phrases he chose to urge prompt passage of the Marshall Plan were memorable and inspiring: an act of "American intelligent self-interest . . . a mighty undertaking worthy of our faith . . . a welcome beacon in the world's dark night . . . a plan for peace, stability, and freedom . . ." Holding forth for more than an hour and a quarter, Vandenberg concluded his speech with a rhetorical flourish. "There is only one voice in the world," he declared, that can enable the survival of Western Europe. "It is our voice." The Marshall Plan, he predicted, "can be the turning point in history for 100 years to come. If it fails, we have done our final best. If it succeeds, our children and our children's children will call us blessed. May God grant his benediction upon the ultimate event."[74]

"Senators and spectators sprang to their feet in unrestrained applause," wrote Felix Blair of *The New York Times*.[75] Some called it "the climactic role of Vandenberg's career."[76] Marshall said the speech was a "masterpiece."[77]

As the debate on the floor of the Senate began, the British, French, and Benelux nations, meeting in London, announced plans to formally incorporate western Germany into the Marshall Plan and establish a West German federal government. It was a bold and historic decision that vastly strengthened Western Europe and was therefore regarded by the Soviets as a direct threat to their security. In a cable to the army intelligence director, Lucius Clay, military governor in Berlin, predicted that war might "come with dramatic suddenness."[78] It was leaked and widely circulated in Washington.

With these developments in the headlines, the debate in the Senate droned on. For the most part Vandenberg fended off crippling amendments and other attacks by the opposition. He enlisted Marshall to speak to Republican senator Homer Capehart of Indiana, the so-called father of the jukebox industry, about his proposal for the Reconstruction Finance Corporation to provide business loans to the Western European states instead of direct government aid. Marshall persuaded Capehart to back off, telling him that his amendments would completely undermine confidence in the good faith of the U.S. and the progress that the Europeans had made during the previous eight months.

The most serious challenge during debate over the Marshall Plan was mounted by archconservative Senator Bob Taft, a candidate for the Republican ticket in 1948, who wielded considerable influence over other senators, especially on domestic issues. At five p.m. on March 12, the last day for debate, he introduced an amendment to cut authorization for first-year funding from $5.3 billion to $4 billion, assuring Vandenberg that if his amendment was adopted he would vote for the Marshall Plan. Vandenberg held firm, famously responding to Taft's proposed cut, "When a man is drowning 20 feet away, it's a mistake to throw him a 15-foot rope."[79] The Michigander held his supporters in line and quickly moved for a vote. Taft's amendment was defeated 56-31.

The next day Vandenberg delivered a powerful closing argument, focusing on the threat posed by Stalin's westward expansion, namely the Soviet-inspired Communist takeover of the Czech government and its relentless pressure on Finland to agree to a mutual defense pact (Finland agreed on April 6, though she retained her independence). His argument was buttressed by growing fears in the halls of Congress, stoked by Clay's leaked cable, that war was more than a possibility. Finally, at five past midnight on Sunday, March 14, the Senate voted 69-17 in favor of the European Cooperation Act of 1948. Thirty-one Republicans, including Taft, and thirty-eight Democrats voted for the bill. Perhaps it was the fear of war, but given the partisanship that has divided the U.S. Senate in recent years it is difficult to imagine how Republicans and Democrats, driven by such different platforms and ideologies, could coalesce, as they did in the spring of 1948, and vote so overwhelmingly to pass the risky and enormously expensive Marshall Plan.

With whispers of war in the air, the scene shifted to the House of Representatives. Truman's advisers decided the time was ripe for the president to demonstrate his leadership and urge the House to act quickly. Plus, a forceful speech would kick off his uphill campaign for the presidency. On Saint Patrick's Day the president addressed a joint session of Congress. "There are times in world history," Truman declared, "when it is far wiser to act than to hesitate." Everyone in the chamber knew he was talking about the Marshall Plan. "There is some risk involved in action—there always is. But there is far more risk in failure to act."[80] On the same day or earlier that week, Marshall, with Lovett in tow, urged Chairman Charles Eaton (R-NJ), a Canadian-born Baptist minister, as well as members of his House Foreign Affairs Committee, to avoid unnecessary amendments to the European recovery bill and get it to the floor for debate as soon as possible. By a narrow vote of 11-8, the bill was reported out of committee on March 20 with a recommendation that it be passed by the full House in order to "reverse the wave of Communism in Europe." The momentum was behind swift passage. However, the tipping point may have been a letter from former Republican president Herbert Hoover that caused wavering lawmakers to make a "'stampede for the bandwagon.'" In Hoover's letter, read on the floor of the House by Representative John Vorys of Ohio, the ex-president announced that he had withdrawn his opposition to the Marshall Plan and decided to endorse it as "a major dam against Russian aggression."[81] On the last day of March, while Marshall was in Bogotá, Colombia, attending a conference of Latin American states, the House, in a voice vote, approved the Marshall Plan by a lopsided margin of 329–74. Again, it was bipartisan. The *Washington Post* reported that "in a seething and excited House, shouts of 'aye' came from one Republican after another who had seldom, if ever, voted for any international legislation."[82]

Differences between the House and Senate bills were resolved in conference. On April 3, 1948, after returning to Washington from William and Mary College, where he received an honorary degree, Truman signed the Foreign Assistance Act of 1948 (formerly, the European Cooperation Act of 1948) into law. It authorized a total of $6.2 billion—$5.3 billion for European recovery (the Marshall Plan) and the rest for aid to China, Greece, and Turkey and for international child relief. From Bogotá, Secretary Marshall issued a press release. "The leaders in the Congress and the membership generally have faced a great crisis with courage and wisdom and legislative skill, richly deserving of the approval and the determined support of the people."[83]

Within a day or two of Marshall's press release, a message of resurrection arrived at Dodona. Allen's widow, Madge, had written to George and Katherine about a surprise weekend visit by Captain Geoff Wiles, the close friend of Allen's who fought alongside him at Cassino. Wiles was a "sweet person, very young, just 30," wrote Madge. He had come all the way from New Zealand to meet Allen's family and to tell young Tupper, Allen's son, about the love and respect he had for his father. They played in the yard behind the house on Volta Place for an entire afternoon. Wiles built a hutch for Tupper's two Easter rabbits, she wrote. "He was looking forward to meeting the two of you." He would have loved to tell you "what a superb soldier Allen was."[84]

At the moment of Marshall's greatest peacetime achievement, Madge's letter reminded Katherine and George of what they had lost. Yet it assured them that after they were gone, Allen would live on through the lives of his wartime friend Wiles and his little boy.

*   *   *   *   *

While the passage of the Marshall Plan was hailed as a singular triumph, the legislative process was by no means over. It was one thing for Congress to *authorize* the expenditure of up to $5.3 billion for the European recovery program in the first year. It was quite another for it to *appropriate* all or some of those dollars to the authorized program so they could be spent. The idea behind this two-step process—involving separate bills, each of which must traverse arduous paths through Congress before reaching the president's desk—was to make spending harder, normally a good idea.

Fortunately, Paul Hoffman, the new administrator of the ECA, was able to start implementing the Marshall Plan without delay. Senator Vandenberg long ago had found dollars in the projected FY48 budget surplus that could be spent immediately by Hoffman without needing to await completion of the appropriations process.[85] Only eleven days after Truman signed the bill authorizing the Marshall Plan, the victory ship *John H. Quick*, named after a marine who won the Medal of Honor at Guantánamo Bay in the Spanish-American War, set sail from Galveston, Texas, loaded with grain. The *Quick* was the first in a fleet of five American ships owned by the Luckenbach Steamship Company to carry fifty-four thousand tons of grain, fertilizer, and a variety of other Marshall Plan necessities across the Atlantic to France. Before long 150 ships, chartered and paid for by Hoffman's ECA, were on the high seas carrying cargoes to harbors at Bordeaux, Liverpool, Rotterdam, and Genoa.

The psychological effect of the first American ships arriving at ports on the continent, along with the promise of what was to come, cannot be overstated. For the Europeans and the British, the Marshall Plan revived hope for the future, a sense of confidence that economic and political recovery was indeed achievable. For the first time in years, wrote an *Economist* reporter, "it is fitting that the peoples of Western Europe should attempt to renew their capacity for wonder." For this reason, he wrote, the Marshall Plan "must be seen for what it is—an act without peer in history."[86]

"Honest" John Taber, a lawyer from Aurora in upstate New York and chairman of the powerful House Appropriations Committee, had a different view of the objective of the European Recovery Program and how it should be portrayed. With a voice like a bullhorn, Taber was a fiscal conservative, skeptical to his core of the benefits of foreign aid. In his own words, he was convinced that the plan was nothing more "than an international [New Deal] program to give those foreign countries more than they need."[87] Through his power over the purse, he set out to cripple the Marshall Plan, even though it had been authorized by Congress and signed into law by the president. On June 3, Taber's committee slashed the plan's first year's authorized funds of $5.3 billion by about 25 percent. The following day, the House approved the drastic cut by voice vote.

Once the House voted, all eyes were focused on the Senate Appropriations Committee. Marshall called a press conference with the hope that his views would influence the committee. He told the reporters that the appropriation reductions approved by the House would "alter the European Recovery Program from one of reconstruction to one of mere relief." Furthermore, it would have a "most serious effect" on "the political situation in Europe."[88]

Vandenberg was not as diplomatic. He was fighting mad over the House vote. In a departure from tradition, he requested and was granted an opportunity to testify before the Senate Appropriations Committee for the purpose of attacking the House cutbacks. It was "an angry, impassioned appearance," wrote Vandenberg's son, "a scorching assault" on the "'meat-axe approach' of the Taber group."[89] Setting aside his emotion, Vandenberg made a compelling point: the appropriations process should not be used as a backdoor way to reverse a major policy decision already made by Congress and the president. Marshall's calm, understated testimony followed that of Vandenberg. After patiently and at some length reiterating the care exercised by teams of experts that went into paring down the final first-year funding request, Marshall told the senators that in his opinion the reductions voted by the House would "ruin" the promise of the European recovery plan, undermine its "psychological effect," and set it on a calculated course "for failure."[90]

It is impossible to know which of the two styles of advocacy was most effective. Perhaps it was the combination that persuaded Chairman Styles Bridges (R-NH) and a majority of the senators on his appropriations committee. Two days later the committee restored all but $245 million of the $5.3 billion requested for the first year. The Senate as a whole voted overwhelmingly to endorse the restoration. In the ensuing Senate-House conference a compromise was worked out that allowed Taber to save face. However, the spending level that the Senate wanted essentially remained intact. The *Economist* wrote, "Mr. Taber's raid on the funds for ERP [European Recovery Program] has been beaten back. The confidence of those who believed in the ability of America's responsible leaders to overcome the ignorant and obstinate obstruction of the isolationist fringe is now re-warded."[91]

Shortly before dawn on June 20, with Congress rushing to adjourn and the Republican national convention about to convene in Philadelphia, the legislative process that was sparked by Marshall's speech at Harvard a year earlier, and which officially began in December, at last came to an end. By roll call vote in the House, followed by voice vote in the Senate, the conference report on appropriations was approved. The spending bill was ready to be signed by the president.

That morning Marshall and his wife checked in to Walter Reed Army Hospital for their annual physical examinations. There is no evidence of Marshall's reaction when he received the good news that Congress had voted to restore funding and that the long fight was finally over. Nor is there any record of his reaction when he received unsettling news a day or two later. The doctors "found a growth"—a renal tumor—on his "enlarged right kidney." The kidney would have to be surgically removed.[92]

*   *   *   *   *

Due to forthcoming talks to establish a North Atlantic defense pact (ultimately NATO, the North Atlantic Treaty Organization) and UN meetings in New York and Paris in the fall of 1948, Marshall insisted that his kidney operation be postponed. With a full plate in front of him it was fortunate that he was not also responsible for the implementation and administration of the Marshall Plan. Those duties were lodged in the more than capable hands of Paul Hoffman, administrator of the ECA. By the end of the plan's first fiscal year, June 30, 1949, Hoffman's ECA reported to Congress that the Western European nations had already notched impressive gains in productivity as a result of the "flow of United States dollars" and the self-help measures taken by the countries themselves.[93] Prime Minister Clement Attlee of Great Britain wrote a note of appreciation to Truman. "[D]uring the last year the whole economic scene in Western Europe has been transformed to a degree that must astonish all of us when we recall the uncertainties and perils of the immediately preceding years."[94]

Midway through 1950, the Korean War broke out. The intervention of the Chinese in November marked the beginning of the end for the Marshall Plan. Once it became clear that an early peace was not in sight, the funding for the Marshall Plan was terminated, effective as of the end of 1951, six months earlier than originally planned. With American armed forces tied down in the Far East, the military defense of the Western European states against Soviet aggression was seen by the U.S. as a greater priority than the continuation of efforts to achieve economic recovery.

Notwithstanding its early termination, the total amount actually provided by the Marshall Plan to help finance the recovery of Western Europe was $13.2 billion, $4 billion less than Truman requested. In today's dollars, the amount spent by the U.S. on the Marshall Plan would be approximately $135 billion; as a percentage of GNP (5.2) it would exceed $800 billion. By any standard, the amounts spent were a heavy burden for U.S. taxpayers.[95]

In its final press release at the end of 1951, the ECA summarized its view of the accomplishments of the Marshall Plan "in cold statistics." Industrial production in Western Europe, it proudly noted, was "64 percent above 1947 and 41 percent above prewar levels." The production of steel "doubled in less than four years." Coal output was slightly less than it was before the war, but it was "27 percent higher than in 1947." Production levels of aluminum, copper, and cement, and levels of food production were all substantially above 1947 and prewar levels.[96]

While the cold statistics were impressive they do not necessarily prove that recovery was attributable to the Marshall Plan. Nor do they support the messianic notion that the plan saved Europe. After all, the $13.2 billion provided by the U.S. was little more than the equivalent of about 2 percent of Western Europe's national income from 1948 to 1951. Moreover, it was obvious that the amazing economic miracle in West Germany had more to do with the success of U.S. measures to block collection of Germany's massive debt and reparations obligations, as well as General Lucius Clay's introduction of currency reform, than the comparatively small amount of relief provided by the Marshall Plan.

Since the 1980s, economists in Europe and the U.S. have debated the causal relationship between features of the Marshall Plan and the recovery of production and investment in Western Europe. Revisionist Alan Milward downgraded the Marshall Plan's importance, arguing that Great Britain and Western European nations could have financed their own recovery programs without U.S. aid by maintaining food consumption at 1947 levels and that trade with West Germany could have functioned as a substitute for the dollar-based Marshall Plan. Milward contended that it might have taken a bit longer, but the Western European states would have figured out a way to recover without Marshall Plan aid.[97]Benn Steil, chief economist at the Council on Foreign Relations, dismissed Milward's thesis as "farfetched," relying as it did on lower levels of food consumption and more trade with West Germany. He opined that the Marshall Plan, standing alone, made a positive contribution to the recovery of Western Europe because it "helped to close the dollar gap by engineering Germany's revival as western Europe's primary capital goods supplier," thus replacing the United States.[98] But Steil persuasively argues that without a military security pact to contain Soviet aggression and the spread of communism, the Marshall Plan probably would not have succeeded in achieving its goal of reviving the economies of Western Europe.

The debate among economists as to the causes of postwar European recovery will probably never be resolved. From a historian's viewpoint, the most that can be said is that the Marshall Plan provided breathing room, a cushion of resources, perhaps even the "crucial margin" of aid.[99] However, there were three consequences of the plan that appear to be beyond dispute. The first was the enormous "psychological boost" that it "gave to a recovering Europe," as John Agnew and Nicholas Entrikin wrote in *The Marshall Plan: Model and Metaphor* and as George Kennan had predicted.[100] Vernon Walters, who worked at the ECA in Paris with Averell Harriman, agreed. He said that "the most important achievement of the Marshall Plan was not so much the material aid it gave as the rekindling of hope, the rekindling of energy."[101] At a critical time, beginning before the first shipload of goods even arrived, there is no question that the Marshall Plan boosted confidence and raised the morale of its European recipients.

The second consequence was the contribution of the Marshall Plan to cooperation and trade liberalization among the Western European states and the resulting divide with the Soviets and their satellites. Cooperation in the West was a long way from integration or a single market. But it set the stage for future unification and decisions by West Europe states to side with the U.S. in the Cold War against the Soviet Union (though the plan failed to lure satellites out of the Soviet orbit, which was one of Kennan's objectives).

The third consequence was an urgent request to Marshall by the British foreign secretary asking the U.S. to join the UK and Western European nations in a mutual defense pact to deter the Soviet Union from dominating Europe and to allow democracy and free enterprise to flourish. Marshall responded on March 12, 1948, saying the U.S. was prepared to discuss the "establishment of an Atlantic security system." Reluctantly, Marshall and the president had come to the conclusion that in order for the Marshall Plan to achieve its vision of a new Europe, the U.S. would have to commit to a military alliance, an alliance that became known as the North Atlantic Treaty Organization.[102]

In memory and myth the Marshall Plan endures as America's most successful foreign policy initiative in history, rivaling that of the Monroe Doctrine or the Louisiana Purchase. Perhaps it endures because it speaks to a moment in the American story when it was the right and honorable thing to do. Or maybe it endures because it was such a monumental and risky undertaking, an act of unprecedented altruism, yet equally motivated by intelligent self-interest.

Understandably, the collective memory of the man whose name will forever be linked with the plan has faded. Few recall the critical role he played in the conception and birth of what became known as the Marshall Plan and the promotion of its bipartisan passage through Congress. In part, this is due to the character of George Marshall. He was selfless, self-sufficient, and private, a magnanimous person who found incentive and reward deep within himself. He did not seek or require praise. Except for the very few who were close to Marshall, he seemed solitary and detached, always reserved and dignified. Since the plan that bore his name had many fathers, Marshall never claimed authorship. He never referred to it as "the Marshall Plan." Yet it was he who chose and trusted the talented individuals whom he then credited with helping him shape, articulate, and promote the ideas that became the plan—namely, Kennan, Acheson, Clayton, Bohlen, Lovett, and Harriman. And it was Marshall who befriended and gained the lifelong respect of Senator Arthur Vandenberg, the indispensable isolationist-turned-internationalist who shepherded the European recovery legislation through Congress.

When Marshall returned from the Moscow conference in April 1947, he believed that unless something was done to help the Western European economies recover from the war, the peace that his armies had fought and died for would never be achieved. Stalin and the Communist Party, he was convinced, intended to exploit the chaos and dominate much of the rest of Europe. By the time the last of the Marshall Plan dollars were spent in 1952, the West was divided from the East, each backed by military alliances. The United States and the Soviet Union were engaged in a nuclear arms race, restrained only by the fear of mutual assured destruction. It was nowhere near the kind of peace that Marshall envisioned in 1945 when American troops linked up with their Russian counterparts and shared vodka and whiskey on the banks of the Elbe. Nevertheless, his plan was a signal accomplishment. The Western European states, including West Germany, were well on their way to full recovery. The Soviet Union would remain a threat. However, it would not dominate Europe.

CHAPTER 16

Showdown in the Oval Office

George and Katherine cherished their weekends at Dodona, especially in the spring, the two of them working together in the garden, followed by a simple candlelit dinner on the patio. Normally they would turn down invitations to dine in town. Saturday, May 8, 1948, however, was a special occasion. It was President Harry Truman's sixty-fourth birthday.

At around eight p.m., Secretary and Mrs. Marshall arrived at the 1925 F Street Club, a yellow Greek Revival house named for its street address that was located a few blocks west of the White House (today, the residence of the president of George Washington University). Attorney General Tom Clark had invited about forty close friends and supporters of the president to participate in the celebration. Truman needed an emotional lift. His approval rating was hovering at 36 percent, a record low that no chief executive would sink to until the presidency of Donald Trump. Republicans controlled Congress. His own party was imperiling the president's effectiveness, having helped to override his veto of what he termed a "rich man's" tax bill. In the presidential sweepstakes, Truman trailed in the polls behind Dewey, Vandenberg, and MacArthur. Columnist Arthur Krock had written that Truman's "influence is weaker than any President's has been in modern history."[1]

After-dinner toasts were proposed by Attorney General Clark and others, but it was Marshall's unexpected and deadly serious tribute that silenced the room, leaving the president almost speechless. "I cannot recall that there has been a President in our history," said Marshall, his eyes fixed on Truman, "who has more clearly demonstrated courageous decision, and complete integrity in his decisions than the Birthday guest of honor tonight. I ask you all to drink to the health of the President and to the courage with which he has fought for the peace and good of all mankind."[2] Air Force Secretary Stuart Symington, one of the guests, told a *Time* magazine reporter that "Truman flushed at the tribute, rose to respond but was unable to compose himself." Several seconds passed. "He finally gestured toward Marshall and said simply: 'He won the war.'"[3]

Marshall never doubted Truman's courage. Four days later, however, in a face-to-face confrontation in the Oval Office, he angrily questioned the president's integrity, warning him that he was on the verge of undermining the "great dignity of the office of the President" in a "transparent dodge to win a few [Jewish] votes."[4] The epic clash involved whether the United States should be the first to recognize the new sovereign state of Israel.

* * * * *

Marshall was generally aware of the history of efforts since the late nineteenth century to establish a Jewish state in Palestine. It was well known that in 1917 Lord Balfour, the British foreign secretary, pledged his country's support for a Jewish "national home" (the Balfour Declaration); and that after World War I the League of Nations conferred on Great Britain a mandate to govern Palestine with the understanding that it would be made ready for independence in due course. As noted in an earlier chapter, in February 1944, when Marshall was chief of staff, he was asked by a Senate committee to express his views in a closed session on whether the U.S. should advocate for a Jewish state in Palestine (not during the war, he counseled). To prepare for his appearance before the committee, he renewed his understanding of the 1939 white paper prepared by the government of UK Prime Minister Neville Chamberlain that called for an "independent Palestine" within ten years, instead of a national home for Jews, and imposed strict limits on Jewish immigration. And he updated his knowledge of the politics and violence surrounding the Palestine question that persisted during the war.

In January 1947, just after Marshall arrived at the State Department from his year in China, Fraser Wilkins, the Palestine desk officer, briefed the new secretary of state on American policy in Palestine. Based on a memorandum that Wilkins delivered to Marshall, the policy at that time was to support "full independence" of the people of Palestine "in one or more states." The U.S. could support a two-state solution, but only if "a workable partition" would satisfy the national aspirations of both Jews and Arabs. The devil was clearly in the details of these equivocal pronouncements. As to immigration, the Truman administration's policy was specific—a call for "immediate transfer" of 100,000 Jews from Europe to Palestine and liberalization of immigration laws in the U.S. and other nations. The opening sentence of Wilkins's memorandum told Marshall what he probably already knew: "The Palestine question is one of the most difficult problems with which the Department is faced."[5]

During the first eight months of 1947, Marshall was kept abreast of these problems by Wilkins and others. However, due to the six weeks of meetings in Moscow, the development of the Marshall Plan, the beginning stages of the Cold War, and the conference of Latin American nations in August, he devoted little attention to the Palestine question. In the meantime, the pressures on the British to keep order in Palestine while trying to find an acceptable solution to some form of self-government by the Arabs and Jews became unbearable. Since the time of the Balfour Declaration the proportion of Jews to Arabs in the mandated territory had grown exponentially (from roughly 8 percent to almost 50 percent). The Arabs clamored for tighter restrictions on immigration while the World Zionist Congress and American politicians, reacting to the horrors of the Holocaust and the pleas of the survivors, pressured the UK for almost unlimited immigration. Passions were inflamed. As a consequence, the British were faced with Jewish and Arab terrorism and guerrilla warfare in Palestine. The government of Prime Minister Clement Attlee threw up its hands. On April 2, 1947, it officially turned the future of Palestine over to the United Nations. The UN promptly established a committee to investigate the issues and propose a solution. The committee's recommendation was to be voted on by the UN General Assembly at its second annual meeting in the fall of 1947.

After deliberating all summer, the UN Palestine committee produced a majority report, backed by seven of its eleven members, and a minority report. The majority recommended partition—that the Palestine mandate be divided into two autonomous states, one Jewish and the other Arab. The plan provided for an "economic union" of the two states and a five-member UN commission to assist in establishing provisional governments in each state. During the proposed two-year transitional period, 150,000 Jews were to be admitted to settle on land allocated to the new Jewish state. The minority recommended transition over a three-year period to a single Swiss-style federated state for both Arabs and Jews with Jerusalem as its capital. Neither report addressed the critical question of how the respective recommendations would be enforced.

* * * * *

With the fate of Palestine and a national homeland for the Jews in the balance, Secretary of State Marshall was among the hundreds of delegates to the fledgling UN from all over the world that checked into New York City hotels during the second week of September to attend the 1947 General Assembly. For the first time Marshall was fully engaged in the Palestine question. On the morning of September 15, two days before the Assembly opened, he convened a top secret meeting of the Truman-appointed delegates to the UN, among them Eleanor Roosevelt, John Foster Dulles, General John Hilldring (former assistant secretary of state for occupied areas), and UN ambassador Warren Austin (former Vermont senator). Loy Henderson, an expert on the Middle East who was chief of the State Department's Office of Near East Affairs, was invited by Marshall to sit in. Recalling the meeting years later, Mrs. Roosevelt remarked that Marshall "was a magnificent presiding officer" with an "extraordinary quality of patience."[6]

Knowing that Henderson opposed partition, Marshall asked him to speak first. Henderson was described by Chip Bohlen as "absolutely incorruptible," a man of the "highest character" who "always spoke his mind, a practice that did not make him popular."[7] Clark Clifford, the forty-year-old smooth-talking special counsel to Truman, wrote that Henderson belonged to "a group of Mideast experts in the State Department who were widely regarded as anti-Semitic," though Clifford was quick to add that he had no "firsthand evidence."[8] As Henderson later recalled to his interviewer, he told Marshall and the UN delegates that partition would result in years of "bloodshed and suffering," damage America's relations with the Arab world, and might even deprive the U.S. of access to Middle East oil, which would threaten success of the Marshall Plan. According to Henderson, Eleanor Roosevelt belittled his advice, saying, "Come now, come, Mr. Henderson. I think you're exaggerating the dangers."[9] Henderson remembered that General Hilldring spoke up and expressed his agreement with Mrs. Roosevelt, while the others, including Marshall, did not react.

Notwithstanding Henderson's views, it is apparent from the minutes of the meeting that Marshall supported the concept of partition from the beginning to the end of the session. Nevertheless, he believed it would be a mistake to take an unequivocal position favoring a separate Jewish state because it would deprive his delegates of flexibility and maneuvering room during the debates and backroom lobbying that was bound to take place during the days and weeks leading up to the actual vote. A strong stand at the outset, he argued, could drive the Arabs into the arms of the Soviet Union and might obligate the U.S. to "put troops into Palestine" to enforce partition. Ambassador Austin, who actually had serious reservations about the wisdom of partition, said he "stood with the Secretary" on this tactic. Eleanor Roosevelt pushed back. She suggested that it was important for the U.S. to clearly express its support for the majority recommendation because it would "promote the success" of the UN and strengthen it in "the minds of the American people."[10]

Mrs. Roosevelt's point must have resonated with Marshall. In his address to the General Assembly on September 17, his first speech in the United Nations, Marshall went out of his way to give it a boost by commending the quality of the work of the Palestine committee, though its recommendations were not unanimous. He followed the compliment with an announcement that he and the American delegation "gave great weight" to the majority report favoring partition, but that a "final decision" by the U.S. on the matter would have to await further deliberations and debate.[11]

Not surprisingly, Marshall's attempt to remain noncommittal, while thumbing the scales toward partition, was interpreted by the Arab world as an endorsement of partition. Speaking for the Arab delegations, Faris Bey el-Khouri of Syria told Marshall that establishment of a Jewish state was unacceptable. It "would end up in bloodshed and disaster."[12] Responding on behalf of the Palestinian Arabs, Jamal al-Husayni, a relative of the Grand Mufti of Jerusalem and well-known Nazi collaborator, angrily pledged to defend "every inch" of Palestine "with the last drop of our blood."[13] On the opposite side, many Zionists were disappointed at Marshall's failure to clearly state his support for partition on the eve of the General Assembly deliberations. However, Moshe Shertok and the Jewish delegation to the UN that he had organized were, according to Shertok's biographer, "encouraged by Marshall's seeming readiness at that early stage to support a partition resolution."[14] Shertok, who later changed his surname to Sharett, was the political and foreign policy director of the Jewish Agency for Palestine, the Jerusalem-based organization chaired by David Ben-Gurion that served as the de facto government of what would become the nation of Israel. A gifted politician who would become Israel's second prime minister in 1954, Shertok knew how to play the long game. He understood that Marshall's statement was designed to buy time, during which the American delegation would try to come up with proposals to placate Arab opposition. Known for his charm, sparkling dark eyes, and distinctive mustache, Ukranian-born Shertok, who emigrated to Ottoman Palestine in 1906, would soon emerge as the most effective Jewish leader and lobbyist at the UN during the tumultuous period that led to statehood.

In mid- to late September, while Marshall was shuttling from his hotel in Manhattan out to Flushing Meadows and Lake Success, where the UN was temporarily headquartered, he phoned his old friend Rose Page Wilson and told her he would like to stop by for a "flying visit." At the time, Rose, her husband, and their two baby boys were living at Kings Point on Long Island, a short distance from Lake Success. As Rose recalled in her memoir, when Marshall arrived one afternoon at her family's house in the country they had drinks on the porch and she fixed him a supper of "scrambled eggs, cheese toast, and fruit." Afterward, as she walked Marshall to his car so he could rush back to New York, she remembered saying, "'Colonel Marshall, don't let those Russians get you down.'" She was just guessing that the Russians were on his mind. She had no idea that Marshall was worried that the Soviets might try to establish an influential position in the Middle East by moving troops into Palestine to enforce partition. "He kissed me goodbye and drove off," she wrote.[15]

The first known meeting between Marshall and Moshe Shertok took place on September 26, 1947. Shertok asked for the interview because he had heard that the secretary met secretly with Arab delegates (true) and was wavering in his support for partition. Gabriel Sheffer, Shertok's biographer, wrote that the Jewish delegation to the UN had prepared in advance a "psychological profile of Marshall." Guided by this profile, which suggested that Marshall would not likely be swayed by traditional lobbying tactics, Shertok and Rabbi Abba Hillel Silver, the American chair of the Jewish delegation from Cleveland, began the meeting with a simple but blunt request. They asked Marshall to "confirm or deny" that he was a firm supporter of partition. This "maneuver succeeded," wrote Sheffer. Marshall's "exasperated reaction to this undiplomatic query"—declaring that he remained committed to partition—seemed "genuine enough" to both Shertok and Silver. Marshall did not, however, disclose the tactics that the American delegation planned to use during the forthcoming UN debate.[16]

Given the strong opposition by Loy Henderson and many other influential voices in the State Department, Pentagon, and the CIA, it is tempting to suggest that Marshall harbored private doubts about the wisdom and workability of partition, especially because there was no mechanism that had been proposed for enforcement. Doubts would surface later, but at the time, the fall of 1947, there is no evidence that Marshall had reservations. In any event, the president settled the issue. In early October he "instructed" Marshall and Lovett to support partition, provided it was made clear that the U.S. would not take the lead in deploying troops to enforce the UN resolution.[17] Shortly thereafter Herschel Johnson, the deputy U.S. ambassador to the UN, formally announced United States support for partition along with a call for increased immigration to Palestine. To the surprise and relief of Marshall and most of the General Assembly the Soviets affirmed their support two days later, though they would insist on an immediate withdrawal of the British from the mandate, which seemed calculated to sow disorder in Palestine.

The Arabs prepared for all-out war against the Jews in the Holy Land. King Ibn Saud of Saudi Arabia warned Truman that "the dispute between Arab and Jew will be violent and long-lasting and without a doubt will lead to more shedding of blood." He vowed that even if the Jews succeeded in establishing a state, "the Arabs will isolate such a state from the world and lay siege to it until it dies by famine."[18] In a desperate attempt to avert war by enticing the Arabs to enter into negotiations, Marshall ordered the U.S. delegation to introduce an amendment to the majority plan for partition. The amendment proposed to move certain territories from the Jewish state to that of the Arabs, most importantly the southern portion of the Negev region of Palestine. Negev is a 4,700-square-mile inverted triangle of rocky desert that extends from the city of Beersheba along its base in the north to the town of Eilat at its tip in the south. Marshall claimed that this arid land, which was a "historic land bridge" that connected Arabs in the east with the Egyptian Sinai Peninsula to the west, was "overwhelmingly Arab" and suitable only for "marginal cultivation and seasonal grazing." On the other hand, Shertok and Ben-Gurion attributed extreme strategic importance to the Negev because Eilat at its southern terminus was situated on the coast of the Gulf of Aqaba. The gulf led to the Red Sea and beyond it to trading ports in East Africa, India, and Southeast Asia. If the Egyptians should bar the new Jewish state from access to the Suez Canal, the Gulf of Aqaba would be the only outlet to the eastern half of their world.[19]

Looking back, it is difficult to understand why Marshall thought this last-minute offer of territory had the slightest chance of bringing the Arabs to the table. They were already on record as being implacably opposed not only to a separate Jewish state but also to a federated state for both Jews and Arabs (the minority recommendation). Moreover, Herschel Johnson and General Hilldring, two key American delegates, warned Marshall that his proposal might backfire because it would cast doubt on the justice of the partition plan. Wavering states might decide to cast negative votes, and the U.S. could be blamed for the defeat of partition.

The heat was on Shertok and his political representative in Washington, Eliahu Epstein (later changed to Elath). With only days before the UN General Assembly was scheduled to vote, they had to find a way to force Marshall to withdraw his territorial giveaway. President Truman, ultimate arbiter of U.S. foreign policy, was the one person who could do it. How could they get through to him most effectively? Either Shertok or Epstein, or perhaps the two of them together, came up with the answer: Chaim Weizmann, the grand old architect of the Balfour Declaration who recently stepped down, or had been removed, from the presidency of the World Zionist Organization. Weizmann, almost seventy-three and in failing health, had just arrived at the Waldorf-Astoria Hotel in New York and was preparing to address the General Assembly. Shertok (or more likely Epstein) phoned Weizmann, who was delighted to be called out of retirement, eager to meet with the president. At Epstein's request, David Niles, a fervent Zionist Truman had inherited as an aide from FDR, arranged for Truman and Weizmann to get together. Inside the Oval Office, Weizmann spread out a map of Palestine on the president's desk. Knowing that Truman had spent years working on a farm in the American Midwest, Weizmann, a brilliant scientist with a PhD in chemistry, spoke about how the Jews would use new desalinization technology to transform the desert into productive farms. As to the waters in the Gulf of Aqaba off the town of Eilat, Weizmann explained that they could easily be dredged and made into a deepwater harbor that could accommodate large cargo ships. This was important, said Weizmann, because if "the Egyptians chose to be hostile to the Jewish state," a harbor at Eilat leading to the Red Sea would serve "as a parallel highway to the Suez Canal."[20] Weizmann was responding directly to the sentence in Marshall's instructions to the American UN delegation where he said, "The possibility of developing any part of Palestine bordering on the [Gulf of Aqaba] as a port is open to serious doubt . . ."[21]

By most accounts Weizmann's presentation on November 19 was persuasive. Any lingering doubts Truman had about retaining the southern Negev in the proposed Jewish state were probably dissipated by a political strategy memorandum he received that day dealing in part with the importance of the New York Jewish vote in the 1948 presidential election. The memo, signed by Clark Clifford, but mostly written by former FDR aide James Rowe, suggested that the president should not approach "the Palestine problem" on the basis of "political expediency." However, a few paragraphs later the memo stressed the importance of the Jewish vote. With the exception of Woodrow Wilson in 1916, wrote Clifford, "no candidate since 1876 has lost New York and won the presidency, and its 47 [electoral] votes are naturally the first prize in any election."[22] Later that afternoon, it appears that Truman decided to reverse Marshall's instruction to transfer most of the Negev to the Arabs. His approach, however, was anything but bold and determined. He could have summoned Marshall to the White House since the Secretary was in Washington on November 19, preparing to leave the next day to attend the Council of Foreign Ministers conference in London. For some reason, however, Truman chose not to, perhaps because he preferred to avoid a confrontation. Instead, at about three p.m., he telephoned delegate Hilldring in New York. At that moment Hilldring and Herschel Johnson were in the lobby of the Sperry Gyroscope building at Lake Success about to formally present the U.S. position on the Negev, as instructed by Marshall, to Moshe Shertok and the Arab delegates. According to one of the two contemporaneous memos recounting the conversation (neither of which were written by the participants), after Hilldring indicated that he was not "happy" with the Negev instruction, the president simply said that "nothing should be done to 'upset the apple-cart.'" Whose "apple-cart" was he referring to? Was it Truman's? Was it Marshall's? Or was it the cart of the Jews or that of the Arabs? He didn't say. This was a moment when Truman was far from being direct and decisive, traits he was known for. The other memo of the conversation, written by Chip Bohlen to Bob Lovett, said that Truman did not issue a "direct instruction," but somehow he "made it plain" to Hilldring that he "wished" the U.S. delegation "would go along with the majority report" on the Negev, meaning keep it in the Jewish state.[23] Faced with competing applecarts, a wish from Truman, and an explicit instruction from the secretary of state, Hilldring and Johnson wisely declined to take a position when they met a few minutes later with Shertok and the Arab delegates.[24]

That evening, in a telephone conversation with Lovett, the president claimed that he did not intend to overrule or otherwise "change" Marshall's instructions concerning the Negev.[25] If so, then what was the purpose of his ambiguous comment to Hilldring? Was he trying to shift responsibility to Hilldring for reversing Marshall's instructions? Assuming the two memos are accurate, Truman either forgot what he actually said to Hilldring or was being deliberately opaque. As will be seen, through lapses in memory or episodes of miscommunication, the president (or his White House staff) would continue to create confusion and messy mix-ups for Marshall and the UN delegation as they grappled with the Palestine question through the winter and into the spring of 1948.

While Marshall was in London attending the foreign ministers' conference, Lovett, as acting secretary of state, authorized the American delegation to withdraw the amendment proposing that the southern Negev be transferred to the Arab state. Whether he consulted Marshall or received another signal from Truman is not known. In a speech by Herschel Johnson to the UN on November 22, Marshall's instruction was officially reversed. Shertok and the Jewish Agency were immensely relieved. Loy Henderson predicted grave problems. There is no record of Marshall's reaction.

The vote in the General Assembly on partition was set to take place on November 25. During the tense days leading up to the vote, Shertok and his entire delegation, as well as the delegations of the Arabs and British, conducted intense lobbying campaigns in New York hotels and buildings that housed the temporary headquarters of the UN at Flushing Meadows, just south of LaGuardia Airport, and in the Sperry plant at Lake Success twelve miles to the east. In Washington, Epstein worked the halls of Congress and the White House. By the day of the scheduled vote it was apparent that the proponents of partition were one vote short of the two-thirds majority of

those voting that was required for adoption. To buy more time, the Jewish
Agency organized a filibuster, which delayed the vote until November 29,
the Saturday after Thanksgiving. The Truman administration had originally
balked at lobbying other countries to vote for partition or to abstain. Indeed,
Marshall instructed his delegation to refrain from lobbying. However, after
Marshall departed for the UK, the president, under extreme pressure from
the Zionists, relented. "Get busy," he ordered. "[T]here would be hell if the
voting went the wrong way."[26]

In London, Marshall was getting an earful from British foreign secretary
Ernest Bevin. After dinner on the evening of November 25, Bevin informed
Marshall that he had directed his UN delegation to abstain from voting for
partition. Bevin and his government regarded the partition proposal as a
hodgepodge that would never work, mainly because the population of Arabs
to be included in the so-called Jewish state was at least 40 percent of the
total. The British hoped that partition would not come to pass. They had
no interest in helping it succeed, especially if it involved British military
intervention. Moreover, Bevin pointed out that "the anti-Jewish feeling in
England . . . was greater than it had been in a hundred years." He told Marshall that this was due in part to the recent execution of two British sergeants
in Palestine by Jewish terrorists, a brutal tragedy "that will never be forgotten." Bevin fumed over unfair "Jewish influence from the United States" that
frustrated his efforts to solve the Palestinian problem prior to referring responsibility for the mandate to the UN. He claimed that Jewish groups em-
igrating to Palestine from the Balkans were infiltrated by "many indoctrinated
Communists."[27] And he passed on complaints from the Arabs that the
Americans were pressuring other countries, especially those in Latin America, to vote for partition.

Three days later Marshall sent an urgent message to Bob Lovett: if partition is voted in, the British will end their mandate over Palestine at midnight on May 14, 1948 (six p.m. Washington time), much earlier than their
original deadline.[28] Not only that, the British insisted that the five-member
UN commission sent to assist in governance should not plan to arrive in
Palestine before May 1. This would leave very limited time to set up new
administrative machinery.

On Saturday afternoon, November 29, the UN General Assembly reconvened at Flushing Meadows in the New York City Building, a large

neoclassical structure originally built as the city's pavilion for the 1939 World's Fair. Assembly Hall was packed with UN delegates wearing headphones. Alexandre Parodi, a French delegate, reported that there was no chance of compromise. On behalf of the Americans, Herschel Johnson called for a vote on partition. In a rare show of support, his motion was seconded by young Andrei Gromyko, the Soviet Union's permanent representative to the UN General Assembly. President Dr. Osvaldo Aranha of Brazil polled each of the delegations. The vote was 33–13, with ten abstentions and one absentee. Since more than two-thirds of those who voted cast their votes in the affirmative, the proposal to partition Palestine into two states, one Arab and the other Jewish, was approved. As soon as the Arab delegates heard the results, they began to walk out. Journalist Ruth Gruber wrote that the faces of Azzam Bey of Egypt and Prince Faisal of Saudi Arabia (son of King Ibn Saud) were "twisted with anger" as they beckoned "delegates from the other Arab states to follow them." Azzam Bey shouted in accented English, "Any line of partition drawn in Palestine will be a line of fire and blood."[29] Trygve Lie, the Norwegian secretary general of the UN, gave a farewell speech. The historic second session of the General Assembly concluded at 6:57 p.m.

Moshe Shertok wrote that "on that sleepless Saturday night, Jews all over the world were sitting attached to their radios, counting one by one the votes of the world's nations . . ."[30] One newspaper reported that "semi-hysterical Jewish crowds in Tel Aviv and Jerusalem were still celebrating" the partition vote at dawn. "Great bonfires at Jewish collective farms in the north were still blazing."[31] Menachem Begin, future prime minister of Israel, was not among the celebrants. Begin was the leader of the Irgun, an organization in Palestine that supported terrorism as a tactic to gain statehood. He predicted a war "for our existence and future."[32] David Ben-Gurion hailed the vote and praised Moshe Shertok's political achievement. However, he warned that there could be no "stable and strong Jewish state" as long as its Arab population was such a high percentage of the total.[33]

In Manhattan, thousands of Jews celebrated the vote at a mass meeting in the Saint Nicholas ice/boxing arena that spilled outside onto West 69th Street. Elderly Chaim Weizmann, regarded by Ben-Gurion as the "greatest Jewish emissary to the Gentile world," was ushered inside and accorded a hero's welcome.[34] A *New York Times* headline said that Weizmann was proposed that night to become the first president of the new Jewish state.[35]

Shertok too was greeted by enthusiastic cheers. There were many in the arena who said that he should be the new nation's first foreign minister or ambassador to the United States.

Historian John Judis characterized the partition proposal as a "monstrosity" and the UN vote "a fiasco."[36] The adjectives were overblown, but Judis was essentially correct. The partition plan stipulated that the Arab state was to consist of three noncontiguous areas in the Palestine mandate, namely a relatively large central section bordered by the west bank of the Jordan River (the West Bank), a part of western Galilee, and a strip along the southern Mediterranean coast and the Egyptian border (the Gaza Strip), plus two city enclaves (Jaffa and Safed). The Jewish state included the coastal plain (from Haifa south to Rehovot), most of the Negev down to Eilat, and the fertile eastern Galilee. Jerusalem and its holy places were to remain under UN control. Given this patchwork in an area the size of Vermont and the fact that the Arabs would comprise more than 40 percent of the population of the Jewish state, the idea that Arabs inside the borders of a Jewish nation and their surrounding brothers and sisters could live in harmony with the Jews was wishful thinking at best. The Arabs had long made it known that they would not tolerate the existence of a Jewish state in their midst. The British signaled that they would not lift a finger to help make the partition proposal work. And due to the need to contain Soviet-inspired aggression in central and Eastern Europe as well as the potential loss of access to Middle East oil, the Truman administration was reluctant to commit military forces to enforce partition in Palestine. Perhaps "fiasco" is too strong a word for the UN proceedings. However, there was little doubt that a bloody war was in the offing.

Nevertheless, the UN vote for partition in November of 1947 was a watershed moment. For the first time the United Nations, the world's peacekeeping authority, recognized the validity of a sovereign Jewish state. Thirty-three nations, including not only the U.S. and Canada but also France, Belgium, Norway, the Soviet Union, Byelorussia, Poland, Czechoslovakia, Brazil, South Africa, Australia, and the Philippines went on record as supporting a two-state solution and the historic roots of both Muslims and Jews in the city of Jerusalem. Moreover, the backing of these nations and the rest of the thirty-three provided invaluable momentum to the struggle of the Jews for statehood.

The UN vote strengthened the moral authority and credibility of the Jewish Agency. At the same time the idea of partition would eventually divide the Arabs. Rather than adhering to a coordinated strategy for surrounding, attacking, and defeating Israel in the 1948 war, King Abdullah of neighboring Transjordan decided to direct the Arab Legion, the only effective Arab fighting force, toward the large central region west of the Jordan River that was to be the core of the new Arab state. By occupying the West Bank, Abdullah's aim was to effect partition, not prevent it. As a result, Egypt's leadership became more concerned about a Jordanian takeover than destroying the Jews. Instead of concentrating all of its military power against the Jewish defenders on the coastal plain, Egypt split its forces, sending some to the West Bank to head off Abdullah's armies.

According to David Horowitz, director of the economic department of the Jewish Agency, if the UN partition resolution had been voted down there is no doubt that it would have led "to our political and physical" defeat.[37] For this reason alone, the affirmative vote by the UN for partition must be regarded as a significant milepost on the road to Jewish statehood.

* * * * *

While the secretary's attention during the first six weeks of 1948 was focused almost exclusively on selling the Marshall Plan, George Kennan and his staff, in close collaboration with Loy Henderson, were busily reassessing the U.S. stance on partition in light of American security interests. Kennan, most professionals in the State Department, and the entire U.S. defense and intelligence establishment believed that partition in the near term would draw the nation into a war with the Arabs, which could result in denial of access to oil and weaken U.S. ability to contain the Soviets in Europe. In a working paper submitted to the recently formed National Security Council (NSC), which included Secretary Marshall, Kennan wrote that there were three alternative courses that the U.S. could "pursue with respect to the problem of Palestine."[38] At the next meeting of the NSC they were summarized by Marshall as: (1) "direct abandonment of American support" for the partition plan approved by the General Assembly; (2) "vigorous support for the forcible implementation of the partition plan by the UN Security Council . . . which would involve the use of substantial American forces, either unilaterally or jointly with Russia"; or (3) reference of the entire matter "back to the General Assembly" coupled with an "attempt to reshape the policy, not surrendering the principle of partition but adopting some temporary expedients such as a trusteeship . . ." Since abandonment was morally and politically unacceptable and the deployment of American armed forces could result in war against the Arab world with consequent loss of access to oil and military bases in the Middle East, Marshall leaned toward the third alternative—a temporary trusteeship of Palestine, perhaps administered by the UN or jointly by the United States, the UK, and France. When James Forrestal observed that the U.S. would have to reinstitute "selective service"—that is, the draft—in order to have enough troops to enforce partition while protecting the nation's security interests in Europe and elsewhere in the world, Marshall tipped his hand. According to Forrestal, Marshall responded, "We are playing with fire while we have nothing with which to put it out."[39] Marshall would later say he had not made up his mind. However, everyone in the room knew where he was headed, though curiously no one from the White House attended that meeting. As far as Marshall was concerned, temporary trusteeship was the preferred option.

Meanwhile, the time was fast approaching when the American delegation to the UN would be required to state its position to the Security Council on whether the council should enlist armed assistance from member nations to carry out the partition resolution or whether other alternatives should be considered. At half past noon on February 19, five days before the head of the U.S. delegation, Ambassador Warren Austin, was to address the council, Marshall met with the president in the Oval Office (his usual Thursday appointment). Knowing that Truman would leave the next day for a long Caribbean cruise aboard the *Williamsburg*, Marshall told him that a draft statement for Austin to deliver to the council would be sent to his ship over the weekend for his review. Truman assured Marshall that whatever he recommended as the right approach, he should feel free to "disregard all political factors."[40] This was an obvious reference not only to the fact that 1948 was an election year but more particularly to fresh press reports stating that because Truman was thought to be waffling on the partition issue, the Democratic nominee to fill a congressional seat in a predominately Jewish district in the Bronx had just been handily defeated in a special election. The winner's campaign slogan was "Peace, Prosperity and Palestine."[41] By mid-February, partition, by force if necessary, and the establishment of a Jewish state were supported by *The New York Times*, virtually all Jewish leaders and groups in the U.S., and most American Jews.

The working draft and then the final draft of Austin's statement to the Security Council—prepared by Lovett, reviewed by Marshall, and sent to the president during the next few days—were premised on a deliberately narrow interpretation of Articles 39, 42, and 24 of the United Nations Charter, an interpretation that was recommended, wrote Marshall, "by [unnamed] men of some international legal understanding."[42] The two drafts asserted that the UN Security Council was authorized to enlist armed forces of its member states to keep the peace, but not to enforce partition. This interpretation ignored the fact that in Palestine, enforcement of partition was itself a peacekeeping action. The peace simply could not be kept without forcing the separation of the warring parties into two states. Thus, under the interpretation clumsily set forth in Austin's final statement, the use of armed forces by the UN to keep the peace in Palestine would be impermissible because they would necessarily be aimed in part at enforcing partition or perceived as doing so.[43]

Ben Cohen, one of the brightest lawyers on Truman's White House staff, called Austin's statement "legal sophistry."[44] A *Stanford Law Review* note criticized the interpretation as overly narrow and predicted that it would damage the prestige and effectiveness of the UN.[45] Secretary General Trygve Lie agreed. Nevertheless, this dubious interpretation served the objectives of Lovett and Marshall. From their non-lawyer perspective, the Security Council was powerless to use armed forces because by keeping the peace it would also be enforcing partition. Without force, the two of them were convinced that partition could not be achieved. Their yet-to-be-revealed so-called solution? Temporary UN trusteeship or some other alternative.

Apparently, neither the president nor Special Counsel Clark Clifford, a skilled trial lawyer who was also on the cruise, appreciated the implications of what Lovett and Marshall were actually proposing. Truman instructed that the final draft of Austin's statement be softened so as to not recede on what he and Clifford viewed as their position on partition (i.e., that if necessary the UN could raise a "police force" of its members to enforce partition).[46] His instruction was misunderstood or possibly ignored by Marshall, Lovett, or their subordinates. When the Lovett/Marshall interpretation of the UN Charter was repeated in the final draft, the president nevertheless radioed his approval. In fact, on February 24, hours after Austin delivered his statement to the Security Council, Truman issued a press release confirming that the U.S. position on partition was "accurately presented by Ambassador Austin."[47] This meant that Truman was not paying attention or did not understand the import of Austin's statement.

The distractions of the Caribbean cruise and the absence of personal contact between Marshall and Lovett on the one hand and Truman and Clifford on the other no doubt contributed to the misunderstandings. No one, however, can be held blameless.

Astute observers realized at once that Austin's statement to the Security Council laid the groundwork for a fundamental change in the U.S. position on partition. From the full-throated support for partition that it had advocated before the General Assembly in November of 1947, the Truman administration appeared to be backing away—that is, receding—by claiming that the UN Security Council did not have authority to enforce the partition resolution. In a letter to the president, Senator Francis Myers of Pennsylvania wrote that "because of sloppy draftsmanship, perhaps purposely so," Austin's speech gave the impression that the U.S. was "selling out the Jewish people and undercutting the UN structure."[48] Freda Kirchwey, the influential editor of *The Nation*, a pro-Zionist weekly, sent a telegram to Truman the day after Austin's statement advising him that "Lovett has told selected group newspaper people this [Austin's] statement is preparation for American effort to revise partition resolution in which you played leading role." She could not believe that the president "could conceivably be partner to such action."[49]

* * * * *

Along with Mrs. Truman and her daughter Margaret, Marshall was at National Airport to greet the president when he arrived from Key West following his two-week cruise. An hour or so later Marshall and Lovett briefed Truman on Palestine in the Oval Office, informing him that there were not enough votes in the Security Council to pass a resolution favoring partition absent the use of force. Consequently, the council would most likely refer "the Palestine problem" back to the General Assembly "for fresh consideration."[50] There is no evidence that Marshall or Lovett used the word "trusteeship," but an alternative like that was certainly implied.

By this time Clark Clifford was aware that Marshall's State Department was intent on reversing Truman's public position in favor of partition, as expressed when he instructed the American delegation to vote for partition in November 1947. With the help of White House staffers Max Lowenthal and David Niles, Clifford crafted two memos to the president arguing that the establishment of a Jewish state should and must be pursued without re-gard to whether the UN had the power to enlist military forces to enforce partition. Knowing that the president wanted to avoid the appearance of acting for political reasons, Clifford advised Truman that his recommenda-tions favoring Jewish statehood were not influenced by the fall election. Yet he made subtle allusions to the importance of domestic politics. Indeed, Clifford's second memo was delivered to Truman on March 8, the day he announced he would run for the presidency.[51]

Five days later, fifty-seven-year-old Eddie Jacobson, one of the presi-dent's closest friends, showed up at the West Wing, unannounced. Jacobson had known Truman since they served together in the fall of 1917 at Fort Sill, Oklahoma, during World War I. One of Lieutenant Truman's duties as an officer was to run the regimental canteen. In an effort to make it a financial success, he assigned Sergeant Edward Jacobson, who had clerked for six years in a Kansas City clothing store, to take command of the day-to-day operation of the canteen. "I have a Jew in charge of the canteen by the name of Jacobson and he is a crackerjack," wrote Truman to Bess Wallace, his future wife.[52] They became best friends. After the Great War the two of them formed a partnership, Truman & Jacobson, and opened a men's store in Kansas City that was initially successful but eventually had to be closed, deep in debt as a consequence of the 1921 recession. Like Truman, Jacob-son bounced back. By March 1948, he was a successful and respected Kan-sas City businessman.

At the instance of Shertok's Jewish Agency, Jacobson had been asked to persuade the president to meet again with Chaim Weizmann. The agency was acutely aware that Marshall and Lovett were pressing for a reversal of the administration's position on partition and that Truman seemed to be vacillating. Since Weizmann had previously changed Truman's mind on the Negev issue, it was thought that he could stiffen Truman's resolve to insist on partition and the prompt establishment of a Jewish state. Perhaps Jacob-son, son of immigrants from Lithuania who had long been a supporter of a Jewish homeland, could set up a face-to-face session between Weizmann and Truman. Time was running out. The mandate was set to expire at mid-night on May 14.

Matt Connelly, Truman's appointments secretary, greeted Jacobson and showed him into Truman's office. March 13 was a quiet Saturday. The phones were not ringing. For a few minutes the two old friends talked about personal matters. Before long, Jacobson brought up the subject of Palestine. According to Jacobson's account, he told Truman that he could not understand why he refused to meet with Dr. Weizmann, by then "an old and a sick man" who had "made his long journey" all the way to the U.S. especially to see him and plead the cause of the Jewish people. Jacobson recalled that Truman became tense, abrupt, and bitter. He complained about "how disrespectful and how mean certain [American] Jewish leaders" had been toward him when pestering him incessantly to come out foursquare for partition. His "dear friend, the President," Jacobson recalled, "was at that moment as close to being an anti-Semite as a man could possibly be."

Jacobson said he was "crushed," about to give up, when he glanced over at a small bronze statue of Andrew Jackson mounted on a horse that stood atop a table. Truman was a great admirer of Jackson, a student of Jackson's life and Jacksonian democracy. Pointing to the statue, Jacobson said, "Harry, all your life you have had a hero . . . Well, I too have a hero, a man I never met, but who is, I think, the greatest Jew who ever lived." Just because "you were insulted by some of our American Jewish leaders," said Jacobson, "you refuse to see" Weizmann, even though you know he had "absolutely nothing to do with these insults."

Jacobson stopped talking. Truman said nothing. He drummed his fingers on his desk, "gazing out the window." Jacobson wrote that he recognized "the sign. I knew that he was changing his mind." Truman swung around, looked Jacobson straight in his eyes, and said, "You win, you baldheaded son of a bitch. Tell Matt [Connelly] to arrange this meeting as soon as possible after I return from New York on March 17."[53]

* * * * *

To avoid being seen by reporters, Chaim Weizmann entered the White House through the East Gate at about noon. The president ordered that the meeting be kept secret. No one in the State Department, including Marshall, was informed. Truman and Weizmann talked for forty-five minutes, though the revered Zionist leader was scheduled for only a quarter of an hour. Weizmann spoke about the possibilities for "industrial activity" in Palestine and the "need for land," including the Negev, if Jewish refugees from Europe were to have enough room to raise their families, support themselves, and establish a homeland.[54] As to the elephant in the room, the crucial question of whether Truman would go all-out in support of partition, the record is muddled. On the one hand, Weizmann wrote in his 1949 autobiography that the president "indicated a firm resolve to press forward with partition." Based on her diary entries, Weizmann's wife, Vera, backed this assertion in her as-told-to memoir.[55] On the other hand, in his memoir that was published years later, Truman wrote that he "felt" Weizmann left his office with a "full understanding" of his policy. Yet the memoir is not at all clear on whether the president supported vigorous implementation of partition at that time or whether he backed the expedient of a temporary trusteeship, as he suggested in the very next paragraph.[56] By describing what he felt Weizmann understood, instead of the words he remembered using, it appears that Truman chose to deliberately gloss over his actual policy stance.

Whatever Truman said or didn't say, there is little doubt that Weizmann left the White House with the impression that Truman was a resolute supporter of partition. Shertok and his colleagues at the Jewish Agency in New York eagerly accepted his assessment.

While Truman chose not to tell Marshall about his meeting with Weizmann, Marshall neglected to inform Truman that he had just instructed Ambassador Warren Austin to deliver a statement to the UN in favor of temporary trusteeship. As will be seen, these twin oversights led to anger, embarrassment, and charges of ineptness.

*   *   *   *   *

Two days before Truman secretly met with Weizmann, Marshall had advised Austin that it was time for the Security Council to "dispose" of the partition issue. His timing was based on the same flawed legal interpretation that he and Lovett had advanced in February.[57] It was "apparent," wrote Marshall to Austin, that due to the growing threat to peace in Palestine, the Security Council was on the verge of having to enlist armed forces to stop the violence. It followed from this, he reasoned, that partition would have to be abandoned, at least for the time being. Otherwise, the use of armed forces to keep the peace would be construed "by a majority of the people of Palestine as a covert method of carrying out partition by force"—an action that the UN Charter, at least under the Marshall/Lovett interpretation, did not permit. Having already received approval from Truman (on March 8) to inform the Security Council "when and if necessary" that the U.S. was in favor of a temporary trusteeship as an alternative to immediate partition, Marshall ordered Austin to deliver the news as soon as possible. "The time factor is imperative and Council must act without delay," he wrote.[58] Marshall mistakenly assumed that there was no need to alert Truman.

Friday, March 19, was the earliest date the UN Security Council could meet. That day would be remembered by Moshe Shertok and his colleagues as "Black Friday." As instructed by Marshall, Warren Austin informed the Council that the U.S. government had decided to withdraw its support for immediate partition and was recommending a "temporary trusteeship" in order to afford Jews and Arabs an opportunity to reach an agreement on the future government of Palestine.[59] Believing he had been blindsided, Truman was furious. He either forgot about his prior approval or was angry because he was not given advance notice. "The State Department pulled the rug from under me today," he wrote in his diary. "I am now in the position of being a liar and a double-crosser."[60] Clark Clifford was livid. He blamed Marshall. "Marshall didn't know his ass from a hole in the ground," he said.[61] Shertok and Ben-Gurion, together with Jews and their leaders everywhere, regarded the reversal of policy as a shocking betrayal. Trygve Lie, the UN secretary general, said the U.S. position was a rebuke to the UN itself. *The New York Times* condemned Austin's speech, calling it the "climax to a series of moves" by the Truman administration, "which has seldom been matched for ineptness." And the *Times* picked up on an argument by Rabbi Silver that exposed a gaping hole in Marshall's rationale for recommending trusteeship as an alternative to partition: as with partition, armed forces would be necessary to affect and sustain a trusteeship. Thus, if partition had to be jettisoned in order for the UN to be clearly empowered under the UN Charter to enlist armed forces of its members to keep the peace, trusteeship would likewise have to be abandoned. Indeed, as the *Times* pointed out, trusteeship might "well require an even larger armed force than would be required for partition."[62]

On Black Friday Marshall was in Los Angeles selling the Marshall Plan. The next day, after giving a talk at UCLA, he digested several newspaper reports and editorials. Austin's speech was regarded as a "bombshell" by *The New York Times*.[63] Jewry in the U.S. and around the world characterized the statement as a betrayal. Arab leaders were heartened, hoping that partition was at last a dead issue. Marshall called a press conference and took full responsibility for Austin's statement. A temporary trusteeship "was the wisest course to follow," he explained, because it would give the UN time to negotiate a truce, "bring the fighting to an end," and save lives. "I recommended it to the President and he approved my recommendation."[64]

The Monday after Black Friday Truman calmed down. He was initially angry because he thought he had never endorsed the trusteeship alternative. However, over the weekend Clifford, or possibly his assistant George Elsey, persuaded the president that he had in fact approved the substance of Austin's speech, though perhaps not the complete text. When Marshall, having returned from the West Coast, met with Truman in the White House, the president admitted to him that he had previously "agreed" with Austin's proposed statement to the Security Council. However, he was "exercised" because no one told him in advance that the statement was about to be delivered. Truman said that if he had been given notice, "he could have taken certain measures to have avoided the political blast of the press."[65] For example, he could have told Weizmann that his policy was merely to delay but certainly not abandon partition; and he could have given a live press conference or issued an explanatory press release at about the same time Austin made his statement to the Security Council.

It was obvious to staffers in the White House and at the Democratic National Committee (DNC) that Austin's surprise statement to the UN and the storm of adverse press would reduce Truman's favorability percentage even further and could cost him the presidency. On March 24, the president called a meeting, the ostensible purpose of which was to discuss next steps and develop a statement to the press that he could use to contain the damage. When Marshall walked into the Cabinet Room he was disappointed but not surprised to see that he and his colleagues from State were outnumbered by the presence of Clifford and five other White House and DNC political operatives. The minutes do not capture the tension that existed in the room. On the subject of next steps, Marshall reported that the State Department was trying to negotiate a truce. The political attendees, mindful that Marshall had failed in China, thought this was a waste of time. They wanted to lift the U.S. embargo on arms sales as soon as possible, which of course would have only exacerbated the fighting.[66] Truman's impatience with the bickering was leaked to a *Time* magazine reporter. "This gets us nowhere," he reportedly said. "All I want is a statement I can read tomorrow at my press conference."[67]

Truman's press statement the next day tried to have it both ways. "Trusteeship" was not proposed as "a substitute for the partition plan," it said, but merely as a temporary "effort to fill the vacuum" that would be created when the British mandate expired at midnight on May 14. This was intended to convey the thought that partition—establishment of a sovereign Jewish state and a separate state for Palestinian Arabs—remained the ultimate goal. In the next sentence, the press statement said that "trusteeship does not prejudice the character of the final political settlement." This point obviously opened the door to a one-state solution or some other political settlement that would not involve partition and a separate Jewish state.

Truman was known for plain speaking. However, his press release, drafted by Clifford, was anything but. Moreover, in addressing the use of force, Truman's release, in a backhanded way, endorsed the UN Charter interpretation first advocated by Marshall and Lovett in February and in addition said that in any case American troops would not be used in Palestine "as a matter of national policy."[68]

Just as Truman's press release did little to repair the negative political fallout from Austin's statement to the UN, Marshall's effort to arrange a truce came to naught. On March 26, he and Lovett met with Shertok and his Washington-based colleague, Eliahu Epstein. No truce was possible, said Shertok, as long as any of the Arab troops from Syria, Lebanon, Transjordan, and Iraq remained in Palestine. Shertok told Marshall that even if the Arab forces were tempted to withdraw, the Jews would still continue to prepare to take over governance of the territories allocated to them under the partition plan. The Arabs would not let this happen without a fight. Asked by Marshall whether the Jews had the "ability" to defend themselves, Shertok said they were prepared to fight on their own "indefinitely," though they "were in desperate need of arms." The only "solution" to the Palestine problem, Shertok said, was a UN "international police force" to maintain peace and enforce partition. With evident contempt, Shertok pointed out that such a force was "non-existent today as it was in November of 1947," presumably because of the crabbed interpretation of the UN Charter that prevented it from being organized and deployed.[69]

* * * * *

Marshall left the handling of truce and trusteeship negotiations to Bob Lovett and others in the State Department. On Easter morning he and his party departed National Airport for close to a monthlong conference of the American States in Bogotá, Colombia. The long-overdue talks were supposed to focus on economic assistance and development. Marshall had been warned by the U.S. ambassador, however, that "Communists and left wing liberals" might try to sabotage the conference in order to "embarrass Colombian Government and create difficulties among American republics."[70] Violence was more than just a possibility. He and Katherine decided that instead of accompanying him on this trip she would drive from Pinehurst up to Leesburg in mid-April and open Dodona for the season.

The secretary was pleased to be out of Washington. On his first full day he strode alone through the streets of the capital city to attend the Te Deum mass at the Metropolitan Cathedral. But in less than forty-eight hours he was drawn back into the Palestine problem. During a dinner on April 1 and a lunch the next day Byron Price, a top UN official, told Marshall that his failure to help create a "UN security force" to enforce partition was in his opinion and that of Secretary General Trygve Lie, "seriously threatening the life of UN." Marshall radioed a note to Lovett imploring him "to do something to get ourselves popularly understood."[71] The problem, as both he and Lovett knew, was that the U.S. would have to supply upward of 50,000 men to such a security force, or so they thought, leaving virtually no ground force reserves available to deter the Soviet Union and other Communist regimes that were on the march elsewhere in the world. It was a matter of priorities. How could this pragmatic point be put across without appearing to ignore the Holocaust and the moral cause of the Jewish people? Marshall had no guidance for Lovett other than to "do something."

For Marshall, the first week in Bogotá was devoted to visiting the other delegations and exchanging preliminary views. The only outside distractions were daily reports from Berlin and Washington advising the secretary of a potential crisis with the Soviet Union. Due to a provocative speech by Truman condemning the Soviets as obstacles to peace and a mutual defense pact signed by members of the Western bloc in Europe, the Soviet deputy military governor in Berlin had retaliated by announcing a series of restrictions on rail and highway traffic between the western zones of Germany and Berlin. It was the beginning of an effort to block the U.S. and its western allies from access to Berlin, an enclave surrounded by the Soviet-controlled eastern zone that was more than one hundred miles from the western zones. Assured by Lovett and Lucius Clay that they could manage the restrictions without starting a shooting war, Marshall saw no need to become personally involved until he returned to Washington.

The violence in Bogotá that Marshall had been warned about was triggered on the afternoon of April 9 while he was having lunch at a private home beyond the city center. A call came in from the embassy reporting that Jorge Eliécer Gaitán, popular leader of the liberal opposition party, had been shot and killed downtown. Mobs quickly formed. The murderer was chased down, beaten to death, and hung from a streetlamp. Gaitán's followers took over several radio stations and broadcast accusations that Americans were responsible for his assassination. Marshall and the others with him could hear gunfire in the streets. One of Marshall's aides called the Ministry of War and asked that troops be sent to defend the secretary of state. Late in the afternoon a detachment of thirteen arrived. Marshall sat calmly near a window in the living room reading a western novel. As darkness descended, he summoned the officer in charge of the Colombian troops that were stationed outside. Through an interpreter Marshall said, "If I remember my small-unit tactics correctly, when you are defending a perimeter, what you do is to garrison that perimeter lightly and place a large, centrally located, mobile reserve at a point where it can move rapidly to any threatened point on the perimeter." The officer, who had very few men, asked Marshall how he would do it. Marshall responded, "Put one man at the front door, one man at the back door, and all the others in the garage where they can keep warm tonight. That's the way the United States Army would handle it."[72] Marshall was pleased to remember the lessons he learned in the Philippines and the tactics he taught at Fort Benning.

By eleven that night the Colombian army had regained control. Speaking to the conference delegates a few days later, after the uprising had been quashed, Marshall stated that the situation in Bogotá followed "the same definite pattern . . . which provoked strikes in France and Italy . . . This is a world affair—not merely Colombian or Latin American."[73]

* * * * *

While Marshall was in Colombia the Jewish armed forces in Palestine, the Haganah, received the first of many shipments by air and sea of machine guns, rifles, ammunition, and fighter aircraft from Czechoslovakia that they desperately needed in order to conduct offensive operations (the U.S. had embargoed the sales of arms to the Jews and Arabs in the Middle East). Ben-Gurion reported to Shertok that "the military situation has changed radically in favor of the Jews."[74] As a result, the attitude in Washington and New York shifted from truce and trusteeship—alternatives that had gained very little traction—to the question of whether to recognize a Jewish state when the British mandate expired. Even if it would not last, partition through force of arms appeared inevitable. On April 9, Chaim Weizmann put the issue to Truman in stark terms. "The choice for our people, Mr. President, is between statehood and extermination," he wrote. In other words, truce and temporary trusteeship were off the table. "History and providence has placed this issue in your hands," he told the president. "I am confident that you will yet decide in the spirit of the moral law."[75]

After speaking personally with Weizmann in New York, Eddie Jacobson was admitted through the East Gate of the White House and met secretly with Truman on Sunday, April 11. "It was at this meeting," Jacobson wrote, "that I also discussed with the President the vital matter of recognizing the new [Jewish] state, and to this he agreed with his whole heart" (underlining in Jacobson's original letter).[76] Twelve days later, the day before Marshall returned to Washington, Truman reportedly sent a message to Weizmann through Judge Sam Rosenman (former FDR aide) that "he would recognize the Jewish state as it was proclaimed."[77] Truman did not share with Marshall the commitment he made to Jacobson or the message that he asked Rosenman to pass on to Weizmann.

If, as appears from the foregoing, Truman had made up his mind by the end of April to recognize a new Jewish state, he proceeded to mislead Marshall and the State Department. Based on a memorandum written by Dean Rusk, head of State's Office of UN affairs, the president instructed Rusk during a meeting on April 30 to inform Marshall "that he (the President) was ready to take whatever steps the Secretary thought would hasten the completion of a truce." When Rusk asked Truman what he would do if the Arabs accepted a truce but the Jews would not, Truman "replied that 'if the Jews refuse to accept a truce on reasonable grounds they need not expect anything else from us.'" Marshall initialed Rusk's memo, indicating that he had read it.[78]

Four days later the Jewish Agency rejected State's latest truce proposal, making it clear that the Jews intended to establish a "separate state by force of arms."[79] Having just provided assurance to Marshall and Rusk that the Jews could not "expect anything else from us," Truman was caught in another lie. He had already decided to grant a critically important something "else" to the Jews—U.S. recognition of their new state. Therefore, he was going to have to renege on his assurance to Marshall and Rusk.

*   *   *   *   *

The day before Truman's birthday party at the 1925 F Street Club, Clark Clifford and the president sat down in the Oval Office for their "customary private day-end chat." The subject was Palestine. The British mandate was set to expire in seven days—midnight, May 14. Clifford handed Truman a statement that he wanted the president to read on May 13, his next scheduled press conference. If delivered, the draft statement would announce Truman's intention to recognize the new Jewish state as soon as its existence was declared by its provisional government in Palestine on May 15. Clifford's rationale, based on notes that he had jotted two days earlier, was that a Jewish state was "inevitable." Indeed, the UN's partition plan would become a fact as of the first minute after midnight on May 15. Why shouldn't the U.S. be the first to recognize the new nation?[80]

Sensing that Marshall had "strong feelings" concerning the issue of immediate recognition, Truman "picked up the telephone to get his views." Listening to Truman's end of the conversation, Clifford "could tell that Marshall objected strongly to the proposed statement." Truman listened politely but did not disclose his position. He asked that Marshall, along with Lovett, meet with him on May 12.

After Truman hung up, he said that he "was impressed with General Marshall's argument that we should not recognize the new state so fast." He told Clifford that he would like him to "make the case in favor of recognition" at the meeting on May 12 with Marshall and Lovett. "You know how I feel. I want you to present it just as though you were making an argument

before the Supreme Court of the United States . . . I want you to be as persuasive as you can possibly be."[81] To an interviewer, Clifford recalled Truman ending his instructions by saying, "But the person I really want you to
convince is Marshall."[82]

Clifford would have his showdown with Marshall on May 12. But Moshe
Shertok was given one last shot at the secretary before rushing back to Palestine to make plans to announce the new Jewish state. On Saturday afternoon, May 8, he and Eliahu Epstein were shown into the secretary's office.
Marshall was there along with Lovett and Rusk. Shertok began by assuring
the Americans that, contrary to rumors, the time for talking about truce and
a postponement of statehood had ended. His people had waited for centuries. It was "either now or never." Shertok's hope was that once he drove
home the fact that the Jewish Agency was dead serious—that it was actually
going to declare statehood within the first minute of May 15—Marshall and
his colleagues would change their minds. Lovett and Rusk argued with
Shertok for more than an hour. After a call was made to delay the departure
of Shertok's plane, Marshall weighed in. "He wanted to warn us," recalled
Shertok, not to place too much reliance on temporary military success. Marshall spoke of his experience with Chiang and Mao in China. Each time he
was on the verge of reaching a truce, the side that had scored the most recent
battlefield success would back off, believing it had more to gain by continuing the fighting. Marshall told Shertok that he and his people were "taking
a gamble." If they succeeded, "well and good." But what if "they failed"?
They could not "expect help from the United States."[83]

Shertok left the meeting knowing that he had not changed Marshall's
mind. By all accounts Marshall never even hinted that the U.S. would recognize the new Jewish state. The most he did was to express sympathy with
the Jewish quest for statehood. "[H]e wished us well," wrote Shertok.

In New York, while waiting for his overseas flight, Shertok was called to
the telephone. It was Chaim Weizmann. He asked Shertok to carry a message to Ben-Gurion in Tel Aviv. "Proclaim the Jewish state, now or never!"[84]

* * * * *

At four o'clock on the afternoon of May 12, four days after Marshall silenced
the room at Truman's birthday celebration and just fifty hours before the
British mandate in Palestine was set to expire, the secretary entered the

Oval Office. Chairs were arranged in a semicircle facing the president's desk. Marshall and Lovett took seats to the right; Clark Clifford was seated in the center, notes in the breast pocket of his elegant suit, with David Niles and Matt Connelly to his left. State Department aides Fraser Wilkins and David McClintock sat behind Marshall and Lovett. In his memoir, Clifford called the meeting "Showdown in the Oval Office," a historic hour when "the Truman administration faced a decision whose consequences are still with us today."[85]

From a swivel chair behind his desk, Truman looked across to Marshall and Lovett. Without mentioning the issue of recognition, he asked them to begin by bringing the group up to date on negotiations with the Jews and Arabs. Lovett reported that truce and trusteeship were taken off the table due to "recent military successes" by Jewish forces and a belief by Shertok and the Jewish Agency that they could cut a "behind the barn deal" with King Abdullah whereby the Arab Legion would take over the Arab portion of Palestine but leave the Jews in possession of the territory they already occupied. Marshall intervened. He told Truman and the others what he had said to Shertok—"that it was extremely dangerous to base long-range policy on temporary military success" and that "they were taking a gamble." Marshall also informed the group that he placed Shertok on notice that if the Jewish armed forces faced setbacks and "came running to us," they would get no help from the United States.[86] He concluded by recommending that the U.S. continue to pursue truce and trusteeship and defer a decision on recognition.

The president signaled Clifford that it was his turn to speak. He began by pointing out that the efforts of the State Department to secure a truce and establish a trusteeship had failed. By Lovett's own admission, they were off the table. Be realistic, argued Clifford. "Partition into Jewish and Arab sectors has already happened." Given this fact, the president should recognize "the Jewish state immediately after the termination of the British Mandate on May 14. This would have distinct value in restoring the President's position for support of the partition of Palestine."[87]

To the sensitive ears of Marshall, Lovett, and the two State Department aides, the phrase "distinct value in restoring the President's position" could only mean domestic political value. Indeed, in McClintock's memo of the meeting he quoted Clifford as saying Truman's policy in support of partition and immediate recognition was "firmly based upon a consideration of the favorable political implications."[88]

Clifford's next sentence confirmed their suspicions. The president, he said, should announce his intention to recognize the new Jewish state "at his press conference tomorrow [May 13]," before the "Soviet Union or any other nation" does so.[89] By stealing a march on the Soviets and being the first to recognize the Jewish state, it appeared to Marshall and his State Department colleagues that Clifford was intent on having the president squeeze maximum home-front political value from his recognition decision. Everyone in the room knew that the presidential election would take place in less than six months.

The special counsel's final arguments were his most eloquent. He appealed to the promise of the Balfour Declaration, the horrors of the Holocaust, and the "great moral obligation" of Americans "to oppose discrimination such as that inflicted on the Jewish people."[90] In his rich, honeyed voice, Clifford cited from memory the verse from Deuteronomy that Jews regard as the biblical validation of their claim to a homeland in Palestine:

"Behold, I have set the land before you: go in and possess the land which the Lord sware unto your fathers, Abraham, Isaac, and Jacob, to give unto them and to their seed after them."[91]

While Clifford was making his points, he "noticed Marshall's face reddening with suppressed anger."[92] Suddenly Marshall interrupted, sounding, as Clifford recalled, "like a righteous God-damned Baptist."[93]

"This is just straight politics," said Marshall. "I don't even understand why Clifford is here. This is not a political meeting."[94]

Barely audible, Truman responded. "General, he is here because I asked him to be here."[95]

Lovett jumped in, pouncing on Clifford's recommendation that Truman should announce his recognition decision on the morrow, before the Jewish state even existed. He said that such a move would be "highly injurious" to the UN, especially since the General Assembly "was still considering the question of the future government of Palestine." Underscoring Marshall's point about the influence of politics, Lovett said that immediate recognition of the new Jewish state would be viewed as "a very transparent attempt to win the Jewish vote" that would harm the "prestige of the President" and probably "lose more votes than it would gain." Finally, Lovett argued that premature recognition of the Jewish state would be like "buying a pig in a poke." He read out loud parts of intel reports indicating that the Soviets had been sending Jewish/Communist agents into Palestine. "How [do] we know what kind of a Jewish State would be set up?" he asked rhetorically.[96]

When Lovett finished, Marshall piled on, his temper barely under control. According to a written account of Marshall's words, which he insisted be inserted into the official record, the secretary warned the president that recognition of Jewish statehood, as recommended by Clifford, would be seen as a "transparent dodge to win a few votes." Clifford's counsel, said Marshall, was "based on domestic political considerations" and would diminish the "great dignity of the office of the President." The secretary looked directly at Truman, just as he did when he lauded his "complete integrity" a few days before in the midst of his birthday toast. He said, "*If* [you] *follow Mr. Clifford's advice and if in the elections I were to vote, I would vote against the President.*"[97]

It was "the sharpest rebuke *ever* for [Truman]," recalled Clifford.[98] Yet the president revealed no emotion. Everyone in the room was stunned.

Marshall glared at Clifford. Clifford thought to himself that if Marshall's statement became public, "it could virtually seal the dissolution of the Truman Administration and send the Western Alliance [forerunner of NATO], then in the process of creation, into disarray." It would cause Truman to lose the upcoming election.

Truman knew that he could not risk losing Marshall. Signaling that the meeting was over, Truman rose and walked over to the secretary. He could see that Marshall was still seething, perhaps even a bit embarrassed that he had caused such a scene. "I understand your position, General, and I'm inclined to side with you in this matter," he fibbed.

Truman and Clifford lingered in the Oval Office for a few minutes after everyone else had left. Based on the president's last comment to Marshall, Clifford thought he had lost the argument. Truman tried to cheer him up. "That was rough as a cob," he quipped, invoking an old Missouri farmer's expression. "I never saw the General so furious," said the president. However, he made it clear that he had not changed his mind and he wanted Clifford to keep Marshall from going public. "[L]et the dust settle a little," he advised Clifford, "but be careful. I can't afford to lose General Marshall."[99]

Clifford could not approach Marshall directly. Since they were no longer on speaking terms he needed an emissary. Fortunately, Bob Lovett offered his services. Within an hour after the disastrous Oval Office meeting adjourned, Lovett telephoned Clifford at his office in the White House. "It would be a great tragedy if these two men were to break over this issue," he said. "Can you drop by my house on your way home for a drink tonight?" During the evening and all the next day, Clifford and Lovett tried to find a way to avoid a breakup. Clifford began by telling Lovett that Truman had been persuaded by arguments of Lovett and Marshall during the Oval Office meeting that it would be a mistake to announce recognition on the 13th, before statehood was declared. Thus, if the prospect of premature recognition triggered Marshall's outburst, it was no longer an issue. However, Clifford said Truman remained adamant that he intended to recognize the new state as soon as it came into existence and the U.S. government was presented with an official request for recognition. "The thing for you to do," said Clifford to Lovett, "is to persuade General Marshall that he's wrong" to oppose immediate recognition.[100] "[I]f anyone is going to give, it is going to have to be General Marshall."[101]

Knowing he had little chance of persuading Marshall that he was wrong, Lovett came back on the 13th with a proposal to delay recognition. This was progress, an indication that the secretary might agree to recognition down the road. Clifford would not agree to any delay. His explanation, according to Lovett, was that the timing of recognition was of the "greatest possible importance to the President from a domestic point of view."[102] If these were the words that Clifford actually used, election year politics was clearly behind the presidential decision for early recognition.

The morning of the 14th dawned with no resolution in sight. Realizing that Lovett would never persuade Marshall to support immediate recognition, Clifford altered his approach. He informed Lovett that all Truman was asking was that Marshall agree to refrain from publicly opposing the president's decision. Lovett said he would take this proposal to Marshall. Time was running out and there was much to do. At six p.m. in Washington, which was midnight in Tel Aviv, the mandate would expire and the provisional government would promptly declare the existence of a new state—the name "Israel" had not yet been decided upon. While waiting for a response from Lovett, Clifford telephoned Epstein and asked him to prepare and deliver a letter to Truman by noon, with a copy to Marshall, formally requesting the

U.S. government to recognize the new Jewish state. Meanwhile, Clifford worked on drafts of Truman's reply and a presidential statement to be issued after six p.m.

Late that morning Clifford was getting anxious. Having not heard back from Lovett, he called and asked him whether he and Marshall had had an opportunity to talk. As if the passage of time was not his slightest concern, Lovett demurred and suggested that the two of them meet for lunch at the F Street Club. Clifford had little choice but to agree. Over lunch, which dragged on until after two o'clock, Lovett once again pressed hard for a delay. What difference does a few days make, he argued. Clifford kept his cool and remained firm, saying the president was worried about leaks and that the timing of recognition was of supreme importance. There would be no delay. As professionals, the two of them went over the draft letters and the presidential statement, though Lovett was in profound disagreement with the president's decision. They noticed that in the letter Epstein prepared asking for recognition, the term "Jewish state" had been lined out and the new name "State of Israel" had been written in by hand. At the Tel Aviv Museum of Art where Ben-Gurion, Shertok, and the rest of the Jewish leaders were meeting, they had voted by a majority of seven to adopt the name Israel and promptly radioed it to Epstein.

At four o'clock Lovett finally called Clifford with the news he had been waiting for. "I've had a good talk with General Marshall," he said.[103] "He cannot support the President's decision, but he has agreed that he will not oppose it."[104] When asked years later what he said to Marshall to persuade him, Lovett responded, "I told him it was the president's choice."[105] It followed, therefore, that Marshall's choice was either to loyally carry on or resign. As Marshall said in the presence of Dean Rusk and others, "You don't accept a post of this kind and then resign when the man who has the Constitutional authority to make a decision makes one that you don't like."[106] Marshall continued to serve, keeping his opinions to himself.

The White House made one concession to the State Department. Recognition would be de facto, not de jure, which meant that the U.S. would merely acknowledge the existence of a new Jewish state and that its provisional government could carry out its obligations. De jure status would recognize borders and permit ambassadors to be exchanged. It could be conferred at a later date.

Israel's Declaration of Independence was proclaimed to the world by David Ben-Gurion at 12:01 a.m. Tel Aviv time on May 15 (6:01 p.m. on May 14 in Washington). Among its provisions was a guarantee of "complete equality of social and political rights to all of its inhabitants irrespective of religion, race or sex."[107] Truman's statement was read to the White House press corps by press secretary Charlie Ross at 6:11 p.m. "The United States recognizes the provisional government as the de facto authority of the new State of Israel."[108]

Truman's announcement stunned almost everyone. At the UN in Flushing Meadows the American delegates, still pursuing truce and trusteeship, were completely surprised and thoroughly outraged. Ambassador Austin had been notified scarcely fifteen minutes before the announcement. He was so disheartened that he departed the General Assembly and went home without informing the other delegates. Dean Rusk, future secretary of state under Presidents Kennedy and Johnson, received a call from Marshall. "Rusk," he said, "get up to New York and prevent the US Delegation from resigning *en masse*."[109] Eleanor Roosevelt complained to Marshall that the U.S. policy of "going it alone" without consultation had undermined the UN and eroded trust in the leadership of the United States. In his letter of reply Marshall said he was aware of the unfortunate and regrettable effect that the announcement would have on the U.S. delegates, but "[m]ore than this I am not free to say."[110] This was Marshall's way of telling the former first lady that he disagreed with the way the matter was handled by the White House.

In the early hours of Saturday, May 15, the last British official boarded a cruiser in Haifa and departed Palestine. At dawn on the Sabbath, the day of rest and worship, Egyptian bombers appeared over Tel Aviv. The armies of Lebanon, Syria, Iraq, Egypt, and Transjordan began their invasion (though King Abdullah of Jordan only took control of the West Bank, having agreed to stop short of Jewish territory). The Arab-Israeli War of 1948 was officially under way.

Inside the White House, Truman walked into a roomful of jubilant aides. He spotted diminutive Max Lowenthal, the behind-the-scenes author of Clifford's memos to Truman arguing for immediate recognition. Truman asked him why he was so happy. "I am smiling because you are going to win the presidency."[111] At 2210 Massachusetts Avenue on Embassy Row a handmade flag appeared outside the Jewish Agency's Washington headquarters.

It was emblazoned with a Star of David against a white background and bordered at top and bottom by two sky-blue stripes symbolizing the stripes on a *tallit*, the traditional Jewish prayer shawl.

* * * * *

In the decades since Truman's courageous decision to be the first to recognize the State of Israel, Marshall's opposition, not to mention his judgment, has been questioned. His adamant resistance was regarded as bloodless—lacking sympathy and compassion for the survivors of the Holocaust and their quest for a homeland. There are those within and outside the Jewish community who are convinced to this day that Marshall's opposition to immediate recognition was motivated by anti-Semitism, his own and the views of a formidable group of foreign policy "wise men" who arguably influenced him.[112] This belief was no doubt shaped by a one-sided, best-selling book authored by Clark Clifford "with" Richard Holbrooke, published in 1991, and a column written in 2008 by Holbrooke, by then a celebrated diplomat, that was published in the *Washington Post*.[113] Taken together, these publications suggest, without ever using his name, that Marshall was among the cohort of anti-Semitic policy makers who inhabited America's national security and foreign policy establishments in 1948.

Was anti-Semitism—hostility toward or prejudice against Jews—among the motives underlying Marshall's opposition to the immediate recognition of Israel in May 1948? No one will ever know for sure what was in his mind at the time.

Looking back, arguments can be made that prejudice was a factor. In February 1948, Marshall signed on to a narrow interpretation of the UN Charter that was recommended by Lovett after he consulted, according to Marshall, with "men of some legal understanding."[114] This controversial interpretation rendered the Security Council powerless to enforce the partition of Palestine. Anti-Semitism on the part of Lovett and the mysterious men of "legal understanding," as well as Marshall himself, could have been behind this interpretation, which, of course, left it to the outnumbered Jews to unilaterally declare statehood and fight alone against the Arab armies. Similarly, latent hostility to Jews could have been responsible for the virulent outbursts by both Lovett and Marshall at the meeting on May 12 when they accused the president of engaging in a transparent attempt to win the Jewish vote. Marshall in particular had years of experience dealing with presidents and their wily political advisers whose decisions, foreign and domestic, were often politically motivated. Why was he so red-faced, righteous, and furious? After all, a president running for election is in the business of attracting voters. Why not Jewish voters?

The bulk of the evidence of what Marshall said and how he acted, however, points to the conclusion that anti-Semitism was not a material factor. According to all contemporaneous accounts of those who participated in the decision by Truman to recognize Israel, Marshall was against immediate recognition because he believed that UN and U.S. diplomats should be given more time to negotiate a truce and trusteeship; that the Jews in Palestine would likely be defeated on the battlefield; that American armed forces would be drawn into the conflict; that the Arabs would be driven into the arms of the Soviets; that the U.S. might be denied access to Middle East oil; and that election year politics was the main reason behind the rush to be the first to recognize the new Jewish state. At no time did the secretary utter words of prejudice or hostility toward Jews. If anything, his worry that they might be defeated in battle indicates that he was trying to protect them from being annihilated or driven out of Palestine. Also, Marshall failed to even mention the fact that hundreds of thousands of Palestinians would be displaced by the emergence of the new Jewish state and forced into refugee camps. If he was motivated by anti-Semitism it would have been logical for him to have used this prospect as an argument against recognition.

As to Marshall's angry eruptions on May 12, it is equally arguable that they had nothing to do with anti-Semitism, though they probably confirm the existence of a couple of Marshall's blind spots—an arrogant contempt for the concerns of politicians and a tendency, noted by Clifford, to come across as "a righteous [expletive deleted] Baptist." This was not the first time that Marshall was close to resigning over a presidential decision that he thought was motivated by partisan politics. As will be recalled, Marshall was convinced in August 1942 that FDR's decision to invade North Africa by November, instead of waiting until 1943 to assault northwest France, was based on domestic political considerations—a desire to influence the midterm elections and a perceived need to "keep the people entertained."

If Marshall is to be faulted for his opposition to the immediate recognition of Israel, it should not be attributed to anti-Semitism or an overreaction to the influence of partisan politics. Rather, it was his judgment, and that of the entire U.S. national security establishment, that can be questioned. Almost everything Marshall and his colleagues warned would happen in the event of immediate recognition failed to come to pass. The Jews were not driven into the sea by the Arabs. U.S. armed forces were not dragged into the war. Access to oil was not limited or cut off. The Soviets did not gain influence in the Middle East at the expense of the United States. And America's influence in the region was not doomed.

But in one important respect Marshall's judgment was vindicated. Partition would not resolve hostilities between Jews and Arabs. The Arabs would deny Israel's right to exist. There would be no end to the fighting.

Chapter 17

We Will Not Be Coerced

During the last days of June and the first week of July 1948, America teetered on the precipice of war with the Soviet Union. The flashpoint was Berlin. The fuse had been ignited months earlier by questions concerning the future of Germany that begged for prompt answers and decisive action. Should the U.S. abandon hope that Germany would be reunited? Did it have any alternative but to accept the east-west division and to work to integrate the economy and politics of West Germany with Western Europe? Did the Soviets intend to draw the western zones of Germany into their orbit? If so, this would pose "the greatest threat to security of all Western Nations, including the US," wrote Secretary Marshall in February 1948.[1] He would risk war to stop them.

By June, U.S. policy makers and their Western European counterparts finally made some choices. They agreed to merge their three zones into a single West German state. Their plan was to integrate the new state into the Western European community of nations, fit it into the Marshall Plan, and stabilize its economy through currency reform. As if these moves were not provocative enough, Marshall assigned Undersecretary Bob Lovett to help Senator Arthur Vandenberg draft and pass the so-called Vandenberg Resolution, the precursor of the North Atlantic Treaty Organization (NATO). The Vandenberg Resolution, officially designated Senate Resolution 239, authorized the U.S. under Article 51 of the UN Charter to enter into regional and other collective "self-defense" alliances, provided its national security was threatened.[2] On June 11, 1948, the Senate, after a single day of debate, approved the resolution by an overwhelming bipartisan vote. It was obvious to Joseph Stalin, his comrades in the Kremlin, and the rest of the world that the Vandenberg Resolution was aimed at a military alliance of the United States with the non-communist nations in Europe.

It was currency reform, however, not the Vandenberg Resolution, that pushed the Soviets and the U.S. to the brink of war. "Currency," as Daniel

Yergin wrote in *Shattered Peace*, is a "symbol of sovereignty and a mechanism for exercising sovereignty."[3] On June 18, General Lucius Clay announced that the Western allies would begin circulating the "west mark" (eventually the deutsche mark) into West Germany, but not the western sectors of Berlin. As expected, the Soviets retaliated, declaring that they would introduce their own currency, the "ostmark," into East Germany and all of Berlin, including the western zones of the city that had been allocated to the Allies. This attempt to exercise sovereignty over West Berlin could not be tolerated. On June 23, the western allies announced that they would circulate the west mark in their sectors of Berlin. The next day, the same day that Governor Dewey accepted the Republican nomination, Stalin made a decision that he would later regret. He ordered that all overland access to West Berlin from West Germany via roads, rail, and canals be blockaded. Electricity from East Berlin was shut off. With little more than a month's supply of coal and food, 2.4 million West Berliners were threatened with a complete lack of electric power and, much worse, starvation.

The west mark triggered the crisis. But it was clear that Stalin intended to force the Americans and their allies out of Berlin and perhaps out of West Germany as well. The situation was fraught with danger. In Berlin, Clay regarded the blockade as an act of war. Though the Red Army in and around Berlin far outnumbered Allied ground forces, Clay repeatedly recommended that the Western allies should try to break the blockade by sending armored convoys by rail or autobahn into West Berlin. This risked a shooting war with little prospect of success. The alternative was to mount a humanitarian airlift to supply the beleaguered Berliners with food, fuel, and other necessities. An airlift was less likely to be challenged by the Soviets because access by air through three twenty-mile-wide air corridors was guaranteed by a written agreement, whereas overland access was pursuant to an oral understanding that the Soviets claimed was no longer operative. Accounts differ as to who originated the airlift idea—Clay, Lovett, and an RAF officer named Reginald Waite were the main claimants—and who in Washington approved it. Suffice it to say that Clay prevailed upon General Curtis LeMay, commander of U.S. air forces in Europe, to assign his entire fleet of C-47 transports to what became known as the Berlin airlift. When Clay asked LeMay whether his planes could carry coal, LeMay replied, "We can haul anything."[4] On June 26, Clay ordered the first flight of 32 C-47s, collectively carrying eighty tons of milk, flour, and medicine, to fly more than one hundred miles from airfields in West Germany over Soviet-occupied East Germany and drop off their cargoes at Tempelhof Airport in West Berlin. Shortly thereafter British Yorks and Dakotas (Douglas DC-3s) joined the airlift, flying their cargoes into the British sector of Berlin from airports near Hamburg.

Two days after the Berlin airlift began Marshall was again out at Walter Reed being examined by kidney specialists. At a meeting with Lovett and Forrestal in the White House, Truman essentially confirmed the policy regarding Germany that Clay and LeMay had already implemented. According to Forrestal's diary, Truman cut off all further "discussion" as to whether or not the U.S. and its allies would stay in West Berlin. We are "going to stay, period," he reportedly said.[5] That evening Lovett briefed Marshall on the president's decision.

The doctors permitted Marshall to attend the cabinet meeting on Friday, July 2, the first time in several days that he had seen the president. Marshall reported that B-29 strength in West Germany was being beefed up "from one squadron to a group" and that the British had accepted the U.S. offer to send "two additional B-29 groups" to the UK. At the time a single group of the B-29 heavy bombers consisted of approximately thirty planes. The rationale for substantially increasing the number of B-29s in England and Germany was deterrence. The Soviets knew that the high-altitude, long-range superfortresses could easily reach Moscow and other targets deep within Russia and that they were the type of plane that delivered atomic bombs to Hiroshima and Nagasaki (they might not have known, however, that the B-29s sent to Germany and the UK had not been fitted to carry atomic bombs). Marshall believed that the presence of the B-29s would deter the Red Army from trying to shoot down the C-47s or otherwise prevent them from landing in Berlin. At the same time the arrival of the huge bombers at bases in England and West Germany would quickly become known to the public. There was a risk, Marshall warned Truman, that the presence of the B-29s would be regarded as a "provocative act" that might backfire and cause the Soviets to initiate hostilities. It was a delicate balance, said Marshall. Truman raised no objection.[6]

Shortly after the cabinet meeting broke up, Marshall met at the State Department with the print press and network radio reporters. It was time to try to dispel rumors about his health that had been flying around Washington. He began with a lame attempt at humor, saying he had learned, presumably through press reports and the rumor mill, that he "was supposed to be seriously ill or approaching death—I don't know which." At that point Marshall went off the record, a technique he frequently used to bring reporters into his confidence, trying to make them feel that he was about to disclose deep state or personal secrets. His so-called secret was that he had undergone a "physical examination," at "doctors' urging" that was "not yet finished," that he was going back to the hospital that afternoon, and that he would have to "report in again" during the following week. He said nothing about his enlarged kidney or the renal tumor.

A reporter interjected. "Mr. Secretary, while you are talking OFF THE RECORD . . . one report which was widely circulating was that your health had turned out to be not so good and that you were resigning because of it." Marshall's answer: "Well, I had no thought of resigning now. I felt very well when I went into the hospital and I feel very well now." He continued, reminding the press that he was still off the record. "I got out on Saturday [June 26], so I did a six-hour day out in the hot sun . . . real work, not pleasant . . . and I did the same on Sunday from nine o'clock to half past one . . . The temperature was 92. I challenge anybody after two hours to do what I was doing . . ."

"What sort of work was that?" asked another reporter. "It involved pick-ax, shovel, wheelbarrow," responded Marshall, "and I believe, some back seat driving," the last another attempt at humor.[7]

Marshall may not have flat-out lied. But he certainly didn't tell the whole truth. By the time of the press conference he knew that the doctors had recommended that the large tumor and perhaps all or part of his enlarged kidney would have to be surgically removed (though they went along with his request that the operation could be postponed so he could deal with the Berlin crisis and attend the UN meetings in Paris in the fall). On the other hand, he was probably being truthful when he said he worked hard the previous weekend in ninety-degree heat. The day of his press conference Marshall wrote Rose Page about how, like the Indians, he had buried fish heads under the corn he planted the past weekend and that "every cat in Leesburg descended on me . . . and practically dug up the foundations of the house getting at the fish heads." On "second thought," he joked to Rose, "the corn was sent to me by Henry Wallace, so perhaps the cats were after that."[8] Marshall loved to make fun of Wallace, FDR's eccentric vice president who had made millions developing hybrid corn, and was running for president that year against Truman as a far-left Independent.

* * * * *

By the second week of July the Anglo-American airlift gathered strength, delivering an average of 1,000 tons per day to the U.S. and British sectors of Berlin. General LeMay scraped together about 70 C-47s. Clay and LeMay persuaded Chief of Staff Omar Bradley and others to dispatch two groups of the newer four-engine C-54 Skymasters to airfields in West Germany. The British added Short Sunderland flying boats to their fleet of Yorks and Dakotas. It was an impressive beginning, but it was hardly enough. To sustain a population of more than two million through the winter, it was estimated that an average of about 5,000 tons of food, medicine, coal, gasoline, and other supplies would have to be landed each day.

Several top officials in Washington doubted that the airlift would work. Cornelius Vanderbilt Whitney, assistant secretary of the air force, told the NSC on July 17 that "the airlift was doomed to failure."[9] Lovett called it "unsatisfactory" and only a "temporary expedient."[10] Forrestal worried that the airlift would stall in late October when winter weather would cause flights to be canceled. Marshall disagreed. At a meeting with Truman and Forrestal in the White House on July 19 that Forrestal summarized in his diary, Marshall calmly advised the president to stay the course. If we remain firm, the Soviets will back down, he counseled, just as they had done when the administration's policies managed to contain them in Greece, France, and Italy. Forrestal reminded Marshall that available American ground forces were inadequate to defend Berlin. Marshall responded by saying that the U.S. was "much better off" than it was in 1940.[11] In his diary that night, Truman wrote that Forrestal "wants to hedge—he always does." The president agreed with Marshall. "We'll stay in Berlin—come what may," he wrote. "I don't pass the buck, nor do I alibi out of any decision I make."[12]

The July 19 meeting in the Oval Office that had begun at noon lasted less than an hour. Marshall and the others had to rush across Memorial Bridge to Arlington National Cemetery. A horse-drawn caisson bearing General Pershing's flag-draped casket was already leaving the Capitol, slowly leading a massive procession in the rain down Constitution Avenue toward Arlington. At age eighty-seven, Pershing had died at Walter Reed Army Hospital, where he had been a patient since 1941. Born less than two months before Lincoln was first elected president, "Black Jack" Pershing was Marshall's mentor, one of his closest friends. Marshall visited him regularly, sometimes weekly, during the years he lived at Walter Reed. At Pershing's request Marshall was in charge of the funeral plans—a "purely military one as Pershing had insisted."[13]

After a brief stop at the Tomb of the Unknown Soldier and an Episcopal funeral service at the Memorial Amphitheater, Marshall accompanied the procession to the gravesite on what later became known as Pershing Hill. There, as Pershing requested, the General of the Armies was buried beneath a simple white stone near the identical markers of the troops he had served with thirty years before.

Two days later Marshall publicly challenged the Soviets. At a press conference a reporter asked him to comment on "widespread fears of war" over the Berlin blockade and airlift. "We will not be coerced or intimidated in any way," he responded. ". . . I repeat again, we are not going to be coerced."[14]

* * * * *

Marshall spent the rest of the summer of 1948 working at the State Department. On weeknights he stayed in DC on Volta Place with Allen's widow, Madge, and her son Tupper. During most weekends he was out at Dodona with Katherine. By the end of August the Berlin airlift appeared to be succeeding. Each day about 1,500 flights were disgorging more than 4,500 tons of cargo in West Berlin, not quite enough to sustain Berliners through the winter but getting close to the target of 5,000 tons per day. There were snafus, accidents, and setbacks along the way, but overall it was a spectacular success, a masterful combination of logistics, teamwork, and coordination with the British.

Throughout August and into September, talks in Moscow between the three allied ambassadors and Molotov and Stalin to settle the Berlin crisis went nowhere. According to Chip Bohlen, the State Department's expert on Soviet affairs, Stalin would not lift the blockade unless the Allies agreed to "abandon the idea of forming a West German government." This was a price that the secretary and the president "would not pay."[15] Forrestal pressed both Marshall and Truman for "resolution of the question" of whether the

U.S. would use the atomic bomb if war broke out. The answer he got was conditional. The president "prayed that he would never have to make such a decision," wrote Forrestal in his diary, but said that "if it became necessary" he would not hesitate to use it.[16]

While Katherine was at Oyster Bay on Long Island with Belle Roosevelt (widow of Kermit Roosevelt, who had committed suicide), Marshall spent four days in an air-conditioned suite at Walter Reed for "the continuation of tests."[17] X-rays showed his right kidney to be pear-shaped, with a large tumor and multiple cysts. Again, there is no indication that the doctors were concerned about possible malignancy. They concluded that surgery to remove Marshall's kidney could be delayed until after he returned from the UN General Assembly meetings in Paris that were scheduled to begin in late September. He was discharged from the hospital on August 30. It is probable that around this time Marshall let Truman know that he intended to resign as secretary after the election, due in part to the need to recover from his planned operation. In a September 2 letter to actor Walter Huston, who Marshall had befriended during the war, the secretary indicated that he had an agreement with Truman that he would stay until the end of 1948.

* * * * *

At the beginning of September, with the election only two months away, pollsters and pundits had already concluded that Governor Dewey, the Republican nominee, would easily win the presidency. Elmo Roper announced that his latest poll showed Dewey with a 41 percent to 33 percent lead in the popular vote over Truman. "Only a political convulsion," he said, would keep Dewey from the White House.[18] At the Democratic convention in July, the "Dixiecrats" had walked out to protest the civil rights platform that Truman supported. The candidate of the southerners' newly formed States' Rights Party was Governor Strom Thurmond of South Carolina. Former vice president Henry Wallace was the standard-bearer for the left-leaning Progressive Party, the party of "peace and the common man." Split three ways, the Democratic coalition that elected Roosevelt four straight times was a shadow of itself.

Truman's only hope was to relentlessly attack the Republicans for the high cost of living and take his "party of the people" case directly to the voters. A crowd of a hundred thousand had turned out to see him on Labor Day in Detroit's Cadillac Square. Truman was confident that he could continue to draw tremendous crowds right up to election day if he had the time, stamina, and wherewithal to crisscross the country and talk to the people at every whistle-stop.

The only thing holding him back was money. The DNC was virtually broke, having encountered difficulty raising funds for what most Democrats regarded as a losing ticket. Seventy-seven-year-old Bernard Baruch infuriated Truman when he politely but firmly refused to help raise funds for the president's campaign. By today's standards it is hard to believe, but in early September 1948, just sixty days before the election, no one had stepped forward to chair Truman's finance committee. Finally, at the suggestion of several supporters, Truman persuaded Colonel Louis Johnson of West Virginia to serve as chairman. (As will be recalled, Johnson began an up-and-down relationship with Marshall before the war when, as FDR's assistant secretary of war, he claimed credit for promoting Marshall to deputy chief of staff.) Johnson was an experienced fund-raiser, wealthy in his own right. He immediately put his own assets on the line by signing a personal note for $100,000.

Thanks to the efforts of Johnson and other major donors, Truman's soon to be famous whistle-stop campaign began on schedule. On Friday, September 17, the *Ferdinand Magellan*, the president's 142-ton private railroad car, pulled out of Washington's cavernous Union Station, coupled at the end of a seventeen-car train. Standing on the rear platform, Truman posed for photos with vice presidential nominee Alben Barkley. "I'm going to fight hard. I'm going to give 'em hell," he reportedly said.[19] Six stops and six speeches later Truman spoke before a crowd of 75,000, mostly farmers, at the National Plowing Contest in Dexter, Iowa.

Out on the hustings Truman said little about the Berlin airlift and the possibility of war with the Soviet Union. Likewise, Dewey was largely silent. Henry Wallace, however, had a good deal to say about Truman's foreign policy. He accused the president of deliberately creating a climate of fear in the world and leading the nation toward war. Branding Truman a warmonger, Wallace denounced the Truman Doctrine, the multibillion-dollar Marshall Plan, and Marshall's pet proposal for universal military training, which had been endorsed by Truman. Albert Carr and David Noyes, two of Truman's aggressive speechwriters who were on the president's train during his whistle-stop tour, believed that Wallace's promises to deliver a "century of peace" were resonating with voters. They knew that Wallace's appeal to a significant slice of Democratic voters could cause Truman to lose the election. Carr was an economist, educated at the University of Chicago, Columbia, and the London School of Economics. Noyes was a journalist, small-town newspaper publisher, and advertising executive. Near the end of September, as the campaign train was heading back toward Washington, the two speechwriters hatched the idea for an election-winning "October surprise." Although Truman had narrowed the gap with Dewey, fifty of the most prominent newspaper editors and columnists and most everyone else who paid attention still thought he would lose. Carr and Noyes were convinced that Truman needed to make a bold move and that he needed to do it soon. As will be seen, Truman agreed to help orchestrate their explosive surprise.

*　*　*　*　*

While Truman was in the first stages of his sixteen-day whistle-stop tour, George and Katherine were settling into the American Embassy residence in Paris, courtesy of Ambassador and Mrs. Jefferson Caffrey. "We are luxuriously established and have great privacy, eating most of our meals in our sitting room," wrote Marshall to Madge.[20] The secretary and Mrs. Marshall arrived in Paris on the morning of September 20 after an overnight flight from Washington, accompanied by a young doctor assigned to monitor Marshall's health. Though Marshall was there to represent the U.S. at the third convening of the UN General Assembly and at overlapping sessions of the Security Council, he and his wife made arrangements for some private road trips. Marshall knew that this would probably be his last trip abroad as secretary of state, or perhaps ever. He and Katherine planned to relax as much as possible and enjoy their time together.

First, however, the secretary had to deal with his counterparts, Ernest Bevin and Robert Schuman, the foreign ministers of Great Britain and France. Over the past three weeks the temperature of the crisis in Berlin had risen. The secretary was at the point where he wanted to break off the fruitless talks with Stalin and Molotov aimed at ending the blockade. Since the crisis threatened the peace, he believed the issue should be submitted to the UN for debate and settlement. Bevin and Schuman insisted on a more cautious approach. They worried that a sudden break, coupled with a threat to take the matter to the UN, might provoke a shooting war. Marshall felt that yet another round of talks would send the wrong signal to the Soviets, but he could not afford to part ways with his two main allies. At a meeting at the Quai d'Orsay on September 21 with Bevin, Schuman, and their aides, Marshall was direct. The Berlin blockade was no longer the "fundamental issue," he declared. Due to the success of the airlift, "[w]e have broken the blockade." Throughout Eastern Europe, he argued, "the Russians are retreating . . . We have put Western Germany on its feet and we are engaged in bringing about its recovery in such a way that we can really say that we are on the road to victory." This was an obvious but deliberately unstated reference to the success of the European Recovery Program, the so-called Marshall Plan. Stand firm with me, Marshall pleaded. We have them on the run.

Bevin and Schuman were still not persuaded. They insisted on making one more "approach to the Russians" with the hope of achieving a settlement.[21] Marshall had no choice but to accede. However, he extracted a concession. If the Soviet reply was not satisfactory, the British and French governments would agree, along with the U.S., to submit the Berlin matter to the UN Security Council. As expected, the Soviet reply was unsatisfactory. In identical letters delivered to the UN secretary general on September 29, Marshall, Bevin, and Schuman requested an early meeting of the Security Council. By a vote of 9 to 2, with the Soviet Union and Ukraine voting no, the Berlin question was placed on the Security Council agenda (because it was a procedural matter, it could not be vetoed).

Meanwhile, during one of the free moments at the end of September, probably when Truman's campaign train was in Kentucky or West Virginia on the way back to Washington, the two speechwriters, Carr and Noyes, huddled with Matt Connelly, Truman's appointments secretary. They had a daring and unorthodox idea that could swing the election in the president's favor. The president, they recommended, should announce via nationwide radio broadcast that he was sending Chief Justice Fred Vinson to Moscow to meet face-to-face with Joseph Stalin. And he should say to the American people that the purpose of the mission is to persuade the Soviet Union (and show the world) that the United States would spare no effort to achieve peace. The speech and the mission, they told Connelly, would convince Wallace-leaning voters that the president was committed to peace, calm fears that the Berlin crisis would result in war, and demonstrate that Truman was the commander in chief best able to deal with Soviet aggression.

Connelly passed the Carr/Noyes idea on to Truman who, according to Clifford, liked it "from the moment he heard it."[22] Three years earlier Truman had sent Harry Hopkins to meet face-to-face with Stalin. Since Hopkins succeeded in easing tensions, albeit briefly, Truman thought Vinson stood a good chance of achieving a breakthrough as well. On Sunday, October 3, the president asked Vinson to drop by the White House for a talk. When Truman explained what he had in mind, it left Vinson breathless. In the first place, as he reminded Truman, he was chief justice of the Supreme Court, bound by his personal code of ethics to confine himself to matters relating to the court and to steer clear of politics, particularly in an election year. Moreover, he had no background in Soviet affairs and diplomacy and little knowledge of the Berlin crisis. No one knows for sure what Truman said, but by the end of the day Vinson agreed to go to Moscow, perhaps having been ordered by his old friend the president. As soon as the chief justice left, Truman instructed Charlie Ross, his press secretary, to arrange for the radio networks to set aside a half hour on the evening of October 5 "for a public statement of major importance."[23]

Incredibly, it was not until the morning of Truman's proposed address to the nation that the White House notified the State Department of its plans. Bob Lovett, who was in his Foggy Bottom office, was the first to get the word. A teletype message from one of Truman's aides asked Lovett to review and comment on a draft letter from Truman to Stalin explaining the purpose of Vinson's mission and to make arrangements with the Kremlin for Stalin to meet with Vinson. As Lovett recounted later, he immediately "picked up the White House phone" and said, "'Mr. President I've got to see you right away, urgent.'" For the first and only time, said Lovett, he asked his driver to turn on the "red light" mounted atop the car roof, activate "the siren," and get him to the White House as fast as he could.[24]

According to Lovett, as soon as the president received him that morning, he bluntly declared that what Truman was proposing was "utterly impossible." When Truman asked him to explain, Lovett told him that if he went ahead with the Vinson mission, it would undermine Marshall's efforts to reach a solution to the Berlin crisis via the UN, alienate the British and French governments, and might precipitate Marshall's resignation. Perhaps for the first time Truman understood and appreciated at least some of the diplomatic machinations in Paris that Marshall was overseeing. He concluded that Lovett was right. He told Charlie Ross to cancel the airtime that he had arranged with the radio networks.

Before he knew for sure that the Vinson mission was canceled, Lovett either telephoned Marshall or radioed a message to the embassy in Paris alerting the secretary and his aide, Marshall Carter, of what the president was proposing. Marshall and Carter went to the embassy's communications center, where they read the same messages that caused Lovett to race to the White House. As Carter recalled to his interviewer, like a "good staff officer" he began writing a reply that Marshall could send to the president. His first sentence began "Never in the history of diplomatic negotiations in the United States has a more fatal proposition been proposed for the peace of the world . . ." Marshall took "one look" at Carter's draft reply, "threw it aside," and wrote down his own reply. It said, as Carter recalled, "I understand what's worrying you Mr. President and I am coming home immediately."[25]

There are few moments in Marshall's long career that could match the magnanimity that he revealed in this simple message. He could have expressed resentment and outrage, in accordance with Carter's suggestion. He could have threatened to resign, as Lovett warned. Instead, he was forgiving. He thought not about himself but about all of the burdens, domestic and foreign, that Truman was shouldering as he struggled against all odds to win the presidency in his own right. George Marshall was generous, "a great-souled man."[26]

In addition to informing Truman that he would be returning to Washington, Marshall explained during a teletype conference on October 5 the reasons why he opposed the Vinson mission. Truman assured him that the mission had been or would be canceled. It was decided that the president would send his own plane, the *Independence*, to pick Marshall up in Paris and bring him to Washington on the weekend of October 9.

If the Vinson mission had been launched as planned, the term "October surprise" might have entered the political lexicon in 1948. According to *New York Times* language expert William Safire, the term was not coined until twenty years later when William Casey, then a Nixon aide, mused that President Lyndon Johnson might pull off an "October surprise" by agreeing to a last-minute Vietnam peace deal in order to give Hubert Humphrey a leg up in the presidential race against Nixon.

While Marshall was flying to the U.S. capital and Katherine was touring the "Normandy landings," the tale of the botched Vinson mission was leaked, possibly by one of the radio networks that had been asked to air (and then cancel) the president's announcement.[27] The press had a field day, accusing Truman of staging a desperate election-eve gambit that had to be aborted when Marshall found out about it. Rumors ran rampant that Marshall was coming home to resign as secretary of state. In his memoir, Clifford, who claimed that he had opposed the Vinson mission, wrote that "it was the worst mistake of the Truman campaign."[28] Fortunately, however, Dewey did not exploit the blunder, apparently confident that he was far ahead and would easily win the election.

Truman greeted Marshall at National Airport when he landed shortly after ten a.m. on Saturday, October 9. Marshall and Lovett met with Truman in the Oval Office at eleven and again at three in the President's Study. To the president Marshall presented an overview of the Berlin crisis as well as the Security Council proceedings, and a broader analysis of the state of U.S.-Soviet relations. He explained in some detail why he opposed the Vinson mission. He graciously apologized for not keeping Truman better informed and took some of the blame for contributing to the president's belief that a direct approach to Stalin, such as the Vinson mission, was more likely to achieve results than the multilateral efforts being pursued at the UN by Marshall and his British and French allies. Contrary to some press reports Marshall did not offer his resignation, although he may have reiterated his plan to step down after the election.

At 5:45 that afternoon, Marshall gave a press and radio news conference, the apparent purpose of which was to dispel rumors and press reports that there was a growing rift between him and the president on U.S. foreign policy, particularly the Berlin crisis and other matters before the UN. "There is no foundation" for these claims, he said. "Such statements can do no good and they certainly can do a great deal of harm and I deplore them." Going off the record, as was his wont, Marshall told the reporters that he doubted they even vaguely appreciated the "red hot" tension that pervaded the UN meetings in Paris and the "delicacy of the situation."[29]

The day before Marshall returned to Paris, he demonstrated what Chip Bohlen called "his great human qualities." While meeting with Beetle Smith at the State Department the secretary heard that Bohlen's two-year-old son, Charlie, was in the building with the woman who was taking care of him while Bohlen and his wife were in Paris. Sensitive to the fact that the Bohlens had not seen their son in several weeks, Marshall arranged for a State Department photographer to take a snapshot of Charlie sitting on the secretary's knee. As soon as Marshall returned to Paris he handed the photo to the Bohlens. According to Chip, he said, "This is how Charlie looked yesterday."[30]

The Berlin blockade was eventually resolved not at the UN but by the success of the massive airlift conceived and managed by the U.S. and Great Britain. After Marshall returned to Paris, a resolution proposed by "neutral powers" aimed at resolving the crisis was debated at the Security Council. This resolution, supported by the United States, the UK, and France, was put to a vote on October 25. It received nine affirmative votes, but was vetoed by the Soviet Union.[31] In 1949, after Marshall resigned as secretary of state, Stalin began to realize that the blockade was doing the Soviets more harm than good. His regime was viewed by the world as heartless and the blockade as feckless. The airlift made a laughingstock of the Red Army's attempt to strangle the city. Stalin signaled that he was willing to negotiate. The four powers began talks in April. The Soviet blockade ended on May 12, 1949, almost a year after it began. When they heard the news, Chip Bohlen and Dean Acheson, Marshall's successor as secretary of state, broke out a bottle of champagne.

*　*　*　*　*

Following passage in June of the Vandenberg Resolution, which authorized the U.S. to enter into self-defense alliances, Marshall assigned Undersecretary Lovett to conduct "top secret exploratory talks" in Washington with representatives of Britain, France, Canada, Belgium, and the Netherlands concerning, among other things, "estimates of Soviet intentions" and an association by the U.S. with existing "European security arrangements" (meaning the so-called Brussels Treaty between the UK, France, Belgium, the Netherlands, and Luxembourg that Marshall had lent his encouragement and support to in March).[32] Over the summer and into September, Lovett's group put together an outline and guiding principles for a North Atlantic mutual security agreement.

Marshall was kept apprised of these developments by Lovett. Within a day or two after returning to Paris from his weekend in Washington, Marshall tasked himself with the job of persuading additional Scandinavian members to join the proposed North Atlantic alliance. On October 13, he sat down with Foreign Minister Bo Undén of Sweden. As recorded in the minutes, Marshall's arguments to Undén reveal his perception of the existential threat posed by the Soviet Union and why he believed a strong alliance to meet the threat was necessary. He said that because the Soviet Union was "utterly ruthless and devoid of all human decencies," the Swedish people and those throughout the rest of the world were confronted with the prospect of being ruled against their will by a "police state." The key to stopping this "ruthless force," he argued, was unified "military assistance," just as a unified approach by the Western European states was essential to the success of the European Recovery Program.[33] To put it another way, Marshall was arguing that because of the Soviet threat a North American military alliance was a necessary complement to the economic recovery of Western Europe.

By the end of October the five nations that had signed the Brussels Treaty agreed in principle to negotiate a North Atlantic pact with the United States and Canada. They proposed that talks take place in Washington on a date set by the U.S. In light of the elections on November 2, everyone understood that negotiations would not begin until a new Congress was convened and a new president—either Truman or, more likely, Dewey—was inaugurated. Because Marshall officially stepped down in January, he did not oversee the negotiations or participate in the deliberations leading to approval of the North Atlantic Treaty and the formation of NATO in 1949.

Late in life Marshall claimed, with an uncharacteristic lack of modesty, a large slice of credit for the origination of NATO. In 1956, three years before his death, Marshall told his interviewer, "I started NATO, actually, from the first jump."[34] Actually, the "first jump" toward NATO was a general suggestion by British foreign secretary Ernest Bevin to Marshall on December 17, 1947, as to which Marshall, according to the minutes of their conversation, gave only mild encouragement and did not affirmatively support.[35] It was not until March 1948 that Marshall, at Bevin's urging, seized on the idea of a North Atlantic military alliance. From that time forward, he was a strong proponent of NATO. "I got every living soul," Marshall recalled, "one after the other, in [sic] talk to me personally on the thing [NATO] and to get them stirred up to do this business."[36]

*   *   *   *   *

For George and Katherine, the side trips during the nine weeks they were headquartered at the embassy in Paris were memorable. On the first weekend in October they drove out to see the northernmost Meuse-Argonne battlefields, "a glorious trip," wrote Katherine. "He wanted to show it all to me. I never saw anyone enjoy a trip more."[37] The highlight was a return on a peaceful Sunday morning to Gondrecourt, where then captain Marshall had lived for six gloomy months during the Great War with a family headed by Madame Jouatte, who Marshall described in his World War I memoir as "a rather homely, vigorous French woman of forty-five years," and her husband, "a little weazened fellow, who looked like a scoundrel—and later proved to be one." While billeted through the winter of 1917–18 in a tiny room on the second floor with a "Napoleonic type bed" and eating downstairs with three other messmates (one of whom was the son of Victor Hugo), Marshall and Mme. Jouatte formed a close friendship. He was endeared to her and she to him.[38] They kept in touch by occasional letters, but had not seen one another in thirty years. George and Katherine arrived unannounced in the square in front of her house. He stepped out of the car. "She came out of her doorway in an old wrapper and carpet slippers," recalled Marshall. When she recognized him, "she dashed at me and threw her arms around my neck and kissed me on both cheeks. So I embraced her and I kissed her, and we had a great scene out there with all the people in the square cheering."[39] Katherine wrote that Mme. Jouatte kept saying, "Mon dieu, it can't be, it can't be."[40] Marshall described it as "a very affecting meeting," a phrase which for him meant freighted with emotion.[41]

There were other enjoyable side trips in the fall of 1948—a two-day jaunt to the Picardy region and another to London that included lunch with the Churchills—but the one that meant the most to Katherine was the trip to Italy. On the afternoon of October 18, Marshall asked the pilot of the Sacred Cow, FDR's old plane with its broad picture window, to fly low over Monte Cassino, up the Liri Valley, over the hills to Anzio, and then into Rome. As they flew, George pointed out and described for Katherine the places where Allen lived and fought. Early the next morning the two of them drove south to the Alban Hills for a twenty- or thirty-minute audience with Pope Pius XII at his summer residence, Castel Gandolfo. Interestingly, Marshall brought up the atomic bomb, its value as a deterrent to Soviet aggression (the Russians did not yet have a serviceable atomic bomb), and the fact that Truman had the sole responsibility for deciding whether to actually use it. Marshall expected that the pope might comment on the morality of using this awesomely powerful weapon to instantly incinerate hundreds of thousands of human beings. However, the pope said nothing. In fact, according to Marshall's memorandum of the conversation, he "seemed to indicate general approval" of all that Marshall said. Turning to Katherine, the pope expressed condolences with respect to the death of her son. In a letter to Madge (Allen's widow) about their papal audience Marshall wrote that when the pope "learned that Allen had been killed in the approach to the town and hill on which the [Castel Gondolfo] is located he was very impressive in his attitude and statements to her."[42]

After their audience, George and Katherine motored south, stopped for a time at the approximate place where Allen was killed, and continued down into Anzio. In his letter to Madge, Marshall wrote that the town had been "rehabilitated into a lovely sea side resort," though the "cemetery was in a state of reconstruction . . . but not too bad in appearance."[43] Marshall, of course, had already been to Allen's gravesite, but Katherine had not. He knew how emotional it would be for her to see the marker bearing the name "Allen Tupper Brown," the sweet boy she called Beau. And he knew that she was still considering whether to have Allen's remains disinterred and brought back to Dodona, where he had nailed the horseshoe points down, then up, the evening before going off to war.

A few years later Katherine described what she saw and felt when she approached Allen's grave. "As I knelt down to place a wreath, two soldiers stood beside me. They laid a blanket of roses over his grave . . . I felt resigned for the first time that he should remain so far from the land he loved. It seems to me that it was as it should be. I felt that his last resting place should be with his comrades where his life had counted the most, for they had given a country liberty and a people freedom."[44]

* * * * *

Back in Paris, the UN General Assembly reconvened at the Palais de Chaillot. Secretary Marshall spent hours sitting in plenary sessions with plenty of downtime to write letters to Madge and his sister. When not at the General Assembly, he met with Bevin, Schuman, and Shertok and sent messages to Lovett concerning the Berlin crisis, UN truce resolutions designed to stop the fighting in Palestine, and whether Italy would decide to join the North American security pact. Marshall and the other U.S. delegates to the UN were careful to avoid saying or doing anything that might tip the elections in America one way or the other. Truman's aides in the White House, as well as Dewey's team in Albany, were keeping close watch over developments in Paris.

A photograph of Marshall, UN ambassador Warren Austin, and Republican delegate John Foster Dulles, taken in Paris the day after the election, shows them sitting around a radio listening to the election returns. The photo op must have taken place in the morning because Dulles looks elated, no doubt believing that Dewey was on the verge of victory and that he would become the next secretary of state. When Dewey conceded the race to Truman at 11:14 a.m. East Coast time it was late afternoon in Paris. By then, the expression on Dulles's face was anything but elated.

Truman's come-from-behind victory in 1948 was astonishing, arguably the most surprising in the history of presidential politics. Donald Trump's narrow electoral win in 2016, though shocking to many, was not as surprising as Truman's. In the days leading up to Trump's election, virtually all pollsters concluded that Hillary Clinton's margin of victory had narrowed considerably and that it was almost a dead heat. By contrast, in Truman's case none of the experts predicted that he had come close enough in popular or electoral votes in the final days to actually pull off a win, particularly because the Democratic party was split three ways.

As it turned out, Truman was victorious in 28 states with a total of 303 electoral votes, three less than Trump, while Dewey carried 16 states, Thurmond captured 4 southern states, and Wallace did not win a single state. If it is true, as many suspected, that Truman recognized Israel in order to garner New York's 47 electoral votes, the strategy failed. Though he came very close, the president lost New York because of Wallace's strong showing, which enabled Dewey to score a narrow victory. Clark Clifford commented later that it was a "mistake" for Truman not to spend more time in New York.[45]

The next day Marshall wrote Truman that he "put over the greatest one man fight in American history. You did exactly what you told me and what nobody else believed possible."[46] It is evident from this telegram that Marshall had great respect for Truman's courage and political acumen. It is also apparent that by this time he had set aside his misgivings about Truman's integrity that had spilled out during the angry confrontation in May when he accused the president of choosing to recognize Israel for domestic political reasons—that is, the Jewish vote. Did this mean that Marshall came to believe that Truman was right to immediately recognize Israel on May 15? It's possible. After all, five months had gone by and all efforts to end the fighting had failed. Marshall might have decided that truce or trusteeship was never in the cards. Or he could have taken the long view, concluding that the country was simply better off with Truman as president. Perhaps he came down from his high horse of righteousness, persuaded that there are times when political expediency is excusable in order to achieve an objective that best serves the national interest.

Given Marshall's unpleasant encounters with Dewey in 1944, he was clearly pleased that Truman won the presidency. But from a personal standpoint the fact that the Democrats recaptured both houses of Congress—with fifty-four seats in the Senate and an overwhelming majority in the House—was even better news. Up until the election Truman counted on Marshall's reputation as a nonpartisan to steer matters through the Republican-dominated Congress. Now his presence in the Truman administration was nowhere near as important. He could retire as secretary of state without feeling that he was letting the president down.

Truman had other ideas. Marshall thought he had an understanding with the president that he would not resist his resignation. However, on November 6, in the second sentence of a letter to Marshall thanking him for his congratulatory telegram, Truman wrote, "Please don't go out on a limb about the future until you and I can have a heart to heart conversation. I have some things in mind that need your advice and judgement."[47] Marshall claimed that he did not receive Truman's letter until November 13. In the meantime, he made a remark at a press conference in Paris suggesting that he was sticking to "his original intention to resign from the Cabinet by January 20." The day he received Truman's letter about not going out on a limb, he issued a press release saying that he was misinterpreted. "I would never take a decision of this nature without discussing it with the president," said the release. The concluding clause—"and he and I have never discussed the matter"—was almost certainly untrue.[48]

While Marshall wasn't sure what the president had in mind for him, he told Truman that he would be returning home to Washington on November 22. And he went ahead with plans for surgery to have his diseased kidney removed at Walter Reed shortly after Thanksgiving. In a letter to

Madge, Marshall wrote that the operation would either give him a "permanent 'out,'" with the hope that his successor would be named in December,
or at least "a pleasant period of convalescence" before having to return to
Paris as secretary of state or whatever else the president wanted him to do.
"My future plans remain in doubt," he lamented.[49]

Truman was waiting at National Airport when the Sacred Cow landed on
the Monday of Thanksgiving week. Katherine went directly out to Leesburg,
while George rode with the president across the Potomac to the White
House. At some point during the next three days, Truman must have had the
"heart to heart" talk about Marshall's future that he had insisted upon. But
there is no contemporaneous record of whether he pressed Marshall to stay
on as secretary or to accept another post and how Marshall reacted. All that
is known is that Marshall spent nights at Walter Reed so the doctors could
conduct tests and examinations in preparation for his kidney operation and
that he was terribly busy, "the busiest [time]," he told reporters on Wednesday, that he had "ever had in Washington."[50] On Thanksgiving Day, he took
a break with Katherine. They traveled in a private car of the Southern Railway to Roanoke, where Katherine had attended Hollins College. There they
saw VMI beat VPI (predecessor of Virginia Tech) in football. In a letter to his
sister, Marshall proudly wrote that he had played for VMI (left tackle) against
VPI "on Thanksgiving Day forty-eight years ago—and we won."[51]

Four days before his operation Marshall received a distinguished visitor
in his suite at Walter Reed: Madame Chiang Kai-shek, wrapped against the
cold in her beaver coat. During the year since he last saw her the military
situation of the Nationalists had deteriorated. The Communists controlled
much of the north and west. In the last four months they had seized 75 percent of Chiang's U.S.-financed weapons and neutralized half of his fighting
forces. Communist armies had swept south and were approaching Nanking.
American Embassy personnel in the capital were beginning to leave. Marshall was under the impression that more than thirty Nationalist divisions
had surrendered to the Communists. It was only a matter of a few weeks
before Mao Zedong would rule all of China north of the Yangtze.

As far as Madame and the Generalissimo were concerned, the political
landscape in America had also deteriorated. They had hoped that Dewey
would win and that the Republicans would retain control of Congress. Indeed, through Madame's brother-in-law, H. H. Kung, it was believed that

the Nationalists contributed $2 million to the Dewey campaign. With the sweeping defeat of the Republicans, the odds of getting additional support and military aid from the U.S. had worsened. Truman had already declined to act on the Generalissimo's plea for aid. And he refused to invite Chiang to come to Washington to make his case in person. His wife took it upon herself to make an unofficial visit.

Marshall knew that Madame Chiang had come to his hospital room to make a desperate appeal for aid on behalf of her husband. Premised on the argument that if Communism prevailed in China, the rest of the Asian states would follow like cascading dominoes, Madame quickly got to the point. She asked that the White House issue a statement of support for the Nationalist government in its fight against Communism in the Far East; that the U.S. send a "spark plug" in the person of an outstanding American general to take control of the war against Mao; and that it provide upward of $1 billion of emergency aid for each of the next three years, plus military advisers. Marshall listened politely, showing (or more likely feigning) sympathy and concern. But he was far from encouraging. Marshall told Madame that Truman had already ruled out making a public statement of support for the Nationalists because it "would have to be so watered down that it would do more harm than good." Referencing his "own experiences" in China, Marshall said that the idea of sending a prominent U.S. general to run the war against the Communists was a nonstarter because such a person would have to virtually take "over the Chinese Government."[52] Finally, there was little chance, he told her, that a Congress controlled by the Democrats would pass a substantially increased economic aid package, let alone one that came remotely close to $3 billion over three years.

After four hours of discussion, Mayling returned empty-handed to Dodona. At Katherine's invitation, she lived there as a houseguest along with her two secretaries for the next month while lobbying Marshall and sympathetic members of Congress and waiting for an invitation to meet with Truman. The two women had become fast friends when they spent the summer and fall of 1946 together on the mountaintop at Kuling. They had remained in touch by letter after Katherine and George left China in early 1947.

The operation went well, reported Colonel Clifford Kimbrough, the surgeon who removed Marshall's right kidney on December 7. Half of his enlarged kidney was found to be "occupied and destroyed by cysts" and "there was no evidence of malignancy."[53] A week later, he was still not up and walking. In a letter to his sister, Marshall remarked that his convalescence was satisfactory, but "a rather painful business at times." He seemed more concerned about the strain on Katherine, who felt the need to visit him at the hospital every other day while looking after Madame Chiang and also suffering from painful shingles. Katherine "always does get the short end of the deals," he wrote.[54]

To cheer George up, Mayling wrote him a mock battlefield report from the "Dodona front." Addressing Marshall as "General Flicker," his boyhood nickname that suggested fecklessness, she accused him of "lolling in 'silken sheets'" while she was forced to dig "trenches" in the garden and spend "harrowing hours" doing "kitchen duty" under the "Deputy Commander," who Marshall knew from years of experience was his wife.[55]

Madame Chiang's last conversation with Secretary Marshall was dead serious. It took place three weeks after his operation when he was still at Walter Reed. By that time Marshall knew that Madame had already met with the president at Blair House and that Truman had promised her nothing. Marshall was prepared for a desperate gambit. She didn't disappoint. Madame told Marshall that she had just received a message from her husband. Unless American aid was promised immediately, the message said, the Generalissimo was going to "step aside" and make way for members of his government to negotiate "peace with the Communists" through the offices of the Soviet Union. Marshall calmly explained that while he was recovering from surgery he was not "officiating" as secretary of state.[56] If she wanted Chiang's message and any of her other requests to be given serious consideration she should make sure they were all in writing and delivered to Bob Lovett.

That afternoon, December 27, Madame Chiang met with Lovett. She showed him her husband's message and handed him a memo setting forth her requests for U.S. support. Lovett agreed to discuss the Generalissimo's message and her requests with Truman. Otherwise, he made no commitments. Neither the president nor Marshall, in his official capacity, met with her again. In early January, Madame left Washington for her brother-in-law's estate in Riverdale, New York. Her plan was to try to mobilize pro-Chiang support in the U.S. by appealing to journalists, sympathetic politicians, members of the military, and church leaders—the so-called China Lobby. She would never return to her native land.

On January 21, Chiang resigned as president, though he held on to the essential reins of power by remaining head of the KMT (the Nationalist political party) and commander in chief of the armed forces. He was obviously hedging his bets. Chiang retreated to his ancestral village south of Shanghai, telling his wife he needed a rest. The Nationalist government, under acting president Li Zongren, moved from Nanking south to Canton.

Marshall was released from the hospital near the end of December. He and Katherine immediately flew to Pinehurst. His letter of resignation was reluctantly accepted by the president. "I had hoped," wrote Truman, "that with medical treatment and rest and recuperation you could continue in office. I am, however, unwilling to assume the responsibility of further jeopardizing your health."[57] At a press conference on January 7, Truman announced the resignations of both Marshall and Lovett and the appointments of Dean Acheson as secretary of state and James Webb as undersecretary, all effective on January 20, 1949.

Acheson, who had served for six months as Marshall's undersecretary and was about to be his successor, paid tribute to Marshall as only he could. "To say what makes greatness is very difficult," he wrote. "But when one is close to it one knows. Twice in my life it has happened to me. Once with Justice Holmes and once with you. Greatness is a quality of character and is not the result of circumstances. It has to do with grandeur and with completeness of character."[58]

* * * * *

Marshall's convalescence was unexpectedly slow and painful. A press photograph taken at Pinehurst on January 7, the day Truman announced Marshall's resignation, shows him standing unsteadily, his face much thinner and his buttoned suit coat looking two to three sizes too large. As he remarked in a letter to Madge, his "feeble appearance" was accentuated by the fact that he was gripping a wooden cane.[59] For almost three months, as Marshall recuperated at Pinehurst, on the beach in Puerto Rico, and at a guesthouse in New Orleans owned by his VMI roommate, he complained of painful swelling on his right side—"about six inches"—which Dr. Kimbrough assured him was "normal anticipated neuritis of the twelfth nerve."[60]

In Washington, as Inauguration Day approached, the president laid the groundwork for another change in his cabinet that would have fateful consequences for Marshall—but not until the summer of 1950. Truman had come to the conclusion that James Forrestal, the nation's first secretary of defense, had to be replaced because, as he wrote several months later, "Forrestal was cracking up under the pressure of reorganizing the defense departments."[61] A year and a half earlier the National Security Act of 1947 abolished the old War and Navy Departments and merged their functions and responsibilities—army, navy, and air force, each with a separate secretary—into a single umbrella entity. Given the grand title "Secretary of Defense," Forrestal's job was to manage the reorganization and unify the formerly separate branches of the nation's armed services. This turned out to be an almost impossible task because the legislation deprived him of chain-of-command authority over the secretaries of the three branches, who were permitted to report directly to the president. Forrestal's logical replacement was big, bald Louis Johnson. Unlike Forrestal, he was decisive, tough-minded, and mean, qualities that Truman believed were needed to get the unification job done and to help him cut the defense budget. As assistant secretary of war under FDR, Johnson had extensive experience managing military brass. Having just finished raising the money that enabled Truman to win the election, Johnson made it known personally and through White House surrogates and reporters that he badly wanted the job.

According to Forrestal's biographers, Truman told Forrestal in a private talk on January 11 that he planned to replace him and nominate Johnson as secretary of defense. Forrestal was devastated. The next afternoon, Truman made a surprise visit to Pinehurst. It is likely that Truman asked Marshall's advice about the appointment of Johnson, though there is no record of what they actually discussed. A week later Truman and Johnson agreed that the change would not be announced until around the first of March. Johnson needed time to familiarize himself with the duties of the defense secretary and to sever his ties with Convair, an aircraft manufacturer that was trying to sell B-36 bombers to the government.

Scarcely three months later, Forrestal shocked the nation when he tried to hang himself and then fell to his death from the top floor of Bethesda Naval Hospital, where he had been hospitalized for severe mental illness. Moments before his death he was copying Sophocles's poem "The Chorus from Ajax," in which Ajax, forlorn and "[w]orn by the waste of time," contemplates suicide.[62] At Arlington National Cemetery, Marshall served as one of James Forrestal's honorary pallbearers.

When Marshall heard or read in early March that the president had actually decided to nominate Johnson as secretary of defense, he included a handwritten note to Johnson in an envelope sent to his secretary, Sally Chamberlin. The note to Johnson that Chamberlin typed up and sent out under Marshall's name was eerily prophetic. "Congratulations on your appointment," it began. Recalling his experiences with Johnson when he was assistant secretary of war, Marshall wrote, "I have always felt . . . that you produced much needed aggressive action along with an unusually clear understanding of what was needed. I felt then and still think that you would have been one of the great outstanding figures of the war years *if you had confined yourself to the job* . . . I have an earnest hope that you will give the country what is so urgently needed [italics added]."[63] This was a blunt warning that Johnson should not use the secretary of defense post as a stepping-stone to the presidency, a political ambition that Johnson was known to have harbored ever since Roosevelt passed over him to nominate Stimson as secretary of war in 1940.

Unfortunately for Johnson, his ambition rendered him incapable of following Marshall's advice. As a consequence, duty would eventually call Marshall back into his third shooting war.

* * * * *

Sometime in early March, recalled Marshall, the president "brought up the subject" again.[64] The "subject" was whether Marshall would be willing to take over the presidency of the American National Red Cross, an appointment that Truman was empowered to make. Basil O'Connor, Roosevelt's close friend who helped establish the Warm Springs foundation, had headed the Red Cross since 1944. After the war, hundreds of volunteers throughout the U.S. who ran the local chapters and did the fieldwork began complaining about the small number of elites that actually governed the Red Cross and O'Connor's imperious management of the vast organization. In 1947, Congress responded by expanding the size of the governing board and requiring, among other reforms, that 60 percent of its members be elected by chapters and blood service regions. As a result of those reforms, the leadership of the Red Cross was broadened and those who labored in the hinterlands were given a greater voice in policy making and governance. However,

O'Connor hung on as president, continuing to maintain a tight grip on the millions contributed to the Red Cross and deciding how the funds were spent. When he traveled it was always first-class, surrounded by aides as if he were a four-star general.

Truman was anxious to make a change. In light of Marshall's support of the Red Cross during the war, his effectiveness in selling the Marshall Plan, and his stature in America, Truman believed Marshall was the perfect choice to tamp down dissension and restore morale among the ranks of the Red Cross volunteers.

"I told the President," wrote Marshall, "that I appreciated the compliment he was paying me and that Mrs. Marshall and I would talk the matter over as we had done four years before." (Truman first mentioned the Red Cross post as a possibility in November 1945, a few days before Marshall retired as army chief of staff.) George and Katherine talked it through. Both agreed that the Red Cross was "a great humanitarian organization" and that if Marshall were to take on any active engagement following his recuperation, the presidency of the Red Cross "was by far the most satisfying opportunity."[65] Marshall credited Katherine with making the final decision. Sitting on boards and commissions was not enough, she reasoned. He needed to be active and he needed a new challenge. She knew her man.

By letter dated March 15, Marshall told Truman he was prepared to accept the Red Cross appointment as early as May 1, or "whatever later date meets your convenience."[66] Truman did not respond. Six weeks later, Marshall begged off a request by the Episcopal Bishop of Washington that he become trustee of the National Cathedral, writing, "I probably will be appointed head of the American Red Cross in the near future."[67] Still no word came from the White House about the appointment. George and Katherine finalized plans to vacation for the month of August at a "camp" formerly owned by J. P. Morgan (renamed "Camp Uncas") on Racquette Lake in the Adirondacks. Katherine had invited Madame Chiang to join them there.

Why the delay? Most likely because O'Connor wanted to mark his departure by making a splash at the annual Red Cross convention in Atlanta that was not held until the end of June. The theme of his keynote speech at the convention was an enthusiastic yes to the rhetorical question that served as the title of his address: "Can the Red Cross Survive?"[68] If it were not for the record-breaking summertime outbreak of polio that demanded

O'Connor's full-time attention to his other vocation, fund-raising for the National Foundation for Infantile Paralysis (the March of Dimes), he might have continued to resist the not-too-subtle hints coming from the White House that it was time to step down. As it was, he finally submitted his resignation in September, which allowed Truman to appoint Marshall to replace him, effective October 1, 1949.

The press releases announcing Marshall's appointment were completely overshadowed by two developments that shifted the global balance of power and to this day have posed a threat to U.S. security. On September 23, Charlie Ross called the press corps into the Blair House briefing room and distributed a mimeographed statement from the president. (Due to reconstruction of the White House, Truman and his staff had moved into nearby Blair House on Jackson Square.) The words that jumped out were "We have evidence that in recent weeks an atomic explosion occurred in the USSR."[69] Truman didn't use the word "bomb," but everyone knew that the U.S. no longer had a monopoly on atomic bombs. *Newsweek* called it "the biggest news since the close of the Second World War."[70] Seven days later, in Tiananmen Square, Mao Zedong climbed the stone steps of the Gate of Heavenly Peace. To the crowd of revolutionaries below, including one of Madame Chiang's sisters, who defied her family, Mao announced that "the People's War of Liberation has been basically won ... This government is the sole legal government representing all the people of the People's Republic of China."[71]

*   *   *   *   *

In Washington, across from the Ellipse, a crowd of staffers gathered around the entrance to the white marble headquarters of the American Red Cross. They sighted the general's car as it came down 17th Street and slowed to a stop. Marshall stepped out, followed by O'Connor and James Nicholson, the executive vice president and general manager of the Red Cross. The general was tanned and relaxed, every strand of his whitening hair brushed and shining. His face broke into a broad smile as he briskly ascended the steps under the temple portico. Inside the building he was greeted with applause and the popping of flashbulbs. At the top of the landing leading to his second-floor office he quieted the crowd and simply said "Thank you" two or three times.[72]

Marshall went right to work. During the first three weeks he learned that the American Red Cross was actually a network of 3,700 local chapters and about two dozen blood service regions. The organization was originally founded in 1881 by Clara Barton. Its post–World War II mission was to provide domestic and international disaster relief, furnish various forms of support to the U.S. military, operate a national blood program, and render emergency relief abroad pursuant to the dictates of the Geneva Convention. In 1949-50, the Red Cross had about 5,000 employees, though the bulk of its work and its successes or failures were largely dependent on the services of tens of thousands of volunteers. Most of its financial support came from voluntary contributions by citizens and foundations and from cost-recovery charges for services, such as the provision of blood and blood products and health and safety training courses.

The general's first move in his new job was a highly publicized cross-country "listening trip" with the aim of restoring morale among the volunteers and employees. On the morning of October 24, Marshall, along with two top officials of the Red Cross, departed National Airport in a converted Martin B-26 bomber. For the next six days he visited 15 cities, discussed Red Cross plans with the heads of 158 chapters, shook hands and broke bread with hundreds of employees and volunteers, and held press conferences at every stop. Several news articles expressed surprise at Marshall's vigor—"the bounce in his step" that "left local Red Cross personnel and civic leaders spinning in their tracks."[73] At meetings with the chapter leaders, Marshall encouraged them to speak openly about their concerns. He listened and learned.

By all accounts, Marshall's coast-to-coast blitz in October 1949 and another flying trip in 1950 (30,000 miles from mid-January to early March) were public relations successes. They boosted the morale of the volunteers, employees, and chapter leaders. Moreover, they provided platforms for Marshall to promote the value of the Red Cross and to respond to complaints from the media and servicemen about some of its shortcomings (e.g., delays in responding to disasters; charging servicemen for food, lodging, and donated cigarettes; breakdowns in providing overseas telephone services to servicemen).

During trips around the country and in nationwide radio addresses, Marshall used his bully pulpit as president to propose improvements in the operations and services of the Red Cross. For example, in speeches and articles aimed at chapter heads, Marshall pressed for a "much stronger volunteer effort" to recruit volunteers from the ranks of the Junior Red Cross (19 million members) and from the large pool of "young women" who he said represented "greatest potential for vigorous and enthusiastic action in the whole Red Cross scene."[74] Marshall told an American Legion audience that the Red Cross could and would do more to assist the Veterans Administration by visiting and counseling "mentally disturbed" veterans.[75] And he cautioned chapters against weakening their fund-raising efforts and the "national status of the Red Cross" by partnering with local organizations like "community chests."[76] Yet there is no evidence that programs were instituted to accomplish any of these objectives. Nor is there a basis for claims made by two of Marshall's biographers that he "put reforms in place" to "broaden the organization's leadership" and "untangle overcomplicated lines of authority."[77] The reforms were legislated by Congress before Marshall arrived.

In one vitally important respect, however, Marshall engineered a reorganization that changed the face of the Red Cross. On July 11, 1950, two weeks after the outbreak of the Korean War, Marshall spent part of the day at Harvard Medical School with Dr. Edwin Cohn, one of the world's foremost medical researchers on the components of human blood. With Marshall at Cohn's elbow and asking questions, Cohn and his colleagues demonstrated a device that could rapidly fractionate blood into a number of new, potentially lifesaving derivatives. That evening, at the Harvard Club in Boston, Marshall addressed Dr. Cohn and a group of scientists, doctors, and representatives of government agencies with expertise in blood and blood derivatives. Referencing the growing danger to the "national welfare and security" posed by the Korean War and the Soviet nuclear threat, Marshall announced that the peacetime National Blood Program of the Red Cross had been made "a separate service," reporting directly to him. The Red Cross, Marshall declared, was about to be officially designated by Secretary of Defense Louis Johnson as the entity responsible for meeting the needs of the U.S. armed forces and civil defense for blood and blood derivatives. In effect, the relationship that the Red Cross had with the War and Navy Departments during World War II with respect to blood and blood products was being reestablished with the Defense Department. Marshall also reported that to "realize the goal of a truly national program," an agreement had been reached between the Red Cross, other nonprofit blood banks in the U.S., and the American Medical Association—the "Boston Agreement"—whereby they would cooperate with one another on blood procurement, storage, processing, and preparation for shipment.[78] Thus, it was on Marshall's watch and probably due to his leadership that the mission of the Red Cross National Blood Program was greatly expanded to embrace not only the supply of blood and blood products for civilian purposes but also for military use in the Korean War.

Eleven days later, Marshall notified Johnson that the Red Cross would immediately increase its blood collections. Soon thereafter it began sending whole blood to a temporary processing laboratory at a U.S. naval hospital in Oakland, California. The first shipment of blood from the U.S. for soldiers wounded in Korea left the laboratory on August 26, 1950, and was flown to Japan. From then until February 1954, more than 340,000 pints were flown to Japan for transshipment to medical units of the United Nations in Korea. Near the end of the war, Dr. Melvin Carsberg, head of the Office of Medical Services, reported that the rate of death from combat wounds dropped from 4.5 percent during World War II to 2 percent in the Korean War. In addition, his statistics showed that 85 percent of the wounded in Korea returned to active duty, compared to 77 percent in the Second World War.[79] Evacuation helicopters and advances in medicine and surgery obviously had much to do with these declines. Nevertheless, the availability of whole blood, plasma, and other blood derivatives supplied through the Red Cross National Blood Program had a significant role in saving lives and sending servicemen home.

*   *   *   *   *

On Saturday morning, July 1, 1950, before much blood had been spilled in Korea, Marshall received a call at Dodona. Dean Acheson, his successor as secretary of state, informed Marshall that the president had just approved a request by General MacArthur, commander of all U.S. forces in the Far East, to deploy army ground troops in South Korea for the purpose of mounting a counteroffensive against the North Korean invaders. America was thus committed to a land war in Asia, he said, a step that could lead to war with the People's Republic of China or the Soviet Union, or perhaps even the two of them at once. Acheson needed Marshall's advice.

Around one o'clock that afternoon Acheson arrived at Dodona, bringing with him Averell Harriman and Chip Bohlen, who had recently flown in from Paris, and George Kennan, who was about to leave the State Department, but agreed to stay on through August as counselor on Soviet affairs because of the outbreak of the Korean War. Out on the lawn, under the big oaks, the so-called wise men filled Marshall in on the events of the previous week, beginning with the first meeting at Blair House on Sunday evening, June 25, when Truman made it clear that while the U.S. would work through the UN he would not let the North Korean attack succeed. "By God, I am going to let them have it," he was purported to have said.[80] According to Kennan's diary, Marshall "listened very attentively and silently, as he always does . . . and then gave us his views vigorously and without hesitation." He began by saying that "there could be no doubt about the proper course for us to pursue . . . We had begun this thing; now we had to go through with it." Marshall confessed that his "greatest worry" was Western Europe, the area of "real strategic importance," but the wise men assured him that U.S. action in Korea would not cause the Soviets to attack in Europe nor would it weaken the North Atlantic alliance. As to MacArthur's request for additional troops, Marshall observed that it was a "common failing for commanders to ask for more than they needed." MacArthur, he said, "should be told to do this job with what he had." Someone in the group, probably Harriman, suggested that the "defense establishment," meaning Louis Johnson, had gone out of its way to undermine Acheson. Among other things, Marshall was told that Johnson and his supporters were spreading the word throughout Washington that when Acheson gave a speech declaring that Korea was outside the U.S. defensive perimeter and expressed his opposition to military assistance to Formosa, he encouraged not only North Korea but world communism itself to advance aggressively into the free world. According to Kennan, Marshall reacted by saying he was "deeply disturbed" to learn of Johnson's "attitude," though he could not have been surprised.[81] At the time, no one came out and said it, but Marshall's esteemed visitors must have conveyed the impression that they were on the verge of advising the president to fire Johnson and that they wanted Marshall to support them.

A few days later, in a chatty letter to Senator Vandenberg, who was in Grand Rapids battling lung cancer, Marshall referenced the identity of the four men who showed up for lunch at Dodona, without providing details.

"You can imagine the character of the discussion," he hinted, knowing that Vandenberg would probably guess what they talked about. "Now for a man who is trying to devote himself to Red Cross and keep out of governmental things," wrote Marshall, "I certainly found myself up to the neck in this situation."[82]

CHAPTER 18

Distressing Necessity

Early on the morning of July 4, 1950, before the Marshalls had gotten out of bed, the president called. Would it be okay, he asked, if he and his daughter Margaret drove out to Dodona? About an hour later they arrived, with Margaret, as usual, behind the wheel. Scarcely anyone at Blair House knew where the two of them had gone.

Truman had not quite made up his mind. With the nation once again at war, he was giving serious thought to asking Louis Johnson for his resignation as defense secretary. He wanted to know whether Marshall would be willing, if and when the time was right, to take Johnson's place. Truman's main problem with Johnson was that he seemed incapable of confining himself to his job, the same shortcoming that Marshall identified in his March 1949 letter of advice to Johnson. Fueled by his ambition to become president, Johnson had convinced himself that Truman was being ill-served by Secretary of State Dean Acheson. He was using every opportunity to bad-mouth Acheson to members of the press, especially Drew Pearson, and sometimes to government officials he barely knew. In his diary, Truman wrote that "Louis . . . tried to . . . blow himself up and everyone else down, particularly the Secretary of State."[1]

For months, Truman had tolerated Johnson's boorish efforts to undercut Acheson, yet a shocking incident a few days prior to Truman's visit to Dodona hastened the man's ultimate downfall. Averell Harriman had stopped by Johnson's office at the Pentagon one morning to catch up on developments in Korea. In the midst of their chat Johnson accepted a telephone call from Senator Robert Taft (R-OH) one of Truman's most outspoken critics, who had delivered a speech a day earlier lambasting the president for not seeking congressional approval before entering the war and calling for Acheson's resignation. Harriman told Truman he was stunned when he heard Johnson praise Taft for his speech, especially the senator's demand for Acheson's resignation. When Johnson hung up, he turned and reportedly said to Harriman that if we can "get Acheson out," he, Johnson, would personally "see that Harriman was made Secretary of State."[2]

Johnson had made a monumental misjudgment. He was under the impression that Harriman's well-known desire to be secretary of state would outweigh his loyalty to Acheson and the president. Instead of conspiring with Johnson, Harriman, "white-faced and upset," went directly to Truman.[3] It was Harriman's tale of Johnson's perfidy that motivated Truman to call Marshall on the morning of the 4th of July.

Truman remained at Dodona until noon, talking with Marshall about a litany of subjects ranging from China to MacArthur to his troubles at the Defense Department, the latter topic indicating that the president brought up the problems he was having with Johnson and probably asked Marshall whether he would consider replacing him. A letter that Marshall wrote to Rose Page three weeks later suggests that he told the president that if he decided to relieve Johnson, he was willing to serve. Referring to the Korean War crisis and the possibility of being "called again into public service," Marshall confessed to Rose that "I hope to get by unmolested, but when the President motors down and sits under our oaks and tells me of his difficulties, he has me at a disadvantage."[4]

Marshall was not yet secretary of defense, but he quickly found himself immersed in Korean War discussions. The day after Truman's visit, Frank Pace, the thirty-seven-year-old secretary of the army, a rising star in the Truman administration who had been in office only for two months, asked Marshall to stop by the Pentagon for a briefing on the war.[5] Pace's boss, Louis Johnson, was nowhere to be seen. Thereafter, Marshall had a late lunch with Truman, General Omar Bradley, Admiral Forrest Sherman, and Dwight Eisenhower, who told the president that he believed the military was "not moving fast enough" to meet the crisis in Korea. Both he and Marshall stressed the need for "speed and strength" and recommended, in effect, "all-out mobilization."[6]

* * * * *

The Korean Peninsula, jutting like a thick thumb some 600 miles southward from the northeast coast of Asia, has had a challenging history. Bordering in the north on superpowers China and Russia, and just a short distance from Japan, Korea has suffered roughly nine hundred invasions over the last two thousand years. In 1910, following its victory in the 1904–1905 Russo-Japanese War, the Japanese empire annexed the entire Korean Peninsula. Four years later, First Lieutenant Marshall traveled with his first wife, Lily, and his Japanese army hosts up through Korea and toured the Manchurian battlefields of that war, a conflict largely forgotten by most Americans.

For the ensuing thirty-five years Japan virtually enslaved the Korean people, its brutal colonial government intent on stamping out Korean identity and exploiting its resources. In early August 1945, as World War II was drawing to a close and Japanese resistance was collapsing, the Soviet Union declared war on Japan. Joseph Stalin ordered troops to move into Manchuria and the northern part of Korea. When the Japanese sued for peace on August 10, the U.S. was concerned that the Soviets would try to occupy all of Korea. To block further Red Army advances, the U.S. prepared to land troops in southern Korea and proposed the establishment of a line of demarcation that would divide Soviet and American forces. Japanese troops on the north side of the line were to surrender to the Red Army, while those on the south side were to surrender to the Americans. On the night of August 10–11, 1945, during an emergency meeting of the State-War-Navy Coordinating Committee in Washington, two young army officers—Dean Rusk, future secretary of state, who was on Marshall's staff, and Charles Bonesteel, who would later become military commander in Korea—were asked by Assistant Secretary of War John J. McCloy to slip into an anteroom, decide on a boundary line, and come out with a recommendation. Using a *National Geographic* map, they settled on the 38th parallel as the east-west line across the peninsula that would divide North and South Korea. They recommended this line, explained Rusk, because they felt it important to include "Seoul, the capital, in the American sector."[7] The Soviets accepted the line without argument or hesitation. To this day, a 160-mile line approximating the path of the 38th parallel, which is straddled by a 2.5-mile strip of no-man's-land known as the demilitarized zone (DMZ), marks the boundary between North and South Korea. In 1950, about 9 to 10 million people lived in the industrial north and 20 to 21 million in the largely rural south.

Surprisingly, the Soviets in September 1947 proposed to withdraw their occupying forces in the north if the U.S. did the same in the south. Since the Joint Chiefs of Staff (then chaired by General Eisenhower), along with George

Kennan and Secretary of State Marshall, privately concluded that the U.S. had "little strategic interest in maintaining the present troops and bases in Korea," the Truman administration readily agreed.[8] The Soviets pulled out by the end of 1948 and most of the Americans were gone by the summer of 1949.

With the question of who would run the country left up in the air, the United Nations, at the instance of the United States, proposed free elections throughout Korea with a view of unifying the entire peninsula. The north, controlled and supported by the Soviets, boycotted elections and installed as their leader thirty-six-year-old Kim Il-sung, the first of the Kim dynasty, a hard-core Communist who fought the Japanese in Manchuria during World War II and probably attended military schools in Moscow. The south conducted elections in May 1948 and established the Republic of South Korea. Their leader was Syngman Rhee, an eccentric seventy-three-year-old right-wing anti-Communist who had lived in the U.S. for forty years and held degrees from Harvard, Princeton, and George Washington University. In their inauguration addresses both Rhee and Kim pledged to reunite the peninsula under their own form of government. They each threatened to invade the other.

Militarily, the Koreans in the north were stronger than those in the south. When the Soviets pulled out they left behind a well-trained and well-equipped army and air force of some 135,000 men, called the North Korean People's Army (NKPA), including a newly formed armored division soon to be supplied with 150 Russian T-34 tanks. The Americans left behind 500 U.S. military "advisers" whose mission was to double the strength of Syngman Rhee's 50,000-man Constabulary Regiments and turn them into an eight-division Republic of Korea (ROK) army. However, because the U.S. joint chiefs feared that Rhee would invade the north and drag the U.S. into a war, they rejected his requests for American-built tanks, mobile artillery, and aircraft.

Since Kim Il-sung's rise to power in the fall of 1948, he repeatedly requested support from his Soviet sponsor for an invasion of the south to unify Korea. In January 1950, Moscow finally gave him the "green light." Stalin had been reading the tea leaves. Top secret studies by the NSC and the joint chiefs, purloined by British spies, indicated to him that the U.S. did not regard Korea to be of enough strategic importance to be worth defending. Then on January 12,

Secretary of State Acheson declared publicly that the American "defensive perimeter" did not extend to Korea. As a result, it appeared to Stalin that by using North Korea as his proxy he could open a "second front" for Communist expansion in East Asia and the U.S. would not respond militarily. After all, the Americans had done nothing in 1949 to help Chiang Kai-shek's Nationalists escape defeat at the hands of the Chinese Communists. Hearing no objection from Mao Zedong, Stalin gave Kim Il-sung the go-ahead. Kim assured Stalin that "[t]he attack will be swift and the war will be won in three days."⁹

Shortly thereafter, Stalin encouraged Ho Chi Minh to step up his offensive against the French in Indochina (today Vietnam), thus expanding the Communist second front in Asia and at the same time compensating for Soviet setbacks in Europe (e.g., the Berlin airlift). Stalin's strategy had the advantage of substituting the revolutionary ambitions of Kim Il-sung and Ho Chi Minh for direct Soviet involvement. And, as Cold War historian John Gaddis wrote, "The Chinese, still eager to legitimize their revolution by winning Stalin's approval, were more than willing to provide backup support if and when needed."¹⁰

Beginning in February 1950, the signs of a buildup for an early summer attack by the North Koreans across the 38th parallel were abundant. Donald Nichols, a young American air force intelligence operative assigned to advise Syngman Rhee, sent dozens of reports detailing the preparations for and the precise timing of an invasion by the North Koreans to air force headquarters in Tokyo and to General Charles Willoughby, chief of intelligence for General MacArthur in the Far East Command. Some of Nichols's reports, including one predicting the inevitability of an attack, reached the joint chiefs and the State Department in Washington. In late May an informant told Willoughby's staff about the formation of a new North Korean tank brigade near the frontier consisting of 10,000 men, 180 light and medium tanks, artillery, antitank guns, and motorcycles. Three days before the attack, Nichols reported that more than two dozen truckloads of North Korean troops were moving toward the 38th parallel "for the purpose of preparing to invade South Korea."¹¹ For a variety of reasons none of these reports were taken seriously.

*   *   *   *   *

At about 3:30 a.m. on Sunday, June 25 (Seoul time), North Korean artillery commenced firing. Seven divisions of NKPA troops, spearheaded by T-34 tanks and supported by about 100 Soviet aircraft, streamed south across the

38th parallel. Two divisions headed straight for Seoul. Captain Joseph Darrigo, one of the senior U.S. military advisers to the South Korean (ROK) army, was awakened by the artillery fire. He drove his jeep into the center of the border town of Kaesong. When he arrived, he observed a fifteen-car train pull into the railroad station bearing a NKPA infantry regiment, with many soldiers on the roof and clinging to the sides. Sometime during the night they had relaid the tracks. Darrigo knew right away that this was no minor border skirmish.

The ROK regiment that Darrigo was responsible for training and advising was outflanked. The rest of the poorly equipped ROK forces were caught by surprise. Confronted by the overwhelming firepower and speed of the Russian T-34 tanks, most units panicked and fled southward. In Tokyo, at six o'clock that evening, General MacArthur, supreme commander of Allied powers, projected an attitude of unconcern. "This is probably only a reconnaissance in force," he reportedly said to a group of visitors. "If Washington only will not hobble me, I can handle it with one arm tied behind my back."[12]

Though MacArthur would complain later that he was hobbled, he could not make that claim at the outset. On Sunday afternoon in the U.S., while Truman was flying from his home in Independence, Missouri, to Washington, the UN Security Council convened in Lake Success at the request of Secretary of State Acheson and voted unanimously to condemn the invasion and to call for a cease-fire and the withdrawal of North Korean forces to the 38th parallel. Andrei Gromyko, the Soviet representative to the Security Council, was not present to veto the UN actions; he had been recalled to Moscow months earlier in protest to the UN's refusal to seat the Chinese Communists. When the president met with Acheson, Johnson, and the joint chiefs at Blair House on Sunday evening, it was apparent within the first few hours that American military power, backed by the UN, would come to the defense of South Korea even though the region was deemed not essential to the strategic interests of the United States. Like Pearl Harbor, the brazen attack was a shock to the president and everyone in the room, an affront to the structure of collective security that the Truman administration was advocating in Europe and elsewhere. Memories of the aggressive acts by totalitarian regimes against small states in the 1930s that led to World War II were still fresh. To a man, the president and the rest of his team agreed that this was the time and place to draw a line. "We can't let the UN

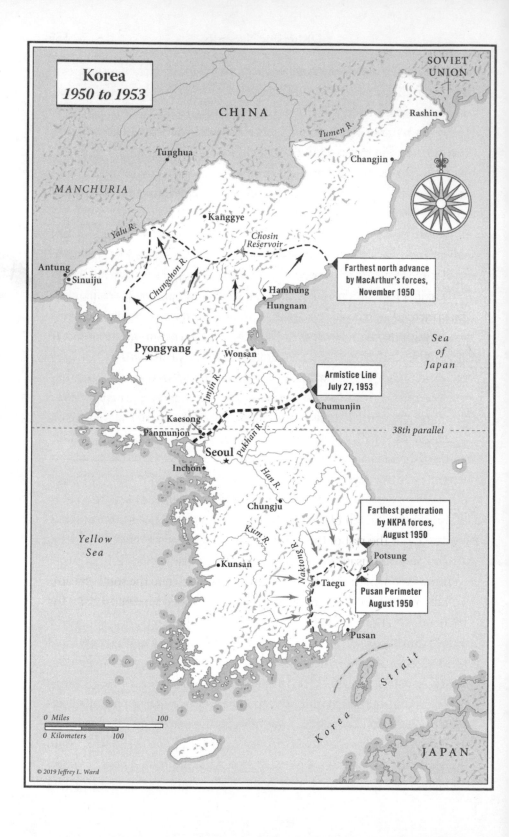

Korea
1950 to 1953

SOVIET UNION

CHINA

MANCHURIA

Tumen R.

Rashin •

Tunghua •

Changjin •

Kanggye •

Chosin Reservoir

Antung •

Yalu R.

Sinuiju •

Chungchon R.

Farthest north advance
by MacArthur's forces,
November 1950

Hamhung •
Hungnam •

Sea of Japan

Pyongyang ★

Wonsan •

Imjin R.

Armistice Line
July 27, 1953

Chumunjin •

Kaesong •

Panmunjon •

- - - - - - - 38th parallel - - - - - - -

Seoul ★

Pukhan R.

Inchon •

Han R.

Chungju •

Farthest penetration
by NKPA forces,
August 1950

Yellow Sea

Kum R.

Naktong R.

Potsung •

Kunsan •

Taegu •

Pusan Perimeter
August 1950

Pusan •

Korea Strait

0 Miles   100
0 Kilometers   100

JAPAN

© 2019 Jeffrey L. Ward

down," Truman kept repeating.[13] Instead of asking Congress for a war resolution or declaration, the president decided that he was empowered as commander in chief to deal with what he thought would be a short-term emergency without seeking congressional approval.

By the second week of July, MacArthur had gotten much more than he asked for. As supreme commander of all U.S. forces in the Asia Pacific, he was authorized by Truman to deploy in South Korea "any and all ground forces under his command."[14] In addition, MacArthur was appointed commander in chief, UN Command, which meant that he commanded the soldiers and ships of a dozen nations under a UN resolution authorizing the use of force to expel North Korea from south of the 38th parallel. On July 15, President Rhee entrusted MacArthur with overall command of all South Korean armed forces.

Throughout July, elements of the U.S. Army's 24th and 25th Infantry and 1st Cavalry Divisions—the so-called United Nations ground forces—attempted to slow the enemy attack. However, in spite of brave fighting they were forced to fall back toward the southeast corner of the peninsula. At the same time, North Korean forces were funneled down the western fringes, largely unopposed. As they approached the southern coast they wheeled east, flanking the U.S. forces from the left. On August 1, the U.S. divisions, with their backs to the Sea of Japan, were ordered to withdraw farther behind the Naktong River and defend what became known as the "Pusan perimeter," a little patch of Korea named for the port city at the tip of the peninsula. For the rest of the summer, the U.S. Army fought desperately, trying to prevent Pusan from becoming an American Dunkirk.

As the cream of the NKPA was being sucked down to the southern limits of the peninsula, General MacArthur envisioned an opportunity for American power to reunite the country. With a surprise amphibious landing far to the northwest at Inchon, combined with the insertion of additional Eighth Army reinforcements at Pusan, he could entrap and destroy the NKPA. As early as July 13, MacArthur outlined his grand plan to Lightning Joe Collins, army chief of staff. MacArthur's plan was met with skepticism because it required a daylight landing at high tide on mud flats (no beaches), the capture of a fortified island in the middle of the shoal-laden approach to the harbor, and the scaling of twelve-foot-high seawalls. Surprise would be impossible.

* * * * *

With the military situation in Korea deteriorating, Truman allowed Louis Johnson to stay on, at least for the time being. If he fired his secretary of defense while U.S. troops were besieged at Pusan, pundits and the American public might sense panic and disarray in the Truman administration. Plus, he harbored second thoughts about pulling the trigger. Johnson was being crucified in the press for aggressively slashing the military budget, which allegedly led to the desperate predicament of U.S. troops at Pusan and the prospect of a humiliating evacuation or surrender. Truman struggled with whether it was fair to dismiss Johnson and add to his shame when it was he, the president, who ordered him to cut the budget.

Marshall left instructions with one of Truman's aides as to how he could be reached if needed. Having turned down invitations to vacation at Jackson Hole, Nantucket, and the Adirondacks, the Marshalls accepted an offer from their old friend Charles Haffner, CEO of R. R. Donnelly Company, whom they had met when they lived in Chicago and George managed the Illlinois National Guard during the 1930s. They planned to spend August as Haffner's guests at the Huron Mountain Club, a 24,000-acre preserve of pristine lakes and forests on the southern shore of Lake Superior, founded around 1890 by Cyrus McCormick and other industrialists. The club had fifty regular members, each of whom owned a "cabin" along the shores of the big lake or the Pine River. The Marshalls stayed in a cabin owned by Victor Elting and took their meals with other members and their guests in the Huron Mountain clubhouse. For the next four weeks, they relaxed, Katherine suffering from shingles and occasional headaches, and George fishing for bass and trout almost every day in the small lakes and streams.

The call came at ten o'clock on Saturday night, August 26, 1950. Because there were no telephones on club property, Marshall was driven five miles through the forest on winding dirt and gravel roads to the tiny village of Big Bay, scene of the murder that inspired the book and film *Anatomy of a Murder*. With a note of urgency in his voice, Truman asked Marshall to stop by his office when he returned to Washington. He said nothing of what he wanted to discuss, but Marshall knew what was on his mind. The president was ready to replace Louis Johnson as secretary of defense. Aware that anything he said would be overheard by the locals who were loitering nearby,

Marshall uttered one- or two-word responses. The next day Marshall wired his aide, Major C. J. George, informing him that he and Mrs. Marshall would depart the club a day earlier than planned and to advise Matt Connelly, the president's appointments secretary.

Marshall could never have guessed what led up to Truman's Saturday night call and the consequences it would have for him. Early that morning at Blair House, Truman read with rising anger an advance copy of a statement by MacArthur to the forthcoming Chicago convention of the Veterans of Foreign Wars (VFW) that had already gone out over the wire services. The tenor of MacArthur's message created the impression that the U.S. desired to use Formosa, Chiang's Nationalist redoubt, as a military base and that those who opposed all-out defense of the island lacked "dynamic leadership" and did "not understand the Orient."[15] It was a direct challenge to Truman's leadership and to his carefully crafted policy to avoid any actions suggesting that he might back Chiang in a renewed war against the Chinese Communists, which in turn could drag the U.S. into a world war.

A few minutes later, Secretaries Acheson and Johnson, the joint chiefs, and a few others arrived for a previously scheduled meeting to discuss the next steps in the Korean war. According to General Bradley, chairman of the joint chiefs, Truman began by reading MacArthur's statement aloud, "his lips white and compressed." Bradley wrote that he was "shocked." To him "the message seemed the height of arrogance."[16] A partial account of the meeting states that the president "instructed Secretary Johnson to issue an order to General MacArthur" to withdraw his message to the VFW.[17] Believing Johnson would carry out his directive, Truman set aside his anger and proceeded to the main subject of the Saturday morning meeting— MacArthur's plan for an amphibious landing at Inchon. General Collins and Admiral Sherman had just returned from a full-scale review with MacArthur and his staff in Japan. Truman wanted to hear their views and those of the other chiefs on the advisability of proceeding with the audacious plan. Collins and Sherman expressed doubts about the wisdom of the plan and its prospects for success. Bradley added his own misgivings. As a group, wrote Bradley, the joint chiefs were "inclined toward postponing Inchon" until "they were certain" that U.S. forces in the south could hold Pusan.[18] It appeared, however, that the president had already made up his mind. As he wrote in his memoir, Truman regarded MacArthur's plan as "a daring

562   GEORGE MARSHALL

strategic conception" and he "had the greatest confidence it would succeed."[19] None of the chiefs raised objections. At the urging of the president
they sent MacArthur a tentative okay, suggesting that he should consider
landing at places other than Inchon.

Two or three hours after the Saturday morning meeting adjourned, Truman learned that Johnson was trying to "weasel" out of ordering MacArthur
to withdraw his statement to the VFW.[20] In a flurry of phone calls to and
from Acheson and Harriman, Johnson claimed he was worried that MacArthur would be embarrassed and might resign (in fact, Johnson agreed with
much of what MacArthur had written to the VFW). Johnson asked Acheson
point-blank whether the U.S. civilian leadership should "dare" to insult or
demean MacArthur by sending the order. Truman was furious. He called
Johnson, dictated an order to MacArthur to withdraw his VFW statement,
and told Johnson to send it at once.

Saturday, August 26, turned out to be quite a day. The VFW episode
caused the president to turn the corner on Johnson. As Truman's daughter
put it, Johnson was an "obstructionist force in the government."[21] He would
have to go. The statement to the VFW also confirmed what Truman had
always suspected: MacArthur could not be trusted. He was disloyal to his
commander in chief. Yet at the same time Truman believed that MacArthur
was a gifted and visionary military commander. Ignoring the misgivings of
his joint chiefs, he went ahead and approved MacArthur's risky plan to land
at Inchon. No wonder Truman summoned Marshall from Big Bay to Washington at the end of that day. Like Franklin Roosevelt when he gave the
Overlord command to Eisenhower, Truman needed Marshall at his side.

* * * * *

After returning from the Huron Mountain Club, Marshall slipped into Blair
House alone at noon on September 6. Truman began by telling him that he
was going to demand Johnson's resignation. He asked Marshall whether he
would be willing to serve as secretary of defense through the current "crisis"—
meaning the Korean War. As Truman wrote the next day in a letter to his
wife, Marshall responded, "Mr. President, you have only to tell me what you
want, and I'll do it. But I want you to think about the fact that my appointment may reflect upon you and your administration. They [the China
Lobby] are still charging me with the downfall of Chiang's government in

China. I want to help, not hurt you." To his wife, Truman added, "Can you think of anyone else saying that? I can't and he's of the *great*."[22]

Marshall had only two conditions. First, he would serve for six months to a year. And second, he asked Truman to appoint Bob Lovett as deputy secretary of defense, provided he could be persuaded to sign on. Aware that Marshall was almost seventy, Truman agreed.

Despite his vaunted reputation for decisiveness it took Truman another six days before he cornered Johnson and forced him to resign. Following the cabinet meeting on the afternoon of September 12, Johnson finally handed his resignation letter to Truman. "Louis," the president reportedly said, "you haven't signed this—sign it." Johnson made a final appeal, saying he didn't think the president would "make him do it." Weeping openly, he signed. As he handed the letter to Truman, he said in a barely audible voice, "You are ruining me." Truman could only come up with a bromide. "This hurts me more than it does you, Lou."[23] Johnson departed without another word. As soon as he left, Truman picked up the phone and called Marshall. By seven p.m. Johnson's signed letter of resignation, Truman's acceptance, and Marshall's nomination as secretary of defense had been released to the press. In less than forty-eight hours, MacArthur's invasion of Inchon was set to begin.

Wearing sunglasses and his old crushed garrison cap, MacArthur was already aboard the cruiser *Mount McKinley* in the Sea of Japan on his way to Inchon with an armada of more than 200 ships and 70,000 men. A few days before departing, he called in a group of reporters. "I'm going on a little operation and I'd like to have you boys with me." At Sasebo, the Japanese port closest to Korea, he invited the press corps to join him on the *McKinley* and to be briefed by him. "The history of war," he told them, "proves that nine times out of ten an army has been destroyed because its supply lines have been cut off." The objective of the forthcoming invasion, he said, was to seize Seoul, cut off supplies to the enemy fighting around Pusan, and annihilate the North Korean armies. A reporter asked whether the Chinese Communists would intervene. If they do, MacArthur replied, "our air will turn the Yalu River into the bloodiest stream in all history."[24]

In Washington, hours after the 1st Marine Division landed at Inchon, Marshall faced the first of two hurdles that had to be surmounted before he could be sworn in as secretary of defense. To guarantee civilian control of the military, a provision of the 1947 National Security Act barred any citizen from becoming secretary of defense if he or she had served on active duty as an officer in the armed services during the past ten years. Since it obviously applied to Marshall, the law had to be waived by both houses of Congress. The debate in the House of Representatives was brief, the only excitement occurring when Dewey Short of Missouri, known for his colorful oratory, brought Republicans to their feet by declaring that Marshall was a "catspaw and a pawn" who was being brought back "to bail out desperate men who were in a hole," an obvious reference to Acheson, Johnson, and Truman.[25] In the Senate on the same day, September 15, the debate went on for hours and was highly partisan. With midterm elections looming, a group of Republican senators took advantage of the debate to use the Marshall appointment as a vehicle to criticize Truman and Acheson for "losing" China to the Communists and for allowing the State Department to be infiltrated by Communists. But it was Republican Senator William Jenner, a Hoosier original, who stole the headlines with his personal attack on Marshall himself, a dress rehearsal for the vicious charges that Senator Joseph McCarthy would level against Marshall a year later. In an hour-long speech that was delivered "at times in shouts and half-screams," Jenner alleged that Marshall was "not only willing, he is eager to play the role as front man for traitors. The truth is this is no new role for him, for General George C. Marshall is a living lie . . . an errand boy, a front man, a stooge or a conspirator for this Administration's crazy assortment of collectivist cutthroat crackpots and Communist fellow-travelling appeasers." (When Marshall heard of this attack a day or so later, he remarked, "Jenner? Jenner? I do not believe I know the man.")[26] Massachusetts senator Leverett Saltonstall, a Republican blue blood whose ancestry can be traced to the *Mayflower*, was enraged. "I wish I had the vocabulary to answer the statement that General Marshall's life is a lie," he said, "because if ever there was a life spent in the interest of our country, a life that is not a lie, it is the life of George C. Marshall."[27] Several other senators who opposed amending the National Security Act distanced themselves from Jenner's personal attack.

By the end of the day, the House voted 220–105 to waive the provision of the 1947 law that barred Marshall from becoming secretary of defense, making it clear that it applied to him only and not to any future officer who a president might want to appoint as secretary of defense. A few days later, the Senate, by a vote of 47–21 with twenty Republicans opposing, accepted the House waiver, including the amendment saying it was supposed to be a one-time exemption (in 2017, Congress made it a two-time exemption by waiving an updated version of the 1947 law to permit four-star General James Mattis to serve as secretary of defense).

The other hurdle that stood in the way of Marshall's appointment was the Senate confirmation hearing and floor debate on September 19. The hearing before the Armed Services Committee lasted for only fifty-five minutes. Once again Senator Jenner, though not a committee member, was the source of controversy. Marshall sat at the end of a long table facing Jenner, who had asked that the chairman of the committee, Senator Millard Tydings (D-MD), read a list of thirteen "questions" that Jenner had written. The majority of Jenner's "why did you beat your wife" questions were designed to score political points, not to elicit information. For example, Marshall was asked why he didn't protest when President Roosevelt at Tehran, Yalta, and Potsdam "handed half the world on a silver platter to Stalin," and whether he favored the surrender of "American sovereignty" to the UN. Marshall gazed impassively at Jenner when the questions were read, occasionally breaking into a smile or chuckling when a question was particularly outrageous and self-serving. Jenner's question disparaging Marshall's 1946 mission to China was actually helpful because it allowed Marshall to present a succinct summary of the purpose of the mission, what he tried to accomplish while there, and why it failed.[28] The committee went into executive session and voted 9–2 to confirm Marshall as secretary of defense. Late that afternoon, the Senate, with little debate, approved confirmation by a vote of 57–11.

* * * * *

While Marshall's nomination was wending its way through Congress, the execution of General MacArthur's bold plan to rout and destroy North Korea's armies turned out to be a stunning success. By midnight of D-Day, September 15, the 1st Marine Division landed 13,000 troops and tons of weapons and equipment at Inchon. Casualties were extremely light (a total of only 174, 21 of whom were killed). Resistance was negligible. As MacArthur had predicted, the North Koreans were caught by surprise. During the next two days the jarheads moved inland, captured Kimpo Airfield, and prepared to liberate Seoul. On the third day, the 7th Marines came ashore at Inchon, consolidated the beachhead, and deployed inland to the southeast, protecting the right flank of the 1st Marines. In describing the Inchon operation, Omar Bradley went overboard. Perhaps because he preferred a different location for the landings and had warned of disaster, he called the operation both a "military miracle" and "the luckiest military operation in history."[29]

The other part of MacArthur's plan—a breakout by the reinforced Eighth Army from the Pusan perimeter in the south—was delayed by almost a week due to fierce resistance by the North Koreans. As the NKPA units became aware of the invasion of Inchon in the north and the possibility of being trapped, they began withdrawing. Finally, on September 22, the day after Marshall was sworn in at the Pentagon, the perimeter collapsed, allowing leading elements of the Eighth Army's four divisions to dash at top speed northwest toward Seoul and west toward Kunsan on the coast, while six ROK divisions sped in two columns up the east side of the peninsula, completely unopposed. Four days later, near Osan, just a few miles south of Seoul, units of the 7th Marines that had landed at Inchon linked up with the 1st Cavalry, which had broken out of Pusan. The North Korean armies fled north in total disarray. Half were trapped south of the 38th parallel by the pincers that closed in on them. Seoul fell to the American marines on September 26 and 27. By the first of October, South Korea was under UN control.

The time had come for a major decision. Truman's original objective when he chose to intervene militarily was to drive the North Korean invaders out of South Korea and restore the status quo. Now that between 25,000 and 30,000 North Korean soldiers were fleeing north with most of their senior officers, the question was whether MacArthur's UN forces should cross the 38th parallel, destroy the remainder of the NKPA army, depose Kim Il-sung and his Communist regime, and unify the peninsula under Syngman Rhee's democratic government.

As the newly confirmed secretary of defense, Marshall was the last link in the chain of recommendations from the joint chiefs and the State Department that led to a presidential directive authorizing MacArthur to conduct military operations north of the 38th parallel. Though Marshall was not a particularly zealous advocate of invading North Korea, he supported the idea that field generals, in this case MacArthur, should be free to continue in hot pursuit of the fleeing enemy. Therefore, on September 27, Marshall approved and forwarded to Truman a "draft directive," prepared by the joint chiefs and concurred by Secretary Acheson, that permitted MacArthur to pursue and destroy the enemy. The directive, however, limited his authority in three important and somewhat ambiguous respects. First, if "major" Soviet or Chinese Communist armed forces intervened or threatened to intervene in North Korea, MacArthur was to report to Washington (the term "major" was not defined). In the case of an armed intervention by the Soviets, MacArthur was to assume the "defensive," but if it was the Chinese, the directive, oddly, did not instruct MacArthur as to what he was supposed to do. Second, "under no circumstances" were MacArthur's "forces," presumably including warplanes as well as ground troops, to cross the Manchurian and Soviet Union borders of Korea. And third, "as a matter of policy," no "non-Korean ground forces" were to be used in the "northeast provinces bordering the Soviet Union or in the area along the Manchurian border." A "political guidance" paragraph added by Acheson's State Department advised MacArthur that the political future of the north, including occupation policy, would have to await UN action "to complete the unification of the country."[30]

The directive was approved by the president and sent by the joint chiefs to MacArthur on the same day, September 27.

Around the time MacArthur, as head of all UN forces, was informed of the presidential directive that he was authorized to cross the 38th parallel, Marshall was receiving press reports of an announcement by General Walton "Johnnie" Walker that he intended to halt his Eighth Army at the line of demarcation and await a UN instruction that authorized him to cross over to North Korea. Walker's suggestion that his troops could not cross without UN authorization was at odds with Truman's directive to MacArthur. Marshall understood that due to the likelihood of a Soviet veto, the president did not want to risk a vote in the UN Security Council on whether the 38th parallel could be crossed. Truman preferred to bypass the question of advance UN approval by taking the position that MacArthur deemed it militarily necessary to cross the parallel. For these reasons, Marshall took it upon himself to send an "eyes only" cable to MacArthur on September 29 saying that rather than pausing to await UN approval, MacArthur and his field commanders, including Walker, should "feel unhampered tactically and strategically to proceed north of the 38th parallel."[31] MacArthur replied the next day, saying, "Unless and until the enemy capitulate I regard all of Korea open for our mil operations."[32] Marshall made no further response.

Taken out of context, the quoted language in Marshall's message and MacArthur's response (with no pushback) could be taken to indicate that the three conditions imposed on MacArthur by the presidential directive were no longer operative—that he was literally free to fight in the north until the enemy was defeated without regard to intervention by China and the Soviet Union or the proximity of their borders. To Marshall's regret, MacArthur and his supporters subsequently seized on these documents to defend against charges that he exceeded his authority.

* * * * *

As General "Lightning Joe" Collins later lamented, he and the other joint chiefs were "overawed" by MacArthur's success at Inchon and how quickly he turned defeat into apparent victory.[33] Marshall was by no means immune from being caught up in the excitement of the moment. On September 30, he wrote an uncharacteristically effusive note to MacArthur, calling his "courageous campaign" in Korea a "daring and perfect strategical operation which virtually terminated the struggle."[34] In his voluminous correspondence throughout three wars and hundreds of interwar training exercises, Marshall was never known to have conferred the word "perfect" on another commander's performance. "Thanks, George," MacArthur responded, as if this were a routine compliment. And then, picking up on the word that Marshall used, MacArthur wrote that the two of them had always worked in "perfect unity" and he inferred that this was the kind of relationship that would continue to exist in their future "martial endeavors."[35]

Unity, though not perfect, would prevail, at least for the time being. During the first ten days of October, while MacArthur's generals were implementing his unorthodox plan to cross the 38th parallel and march north in two widely separated columns, the Chinese Communists were threatening to intervene in the defense of their neighbor. Truman, Acheson, and the CIA discounted the threats, regarding them as propaganda or bluffs. The joint chiefs, realizing that the September 27 presidential directive did not instruct MacArthur on the actions he should take in the event of Chinese intervention, worked up a supplemental directive and asked Marshall to present it to Truman. After it was approved and dispatched without change, the joint chiefs' codicil informed MacArthur that in the event of "open or covert" intervention by "major" Chinese Communist units "anywhere in Korea" he was to continue to engage them as long as his forces had "a reasonable chance of success," and, in any case, he was to "obtain authorization from Washington prior to taking any military action against objectives in Chinese territory."[36]

With Inchon a success and victory believed to be at hand, Truman's political advisers pressed him to set up a face-to-face meeting with MacArthur in the Pacific, similar to Roosevelt's meeting with MacArthur in Honolulu when he was running for his fourth term in the summer of 1944. "The thought was that it was good election-year stuff," recalled Charles Murphy, who had replaced Clark Clifford as Truman's special counsel.[37] Midterm elections in 1950 were set to take place on November 7. While Marshall and Acheson saw no need for such a meeting, the president, who had never met MacArthur, believed some good could come of it. In late September or early October, Truman asked Marshall to invite MacArthur to meet him in Hawaii. Marshall told the president that since UN forces would be attacking Pyongyang, the heavily defended North Korean capital, and at the same time risking a dangerous amphibious landing on the east coast at Wonsan, MacArthur might not want to travel so far. He advised that if there was to be a meeting, it should take place at Wake Island, which was 2,200 miles closer to Far East headquarters in Japan. Truman and MacArthur agreed.

MacArthur was sitting in a jeep on the airstrip on tiny Wake Island at 6:30 a.m. on October 15 when the president, followed by Rusk, Pace, Bradley, and several others, started down the exit ramp of the *Independence*. By the time Truman stepped onto the tarmac, MacArthur was there to greet him. Instead of saluting his commander in chief, he held out his hand. The two of them gripped, pumped, and grinned for the benefit of the photographers. Marshall did not make the trip, explaining that someone in authority needed to be at the Pentagon in case of an emergency elsewhere in the world. Acheson's reason for skipping the meeting was more colorful. "While General MacArthur had many of the attributes of a foreign sovereign," he wrote, "it did not seem wise to recognize him as one . . . The whole idea was distasteful to me."[38]

After Truman and MacArthur met alone for about forty minutes during which MacArthur apparently apologized for his VFW statement, the meeting of the principals and all of their advisers and aides took place in a one-story pink cinder-block shack near the beach. MacArthur was full of good news. According to shorthand notes taken by Vernice Anderson, a State Department stenographer, and others, he began by declaring that "formal resistance will end throughout North and South Korea by Thanksgiving," and that he hoped "to withdraw the Eighth Army to Japan by Christmas." Eventually, Truman posed the key question: "What are the chances for Chinese or Soviet interference?" MacArthur responded, "Very little." Puffing on his pipe, he confidently went on, "[w]e are no longer fearful of their intervention." The Chinese Communists, he said, could only put "50/60,000" troops across the Yalu River and "they have no Air Force." If they "tried to get down to Pyongyang there would be the greatest slaughter." As to the Russians, "they have no ground troops available for North Korea." The Russian air force is "fairly good," and could provide "air support" to the Chinese, he said, "but the coordination between the Russian air and the Chinese ground would be so flimsy that I believe Russian air would bomb the Chinese as often as they would bomb us . . . I believe it just wouldn't work."[39]

With the benefit of hindsight, MacArthur's statements about Chinese intervention would be regarded as wildly optimistic. However, his complacency was consistent with CIA assessments and the majority view in Washington at the time. It was probably for this reason that no one in the room asked follow-up questions or otherwise challenged MacArthur on the odds of intervention by the Chinese and an early end to the war. The formal part of the conference adjourned at 9:12 a.m. (Wake Island time), scarcely an hour and a quarter after it began.

* * * * *

Just a few days after Truman returned from Wake, with hopes high for an end to the fighting by Thanksgiving, Mao Zedong finalized his decision. As promised, he would come to the aid of Kim Il-sung even though Stalin refused to contribute not only ground troops but air support as well. At dusk on October 19, the first of eighteen Chinese Communist infantry divisions (180,000 soldiers) under the command of General Peng Dehuai began crossing Yalu River bridges into North Korea. Over the next two weeks they marched across at night, undetected, taking cover each morning before dawn. The United States and the Peoples Republic of China were on a collision course.

Unaware that Chinese divisions were crossing the Yalu in force, MacArthur issued a battle order that violated the spirit, and arguably the letter, of the September 27 directive recommended by Marshall and approved by the president that authorized him to pursue North Korean forces north of the 38th parallel. On October 24, in a final push to destroy the enemy, MacArthur ordered his American field generals to "use any and all ground forces . . . as necessary to secure all of North Korea."[40] In so doing, he unilaterally lifted the provision in the presidential directive that precluded him from using "non-Korean ground forces" near the Manchurian (Chinese) and Soviet borders. The joint chiefs in Washington reacted quickly, cabling MacArthur that his new order was "a matter of some concern here," since it was "not in consonance" with the restrictions against use of non-Korean troops set forth in the presidential directive.[41] Asked to explain his reasons, MacArthur shot back a reply that Omar Bradley, chairman of the joint chiefs, characterized in his memoir as "shocking" and "evasive, if not untruthful." Among other excuses, MacArthur claimed that the subject of using American troops near the northern borders was discussed and approved at the Wake Island conference. Bradley, who was there and reviewed all of the notes of the participants, wrote that he was "certain the subject was never raised."[42] MacArthur also argued that Marshall's letter of September 29 saying that he and his field generals should "feel unhampered" about crossing the 38th parallel gave him license to ignore the restrictions against using American forces in the far north near the Manchurian and Soviet borders.[43] MacArthur knew full well that Marshall's note did not authorize a sweeping drive to the borders of North Korea. It merely clarified that MacArthur and his generals should feel free to cross the 38th instead of pausing there to await a UN vote.

Nonetheless, the joint chiefs chose not to countermand or further question MacArthur's order. Whether Marshall or Truman, the only ones with higher authority who could have intervened, had any knowledge of the exchanges between the joint chiefs and MacArthur is not known. In his memoir, Bradley said it was "really too late" for the joint chiefs to do anything about the order because U.S. ground forces were already advancing close to the Manchurian and Soviet borders.[44]

Over the next several days it became apparent to MacArthur in Tokyo, and Marshall and the joint chiefs in Washington, that well-trained and well-led Chinese Communist regulars had crossed into North Korea. Initially, they surprised and attacked a ROK division near Onjon and then another at Unsan. Chinese infantry annihilated elements of the U.S. 1st Cavalry Division on November 1. In a "not to worry" tone, MacArthur confidently assured the joint chiefs that the Chinese intervention was more likely a low-key operation than a "major" commitment of ground forces. On the morning of November 6, Undersecretary of Defense Bob Lovett was informed that MacArthur had ordered a massive air attack that included a mission to bomb and destroy the southern ends of bridges that spanned the Yalu River from the town of Sinuiju in Korea to Antung in Manchuria. The American B-29s were scheduled to take off in just a few hours. Lovett realized at once that the attack could have disastrous international consequences and needed to be permanently aborted, or at least postponed. There was a very real danger that bombs would fall in Manchuria (the border ran along the middle of the Yalu) and possibly on the city of Antung itself, which would violate a commitment that the U.S. made to consult with the British in advance of operations affecting Manchuria. Moreover, if U.S. bombs were accidentally dropped on Manchurian territory, such an action would jeopardize the chances that the UN might vote favorably on a pending resolution calling on the Chinese to cease intervention.

From the State Department, where he was conferring with Rusk and Acheson, Lovett called Marshall, who advised that the bombing mission was "unwise unless there was some mass movement across the River, which threatened the security" of MacArthur's troops.[45] The president, contacted by Acheson while traveling home to Independence to cast his vote in the midterm elections, agreed to a postponement. In addition, he ordered that the joint chiefs ask MacArthur to explain his "reasons" for bombing the Yalu bridges near Sinuiju.[46] The chiefs passed along Truman's request and, on their own initiative, broadened the scope of the bombing pause by requiring MacArthur to "postpone all bombing of targets within five miles of Manchurian borders."[47] With little more than an hour before takeoff, the mission was aborted.

As Bradley wrote in his memoir, no one in Washington was prepared for the "ferocity of the blast that came back from MacArthur at about eight o'clock" on the night of November 6.[48] "Men and matériel in large force are pouring across all bridges across the Yalu," the message began, and "this movement . . . threatens the ultimate destruction of the forces under my command." Bradley was stunned because it was a complete reversal from what the joint chiefs had been told two days earlier. The remainder of the message was equally disturbing. Claiming that the order of the joint chiefs suspending bombing would have calamitous consequences, MacArthur made it clear that not only was he asking the chiefs to reconsider, he was also demanding that the matter be brought to the "immediate attention of the President."[49] Unless this was done, he warned, he would not accept responsibility. It was an extraordinary rebuff to the authority of the joint chiefs. Bradley wrote that "it was a grave insult to men who were his legal superiors, including George Marshall."[50]

At about 9:20 that evening Bradley convened a meeting of Marshall, Lovett, Acheson, Rusk, and the joint chiefs. Faced with MacArthur's cable saying the Yalu bridges needed to be bombed immediately or his forces faced destruction, the group had little choice but to authorize the mission despite possible adverse effects on the UN resolution calling for withdrawal of the Chinese (subsequently vetoed by the Soviet Union) and on relations with the British. Bradley phoned Truman at his home in Independence, read him the text of MacArthur's message, and informed him that Marshall, the State Department, and the joint chiefs all recommended resumption of the bombing mission. Truman gave the go-ahead. For the next hour or so the group worked on a message to MacArthur that authorized bombing near the Manchurian frontier, including targets at the Korean end of the Yalu bridges, and cautioned him "that it is vital in the national interest of the US to localize the fighting in Korea." As a matter of national policy, he was to take "extreme care" to avoid doing anything on the ground or in the air that would widen the war.[51]

Once the message to MacArthur was finished, the group turned to a discussion of the Korean situation in general and reached a "consensus." It was this part of the late-night meeting that Bradley believed to be one of the "most important" of the war. In the event of the worst case—that the Chinese intervention was in fact massive and they intended to drive MacArthur south to the 38th parallel or perhaps even farther—the conferees agreed, after weighing pros and cons, that they would order MacArthur to pull back to the narrow "waist" of Korea (the Pyongyang-Wonsan line) and allow the diplomats to negotiate a cease-fire via the UN.[52]

General Bradley subsequently expressed profound regret that Secretary Marshall, the top State Department officials, and the joint chiefs, having reached a consensus that night, failed to seize control of the war. In retrospect he was right. However, at the time no one in Tokyo or Washington had reliable intelligence as to the size of the forces the Chinese were sending across the Yalu River. MacArthur was telling Washington that there were between 25,000 and 30,000 Chinese soldiers in North Korea and that they could be readily defeated. A dispatch from Tokyo reported that Chinese and also NKPA troops had broken off contact with MacArthur's Eighth Army and X Corps and had vanished. In fact, there were 300,000 Chinese troops in North Korea by mid-November. Their objective was unknown. It was, wrote Bradley later, "our greatest battlefield intelligence blunder since the Bulge."[53]

Like everyone else, Marshall was blinded by the lack of credible intelligence. On November 7 he wrote a soothing letter of support to MacArthur, the same kind of note he used to write to Eisenhower, suggesting that he understood why MacArthur bridled at limitations placed on him by the joint chiefs. At the same time he warned that a widening of the war could lead to "world disaster." MacArthur responded with warmth, writing that he was in "complete agreement with the basic concept of localizing, if possible, the Korean struggle."[54] Two days later at an afternoon NSC meeting, Marshall agreed that pending clarification of Chinese strength and intentions, MacArthur's mission "should not be changed." In other words, MacArthur should be allowed to resume his ground offensive to defeat all hostile forces in North Korea so long as there appeared to be a "reasonable chance of success."[55]

During the next nineteen days Marshall expressed concerns to the joint chiefs about the gap between the Eighth Army and X Corps that left their flanks unprotected, the dispersion of U.S. forces in the northeast, the establishment of enemy strong points on key terrain features, and the lack of good intelligence about the Chinese. But he did not communicate his misgivings to MacArthur, nor did he insist that the joint chiefs take a firmer stand. When asked by Acheson why he was not more actively involved, Marshall replied that he was no longer army chief of staff. As a "civilian" secretary of defense, he believed that he should not meddle in the decisions of a field commander. In a letter to Clay Blair, the coauthor of Bradley's memoir, Forrest Pogue commented, "If Secretary Stimson had sent 'firm messages' to

Ike and MacArthur [in World War II] Marshall would have exploded."[56] And even if Marshall had been army chief of staff at the time, he still would have been reluctant to interfere. He was always a firm proponent of the principle that once a field commander's mission has been defined, "there must be no interference with his method of carrying it out."[57]

*   *   *   *   *

"TOP SECRET FLASH . . . We face an entirely new war." The cable from MacArthur arrived at the Pentagon at 4:46 a.m. on November 28, 1950.[58] It was delivered to General Omar Bradley at Quarters One.

Four days earlier MacArthur had mounted what he believed would be his war-ending offensive. To reporters that day he declared, "I hope to keep my promise to the G.I.'s to have them home by Christmas."[59] Invisible in the rugged mountains of North Korea, the Chinese Communist regulars had been waiting patiently. To the west, an estimated force of 180,000 faced Johnnie Walker's Eighth Army. Far to the east, some 120,000 Chinese were poised to hit General Edward "Ned" Almond's X Corps. On the night of November 24, they struck, not just by headlong frontal assaults but also by finding soft spots in exposed flanks and moving in behind American and ROK units to sow confusion and cut off retreat. By the third day, as Bradley wrote, "it was clear to Walker and Almond that they had been ambushed by massive Chinese forces and that the entire UN ground force was in danger of piecemeal envelopment."[60]

Bradley called the president at 6:15 a.m. and read him the entire contents of MacArthur's message. It was a "new war," wrote MacArthur, because his "present strength of force" was not sufficient to meet that of the Chinese. Their objective, he said, was "complete destruction" of all UN forces in Korea. In a rare show of humility, MacArthur admitted that since the new picture raised "world embracing considerations," the grand strategy for managing the conflict was beyond his authority as a "Theater Commander." For the near term, he concluded, his plan was to "pass from the offensive to the defensive."[61] It was a dramatic turn of events.

Shocked at this completely unexpected news, Truman convened an extraordinary afternoon session of the NSC in the Cabinet Room. Marshall had spent most of the morning with the civilian service secretaries, the joint chiefs, Rusk, and Harriman formulating his views so he could present the president with the best possible advice. It was at this NSC meeting—one of the most important of the Truman presidency—that Marshall demonstrated why Truman and his predecessor wanted to have him in Washington sitting beside them when major decisions affecting the security of the Republic had to be made.

After a briefing by Bradley on the military situation in Korea, the president turned to Marshall. His first and most salient point was that the U.S. on its own or as a member of the UN should do everything in its power to "limit" the war. And, as a logical and essential corollary, it should take no actions that might broaden the war. "We should not go into Chinese Communist territory and we should not use Chinese Nationalist forces," he counseled. "To do this would be to fall into a carefully laid Soviet trap." If the U.S. should get bogged down in a war in China with the Chinese Communists, he warned, its power to contain the Soviet Union in Europe and elsewhere would be weakened. With that in mind he advocated "a more rapid buildup" of U.S. forces in Europe, combined with pressure on Congress to provide funding to "accelerate" a program of rearmament. Underlying this advice was Marshall's conviction that it was aggressive actions by the Soviet Union in Europe, not China or North Korea, that posed the greatest threat to America's national security.

With respect to force levels in Korea, Marshall recommended an increase in the number of non-American UN troops, suggesting that MacArthur would have to get along with the U.S. forces he already had, at least for the time being. Vice President Alben Barkley pressed Marshall, asking him what he would do if the Chinese Communists "put even more men" into North Korea. Marshall said he couldn't give an immediate answer. All he could say was that the U.S. should "avoid getting sewed up in Korea," and should seek to "get out with honor." Marshall said he assumed that MacArthur would "withdraw his advanced forces" and "hold a line" farther south, but it would not be "helpful to interfere" with such tactical decisions.

At the conclusion of the NSC meeting, Truman was asked whether he wished to have "any decisions recorded." His answer was "no."[62] Though not recorded, historic decisions were in fact made. First, the president and his national security team decided not to allow the crisis in Korea to morph into a war in China, which might in turn flare into a third world war. Second, they agreed that to contain the Soviet Union, U.S. defense expenditures

Distressing Necessity

577

would have to be substantially increased. And finally, under the auspices of the UN it was determined that America would wage a limited war in Korea with the objective of reaching a diplomatic settlement.

* * * * *

For the next six weeks MacArthur's UN forces in Korea stood on the brink of disaster. On the east side of the peninsula, X Corps, which included the 1st Marine Division, withdrew from the Chosin Reservoir in the bitter cold and snow to the port of Hungnam on the Sea of Japan. On Christmas Eve, under the protection of naval gunfire and carrier-based aircraft, the last of the divisions was safely evacuated by sea to Pusan in the far south. Approximately 105,000 UN troops, along with thousands of vehicles and Korean civilians and a third of a million tons of supplies, were shipped out of Hungnam harbor on 193 navy transports.

Over on the west side, the Eighth Army, under General Walker, withdrew south pursuant to orders to establish a defensive line across Korea at the most advantageous position. On December 23, Walker was killed instantly when he was thrown from his open jeep after being hit by a Korean truck. He was the highest-ranking U.S. general to be killed in Korea. Almost immediately, Collins, Marshall, and Truman approved MacArthur's request to appoint General Matthew Bunker Ridgway, a brilliant leader of airborne troops during World War II, to replace Walker. Ridgway was known as a "Marshall man," having served under him as a company commander in Tientsin, China, a student at Fort Benning, and a staff officer during military maneuvers in the Midwest prior to World War II. He was an early entry in Marshall's mythical black book. Ridgway took command of the Eighth Army near the 38th parallel the day after Christmas. In contrast to Walker, MacArthur gave Ridgway complete discretion to attack, defend, or withdraw as he saw fit. "The Eighth Army is yours, Matt," said MacArthur. "Do what you think best."[63] On New Year's Eve the Chinese tested the brand-new commander. They attacked the Eighth Army along a 44-mile-long front. Ridgway deliberately fell back and established a bridgehead around Seoul. But two days later he was forced to abandon the capital and withdraw south of the Han River, where he established a new defensive line.

Sensing that he could be made the scapegoat for the looming defeat,

MacArthur tried to shift blame to the Truman administration, complaining in an interview published in early December by *U.S. News & World Report* that restrictions preventing "hot pursuit" of Chinese aircraft and bombing of bases in Manchuria posed "an enormous handicap, without precedent in military history."[64] In a message on the same date to the president of the United Press, MacArthur suggested that "selfish" and "short-sighted" views of U.S. allies, probably meaning the British, were responsible for limits on his operations in North Korea.[65] Truman was livid. "I should have relieved General MacArthur then and there," he wrote in his memoir.[66] Instead, he tried to muzzle him. On December 5, the president directed that all statements concerning foreign or military policy by any public official, including military commanders, must be cleared in advance by the Defense or State Departments and submitted to the White House. The joint chiefs made sure MacArthur received a copy.

On January 10, 1951, probably the low point of the Korean War for Marshall and the Truman administration, MacArthur sent a cable to Washington that, in the words of joint chiefs' historian James Schnabel, "produced profound dismay."[67] It was cleverly written, but in essence it was an argument in opposition to orders by the administration requiring MacArthur's UN troops to find and hold a line in Korea while the diplomats broker a political settlement. The only viable choices, claimed MacArthur, were either "evacuation" of UN forces from the peninsula, which he knew was a nonstarter, or all-out war with Red China, obviously his preferred choice. To ask his "tired" troops to hold a line in Korea and "trade life" for an undefined "political policy" was "untenable," he argued. "Their morale will become a serious threat to their battle efficiency."[68] Secretary Acheson wrote that MacArthur's cable was nothing more than a "posterity paper," designed to absolve "himself of blame if things went wrong" and to put "maximum pressure on Washington to reverse itself and adopt [MacArthur's] proposals for widening the war against China." He was convinced that MacArthur was "basically disloyal to the purposes of his Commander in Chief." Acheson recalled that when Marshall read the sentence in the cable about poor morale "he remarked to Dean Rusk that when a general complains of the morale of his troops, the time has come to look into his own."[69]

Marshall obtained permission from Truman to send army chief of staff

Joe Collins and air force chief Hoyt Vandenberg (nephew of Senator Arthur Vandenberg) to Korea to make an on-site assessment. On January 17, Collins wired a brief flash to Bradley that painted a picture opposite to that described by MacArthur. "Eighth Army in good shape and improving daily under Ridgway's leadership," he wrote. "Morale very satisfactory considering conditions . . . Eighth Army . . . prepared to punish severely any mass attack."[70] Bradley took this optimistic message to Marshall, who read it to Truman over the telephone. Word spread through the upper levels of government. It "was a tremendous relief" and marked a "turning point" in the war, wrote Bradley.[71] Marshall did not reveal his feelings. However, like Truman and the rest of his administration, he must have lost faith in MacArthur's judgment.

During the ensuing two months Ridgway was transformed by war correspondents into a national celebrity, appearing on the cover of *Time* magazine for the second time (the first was in April 1945 when he was wounded leading Operation Varsity, a massive airborne jump into Germany). Beginning from positions along a wavy west-east line far to the south of the 38th parallel, Ridgway mounted a series of counterattacks by the Eighth Army that shattered the better part of fourteen Chinese Communist divisions— nearly half of the forces that the Chinese committed to Korea the previous November. The remainder, along with NKPA divisions, withdrew to their previous defensive positions. After delays due to unusual February rains and logistical problems, Ridgway launched Operation Ripper, which was a smashing success. His I Corps made a surprise crossing of the Han River, outflanked Seoul, and captured high ground to the east of the capital. Forced to choose between attacking I Corps and abandoning Seoul, the enemy fled the city. To the east, IX Corps, with the 1st Marines leading the way, fought much farther north to Chuncheon, close to the 38th parallel.

On March 15, a ROK unit raised the South Korean flag above the rubble of Seoul, the fourth time the city had changed hands. Marshall, whom Ridgway revered, wrote a newsy letter that began by complimenting him on "the magnificent job" he had done "amidst many hardships," and went on to thoughtfully report that Penny, Ridgway's wife, "and little Matt are getting along in splendid fashion."[72]

* * * * *

Heartened by the fact that Ridgway had driven the Chinese Communists back to the 38th parallel, the Truman administration, in consultation with its UN allies, decided that the time was ripe to pause and focus efforts on a political settlement of the war. On March 20, the joint chiefs, with the approval of Marshall, Acheson, and Truman, cabled MacArthur to inform him that the president would shortly announce publicly that the United Nations was prepared to enter into negotiations with Chinese and North Korean representatives. MacArthur was further advised that while these diplomatic efforts were developing, there was a "strong UN feeling" that he should not "advance with major forces north of 38th Parallel."[73]

MacArthur must have been outraged when he read the chiefs' cable. Any hopes he had of convincing Washington to widen the war so that he could advance without restriction to the Yalu River and reunify the peninsula were dashed. Four days later, while MacArthur was in Korea, his staff in Tokyo issued a communiqué under his name that was designed to preempt Truman's imminent announcement of a peace initiative. MacArthur began by taunting if not insulting Chairman Mao and his Chinese Communists for their lack of "industrial capacity" and their "military weaknesses." He threatened to expand the war against China to its "coastal areas and interior bases." And he took it upon himself to declare that he, not the president, stood ready to "confer in the field with the Commander-in-Chief of the enemy forces in an earnest effort" to realize the "political objectives of the United Nations in Korea . . . without further bloodshed."[74]

MacArthur's communiqué was an astonishing rebuke, "a challenge to the authority of the president under the Constitution," as Truman later wrote, a breach of the principle of civilian control over the military, and a clear violation of the president's order of December 5 that public statements on foreign policy be approved in advance.[75] To his daughter Margaret, Truman reportedly said, "I couldn't send a message to the Chinese" after MacArthur's communiqué. "He prevented a cease-fire proposition right there."[76]

Truman made up his mind. General MacArthur would have to be relieved. However, he was talked out of taking such drastic action, at least for the time being, by Acheson, Rusk, and Lovett (Marshall was at Pinehurst for the Easter weekend). MacArthur's offer of peace negotiations was playing well in the press, they said. Firing MacArthur at this moment would put the president "on the side of sin."[77] Moreover, they could assure UN diplomats behind the scenes that MacArthur's statement did not reflect the president's position. Truman was persuaded that a reprimand rather than dismissal was the prudent action to take. He dictated a message to MacArthur reprimanding him for violating his December 5 directive (concerning advance approval of public statements) and ordering him to immediately report to the joint chiefs any request by an enemy military leader for an armistice or other peace overture. Acheson wrote that the president's message "laid so plainly the foundation for a court-martial as to give pause even to General MacArthur."[78]

The president took his time, confident that MacArthur would hurl an even more blatant challenge to his authority. On Thursday afternoon, April 5, Roger Tubby, a new assistant press secretary, burst into the Oval Office with a ticker bulletin in his hand. "Mr. President," he said, "this man is not only insubordinate, but he's insolent, and I think he ought to be fired."[79] Truman read the bulletin. It was a letter written by MacArthur to House minority leader Joe Martin (R-MA), one of Truman's most virulent critics, that Martin had read on the floor of the House and released to the press earlier that day. In the letter, MacArthur wrote that he agreed with Martin that the U.S. should encourage Chiang's Nationalist forces on Formosa to attack the Chinese mainland, a step that the Truman administration had repeatedly refused to take because it would result in a full-scale war with Red China and possibly trigger a world war. In the next paragraph MacArthur denounced the fundamental principle underlying Truman's foreign policy, the "Europe first" policy advocated and for the most part adhered to by Roosevelt and Marshall ever since the 1941 Pearl Harbor attack. The place to defeat the "Communist conspirators" is "here in Asia," wrote MacArthur, not in Europe. If we win the war in Asia, he pronounced, "Europe most probably would avoid war." His concluding words—"There is no substitute for victory"—made clear that MacArthur not only disagreed with, he also held in contempt Truman's effort to broker a diplomatic settlement of the Korean War.[80]

The president phoned Marshall to get his reaction. Lovett recalled that when Marshall heard Truman repeat the substance of MacArthur's letter to Martin, who was "the leader of the opposition," he was "revolted."[81]

"This look [*sic*] like the last straw," Truman angrily scribbled in his diary. "Rank insubordination . . . I've come to the conclusion that our Big General in the Far East must be recalled," he wrote. However, "I don't express any opinion or make known my decision [while my advisers deliberate]."[82] His aim was to wait until he received a unanimous recommendation from his four key advisers—Marshall, Acheson, Harriman, and Bradley—before disclosing his decision to relieve MacArthur. Given the political firestorm that he knew would follow he could not afford to have any "no" votes, abstentions, or doubts leaked from his advisers or their aides.

The president called the "Big Four" together on Friday April 6 to test the waters. Acheson left no doubt where he was coming from: MacArthur should be relieved of command and brought home. Warning that Truman would have a major battle on his hands, the only issue, wrote Acheson, was how to manage MacArthur's firing so as to minimize the fallout. On the other hand, Marshall was not close to pulling the trigger. Worried about the effect on troop morale and on appropriation requests pending in Congress, Marshall counseled caution. The president asked him to take time to review all of the relevant messages from MacArthur, which he did. Later that afternoon, the Big Four met in Marshall's office. Marshall proposed that rather than firing MacArthur outright, he should be called home "for consultation and reaching final decision after that." Recalling MacArthur's "histrionic abilities" and "prestige," Acheson was strongly opposed, writing that this would play into the hands of Senator McCarthy and the other "primitives" on the "extreme Republican right" who were trying to get Truman impeached.[83] Marshall backed down.

The next day, Saturday, the four advisers met briefly with Truman in the morning and asked him to postpone a decision until Monday. Army Chief of Staff Collins, who was in Alabama at the Air War College, would be flying back to Washington Saturday night. Bradley and Marshall needed to have Collins's views before they would be ready to make a recommendation. That afternoon Bradley and Marshall searched for an alternative to dismissal. They were concerned that if MacArthur was fired for "insubordination" or willful violation of a direct order, it could lead, as Bradley wrote, "to myriad legal entanglements, perhaps even—God forbid!—a Billy Mitchell-type court-martial."[84] As Bradley wrote, they were also concerned about a "larger point." Since MacArthur was a darling of the right and a potential candidate for the presidency in 1952, a recommendation by the joint chiefs to relieve MacArthur could and probably would be construed as politically motivated. Marshall and Bradley wanted to do everything in their power to avoid "politicizing" the joint chiefs, a prospect that they regarded as a serious danger to the security of the nation.[85]

In his memoir Bradley speculated that Marshall may have sought an alternative to dismissal of MacArthur for personal reasons. Marshall had made it known that he expected to retire in September. Why would he want to end his career by enduring a new round of vicious personal attacks by the likes of Senators McCarthy and Jenner? It had long been rumored that Marshall and MacArthur were bitter rivals. Why should Marshall open himself up to charges that he masterminded the firing of MacArthur as a petty act of revenge? Since Bradley knew and worked with Marshall for more than two decades, there was perhaps more than a grain of truth to his conjecture.

At a few minutes after four o'clock on Sunday afternoon, the joint chiefs filed into Marshall's office at the Pentagon. They were a "sad and sober group," wrote Collins. Marshall asked each to state his views separately. Collins simply said that the president was entitled to have a commander whose views were "in consonance" with the "policies of his government."[86] The chiefs were unanimous. If the president decided to relieve MacArthur, each of them would concur. Bradley, as chairman, summarized their reasoning, which he later reduced to writing. MacArthur should be relieved, not for "insubordination," a legally freighted term, but because he was "not in sympathy with the decision to try to limit the conflict to Korea"; his actions jeopardized "civilian control" of the military; and he failed to comply with the president's December 5 directive to clear statements of policy before making them public.[87] Marshall made no comment of his own except to direct Bradley to state the views of the joint chiefs to the president in the morning. Collins wrote that this was Marshall's usual practice when he received staff reports orally.

The Big Four convened in the president's study at nine o'clock on Monday morning. Bradley reported that the joint chiefs were unanimous: MacArthur should be relieved of all of his commands in the Far East. Marshall finally spoke up. He agreed. Acheson and Harriman likewise concurred. Up until that time the president had not disclosed his decision, but everyone in the room knew what it was. General MacArthur had to go.

Truman explained that he had made up his mind almost two weeks earlier when MacArthur issued the communiqué undermining his peace initiative. As to who should replace MacArthur as Far East commander in Tokyo, Bradley said that Matt Ridgway was the first choice of Marshall and the joint chiefs. They also recommended that James Van Fleet should replace Ridgway as commander of the Eighth Army in Korea.

Truman instructed Bradley to draw up the necessary papers. However, in view of MacArthur's fifty years of service to the nation, he made it clear that the process of relieving him of his commands should be carried out with courtesy and dignity. At Marshall's suggestion, top secret plans were put in place to have Secretary of the Army Frank Pace, who happened to be in Korea, deliver the relief orders personally to MacArthur in Tokyo prior to the public announcement to be made by Truman from the White House. The president agreed that this would be the most respectful and least embarrassing way to deliver the news to the proud general.

Marshall's carefully laid plans were thrown into disarray late on the afternoon of April 10 when reporters with the *Chicago Tribune* called Bradley and the White House press office for a comment on rumors that MacArthur had been relieved of command. By that time, Truman's relief orders had already been radioed in encoded form to Pace, who was still in Korea, but they were not to be delivered to MacArthur at his headquarters in the Dai-ichi Building for several hours. White House press aides assumed that the leak came from Tokyo, not Washington, and that MacArthur was on the verge of pulling off a clever public relations masterstroke by resigning himself and issuing a press release critical of the administration before Truman could announce that he had been fired. According to Truman aide George Elsey, the White House was "panicked by the fear that MacArthur might get the jump."[88] Should Truman stick to the plan or should he release the news before MacArthur stole the show by resigning? Calls went out to the Big Four. Marshall, who was at a movie with Katherine, couldn't be reached. The other three rushed to the White House. At ten p.m., Acheson, Harriman, and Bradley, plus Dean Rusk and Joe Short (the new press secretary), got Truman out of bed at Blair House where he was living because the White House was being renovated. "They caught me in my pajamas," Truman said the next day. "I authorized Bradley to send an urgent wire directly to MacArthur. And I told Joe Short to announce MacArthur's relief and Ridgway's appointment right away. I wasn't going to let the SOB resign on me. I wanted to *fire* him."[89]

When Marshall returned from the movies he was advised of the change of plans. He cabled Pace, telling him it was no longer necessary to deliver the relief orders to MacArthur but that he should still proceed to Tokyo "to assist Ridgway in assuming . . . his [new] command."[90]

Select members of the Washington press corps had to be roused from sleep or tracked down at bars and nightclubs by the White House switchboard. By one a.m. on April 11, they gathered in Short's office. He began by reading a terse statement by the president. "With deep regret I have concluded that General of the Army Douglas MacArthur is unable to give his wholehearted support to the policies of the United States Government and the United Nations in matters pertaining to his official duties . . . I have, therefore, relieved General MacArthur of his commands."[91] Short handed out mimeographed copies of the relief orders and seven background documents that were intended to substantiate Truman's reasons for firing MacArthur.

In Tokyo, MacArthur was hosting a lunch at the U.S. Embassy for Senator Warren Magnuson (D-WA) and others. Sometime after two p.m., his wife, Jean, entered the dining room and whispered in his ear the news that one of MacArthur's aides had just heard on the radio and passed on to her. MacArthur's face froze. He was heard to say, "Jeanie, we are going home at last."[92]

* * * * *

The angry outcry throughout the United States at the news that Truman fired MacArthur was beyond all expectations. "Seldom has a more unpopular man fired a more popular one," wrote *Time* magazine.[93] A Gallup poll reported that two out of three Americans disapproved Truman's relief of MacArthur. The reaction was partisan and menacing. Prominent Republicans called for Truman's impeachment. Senator Richard Nixon stopped short of impeachment. Instead, he moved to censure Truman and reinstate MacArthur. The legislatures of the states of California, Illinois, Michigan, and Florida voted to condemn the president's action.

MacArthur's twin-tailed Constellation, the *Bataan*, touched down at National Airport fifteen minutes after midnight on April 19. He had been away from the United States for almost a decade and a half. Waiting for him on the darkened tarmac were George Marshall; the joint chiefs; General Jonathan "Skinny" Wainwright, who was captured and held by the Japanese as a POW for three years after MacArthur left Corregidor; Congressman Joe Martin, who made public the letter that led to MacArthur's downfall; and Truman's military aide, Major General Harry Vaughan. As MacArthur descended the ramp, he spotted Marshall and thrust out his hand. "Hello, George," he shouted. "How are you?"[94] They clasped hands for the photographers. A cheering crowd estimated at 12,000 surged forward.

About twelve hours later, half past noon, MacArthur stood at the rostrum in the House of Representatives waiting for the thunderous applause to die. He was wearing a trim, waist-length "Eisenhower" military jacket without medals or ribbons. The only decorations were five stars attached to his collar. Due to his jet-black hair (which some said was dyed), unlined face, and erect posture, MacArthur looked younger than his seventy-one years. Peering down at the front row he could see that Marshall, the rest of Truman's cabinet, the joint chiefs, and the Supreme Court justices were conspicuously absent. Seated in the places normally reserved for them were Jean, his son Arthur, and a number of MacArthur's friends and supporters.

In addition to those on the House floor and in the jam-packed gallery, a record 20 to 30 million Americans watched on television as MacArthur began his memorable address to this joint session of Congress. Gifted with a rich voice and a skilled actor's sense of timing, it took only a few minutes for MacArthur to mount a full-scale attack on the "Europe first" policy advocated by the Truman administration and its corollary, a limited war in Asia. "There are those who claim," intoned MacArthur, that U.S. military "strength is inadequate" to contain the Soviet Union in Europe and at the same time fight an all-out war against Red China in Asia. As if the facts concerning U.S. strength didn't matter, MacArthur charged that those making such claims were nothing more than "defeatists." And he didn't have to name names.[95] The millions watching and listening to him knew that the so-called defeatists were Marshall, Acheson, and Truman. By preventing him from widening the Korean War, alleged MacArthur, they were "appeasing" communism in Asia while prioritizing the defense of Europe (MacArthur sprinkled the loaded A-word throughout his speech).

Reduced to its essence, MacArthur's thirty-four-minute speech eloquently made his case for "Asia first," a complete reversal of the administration's policy. In doing so, he also made the case for why Truman had to fire
him. A man of the Orient, MacArthur was never "in sympathy" with his
commander in chief's national security policy.

General Bradley, who watched MacArthur's speech on television at the
Pentagon, wrote that it was one of the "most moving speeches" he had ever
heard. Nevertheless, he noted three misstatements, each incorrectly suggesting that the joint chiefs approved proposed actions by MacArthur, that
he found "quite disturbing."[96] The most troubling was a claim by MacArthur
that Bradley and the joint chiefs "fully shared" his view that Chiang's Nationalist forces on Formosa should be encouraged to invade mainland China
and that the U.S. should provide them with "logistical support." This was an
outright lie. Still, like almost everyone who heard or saw MacArthur's performance that day, Bradley was "touched deeply" by MacArthur's sentimen-
tal peroration that perfectly fit the emotions of the occasion: "The world has
turned over many times since I took the oath on the plain of West Point . . .
But I still remember the refrain of one of the most popular barracks ballads
of that day, which proclaimed most profoundly that—'Old soldiers never die;
they just fade away.' And like the old soldier of that ballad I now close my
military career and just fade away—an old soldier who tried to do his duty as
God gave him the light to see his duty. Good Bye."[97]

The sustained applause in the chamber and the public adulation during
the next few days were overwhelming. "We saw a hunk of God in the
flesh, and we heard the voice of God," exulted Congressman Dewey
Short. Former president Herbert Hoover exclaimed that MacArthur was
"the reincarnation of Saint Paul into a great General of the Army who
came out of the East."[98] Truman was not among those who were touched.
He claimed that he did not watch or listen to the speech, but read it later.
He told an aide that he thought MacArthur's speech was "a bunch of
damn bullshit."[99]

Immediately following MacArthur's speech several congressmen
pressed for a joint congressional investigation of his dismissal by the president. Republicans had high hopes that MacArthur might emerge as their
standard-bearer in 1952.

* * * * *

Two weeks later, on the morning of May 3, the voice of God was about to confront deft cross-examination in the marble Caucus Room of the Senate Office Building. Seated at a small desk, with his aide Courtney Whitney to his left, MacArthur faced a tableful of senators in front of him and equally laden tables on each side, microphones at the ready. Flashbulbs littered the carpet. The closed-door hearings of the Senate Armed Services and Foreign Relations Committees were gaveled to order by Senator Richard Russell Jr., a highly respected conservative Georgia Democrat who was ideologically closer to most Republican senators than he was to liberal Democrats. Russell made it clear to his colleagues that the hearings on the relief of MacArthur were to focus on substance—matters of vital importance to national security. To limit histrionics, reporters and TV cameras were barred from the Caucus Room, though edited transcripts were distributed to the press every evening.

Midway through the afternoon of the first day, Russell turned the questioning over to the junior senator from Connecticut, Brien McMahon. A graduate of Yale Law School, McMahon was appointed at age thirty-one to head the Criminal Division of the U.S. Justice Department, where for six years he tried high-profile "gangster" cases and the landmark Harlan County Coal Miners' case, involving the right of labor to form unions under the Wagner Act. Elected to the Senate as a Roosevelt Democrat at age forty-four, he had become an expert in foreign affairs.

In contrast to other committee members who fawned over MacArthur at the outset of their questioning, McMahon brusquely seized control of his witness: "I will make no apology for the time that I take because we are here discussing the survival of our Nation, which means the future of civilization itself." MacArthur must have realized that he was in for a long afternoon. McMahon's first question went to the heart of why Marshall and the joint chiefs supported Truman's decision to relieve MacArthur. "General," McMahon asked, "we are faced, are we not, with a global problem in the ambitions of Communist Russia?" McMahon knew how MacArthur would respond and he delivered on cue. "Unquestionably," said the general. Once MacArthur conceded that the Soviets were the principal threat, McMahon set the hook. He skillfully marched him through a series of questions that caused him to admit that as a "theater commander" he had no responsibility for and thus little if any knowledge about global defense, the defense of Western Europe, or the defense of America in the event the Soviet Union should decide to make war. When MacArthur asserted his belief that his actions in Korea and Manchuria would not "necessarily" bring the Soviets into the war, McMahon shot back, "You could be wrong about it, couldn't you?" MacArthur responded, "Most assuredly." McMahon paused for effect, knowing that he had set MacArthur up. The forthcoming testimony of Marshall and the joint chiefs, who actually had the responsibility for global defense and had intelligence about Soviet intentions, would establish with scarcely any doubt that Truman was right to fire MacArthur. McMahon made sure Russell and the other twenty-four members of the two committees were listening, and then said, "General, I think you have made the point very well that I want to make; that the Joint Chiefs of Staff and the President of the United States, the Commander in Chief, has to look at this thing on a global basis and a global defense. You as a theater commander by your own statement have not made that kind of study [of the "global problem"], and yet you advise us to push forward with a course of action that may involve us in that global conflict."[100]

Picking up on McMahon's cross-examination in his opening statement on May 7, Marshall brought the voice of God down to earth. MacArthur's responsibilities were those of a "local theater commander," explained Marshall. However, the joint chiefs, the secretary of defense, and the president were responsible for determining the locus of the primary threat to the "total security of the United States," and "how and where we must gain time to grow stronger." MacArthur's words and actions would have us, warned Marshall, "carry the conflict beyond Korea" into mainland China. This would risk not only an "extension of war with Red China," it would also "expose Western Europe to attack by the millions of Soviet troops poised in Middle and Eastern Europe." Left unsaid was the obvious fact that no one in the Truman administration was willing to assume those risks.

It was one thing for a theater commander like MacArthur to complain to his superiors because they prioritized another theater, said Marshall (during World War II he characterized this naturally occurring phenomenon as "a case of localitis"). It was quite another—and "wholly unprecedented"—for MacArthur to "publicly" express his "displeasure at and his disagreement with the foreign and military policy of the United States." Since it was therefore apparent that MacArthur was "out of sympathy" with the policies of the U.S., "there was no other recourse but to relieve him," concluded Marshall.[101]

As far as Marshall was concerned, his testimony should have ended then and there. At age seventy he tired easily. However, even though he was compelled to endure another six days of endlessly repetitive and hostile questioning, he did not falter. After Marshall was finally dismissed, Bradley, the joint chiefs, Acheson, and other witnesses carried on for six weeks. Passions gradually cooled. The point that McMahon established through MacArthur's own words and which Marshall drove home in his opening statement survived intact. Most who paid attention agreed that Truman's decision to relieve MacArthur was warranted. Though eight of the twenty-six members of the joint congressional committee wrote a minority report that was critical of the Truman administration, the majority decided to let the record—3,691 pages—speak for itself. By far the most-quoted line that emerged from the hearings was uttered by General Bradley on May 15. MacArthur's "strategy," he famously said, "would involve us in the wrong war, at the wrong place, at the wrong time, and with the wrong enemy."[102]

*　*　*　*　*

While most historians would agree that Marshall's testimony was instrumental in justifying Truman's decision to relieve MacArthur, the question lingers: Why didn't Marshall weigh in much earlier? Acheson refused to buy Marshall's initial explanation—that, as a "civilian" secretary of defense, he was hesitant to interfere with the decisions of a field commander. In a letter to Paul Nitze, the State Department's head of policy planning who succeeded George Kennan, Acheson aptly criticized Marshall's months of relative silence concerning MacArthur's actions as a "curious quiescence."[103] It was perhaps curious to Acheson, but not to Marshall. As Marshall stated at the beginning of his opening statement, the relief of MacArthur was a "distressing necessity" because MacArthur was a highly respected "brother Army officer."[104] The distress was due to Marshall's "institutional mindset," a hallmark of his character.[105] General of the Army Douglas MacArthur was a national hero. Like George Patton, who was likewise controversial, MacArthur's bravery and leadership in two world wars were woven into the fabric of the army. Aware that firing MacArthur, former chief of staff and superintendent of West Point, could severely tarnish his beloved institution, Marshall gave in to an unrealistic hope that MacArthur could be talked into changing his ways or that the fortunes of war would render his relief unnecessary. It was one of his "weakest moments," wrote David Halberstam.[106] That's why it was so distressing to him when he was finally compelled to acknowledge that his brother officer had to be fired.

* * * * *

By the end of May, U.S. war objectives in Korea had been radically altered by the NSC and approved by the president. The goal was no longer to unify the peninsula by force. Instead, General Ridgway was ordered to continue to inflict maximum losses on the NKPA and Chinese Communist forces with the aim of creating conditions favorable to a diplomatic settlement. In early June Trygve Lie of the UN and Dean Acheson publicly called for a cease-fire at or near the 38th parallel. George Kennan, who was at Princeton's Institute for Advanced Studies, was deputized to discuss a possible cease-fire with Yakov Malik, the Soviet ambassador to the UN. On June 5, during Kennan's second session at Malik's home on Long Island, the ambassador made a surprising statement. The Soviet government, he informed Kennan, "wanted a peaceful solution of the Korean question—and at the earliest possible moment."[107]

Aware that the odds of truce talks had improved, Marshall made arrangements for a secret flight to Korea. According to the official history of the Office of the Secretary of Defense, "he wanted particularly to greet and encourage Ridgway" who, according to Marshall Carter, was probably "the single officer in the whole military establishment that the secretary most admired."[108] After delivering a commencement address at Washington University in St. Louis, in order to fool the press Marshall swapped planes with a general who was on his way back to Washington. Only a handful of people knew that Marshall and his aide, Colonel Marshall Carter, were headed to Korea. Once they arrived in Seoul, about midday on June 8, Marshall, along with Ridgway and his public relations officer, Colonel James Quirk, boarded a small "light aircraft" for "a tour of the front line units." Ridgway, whose men nicknamed him "Old Iron Tits" because he typically appeared with matching grenades dangling from his chest straps, was delighted to host

Marshall's visit. According to Ridgway, the weather was "foul" with "lots of turbulence," so he suggested to Marshall that they continue the tour in jeeps.[109] Marshall insisted on flying. In a letter to his wife, Quirk wrote that "it was so dangerous it was silly, but Generals are like that. They think they always have to be braver than everyone else and they get away with it."[110] In a "green camouflaged army tent on the western front," Marshall met with General James Van Fleet, head of the Eighth Army, Lieutenant General Frank Milburn, commander of I Corps, and "several division commanders," while artillery thundered in the distance and "fighter planes droned overhead." By the end of the afternoon Marshall visited with "all corps commanders," most of the other "division commanders," and "all but two of the commanders of foreign units."[111]

The generals with whom Marshall spoke soon realized he was not there to deliver orders or to discuss the possibility of a cease-fire. He had come to boost morale, to provide encouragement, and to let them know that he and the brass back in Washington appreciated their sacrifices and backed them to the hilt. There is no known record of how he was perceived by the many commanders who spoke with him or by the more cynical GIs who glimpsed him from afar. A photo depicts Marshall striding past a white-gloved army honor guard in Hongcheon, holding his hat over his heart. For almost fifty years, he had inspected troops at home and on distant battlefields. But sadly, this was the last time the "old man" was to mix with his soldiers at an active battlefront.

Marshall was back in Washington just in time to hear about Senator Joseph McCarthy's bitter diatribe against him, which the Wisconsin senator read from the empty floor of the Senate to reporters in the gallery. Furious at Marshall's testimony supporting the president's decision to fire MacArthur and blaming the secretary of defense for the bloody stalemate in Korea, McCarthy charged, among many other things, that "it was Marshall's strategy for Korea which turned that war into a pointless slaughter." And "it was Marshall" who fixed the 38th parallel "as the dividing line for Korea, a line historically chosen by Russia to mark its sphere of influence in Korea."[112] Marshall declined to respond to these lies, creating the impression that he was not affected by McCarthy's slanderous accusations. To Rose Page, he repeated an old joke that he thought was an appropriate retort to McCarthy:

"As the street cleaner said to the elephant, 'That's enough out of you.'"[113] However, as Mark Stoler and other Marshall biographers have suggested, McCarthy's attacks "may have reinforced" Marshall's "determination to retire as soon as possible."[114]

Nine days after McCarthy's attack on Marshall, prospects for a negotiated peace gained momentum. On June 23, the Soviet Union, via a UN-sponsored radio broadcast, publicly declared that talks for a cease-fire and armistice should begin. Ambassador Alan Kirk reported from Moscow that the Chinese government in Beijing supported the move to end the costly war because it was undermining its economic plans. To solve the problem of establishing contact with the North Korean and Chinese forces in the absence of diplomatic channels, Ridgway was instructed to send messages to the NKPA and Chinese Communist commanders in Korea inviting them to begin talks aboard a neutral Danish hospital ship in the Han River southwest of the town of Kaesong. The Chinese and North Korean commanders promptly replied. It was agreed that cease-fire negotiations would commence on July 10, not aboard ship but on or near the 38th parallel just south of Kaesong. Fighting was to continue except in the immediate area of the talks.

On-again, off-again negotiations proceeded slowly for the next two years. The fighting finally ended when the parties signed an armistice agreement on July 27, 1953, in the nearby village of Panmunjom (the site of the negotiations was changed in October 1951 after the North Koreans claimed that the original locale had been bombed). Of the approximately 1.8 million Americans who fought in the Korean War, 33,652 were killed in action; 92,134 were wounded; and 7,747 are listed as still missing or not accounted for. The South Koreans sustained about 300,000 military and roughly a million civilian casualties (killed, wounded, and missing). Estimated casualties suffered by the Chinese Communist armies ranged from a low of 360,000 to a high of a million and a half. In North Korea, B-29 bombers laid waste to the infrastructure, pulverizing bridges, power plants, railways, roads, and towns. Casualties of the NKPA approached 500,000, while millions of civilians fled south or vanished. Almost every year since 1953, the North Korean leaders Kim Il-sung, Kim Jong-il, and Kim Jong-un, respectively, have celebrated the July 27 armistice with a "Victory Day" military parade in Pyongyang.

* * * * *

"We are having the most restful and delightful" vacation, wrote Katherine. "We are very lazy and fish, canoe and bathe when we feel like it—or just sit in the sun on the beach."[115] Harold Dodds, the popular president of Princeton, loaned Katherine and George his cottage on Cape Cod's Waquoit Bay for the month of August while he was away in Great Britain. Marshall was bone-tired. With the relief of MacArthur, Ridgway in firm command, cease-fire talks under way, and Congress in recess, there were no looming crises that obligated Marshall to remain in the sweltering capital. And even if something did come up, Undersecretary Bob Lovett was perfectly capable. He was ready to take over as secretary whenever Marshall decided to step down.

Shortly after Marshall returned to the Pentagon he wrote a fatherly tongue-in-cheek "order" to Lovett, the first written clue that he was about to resign. Informing Lovett that he had "no recourse but to comply," Marshall directed the undersecretary to place himself under the "exclusive control" of his wife and vacate the Pentagon for a four-day weekend "for pleasure and divertissement." Marshall reminded Lovett that when the Germans overran Western Europe in 1940, Henry Stimson, as secretary of war, sent him a very similar order because he knew that Marshall needed a break before shouldering the enormous responsibility of building an army from scratch to defeat the Nazis. "If Stimson could issue such a directive and get away with it," wrote Marshall, "I think I have strong precedent for this action."[116]

It is likely that Marshall had already discussed with Lovett the fact that he was about to step down. However, like Stimson's order in 1940, Marshall wanted to leave Lovett with a written memento of their close relationship that he knew the younger man would cherish, just as Marshall cherished the letter Stimson wrote him a decade earlier. Moreover, he sincerely felt that Lovett, whose health was precarious, needed to get some rest before inheriting his job and all of the responsibility it entailed.[117]

Marshall's letter of resignation, submitted to the president "in late August or early September," specified that it was to take effect on September 12.[118] On that morning, he met individually with staffers, a few members of the press, and several others, explaining to each that he was leaving for personal reasons, and not because of any disagreements with the president. Marshall's last official act was to compliment Acheson for concluding the

Japanese peace treaty (formally, the Treaty of San Francisco) negotiations. Acheson replied, writing that Marshall's presence as secretary of defense "during the last year of grave peril to our country . . . steadied all of our vital actions and decisions . . ."[119]

*   *   *   *   *

Three authors who pieced together a recent biography of Marshall disagreed with Acheson, writing that Marshall's achievements during his year as secretary of defense "were meager."[120] The record belies this assertion. His mere presence in the top job at the Pentagon restored the relationship between Defense and State that Louis Johnson had poisoned. When Marshall took over the Department of Defense after a period of downsizing, he was tasked to rebuild America's military strength so that the U.S. could prevail in Korea and deter the Soviet threat in the West. One of his first moves was to recruit and fight for Senate confirmation of Anna Rosenberg, an expert on labor relations, to become his assistant secretary for manpower. Because she was a woman, Jewish, a New Dealer, and (falsely) suspected of being a Communist, witnesses testifying before the Senate Armed Services Committee fiercely resisted the appointment. Marshall would not be denied. By presenting her side of the case to the senators, he eventually secured her confirmation. By the time Marshall resigned, he and Rosenberg doubled the strength of U.S. armed forces to 3.4 million men and women, and they did it in less time than the mobilization Marshall oversaw at the beginning of World War II. Moreover, with her help, Marshall succeeded in persuading Congress to extend the draft for an additional two years, and to approve the activation of four more divisions for Europe, though he failed to convince it to implement a program of universal military training, a concept that he had been advocating since the early 1920s as an alternative to a large standing army.

Marshall's most significant achievement as secretary of defense, however, was his steadfast adherence to the "Europe first" strategy as essential to America's national security. Marshall was convinced that because Soviet aggression aimed at the domination of Europe threatened the revival and growth of the economies of America's principal trading partners, the first priority of the U.S. should be to provide military troops, armaments, and economic assistance to those partners. As a consequence, during the "Great Debate" in Congress over sending troops and military aid to NATO, as well as the hearings concerning the relief of MacArthur, Marshall's testimony in 1951 was pivotal. If Europe should fall, he warned, "there would be built up, under the Soviets' domination, a productive power that would exceed ours . . . We would have the Atlantic dominated on the far side by governments hostile to our purpose . . . It would put us in an extremely perilous situation . . . and our national existence would be threatened."[121] Marshall's words, backed by his reputation as an apolitical straight shooter, convinced Congress to allocate the bulk of its military and economic assistance to Europe.

* * * * *

With no ceremony, Marshall left the Pentagon and headed out to Leesburg. This time his retirement was permanent. He had defended the nation for fifty years. Katherine and the Dodona gardens were beckoning.

Epilogue

WE COMMEND THY SERVANT GEORGE

On the morning of November 28, 1953, George Marshall arrived at Pier 84 in Manhattan. Looming above him was the *Andrea Doria*, pride of postwar Italy, widely regarded as the most beautiful ocean liner ever launched. As he mounted the gangway he looked tired and weak, having still not recovered from what he described as a "virus-flu" that rendered him bedridden and coughing almost continuously since the last week of September. The New York press had been alerted that Marshall was on his way to Norway to accept the Nobel Peace Prize for his sponsorship of the European Recovery Program—the Marshall Plan. In a room set aside aboard the ship for a televised press conference, Marshall told reporters that he was highly honored to accept the award, not for himself but because it was a "tribute to the whole American people." A great many individuals contributed to its success, he said, and if anyone should be singled out it should be "the late Senator Vandenberg," who had succumbed to lung cancer in 1951.[1]

Marshall's doctors had persuaded their seventy-two-year-old patient to take the southern route to Europe, hoping he could relax on deck in the warmth of the sun and recuperate, while spending part of the eight-day voyage writing the lecture he was obliged to deliver in Oslo. As it turned out, the crossing was cold and damp, Marshall later wrote to Truman, and he found it "utterly impossible to concentrate" on his speech. He arrived in Naples without having written a single line.[2] In a letter to Katherine, who was not up to joining her husband on the trip, George wrote that his aide, Colonel C. J. George, "watches over me like an old hen, helps me in dressing and undressing and steadies me in walking about the boat."[3]

From Naples, Marshall and C. J. George flew to Paris, where they stayed for a few days at the residence of the supreme allied commander of Europe for NATO, General Alfred Gruenther. Marshall wrote Katherine that the morning after he arrived, he "grit [his] teeth" and spent an hour and a quarter dictating a draft of his Nobel lecture.[4] Colonel Andrew Goodpaster, who held a PhD in international relations and would rise to become commander of NATO in 1969, was serving at the time as special assistant to Gruenther. Because Goodpaster had worked with Marshall previously, he was dispatched to Marshall's bedroom to help with the speech. Instead of a draft, Goodpaster found that Marshall had only "jotted down a few thoughts on some note paper." After discussing Marshall's ideas, Goodpaster emerged with a rough outline. "I had never seen the general so tired," he recalled. By their third meeting the speech was all but finished and Marshall's "health had improved greatly."[5]

The first afternoon of the two-day awards ceremony at Oslo University's Festival Hall was marred by protest. As Marshall was called forward by Gunnar Jahn, chairman of the Nobel Committee, to receive the Nobel medal, three communist journalists in the balcony began screaming "Murderer! Murderer!" while showering the audience below with propaganda leaflets accusing Marshall of war crimes.[6] Clad in cutaway and striped pants, Marshall looked on matter-of-factly, his face betraying little emotion. Up in the balcony, the agricultural attaché of the U.S. Embassy bear-hugged one of the protesters and yanked him back from the railing by his hair. The pilot of Marshall's plane, also nearby, slugged him in the mouth.[7] While the protester was being turned over to the police and the other two fled, Norway's King Haakon VII stood and led the entire audience in a thunderous ovation.

The following evening, Marshall approached the podium in Festival Hall and waited for the applause to subside. He began his Nobel lecture with an honest acknowledgment that he "lacked the magic and artistry" of Winston Churchill, who had been awarded the prize for literature the day before in Stockholm. In contrast to the style of England's great orator, Marshall said that his views concerning the "cause of peace" would be phrased in the plainest possible terms.

Marshall was upfront about the controversy surrounding his selection. Given the protests the previous day, it was obvious that there were many who felt that Alfred Nobel's peace prize should not have been awarded to an individual who spent most of his adult life either waging or preparing for war. Marshall made no excuses. He defended his role in rebuilding America's postwar military strength to deter the Soviet Union and to repel the invasion of South Korea. To maintain the peace, he declared, a "very strong military posture is vitally necessary today."[8] Fifty-six years later another American had to confront even greater controversy that swirled around his selection. Newly elected president Barack Obama conceded at the outset of his Nobel lecture that he had done little to promote world peace and could not be compared with the likes of "Marshall and Mandela." Yet he too launched into a full-throated defense of American military power as a vital element in promoting "peace and prosperity."[9]

Beyond military strength as a guarantor of peace, the remainder of Marshall's lecture focused on a handful of other factors essential to achieving peace. For the most part, these consisted of vague platitudes. Twice he advised that the most important single factor would be "a spiritual regeneration" that would establish "good faith" among nations and men. However, he offered no specifics. He spoke about how improvements in education and the spread of democracy would lead to peace. Again, he offered nothing about how to achieve these lofty goals.

Nevertheless, Marshall's lecture touched on one important point, not picked up in press reports, that resonates today. America has a built-in "advantage in the quest for peace," he said. Immigrants "now constitute an organic portion of our population." As a consequence, he argued, Americans have acquired a "concern for the problems of other peoples," a "deep urge to help the oppressed," and a "readiness to cooperate" with other nations in preserving peace. This cooperative attitude, declared Marshall, "is one of the great and hopeful factors of the world today."[10]

* * * * *

The Nobel Peace Prize was but one of the countless accolades that Marshall received during and after his fifty years of continuous service to the nation. But the praise that best captured the man and the unparalleled sweep of his career was the citation set forth in the honorary degree conferred by Harvard in 1947: "To George Catlett Marshall, an American to whom Freedom owes an enduring debt of gratitude, a soldier and statesman whose ability and character brook only one comparison in the history of this nation."[11] The operative words in this tribute are "ability" and "character." It is those qualities possessed by Marshall that enabled Harvard's president, James Conant, to make the audacious yet credible claim that he was the only solider-statesman in the history of America worthy of being compared favorably with George Washington.

Ability is a quality of human nature—an ambitious side of it, to be sure—that facilitates achievement. By this definition, Marshall's abilities as both soldier and statesman were prodigious. In the Second World War he was responsible for organizing, equipping, and supplying an army and air force of 8.3 million men and women; he selected and mentored many of the top commanders; and he was usually the dominant voice in conferences with allied military and political leaders concerning the strategies and deployment of forces across the globe that resulted in victory. As secretary of defense, Marshall, aided by Anna Rosenberg and Bob Lovett, oversaw the rebuilding of the depleted postwar armed forces, increasing military manpower from 1.4 million men and women as of June 30, 1950, a few months before he took over, to a total of 3.5 million three years later, enough to contain Soviet aggression in Europe and at the same time end the fighting in Korea at the 38th parallel with a negotiated truce. In the Great War, Marshall planned and executed the sixty-mile nighttime movement of more than half a million men, together with guns and supplies, so that they were in place to fight the decisive battle that led to the armistice—the forty-seven-day Meuse-Argonne offensive. Were it not for the Meuse-Argonne victory, it is likely that the war would have ended with Imperial Germany as the preeminent power in Europe, in control of the greatest concentration of European industry on its side of the Rhine.

In an attempt to describe Marshall's ability to manage "great affairs of state," Dean Acheson wrote that Marshall was "richly endowed," having mastered the art of "judgment in its highest form"—the capacity to weigh a "wide scope" of relevant facts and to apprehend "imponderables."[12] The quintessential example of what Acheson meant was Marshall's decision to ask a Republican-controlled Congress, at a time when the U.S. was already saddled with wartime debt, to spend several billions to revive the economies of Western Europe on the theory—the imponderable—that it would both contain the Soviet Union and be repaid in future trade with American companies. Secretary of State Marshall returned from Moscow in the spring of 1947 with a general notion that the U.S. should take the lead in providing such assistance. To put meat on the bones, he selected George Kennan and others to develop a plan. Once an outline was prepared, it was Marshall who dictated the time and place to deliver the low-key speech that launched what became known as the Marshall Plan. For the next several months, Secretary Marshall, with the help of Senator Vandenberg, stumped the country and lobbied Congress to enact the European Recovery Program into law. There was no one in public life other than Marshall who had the ability and credibility at home and abroad to lead the effort.

Strong moral "character" was the other praiseworthy quality possessed by Marshall that caused Harvard's president to place him at the elbow of George Washington. Marshall's character took shape at the Virginia Military Institute when he was barely twenty years old. "What I learned at VMI," he later recalled, "was self-control, discipline so that it was ground in."[13] He learned to renounce fleeting pleasures in order to enjoy more rewarding ones later, such as the lasting inner contentment that comes from earning the respect and admiration of one's peers or from serving a higher cause. He also began a lifelong struggle to contain his explosive emotions. Forty years on, during the dark days after Pearl Harbor, he was still fighting to achieve self-mastery, confessing to Katherine during a winter walk that he could not allow himself to "get angry" or "appear tired," that he "cannot afford the luxury of sentiment," and that above all he must keep his brain clear.[14] At age seventy-five Marshall told an interviewer that his "hardest job in public life" was to control his "temper," though there were moments, notably in the presence of Clark Clifford and Harry Truman, when he failed miserably.[15]

A fifteen-minute conversation between Marshall and President Roosevelt that took place in Cairo at midday on December 5, 1943, laid bare the nature of Marshall's character. Asked by the president whether he wished to command OVERLORD—the invasion of Western Europe that he had been advocating for almost two years—Marshall declined to venture an opinion or to express his desire. Instead, he told his commander in chief that he should feel free to act in the best interests of the country and not to consider his, Marshall's, feelings. The command of OVERLORD went to Eisenhower, his springboard to the presidency, although if Marshall had asked, it surely would have gone to him. Many were convinced that Marshall was crushed. Yet he never made known his feelings. This was his selfless nature, the moral code that he lived by.

Beyond self-mastery, a hallmark of Marshall's character, especially as he matured, was magnanimity, a word indicating that he was high-minded, free from petty resentfulness—a derivation of two Latin words, *magnus* and *animus*, which when translated mean "great-souled." Marshall evidenced the magnanimous aspect of his character the day after the president decided that Eisenhower would command OVERLORD. At the bottom of a copy of FDR's signed order, Marshall handwrote a note to his protégé: "Dear Eisenhower: I thought you might like to have this as a memento. It was written very hurriedly by me as the final meeting broke up yesterday."[16] Eisenhower cherished the note. He understood at once the noble generosity of Marshall's gesture.

A few years later, Marshall raised himself to the heights as a great-souled leader. During the 1948 presidential election campaign, when Secretary of State Marshall was in Paris locked in negotiations aimed at submitting the Berlin crisis to the UN Security Council, he learned that President Truman was on the verge of undermining him by sending an inexperienced envoy to Moscow to appeal directly to Joseph Stalin. Marshall could have resigned in anger or at least threatened to resign. Instead, he thought of the pressures and demands on Truman as he fought against heavy odds to be elected in his own right to the presidency. He dashed off a note to the White House. "I understand what's worrying you Mr. President and I am coming home immediately."[17] This was an act of magnanimity on a grand scale. It was the mark of a great man.

In his biography of George Washington, Chief Justice John Marshall singled out the first president's Athenian magnanimity as one of his most significant virtues. Washington, he wrote in the early 1800s, "had the magnanimity to pursue [America's] real interests in opposition to its temporary prejudices, and in more instances than one, we find him committing his whole popularity to hazard, and pursuing steadily the course dictated by a sense of duty."[18] Harvard's president had this quality of character in mind when he prepared the honorary degree citation in 1947 comparing Marshall favorably with the father of our country.

* * * * *

On a November afternoon in 1958, Rose Page paused at the door of Marshall's tiny bedroom at Liscombe Lodge, the one-story house on Linden Avenue in Pinehurst where George and Katherine were living. "Colonel

Marshall," as Rose always called him, was sitting up in bed, dressed in a dark blue dressing gown. Rose was shocked at his appearance. She hadn't seen him for almost two years. Marshall's "skin was stretched tightly across his jutting cheekbones," she later wrote, and his hair was "dead white." He had become an "old man." She realized at once that he was never going to get well.

The two old friends reminisced for hours. "You know," Marshall said, "I was thinking of my father" and how in the winter, "when I was very small, he would take me tobogganing down a snowy hill in the center of Uniontown." Rose, who had been told by Marshall's first wife that his father never appreciated him, replied, "I'm sorry your father didn't live long enough to know what a great son he had. He would have been very proud of you."

"I'd like to believe," remarked Marshall in all seriousness, "that he would have approved of me."[19]

In early 1959, Marshall suffered the ravages of a series of strokes. His vision and speech were impaired. He was confined to bed or a wheelchair, frail and unable to walk on his own. He could no longer read. In March, he was transferred to Walter Reed in Washington. Visitors stopped by to boost Marshall's spirits, including Anna Rosenberg, Vice President Richard Nixon, Mamie Eisenhower, and the Maxwell Taylors, who brought home-made cookies and a cake. On May 5, President Eisenhower and eighty-four-year-old Winston Churchill came to pay their respects, but Marshall, virtually comatose, was unable to recognize either of them. Churchill watched him from the doorway, tears welling in his eyes.

Over the summer, Marshall lost his hearing, sight, and speech. He fell into a permanent vegetative state, kept alive only by tubes and a mighty constitution. In early September, Katherine moved to an apartment at 1900 Q Street and informed C. J. George that she had no intention of returning to Dodona. Her daughter, Molly Winn, along with her husband and children, were already living there and would soon purchase the manor house.

Eight minutes after six o'clock on the evening of October 16, 1959, Marshall passed away. His orderly, Sergeant William J. Heffner, was with him until the end, seated vigilantly in a straight-backed chair next to his bed.

According to the death certificate, General of the Army George C. Marshall died of a "cerebrovascular accident due to hypertension."[20]

Marshall left oral and written instructions concerning his funeral, which for the most part were followed. Unlike Pershing's funeral, which he had planned, there was to be no lying in state in the Capitol Rotunda, no service at the National Cathedral, no horse-drawn caisson, riderless horse, and muffled drums proceeding down Pennsylvania Avenue, and not a single eulogy. He provided a short list of pallbearers. Interment was to be private, family only.

As instructed, the funeral was held at the Old Post Chapel at Fort Myer, a short walk from the stables that Marshall had frequented almost every morning when he served as chief of staff for Pershing, and then later for the entire U.S. Army. Inside the crowded chapel, waiting for the service to begin, Rose Page watched as former president Truman and then President Eisenhower walked down the center aisle to the front pew on the left, shook hands, and sat side by side. "Mrs. Marshall came down the aisle on Colonel Winn's arm," wrote Rose. "She was heavily veiled," grief-stricken over yet another great loss. In addition to George, to whom she was devoted for twenty-nine years, she had lost her sister Allene, her sons Clifton (to lung cancer) and Allen, and her first husband.

The brief funeral service, from the 1789 Book of Common Prayer, was conducted by Luther Miller, whom Marshall had known since they served together with the 15th Infantry in Tientsin, China. Near the end, the portion called "The Commendation," where the living say farewell to the departed, Miller made one of his few references to Marshall by name, saying "We commend thy servant George."[21] In Marshall's case, the word "servant" was particularly apt.

Following the service, Marshall's family—including Allen's widow, Madge—the pallbearers, an honor guard, and a few others walked in the autumn sunshine behind the caisson bearing the flag-draped casket, making their way from the chapel to the freshly dug grave in Section 7, downhill from the Tomb of the Unknown Soldier. Marshall's final resting place, overlooking Washington and the Potomac, was not far from the equestrian statue of his friend, Sir John Dill, and the stones beneath, which the remains of Lily and her mother were buried years ago.

* * * * *

Few individuals in American history have thrown a longer shadow over world events than George Marshall. Yet as his shadow wanes, the depth of his moral character endures. It has been said that "if you want to test a man's character, give him power."[22] By quieting his shortcomings, General George Marshall surely passed the test.

Acknowledgments

If it were not for Dick Moe, this book would never have been published. On a Tuesday in the fall of 2014, the two of us met for lunch in Washington. I was discouraged. My initial proposal for writing a new treatment of George Marshall had been rejected by a slew of publishers. I wanted Dick's advice. Dick Moe is one of the wise men in Washington, having served as chief of staff to Vice President Walter Mondale, adviser to President Jimmy Carter, president of the National Trust for Historic Preservation, and author of three acclaimed books. I asked Dick whether I should abandon the Marshall project and focus on another book that I had in mind about a controversial politician from the Midwest. Dick's advice was to stick with Marshall. He put me in touch with his agent, John W. Wright.

Wright's first reaction was both confidence-building and daunting. The subject of George Marshall "interests me greatly," he wrote, but your proposal needs to be entirely "recast to make it more clearly a Life," not just World War II and the death of Marshall's stepson. I was in no position to argue. John Wright represents dozens of award-winning historians. Under his expert guidance I wrote and rewrote my proposal six or seven times. By the time it was ready to be submitted to publishers it had ballooned to eighty pages. As Moe had warned, working with Wright was an exhausting and sometimes frustrating experience, but he is a perfectionist and has an instinct for knowing what publishers want.

Wright's idea of broadening the narrative resonated with Brent Howard, a young editor at Penguin Random House. Howard immediately signaled his enthusiasm by suggesting that I develop "fresh, new insights" detailing Marshall's role in shaping game-changing battles in World War I and his actual plan for a bridgehead in Europe in 1942, information that was hardly touched on by previous biographers. In addition, he pressed me to make the selling of the Marshall Plan, the recognition of Israel, the Berlin airlift, and

Marshall's mission to China "a much bigger part of the book." It was obvious to me that Howard was committed to the project and eager to edit and promote my work.

After reviewing one of my early draft proposals, prolific and prizewinning nonfiction author Evan Thomas said he had faith that I could get behind Marshall's "impenetrable mask," but he cautioned me to avoid making the death of Marshall's stepson "the strategic Rosebud" of the book. I understood at once what he meant, but wonder to this day how he managed to come up with this perfectly delightful phrase.

While I am forever grateful to John, Brent, and Evan, the recasting of my original proposal was a mixed blessing. On the one hand, it meant that it would be another four years before my book would be published, yet on the other it would require a great deal of additional research and digging for important new details, the part of the process I like best. Once again I had a reason for making frequent trips up the Shenandoah Valley to Lexington, Virginia, headquarters of the George Marshall Research Library and home of VMI and Washington and Lee University, a quaint village full of antebellum architecture and the Southern Inn, a restaurant I frequented every night. In the library adjacent to the VMI parade ground, Jeffrey Kozak guided me through the various collections and helped me track down boxes and scrapbooks containing the documents and letters I needed. Mame Warren, who was working on the seventh volume of Marshall's papers, provided me with all kinds of research tips, always with a dash of caustic wit. Rob Havers, president of the George C. Marshall Foundation, was a welcome source of advice and encouragement. Thank you, Jeffrey, Rob, and Mame, for your expertise and support.

Another joy was a return trip to the British National Archives. For ten days I lived at the Coach and Horses pub across from Kew Gardens, a pleasant walk to the Archives. I found the English archivists and their systems for locating materials much easier to work with than those at the U.S. National Archives in College Park, Maryland. The documents, maps, and photos I uncovered relating to the plans to invade the Cherbourg Peninsula in the fall of 1942 proved to be revelatory. Pints at the Coach and Horse were excellent and the pub food was not bad.

The expansion of my proposal gave me another opportunity to visit with Allen Tupper Brown, son of Allen, who was killed in Italy, and stepgrandson of George Marshall. Tupper had previously loaned me a trove of original letters written during World War II, along with the crumpled battle map that was in his father's possession when he was mortally wounded on the road to Rome. In a gristmill above a roaring stream in northwest Massachusetts, the four of us—Tupper, his wife Sandy, my wife Nancy, and myself—enjoyed a long lunch, tales of George and Katherine Marshall, and Tupper's description of how he commemorates his father each 4th of July with a reading of the Declaration of Independence at his farmhouse above the Connecticut River. For the past four years I have been in frequent touch with Tupper to ask questions, check facts, and float ideas. I am ever thankful for his responsiveness, openness, and friendship.

Special thanks go to the archivists in the Manuscript Division and the assistants in the Newspaper Reading Room of the Library of Congress (Madison Building), where I whiled away many days pawing through boxes of documents and squinting at microfilm readers. The experts who deal with the public at the Library of Congress are a national treasure.

I would have liked to return to Hyde Park and the Franklin D. Roosevelt Library, where I had done most of my research for *The Hopkins Touch*, but Bob Clark, a senior archivist there, deprived me of this pleasure. I shouldn't say this, but he answered most of my research questions for this book via email. As a consequence, I could not manufacture an excuse for making the trip. A backhanded thanks to you, Bob. There are few, if any, who know more about the Roosevelt collections than Bob Clark.

I can't say enough about master cartographer Jeff Ward. He did a superb job of developing maps that illuminate the text and help readers understand key events in Marshall's storied career. Thanks, Jeff, for your uncommon skill and attention to detail.

As always, the librarians, IT professionals, and others on the support staff at Steptoe & Johnson, the law firm in Washington, DC, where I practiced for more than twenty-five years, were generous and helpful. Kudos in particular goes to Jacqueline Randolph, my efficient assistant. With a wry sense of humor, she kept me organized and on point.

To guide me through the writing process, Brent Howard proved to be a gentle yet persistent and persuasive taskmaster. "Is this needed?" he would frequently say. Or "Would you consider writing it this way?" He was always right. After two comprehensive line edits that immeasurably improved my manuscript, Brent handed me off to Cassidy Sachs, his diligent editorial assistant; Ted Gilley, a gifted copy editor; and Maria Whelan, an outstanding publicist. They and the rest of the team at Dutton/Penguin/Random House worked tirelessly to finalize and promote the book.

No task is more a true act of generosity and more important to a writer than the critical reading of a manuscript. Fortunately two of the best readers answered my call. Mark Stoler, professor emeritus at the University of Vermont and the leading George C. Marshall historian, spent weeks going over the manuscript and provided me with pages of insightful comments and corrections. As I anticipated, Ellen McNamara, an extraordinarily intelligent and perceptive partner at Steptoe & Johnson, offered a host of proposed corrections and candid comments. Since there are instances in which I have stubbornly resisted their suggested changes, I hasten to point out here that Mark and Ellen are in no way responsible for shortcomings in this book and for the views expressed in it. My profound thanks to the two of them.

While working on this book I was fortunate to be named a nonresident fellow of the German Marshall Fund, an organization founded through a gift from Germany that memorializes its postwar revival via the Marshall Plan and promotes transatlantic exchange. My heartfelt thanks to Karen Donfried, president of GMF; Derek Chollet, executive vice president; and Nicola Lightener, director of Strategic Convening and Operations, for their encouragement and support.

Finally, I am blessed to have experienced the love, encouragement, and support of my wife, Nancy, during the years it has taken me to research and write this book. With scarcely a complaint, she selflessly allowed me the space, time, and silence to devote to this happy effort. I am eternally grateful. "Together wing to wing," my love, "and oar to oar."

A Note on Chinese Names

Throughout the text I have tried to use whichever English version of a Chinese name was in use during the period 1925–1947 and was most familiar to Western readers and publications at the time (e.g., Formosa instead of Taiwan; Chou En-lai instead of Zhou Enlai). The exceptions are Beijing, which was in use at the time but was more familiarly known in the West as Peking or Beiping, and Mao Zedong, formerly Mao Tse-tung.

Notes

Abbreviations

AHEC: Army Heritage and Education Center, Carlisle, PA
Bland, Papers: Larry I. Bland et al., eds., Papers of George Catlett Marshall, Vols. I–VI
BNA: British National Archives, Kew, London
DDE: Dwight David Eisenhower
FRUS: Foreign Relations of the United States
GCM: George C. Marshall
GCML: George C. Marshall Research Library, Lexington, VA
HSTL: Harry S. Truman Library, Independence, MO
JCS: Joint Chiefs of Staff
KM: Katherine Tupper Marshall
KM Interview: Pogue interview of KM, Tape 130, March 15 and 17, 1961, Pinehurst, NC, GCML
Marshall Interviews: Larry I. Bland, ed., Marshall Interviews and Reminiscences for Forrest C. Pogue
LOC: Library of Congress, Washington, DC
Marshall Memoirs: GCM, *Memoir of My Services in the World War, 1917–1918*
NA: National Archives, College Park, MD
NYT: *New York Times*
OH: oral history
PHA: Pearl Harbor Attack, Hearings Before Jt. Comm. on Investig. 79th Cong. 1st Sess.
Pogue, I–IV: Forrest C. Pogue, *George C. Marshall*, Vols. I–IV
PPA: Public Papers and Addresses of the Presidents
Stoler, *Papers*: Mark A. Stoler et al., eds., *Papers of George Catlett Marshall*, Vol. VII
Wilson: Rose Page Wilson

Prologue: Sacred Trust

1. Marshall's speech at Uniontown homecoming, September 9, 1939, Bland, Papers, I:8–9, GCML.
2. Marshall Interviews, Tape 2M, 45–46, GCML. In Pogue's biography, he suggests that it was "unlikely" that Marshall's appointment to sit for the examination resulted from his lobbying of McKinley and others in Washington. Pogue speculates that since appointments needed to be approved by the two Pennsylvania senators, Matthew Quay and Boies Penrose, Marshall's father or one of his friends must have persuaded them to put young Marshall on their lists of appointments. Pogue, *Marshall*, I:65.

3. Acheson, *Present at the Creation*, 140.
4. Pogue, interview with Rayburn, November 6, 1957, Notes 152N, Copy 2, at 3, GCML.
5. Mosley, *Hero for Our Times*, 523.
6. Stoler, *Marshall: Soldier-Statesman* (1989); Cray, *General of the Army* (1990).
7. Two deeply researched and scholarly books, one focusing entirely on the Marshall Plan and the other detailing Marshall's one-year China mission, were published in 2018: Steil, *Marshall Plan*; Kurtz-Phelan, *China Mission*.
8. Hilldring, tr. no. 42; Pogue interview, March 30, 1959, GCML.

Chapter 1: Harvest of Death

1. Arnold, *Global Mission*, 44.
2. Ibid.
3. Bland, Papers, I:76-78, GCML.
4. Frye, *Marshall*, 110; Bland, Papers, I:103-4, GCML.
5. Acheson, *Present at the Creation*, 140-41.
6. In the first episode, GCM collapsed in the street in New York as a result of "acute dilation of the heart." Bland, Papers, 1:80, GCML. GCM's sister Marie said it happened while GCM was visiting Lily's sister. "He had overworked and he just fell in the street from the strain." Interview of Mrs. John J. Singer, February 2, 1960, GCML. The second attack was regarded as "subacute," but it required hospitalization, two months of sick leave, and two more months of regular leave. See also Gosling, *Before Freud: Neurasthenia and the American Medical Community, 1870-1910*.
7. Bland, Papers, I:81-84, GCML.
8. Marshall Interviews, 21, GCML.
9. Ibid.
10. Wilson, *Marshall Remembered*, 175.
11. Mitral regurgitation is a leakage of blood backward through the mitral valve of the heart.
12. Jeffers with Axelrod, *Marshall: Lessons in Leadership*, 10.
13. Wilson, *Marshall Remembered*, 175.
14. Marshall, "Forgotten Scenes of Heroism," and report of visit to Manchurian battlefields, with recommendations, Marshall Papers 1/9, GCML.
15. Keegan, *First World War*, 52.
16. Grey of Fallodon, *Twenty-five Years, 1892-1916*, 20.
17. Kershaw, *Hitler: 1889-1936*, 92.
18. Woodrow Wilson speech, May 10, 1915, PPA Woodrow Wilson, XXXIII: 147-49.
19. The National Defense Act of 1916 was enacted on June 3, 1916. The Naval Appropriations Act of 1916, a five-year navy construction program, was signed into law on August 20, 1916.
20. Jeffers with Alexrod, *Marshall*, 29.
21. Cooper, *Woodrow Wilson*, 341-42, 352, 359-60.
22. The origin of the term "doughboy" as applied to the U.S. infantry is not clear. Accounts from the Mexican-American War suggest that it might have come from the

dough-cake look of the buttons on the uniforms of foot soldiers or the flour and rice field rations baked in campfire ashes. Another explanation is that the term derived from the chalky desert dust resembling unbaked dough that covered those who fought with Pershing against Pancho Villa. At first the soldiers were called "adobes," then "dobies," and finally when they were shipped to France, "doughboys."

23. Palmer, *Newton D. Baker*, I:170-71. But see Cooper, *Woodrow Wilson*, where Pershing was supposedly told, somewhat contradictorily, that until he had enough troops to operate independently he should "cooperate as a component of whatever army you may be assigned to by the French government." Ibid., 402.
24. Pershing, *Experiences*, I:37.
25. Bland, Papers, I:104, GCML.
26. Marshall, *Memoirs*, 3. During the five years when GCM served in Washington as General Pershing's aide (1919-1924), he wrote an account of his World War I experiences. After GCM died, his wife, who knew about the memoir, was under the impression that it had been destroyed. However, her daughter, Molly Brown Winn, discovered a copy in the attic at Dodona and arranged for it to be published in 1976.
27. Marshall, *Memoirs*, 6.
28. Marshall, Interviews, 189, GCML.
29. Society of the First Division, *History of the First Division*, Foreword by Pershing, xv.
30. Marshall, *Memoirs*, 11.
31. Marshall Interviews, 191, GCML.
32. Marshall, *Memoirs*, 12. The disastrous defeat, led by General Nivelle, took place at Chemin des Dames on the Aisne River. After the defeat, General Philippe Pétain relieved Nivelle, ended the passive resistance of the troops, and began restoring morale.
33. Pershing, *Experiences*, I:152.
34. Harbord, *American Army in France*, 190.
35. Marshall Interviews, 196, GCML.
36. Ibid., 197.
37. Ibid.
38. Caffey to Pogue, January 14, 1961, GCML.
39. Marshall Interviews, 198, GCML.
40. Ibid.
41. Ludendorff, *War Memories, 1914-1918*, II:537.
42. Marshall, *Memoirs*, 62.
43. Ibid., 365; Smythe, *Pershing*, 101.
44. Marshall, *Memoirs*, 79.
45. Pershing, *Experiences*, I:365.
46. Marshall Interviews, 198, GCML.
47. Pershing, *Experiences*, I:394; "Speeches," Pershing Papers, LOC.
48. Davenport, *First Over There*, 90.
49. Marshall, *Memoirs*, 84.
50. Ibid., 89.
51. Ibid., 90.
52. Bullard, *Fighting Generals*, 45.
53. Nelson, *Five Lieutenants*, 199, 247.

54. Marshall, Field Order No. 18, May 20, 1918, with Annexes May 22 and Amendments to May 24, RG 120, Entry 1241, B-16 and 18, NA.
55. Davenport, *First Over There*, 110.
56. Marshall, *Memoirs*, 93.
57. Ibid.
58. Ibid., 94.
59. Ibid., 94-95.
60. Nelson, *Remains of Company D*, 87-88; Davenport, *First Over There*, 143.
61. Daniel Sargent, "Cantigny," unpublished account, 12, Army War College, Carlisle, PA.
62. Marshall, *Memoirs*, 95.
63. James Hopper, "Our First Victory," *Collier's*, August 24, 1918.
64. Marshall, *Memoirs*, 95.
65. Ibid.
66. Marshall memo: Report of Incidents Immediately Prior to and During Operation Against Cantigny carried out May 28, 1918, May 29, 1918, RG 120, Entry 1241, B-42, NA.
67. Marshall, *Memoirs*, 96.
68. Marshall memo, May 29, 1918, RG 120, Entry 1241, B-42, NA.
69. Rosenbaum to Redwood's mother, Redwood Papers, 1917-1918, Mss. 1530.3, Maryland Historical Society, Baltimore, MD.
70. Marshall, *Memoirs*, 96-97.
71. Message from Ely, May 29, 1918, 8:55 p.m., 1st Artillery Brigade Records for Cantigny Operation, RG 120, Entry 1241, B-66, NA.
72. "History of First Division," RG 120, Entry 1241, B-6, 25, NA.
73. Marshall, *Memoirs*, 99.
74. Jeffers, *In the Rough Rider's Shadow*, 97.
75. Page, *Our 110 Days' Fighting*, 29.
76. Payne, *Marshall Story*, 69.
77. Bland, Papers, I:144, n. 14, GCML.
78. Marshall Interviews, 214-15, GCML.
79. Marshall, *Memoirs*, 117.

Chapter 2: Rumours of Peace

1. Marshall, *Memoirs*, 139.
2. Ibid., 137.
3. Ibid., 138-39. At the time, Pershing was commander in chief of both the AEF and the First Army.
4. Manchester, *American Caesar*, 103.
5. Marshall, *Memoirs*, 146.
6. Manchester, *American Caesar*, 71.
7. Diaries of Dr. Crile, Crile Papers, Western Reserve Historical Society, Cleveland, OH.
8. Casey, *Cannoneers Have Hairy Ears*, 161.
9. Marshall, *Memoirs*, 152.
10. Truman to Elizabeth (Bess) Wallace Truman, November 23, 1918, HSTL.

11. Miller, *Plain Speaking*, 101, 103.
12. Marshall, *Memoirs*, 156.
13. "Notes on World's War," Roy V. Myers Papers, AHEC, Carlisle, PA.
14. Pershing, *Experiences*, II:285-86.
15. Lecture by General Drum, Drum Papers, AHEC, Carlisle, PA.
16. Rickenbacker, *Flying Circus*, 269.
17. Truman to Elizabeth (Bess) Wallace Truman, November 23, 1918, HSTL.
18. Smith, "History of 305th Ammunition Train, 80th Division—U.S. Army," 8, in author's possession; Stultz, Division Historian, *History of the 80th Division, AEF in World War I*, 352.
19. Patton to Beatrice Patton, September 28, 1918, Patton Papers, LOC.
20. Statement by Edwards, "Gallant and Exemplary Conduct," Patton Papers, LOC.
21. Extracts from after-action reports of Edwards and Angelo, Patton Papers, LOC.
22. Patton, "My Father as I Knew Him," Patton Papers, LOC.
23. Patton to Beatrice Patton, September 28, 1918, Patton Papers, LOC.
24. Marshall, *Memoirs*, 164-67.
25. Kershaw, *To Hell and Back*, 61.
26. Callwell, *Field-Marshall Sir Henry Wilson*, II:134-35.
27. Marshall, *Memoirs*, 169.
28. MacArthur, *Reminiscences*, 66.
29. Manchester, *American Caesar*, 106.
30. MacArthur, *Reminiscences*, 66.
31. Pershing, *Experiences*, II:367.
32. Pershing to Allied Supreme War Council, October 30, 1918, United States Army in the World War, X, 28-30.
33. Marshall, *Memoirs*, 179.
34. Ibid., 178-79.
35. Remarque, *All Quiet on the Western Front*, 295, 296.
36. Marshall, *Memoirs*, 189-90.
37. Ibid.
38. Pogue, I:187.
39. The record is not clear on whether Conner was in fact speaking for Pershing. Pogue was of the opinion that Pershing wanted to take Sedan. He also wrote that Marshall recalled after the war that France's General Paul Maistre had "conceded that the military importance of Sedan was such that the Americans should occupy it if they could." Pogue, I:189.
40. Manchester, *American Caesar*, 109.
41. Ibid., 110 and n. 52.
42. Marshall, *Memoirs*, 195.
43. NYT, November 8, 1918.
44. Weygand, *Mémoires. Idéal vécu*, 639, cited in Lloyd, *Hundred Days*, 253, n. 5.
45. Ibid.
46. Marshall, *Memoirs*, 195.
47. Ibid., 196-97.
48. Ibid., 199.
49. Groves, WWI 3345, Army Service Experiences Questionnaire, Veterans Survey Collection, U.S. Army Military History Institute, Carlisle, PA.

50. Weintraub, *Stillness Heard Round the World,* 169.

51. Groover, WWI 2450 (folder 1), "Memoirs of Clare Groover of Service in the U.S. Army," 43, U.S. Army Military History Institute, Carlisle, PA.

52. Woodrow Wilson statement, November 11, 1918, PPA Woodrow Wilson, 53:24.

53. Marshall, *Memoirs,* 203.

54. Pogue, I:189.

55. DDE, *At Ease: Stories I Tell,* 192.

56. GCM, "Profiting by War Experiences," *Infantry Journal,* January 1921, XVII:34-37 at 35.

57. Marshall, *Memoirs,* 79.

58. Bland, Papers, I:202-3, GCML.

59. Marshall Interviews, 239, GCML.

60. Bland, Papers, I:264-66, GCML.

61. The "victory" regiment was a composite regiment whose members were selected because of their "combat records and soldierly bearing." Pogue, I:198.

62. Marshall, *Memoirs,* 217.

63. Ibid., 219-20.

64. NYT, September 2, 1919.

65. GCM to Lily Marshall, November 18, 1917, GCM and KM Collection, GCML.

66. In fact, there is only one other letter between GCM and Lily during their twenty-five years of marriage, an impersonal note concerning GCM's clothing needs, that has survived. It is possible that GCM destroyed all of their correspondence after Lily's death or that KM, GCM's second wife, did so. In a letter to the author, a woman who was briefly married to KM's eldest son wrote that KM was "an experienced letter-burner."

67. Marshall Interviews, 247, GCML.

68. Interview of KM, Tape 139, March 15 and 17, 1961, Pinehurst, NC, GCML.

Chapter 3: I Will Find a Way

1. Wilson, *Marshall Remembered,* 8.

2. Ibid., 1, 4.

3. Ibid., 5.

4. Ibid., 2.

5. Reorganization of Army Hearings, pt. 2: Hearings on S.2691, S.2693, and S.2715 before subcommittee of Committee on Military Affairs, United States Senate, 66th Cong., 1st Sess. (testimony of Col. Palmer, October 9, 1919), 1177.

6. Marshall Interviews, 19, GCML.

7. Testimony of Pershing, October 31, 1919, Reorganization of Army Hearings on S.2691 et al., 1580.

8. Ibid., 1588.

9. Cooper, *Woodrow Wilson,* 565.

10. Pogue, I:211-12.

11. Marshall Interviews, 248, GCML.

12. Ibid., 99.

13. Ibid.; Wilson, *Marshall Remembered,* 73.

14. Marshall, *Memoirs*, 185, 191; Bland, "Fully Equal with the Best," 6, GCML.
15. Marshall Interviews, 99, 98, GCML.
16. Stoler, *Marshall: Soldier-Statesman*, 10.
17. Frye, *Marshall*, 58; Marshall Interviews, 93, GCML.
18. Ibid., 59; ibid., GCML. See also, Stoler, *Papers*, VII:296.
19. Marshall Interviews, 98, GCML.
20. Bland, "Fully Equal with the Best," 11, GCML.
21. Brooks, *Road to Character*, 111.
22. Stoler, *Marshall: Solder-Statesman*, 10.
23. Interview of Mrs. John J. Singer, Notes, 16N, Copy 2, p. 2, GCML.
24. Bland, "Fully Equal with the Best," 13, GCML.
25. Marshall Interviews, 91, GCML.
26. Ibid., 102.
27. Pogue, I:68.
28. Bland, "Fully Equal with the Best," 29, GCML.
29. The Kellogg-Briand Pact, signed by Germany, France, Italy, Poland, the United Kingdom, and a host of other nations (but not the Soviet Union) in 1928, renounced the use of war to settle disputes.
30. Bland, Papers, I:235-44 at 241 (lecture at Army War College), GCML.
31. Wilson, *Marshall Remembered*, 84, 86-88.
32. Ibid., 135, 144.
33. Mitchell, *Ridgway: Soldier*, 35.
34. Ibid.
35. Bland, Papers, I:270, GCML.
36. Lily Marshall to Hughes, November 25, 1926, GCML.
37. Frye, *Marshall*, 191.
38. Stoler, *Marshall: Soldier-Statesman*, 54.
39. Bland, Papers, I:275-76, GCML.
40. Mitter, *Forgotten Ally*, 49.
41. Bland, Papers, I:293-98, GCML.
42. FRUS, 1927, 2:99.
43. Ibid.
44. Bland, Papers, I:310-12, GCML.
45. Ibid., 312-14.
46. Ibid., 314-15.
47. Skutt, *George C. Marshall, Reporting for Duty*, 73, GCML.
48. Bland, Papers, I:314-15, GCML.
49. Death certificate described cause of death as myocarditis, chronic with auricular fibrillation—goiter, adenomatous, toxic secondary/contributory. It listed her age as forty-four, although she was at least fifty.
50. Wilson, *Marshall Remembered*, 155.
51. Hayne to Puryear Jr., March 7, 1963, Reminiscences File, GCML; Pogue, I:246; Hayne OH by Edgar F. Puryear, June 17, 1975, F-14, GCML.
52. Wilson, *Marshall Remembered*, 158, 159.
53. Bland, Papers, I:315, GCML.
54. Ibid., 315-16.

Chapter 4: Hands on Benning

1. Bland, Papers, I:383, GCML.
2. Ibid., I:316. "Aunt Lottie," Mrs. Thomas Coles, was related to Lily by marriage. She was married to the brother of Lily's father, Walter Coles III.
3. GCM to Heintzelman, December 18, 1933, GCML; Pogue, I:250.
4. Spalding, *Georgia: WPA Guide to Its Towns and Countryside*, xi.
5. Bland, Papers, I:316–18, GCML.
6. Ibid., I:334–38.
7. Ibid., I:316.
8. Taylor, n.d., Reminiscences File, GCML.
9. Bland, Papers, I:316, GCML.
10. *Columbus Enquirer-Sun*, October 11, 1930. Three white Fort Benning soldiers attacked and inflicted a knife wound on a man identified as a "negro" in downtown Columbus because he refused to "move on" when ordered by the soldiers to do so.
11. Scipio, *Last of the Black Regulars*; Jones Jr., *Last Black Regulars*, U.S. Army War College, Carlisle Barracks, PA.
12. In his biography of GCM, Pogue referenced an instance in which GCM denied a petition by white officers calling for the removal of two black National Guard officers who had been flown in to attend classes at the Infantry School. Pogue, I:260. One of the officers wrote a note to GCM thanking him for his "quiet and courageous firmness." Col. Marcus Ray to GCM, November 4, 1953, GCML. GCM wrote "a very able officer" on this letter.
13. Pogue, I:259.
14. Bland, Papers, I:383, GCML.
15. Wilson, *Marshall Remembered*, 184.
16. Ritchel to Pogue, October 24, 1960, Research File/Benning, GCML. Author's interview of Daniel Croswell, history professor at Columbus State University, February 24, 2016.
17. The history of the Rotary Club of Columbus states that GCM was an active member from 1927 to 1932. http://rotarycolumbusga.org.
18. Spalding, *Georgia: WPA Guide to Its Towns and Countryside*, 214, 219. By coincidence the state supervisor of the Georgia Writers' Project that produced the WPA guide for Georgia was thirty-three-year-old Samuel Yoer Tupper Jr. of Atlanta, a cousin of KM. In the Tupper tradition, Yoer was a writer who by the age of thirty had written two novels.
19. Winn, "Incident at Winn's Hill," articles in *Columbus Ledger* and *Enquirer-Sun*, August 21, 1912; Rose, *The Big Eddy Club*. Four of the alleged perpetrators were brought to trial. After deliberating for less than half an hour, the jury acquitted all four.
20. Lisby and Mugleston, *Someone Had to be Hated: Julian LaRose Harris—A Biography*, 170. Harris, the son of Joel Chandler Harris, who wrote the Uncle Remus stories, admired FDR and visited him occasionally at nearby Warm Springs.
21. KM interview; KM, *Annals*, 2; author's interview of Iva Benjamin Hall Hudson II, February 20 and 22, 2016. Mrs. Hudson's account of the evening, which she learned from her husband, who was there, differs from that of KM. Mrs. Hudson said that GCM, not Tom Hudson, was to pick up KM and her daughter and drive them the short distance to the Hudsons' for the dinner party. When Edith called to give GCM

directions, he waved her off, saying that since he "managed to guide armies" across the roads of France, he would have no problem getting around Columbus. Nevertheless, he was twenty minutes late and Tom had to go looking for him.

22. KM interview; KM, *Annals*, 3.
23. KM interview.
24. Much of the information about KM's years at Hollins and onstage comes from an unpublished monograph by Mary Catherine Santoro, "First Lady of the Army: The Life and Times of Katherine Tupper Marshall," May 1, 1999.
25. Pogue Notes Collection, F-PN79, GCML.
26. KM interview.
27. Ibid.
28. Ibid.
29. Derwent, *Derwent Story*, 35-36.
30. KM inteview.
31. Ibid.
32. In her interview, KM said Dr. Kelly was a "kidney specialist." KM interview.
33. Ibid. There appears to be no other information concerning the cause and nature of the pain, nor is there evidence of a recurrence after 1911.
34. Ibid.
35. Wedding announcement, NYT, October 1, 1911.
36. KM interview.
37. Ibid.
38. Ibid.
39. Ibid.
40. *Columbus Enquirer-Sun*, October 14, 1930. Article says KM returned in the spring of 1930 at the time of the performance of Allene's play, *The Creaking Chair*, at the Little Theater in Columbus.
41. KM, *Annals*, 3.
42. GCM to Pershing, n.d., but probably August 1930, Pershing Papers, LOC.
43. *Columbus Enquirer-Sun*, October 17, 1930; KM, *Annals*, 5, 7.
44. Bland, Papers, I:358, GCML.
45. Pogue, I:268.
46. Cray, *General of the Army*, 111.
47. Bradley and Blair, *General's Life*, 69.
48. Bland, Papers, I:370, GCML.
49. Letter, September 10, 1962, from Partridge, former secretary of the Fort Benning Infantry School, to Puryear, F-15-16, Reminiscences File, GCML.
50. PPA, Franklin D. Roosevelt, I:639-47. President Bill Clinton used these lines in his 1992 inaugural address.
51. Hessen, *Berlin Alert*. At GCM's request, Smith spent the summer of 1931 attending maneuvers of the First German Division in East Prussia. When he returned, he gave several lectures at Fort Benning on the methods used by the Germans in training their armies and how they dealt with the limitations imposed by the Treaty of Versailles. Ibid., xv.
52. Bland, Papers, I:387-88, GCML.
53. Ibid., 482-84. Smith was responding to a letter from GCM. Ibid., 479 (no. 1-392).

Chapter 5: God Help Us All

1. KM, *Annals*, 24.
2. White House memo for President Roosevelt from Senator Neely, April 27, 1938, OF 25-A, "War Department," "Endorsements for Assistant Secretary," FDRL.
3. Pearson and Allen, "The Merry-Go-Round," *Akron Beacon Journal*, December 1, 1938.
4. KM, *Annals*, 41.
5. Shirer, *Berlin Diary*, 126.
6. Report by Colonel Wilson, RG 407, War Department, Office of Adjutant General, Central Files, 1926-39, B-2737, NA.
7. Bland, Papers, I:636-37, GCML.
8. KM, *Annals*, 34.
9. Manchester and Reid, *The Last Lion*: "Alone," 358.
10. Ibid., 356.
11. FRUS, 1938, 1:688; Ickes Diary, 2:468.
12. Blum, *Morgenthau Diaries*, II:46; memoranda by Johnson and Craig, October 15, 1938, B-34, Johnson Papers, University of Virginia; Frye, *Marshall*, 248. Frye based his dialogue on one of the persons present.
13. Blum, *Morgenthau Diaries*, II:48-49; quoted in Reynolds, *Munich to Pearl Harbor*, 45-46 (emphasis added).
14. Notes by Arnold, November 15, 1938, OF 25-T, Army Chief of Staff, B-6, FDRL.
15. Marshall Interviews, 108-9, GCML.
16. Ibid., 109.
17. Unger, D. and I., with Hirshon, *George Marshall*, 83.
18. Bland, Papers, I:654-55, GCML; Roosevelt to Pershing, December 3, 1938 ("I am having a study made"), Correspondence files (Marshall, Roosevelt), Pershing Papers, LOC.
19. Interview of General James Burns. Watson, *Chief of Staff: Prewar Plans and Preparations*, 142.
20. Sherwood, *Roosevelt and Hopkins*, 2-3.
21. Ibid., 80, quoting Hugh Johnson.
22. Ibid., 101.
23. Ibid.
24. Bland, Papers, I:638-39, GCML.
25. Ibid., I:682-84.
26. Ibid. Marshall's blood pressure was 132 over 78. Without socks he was five feet eleven and three-quarter inches tall and weighed 175 pounds.
27. Wilson, *Marshall Remembered*, 231.
28. Olson, *Those Angry Days*, 200.
29. GCM to Pershing, January 16, 1939, Correspondence (Marshall file), Pershing Papers, LOC.
30. Olson, *Those Angry Days*, 200.
31. Drum Papers, B-23, B-9, ACEH, Carlisle, PA.
32. Ibid., B-23.
33. Ibid., B-9.
34. Tugwell, *Brains Trust*, 434.

35. Transcript of conference with Senate Military Affairs Committee, January 31, 1939, PPF 1-P, B-252, FDRL.
36. *Life*, February 13, 1939, at 19.
37. Schewe, ed., *Franklin D. Roosevelt and Foreign Affairs*, 13:243.
38. Ibid., 273.
39. Baynes, ed. *Speeches of Adolf Hitler*, I:737–41. The speech was delivered on January 30, 1939, the sixth anniversary of Hitler's ascent to power.
40. Reynolds, *Munich to Pearl Harbor*, 61. From February 18 to March 3, 1939, FDR was in the Caribbean aboard the *Houston* observing the naval exercises.
41. Pogue, I:330; *Life*, January 3, 1944, 7; Mosley, *Hero for Our Times*, 127.
42. Williams, Reminiscences File, GCML.
43. "Conversation with Secretary Marshall in His Office at the State Department," July 23, 1947, Sherwood Papers, Houghton Library, Harvard.
44. Bland, Papers, I:714, GCML.
45. Correspondence (Marshall), Pershing Papers, Library of Congress.
46. KM, *Annals*, 54.
47. The Pact of Steel was signed by foreign ministers Galaezzo Ciano of Italy and Joachim von Ribbentrop of Germany on May 22, 1939.
48. Alsop and Kintner, *American White Paper*, 46.
49. Patton to Beatrice A. Patton, July 27, 1939, Patton Papers, LOC.
50. Speer, quoted by Sereny, *Albert Speer: His Battle with Truth*, 207.
51. Reynolds, *Munich to Pearl Harbor*, 62.
52. Dallek, *Franklin D. Roosevelt*, 351, quoting J. Pierrepont Moffat, assistant secretary of state for Western European Affairs.
53. Note dictated by FDR in bed at 3:05 a.m. on September 1, 1939, PF Files, FDRL.
54. Alsop and Kintner, *American White Paper*, 1.
55. Bland, Papers, II:59–61, GCML.

Chapter 6: A Time to Plant

1. "Gen. and Mrs. George Marshall Give Garden Party Reception," *Washington Post*, May 11, 1940, 11. See also "Chilean Envoy Receives for 27 Naval Cadets; Gen. Marshall Is Host," *Evening Star*, May 11, 1940.
2. "Marshalls' Guests Pay Tribute as Flag Is Furled at Sunset," *Washington Times-Herald*, May 11, 1940.
3. Bland, Papers, II:163–64, GCML.
4. Marshall Interviews, 610, GCML. Baruch, *The Public Years*, II:278.
5. Morgenthau Jr., Papers, Presidential Diary, 2:291–92, FDRL.
6. Lash, *Roosevelt and Churchill*, 184.
7. Marshall Interviews, 329, GCML.
8. Blum, *Morgenthau Diaries*, II:140–41.
9. Marshall Interviews, 329, GCML.
10. Ibid., 330.
11. Churchill, *Their Finest Hour*, 42.
12. Kimball, *Churchill & Roosevelt: Complete Correspondence*, I:37.
13. Roosevelt, "Message to Congress on Appropriations for National Defense," May 16, 1940, online by Gerhard Peters and John T. Wooley, The American

Presidency Project, http://www.presidency.ucsb.edu/ws?pid=15954. The president sought $546 million for the regular army, not the army air corps. His message called for another $186 million for army aircraft, including 200 B-17 bombers, bringing the army total to $732 million.

14. Churchill, *Their Finest Hour*, 115.
15. Ibid., 118.
16. Holmes, *World at War*, 97.
17. Sevareid, *Not So Wild*, 152.
18. Roberts, *Storm of War*, 74.
19. Smith to chief of staff, June 11, 1940, Office of Chief of Staff, SGS, Binder 4, NA.
20. Blum, *Morgenthau Diaries*, II:151.
21. Bland, Papers, II:246-47, GCML.
22. Pub. L. 76-671, Title I, 14 (a), 54 Stat. 676 (1940).
23. Bland, Papers, II:261-62, GCML.
24. Marshall Interviews, 305, GCML. Palmer, one of Marshall's old friends, was dispatched to assist Clark's Military Training Camps Association (MTCA) in preparing a compulsory service bill to be introduced in Congress. On May 26, Palmer sent Marshall a telegram requesting that two army officers be permitted to confer with the MTCA drafting committee, which Marshall approved on May 27. Bland, Papers, II:224-25, GCML.
25. Olson, *Those Angry Days*, 201.
26. Marshall Interviews, 302, GCML.
27. Marshall Interviews, January 22, 1957, Tape 10M (unedited), 13, GCML. In Clifford and Spencer, *The First Peacetime Draft*, the authors suggest that GCM's judgment was correct. "In light of Congress's longstanding suspicion of army requests for expansion or innovation, the Burke-Wadsworth bill may well have profited from the fact that it did not originate with the 'brass hats.'" Ibid., 52.
28. Frankfurter to Roosevelt, June 4 and 5, 1940, B-98, General Correspondence 1878-1945, Frankfurter Papers, LOC.
29. Bland, Papers, II:246-47, GCML.
30. Woodring to Harris, June 23, 1954, inserted in *Congressional Record*, Vol. C, part 10, 12960, by Senator Joseph McCarthy, August 2, 1954.
31. Stimson and Bundy, *On Active Service*, 331.
32. Woodberry Forest, "Fir Tree," 1934.
33. Bland, Papers, I:I241-42, GCML.
34. Madge Pendleton Interview, Great Projects Film Company Collection, "George Marshall and the American Century," Binder 2, GCML.
35. Watson, *Chief of Staff: Prewar Plans*, 110-11 and n. 62 citing RG 165, WPD 4250-3, NA.
36. GCM to KM, June 28, 1940 (Larry Bland file), Marshall Mss., GCML.
37. Clifford and Spencer, *First Peacetime Draft*, 108.
38. Hearing on Nomination of Stimson to be Secretary of War Before Senate Committee on Military Affairs, 76th Cong. (July 2, 1940); NYT, July 3, 1940; Stimson and Bundy, *On Active Service*, 328-30.
39. Marshall Interviews, 300, GCML.
40. Roosevelt, excerpts from press conference, August 2, 1940, online by Peters and

Wooley, The American Presidency Project, http://www.presidency.ucsb.edu /ws/?pid+15985.

41. *New York Herald Tribune*, August 18, 1940, 40.

42. Roosevelt, excerpts from press conference, August 23, 1940, online by Peters and Wooley, The American Presidency Project, http://www.presidency.ucsb.edu /ws/?pid=15994.

43. KM, *Annals*, 67-68.

44. Stoler, *Marshall: Soldier-Statesman*, 73.

45. Second Supplemental National Defense Appropriations Bill for 1941, Hearings Before the Senate Subcommittee of the Committee on Appropriations, 76th Cong., 21-22.

46. Bland, Papers, II:308-12, GCML.

47. U.S. Department of Commerce, Bureau of the Census, Statistical History of the United States, 736.

48. Bland, Papers, II:336-37, GCML.

49. Doyle, *Inside the Oval Office: The White House Tapes from FDR to Clinton*, September 27, 1940, 11:30 a.m., https://www.nytimes.com/books/first/d/doyle-oval .html.

50. Bland, Papers, II:338-39, GCML.

51. Research note, Miss Lejeune re CCS Papers, 1921-1942, Xerox 3232 at 5, GCML; Marshall to J. McCloy, September 4, 1941, Reel 15, Item 552, GCML.

52. Marshall Interviews, 499-500, GCML.

53. Based on an army intelligence report, GCM wrote that the National Negro Congress, an organization that was pressing for "fair and impartial treatment" of black soldiers, was under "complete control of the Communists." GCM to McCloy, September 4, 1941, Reel 15, Item 552, GCML. See also letter by GCM to Mrs. Egbert Armstrong, May 16, 1941, Bland, Papers, II:318-19, GCML, where he refers to a black soldier at Benning as a "darkey soldier," the only instance in Marshall's extensive correspondence where he used a racial epithet.

54. Stoler, *Allies and Adversaries*, 26.

55. Stark to Secretary of Navy, November 12, 1940, PSF (Safe) Navy, FDRL.

56. Chief of Staff to Secretary of War and Anderson to Chief of Staff, "National Policy of the United States," memos, November 13, 1940, RG 165, WPD 4175-11, NA.

57. Conn and Fairchild, *Framework of Hemisphere Defense*, 89.

58. Lippmann, "The Economic Consequences of a German Victory," *Life*, July 22, 1940, 65-69. Sexton to Chief of Staff, memo, July 22, 1940, Sexton Papers, B-2/F-39, GCML.

59. Bland, Papers, II:360-62, GCML.

60. KM, *Annals*, 80.

61. Wilson, *Marshall Remembered*, 233.

62. KM, *Annals*, 80-81. See also KM's scrapbook no. 1, GCML.

63. Bland, Papers, II:391-92, GCML.

64. Roosevelt, Third Inaugural Address, Rosenman, PPA, Franklin D. Roosevelt, 1941, 3-7.

65. KM, *Annals*, 83.

66. Bland, Papers, II:391-92, GCML.

Chapter 7: The Hour to Reap Has Come

1. Marshall Interviews, 302, GCML.
2. KM, *Annals*, 92.
3. Biennial Report of the Chief of Staff of the United States Army, July 1, 1939, to June 30, 1941, to the Secretary of War, July 1, 1941.
4. Hearings Before Senate Committee on Military Affairs in Connection with Retention of Selectees and Reserve Components in Military Service Beyond One Year, July 9, 1941, 4.
5. KTB OKW. *Kriegstagebuch des Oberkommandos der Wehrmacht: Wehrmachtfuhrungsstab, 1939-1945*. Franfurt am Main, 1965, I:417.
6. Heinrichs, *Threshold of War*, 122.
7. Hachey, "American Profiles on Capitol Hill," *Wisconsin Magazine of History* 57, no. 2 (Winter 1973-1974).
8. Hearings Before Senate Committee on Military Affairs, Retain Selectees in Military Service, July 17, 1941, 39.
9. Hearings Before House Committee on Military Affairs, Remove Restrictions on National Defense, July 22, 1941, 26.
10. Hearings Before Senate Committee on Military Affairs, Retain Selectees in Military Service, July 17, 1941, 24-25.
11. Williams, Reminiscences File, GCML.
12. Marshall Interviews, 303, GCML.
13. Bland, Papers, II:585-88, GCML.
14. KM, *Annals*, 94-95.
15. Marshall Interviews, 285-87, GCML.
16. Notes Relative to President Roosevelt's and Prime Minister Churchill's Conference Held Aboard Ship in Placentia Bay, Newfoundland, between the dates of Aug. 9-Aug. 12, 1941, Arnold Papers, B-2, Reel 2, Manuscript Division, LOC (hereinafter referred to as Arnold notes).
17. Ibid.
18. Danchev, *Special Relationship*, 4-5, 49, 132, 134.
19. Watson, *Chief of Staff: Prewar Plans*, 376-77; General Strategy Review by the British Chiefs of Staff, July 31, 1941, attached to L. C. Hollis to Marshall, August 10, 1941, RG 165, WPD 4402-62, NA.
20. Bland, Papers, II:585-88, GCML.
21. "Statement of Admiral Stark," Arnold notes. Stark's "talking points" were discovered by the author on a separate typed sheet among Arnold's copious notes in the Library of Congress.
22. Sherwood, *Roosevelt and Hopkins*, 358; Hamilton, *Mantle of Command*, 34-35.
23. The unsigned "talking points" were most likely prepared by Stark, GCM, or one of their aides and finalized on the morning of August 11 about an hour before the formal meeting of the Anglo-British chiefs. Arnold's notes indicate that it was then that the Americans "went over the British strategy paper in Admiral Stark's office."
24. Ibid.
25. NYT, August 13, 1941.
26. *Congressional Record*, August 12, 1941, 7075.
27. NYT, August 13, 1941.

28. Symington, *Heard and Overheard*, 210 (emphasis in the original).
29. Watson, *Chief of Staff: Prewar Plans*, 362.
30. Heinrichs, *Threshold of War*, 179.
31. Joint Board Estimate of United States Over-all Production Requirements, September 11, 1941, at 14, PSF Safe File, B-1, FDRL.
32. GCM to Roosevelt, "Ground Forces" memo, September 23, 1941, in PHA, pt. 15, exh. 60, 1636–39.
33. Watson, *Chief of Staff: Prewar Plans*, 354–55n70; Stoler, *Allies and Adversaries*, 54, n. 49.
34. "Ground Forces," memo, PHA, pt. 15, exh. 60, 1636–39.
35. Bland, Papers, II:614, n. 2, GCML.
36. Stimson Diary, September 25, 1941, Yale.
37. Bland, Papers, II:567–68, GCML.
38. MacArthur's letter to GCM is quoted in Manchester, *American Caesar*, 208.
39. Bland, Papers, II:541, n. 2, GCML.
40. Watson, *Chief of Staff: Prewar Plans*, 438–39.
41. Marshall Interviews, 244, GCML.
42. Arnold notes, 3–4.
43. Record of discussion among GCM, Dill, and Brigadier Dykes, August 11, 1941, PREM 3/485/5, PRO, BNA.
44. Stimson Diary, September 12, 1941, Yale.
45. GCM-Smedberg phone transcript, September 21, 1941, OPNAV phone records, Navy Operational Records, Navy Yard, Washington, DC.
46. Sir R. Campbell to FO, September 27, 1941, FO 371/27982, F9976/1299/23, PRO, BNA.
47. Langer and Gleason, *Undeclared War, 1940–1941*, 655.
48. FRUS, Japan, 1931–1941, II:701–4.
49. Tokyo to Washington, November 2, 4, 1941, "Magic" Background of Pearl Harbor, IV, Appendix: no. 20 and m. 25.
50. Bland, Papers, II:660, n. 1, GCML.
51. Heinrichs, *Threshold of War*, 204.
52. Ibid.; Stoler, *Allies and Adversaries*, 60–61, PHA.
53. Osugi, *Shinjuwan e no Michi*, 413.
54. Kazumasa, *Rengo Kantai*, 20.
55. Tolischus, "Japanese Ask U.S. to Reverse Stand or Face Conflict," NYT, November 5, 1941.
56. Bland, Papers, II:676–81, GCML.
57. Ibid., 674–75.
58. Ibid.
59. PHA, pt. 12, 165.
60. Ibid., pt. 14, 1405.
61. Bland, Papers, II:411–14, GCML.
62. PHA, pt. 3, 1148.
63. Stimson Diary, November 25, 1941, Yale. Conspiracy theorists make much of the "maneuver" remark, implying that Roosevelt and his War Cabinet conspired to allow the Pearl Harbor attack to take place so that Congress would approve entry by the U.S. into the Second World War.

64. PHA, pt. 3, 1149.
65. Stimson Diary, November 26, 1941, Yale.
66. Ibid., November 27, 1941.
67. PHA, pt. 11, 5424.
68. Ibid., pt. 7, 3029.
69. Ibid., pt. 14, 1406 (Stark/Kimmel—"war warning"); pt. 7, 3032 (Miles, head of army intelligence—"subversive activities expected").
70. Ibid., pt. 14, 1330.
71. Ibid., pt. 39, 143–45.
72. Ibid., pt. 3, 1421.
73. Ibid., pt. 3, 1422.
74. *Showa Tenno dokuhakuroku*, 89–90.
75. Toland, *But Not in Shame*, 14.
76. Ugaki Diary, December 2, 1941. *Niitaka yama nobore ichi-ni-rei-ya*. This meant that the attack was set for zero hours on December 8 (Japan time).
77. Prange's interview with Schindel, *At Dawn We Slept*, 457n24.
78. PHA, pt. 12, 238–39.
79. *Department of State Bulletin* V, no. 129 (December 13, 1941).
80. PHA, pt. 10, 4662.
81. Prange, *At Dawn We Slept*, 476, based on testimony of Bratton, PHA, pt. 9, 4516 ("relatively unimportant militarily").
82. PHA, pt. 2, 925–26.
83. PHA Report, 223.
84. Ibid., 224.
85. PHA, pt. 9, 4519.
86. Wilson, *Marshall Remembered*, 245.
87. Ungers with Hirshon, *Marshall*, 128–29.

Chapter 8: Germany First

1. Bland, Papers, III:8, GCML. MacArthur received first word of the attack at Pearl Harbor at 3:40 a.m. Manila time. Therefore, he had almost nine hours' advance notice before Japanese bombers and fighters began destroying his air force at 12:30 p.m.
2. Interview of Eleanor Roosevelt, Graff Papers, FDRL.
3. Churchill, *Grand Alliance*, 605, 608–9.
4. Keegan, *Second World War*, 240.
5. PPA, Franklin D. Roosevelt, 10:532.
6. DDE, *Crusade*, 14.
7. DDE, interview by Pogue, DDE Library, 20.
8. Ricks, *Generals*, 45.
9. DDE, interview by Pogue, DDE Library, 20.
10. DDE, *Crusade*, 21–22.
11. Pogue, II:238.
12. Kimball, *Churchill & Roosevelt*, I:283–84.
13. Stoler, *Marshall: Soldier-Statesman*, 90.
14. King is alleged to have said that "when the going gets tough they send for the sons-of-bitches," meaning him. Pogue, *Marshall*, III:7.

15. KM, *Annals*, 102.
16. FRUS, Conferences at Washington, 1941-1942, 93.
17. Stimson Diary, December 27, 1941, Yale.
18. Pogue, II:280.
19. Marshall Interviews, 595, GCML.
20. Moran, *Churchill: Taken from the Diaries*, 20, 22.
21. Churchill, *Grand Alliance*, 674.
22. Stimson Diary, December 29, 1941, Yale.
23. Buell, *Master of Sea Power*, 169.
24. Churchill, *Grand Alliance*, 705.
25. Sherwood, *Roosevelt and Hopkins*, 472.
26. Marshall Interviews, 599, GCML.
27. Sherwood, *Roosevelt and Hopkins*, 472.
28. Ibid., 472, quoting Hopkins's Arcadia notes.
29. Stoler, *Marshall: Soldier-Statesman*, 90. In *Mantle of Command*, Hamilton writes that the president created the CCS and suggests that he drove through the concept of unitary command against the opposition of the prime minister. See 139-40. This misstates the pivotal role of Marshall.
30. Wilson, *Marshall Remembered*, 246.
31. KM, *Annals*, 109, 110.
32. James, *Years of MacArthur*, 2:91-92.
33. Quezon to Roosevelt, dispatched as part of MacArthur to GCM, February 8, 1942, RG 4, B-15/F-1, NA.
34. Ibid., MacArthur to GCM.
35. Stimson Diary, February 9, 1942, Yale.
36. Roosevelt to MacArthur, February 10, 1942, RG 2, B-3/F-1, NA.
37. Pogue, II:247-48. (Pogue cites his interview of November 14, 1956, as source for the GCM quote, but there is no record of any such interview.)
38. Limerick poem by Idaho-born Frank Hewlett, Manila bureau chief for United Press, the last reporter to leave Corregidor before it fell to the Japanese.
39. Roosevelt to Quezon, February 10, 1942, RG 2, B-3/F-1, NA.
40. Petillo, *MacArthur: The Philippine Years*, 208, n. 112, n. 113.
41. MacArthur biographer Arthur Herman asserted without citation that Marshall "certainly" knew all about the funds transfer and "let it happen." Another MacArthur biographer, Walter Borneman, speculated that the chief of staff "was not in the loop." No one has found any evidence that Marshall was involved or had knowledge of the funds transfer during the time it took place.
42. Memo by DDE, June 20, 1942; Ferrell, *Eisenhower Diaries*, 63.
43. MacArthur, *Reminiscences*, 142, 143.
44. Ibid., 145; reported in the *Chronicle* (Adelaide), March 26, 1942.
45. General Orders No. 16, War Department, April 1, 1942.
46. Sydney *Morning Herald*, March 27, 1942, 4.
47. Matloff and Snell, *Strategic Planning*, 1941-42, 183-84; Strange, "Cross-Channel Attack," 85-88, App. B, 470-76.
48. Roll, *Hopkins Touch*, 185-86; Arnold memo, April 1, 1942, Conference with President, B-180, Conference File, White House, 1942 Apr-May, Arnold Papers, LOC.

49. Stimson Diary, April 1, 1942, Yale.
50. Kimball, *Churchill & Roosevelt*, I:437.
51. Ibid., 441.
52. NYT, April 6, 1942.
53. Clipping, Hopkins Papers, B-308, book 5, FDRL.
54. KM, *Annals*, 112.
55. DDE to Chief of Staff, March 25, 1942, OPD 381, Bolero Sec.1, NA.
56. Danchev and Todman, *War Diaries of Alanbrooke*, 246.
57. Sherwood, *Roosevelt and Hopkins*, 523, quoting Hopkins's notes.
58. Danchev and Todman, *War Diaries of Alanbrooke*, 249.
59. Sherwood, *Roosevelt and Hopkins*, 527.
60. COS (42) 97 (0), 13 April 1942, Comments on Marshall memorandum. CCS 381 (3-23-42) pt. 3, RG 218, MM, NA.
61. Marshall Interviews, 584–85, GCML.
62. Mountbatten, interview by Pogue, Tapes 83 and 84, Copy 2, May 4, 1961, GCML.
63. FRUS, 1942, General; the British Commonwealth; the Far East, I:633–34.
64. Sherwood, *Roosevelt and Hopkins*, 531.
65. Ibid.
66. Hamilton, *Mantle of Command*, 252–53.
67. Kimball, *Churchill & Roosevelt*, I:448.
68. Roberts, *Masters and Commanders*, 151, citing GCM to McNarney, April 12, 1942, Marshall Papers, Verifax 631-60, GCML. GCM also sent a radiogram on April 12 informing McNarney that "Naval Person told me he accepts our proposal." Bland, Papers, III:159–60, GCML.
69. CAB 69/4/59; CAB 69/4 Defence Committee No. 10 (1942), 14/4/1942, BNA.
70. Ibid.
71. Gilbert, *Churchill: A Life*, VII:89.
72. Bland, Papers, III:162–63, GCML.
73. Loewenheim, ed. *Roosevelt and Churchill*, 209.
74. Churchill, *Hinge of Fate*, 324.
75. Lord Ismay, interview by Pogue, October 18, 1960, GCML.
76. Ismay, *Memoirs of Lord Ismay*, 249–50.
77. KM, scrapbook no. 4, B-22, 30, GCML.
78. Atkinson, *Army at Dawn*, 141.
79. Truscott, *Command Missions*, 18–19.
80. Ibid., 22.
81. Ibid., 23.
82. Bland, Papers, III:183–86, GCML.
83. Ibid.
84. Roosevelt to GCM, May 6, 1942, PSF Departmental (War), Roosevelt Papers, FDRL; Bland, Papers, III:186, n. 3, GCML.
85. Roosevelt for SW, C of S, Arnold, SN, King and Hopkins, 6 May 1942, PSF "Gen. Geo. C. Marshall, 1942" [Closed], FDRL.
86. Speech to Graduating Class, United States Military Academy, May 29, 1942, no. 3-205, Marshall Papers Pentagon Office Collection, Speeches, GCML.

Chapter 9: Hardest Fought Debate

1. Keegan, *Second World War*, 316.
2. Danchev and Todman, *War Diaries of Alanbrooke*, 265.
3. Churchill, *Hinge of Fate*, 381–82. On March 7, 1942, Roosevelt had recommended "the temporary shelving of Gymnast" and said he was "becoming more and more interested in the establishment" of a "new front" in Western Europe "this summer." Kimball, *Churchill & Roosevelt*, 1:392–93, 398–99.
4. Churchill, *Hinge of Fate*, 383, 384.
5. Stimson Diary, June 21, 1942, Yale.
6. Matloff and Snell, *Strategic Planning*, 1941–42, 244.
7. Ibid., 237.
8. Military Intelligence Service, no. 120, July 11, 1942, G-2 Reports, B-67, Map Room, FDRL. See also MID reports, Nos. 110 and 119, July 1 and July 10, 1942, G-2 Reports, B-67, Map Room, FDRL.
9. Bland, Papers, III:273–75, GCML.
10. Parkinson, *Blood, Toil, Tears and Sweat: War History from Dunkirk to Alamein*, 438.
11. Cray, *General of the Army*, 328.
12. KM, *Annals*, 110.
13. Matloff and Snell, *Strategic Planning*, 1941–42, 268.
14. Ibid., 269.
15. Marshall Interview Notes, 593, 602, GCML.
16. Matloff and Snell, *Strategic Planning*, 1941–42, 270.
17. Stoler, *Allies and Adversaries*, 80, 84.
18. Stimson Diary, July 15, 1942, Yale.
19. Roosevelt was concerned that the recommendation by GCM and King of a turn to the Pacific would appear to historians and others in later years to be an "abandonment of the British." Consequently, he requested them to alter their written recommendation. GCM resisted, believing the U.S. could not fairly be accused of outright abandonment, because he would provide for adequate ground troops and air assets to be left behind for the defense of Britain. Fortunately, the written record was not altered. Bland, Papers, III:276–77, GCML.
20. Davis, *FDR: War President*, 544.
21. Matloff and Snell, *Strategic Planning*, 1941–42, 272, n. 19.
22. Entire memo quoted in Sherwood, *Roosevelt and Hopkins*, 603–5.
23. Stimson Diary, July 15, 1942, Yale.
24. GCM to DDE, tel., July 16, 1942, OPD Exec. 5, item 9, RG 165, NA.
25. Bland, Papers, III:266–67, GCML.
26. Marshall Interviews, 433, GCML.
27. Churchill, *Hinge of Fate*, 440.
28. Danchev and Todman, *War Diaries of Alanbrooke*, 280.
29. Hopkins to Roosevelt, July 20, 1942, Hopkins Papers, B-298, FDRL.
30. Roll, *Hopkins Touch*, 213.
31. Chandler, *Eisenhower Papers*, I:393–94.
32. Truscott, *Command Missions*, 48–49.
33. Truscott Papers, July 17, 1942. B-10, F-1, GCML.

34. Giumarra, *SLEDGEHAMMER and OVERLORD*, 28.
35. Ibid., 41.
36. C. C. (42) (3rd draft), July 21, 1942, WO 199/3008, BNA.
37. Giumarra, *SLEDGEHAMMER and OVERLORD*, 29; Strange, "Cross-Channel Attack," 1942, 454.
38. Giumarra, *SLEDGEHAMMER and OVERLORD*, 28.
39. Ibid., 28; Dunn, *Second Front Now*, 232.
40. Giumarra, *SLEDGEHAMMER and OVERLORD*, 95, 98.
41. C. C. (42) (3rd draft), July 21, 1942, WO 199/3008, BNA.
42. After day ten, the Allies would run out of their supplies of external drop-tanks, which extended their range. As soon as supplies of drop-tanks were restored, probably sometime during the winter, Allied fighters could remain over the Cherbourg Peninsula for more than fifteen minutes.
43. Danchev and Todman, *War Diaries of Alanbrooke*, 282.
44. Ibid., 283.
45. Chandler, *Papers of DDE*, 403 (Marshall's argument); Revised Minutes of CCS Conference, July 22, 1942, 3:00 p.m., ABC 381 BOLERO (3-16-2-42), sec. 2, RG 165, MM, NA (Churchill's response).
46. Ibid. (Marshall's statement for the record.)
47. Scrapbook no. 4, B-22, 60, GCM and KM Collection, GCML.
48. At the time the War Cabinet consisted of Churchill as minister of defense and chair, Anthony Eden, Stafford Cripps, Clement Atlee, Oliver Lyttelton, John Anderson, and Ernest Bevin.
49. W. M. (42) 94th Conclusions, 22 July 1942-5:30 p.m., CAB 65/31, PRO, BNA.
50. Ibid.
51. C. C. (42) (3rd draft), 30th July 1942, Combined Commanders, Operation "Wetbob" Appreciation, RG 331, SHAEF CC (42) Papers 42-85, B-124, Tab 42, NA.
52. W. M. (42) 94th Conclusions, 22 July 1942-5:30 p.m., CAB 65/31, PRO, BNA.
53. Ibid.
54. Leshuk, *US Intelligence Perceptions of Soviet Power*, 168; see also "Effect of Soviet Collapse," July 15, 1942, PRO WO208 1777 6895/13 M.I. 3c/COL/43/42, BNA.
55. German Luftwaffe Orders of Battle, http://ww2-weapons.com/Armies/Germany/Luftwaffe/1942.htm.
56. W. M. (42) 94th Conclusions, 22 July 1942-5:30 p.m., CAB 65/31, PRO, BNA.
57. Marshall Interviews, 588, 602, GCML.
58. Butcher, *My Three Years with Eisenhower*, 24.
59. Danchev and Todman, *War Diaries of Alanbrooke*, 284.
60. Memo FDR to Hopkins, GCM, and King listing priorities, n.d. but probably July 23, 1942, book 5, folder "Hopkins to London, July 1942," B-308, Sherwood Collection, FDRL.
61. GCM and King memo for the President, July 28, 1942, RG 165, OCS 319.1, NA, the revised draft of which was approved by the prime minister and the War Cabinet. The revised draft was circulated at CCS 94. Portions of CCS 94 are quoted in Matloff and Snell, *Strategic Planning*, 1941-42, 280-81.
62. Thorne, *Allies of a Kind*, 136.

63. Danchev and Todman, *War Diaries of Alanbrooke*, 285.
64. Ibid. There was some question as to whether Churchill expressly approved CCS 94. See Butler, *Grand Strategy*, III, pt. 2, 635-36, 684-85.
65. Hopkins to Roosevelt, July 25, 1942, book 5, folder "Hopkins to London, July 1942," B-308, Sherwood Collection, FDRL.
66. Memo, FDR to Hopkins, GCM, and King, n.d., but it is FDR's reply to Hopkins's message of July 25 in the previous endnote and can be found in book 5, folder "Hopkins to London, July 1942," B-308, Sherwood Collection, FDRL.
67. Matloff and Snell, *Strategic Planning*, 1941-42, 282, n. 50.
68. Kimball, *Churchill & Roosevelt*, II:543.
69. Ibid., I:542.
70. Matloff and Snell, *Strategic Planning*, 1941-42, 282.
71. Ibid., 283.
72. Ibid.
73. Ibid., 283-84.
74. Bland, Papers, III:305, GCML.
75. Letter from Dill to GCM, August 8, 1942, E-15, RG 165, B-8, NA; letter from GCM to Dill, August 14, 1942, E-15, RG 165, B-8, NA.
76. Davis, *FDR: War President*, 551.
77. Hamilton, *Mantle of Command*, 364.
78. Huntington, *Soldier and the State*. For an insightful critique of Huntington's theory of objective control, see Cohen, *Supreme Command*.
79. Sherwood, *Roosevelt and Hopkins*, 9.
80. Memo by GCM quoting report of DDE, Patton, and Clark to Leahy and King, August 17, 1942, B-105, PSF, FDRL; memo for the President from GCM and King, n.d., folder "Marshall, George C. 1941-April 14, 1942," PSF B-3, FDRL.
81. Marshall Interviews, 593, 599, GCML.
82. Kimball, *Churchill & Roosevelt*, 591-92.
83. Guyer and Donnelly, interview of GCM, February 11, 1949, Interviews and Reminiscences, GCML.
84. See, e.g., Steele, *First Offensive*, 157, referencing memo, Marshall to President, June 23, 1942, FRUS, 1942, Conferences at Washington, 1941-1942, 473-75; and Matloff and Snell, *Strategic Planning*, 1941-42, 240-43.
85. Blumenson, *Patton Papers*, 93.
86. Diary, October 21, 1942, George S. Patton Jr., LOC.
87. Farago, *Patton: Ordeal and Triumph*, 195.
88. KM, *Annals*, 129.
89. Marshall Interview Notes, October 5, 1956, 596, GCML.
90. KM, *Annals*, 130.
91. Marshall Interview Notes, November 13, 1956, 622, GCML.

Chapter 10: He Ruleth His Spirit

1. KM, *Annals*, 153.
2. Ibid.
3. Marshall to Lieutenant Allen Brown, June 29, 1942, Marshall-Winn Collection, B-38/F-10, GCML.; memo by GCM, July 28, 1943, directing that Allen be

assigned as replacement to 1st Armored Division (secret order), Marshall-Winn Collection, B-38/F-11, GCML; see also letters from Marshall to Allen dated September 1, 1942, February 26, 1943, and June 16, 1943, GCML.

4. GCM to Brown, July 8, 1943, loaned to author by Tupper Brown (son of Allen) (emphasis added).

5. Matloff and Snell, *Strategic Planning,* 1943–44, 389. A judgment concerning the organization of twelve additional infantry or armored divisions, scheduled to be activated later in 1943, was deferred.

6. Matloff and Snell, *Strategic Planning,* 1943–44, 181.

7. Greenfield, ed., *Command Decisions,* chap. 15, Matloff, "The 90-Division Gamble," 366.

8. KM, *Annals,* 139.

9. Surles, March 8, 1943, quoted in Matloff and Snell, *Strategic Planning,* 1943–44, 117.

10. Fairchild and Grossman, *Army and Industrial Manpower,* 45–46; Matloff and Snell, *Strategic Planning,* 1943–44, 112–17, 179–84; Kennedy, *Freedom from Fear,* 626–31.

11. Resolutions by CCS, May 20, 1943, in FRUS, Conferences at Washington and Quebec, 1943, 281–82.

12. Guyer, Donnelly, interview of GCM, February 11, 1949, at 3, Interviews and Reminiscences, GCML.

13. Matloff and Snell, *Strategic Planning,* 1943–44, 401.

14. FRUS, Conferences at Washington and Quebec, 1943, 467–72.

15. Stimson Diary, August 10, 1943, Yale; Roberts, *Masters and Commanders,* 394.

16. FRUS, Conferences at Washington and Quebec, 1943, 498–503.

17. Stimson Diary, August 10, 1943, Yale.

18. Stimson to Roosevelt, August 10, 1943, quoted in Stimson and Bundy, *Active Service,* 436–38.

19. Ibid., 438.

20. Danchev and Todman, *War Diaries of Alanbrooke,* 441–42.

21. Ibid., 442.

22. FRUS, Conferences at Washington and Quebec, 1943, 866–67.

23. Danchev and Todman, *War Diaries of Alanbrooke,* 442.

24. Danchev, *Special Relationship,* 129–30; Danchev and Todman, *War Diaries of Alanbrooke,* 442–43.

25. *War Diaries,* 443.

26. Ibid.

27. FRUS, Conferences at Washington and Quebec, 1943, 1025 (emphasis added).

28. Danchev and Todman, *War Diaries of Alanbrooke,* 444.

29. Ibid., 446.

30. King, interview, July 31, 1949, B-9, King Papers, LOC; King, "Notes taken from Flight Log no. 3," August 13, 1943 entry, B-4, King Papers, LOC.

31. Danchev and Todman, *War Diaries of Alanbrooke,* 446; Leahy, *I Was There,* 213.

32. Sherwood, *Roosevelt and Hopkins,* 758.

33. Marshall Interviews, 343–45, GCML.

34. KM, *Annals,* 142, 159; Sherwood, *Roosevelt and Hopkins,* 759.

35. Truscott, *Command Missions,* 243.

36. Kennedy, *Freedom from Fear,* 601.

37. Manchester, *American Caesar*, 338.
38. Allen Brown to KM, September 2, 1943, loaned to author; Atkinson, *Army at Dawn*, 508-10.
39. Second Biennial Report of Chief of Staff, July 1, 1941, to June 30, 1943, 35, 39, 75, 77.
40. Bland, Papers, IV:107-8, GCML.
41. Silverman, "At the Water's Edge: Arthur Vandenberg and the Foundation of American Bipartisan Foreign Policy," PhD dissertation, UCLA, 1967, 301.
42. FRUS, Conferences at Cairo and Teheran, 1943, 72.
43. Ibid., 38-39, 110-12.
44. GCM to Sherwood, February 25, 1947, bMS Am1947 (548), Sherwood Papers, Houghton Library, Harvard.
45. Sherwood, *Roosevelt and Hopkins*, 759-60; *Congressional Record*, 78th Cong., 1st Sess., A4001.
46. Bland, Papers, IV:129, GCML.
47. Sherwood, *Roosevelt and Hopkins*, 761.
48. FRUS, Conferences at Cairo and Teheran, 1943, 279-80; Buell, *Master of Sea Power*, 419-20.
49. Hopkins memo to self, n.d., Hopkins Papers, Reel 20, FDRL.
50. DDE, *Crusade in Europe*, 196.
51. Ibid., 224: Ambrose, *Supreme Commander*, 303.
52. UPI dispatch to *Los Angeles Herald-Examiner*, May 24, 1964.
53. Smith, *Eisenhower*, 307.
54. Sherwood, *Roosevelt and Hopkins*, 770.
55. DDE, *Crusade*, 197.
56. Bland, Papers, IV:190-91, GCML.
57. FRUS, Conferences at Cairo and Teheran, 1943, 322-25.
58. Danchev and Todman, *War Diaries of Alanbrooke*, 481.
59. FRUS, Conferences at Cairo and Teheran, 1943, 364.
60. Marshall Interviews, 621, GCML.
61. Danchev and Todman, *War Diaries of Alanbrooke*, 481.
62. FRUS, Conferences at Cairo and Teheran, 1943, 365, 410-11.
63. GCM to KM, November 26, 1943, Marshall-Winn Collection, B-44/F-17, GCML.
64. Allen Brown to Madge, November 26, 1943, loaned to author.
65. Reilly, *Reilly of the White House*, 172.
66. FRUS, Conferences at Teheran and Cairo, 1943, 463, 476.
67. Reilly, *Reilly of the White House*, 177.
68. Harriman, *Special Envoy*, 262-63.
69. Fenby, *Alliance*, 226-27.
70. FRUS, Conferences at Cairo and Teheran, 1943, 494-95 (First Plenary Meeting).
71. Arnold, *Global Mission*, 469.
72. FRUS, Conferences at Cairo and Teheran, 1943, 535 (Second Plenary Meeting).
73. Leahy, *I Was There*, 208.
74. FRUS, Conferences at Cairo and Teheran, 1943, 540-41.
75. Marshall Interviews, 341-42, GCML.

76. Bohlen, *Witness to History*, 149.
77. FRUS, Conferences at Teheran and Cairo, 1943, 469, 584–85.
78. Ibid., 576–77 (Third Plenary Meeting).
79. FRUS, Conferences at Cairo and Teheran, 1943, 681.
80. Tuchman, *Stilwell*, 409.
81. GCM to Sherwood, quoted in Sherwood, *Roosevelt and Hopkins*, 803.
82. Marshall Interviews, 344, GCML. See also Bland, Papers, VI:54, GCML, and Sherwood, *Roosevelt and Hopkins*, 803.
83. Reynolds, *Command of History*, 387–88 and n. 35.
84. Bland, Papers, IV:197, GCML.
85. Eisenhower, *Crusade*, 208.
86. Stimson Diary, December 18, 1943, Yale.
87. King James Bible, Proverbs, 16:32.

Chapter 11: The Road to Rome

1. GCM to KM, December 7, 1943, B-44/ F-17, Marshall-Winn Collection, GCML.
2. KM, *Annals*, 139.
3. Rhoades, *Flying MacArthur to Victory*, 160–61.
4. Interview of McCarthy, January 7, 1981, Beverly Hills, CA, GCML.
5. Cray, *General of the Army*, 439.
6. Marshall Interviews, 244, GCML.
7. Rogers, *Bitter Years*, 61.
8. MacArthur, *Reminiscences*, 183.
9. Manchester, *American Caesar*, 352, 729, n. 156.
10. Pogue, "The Military in a Democracy, a Review: *American Caesar*," *International Security* 3, no. 4 (Spring 1979), 65.
11. Bland, Papers, IV:201, GCML.
12. MacArthur, *Reminiscences*, 184.
13. Allen Brown to Madge, December 17 and 28, 1943, loaned to author.
14. Harris, *Five Came Back*, 333.
15. Interview of McCarthy, January 18, 1961, Notes 115N, Copy 2, GCML.
16. Capra, *Name Above the Title*, 326 (emphasis in original).
17. Harris, *Five Came Back*, 113.
18. Interview of McCarthy, January 18, 1961, Notes 115N, Copy 2, GCML.
19. Zanuck to GCM, December 22, 1943, Pentagon Office, Selected, GCM Papers, GCML.
20. Interview of McCarthy, January 18, 1961, Notes 115N, Copy 2, GCML. For another version of the dinner, see Bland, Papers, IV:226–27, GCML. McCarthy, a 1933 VMI graduate, worked before the war as a press agent for George Abbott, the Broadway producer of *Brother Rat*, a comedy about VMI cadets that was made into a movie in 1938. After the war, McCarthy produced several motion pictures, among them *Patton*, which won the Academy Award for Best Picture in 1971.
21. DDE to GCM, December 29, 1943, DDE Papers,III:1632.
22. Bland, Papers, IV:215, GCML.
23. Morgan, *Past Forgetting*, 166.

24. Note quoted in Smith, *Eisenhower*, 326. Smith wrote that the note was purchased by the Forbes Collection in 1991 and resold in 2002, present provenance unknown. See also Safire, "Indeed a Very Dear Friend," NYT, June 6, 1991.
25. Bland, Papers, IV:231-32, GCML.
26. Ibid., IV:210-11.
27. Cray, *General of the Army*, 444.
28. Patton Diary, December 7, 1943, Patton Papers, LOC.
29. Clark, "General Patton," n.d., subject file, MWC, bio folder, box 70, Citadel, 3; a similar quote is in "Reminiscences of Mark Clark," 1971, Eisenhower Administration OH Project, OH Research Office, Columbia, at 17. For who was there, see memo undated file 8454, PPF, FDR Papers, FDRL.
30. Reilly, *Reilly of the White House*, 188.
31. Bland, Papers, IV:210-11, GCML.
32. Perry, *Partners in Command: Marshall and Eisenhower*, 255.
33. Jeffers, *Taking Command: General J. Lawton Collins*, 7.
34. Marshall Interviews, 346, GCML.
35. Butcher, *My Three Years with Eisenhower*, 467.
36. Eleanor Roosevelt to Lash, December 25, 1943, in Lash, *World of Love*, 104.
37. Churchill, *Closing the Ring*, 432, 436.
38. Ibid., 440-41.
39. Ibid., 441.
40. Butcher, *My Three Years with Eisenhower*, 365.
41. Morison, *History of United States Naval Operations in World War II*, IX:325.
42. Chandler, *Papers of DDE*, III:1775.
43. Bland, Papers, IV:348-50, GCML.
44. Ibid., 358-59, referring to letter from Allen Brown to Madge, January 27, 1944, lent to author by Tupper Brown.
45. Madge Pendleton Interview, Great Projects Film Company Collection, Binder 2, GCML.
46. Allen Brown to Madge, March 19, 1944, typed version provided to author by Tupper Brown.
47. Allen Brown to KM, March 22, 1944, B-44/F-3, GCM Papers, GCML.
48. Allen Brown to GCM, April 1, 1944, George and Katherine Marshall Collection, B-12/F-21, GCML.
49. Bland, Papers, IV:370, 422-23, GCML.
50. Sinclair, "Cassino Fortress," chap. 19 in *The Official History of New Zealand in the Second World War: 19 Battalion and Armoured Regiment*, 389, 394.
51. Hilldring signed "Marshall" to DDE, November 22, 1943, F-6, Evacuation from the Island of Rab, FDRL.
52. Ibid., DDE to AGWAR for Hilldring, December 6, 1943.
53. Ibid., JCS decision of December 15, 1943, quoted in letter from Hull to Embassy London, January 3, 1944 (italics added).
54. Executive Order 9417, January 22, 1944, online by Peters and Wooley, The American Presidency Project, http://www.presidency.ucsb.edu/ws/?pid=16540.
55. Morgenthau Diaries, 1943-45, Reel 25, LOC.
56. Wyman, *Abandonment of the Jews*, 203, citing at n. 45, Morgenthau Diaries, book 694, 190-93, LOC.

57. Morgenthau to McCloy, January 28, 1944, http://www.jewishvirtuallibrary.org /memorandum-asking-commanders-to-cooperate-with-wrb-rescue-operations -january-1944.

58. McNarney to McCloy, January 28, 1944, http://www.jewishvirtuallibrary.org /war-department-memo-on-cooperation-in-rescue-of-jews.

59. "Accomplishments Since February 2, 1944," RG 107, ASW 400.38, War Refugee Board, B-44, NA; War Refugee Board to American Embassy London, February 9, 1944, copy in Stettinius Papers, B-745, War Refugee Board folder, Small Special Collections Library, University of Virginia.

60. Bland, Papers, IV:315–16, GCML.

61. Bendersky, *Jewish Threat*, 309.

62. GCM to KM, December 29, 1943, B-44/F-17, Marshall-Winn Collection, GCML. In a 1956 interview, Marshall could not recall the name of the governor of Illinois who served during the early 1930s so he referred to him as "the Jew Governor," probably because he was the first Jewish person to be elected to that post. His name was Harry Horner. Marshall Interviews, 579, GCML. In 1950, Marshall recruited into the Defense Department, promoted, and befriended a Jewish woman, Anna Rosenberg.

63. Marshall Interviews, 484, GCML.

64. Wyman, *Abandonment of the Jews*, 292.

65. Bird, *Chairman*, 207.

66. Pehle-Jarvik interview, October 16, 1978; Wyman, *Abandonment of the Jews*, 287, n. 138.

67. Leahy Diary, April 8, 1944, Diary B6, Reel 3, Leahy Papers, LOC.

68. Churchill, *Triumph and Tragedy*, 58.

69. Clark, *Calculated Risk*, 268.

70. Clark to Devers, April 6, 1944, GCM to Devers, April 7, 1944 [incorrectly dated March 7, 1944], Entry (UP-UP) 13 MTOUSA Rec. Office of Secretary to General Staff, Formerly Security Classified Cables, B-135, file "MTOUSA Office of Sec. to Gen. Devers," RG 492, NA.

71. Atkinson, *Day of Battle*, 184.

72. Maurine Clark to GCM, February 23, 1944, with Clark's letter dated February 10, 1944, Correspondence, B-61, GCML.

73. *New York World-Telegram* photo, January 17, 1944, B-48/F-10, GCML; KM, *Annals*, 184–85.

74. Bland, Papers, IV:409–10, GCML.

75. Leahy Diary, April 18, 1944, Diary B6, Reel 3, Leahy Papers, LOC.

76. Clark, *Calculated Risk*, 269.

77. Mrs. Doran, Renie Clark's mother, "Momentous Days," Correspondence 1943, October–1944, June, Citadel.

78. Clark, *Calculated Risk*, 270.

79. Stimson for GCM, May 19, 1944, sub: Our Military Reserves, Paper 42, OPD Files, Item 57, Exec. 10, NA. See also Stimson to GCM, May 10, 1944, in Stimson Diary attached to entry of May 11, 1944, Yale.

80. Matloff, "The 90-Division Gamble," chap. 15 in Greenfield, *Command Decisions*, 379.

81. Ibid., 380.

82. Allen Brown to Madge, May 8, 1944, loaned to author by Tupper Brown.
83. Truscott, *Command Missions*, 369.
84. Ibid., 375.
85. Ibid.
86. Operations, 1st Armored Division, WWII Operations Reports, 1941–48, 1st Armored Division, 601–3, May 1944, B-12045, RG 407, Entry 427, NA.
87. Sevareid, *Not So Wild*, 401.
88. Atkinson, *Day of Battle*, 548.
89. Clark, *Calculated Risk*, 280.
90. Saltzman, memo, June, 1, 1944, based on personal investigation of Allen Brown's death by Lieutenant Lowe, GCM and KM Collection, B-41/F-2, GCML. This memo was forwarded to GCM by Tristram Tupper, KM's brother.
91. KM, *Annals*, 195.
92. KM to Madge, May 30, 1944, A. Tupper Brown Letter Collection, GCM International Center, Leesburg, VA.
93. KM, *Annals*, 195.
94. Bland, Papers, IV:468, GCML.
95. Sevareid, *Not So Wild*, 401-2.
96. Clifton Brown to "Mom and Madge," May 31, 1944, National Archives Project, Xerox 2237, GCML.
97. Tristram Tupper to GCM, June 8, 1944, B-41/F-2, GCM and KM Collection, GCML.
98. KM to Allen Brown, May 23, 1944, B-38/F-9, Marshall-Winn Collection, GCML.

Chapter 12: Keep the Main Thing

1. Wilmot, *Struggle for Europe*, 224–25; Atkinson, *Guns at Last Light*, 35.
2. Notes by Robb, SHAEF C of S for Air, sgd rpt, Mon A.M. 5 June 44, RG 331, Hist Div files, NA.
3. Smith, W. B., *Eisenhower's Six Great Decisions*, 53.
4. Brown, *Bodyguard of Lies*, 632.
5. Notes by Robb, 5 June 44, RG 331, Hist Div files, Dept Army, NA.
6. DDE to GCM, Cable S-52591, June 5, 1944, RG 331, SHAEF, NA.
7. Stimson Diary, June 5, 1944, Yale.
8. Bland, Papers, IV:469-70 (emphasis added), GCML.
9. Bohlen, *Witness to History*, 259.
10. Fireside chat on Fall of Rome, June 5, 1944, Rosenman, PPA of FDR, XIII:147-52.
11. Bohlen, *Witness to History*, 259.
12. Goodwin, *No Ordinary Time*, 509.
13. DDE to GCM, June 6, 1944, 8 a.m. local time, https://www.archives.gov/files/education/lessons/d-day memo. See also Chandler, *PPA of DDE*, III:1914.
14. Eisenhower, David. *Eisenhower at War*, 267.
15. Balkoski, *Utah Beach*, 236.
16. Eisenhower, David. *Eisenhower at War*, 267.
17. Ibid., 270.
18. Weigley, *Eisenhower's Lieutenants*, 80.
19. Bradley and Blair, *General's Life*, 251.

20. GCM to KM, "Thursday," n.d., B-44, F-17, Marshall-Winn Collection, GCML.
21. Manchester and Reid, *The Last Lion*, 850.
22. Danchev and Todman, *War Diaries of Alanbrooke*, 556.
23. Eisenhower, David, *Eisenhower at War*, 298.
24. Butcher, *My Three Years with Eisenhower*, 580.
25. Marshall Interviews, 590, GCML.
26. Lord Wilson, interview by Pogue, April 20, 1961, GCML.
27. Chandler, *Papers of DDE*, III:1938-40.
28. Marshall Interviews, 590, GCML.
29. GCM to Madge, June 23, 1944, B-38/F-11, GCML. The actual battle map was lent to the author.
30. KM, *Annals*, 200-3.
31. Marshall Interviews, 597, GCML.
32. Add Mss. 52577/38, Papers of Admiral Lord Cunningham.
33. GCM [Handy] to DDE, Radio no. WAR57012, June 27, 1944, Pentagon Office, Selected, GCM Papers, GCML. See also, Bland, Papers, IV:496-97, GCML.
34. Reynolds, *Command of History*, 452.
35. Churchill, *Triumph and Tragedy*, 716-21, quote at 720.
36. Roosevelt to Prime Minister, June 29, 1944; Churchill, *Triumph and Tragedy*, 723.
37. Butcher, *My Three Years with Eisenhower*, 634-35.
38. Ibid., 639.
39. Kimball, *Churchill & Roosevelt*, III:229.
40. Moran, *Churchill: Taken from Diaries of Lord Moran*, 614.
41. Pawle, *War and Colonel Warden*, 315-16.
42. Mosenthal, "The Establishment of a Continuous Defensive Front by Army Group G," Nov. 1955, OCMH, R-series, #68, 3-11, RG 319, NA.
43. Truscott to Sarah, September 16, 1944, Truscott Papers, B-1, GCML.
44. Churchill, *Triumph and Tragedy*, 100; for Clark's postwar views, see *Calculated Risk*, 294-96.
45. Marshall Interview Notes, October 29, 1956, 612-13, GCML (emphasis added).
46. *Congressional Record*, House, September 11, 1944, 7648-51.
47. PSF Box Navy 62, FDRL; Weintraub, Stanley, *Final Victory*, 155.
48. Marshall Interviews, 409, GCML.
49. Bland, Papers, IV:605, GCML.
50. Statement for record of participation of Carter Clarke, in transmittal of letters from GCM to Dewey, latter part of September 1944, RG 457, NA [Studies on Cryptology, SRH-043].
51. Bland, Papers, IV:607-11, GCML.
52. Statement for record of Clarke in transmittal of letters from GCM to Dewey, RG 457, NA.
53. Bland, Papers, IV:607-11, GCML.
54. Smith, *Dewey and His Times*, 429-30.
55. Sherwood, *Roosevelt and Hopkins*, 827.
56. Leahy, *I Was There*, 278.
57. PHA Part 39, 144-45.
58. Stimson Diary, November 21, 1944, Yale.
59. PHA Part 12, 261. This is sometimes referred to as the "bomb plot" message.

60. PHA Part 9, 4534, 4526, 4534, 4563–64; PHA Part 2, 886–88, 904, 817.

61. PHA Part 2, 1102.

62. PHA Report, 497–572.

63. Pogue, II:431 (Appendices).

64. KM, *Annals*, 232.

65. Inaugural speech, January 20, 1945, PPA of FDR, 523–25.

66. Bland, Papers, V:58, GCML. See also ibid., 48–49.

67. MacArthur, *Reminiscences*, 216–17.

68. Dunn to GCM, November 8, 1944, and Order of Burial, GCML; letter of Nancy Dill to GCM, November 9, 1944, GCML.

69. KM, *Annals*, 214.

70. Marshall Interviews, 412, GCML.

71. Ibid., 414.

72. Bland, Papers, IV:653–54, GCML.

73. Danchev, *Special Relationship*, 3.

74. Bland, Papers, IV:707–8, GCML.

75. Ibid., 720–21.

76. Cornelius Ryan Papers, Athens, Ohio, DDE, n.d., B-43/F-7, 33.

77. Montgomery to DDE, December 31, 1944, DDE Library, PP-pres. B-83.

78. Butler, *My Dear Stalin*, 280.

79. Marshall Interviews, 591, GCML.

80. Stimson Diary, January 4, 1945, Yale; see also Bland, Papers, V:7–9, GCML.

81. Stimson Diary, January 9, 1945, Yale.

82. Marshall Interviews, 591, 598–99, GCML.

83. Ibid., 591.

84. FRUS, Conferences at Malta and Yalta, 1945, 383–84. The bottom of the memo contains a note by Groves that it was approved by Stimson and Roosevelt on December 30. There is no evidence that the atomic bomb project was mentioned to the British or Soviets at Yalta or to the British at the previous conference at Malta.

85. GCM to KM, February 7, 1945, Marshall-Winn Collection, B-44/F-17, GCML.

86. McCarthy, *America's Retreat from Victory*, 43 (emphasis added).

87. FRUS, Conferences at Malta and Yalta, 1945, 766–71. As the minutes show, the only other participants were the U.S. ambassador to the Soviet Union, Averell Harriman, Soviet foreign minister Molotov, and the two interpreters, Bohlen and V. N. Pavlov.

88. Cray, *General of the Army*, 511.

89. FRUS, Conferences at Malta and Yalta, 1945, 759.

90. Marshall Interviews, 404, GCML.

91. FRUS, Conferences at Malta and Yalta, 1945, 984.

92. Hiss, "Two Yalta Myths," *The Nation*, January 23, 1982, 69.

93. KM, *Annals*, 237–38.

94. GCM to DDE, March 27, 1945, DDE's Pre-Presidential papers, Eisenhower Library.

95. Chandler, *Papers of DDE*, IV:2551.

96. Bland, Papers, V:106–7, GCML.

97. Churchill, *Triumph and Tragedy*, 465.

98. Hassett, *Off the Record with FDR*, 327–28.

99. Personal from President to Prime Minister, April 4, 1945, Map Room Files, B-7, FDRL.

100. Ibid., Prime Minister to Roosevelt, April 5, 1945.

101. Map Room Files, B-14, FDRL.

102. KM, *Annals*, 243.

103. Cray, *General of the Army*, 524, based on Cray's interview of Pasco on January 9, 1986.

104. Truman, *Memoirs*, I:10.

105. Stimson Diary, April 13, 1945, Yale.

106. Millis, *Forrestal Diaries*, April 23, 1945, 48-51.

107. Truman, *Memoirs*, I:246.

108. Bradley, *Soldier's Story*, 589.

109. Chandler, *PPA of DDE*, IV:2696.

110. Bland, Papers, V:171, GCML; Stimson Diary, May 8, 1945, Yale.

111. KM, *Annals*, 251, 252.

112. McCloy, quoting Marshall. Pogue, IV:550n30.

113. Memo of conversation with GCM, May 29, 1945, by McCloy, "Objectives toward Japan and Methods of Concluding War with Minimum Casualties," RG 107, Secretary of War Safe, S-1, NA (emphasis added). At top right there is a handwritten note that says "C/S [chief of staff] has read and has no further suggestions." As noted in the memo, GCM also advocated the use of nonlethal toxic gas, "say on the outlying islands" to take the "fight" out of the Japanese, thus contravening FDR's pledge not to be the first to use "poisonous or noxious gas" in the war. Rosenman, PPA of FDR, 1943, e, 242 (statement of FDR, June 8, 1943).

114. Bernstein, "Looking Back: General Marshall and the Atomic Bombing of Japanese Cities," Arms Control Association, November 2015.

115. Marshall Interviews, 424, GCML.

116. Interim Committee Meeting, 31 May 1945, 1492/196, 11, GCML.

117. Meeting held at the White House on 18 June 1945, at 1530, Miscellaneous Historical Documents Collection, HSTL.

118. Churchill to Truman, May 12, 1945, in Churchill, *Triumph and Tragedy*, 572-73.

119. FRUS, Conference of Berlin (Potsdam), 1945, II:1360.

120. Churchill, *Triumph and Tragedy*, 641, quoting his July 18, 1945, note for the War Cabinet.

121. GCM to KM, July 17, 1945, B-44, F-17, Marshall-Winn Collection, GCML.

122. Birse, *Memoirs of an Interpreter*, 209.

123. FRUS, Conference of Berlin (Potsdam),1945, II:1475-76.

124. Ibid., 340-43.

125. Truman, *Memoirs*, I:416.

126. Zhukov, *Memoirs*, 675; Chuev, *Molotov Remembers*, 56.

127. Exchange of messages between the War Department and GCM, July 24-25, 1945, Manhattan Engineer District Records, RG 77, NA.

128. Hornfischer, *Fleet at Flood Tide: America at Total War*, 434.

129. Groves, *Now It Can Be Told*, 320.

130. Groves to GCM, August 6, 1945, Manhattan District Records, Xerox 1482-89, GCML.

131. White House press release, August 6, 1945, Ayers Papers, Subject File, HSTL.

132. Frank, *Downfall*, 295–96.
133. Bernstein, "The Perils and Politics of Surrender: Ending the War with Japan and Avoiding a Third Atomic Bomb," *Pacific Historical Review* 46 (February 1977), 5.
134. Frank, *Downfall*, 302.
135. Daws, *Prisoners of the Japanese*, 336, 434.
136. Frank, *Downfall*, 287.
137. Marshall Interviews, 425, GCML.

Chapter 13: "Great Hope of China"

1. KM, *Annals*, 258, 263.
2. Bland, Papers, V:366–67, GCML.
3. Music by Vincent Youmans, Lyrics by Leo Robin and Clifford Grey, from the 1927 musical *Hit the Deck*.
4. KM, *Annals*, 282. In interviews she gave on March 15 and 17, 1957, at Pinehurst, KM also vividly recalled humming "Hallelujah" when they arrived at Dodona. Pogue, Interview of Mrs. George C. Marshall, Tape 130, GCML.
5. Truman, *Memoirs*, II:66.
6. Quotes are from KM, *Annals*, 282. The only other account of how she got the news is in a letter dated January 11 or 12, 1946, by John Hart Caughey, Marshall's executive officer in China, to his wife, in which he says Marshall told him that he and Molly kept the president's call to themselves until KM overheard the radio broadcast during dinner. According to Caughey, Marshall said that "Mrs. Marshall must have expected it [the appointment to China] because she without a word merely shed a tear and the party went on with no more ado." Jeans, *Marshall Mission to China*, 71. If GCM said that KM "must have expected it," then he probably told her about the possibility of the appointment while they were driving out to Dodona.
7. Truman, *Memoirs*, II:67.
8. Acheson, *Present at the Creation*, 133.
9. Truman, *Memoirs*, II:65.
10. Wallace, *Price of Vision*, 519.
11. FRUS, Far East, China, 1945, VII:723-24.
12. Truman, *Memoirs*, II:66.
13. Millis, *Forrestal Diaries*, 123.
14. Acheson, *Present at the Creation*, 141.
15. Truman, *Memoirs*, II:68-71. See also FRUS, Far East, China, 1945, VII:770-73, at 772.
16. Truman, *Memoirs*, II:67-68.
17. Ibid., 68-71.
18. FRUS, Far East, China, 1945, VII:770.
19. Truman, *Memoirs*, II:68-71; See also FRUS, Far East, China, 1945, VII:771.
20. Tanner, *Battle for Manchuria*, 83.
21. Kahn, *China Hands*, 184.
22. KM to Frank McCarthy, December 30, 1945, Personal File, GCML.
23. MacArthur, *Reminiscences*, 320.
24. FRUS, Far East, China, 1945, 774-77.

25. Stilwell and White, ed., *Stilwell Papers*, 321–22, 317.
26. FRUS, Far East, China, 1945, VII:748.
27. Bland, Papers, II:293–98, GCML.
28. Melby, *Mandate of Heaven*, 64.
29. Pogue, interview of Robertson, September 6, 1962, GCML.
30. Wedemeyer, *Wedemeyer Reports!*, 363.
31. Ibid., 376.
32. Marshall Interviews, 598, GCML.
33. Beal, *Marshall in China*, 36, 126; Jeans, *Marshall Mission to China*, 120.
34. Taylor, *Generalissimo*, 17.
35. Marshall Interviews, 607, GCML.
36. FRUS, Far East, China, 1945, VII:794–99.
37. Melby, *Mandate of Heaven*, 66–67.
38. NYT, January 1, 1946.
39. John Hersey, "Letter From Chungking," *The New Yorker*, March 16, 1946, 82–86.
40. White, *In Search of History*, 118.
41. FRUS, Far East, China, 1945, VII:800–4.
42. FRUS, Far East, China, 1946, IX:1–2.
43. Ibid., 104.
44. Ibid., 129–30.
45. *Liberation Daily*, CCP newspaper monitored by Foreign Broadcast Information Service, January 12, 1946.
46. FRUS, Far East, China, 1946, IX:373.
47. Byroade OH, September 19 and 21, 1988, HSTL, online at http://www. truman libary.org/oralhist/byroade.htm.
48. FRUS, Far East, China, 1946, IX:206.
49. Chiang Diaries, Hoover, January 22 and 23, 1946, B-45/F-2, Hoover, Palo Alto, CA.
50. FRUS, Far East, China, 1946, IX:148.
51. Ibid., 206.
52. Ibid., 278–89 at 285.
53. Ibid., 291–95.
54. Sheng, *Battling Western Imperialism*, 126.
55. FRUS, Far East, China, 1946, IX:261.
56. Yu, *OSS in China: Prelude to Cold War*, 254.
57. FRUS, Far East, China, 1946, IX:501–2.
58. *Time*, March 18, 1946.
59. Kurtz-Phelan, *China Mission*, 138, based on GCM comments, Secretary's Files 152/4, HST Papers, HSTL.
60. FRUS, Far East, China, 1946, IX:510.
61. Ibid., 511.
62. http://www.winstonchurchill.org/resources/speeches/1046–1963-elder-states man/120-the-sinews.
63. Marshall, "Forgotten Scenes of Heroism," GCM Papers 1/9, GCML.
64. Westad, in Bland, *Marshall's Mediation Mission to China*, 510.
65. Bland, Papers, V:504–7, GCML; NYT, March 17, 1945.
66. FRUS, Far East, China, 1946, IX:576.

67. GCM to Churchill, June 18, 1946, China Mission, General, GCM Papers, GCML. GCM was not able to discuss Churchill's views on the Soviets and Manchuria in person because Churchill needed to return to London before GCM landed in Washington.
68. Bland, Papers, V:516-17, GCML.
69. GCM to Frank McCarthy, February 22, 1946, McCarthy File, GCML.
70. Pogue, Interview of KM, GCML.
71. KM to Frank McCarthy, February 19, 1946, McCarthy Papers, GCML.
72. Pogue, Interview of KM, GCML.
73. Madame Chiang to GCM, April 2, 1946, GCML.
74. FRUS, Far East, China, 1946, IX:735-36.
75. NYT, April 30, 1946. See also *Chicago Daily Tribune*, April 16 and 20, 1946.
76. Van Slyke, *China White Paper*, 149. The formal title of the *China White Paper* was *United States Relations with China, with Special Reference to the Period 1944-1949*. It was published by the Government Printing Office in 1949.
77. KM to Chamberlin, April 24, 1946, KM Papers, GCML.
78. FRUS, Far East, China, 1946, IX:788-90 at 788.
79. Ibid., 802-5 at 805.
80. Ibid., 815-18 at 818.
81. KM to Chamberlin, April 24, 1946, Chunking, and May 7, 1946, Nanking, KM Papers, GCML.
82. Caughey, May 10, 1946, in Jeans, *Marshall Mission to China*, 118.
83. Truman, *Memoirs*, I:553.
84. Newton, *Eisenhower, White House Years*, 81.
85. Chandler, *Papers of DDE*, VII:1085.
86. Bland, Papers, V:571, GCML.
87. Ibid., 576-79 at 578.
88. Ibid.; Fenby, *Chiang Kai-Shek*, 467.
89. Chiang, *Soviet Russia in China*, 166-68.
90. FRUS, Far East, China, 1946, IX:1008-21.
91. Beal, *Marshall in China*, 109.
92. Bland, Papers, V:627-28, GCML.
93. Ibid.
94. Beal, *Marshall in China*, 122.
95. Bland, Papers, V:627-28, GCML.
96. Ibid., 684-85 at 685.
97. Ibid., 698-99 at 699.
98. Ibid., 699-700 at 700.
99. Pogue, Interview of Gillem, Tape 105, Copy 2, June 11, 1962, Atlanta, Georgia, GCML.
100. FRUS, Far East, China, 1946, X:332-41, at 337, 338, 340-41.
101. Bland, Papers, V:714-17, GCML.
102. Melby, *Mandate of Heaven*, 198.
103. FRUS, Far East, China, 1946, X:490-91.
104. Ibid., 544-47.
105. Melby, *Mandate of Heaven*, 212.
106. Beal, *Marshall in China*, 293.

107. KM to Chamberlin, November 22, 1946, in Bland, *Marshall's Mediation Mission to China*, 590.
108. Melby, *Mandate of Heaven*, 113.
109. Marshall Interviews, 607, GCML.
110. Beal, *Marshall in China*, 313.
111. FRUS, Far East, China, 1946, X:583.
112. KM to Chamberlin, July 21, 1946, and December 1, 1946, and to Mr. and Mrs. Coles, August 26, 1946, in Bland, *Marshall's Mediation Mission to China*, 580, 586, 587–88, 590.
113. Jeans, *Marshall Mission to China*, 183.
114. Ibid., 187.
115. Bland, Papers, V:763–67, GCML.
116. FRUS, Far East, China, 1946, X:680.
117. Ibid., 684–85.
118. Chiang Diaries, January 7, 1947, Hoover, Palo Alto, CA; Taylor, *Generalissimo*, 365.
119. Rounds, I:81–82, Butler Library, OH Research Office, Columbia University.
120. *Time*, January 20, 1947, at 34.
121. Jeans, *Marshall Mission to China*, 194.
122. Caughey to Underwood, January 8, 1947, in Jeans, *Marshall Mission to China*, 195.
123. Truman's 1947 diary, entries for January 7, https://www.trumanlibrary.org/diary/transcript.htm.
124. Bland, Papers, V:772–76, GCML.
125. FRUS, Far East, China, 1946, X:624–29.
126. United Press dispatch to *Los Angeles Times*, January 8, 1947.
127. Bland, Papers, V:772–76, GCML.
128. NYT, January 15, 1947.
129. Ibid., January 13, 1947.
130. Caughey to "Darling," his wife, January 8, 1947, in Jeans, *Marshall Mission to China*, 195.
131. *Newsweek*, January 27, 1947, 25.
132. Bland, Papers, VI:3–4, GCML.
133. Ibid., 5.
134. Frank McCarthy to Price, vice president of the Motion Picture Association of America, January 1, 1946, McCarthy Papers, Correspondence, 1946–49, GCML. Marshall wrote that McCarthy suffered from "insomnia," and "nervous exhaustion." Bland, Papers, V:325, GCML.
135. Baxter, "Homo-Hunting in the Early Cold War, Senator Kenneth Wherry and the Homophobic Side of McCarthyism," *Nebraska History* 84 (2003): 119–32; Wiley, *The Lavender Scare*, http://www.edb.utexas.edu/faculty/salinas/students/student_sites/Fall2008/6/.
136. Bland, Papers, V:466–68, GCML. McCarthy never married. His companion for many years was Rupert Allan, a Rhodes scholar and former lieutenant commander in the U.S. Navy during the war (intelligence), who became a prominent publicity agent in Hollywood. McCarthy and Allan lived next door to each other on Sea Bright Place in Beverly Hills.
137. Shepley draft enclosed in Carter Memorandum for GCM, n.d., Secretary of State, General, GCM Papers, GCML.

138. Bland, Papers, VI:8, GCML.
139. Lawrence column, *U.S. News & World Report*, January 22, 1947.
140. Pogue, Interview with Marshall Carter, March 9, 1988, GCML.
141. Memo by Director of Far Eastern Affairs (Butterworth) to Acting Secretary of State, September 28, 1948, https://history.state.gov/historicaldocument/frus1948v07/d373.
142. Melby, *Mandate of Heaven*, 366.
143. *Time*, May 9, 1949, 32.
144. *United States Relations with China, with Specific Reference to the Period 1944–1949* (GPO, 1949), the so-called *China White Paper*.
145. Tucker, *China Confidential*, 62.
146. *Congressional Record*, 81st Cong., 2nd Sess., February 29, 1950, at 1056–57.
147. *Milwaukee Journal*, February 15, 1950.
148. *Congressional Record*, 81st Cong., 2nd Sess., May 9, 1950, at A3426–28.
149. Madison *Capital Times*, April 21, 1950.
150. *Congressional Record*: Proceedings and Debates of the 82nd Cong., 1st Sess., Vol. 97, Part 5 (May 28, 1951–June 27, 1951), 6556–6603.
151. Ignatius, "They Don't Make Them Like George Marshall Anymore," *Washington Post* weekly edition, June 8, 1987, 25.
152. Pogue, *Marshall*, IV:110.
153. Westad, "Losses, Chances, and Myths," *Diplomatic History* 21, no. 1:105.
154. Bidault, *Resistance*, 144.
155. Tuchman, "If Mao Had Come to Washington," *Foreign Affairs* (October 1972). In *The Lost Peace*, Robert Dallek argued that a "greater receptivity to Mao's Communists in 1945 might have averted the later bloodshed between the United States and China in Korea and pressured Moscow into earlier interest in détente, including international control of nuclear weapons." Ibid., 168.
156. Tuchman, *Stilwell and the American Experience in China*, 531.
157. Byroade OH, September 21, 1988, HSTL, http://www.trumanlibrary.org/oralhist/byroade.htm.

Chapter 14: Vision of a New Europe

1. Truman appointment sheet, February 18, 1947, Ferrell, ed., *Off the Record*, 109.
2. Miller, *Plain Speaking*, 250.
3. Acheson, *Present at the Creation*, 213.
4. Marshall Interviews, 561–62, GCML.
5. Acheson, *Present at the Creation*, 214.
6. Gaddis, *George F. Kennan*, 216.
7. Kennan to GCM, 511, February 22, 1946, 9 p.m., Truman Administrative File, Elsey Papers, HSTL.
8. Kennan, "The Sources of Soviet Conduct" ("X" article), *Foreign Affairs* 25 (July 1947): 566–82.
9. Smith to GCM, January 15, 1947, Secretary of State, General, Marshall Papers, GCML.
10. FRUS, Near East and Africa, 1947, V:32–37.
11. Isaacson and Thomas, *Wise Men*, 393.

12. Truman, *Memoirs*, II:103.
13. FRUS, Near East and Africa, 1947, V:60–62.
14. Jones, *Fifteen Weeks*, 139.
15. Acheson, *Present at the Creation*, 219.
16. Jones, *Fifteen Weeks*, 142.
17. Vandenberg Jr., Vandenberg Papers, University of Michigan, 339.
18. Bland, Papers, VI:63, GCML.
19. Clifford, *Counsel to the President*, 136.
20. Acacia, *Clark Clifford*, 70.
21. Bohlen, *Witness to History*, 261.
22. Elsey, *Unplanned Life*, 149 (quoting a talk he gave in 1997 on the fiftieth anniversary of the "Truman Doctrine" speech).
23. Jones, *Fifteen Weeks*, 169, relying on an article by James Reston in NYT, March 11, 1947, quoting Vandenberg.
24. Truman's address before joint session of Congress (the "Truman Doctrine"), March 12, 1947, http://avalon.law.yale.edu/20th_century/trudoc.asp.
25. Clifford, *Counsel to the President*, 137.
26. NYT, March 13, 1947, 1.
27. Smith, *My Three Years in Moscow*, 215.
28. Ibid., 215, 216.
29. *Los Angeles Times*, March 6, 1947.
30. Smith, *My Three Years in Moscow*, 213.
31. Bohlen, *Witness to History*, 262.
32. The Yalta agreements established an Allied Reparations Commission, but it never agreed to the $10 billion amount demanded by the Soviets nor to the details of extracting reparations from Germany's current production.
33. FRUS, Council of Foreign Ministers, 1947, II:255–57.
34. Marshall quote in Smith, *My Three Years in Moscow*, 226.
35. Ibid., 223.
36. FRUS, Council of Foreign Ministers, 1947, II:314.
37. Pogue, *Marshall*, IV:185.
38. FRUS, Council of Foreign Ministers, 1947, II:315.
39. Bohlen, *Witness to History*, 262.
40. Quoted in Yergin, *Shattered Peace*, 300.
41. FRUS, Council of Foreign Ministers, 1947, II:337–44.
42. Smith, *My Three Years in Moscow*, 221.
43. Ibid.
44. FRUS, Council of Foreign Ministers, 1947, II:256.
45. Bohlen, *Witness to History*, 263.
46. GCM to KM, April 17, 1947, Box 44/F-17, Marshall-Winn Collection, GCML.
47. Smith, *My Three Years in Moscow*, 228–29.
48. Pogue, *Marshall*, IV:196.
49. Bohlen, *Witness to History*, 263.
50. Interview of GCM, October 30, 1952, Price Collection, HSTL.
51. GCM's national radio address, April 28, 1947, B-157/F-12, GCM Papers, GCML.
52. Interview of GCM, October 30, 1952, Harry B. Price Papers, HSTL.

53. Kennan, *Memoirs*, I:325–26.
54. Ibid.
55. Acheson, *Present at the Creation*, 230.
56. Ibid., 229; Chace, *Acheson*, 172.
57. Miall OH, HSTL: Interview of Miall by Vandegrift, September 19, 1977, GCML.
58. Acheson, *Present at the Creation*, 230.
59. FRUS, British Commonwealth, 1947, III:223–30.
60. Ibid., 230–32 (italics in the original).
61. Freeland, *Truman Doctrine and Origins of McCarthyism*, 17.
62. NYT, May 25, 1947.
63. Reston, "Washington: The Marshall Plan," NYT, May 24, 1987; Price, interview of James Reston, HSTL.
64. Agnew and Entrikin, *The Marshall Plan Today*, 10.
65. Acheson, *Present at the Creation*, 232.
66. Kennan, *Memoirs*, I:342.
67. Bohlen OH, Price Collection, HSTL. See Summary of Discussion on Problems of Relief, Rehabilitation and Reconstruction of Europe, May 29, 1947, FRUS, British Commonwealth, 1947, III:234–37.
68. Pogue, *Marshall*, IV:209.
69. Acheson, Post-Presidential Memoirs, February 18, 1955, 42, HSTL.
70. Marshall to Carter, May 30, 1947, GCML.
71. Pogue, *Marshall*, IV:210.
72. Bohlen, *Witness to History*, 263.
73. GCM to Kennan, February 17, 1953, Retirement, General, Marshall Papers, GCML.
74. Marshall Interviews, 559, GCML. See also Bland, Papers, VI:149–50 and VII:751–52, GCML.
75. Interview of Miall by Vandegrift, September 19, 1977, GCML.
76. Ibid.
77. Bland, Papers, VI:147–50 (additions, changes, and applause indicated in brackets, GCML. The signed reading copy and audio are available online. http://marshall-foundation.org/marshall/the-marshall-plan/marshall-plan-speech/.
78. Conant, *My Several Lives*, 506.
79. Alsop, *I've Seen the Best of It*, 282.
80. Interview of Miall by Vandegrift, September 19, 1977, GCML.
81. Pogue, *Marshall*, IV:217.
82. Bullock, Alan, *Ernest Bevin: Foreign Secretary 1945–1951*, 405 (quoting speech to National Press Club, April 1, 1949).
83. Acheson, *Present at the Creation*, 234.
84. Vandenberg Jr., Papers of Senator Vandenberg, 374–75, University of Michigan.
85. Clifford, *Counsel to the President*, 144.

Chapter 15: Hope for Those Who Need It

1. Marshall Interviews, 556, 558, GCML.
2. Bland, Papers, VI:153–54, GCML; Vandenberg Jr., Papers of Senator Vandenberg, 375–76, University of Michigan.

3. Bland, Papers, VI:153–54, GCML.
4. Haas, *Harry and Arthur*, 178.
5. Steil, *Marshall Plan*, 123.
6. Narinsky, "The Soviet Union and the Marshall Plan," Cold War International History Project, Working Paper no. 9, p. 51, Woodrow Wilson International Center for Scholars.
7. FRUS, British Commonwealth; Europe, 1947, III:308.
8. Harriman interview with Price, October 1, 1952, Price Collection, HSTL.
9. Bullock, *Ernest Bevin*, 422.
10. Steil, *Marshall Plan*, 135.
11. "Minutes of a Visit to Generalissimo J. V. Stalin on 9 July 1947," *Journal of History and Civilisation in East Central Europe* 32 (1991): 134.
12. Ibid., 135.
13. Lockhart, *Jan Masaryk*, 66.
14. FRUS, British Commonwealth; Europe, 1947, III:327.
15. Ibid.
16. The sixteen states of the Western bloc in 1947 were Austria, Belgium, Denmark, France, Greece, Iceland, Ireland, Italy, Luxembourg, the Netherlands, Norway, Portugal, Sweden, Switzerland, Turkey, and the United Kingdom. Germany, the largest country, was not represented. Issues of its recovery and rehabilitation were not settled. The Eastern bloc consisted of Bulgaria, Czechoslovakia, Hungary, Poland, Romania, Yugoslavia, and Albania. Governance of the Baltic States—Estonia, Latvia, and Lithuania—had been previously ceded to the Soviet Union.
17. Pogue, *Marshall*, IV:175.
18. Quoted in "16 Nations in Paris Launch Aid Conference," NYT, July 13, 1947, 1–2.
19. Isaacson and Thomas, *Wise Men*, 417.
20. Hoopes and Brinkley, *Driven Patriot*, 41, quoting in part. Morison, *Turmoil and Tradition*, 492–93.
21. FRUS, British Commonwealth; Europe, 1947, III:335.
22. Steil, *Marshall Plan*, 108.
23. Ibid., 372–75 and n. 5.
24. Ibid., 383–89.
25. Ibid., 397–405.
26. UK Delegation to Foreign Office, September 11, 1947, FO 371/62582, UE 8507, BNA.
27. FRUS, British Commonwealth; Europe, 1947, III:410–11.
28. Ibid., 423–25.
29. Ibid., 425–28.
30. Committee of European Economic Cooperation, *General Report*, Paris, September 1, 1947, I:1–3, GCML.
31. "16 Nation Aid Plan Signed as Leaders Warn of Collapse," NYT, September 23, 1947.
32. Truman, *Memoirs*, II:117.
33. McNaughton file to Bermingham, October 4, 1947, McNaughton Papers, HSTL.
34. Truman, *Memoirs*, II:117.

35. "Text of Taft's Speech Delivered Before the Ohio Society," NYT, November 11, 1947 (speech was delivered November 10).

36. Diary quoted in Vandenberg Jr., Papers of Senator Vandenberg, 372, University of Michigan.

37. Ibid.

38. Marshall oral interview, Price Collection, HSTL.

39. Report of Herter Committee, May 1, 1948, Prepared by the Executive Secretariat, International Cooperation Administration, September 15, 1956, GCML.

40. Special Message to Congress on First Day of the Special Session, November 17, 1947, online by Gerhard Peters and John T. Wooley, The American Presidency Project, http://www.presidency.ucsb.edu/ws/?pid=12790.

41. Marshall oral interview, Price Collection, HSTL.

42. Bland, Papers, VI:256, GCML.

43. Reston, "Democrats Let Vandenberg Carry Load in Aid Debate," NYT, November 25, 1947, 15.

44. Haas, Harry and Arthur, 191.

45. Millis, Forrestal Diaries, December 10, 1947.

46. Vandenberg Jr., Papers of Senator Vandenberg, 379-80, University of Michigan.

47. FRUS, Council of Foreign Ministers; Germany and Austria, 1947, II:769.

48. Bland, Papers, VI:297-302, GCML.

49. Madge Pendleton Interview, Great Projects Film Company Collection, 13-15, GCML.

50. GCM to Nicholson, January 5, 1948, Secretary of State, General, GCM Papers, GCML.

51. Ibid., GCM to Molly Winn and to DDE, January 5, 1948.

52. Jones, Marshall Plan, 15.

53. Time, January 5, 1948.

54. Marshall Interviews, 527, GCML.

55. Reston, "Marshall Always Patient, but Adamant on His Plan," NYT, January 9, 1947.

56. Bland, Papers, VI:309-19, GCML.

57. Reston, "Marshall Always Patient," NYT, January 9, 1947.

58. Bland, Papers, VI:69-72, GCML.

59. Reston, NYT, January 11, 1948, 1.

60. House of Representatives Committee on Foreign Affairs, Hearings on European Recovery Program, 80th Cong., 2nd Sess., pt. 1, questions of Mansfield to Marshall, 75.

61. Marshall Interviews, 557, 556, GCML.

62. Memo of Press and Radio News Conference, January 28, 1948, RG 59, Office of the Special Assistant to Secretary of State, Verbatim Reports of Press Conferences, NA.

63. Marshall Interviews, 527, GCML.

64. GCM told La Follette that he bought his "helpful suggestions . . . lock, stock and barrel." Marshall to La Follette, February 16, 1948, Secretary of State, General, GCM Papers, GCML.

65. Marshall Interviews, 557, GCML.

66. Bland, Papers, VI:357, GCML.

67. GCM's speech at University of California–Berkeley, March 19, 1948, B-158/F-14, GCM Papers, GCML.
68. Marshall's remarks at UCLA, March 20, 1948, B-158/F-15, GCM Papers, GCML.
69. Jones, *Marshall Plan*, 66.
70. Bland, Papers, VI:385, GCML.
71. *Washington Post*, February 11, 1948, 1, 3.
72. GCM's comments attached to Humelsine to Secretary of Agriculture, November 12, 1947, 711.61/11-1247, Secret, State Department Papers.
73. FRUS, Eastern Europe; The Soviet Union, 1948, IV:739.
74. Vandenberg Jr., ed., Papers of Senator Vandenberg, 389–92, University of Michigan.
75. "Says Peril Near: He Urges Counter-Action to Stop Communism's Westward March," NYT, March 2, 1948, 1.
76. Vandenberg Jr., Papers of Senator Vandenberg, 392, University of Michigan.
77. GCM oral interview, Price Collection, HSTL.
78. Smith, *Papers of General Lucius D. Clay*, Indiana University Press, 568–69. The cable was circulated by Forrestal throughout Washington and leaked by someone to the *Saturday Evening Post*. It is quoted in Millis, *Forrestal Diaries*, 387.
79. Kindleberger, Charles, *Essays in History*, 215.
80. PPA, Harry Truman, 1948, 184–85.
81. "Hoover Supports $5.3 Billion for ERP: Opposition Fading," NYT, March 25, 1948, 1.
82. *Washington Post*, April 1, 1948, 1.
83. GCM press release quoted in "Aid Bill Is Signed by Truman," NYT, April 4, 1948, 1.
84. Madge to GCM and KM, n.d. (must have been written right after Easter, March 28, 1948, when she gave the rabbits to Tupper), B-38/F-8, Marshall-Winn Collection, GCML.
85. Records of Senate Foreign Relations Committee in Executive Session, Foreign Assistance Act of 1948, 80th Cong., 2nd Sess., 297.
86. *The Economist*, April 10, 1948, 119.
87. "House Approves $2,160,000,000 Cut in U.S. Global Aid," NYT, June 5, 1948, 5.
88. Press Conference, June 4, 1948, RG 59, Office of the Special Assistant to the Secretary of State, Verbatim Reports of Press Conference, NA, 59.
89. Vandenberg Jr., Papers of Senator Vandenberg, 396–97, University of Michigan.
90. Bland, Papers, VI:480, GCML.
91. "Dollar Shortage for Ever," *The Economist*, June 25, 1948, 1051.
92. Bland, Papers, VI:491, n. 1, GCML. See also Abstract from Clinical Record of GCM, C. B. Sageman, n.d., GCML.
93. Fifth Report to Congress of Economic Cooperation Administration for the Period April 3, 1948–June 30, 1949, 3, 16–37.
94. Prime Minister of Great Britain to the President, April 3, 1949, HSTL.
95. Steil, *Marshall Plan* book launch, moderated by Richard Haas, https://www.cfr.org/event/marshall-plan-dawn-cold-war-benn-steil. See also Ferguson, "Dollar Diplomacy," *The New Yorker*, August 27, 2007.

96. ECA press release, December 30, 1951, "Achievements of the Marshall Plan," *Department of State Bulletin* 26 (January 14, 1952): 43.
97. Milward, "Was the Marshall Plan Necessary?" *Diplomatic History* 13, no. 2: 231–42.
98. Steil, *Marshall Plan*, 370.
99. Hogan, *Marshall Plan*, 432 (quote by Stephen A. Schuker).
100. Agnew and Entrikin, *The Marshall Plan Today*, 2.
101. Walters, *Silent Missions*, 187–88.
102. FRUS Western Europe, 1948, III:46–48. See also Steil, *Marshall Plan*, 369, and Melvyn P. Leffler, "Divide and Invest," *Foreign Affairs*, July/August, 2018, 170.

Chapter 16: Showdown in the Oval Office

1. NYT, April 4, 1948.
2. GCM to Mrs. Truman, May 10, 1948, containing written draft of GCM's toast to the president. Stoler, *Papers*, VI:449. The quote in the text is taken from this draft. David McCullough, in his biography of Truman, quoted Marshall's words from a version written seven months later by Edward Jones, a *Time* correspondent, who was not at the birthday celebration. See McCullough, *Truman*, 614, and note below.
3. Memo containing draft article from "Eddie Jones" (*Time* magazine domestic correspondent) to "Don Bermingham" (*Time* U.S. and Canadian News Service correspondence), December 18, 1948, McNaughton Papers, HSTL.
4. FRUS, Near East, South Asia and Africa, 1948, V, pt. 2: 975.
5. FRUS, Near East and Africa, 1947, V:1004–5.
6. Pogue interview with Mrs. Roosevelt, March 17, 1958, GCML.
7. Bohlen, *Witness to History*, 125.
8. Clifford, *Counsel to the President*, 5.
9. Henderson, OH by McKinzie, June 14, 1973, at 126, HSTL. On September 22, 1947, Henderson submitted a seven-point memo to Marshall titled "Certain Considerations Against Advocacy by the U.S. of the Majority Plan" that set forth in detail the reasons why GCM and the UN delegation should oppose the partition plan proposed by the UN Palestine committee. FRUS, Near East and Africa, 1947, V:1153–58.
10. Ibid., 1147–50.
11. Bland, Papers, VI:213, GCML.
12. FRUS, Near East and Africa, 1947, V:1159. The conversation took place on September 23, but the memo was prepared on September 26, 1947.
13. NYT, September 30, 1947, 1.
14. Sheffer, *Shertok*, 248.
15. Wilson, *Marshall Remembered*, 366, 329.
16. Sheffer, *Shertok*, 251 and n. 14. In support of the quoted statements, Sheffer cited Agency Executive in New York, 26 Sept. 1947, CZA. Central Zionist Archives, Jerusalem.
17. Truman, *Memoirs*, II:155. See also Judis, *Genesis*, 272, and Michael J. Cohen, *Truman and Israel*, 157 (a different account).

18. FRUS, Near East and Africa, 1947, V:1212–13.

19. Ibid., 1255–56.

20. Weizmann, Chaim, *Trial and Error*, 458.

21. FRUS, Near East and Africa, 1947, V:1255–56.

22. Clifford to Truman, November 19, 1947, Clifford Papers, Box 22, HSTL.

23. FRUS, Near East and Africa, 1947, V:1271–72; and editor's n. 2 referring to memo by Bohlen to Lovett, November 19, 1947, RG 59, Central Decimal File, 867N.01/11-1947, NA.

24. As evidenced by the two memos, American diplomat Dennis Ross was mistaken when he wrote that Truman explicitly instructed that the UN commission's partition plan "should not be changed and the Negev should remain within the Jewish state." Ross, *Doomed to Succeed*, 14.

25. FRUS, Near East and Africa, 1947, V:1272, editor's n. 3.

26. Henderson, OH by McKinzie, June 14, 1973, at 138, HSTL.

27. FRUS, Near East and Africa, 1947, V:1287–89.

28. Ibid., 1289–90.

29. Gruber, *Witness: One of the Great Correspondents*, 158.

30. Sharett, *At the Gates of the Nations*, 152.

31. *Newcastle Morning Herald* (Australia), December 1, 1947.

32. Begin, *Revolt*, 412.

33. Kanj, *Children of Catastrophe*, 5, quoting Ben-Gurion in Masalha, *Expulsion of the Palestinians*, 176.

34. Stern, *Einstein's German World*, 233.

35. NYT, November 30, 1947, 1.

36. Judis, *Genesis*, 277, 283.

37. Horowitz, *State in the Making*, 306.

38. PPS/21, FRUS, Near East, South Asia and Africa, 1948, V, pt. 2: 619–25. This memo was submitted as a "working paper" to the NSC on February 12 with the understanding that it did not necessarily represent the final views of the State Department. Ibid., n. 1. The alternatives in PPS/21 grew out of the analysis in PPS/19, FRUS, 1948, V, pt. 2: 546–54. There is a marginal note on this document written by GCM that says he outlined his position on Palestine to Lovett, but the editors found no record of his position. Ibid., n. 5.

39. Millis, *Forrestal Diaries*, 371–73.

40. FRUS, Near East, South Asia and Africa, 1948, V, pt. 2: 633.

41. Medoff, *Jewish Americans and Political Participation*, 294.

42. FRUS, Near East, South Asia and Africa, 1948, V, pt. 2: 633. The "men" were not "identifiable by the editors."

43. Ibid., 651–54 (final draft) and 640 (working draft).

44. Draft of Cohen's article, March 1, 1948, Cohen Papers, B-8, LOC.

45. Note, "Power of the UN Security Council to Aid Political Settlement with Force," *Stanford Intramural Law Review* (June 1948): 105–18.

46. Truman to Jacobson, February 27, 1948, Jacobson Papers, HSTL. Truman wrote that he did not want to meet with Weizmann or anyone else on the Palestine issue until the UN "has had a chance to act on our suggestion for a police force to enforce partition." This letter indicates that Truman either did not understand or forgot that Austin's statement took the position, advocated by Marshall and Lovett, that the

Security Council was not authorized to enlist armed forces of its members to enforce partition.

47. FRUS, Near East, South Asia and Africa, 1948, V, pt. 2: 651 (president's message); 637-40 (working draft of Austin's statement to UN Security Council); 651-54 (final draft of Austin's statement to UN Security Council).
48. Myers to Truman, March 4, 1948, Subject File, B-160, HSTL.
49. Kirchwey to Truman, February 25, 1948, CZA L35/137.
50. FRUS, Near East, South Asia and Africa, 1948, V, pt. 2: 678-79.
51. Ibid., 687-89 (first memo, March 6, 1948); 690-96 (second memo, March 8, 1948).
52. Truman to Bess Wallace, October 28, 1917, Dear Bess, 233.
53. Thirteen-page typewritten letter by Jacobson to Dr. Josef Cohn, April 1, 1952, at 5, Weizmann Archives Records, Subject File, Relations Between the United States, Palestine, and Israel, HSTL. Instead of the phrase "son of a bitch," the typewritten statement contains a black line, but Jacobson and others who knew Truman believe those were the swear words that Truman actually used.
54. Truman, Memoirs, II:161.
55. Weizmann, Chaim, Trial and Error, 472; Vera Weizmann, Impossible Takes Longer, 228-29.
56. Truman, Memoirs, II:161-62.
57. Trygve Lie, the respected secretary general of the UN, apparently agreed that GCM's reasoning was flawed. He believed the partition plan could and should be effectuated via armed forces. Otherwise, he reportedly said, "the UN would go downhill rapidly to nothing." FRUS, Near East, South Asia and Africa, 1948, V, pt. 2: 719.
58. Ibid., 728-29. Truman's approval of Austin's statement is at Ibid., 697.
59. Ibid., 742-45 (Austin's "mandate speech").
60. HST Diary, March 20, 1948; Ferrell, Off the Record, 127.
61. Clifford quoted in Cohen, Truman and Israel, 193.
62. NYT, March 21, 1948 at 8-E (editorial).
63. NYT, March 20, 1948, 1-3.
64. Bland, Papers, VI:416-18, GCML.
65. Ibid., 418 (memo by GCM for Bohlen, March 22, 1948).
66. FRUS, Near East, South Asia and Africa, 1948, V, pt. 2: 755.
67. Time, April 5, 1948.
68. Statement by the president, March 25, 1948, Official File, 204: Palestine, May 1946-1953, Truman Papers, HSTL.
69. FRUS, Near East, South Asia and Africa, 1948, V, pt. 2: 761-64, summarized in Stoler, Papers, VI:425.
70. FRUS, The Western Hemisphere, 1948, IX:22-23.
71. Bland, Papers, VI:434-35, GCML.
72. Cray's interview of Marshall Carter, March 9, 1988.
73. UP dispatch to Los Angeles Times, April 13, 1948.
74. Yogev, Political and Diplomatic Documents, companion volume, no. 388, at 25.
75. Ibid., no. 364, at 588-90 (Weizmann to Truman, April 9, 1948).
76. Jacobson to Dr. Josef Cohn, April 1, 1952, at 10, Weizmann Archives Records, Subject File, Relations Between the United States, Palestine, and Israel, HSTL.

Jacobson wrote that he met with the president on Monday, April 12, when Truman had a crowded schedule. It is more likely that they met on Sunday, April 11, when Truman had no other appointments. The president's daily calendar does not indicate that Jacobson was there on either of those days.

77. Weizmann, Vera. *Impossible Takes Longer*, 231.
78. FRUS, Near East, South Asia and Africa, 1948, V, pt. 2: 877-79.
79. Ibid., 894-96.
80. Ibid., 906.
81. Clifford, *Counsel to the President*, 5-6.
82. Weisberger, "An Exclusive Interview with Clark Clifford,"*American Heritage* 28, no. 3 (April 1947).
83. This paragraph is a composite of the following two accounts: FRUS, Near East, South Asia and Africa, 1948, V, pt. 2: 972; and Shertok, May 8, 1948, Yogev, *Political and Diplomatic Documents*, no. 483 at 757-69.
84. Weizmann, Vera, *Impossible Takes Longer*, 231.
85. Clifford, *Counsel to the President*, 3.
86. FRUS, Near East, South Asia and Africa, 1948, V, pt. 2: 973-74.
87. Clifford, *Counsel to the President*, 11.
88. Snetsinger, John. *Truman, the Jewish Vote*, 107-8.
89. Clifford, *Counsel to the President*, 11.
90. Ibid., 11-12.
91. Clifford, letter to McCullough quoting Deuteronomy 1:8, King James Version.
92. Clifford, *Counsel to the President*, 12.
93. Clifford quoted in Cohen, *Truman and Israel*, 213.
94. Address by Clifford, American Ditchley Foundation, April 5, 1984; McCullough interview of Clifford.
95. Ibid.
96. FRUS, Near East, South Asia and Africa, 1948, V, pt. 2: 975.
97. Ibid.
98. McCullough's interview of Clifford.
99. Clifford, *Counsel to the President*, 13, 15.
100. Ibid., 15; Clifford OH, April 13, 1971, HSTL.
101. Clifford, *Counsel to the President*, 17.
102. FRUS, Near East, South Asia and Africa, 1948, V, pt. 2: 1006.
103. Interview of Lovett by Isaacson and Thomas, *Wise Men*, 453, and Notes 792.
104. Clifford, *Counsel to the President*, 21.
105. Interview of Lovett by Isaacson and Thomas, *Wise Men*, 453, and Notes 792.
106. Interview of Rusk by Cray, November 25, 1980.
107. Official Gazette, no. 1 of the 5th, Iyar 5708 (14th May 1948).
108. Ross, Alphabetical File, handwriting of Truman, HSTL.
109. Rusk to Franklin, June 13, 1974, in Editorial Note, FRUS, Near East, South Asia and Africa, 1948, V, pt. 2: 993.
110. Mrs. Roosevelt to GCM, May 18, 1948, and response by GCM, May 18, 1948, Stoler, *Papers*, VI:457-58 and n. 1.
111. Lowenthal Papers, May 15, 1948, University of Minnesota.
112. Among the so-called wise men who influenced GCM on the Palestine question were Acheson, Kennan, Lovett, McCloy, Forrestal, and Bohlen.

113. Holbrooke, "Washington's Battle over Israel's Birth," *Washington Post*, Wednesday, May 7, 2008.
114. FRUS, Near East, South Asia and Africa, 1948, V, pt. 2: 633.

Chapter 17: We Will Not Be Coerced

1. FRUS, Germany and Austria, 1948, II:72.
2. S. Res. 239, S. 7791, 80th Cong., 2nd Sess., CR 94, pt. 6 (June 11, 1948).
3. Yergin, *Shattered Peace*, 368.
4. Spiritoffreedom.org: The Berlin Airlift (http://www.spiritoffreedom.org/airlift.html).
5. Millis, *Forrestal Diaries*, 454.
6. Ibid., 455–56.
7. Bland, Papers, VI:490–91, GCML.
8. GCM to Wilson, July 2, 1948, Marshall Collection, B-1/F-54, Correspondence: GCM to Wilson, 1920–1958, GCML; Wilson, *Marshall Remembered*, 331–32.
9. Bradley to Royall, July 17, 1948, CD 6-2-9, folder 1, RG 330, NA.
10. Memo for President, July 16, 1948, B-220, President's Secretary's File, HSTL.
11. Millis, *Forrestal Diaries*, 459.
12. Truman, Margaret, *Harry S. Truman*, 15.
13. Bland, Papers, VI:503, n. 1, GCML.
14. Press and Radio News Conference, July 21, 1948, RG 59, Office of the Special Assistant to Secretary of State, Verbatim Reports of Press Conferences, NA.
15. Bohlen, *Witness to History*, 281.
16. Millis, *Forrestal Diaries*, 486–87.
17. Bland, Papers, VI:541–42, GCML; GCM to Wilson, August 31, 1948, B-139/F-13, Secretary of State, 1947–1949, Correspondence, General, GCM Papers, GCML.
18. "Ordinary Horse Race," *Time*, September 13, 1948.
19. *Time*, September 27, 1948.
20. Bland, Papers, VI:560–61, GCML.
21. FRUS, Germany and Austria, 1948, II:1177–80.
22. Clifford, *Counsel to the President*, 232–33.
23. Truman, *Memoirs*, II:216.
24. Lovett, interview by Pogue, Tape 120, Copy 2, August 28 and 29, 1973, 47, GCML.
25. Carter, interview by Pogue, October 22, 1959, 9, GCML.
26. Brooks, *Road to Character*, 128.
27. Carter, interview by Pogue, October 22, 1949, 9, GCML.
28. Clifford, *Counsel to the President*, 233.
29. Bland, Papers, VI:578–80, GCML.
30. Bohlen, *Witness to History*, 270.
31. FRUS, Germany and Austria, 1948, II:1233–34.
32. FRUS, Western Europe, 1948, III:139.
33. Ibid., 264–66.
34. Marshall Interviews, Tape 19, 561, GCML.
35. FRUS, Council of Foreign Ministers, Germany and Austria, 1947, II:815–22.
36. Marshall Interviews, Tape 19, 561, GCML.
37. KM to Chamberlin, KM Papers, Corres. 1941–49, B-3/F-18, GCML.

38. Marshall, *Memoirs*, 18.
39. Marshall Interviews, Tape 6, 218, GCML.
40. KM to Chamberlin, KM Papers, Corres. 1941-49, B-3/F-18, GCML.
41. Bland, Papers, VI:589, GCML.
42. Ibid., 597.
43. Ibid., 600-1.
44. KM, Gilman Country School Memorial Scholarship Presentation, 6.
45. McCullough's interview of Clifford.
46. Bland, Papers, VI:609, GCML.
47. Truman to GCM, November 6, 1948, Pentagon Office, Selected, GCM Papers, GCML.
48. GCM statement, November 18, 1948, Secretary of State, General, GCM Papers, GCML.
49. Bland, Papers, VI:623, GCML.
50. Ibid., 628-29.
51. Ibid., 632.
52. Ibid., 633-35.
53. Abstract from Clinical Record of Marshall, C. B. Sageman, n.d., GCML.
54. Bland, Papers, VI:637, GCML.
55. Madame Chiang Kai-shek to GCM, "Top Secret Report to General Flicker," n.d. [December 1948], GCM Papers, 60.46, GCML.
56. Bland, Papers, VI:638-39, GCML.
57. Ibid., 645, 647-48.
58. Acheson to GCM, January 10, 1949, Pentagon Office, Selected, GCM Papers, GCML.
59. Bland, Papers, VI:650, GCML.
60. Ibid., 681 and 655n8.
61. Truman, September 14, 1950, PP HST 1950, PSF, Presidential Appointment File, HSTL.
62. McFarland and Roll, *Louis Johnson*, 153.
63. Bland, Papers, VI:671, GCML.
64. Marshall, "My New Job," *Red Cross Courier*, 29, March 1950, 4. Rather than, or perhaps in addition to, bringing up the subject of the Red Cross in March, the president might have brought it up on the afternoon of January 12 when he flew down to Pinehurst and met personally with Marshall. See Stoler, *Papers*, VI:656, and Daily Appointments of Truman, January 12, 1949.
65. Ibid. See also Samuels, "Touring with Marshall of the Red Cross," NYT, February 26, 1950, 27.
66. Bland, Papers, VI:673, GCML.
67. Ibid., 720-21.
68. Rose, David. *Friends and Partners*, 146.
69. PP HST 1949, 485.
70. "Story Explodes Around the World," *Newsweek*, October 3, 1949.
71. Mao Zedong, "Proclamation of the Central People's Government of the PRC," October 1, 1949, Woodrow Wilson International Center for Scholars, History and Public Policy Program Digital Archive. http://digitalarchive.wilsoncenter.org /document/121557.

72. "General Marshall's First Day," *Red Cross Courier* 29, November 1949.
73. Quotes from articles in *San Francisco Chronicle* and *Portland Journal* (Oregon) in "General Marshall's Flying Trip," *Red Cross Courier* 29, December 1949, 4-6.
74. Stoler, *Papers*, VII:120-21.
75. Ibid., 52.
76. Ibid., 119. See also Marshall, "For a Better Understanding," *Red Cross Courier*, 29, July-August 1950, 16.
77. Cray, *General of the Army*, 672-73; Ungers with Hirshon, *Marshall*, 455.
78. Stoler, *Papers*, VII:136-42.
79. Carsberg, press conference, November 17, 1953, Office of Public Information, Office of Secretary of Defense, OSD Hist., RG 330, NA.
80. Donovan, *Tumultuous Years*, 197, quoting Donovan's interview with James Webb.
81. Kennan diary entry, July 1, 1950, Princeton, Kennan Papers, B-232/F 1; Kennan, *Kennan Diaries*, 258-59 (Frank Costiglia, ed.).
82. Stoler, *Papers*, VII:128.

Chapter 18: Distressing Necessity

1. HST Diary, September 14, 1950, in Ferrell, *Off the Record*, 192.
2. McFarland and Roll, *Louis Johnson*, 321; interview with Hechler, June 5, 2003; "That was something that needed to be said," and "see that Harriman was made Secretary of State," Isaacson and Thomas, *Wise Men*, 520; "could get Acheson out," Ferrell, *Truman in the White House: Diary of Ayers*, 361; Donovan, *Tumultuous Years*, 265-66.
3. Fervell, *Truman in the White House*, July 3, 1950, HSTL.
4. Stoler, *Papers*, VII:146.
5. Ibid., 128.
6. Ferrell, *Eisenhower Diaries*, 176; Bradley and Blair, *General's Life*, 538.
7. Rusk, *As I Saw It*, 124.
8. Schnabel and Watson, *Joint Chiefs*, III, pt. 1: 6.
9. Weathersby, "Stalin and the Korean War," in Leffler and Painter, *Origins of the Cold War*, 274-75.
10. Gaddis, *Cold War*, 42.
11. Harden, Blaine, *King of Spies*, 59.
12. Goulden, *Korea: The Untold Story*, 53.
13. Donovan, *Tumultuous Years*, 197.
14. Blair, *Forgotten War*, 84.
15. FRUS, East Asia and the Pacific, 1950, VI:451-53.
16. Bradley and Blair, *General's Life*, 551.
17. FRUS, East Asia and the Pacific, 1950, VI:454.
18. Bradley and Blair, *General's Life*, 547.
19. Truman, *Memoirs*, II:358.
20. Bradley and Blair, *General's Life*, 551.
21. Truman, Margaret, *Harry S. Truman*, 479.
22. Ferrell, *Off the Record*, 189, quoting September 7, 1950, letter from Truman to his wife, Elizabeth (Bess) Wallace Truman.
23. McFarland and Roll, *Louis Johnson*, 345.

24. Handleman of International News Service, quoted in Heinl, *Victory at High Tide*, 76.
25. NYT, September 16, 1950.
26. "Appointment of Marshall to the Office of Secretary of Defense," *Congressional Record*, 96, pt. 11, September 15, 1950, 81st Cong. 2nd Sess., 14913-17, quotes by Jenner at 14915 and 14917; Pogue, *Marshall*, IV:428, quoting Marshall on Jenner.
27. NYT, September 16, 1950, quoting Saltonstall.
28. Hearing Before Committee on Armed Services United States Senate on Nomination of Marshall to be Secretary of Defense, September 19, 1950, 81st Cong., 2nd Sess., quotes at 19-25.
29. NYT, September 21, 1950; Bradley and Blair, *General's Life*, 556.
30. Stoler, *Papers*, VII:168-69; Schnabel and Watson, *Joint Chiefs*, III, pt. 1: 98-100; Schnabel, *United States Army in the Korean War*, III, "Policy and Direction," 181-83.
31. FRUS, Korea, 1950, VII:826, and Stoler, *Papers*, VII:171.
32. Schnabel and Watson, *Joint Chiefs*, III, pt. 1: 103.
33. Donovan, *Tumultuous Years*, 175. See aslo Collins, *War in Peacetime*, 141-42.
34. Stoler, *Papers*, VII: 172.
35. MacArthur to GCM, October 1, 1950, Pentagon Office, Selected, GCM Papers, GCML.
36. FRUS, Korea, 1950, VII:915.
37. Donovan, *Tumultuous Years*, 284, based on Donovan's interview of Murphy.
38. Acheson, *Present at the Creation*, 456.
39. FRUS, Korea, 1950, VII:948-60 (minutes compiled from notes of several participants by General Bradley) at 949, 953-54.
40. Schnabel and Watson, *Joint Chiefs*, III, pt. 1: 118, n. 140.
41. Ibid., n. 141.
42. Bradley and Blair, *General's Life*, 579.
43. Schnabel and Watson, *Joint Chiefs*, III, pt. 1: 118, n. 140.
44. Bradley and Blair, *General's Life*, 579.
45. FRUS, Korea, 1950, VII:1055-57.
46. Ibid., 1057.
47. Ibid., 1057-58.
48. Bradley and Blair, *General's Life*, 585.
49. FRUS, Korea, 1950, VII:1058, n. 1, text of MacArthur's reply reprinted from Truman, *Memoirs*, II:375.
50. Bradley and Blair, *General's Life*, 585.
51. FRUS, Korea, 1950, VII:1075-76.
52. Schnabel and Watson, *Joint Chiefs*, III, pt. 1: 301, n. 15; Bradley and Blair, *General's Life*, 587-88.
53. Bradley and Blair, *General's Life*, 596.
54. Stoler, *Papers*, VII:228-29.
55. Ibid., attached memo of JCS to GCM, FRUS, Korea, 1950, VII:1117-21.
56. Pogue to Blair, August 19, 1982, cited in Bradley and Blair, *General's Life*, 587.
57. Isaacson and Thomas, *Wise Men*, 538.
58. FRUS, Korea, 1950, VII:1237-38.
59. NYT, November 24, 1950.

60. Bradley and Blair, *General's Life*, 597.
61. FRUS, Korea, 1950, VII:1237–38.
62. Ibid., 1242–49.
63. Ridgway, *Korean War*, 83.
64. Interview with MacArthur, *U.S. News & World Report*, December 8, 1950, published in NYT on December 1.
65. Bradley and Blair, *General's Life*, 601–2.
66. Truman, *Memoirs*, II:384.
67. Schnabel and Watson, *Joint Chiefs*, III, pt. 1: 187.
68. FRUS, Korea and China, 1951, Vol. VII, pt. 1: 55–56.
69. Acheson, *Present at the Creation*, 515.
70. Schnabel and Watson, *Joint Chiefs*, III, pt. 1: 437.
71. Bradley and Blair, *General's Life*, 623.
72. Stoler, *Papers*, VII:404–5.
73. FRUS, Korea and China, 1951, VII, pt. 1: 251.
74. Ibid., 265–66.
75. Truman, *Memoirs*, II:442.
76. Truman, Margare, *Harry S. Truman*, 513.
77. Lovett, memo of conversation, March 24, 1951, Acheson Papers, B-66, HSTL.
78. Acheson, *Present at the Creation*, 519.
79. Tubby journal entry, April 5, 1951, Roger Tubby Papers, Yale.
80. FRUS, Korea and China, 1951, VII, pt. 1: 299.
81. Donovan, *Tumultuous Years*, 359, quoting Donovan's interview of Lovett.
82. Truman Diary, April 6, 1951, Truman Papers, HSTL.
83. Acheson, *Present at the Creation*, 521.
84. Bradley and Blair, *General's Life*, 633.
85. Ibid.
86. Collins, *War in Peacetime*, 283.
87. Bradley and Blair, *General's Life*, 634–35.
88. McCullough, *Truman*, 842, quoting McCullough's interview of Elsey.
89. Elsey, *Unplanned Life*, 205 (italics in the original).
90. Pace OH, HSTL.
91. Truman statement and order, April 11, 1951, PPA of the Presidents, http://www.presidency.ucsb.edu.
92. James, *Years of MacArthur*, III:600.
93. *Time*, April 23, 1951.
94. Bradley and Blair, *General's Life*, 639; NYT, April 19, 1951.
95. American Rhetoric: MacArthur—Farewell Address to Congress. http://www.americanrhetoric.com/speeches/douglasmacarthurfarewelladdress.htm.
96. Bradley and Blair, *General's Life*, 639.
97. American Rhetoric: MacArthur—Farewell Address to Congress. http://www.americanrhetoric.com/speeches/douglasmacarthurfarewelladdress.htm.
98. James, *Years of MacArthur*, III:616–17.
99. Quoted in Miller, *Plain Speaking*, 337.
100. Military Situation in Far East, Hearings Before Committee on Armed Services and Committee on Foreign Relations United States Senate, 82nd Cong., pt. 1, 73–103.

101. Ibid., 325.
102. Ibid., pt. 2, 732.
103. Acheson to Nitze, November 1, 1967, Nitze personal papers, Arlington, VA.
104. Stoler, *Papers*, VII:505. Marshall added the two opening paragraphs of his prepared statement, including the term "distressing necessity," as "something of [his] own." Ibid., n. 2. Interview of Marshall by Felix E. Larkin, September 18 and October 23, 1972, OH, HSTL.
105. Brooks, *Road to Character*, 115.
106. Halberstam, *Coldest Winter*, 481.
107. FRUS, Korea and China, 1951, VII, pt. 1: 507-11.
108. Condit, *Test of War*. Vol. II of *History of the Office of the Secretary of Defense*, 114.
109. Ridgway, February 26, 1959, OH Collection, Tape 21, at 35, GCML.
110. Quirk, *Wars and Peace*, 195-96.
111. Commanding General's Journal, June 8, 1951, Korea 1951-1953, Eighth United States Army, Commanding General's Journal, Van Fleet Papers, GCML; "Korean Visit Just Routine, Marshall Says," *Washington Post*, June 9, 1951, 1, 3.
112. McCarthy, *America's Retreat from Victory*, 137.
113. Wilson, *Marshall Remembered*, 355.
114. Stoler, *Marshall: Soldier-Statesman*, 189.
115. KM to C. J. George, August 9, 1951, KM Corres. Collection, GCML.
116. Bland, Papers, VI:614-15, GCML. GCM attached a copy of Stimson's letter to him when he was army chief of staff.
117. Isaacson and Thomas, *Wise Men*, 417.
118. Stoler, *Papers*, VII:629.
119. Acheson to GCM, September 13, 1951, Secretary of Defense, number indexed M200-19-24, GCM Papers, GCML.
120. Ungers with Hirshon, *Marshall*, 490.
121. Stoler, *Papers*, VII:601.

Epilogue: We Commend Thy Servant George

1. Associated Press to *Los Angeles Times*, November 29, 1953; *New York Herald Tribune*, November 29, 1953.
2. Stoler, *Papers*, VII:823-24.
3. Marshall to Mrs. George C. Marshall, At Sea, December 3, 1953, Marshall-Winn Papers, B-44/F-17, GCML.
4. Marshall to Katherine Marshall, December 8, 1953, Marshall-Winn Collection, GCML.
5. Goodpaster, "George Marshall's World, and Ours," NYT, December 11, 1953, A43.
6. Associated Press to *Los Angeles Times*, December 11, 1953.
7. Stoler, *Papers*, VII:817-18.
8. Ibid., 810-15.
9. "A Just and Lasting Peace," Nobel Prize Lecture by Barack Obama, December 10, 2009. www.nobelprize.org/nobel_prizes/peace/laureates/2009/obama-lecture_en.html.

10. Stoler, *Papers*, VIII:810–15.
11. *Harvard Magazine* (May–June 1947), 84.
12. Acheson, *Present at the Creation*, 141.
13. Marshall Interviews, 98, GCML.
14. Katherine Marshall, *Annals*, 110.
15. White, "Marshall at 75: The General Revisited," NYT, December 25, 1955.
16. Bland, Papers, IV:197, GCML.
17. Marshall Carter interview by Forrest Pogue, Tape 119, Copy 2, October 22, 1959, at 9.
18. Marshall, John, *Life of George Washington*, II:446–47.
19. Wilson, *Marshall Remembered*, 388.
20. Statement of Death, issued October 19, 1959, GCM Family, Xerox 2818, GCML.
21. "The Burial of the Dead: Rite One," *The Episcopal Book of Common Prayer*, ratified on October 16, 1789, 170 years prior to the date of Marshall's death.
22. This quote is from an essay about Abraham Lincoln written by Robert Ingersoll in 1884, which is often attributed to Lincoln himself.

Bibliography

Unpublished Sources

American Red Cross Archives, Washington, DC.

Henry H. Arnold Papers, Manuscript Division, Library of Congress, Washington, DC.

Central Zionist Archives Collections, Jerusalem, Israel.

George Crile Papers, Western Reserve Historical Society, Cleveland, OH.

Enoch Pratt Free Library, Baltimore, MD.

First Division Museum at Cantigny, Wheaton, IL.

Lawrence Guyer, "The Joint Chiefs and the War Against Germany," RG 218.2.2, National Archives, College Park, MD.

Hollins University archives, Roanoke, VA.

Interviews by author: Allen Tupper Brown (son of Allen Brown); Dr. Daniel Crosswell; Iva Benjamin Hall Hudson II; Richard Hyatt; Carol Kushner; Clason Kyle; Em Boles Locker; Dr. Michael Rouland; Gabriel Scheffer; John Watling; William "Billy" Winn.

Louis Arthur Johnson Papers, University of Virginia Library, Charlottesville, VA.

George C. Marshall Collection, George C. Marshall Research Library, Lexington, VA.

Marshall-Winn Collection, donated by James Winn, George C. Marshall Research Library, Lexington, VA.

Katherine T. Marshall Collection, George C. Marshall Research Library, Lexington, VA.

Frank McCarthy Papers, George C. Marshall Research Library, Lexington, VA.

National Archives of the UK, Kew, London.

National Archives of the U.S., College Park, MD.

The National World War II Museum and archives, New Orleans, LA.

Ocean Beach Historical Society archives, Fire Island, NY.

Mary Catherine Santoro. "First Lady of the Army: The Life and Times of Katherine Tuppper Marshall," May 1, 1999, Hollins University, Roanoke, VA.

Henry L. Stimson Diary, Manuscript Room, Sterling Memorial Library, Yale University, New Haven, CT.

"George C. Marshall and 'Europe-First,' 1939–1951: A Study in Diplomatic as Well as Military History," rough outline of lecture by Mark A. Stoler, January 4, 2015.

Lucien K. Truscott Jr. Papers, George C. Marshall Research Library, Lexington, VA.

U.S. Army Center of Military History, Collins Hall, Ft. McNair, Washington, DC.

U.S. Army Heritage and Education Center, Carlisle, PA.

Arthur Vandenberg Papers, Bentley Library, University of Michigan, Ann Arbor, MI.

Woodberry Forest archives, Orange, VA.

Books and Articles

Acacia, John. *Clark Clifford, the Wise Man of Washington*. Lexington, KY: University Press of Kentucky, 2009.

Acheson, Dean. *Present at the Creation: My Years in the State Department*. New York: W. W. Norton, 1969.

A.E.F. Society of the First Division, *History of the First Division During the World War, 1917-1919*. Andesite Press, 2015.

Agnew, John, and J. Nicholas Entrikin, eds. *The Marshall Plan Today: Model and Metaphor*. New York: Routledge, 2015.

Alexander, Bevin. *MacArthur's War*. New York: Berkeley Caliber, 2013.

Alsop, Joseph Wright, and Adam Platt. *"I've Seen the Best of It": Memoirs*. New York: W. W. Norton, 1992.

Alsop, Joseph, and Robert Kinter. *American White Paper*. New York: Simon & Schuster, 1940.

Ambrose, Stephen E. *D-Day June 6, 1944: The Climactic Battle of World War II*. New York: Simon & Schuster, 1994.

_____. *Eisenhower: Soldier, General of the Army, President-Elect*. New York: Simon & Schuster, 1983.

_____. *The Supreme Commander: The War Years of Dwight D. Eisenhower*. New York: Anchor, 2012.

Anonymous [Robert Joseph Casey]. *The Cannoneers Have Hairy Ears: A Diary of the Front Lines*. New York: J. H. Sears & Company, 1927.

Applebaum, Anne. *Iron Curtain: The Crushing of Eastern Europe, 1944-1946*. New York: Doubleday, 2012.

Arnold, Henry H. *Global Mission*. New York: Harper and Brothers, 1949.

Atkinson, Rick. *An Army at Dawn: The War in North Africa, 1942-1943*. New York: Henry Holt, 2002.

_____. *The Day of Battle: The War in Sicily and Italy, 1943-1944*. New York: Henry Holt, 2007.

_____. *Guns at Last Light: The War in Western Europe, 1944-1945*. New York: Henry Holt, 2013.

Bakowski, Joseph. *Utah Beach: The Ambitious Landings and Airborne Operations on D-day, June 6, 1944*. Mechanicsburg, PA: Stackpole Books, 2005.

Baruch, Bernard M. *Baruch: The Public Years: My Own Story*. Volume 2. New York: Holt, Rinhart & Winston, 1960.

Baynes, Norman H., ed. *The Speeches of Adolf Hitler, April 1922-August 1939*. New York: Oxford University Press, 1942.

Beal, John Robinson. *Marshall in China*. New York: Doubleday, 1970.

Beevor, Antony. *The Second World War*. New York: Back Bay Books, 2013.

_____. *Stalingrad*. New York: Penguin Books, 1999.

Begin, Menachem. *The Revolt: Story of the Irgun*. New York: Dell, 1978.

Behrman, Greg. *The Most Noble Adventure: The Marshall Plan and How America Helped Rebuild Europe*. New York: Free Press, 2007.

Beisner, Robert L. *Dean Acheson: A Life in the Cold War*. New York: Oxford University Press, 2006.

Bendersky, Joseph W. "From Cowards to Subversives to Aggressors and Questionable

Allies: US Army Perceptions of Zionism Since World War I." *Journal of Israeli History: Politics, Society, Culture* 25, no. 1: 107-29.

_____. *The Jewish Threat: Anti-Semitic Politics of the U.S. Army.* New York: Basic Books, 2001.

Benson, Constance. *Mainly Players: Bensonian Memories.* London: Thornton Butterworth, 1926.

Bernstein, Richard. *China 1945: Mao's Revolution and America's Fateful Choice.* New York: Alfred A. Knopf, 2014.

Beschloss, Michael. *The Conquerors: Roosevelt, Truman and the Destruction of Hitler's Germany, 1941-1945.* New York: Simon & Schuster, 2002.

Bidault, Georges. *Resistance: The Political Autobiography of Georges Bidault.* Westport, CT: Praeger, 1967.

Bird, Kai. *The Chairman: John J. McCloy, the Making of the American Establishment.* New York: Simon & Schuster, 1992.

Birse, Arthur Herbert. *Memoirs of an Interpreter.* New York: Coward-McCann, 1967.

Bix, Herbert P. *Hirohito and the Making of Modern Japan.* New York: Perennial, 2001.

Blair, Clay. *Forgotten War: America in Korea, 1950-1953.* Annapolis, MD: Naval Institute Press, 1987.

_____. *Hitler's U-Boat War: The Hunted, 1942-1945.* New York: Random House, 1998.

Bland, Larry I. *George C. Marshall: Interviews and Reminiscences for Forrest C. Pogue.* Lexington, VA: George C. Marshall Research Foundation, 1996.

_____, ed. *George C. Marshall's Mediation Mission to China, December 1945-January 1947.* Lexington, VA: George C. Marshall Foundation, 1998.

Bland, Larry I., and Sharon Ritenour, eds. *The Papers of George Catlett Marshall*, Vol. 1. Baltimore: Johns Hopkins University Press, 1981.

Bland, Larry I., Sharon Ritenour Stevens, and Clarence Wunderlin, eds. *The Papers of George Catlett Marshall*, Vol. 2. Baltimore: Johns Hopkins University Press, 1986.

Bland, Larry I., and Sharon Ritenour Stevens, eds. *The Papers of George Catlett Marshall*, Vol. 3. Baltimore: Johns Hopkins University Press, 1991.

_____. *The Papers of George Catlett Marshall*, Vol. 4. Baltimore: Johns Hopkins University Press, 1996.

_____. *The Papers of George Catlett Marshall*, Vol. 5. Baltimore: Johns Hopkins University Press, 2003.

Bland, Larry I., Mark A. Stoler, Sharon Ritenour Stevens, and Daniel D. Holt, eds. *The Papers of George Catlett Marshall*, Vol. 6. Baltimore: Johns Hopkins University Press, 2013.

Blum, John Morton, ed. *From the Morgenthau Diaries.* Vol. 3: *Years of War, 1941-1945.* Boston: Houghton Mifflin, 1967.

Blumenson, Martin. *Mark Clark.* New York: Random House, 1985.

_____, ed. *The Patton Papers, 1940-1945.* Boston: Da Capo, 1996.

Bohlen, Charles. *Witness to History, 1929-1969.* New York: W. W. Norton, 1973.

Bonds, John Bledsoe. *Bipartisan Strategy: Selling the Marshall Plan.* Westport, CT: Praeger, 2002.

Borneman, Walter R. *The Admirals: Nimitz, Halsey, Leahy and King—The Five-Star Admirals Who Won the War at Sea.* New York: Little, Brown, 2012.

_____. *MacArthur at War: World War II in the Pacific.* New York: Little, Brown, 2016.

Bradley, Omar N. *A Soldier's Story.* New York: Modern Library, 1999.

Bradley, Omar N., and Clay Blair. *A General's Life.* New York: Simon & Schuster, 1983.

Breitman, Richard. *Official Secrets: What the Nazis Planned, What the British and Americans Knew.* New York: Hill and Wang, 1999.

Breitman, Richard, and Alan J. Lichtman. *FDR and the Jews.* Cambridge: Belknap Press of Harvard University Press, 2013.

Brooks, David. *The Road to Character.* New York: Random House, 2015.

Brown, Anthony Cave. *Bodyguard of Lies.* New York: Harper & Row, 1975.

Buell, Thomas B. *Master of Sea Power: A Biography of Admiral Ernest J. King.* Boston: Little, Brown, 1980.

Bullard, Robert Lee. *Fighting Generals: Illustrated Biographical Sketches of Seven Major Generals in World War I.* Whitefish, MT: Kessinger, 2010.

Bullock, Alan. *Ernest Bevin: Foreign Secretary 1945–1951.* New York: W. W. Norton, 1984.

Butcher, Harry C. *My Three Years with Eisenhower: The Personal Diary of Captain Harry C. Butcher, USNR, Naval Aide to General Eisenhower.* New York: Simon & Schuster, 1946.

Butler, J. R. M. *Grand Strategy,* Vol. 3. London: HMSO, 1964.

Butler, Susan, ed. *My Dear Mr. Stalin: The Complete Correspondence of Franklin D. Roosevelt and Joseph V. Stalin.* New Haven: Yale University Press, 2005.

_____. *Roosevelt and Stalin: Portrait of a Partnership.* New York: Alfred A. Knopf, 2015.

Caddick-Adams, Peter. *Monte Cassino: Ten Armies in Hell.* London: Preface Publishing, 2012.

Cadogan, Sir Alexander. *The Diaries of Sir Alexander Cadogan, O.M., 1938–1945,* ed. by David Dilkes. New York: G. P. Putnam's Sons, 1983.

Callwell, C. E., *Field-Marshal Sir Henry Wilson.* Cassell and Co., 1927.

Campbell, John P. *Dieppe Revisited: A Documentary Investigation.* London: Frank Cass, 1993.

Capra, Frank. *The Name Above the Title: An Autobiography.* Boston: Da Capo, 1997.

Carroll, Andrew. *My Fellow Soldiers: General John Pershing and the Americans Who Helped Win the Great War.* New York: Penguin, 2017.

Chace, James. *Acheson: The Secretary of State Who Created the American World.* New York: Simon & Schuster, 1998.

Chandler, Alfred, ed. *The Papers of Dwight David Eisenhower: The War Years,* Vol. I. Baltimore: Johns Hopkins University Press, 1970.

Chiang, Kai-shek. *Soviet Russia in China.* New York: Farrar, Straus and Cudahy, 1957.

Chuev, Feliks. *Molotov Remembers: Inside Kremlin Politics.* Chicago: Ivan R. Dee, 1993.

Churchill, Winston S. *Their Finest Hour.* Boston: Houghton Mifflin, 1949.

_____. *The Hinge of Fate.* Boston: Houghton Mifflin, 1950.

_____. *The Grand Alliance.* Boston: Houghton Mifflin, 1951.

_____. *Closing the Ring.* Boston: Houghton Mifflin, 1951.

_____. *Triumph and Tragedy.* Boston: Houghton Mifflin, 1953.

Clark, Mark W. *Calculated Risk.* New York: Enigma Books, 2007.

Clifford, Clark, with Richard Holbrooke. *Counsel to the President: A Memoir.* New York: Random House, 1991.

Clifford, J. Garry, and Samuel R. Spencer Jr. *The First Peacetime Draft.* Lawrence: University Press of Kansas, 1986.

Cohen, Elliot A. *Supreme Command.* New York: Anchor Books, 2003.

Cohen, Michael Joseph. *Truman and Israel.* Berkeley: University of California Press, 1990.

Collins, J. Lawton. *War in Peacetime: The History and Lessons of Korea.* Boston: Houghton Mifflin, 1969.

Conant, James Bryant. *My Several Lives: Memoirs of a Social Inventor.* New York: Harper & Row, 1970.

Condit, Doris. *History of the Office of the Secretary of Defense.* Vol. 2: *The Test of War, 1950-53.* Washington, DC: GPO, 1988.

Conn, Stetson, and Byron Fairchild. *The Framework of Hemisphere Defense.* Washington, D.C.: Office of the Chief of Military History, Department of the Army, 1960.

Cooper, John Milton Jr. *Woodrow Wilson.* New York: Vintage, 2011.

Cray, Ed. *General of the Army: George C. Marshall, Soldier and Statesman.* New York: Cooper Square Press, 2001.

Crosswell, D. K. R. *Beetle: The Life of General Walter Bedell Smith.* Lexington: University Press of Kentucky, 2010.

Dallek, Robert. *Franklin D. Roosevelt.* New York: Viking, 2017.

_____. *The Lost Peace: Leadership in a Time of Horror and Hope, 1945-1953.* New York: HarperCollins, 2010.

Danchev, Alex. *Establishing the Anglo-American Alliance: The Second World War Diaries of Brigadier Vivian Dykes.* London: Brassey's, 1990.

_____. *Very Special Relationship: Field Marshal Sir John Dill and the Anglo-American Alliance, 1941-1944.* London: Brassey's, 1986.

Danchev, Alex, and Daniel Todman, eds. *War Diaries, 1939-1945: Field Marshal Lord Alanbrooke.* Berkeley: University of California Press, 2001.

Davenport, Matthew J. *First Over There: The Attack on Cantigny, America's First Battle of World War I.* New York: St. Martin's, 2015.

Davis, Kenneth S. *FDR: The War President, 1940-1943.* New York: Random House, 2000.

Daws, Gavan. *Prisoners of the Japanese.* New York: William Morrow, 1994.

Derwent, Clarence. *The Derwent Story: My First Fifty Years in the Theatre in England and America.* New York: Schuman, 1959.

D'Este, Carlo. *Eisenhower: A Soldier's Life.* New York: Henry Holt, 2002.

_____. *Patton: A Genius for War.* New York: HarperCollins, 1995.

Dimbleby, Jonathan. *The Battle of the Atlantic: How the Allies Won the War.* New York: Oxford University Press, 2016.

Dobbs, Michael. *Six Months in 1945: From World War to Cold War.* New York: Alfred A. Knopf, 2012.

Donovan, Robert J. *Tumultuous Years: The Presidency of Harry S. Truman, 1949-1953.* New York: W. W. Norton, 1982.

Doyle, William. *Inside the Oval Office: The White House Tapes from FDR to Clinton.* New York: Kodansha USA, 2002.

Duffy, James P. *War at the End of the World: Douglas MacArthur and the Forgotten Fight for New Guinea, 1942-1945.* New York: NAL Caliber, 2016.

Dunn, Susan. *A Blueprint for War: FDR and the Hundred Days That Mobilized America.* New Haven: Yale University Press, 2018.

Dunn, Walter Scott Jr. *Second Front Now.* Tuscaloosa: University of Alabama Press, 1980.

Eiler, Keith E., ed. *Wedemeyer on War and Peace.* Stanford: Hoover Press, 1987.

Eisenhower, David. *Eisenhower at War, 1943-1945.* New York: Random House, 1986.

Eisenhower, Dwight D. *Crusade in Europe.* Garden City, NY: Doubleday, 1948.

_____. *At Ease: Stories I Tell to Friends.* New York: Eastern Acorn Press, 1981.

Eisenhower, John S. D. *Yanks: The Epic Story of the American Army in World War I.* New York: Free Press, 2001.

Ellis, John. *Brute Force: Allied Strategy and Tactics in the Second World War.* New York: Viking, 1990.

Elsey, George McKee. *An Unplanned Life.* Columbia: University of Missouri Press, 2005.

Evans, Richard. *The Third Reich in History and Memory.* Oxford: Oxford University Press, 2015.

Farago, Ladislas. *Patton: Ordeal and Triumph.* Yardley, PA: Westholme, 2005.

Fairchild, Byron, and Jonathan Grossman: *The Army and Industrial Manpower.* Washington, DC: Center of Military History, Department of the Army, GPO, 1988.

Fenby, Jonathan. *Alliance: The Inside Story of How Roosevelt, Stalin and Churchill Won One War and Began Another.* San Francisco: MacAdam/Cage, 2006.

_____. *Chiang Kai-shek.* New York: Carroll & Graf, 2003.

Fergusson, Bernard. *The Watery Maze: The Story of Combined Operations.* London: Collins, 1961.

Ferrell, Robert H. *America's Deadliest Battle: Meuse-Argonne, 1918.* Lawrence: University Press of Kansas, 2007.

_____, ed. *The Eisenhower Diaries.* New York: W. W. Norton, 1981.

_____, ed. *Off the Record: The Private Papers of Harry S. Truman.* Columbia: University of Missouri Press, 1997.

_____. *Truman in the White House: The Diary of Eben A. Ayers.* Columbia: University of Missouri, 1991.

Fisher, Ernest F. Jr. *Cassino to the Alps: U.S. Army in World War II.* Washington, DC: Office of the Chief of Military History, GPO, 1977.

Foreign Relations of the United States, 1945–1951. Washington, DC: GPO. http://digicoll.library.wisc.edu/cgi-bin/FRUS/FRUS-idx?type=browse&scope=FRUS.FRUS1.

Frank, Richard B. *Downfall: The End of the Imperial Japanese Empire.* New York: Penguin, 1999.

Freeland, Richard M. *The Truman Doctrine and the Origins of McCarthyism: Foreign Policy, Domestic Policy, and Internal Security, 1946–48.* New York: New York University Press, 1985.

Freidel, Frank. *Franklin D. Roosevelt: A Rendezvous with Destiny.* Boston: Little, Brown, 1990.

Frye, William. *Marshall: Citizen Soldier.* Indianapolis: Bobbs-Merrill, 1947.

Gaddis, John Lewis. *The Cold War: A New History.* New York: Penguin, 2007.

_____. *George F. Kennan: An American Life.* New York: Penguin, 2011.

Gilbert, Martin. *Churchill: A Life.* New York: Henry Holt, 1992.

Giumarra, G. Michael. *D-Day 1942, D-Day 1944: A Comparative Analysis of Operations SLEDGEHAMMER and OVERLORD.* Revised 23 November 2009. www.D-day1942D-day194423Nov09-copy-pdf.2467.

Goodwin, Doris Kearns. *No Ordinary Time: Franklin and Eleanor Roosevelt: The Home Front in World War II.* New York: Simon & Schuster, 1994.

Gosling, F. G. *Before Freud: Neurasthenia and the American Medical Community.* Champaign, IL: University of Illinois Press, 1987.

Goulden, Joseph C. *Korea: The Untold Story.* New York: Times Books, 1982.

Greenfield, Kent Roberts, ed. *Command Decisions.* CreateSpace, 2015.

Grey, Edward, Grey of Fallodon. *Twenty-five Years: 1892-1916.* New York: Frederick A. Stokes, 1925.

Grigg, John. *The Victory That Never Was.* New York: Hill and Wang, 1980.

Groves, Leslie M. *Now It Can Be Told: The Story of the Manhattan Project*. New York: Harper, 1962.

Gruber, Ruth. *Witness: One of the Great Correspondents of the Twentieth Century Tells Her Story*. New York: Schocken, 2007.

Haas, Lawrence J. *Harry and Arthur: Truman and Vandenberg and the Partnership That Created the Free World*. Sterling, VA: Potomac Books, 2016.

Halberstam, David. *The Coldest Winter: America and the Korean War*. New York: Hyperion, 2007.

Hamilton, Nigel. *The Mantle of Command: FDR at War, 1941-1942*. Boston: Houghton Mifflin Harcourt, 2014.

_____. *Commander in Chief: FDR's Battle with Churchill, 1943*. Boston: Houghton Mifflin Harcourt, 2016.

Harbord, James G. *The American Army in France*. New York: Little, Brown, 1936.

Harden, Blaine. *King of Spies: The Dark Reign of America's Spymaster in Korea*. New York: Viking, 2017.

Harmon, E. N., with Milton MacKaye and William Ross MacKaye. *Combat Commander*. Englewood Cliffs, NJ: Prentice-Hall, 1970.

Harper, John Lamberton. *The Cold War*. New York: Oxford University Press, 2011.

Harriman, W. Averell, and Elie Abel. *Special Envoy to Churchill and Stalin, 1941-1946*. New York: Random House, 1975.

Harris, Mark. *Five Came Back: A Story of Hollywood and the Second World War*. New York: Penguin, 2014.

Harrison, Gordon A. *U.S. Army in World War II: Cross-Channel Attack*. Atlanta: Whitman, 2012.

Hart, Liddell B. H. *The German Generals Talk*. New York: William Morrow, 1971.

Hassett, William D. *Off the Record with FDR, 1942-1945*. New York: Enigma Books, 2016.

Hastings, Max. *Inferno: The World at War, 1939-1945*. New York: Vintage, 2012.

_____. *Winston's War: Churchill, 1940-1945*. New York: Alfred A. Knopf, 2010.

Heefner, Wilson A. *Dogface Soldier: The Life of General Lucien K. Truscott*. Columbia: University of Missouri Press, 2010.

Heinl, Robert Debs Jr. *Victory at High Tide: The Inchon-Seoul Campaign*, 3rd ed. Baltimore, MD: Nautical & Aviation Publishing Company of America, 1979.

Heinrichs, Waldo. *Threshold of War: Franklin D. Roosevelt and American Entry into World War II*. New York: Oxford University Press, 1988.

Heinrichs, Waldo, and Marc Gallicchio. *Implacable Foes: War in the Pacific, 1944-1945*. New York: Oxford University Press, 2016.

Herman, Arthur. *Douglas MacArthur: American Warrior*. New York: Random House, 2016.

_____. *Joseph McCarthy: Reexamining the Life and Legacy of America's Most Hated Senator*. New York: Free Press, 2000.

Hessen, Robert, ed. *Berlin Alert: The Memoirs and Reports of Truman Smith*. Stanford: Hoover Institution Press, 1984.

Hogan, Michael J. *The Marshall Plan: America, Britain, and the Reconstruction of Europe, 1947-1952*. Cambridge, UK: Cambridge University Press, 1989.

Holmes, Richard. *The World at War*. London: Ebury Press, 2012.

Hoopes, Townsend, and Douglas Brinkley. *Driven Patriot: The Life and Times of James Forrestal*. New York: Vintage, 1993.

Horowitz, David. *State in the Making*. Westport, CT: Greenwood, 1981.

Huntington, Samuel P. *The Soldier and the State: The Theory and Politics of Civil-Military Relations.* Cambridge: Harvard University Press, 1957.

Isaacson, Walter, and Evan Thomas. *The Wise Men: Six Friends and the World They Made.* New York: Simon & Schuster, 1996.

Ismay, Hastings Lionel. *The Memoirs of General Lord Ismay.* New York: Viking, 1960.

James, Dorris Clayton. *The Years of MacArthur, 1941-1945.* New York: Houghton Mifflin, 1975.

Jeans, Roger B., ed. *The Marshall Mission to China, 1945-1947: The Letters and Diary of Colonel John Hart Caughey.* Lanham, MD: Rowman & Littlefield, 2011.

Jeffers, H. Paul. *In the Rough Rider's Shadow: The Story of a War Hero, Theodore Roosevelt Jr.* New York: Ballantine Books, 2002.

_____. *Taking Command: General J. Lawton Collins from Guadalcanal to Utah Beach and Victory in Europe.* New York: Dutton Caliber, 2009.

Jones, Bruce. *The Marshall Plan and the Shaping of Strategy.* Washington, DC: Brookings Institution Press, 2017.

Jones, Joseph. *The Fifteen Weeks.* New York: Houghton Mifflin, 1965.

Jordan, Jonathan W. *American Warlords: How Roosevelt's High Command Led America to Victory in World War II.* New York: NAL Caliber, 2016.

Judis, John B. *Genesis: Truman, American Jews, and the Origins of the Arab/Israeli Conflict.* New York: Farrar, Straus and Giroux, 2014.

Kahn, Ely Jacques Jr. *The China Hands: America's Foreign Service Officers and What Befell Them.* New York: Penguin, 1976.

Kaiser, David. *No End Save Victory: How FDR Led the Nation into War.* New York: Basic Books, 2014.

Kanj, Jamal. *Children of Catastrophe: Journey from a Palestinian Refugee Camp to America.* Reading, UK: Garnet, 2010.

Kaplan, Lawrence S. *The Conversion of Senator Arthur H. Vandenberg.* Lexington: University Press of Kentucky, 2015.

Keegan, John. *The Face of Battle.* New York: Penguin, 1978.

_____. *The First World War.* New York: Vintage, 2000.

_____. *The Second World War.* New York: Penguin, 1990.

Kennan, George F. *The Kennan Diaries.* New York: W. W. Norton, 2014.

_____. *Memoirs, 1925-1950.* New York: Pantheon, 1983.

Kennedy, David M. *Freedom from Fear: The American People in Depression and War, 1929-1945.* New York: Oxford University Press, 2005.

Kershaw, Ian. *Hitler: A Biography.* New York: W. W. Norton, 2008.

_____. *Hitler: 1889-1936 Hubris.* New York: W. W. Norton, 2000.

_____. *To Hell and Back.* New York: Penguin, 2016.

Kimball, Warren F., ed. *Churchill & Roosevelt: The Complete Correspondence, 1939-1945.* Three vols. edited with commentaries. Princeton: Princeton University Press, 1984.

_____. *Forged in War: Roosevelt, Churchill and the Second World War.* Chicago: Ivan R. Dee, 2003.

_____. *The Juggler: Franklin Roosevelt as Wartime Statesman.* Princeton: Princeton University Press, 1991.

Kindleberger, Charles P. *Essays in History: Financial, Economic, Personal.* Ann Arbor: University of Michigan Press, 1999.

King, Ernest J., and Walter Muir Whitehill. *Fleet Admiral King.* New York: W. W. Norton, 1952.

Kurtz-Phelan, Daniel. *The China Mission: George Marshall's Unfinished War, 1945-1947.* New York: W. W. Norton, 2018.

Lacey, Jim. *Keep from All Thoughtful Men: How Economists Won World War II.* Annapolis, MD: Naval Institute Press, 2011.

Langer, William Leonard, and S. Everett Gleason. *The Undeclared War, 1940-1941: The World Crisis and American Foreign Policy.* Whitefish, MT: Literary Licensing, 2013.

Larrabee, Eric. *Commander in Chief: Franklin Delano Roosevelt, His Lieutenants and Their War.* Annapolis, MD: Naval Institute Press, 1987.

Lash, Joseph P. *Roosevelt and Churchill, 1939-1941.* New York: HarperCollins, 1977.

Leahy, William D. *I Was There.* New York: Whittlesey House, 1950.

Leffler, Melvyn P., "Divide and Invest: Why the Marshall Plan Worked." *Foreign Affairs,* July/August 2018.

Leffler, Melvyn P., and David S. Painter. *Origins of the Cold War: An International History.* New York: Routledge, 2005.

Leighton, Richard M., and Robert W. Coakley. *U.S. Army in World War II: Global Logistics and Strategy.* Vol. I: 1940-1943. Washington, DC: Office of the Chief of Military History, GPO, 1955.

Lengel, Edward G. *To Conquer Hell: The Meuse-Argonne, 1918.* New York: Henry Holt, 2008.

Leshuk, Leonard. *US Intelligence Perceptions of Soviet Power, 1921-1946.* London: Frank Cass, 2003.

Lewin, Ronald. *Ultra Goes to War.* New York: McGraw-Hill, 1978.

Li, Laura Tyson. *Madame Chiang Kai-shek.* New York: Atlantic Monthly Press, 2006.

Liebling, A. J. *The Road Back to Paris.* New York: Modern Library, 1997.

Lloyd, Nick. *Hundred Days: The End of the Great War.* New York: Viking, 2013.

Lockhart, R. H. Bruce. *Jan Masaryk: A Personal Memoir.* New York: Philosophical Library, 1951.

Loewenheim, Francis L., Harold D. Langley, and Manfred Jonas, eds. *Roosevelt and Churchill: Their Secret Wartime Correspondence.* New York: Dutton, 1975.

Ludendorff, Erich. *My War Memories, 1914-1918.* Uckfield, UK: Naval & Military Press, 2005.

MacArthur, Douglas. *Reminiscences.* Annapolis, MD: Bluejacket Books, Naval Institute Press, 1964.

Manchester, William. *American Caesar: Douglas MacArthur, 1880-1964.* Boston: Little, Brown, 1978.

Manchester, William, and Paul Reid. *The Last Lion: Winston Spencer Churchill, Defender of the Realm, 1940-1965.* New York: Little, Brown, 2012.

Marshall, George C. *Memoirs of My Services in the World War, 1917-1918.* Boston: Houghton Mifflin, 1976.

Marshall, John. *Life of George Washington,* 2nd edition. Philadelphia: James Crissy, 1843.

Marshall, Katherine Tupper. *Together: Annals of an Army Wife.* New York: Tupper & Love, 1946.

Matloff, Maurice, and Edwin M. Snell. *U.S. Army in World War II: Strategic Planning for Coalition Warfare.* Washington, DC: Office of the Chief of Military History, GPO, 1953.

Mawdsley, Evan. *December 1941: Twelve Days That Began a World War*. New Haven: Yale University Press, 2011.

McCarthy, Joseph R. *America's Retreat from Victory: The Story of George Catlett Marshall*. Belmont, MA: Western Islands, 1951.

McCollum, Shoshanna. *Fire Island: Beach Resort and National Seashore*. Charleston, SC: Arcadia, 2012.

McCullough, David. *Truman*. New York: Simon & Schuster, 1992.

McFarland, Keith, and David L. Roll. *Louis Johnson and the Arming of America: The Roosevelt and Truman Years*. Bloomington: Indiana University Press, 2005.

Medoff, Rafael. *Jewish Americans and Political Participation*. Santa Barbara, CA: ABC-CLIO, 2002.

Mee, Charles L. Jr. *The Marshall Plan*. New York: Simon & Schuster, 1984.

Meijer, Hendrik. *Arthur Vandenberg: The Man in the Middle of the American Century*. Chicago: University of Chicago Press, 2017.

Melby, John F. *The Mandate of Heaven: Record of a Civil War, China 1945-49*. Garden City, NY: Anchor Books, 1971.

Miller, Merle. *Plain Speaking: An Oral Biography of Harry S. Truman*. New York: Black Dog & Leventhal, 2005.

Millis, Walter, ed. *The Forrestal Diaries*. New York: Viking, 1951.

Mills, Nicolaus. *Winning the Peace: The Marshall Plan & America's Coming of Age as a Superpower*. New York: John Wiley & Sons, 2008.

Mitter, Rana. *Forgotten Ally: China's World War II, 1937-1945*. Boston: Houghton Mifflin Harcourt, 2013.

Moe, Richard. *Roosevelt's Second Act: The Election of 1940 and the Politics of War*. New York: Oxford University Press, 2013.

Moran, Lord. *Churchill: Taken from the Diaries of Lord Moran*. Boston: Houghton Mifflin, 1966.

Morgan, Kay Summersby. *Past Forgetting: My Love Affair with Dwight D. Eisenhower*. New York: Simon & Schuster, 1977.

Morison, Samuel Eliot. *History of United States Naval Operations in World War II*. Chicago: University of Illinois Press, 2001.

Morison, Elting. *Turmoil and Tradition: A Study of the Life and Times of Henry L. Stimson*. Boston: Houghton Mifflin, 1960.

Mosley, Leonard. *Marshall: Hero for Our Times*. New York: Hearst, 1982.

Nelson, Craig. *From Infamy to Greatness*. New York: Scribner, 2016.

Nelson, James Carl. *Fire Lieutenants: The Heartbreaking Story of Five Harvard Men Who Led America to Victory in World War I*. New York: St. Martin's, 2012.

_____. *The Remains of Company D: A Story of the Great War*. New York: St. Martin's Griffin, 2010.

Nitze, Paul. *From Hiroshima to Glasnost: At the Center of Decision—A Memoir*. New York: Grove Weidenfeld, 1989.

Nolan, John. *The Run-up to the Punchbowl: A Memoir of the Korean War, 1951*. Annapolis, MD: Naval Institute Press, 2006.

Olson, Lynne. *Those Angry Days: Roosevelt, Lindbergh and America's Fight Over World War II, 1939-1941*. New York: Random House, 2013.

Overy, Richard. *Why the Allies Won*. New York: W. W. Norton, 1995.

Page, Arthur W. *Our 110 Days' Fighting*. Whitefish, MT: Kessinger, 2008.

Palmer, Frederick. *Newton D, Baker: America at War*. New York: Dodd, Mead, 1931.

Parrish, Thomas. *Roosevelt and Marshall: Partners in Politics and War*. New York: William Morrow, 1989.

Pawle, Gerald. *The War and Colonel Warden*. New York: Knopf, 1963.

Payne, Robert. *The Marshall Story: A Biography of General George C. Marshall*. Uttar Pradesh, India: Lucknow, 2017.

Peraino, Kevin. *A Force So Swift: Mao, Truman, and the Birth of Modern China, 1949*. New York: Crown, 2017.

Perry, Mark. *The Most Dangerous Man in America: The Making of Douglas MacArthur*. New York: Basic Books, 2014.

_____. *Partners in Command: George Marshall and Dwight Eisenhower in War and Peace*. New York: Penguin, 2007.

Pershing, John J. *My Experiences in the World War*. Vols. I and II. New York: Frederick Stokes, 1931.

Persico, Joseph E. *Roosevelt's Centurions: FDR and the Commanders He Led to Victory in World War II*. New York: Random House, 2013.

_____. *Roosevelt's Secret War: FDR and World War II Espionage*. New York: Random House, 2002.

Petillo, Carol Morris. *Douglas MacArthur: The Philippine Years*. Bloomington: Indiana University Press, 1981.

Plotkhy, S. M. *Yalta: The Price of Peace*. New York: Viking, 2010.

Pogue, Forrest C. *George C. Marshall: Education of a General, 1880-1939*. New York: Viking, 1963.

_____. *George C. Marshall: Ordeal and Hope, 1939-1942*. New York: Viking, 1966.

_____. *George C. Marshall: Organizer of Victory, 1943-1945*. New York: Viking, 1967.

_____. *George C. Marshall: Statesman, 1945-1959*. New York: Viking, 1987.

Prange, Gordon W. *At Dawn We Slept: The Untold Story of Pearl Harbor*. New York: McGraw-Hill, 1981.

Public Papers and Addresses of the Presidents: Harry S. Truman, 1945-1953. Washington, DC: GPO, 1966.

Quirk, Rory. *Wars and Peace: The Memoir of an American Family*. New York: Presidio Press, 1999.

Radosh, Allis, and Ronald Radosh. *A Safe Haven: Harry S. Truman and the Founding of Israel*. New York: HarperCollins, 2009.

Red Cross Courier. Washington, DC: American Red Cross Archives (Susan Watson, archivist).

Reeves, Thomas C. *The Life and Times of Joe McCarthy*. Lanham, MD: Madison, 1997.

Reilly, Michael F. *Reilly of the White House*. Andesite, 2015.

Remarque, Erich Maria. *All Quiet on the Western Front*. New York: Ballantine, 1987.

Reynolds, David. *In Command of History: Churchill Fighting and Writing the Second World War*. New York: Basic Books, 2007.

_____. *From Munich to Pearl Harbor: Roosevelt's America and the Origins of the Second World War*. Chicago: Ivan R. Dee, 2001.

_____. *Summits: Six Meetings That Shaped the Twentieth Century*. New York: Basic Books, 2007.

_____. *From World War to Cold War: Churchill, Roosevelt, and the International History of the 1940s*. Oxford, UK: Oxford University Press, 2015.

Rhoades, Weldon E. "Dusty." *Flying MacArthur to Victory.* College Station, TX: Texas A&M University Press, 2000.

Rickenbacker, Eddie V. *Fighting the Flying Circus.* CreateSpace, 2016.

Ricks, Thomas E. *The Generals: American Military Command from World War II to Today.* New York: Penguin, 2012.

Ridgway, Matthew B. *The Korean War.* Cambridge, MA: Da Capo, 1986.

_____. *Soldier: The Memoirs of Matthew B. Ridgway.* New York: Harper Brothers, 1956.

Roberts, Andrew. *Churchill: Walking with Destiny.* New York: Viking, 2018.

_____. *Masters and Commanders: How Four Titans Won the War in the West.* London: Allen Lane, 2008.

_____. *The Storm of War: A New History of the Second World War.* London: Allen Lane, 2009.

Roberts, Geoffrey. *Stalin's Wars: From World War to Cold War, 1939-1953.* New Haven: Yale University Press, 2006.

Roberts, J. M. *The Penguin History of the Twentieth Century.* New York: Penguin, 1999.

Rogers, Paul P. *The Bitter Years: MacArthur and Sutherland.* Westport, CT: Praeger, 1990.

Roll, David L. *The Hopkins Touch: Harry Hopkins and the Forging of the Alliance to Defeat Hitler.* New York: Oxford University Press, 2013.

Rose, David. *The Big Eddy Club.* New York: New Press, 2011.

_____. *Friends and Partners: The Legacy of Franklin D. Roosevelt and Basil O'Connor in the History of Polio.* Boston: Elsevier, 2016.

Ross, Dennis. *Doomed to Succeed: The U.S.-Israel Relationship from Truman to Obama.* New York: Farrar, Straus and Giroux, 2015.

Rusk, Dean. *As I Saw It.* New York: W. W. Norton, 1990.

Samuels, Gertrude. "Touring with Marshall of the Red Cross." *New York Times Magazine,* February 16, 1950.

Schewe, Donald B., ed. *Franklin D. Roosevelt and Foreign Affairs, January 1937-August 1939.* 11 vols. New York: Garland, 1979-1983.

Schnabel, James F., and Robert J. Watson. *The Joint Chiefs of Staff and National Policy.* Vol. 3: 1951-1953. Fort Belvoir, VA: Defense Technical Information Center, 1998.

Scipio, Albert II. *Last of the Black Regulars: A History of the 24th Infantry Regiment, 1869-1951.* Silver Spring, MD: Roman, 1983.

Sereny, Gitta. *Albert Speer: His Battle with Truth.* New York: Vintage, 1996.

Settle, Frank A. Jr. *General George C. Marshall and the Atomic Bomb.* Santa Barbara, CA: Praeger, 2016.

Severeid, Eric. *Not So Wild a Dream.* Columbia: University of Missouri Press, 1995.

Sharett, Moshe. *At the Gates of the Nations, 1946-1949* (Heb.). Tel Aviv: Am Oved, 1958.

Sheffer, Gabriel. *Moshe Shertok: Biography of a Political Moderate.* Oxford: Oxford University Press, 1996.

Sheng, Michael M. *Battling Western Imperialism: Mao, Stalin, and the United States.* Princeton: Princeton University Press, 1997.

Sherwood, Robert E. *Roosevelt and Hopkins: An Intimate History.* New York: Harper & Brothers, 1948.

Shirer, William. L. *Berlin Diary: The Journal of a Foreign Correspondent, 1934-1941.* New York: Alfred A. Knopf, 1941.

_____. *The Rise and Fall of the Third Reich: A History of Nazi Germany.* New York: Simon & Schuster, 1960.

Showa Tenno dokuhakuroku ("Emperor Hirohito's Monologue"), translated by Terasaki Hidenari. *Bungei Shunjū* magazine, 1990.

Skutt, Mary Sutton. *George C. Marshall, Reporting for Duty.* New York: Blue Valley, 2001.

Smith, Adrian. *Mountbatten: Apprentice War Lord.* London: I. B. Tauris, 2010.

Smith, Jean Edward. *Eisenhower in War and Peace.* New York: Random House, 2012.

————. *FDR.* New York: Random House, 2007.

————. *Lucius D. Clay: An American Life.* New York: Henry Holt, 1990.

Smith, Richard N. *Thomas E. Dewey and His Times.* New York: Simon & Schuster, 1982.

Smith, Walter Bedell. *My Three Years in Moscow.* Baltimore: Lippincott, 1950.

————. *Eisenhower's Six Great Decisions: Europe 1944-1945.* New York: Longmans, Green, 1956.

Smythe, Donald. *Pershing: General of the Armies.* Bloomington: Indiana University Press, 2008.

Snetsinger, John. *Truman, the Jewish Vote, and the Creation of Israel.* Stanford: Hoover Institution Press, 1974.

Spalding, Phinizy. *Georgia: The WPA Guide to Its Towns and Countryside.* Columbia: University of South Carolina Press, 1990.

Spector, Ronald H. *Eagle Against the Sun: The American War with Japan.* New York: Free Press, 1985.

Speer, Albert. *Inside the Third Reich.* New York: Macmillan, 1970.

Steele, Richard E. *The First Offensive, 1942: Roosevelt, Marshall and the Making of American Strategy.* Bloomington: Indiana University Press, 1973.

Steil, Benn. *The Marshall Plan: Dawn of the Cold War.* New York: Simon & Schuster, 2018.

Stern, Fritz. *Einstein's German World.* Princeton: Princeton University Press, 2001.

Stimson, Henry L., and McGeorge Bundy. *On Active Service in Peace and War.* New York: Harper & Brothers, 1948.

Stilwell, Joseph W., and Theodore H. White, eds. *The Stilwell Papers.* New York: William Sloane, 1948.

Stoler, Mark A. *Allies and Adversaries: The Joint Chiefs of Staff, the Grand Alliance and U.S. Strategy in World War II.* Chapel Hill and London: University of North Carolina Press, 2000.

————. *Allies in War: Britain and America Against the Axis Powers, 1940-1945.* Great Britain: Hodder Arnold, 2007.

————. *George C. Marshall: Soldier-Statesman of the American Century.* New York: Twayne, 1980.

————. "The 'Pacific First' Alternative in American World War II Strategy," *International History Review* II (1980).

————. *The Politics of the Second Front: American Military Planning and Diplomacy in Coalition Warfare, 1941-1943.* Westport, CT: Greenwood, 1977.

————, ed. *The Papers of George Catlett Marshall,* Vol. 7. Baltimore: Johns Hopkins University Press, 2016.

Strange, Joseph L. "Cross-Channel Attack, 1942: The British Rejection of Operation Sledgehammer and the Cherbourg Alternative." PhD dissertation, University of Maryland, 1984.

————. "The British Rejection of Operation Sledgehammer: An Alternative Motive." *Military Affairs* 46, no. 1 (1982).

Symington, James W. *Heard and Overheard: Words Wise (and Otherwise) with Politicians, Statesmen and Real People.* Dallas: Vellum, 2015.

Symonds, Craig L. *Neptune: The Allied Invasion of Europe and the D-Day Landings*. New York: Oxford University Press, 2014.

Tanner, Harold M. *The Battle for Manchuria and the Fate of China: Siping 1946*. Bloomington: Indiana University Press, 2013.

Taylor, Jay. *The Generalissimo: Chiang Kai-shek and the Struggle for Modern China*. Cambridge: Belknap Press of Harvard University Press, 2009, 2011.

Thompson, Rachel Yarnell. *Marshall: A Statesman Shaped in the Crucible of War*. Leesburg, VA: George C. Marshall International Center, 2014.

Thorne, Christoper. *Allies of a Kind: The United States, Britain and the War Against Japan, 1941-1945*. ACLS Humanities E-Book, 2008.

Toland, John. *But Not in Shame: The Six Months After Pearl Harbor*. New York: Random House, 1961.

Tooze, Adam. *The Wages of Destruction: The Making and Breaking of the Nazi Economy*. New York: Penguin, 2008.

Truman, Harry S. *Memoirs by Harry S. Truman*. Vol. 1: *Year of Decisions*. Garden City, NY: Doubleday, 1955.

_____. *Memoirs by Harry S. Truman*. Vol. 2: *Years of Trial and Hope*. Garden City, NY: Doubleday, 1956.

Truman, Margaret. *Harry S. Truman*. New York: William Morrow, 1973.

Truscott, Lucien K. Jr. *Command Missions: A Personal Story*. New Orleans: Quid Pro Books, 2012.

Tuchman, Barbara. *Stilwell and the American Experience in China, 1911-45*. New York: Macmillan, 1970.

Tugwell, Rexford G. *The Brains Trust: Members and Associates*. New York: Viking, 1968.

Twomey, Steve. *Countdown to Pearl Harbor: The Twelve Days to the Attack*. New York: Simon & Schuster, 2016.

Unger, Debi, and Irwin Unger, with Stanley Hirshon. *George Marshall*. New York: HarperCollins, 2014.

Vandenberg, Arthur Jr., ed. *The Private Papers of Arthur Vandenberg*. Boston: Houghton Mifflin, 1972.

Van Slyke, Lyman P. *The China White Paper*. Palo Alto: Stanford University Press, 1967.

Villa, Brian Loring. *Unauthorized Action: Mountbatten and the Dieppe Raid*. Oxford: Oxford University Press, 1994.

Wallace, Henry A. *The Price of Vision: The Diary of Henry A. Wallace*. New York: Houghton Mifflin, 1973.

Walters, Vernon A. *Silent Missions*. New York: Doubleday, 1978.

Watson, Mark S. *Chief of Staff: Prewar Plans and Preparations*. Washington, DC: U.S. Government Printing Office, 1950.

Wedemeyer, Albert. *Wedemeyer Reports!* New York: Henry Holt, 1958.

Weintraub, Stanley. *15 Stars Eisenhower, MacArthur, Marshall: Three Generals Who Saved the American Century*. New York: NAL Caliber, 2008.

_____. *Final Victory: FDR's Extraordinary World War II Presidential Campaign*. New York: Da Capo Press, 2012.

_____. *A Stillness Heard Round the World: The End of the Great War, November 1918*. New York: Oxford University Press, 1987.

Weigley, Russell F. *Eisenhower's Lieutenants: The Campaign of France and Germany, 1944-1945*. Bloomington: Indiana University Press, 1990.

Weizmann, Chaim. *Trial and Error: The Autobiography of Chaim Weizmann.* New York: Harper, 1949.

Weizmann, Vera. *Impossible Takes Longer.* New York: Hamish Hamilton, 1967.

Westad, Odd Arne. *The Cold War: A World History.* New York: Basic Books, 2007.

White, Theodore H. *In Search of History.* New York: Grand Central, 1978.

White, William S. "Mr. George C. Marshall of Leesburg, Va.," *New York Times Magazine,* August 7, 1949.

Wilmot, Chester. *The Struggle for Europe.* New York: Carroll & Graf, 1998.

Wilson, Rose Page. *General Marshall Remembered.* Englewood Cliffs, NJ: Prentice-Hall, 1968.

Wyman, David S. *Abandonment of the Jews: America and the Holocaust, 1941-1945.* New York: New Press, 1984.

Yergin, Daniel. *Shattered Peace: The Origins of the Cold War.* New York: Penguin, 1990.

Yogev, Gedalia. *Political and Diplomatic Documents of the State of Israel: December 1947-May 1948.* Vienna: World Zionist Organization, 1979.

Yokelson, Mitchell. *Forty-Seven Days: How Pershing's Warriors Came of Age to Defeat the German Army in World War I.* New York: NAL Caliber, 2016.

Yu, Maochun. *OSS in China: Prelude to Cold War.* Annapolis, MD: Naval Institute Press, 1996.

Zhukov, Georgy Konstantinovich. *The Memoirs of Marshall Zhukov.* New York: Jonathan Cape, 1971.

Index

678

Index

"Little Boy" uranium bomb, 367, 369
plutonium bomb tests in New Mexico, 367
Pope Pius XII's response to, 535–36
possibility of use after WWII, 525–26
potential targets, 369
readiness of an, 321, 354–55, 363–64
Soviet detonation of its first, 414–15, 546
support for using, 368
U.S. strategy, 367
Attlee, Clement, 249, 477, 484
Augusta, 162–64, 174, 332
Austin, Warren, 160, 485–86, 497–99, 502–4
Australia, 227–28
Austria
Council of Foreign Ministers conference
(Moscow, 1947), 429–35
Austria-Hungary, 12

Baden, Maximillian von ("Prince Max"),
47, 50, 54
Baker, Newton, 16, 63
Balfour, Lord, 483
Balfour Declaration, 483, 484
Baltic journey to Europe, 16–17
Barkley, Alben, 527, 576
Baruch, Bernard, 316, 527
The Battle of San Pietro (film), 301
Battle of the Atlantic, 307
Battle of the Bulge, 321, 350–53
Battle of the Kursk Salient, 275
Beal, John Robinson, 400, 404
Beaverbrook, Max, 202–3
Begin, Menachem, 493
Belasco, David, 92
Belgium, 133
Bell, Elliott, 345–46
Bell, J. Franklin, 8, 16, 17
Bendersky, Joseph, 315–16
Beneš, Edvard, 470
Ben-Gurion, David, 486–87, 488–89, 493,
503, 508, 516
Benning, Henry, 88
Benson, Frank, 92–94
Bensonian Company, 92–94
Beria, Lavrentiy, 289
Beria, Sergio, 289
Berman, Louis, 95–96
Bernstein, Barton, 364
The Best Years of Our Lives (film), 302
Bevin, Ernest, 432, 441, 443–44, 447–51, 454,
492, 528–29
Bey, Azzam, 493
Bidault, Georges, 418, 444, 447–49
Biddle, Anthony Drexel, Jr., 126
"Big Four" (later United Nations Security
Council), 285

"Big Four" (Truman's advisors), 582–84
"Big Three"
meeting in Tehran, 280, 288–93
Potsdam Conference (Terminal), 366–69
Yalta Conference (Argonaut), 354–56
Bird, Kai, 317
Black, Lieutenant, 52
Blair, Felix, 472
Blanchard, Mrs. William ("Etta"), 90, 96–97
Bland, Larry, 72
Bliss, Robert Woods, 306, 350
blood and blood products, 548–549
Boeing, 173, 175
Bogotá, Colombia, 506–07
Bohlen, Charles ("Chip"), 292, 329–30, 427,
430–31, 432–33, 435, 439, 440, 485, 491,
525, 532–33, 549–50
Bohlen, Charlie, 532–33
Bonesteel, Charles, 554
Boyce, James, 91
Boyce, Ker, 91
Bradley, Kitty, 440–41
Bradley, Omar, 86, 99, 304–5, 332, 335,
351–52, 357–58, 440–41, 524, 561, 566,
571, 572–76, 579, 582–85, 587, 590
Bratton, Rufus, 186, 187–91, 347–48
Brewster, Owen, 348
Bridges, Styles, 476
Bright, Joan, 333–34
Brinkley, Douglas, 452
Britain
ABC talks between Britain and the U.S.,
165–66
aid to Greece and Turkey, 423–26
Arcadia Conference, 195–204
attacks by Germany, 146
Balfour Declaration, 483, 484
British Combined Operations Headquarters
(COHQ), 220, 240–41
desire for control over India, 221–23
expectation of a German attack, 131–32
importance of British survival for the U.S.,
134–35, 149–50
military supplies sold by the U.S., 135–36
Operation GYMNAST, 231–34,
236–37, 239
opposition to the partition of Palestine, 492
response to the Marshall Memorandum,
218–23
as a staging area for Allied forces, 212, 268
U.S.'s continued supplying of matériel to,
150, 153
War Cabinet Defense Committee, 222–23
Brooke, Sir Alan, 218–19, 224, 245–48, 251,
269, 270–73, 286–87, 334
Brookings Institution, 462, 467–68
Brooks, David, 69